COLLEGE STUDENT AFFAIRS ADMINISTRATION

Edited by
Elizabeth J. Whitt

Advisory Board
Rosalind E. Andreas, University of Vermont
Larry Benedict, Johns Hopkins University
Don Creamer, Virginia Tech University
Jon Dalton, Florida State University
Wanda Everage, Drake University
George d. Kuh, Indiana University
James W. Lyons, Stanford University
Marcia B. Baxter Magolda, Miami University
Thomas Miller, Canisius College
Elizabeth M. Nuss, Goucher College
Ernest T. Pascarella, University of Illinois at Chicago
Patrick T. Terenzini, Pennsylvania State University
Larry D. Roper, Oregon State University
John H. Schuh, Wichita State University
Mary Beth Snyder, Oakland University
Lee Upcraft, Pennsylvania State University

ASHE READER SERIES
Bruce Anthony Jones, Series Editor

SIMON & SCHUSTER
CUSTOM PUBLISHING

LB
2341
.C64
1997
Nov 2009
Gift

SIMON & SCHUSTER CUSTOM PUBLISHING
160 Gould Street/Needham Heights, MA 02194
Simon & Schuster Education Group

Copyright Acknowledgments

Contents

PART II CONTEXTS OF COLLEGE STUDENT AFFAIRS ADMINISTRATION

PART III THE EDUCATIONAL PRACTICE OF COLLEGE STUDENT AFFAIRS ADMINISTRATION

ix

Acknowledgments

In a project of this scope, there are many people to thank. First, I would like to express my appreciation to the following for granting permission to reprint copyrighted materials in this *ASHE Reader*: Accelerated Development, American Association of Higher Education, Berrett-Koehler, The Free Press, Harvard University Press, The Johnson Foundation, Jossey-Bass Publishers, Inc., National Association of Student Personnel Administrators, Teacher's College Press, University of California Press, W.W. Norton and Sons, and American Colllege Personnel Association.

I would also like to thank Barbara Townsend, University of Memphis, past Editor of the *ASHE Reader* Series, for her guidance. Special thanks are due Kathleen Kourian of Simon & Schuster Custom Publishing for her encouragement, support, and patience throughout the process of developing and publishing the Reader. Finally, I am grateful to my colleagues who helped in the selection of readings for this volume: Rosalind E. Andreas, University of Vermont; Larry Benedict, Johns Hopkins University; Don Creamer, Virginia Tech University; Jon Dalton, Florida State University; Wanda Everage, Drake University: George D. Kuh, Indiana University; James W. Lyons, Stanford University; Marcia B. Baxter Magolda, Miami University; Thomas Miller, Canisius College; Elizabeth M. Nuss, Goucher College; Ernest T. Pascarella, University of Illinois at Chicago; Patrick T. Terenzini, The Pennsylvania State University; Larry D. Roper, Oregon State University; John H. Schuh, Wichita State University; Mary Beth Snyder, Oakland University; and M. Lee Upcraft, The Pennsylvania State University.

A Note to the Reader

We anticipate that this edition of the *ASHE Reader on College Student Affairs Administration* will be in print for about three years, at which time a revised edition is expected. Your assistance in shaping the contents (e.g., what is particularly useful, what should be added) will be appreciated.

Please send your suggestions, comments, and recommendations regarding this *ASHE Reader* to the editor:

> Elizabeth J. Whitt
> Policy Studies
> College of Education (m/c 147)
> The University of Illinois at Chicago
> 1040 West Harrison Street
> Chicago, IL 60607–7133

Suggestions about other topics that might be addressed by the *ASHE Reader Series*, or other comments about the series should be sent to:

> Bruce Anthony Jones
> Center for Educational Policy Analysis
> University of Missouri–Columbia
> Columbia, Missouri 65211

Introduction

Background of the Reader

The impetus for the development of this ASHE Reader on College Student affairs Administration was a series of discussions between student affairs practitioners and faculty sponsored by the National Association of Student Personnel Administrators (NASPA) in 1993 and 1994. Both NASPA and the discussion participants were concerned about the rapidly changing conditions of undergraduate education on and off campus and what the implications of such change might be for the preparation and ongoing professional development of student affairs administrators. Among the questions considered by the discussants were (1) what should student affairs professionals know and be prepared to do?, and (2) what methods and materials should be used in the preparation and professional development of student affairs staff? Consideration of these seemingly simple, yet truly complex, questions revealed consensus on two key points. First, participants identified what they believed to be the most important arenas of skills and knowledge for student affairs work in this time of change: (1) fostering student learning and development through work with students and development of learning environments, (2) leading and managing learning organizations, (3) engaging in reflective practice, which includes ongoing professional development, (4) facilitating development of diverse learning communities, and (5) conducting ongoing research and assessment of student outcomes and organizational performance. Second, the discussants asserted that the traditional student affairs knowledge bases—however useful—are insufficient for understanding today's students and today's institutions of higher education; what is needed are more complex views of students, institutions, and other contexts of student affairs work, as well as more information about how to develop critical skills and knowledge, from sources outside the student affairs literature. At the same time, participants advocated broader dissemination of student affairs research and writing, especially for student affairs administrators new to the field.

One of the recommendations of the group to respond to these concerns was a means to pull together research and writing from outside, as well as within, student affairs to assist in developing necessary skills and knowledge. This ASHE Reader was the result of that recommendation, and many of the people involved in the NASPA-sponsored discussions served on the advisory board for the Reader.

Purpose of the Reader

The purpose of the ASHE Reader on College Student Affairs Administration, therefore, is threefold. First, the Reader is intended to be used as a text in graduate courses on college student affairs administration. The Reader introduces issues and ideas appropriate to developing an understanding of student affairs as a field and an awareness of the roles, responsibilities, skills, and demands of students affairs professionals. Second, the Reader can be used in continuing professional development efforts, including for college and university administrators unfamiliar with the field and work of student affairs. Third, the ASHE Reader on College Student Affairs Administration is intended to provide a means to critically examine—as well as describe—current issues, trends, and research in the field, as well as its foundations and history.

Overview of the Reader

The Reader is divided into four parts: (1) Foundations of College Student Affairs Administration, (2) Contexts of College Student Affairs Administration, (3) The Educational Practice of Student Affairs Administration, and (4) Professional Development in Student Affairs Administration. A description of each part follows.

Part One: Foundations of Student Affairs Administration

An important aspect of understanding college student affairs administration today is understanding its roots. This section of the Reader provides an overview of, and acculturation to, the past and present of college student affairs. Components of Part One include descriptions and examinations of the history, philosophies and purposes of student affairs administration. The evolution of the field over time, implications of the past for the present and future, and the place of student affairs in the development of higher education in the United States are addressed by the articles offered here.

Part Two: Contexts of College Student Affairs Administration

College student affairs administration is conducted within a variety of contexts inside and outside colleges and universities, and the nature of those contexts has important implications for student affairs practice. Thus, Part Two of the Reader focuses on the institutional and external contexts in which student affairs administration takes place. Topics addressed include the influence of external contexts and constituencies of higher education; descriptions of the institutional structures and cultures within which student affairs exists; and general discussion of the characteristics and needs of undergraduate students.

Part Three: The Educational Practice of College Student Affairs Administration

Because the functions and tasks of student affairs professionals vary with institutional size, type, cultures, and structures, the purpose of Part Three is to examine areas of responsibility and concerns that tend to be common regardless of specific job descriptions. These areas are (1) student learning and development, (2) community development, (3) reflective practice, and (4) research and assessment. Articles in each area challenge the reader to think about these elements of student affairs practice from a variety of perspectives.

Part Four: Professional Development in College Student Affairs Administration

Part Four focuses on issues important to the initial and ongoing development of student affairs professionals. Issues addressed in this section are (1) development of new professionals, (2) professional ethics, and (3) involvement in professional associations and activities.

Even though this Reader is quite long, it provides—at best—a brief introduction to the myriad issues encompassed within each of these areas. The bibliography at the end of the Reader provides many additional readings on the major topics. The editor and advisory board have attempted to blend some of the best works within student affairs with some of the best works from outside the field, and balance useful perspectives from the past with useful perspectives on the present and future. We also hope—in our selection of articles and papers—to challenge the readers of this volume to think in new ways about student affairs roles, responsibilities, and contexts. Because this Reader, like the field of student affairs, is a work–in–progress, we encourage your feedback and reactions to what is included here, as well as what is not.

The ASHE Reader Series

The ASHE Reader Series is a collection of readers on topics of current interest in higher education. Each reader represents a compendium of exemplary published works chosen by scholars who teach and conduct research in these areas. The books are designed to be used as supplementary text material in courses of higher education or as reference works.

TEACHING AND LEARNING IN THE COLLEGE CLASSROOM
Edited by Kenneth A. Feldman and Michael B. Paulsen

A comprehensive review of classic and recent research in the area, TEACHING AND LEARNING IN THE COLLEGE CLASSROOM addresses issues from diverse theoretical and philosophical perspectives. Each section includes quantitative and qualitative research, a separate introductory essay, research reports, literature reviews, theoretical essays, and practitioner-oriented articles. It emphasizes teacher-student and student-student interaction. It considers multicultural and gender issues and contains practical teaching strategies based on research.

Paperbound 704 pages ISBN 0-536-58535-0

ASSESSMENT AND PROGRAM EVALUATION
Edited by Joan S. Stark and Alice Thomas

This reader effectively provides the broad perspective necessary for the study of assessment by consolidating articles from a wide range of sources, some not easily obtained. By addressing such topics as historical and philosophical context and ethical issues, this volume will help readers develop the necessary assessment skills, attitudes and knowledge to conduct and supervise studies and program reviews or to be informed clients inside or outside the academic environment.

Paperbound 832 pages ISBN 0-536-58586-5

COMMUNITY COLLEGES
Edited by James L. Ratcliff

This updated edition includes new information on the diversity of the student population and features a special focus on community college scholarship and faculty renewal. It will give you and your students a review of the current community college systems in American history, philosophy, and purpose: organization, administration, and finance; programs and services; students; professional staff; and the social role.

Paperbound 503 pages ISBN 0-536-58571-7

QUALITATIVE RESEARCH IN HIGHER EDUCATION:
Experiencing Alternative Perspectives and Approaches
Edited by Clifton E. Conrad, Anna Neumann, Jennifer Grant Haworth, and Patricia Scott

Designed to help students and teachers prepare for, enter into, participate in, reflect on, and give voice to the experience of doing qualitative research. Organized around six topics: Explicating Frames of Reference, Approaching Inquiry, Doing Fieldwork, Interacting with Self and Other, Creating a Text, Reading a Text.

Paperbound 600 pages ISBN 0-536-58417-0

WOMEN IN HIGHER EDUCATION: A Feminist Perspective
Edited by Judith Glazer, Estela Bensimon, and Barbara Townsend

Essays representing the best of feminist scholarship in the field of higher education on four main themes: Theoretical and Research Perspectives, Context Historical, Social, and Professional, Institutional, Women in Academe: As Student, Faculty, Administrators, and Trustees, and The Transformation of Knowledge: Circular Change and Feminist Pedagogy.

Paperbound 600 pages ISBN 0-536-58351-0

FOUNDATIONS OF AMERICAN HIGHER EDUCATION
Edited by James L. Bess

A comprehensive introduction to the basics of American higher education—45 articles by some of today's most respected leaders in the field, in six parts: The Scope of Higher Education in American Society, The Participants, The Conduct of Education and Research, The Management of the College or University, Innovation, Change, and the Future, The Study and Practice of Higher Education Administration.

Paperbound 772 pages ISBN 0-536-58013-8

THE HISTORY OF HIGHER EDUCATION
Edited by Lester E. Goodchild and Harold S. Wechsler

Included are an introductory essay on American higher education historiography; introductory overviews of each of the five chronological periods of higher education; in-depth scholarly analyses from journal articles, book chapters, and essays; and the use of primary readings to capture the flavor and meaning of important issues for each period.

Paperbound 675 pages ISBN 0-536-57566-5

ORGANIZATION AND GOVERNANCE IN HIGHER EDUCATION, Fourth Edition
Edited by Marvin W. Peterson, with Associate Editors Ellen E. Chaffee and Theodore H. White

The selections not only reflect the changing views of colleges and universities as organizations, but also highlight the areas of literature applied to higher education that need to be addressed. The text is divided into three parts: Organization Theory and Models, Governance and Management Processes, and Leadership Perspectives.

Paperbound 475 pages ISBN 0-536-57981-4

FINANCE IN HIGHER EDUCATION
Edited by Dave Breneman, Larry L. Leslie and Richard E. Anderson

Practical and theoretical, the selections look at the financial management of colleges and universities, higher education economies, and federal and state policies, and represent a number of divergent perspectives and opinions.

Paperbound 450 pages ISBN 0-536-58352-8

RACIAL AND ETHNIC DIVERSITY IN HIGHER EDUCATION
Edited by Caroline Sotello Viernes Turner, Mildred Garcia, Amaury Nora, and Laura I. Rendón

This reader focuses on racial/ethnic diversity in America's higher education institutions. Diversity is discussed from an historical perspective, providing a context for the many contemporary experiences described in these writings by and about students, staff, and faculty. The selections represent scholars, providing viewpoints of African American, Asian Americans, Native Americans, and Latinos in higher education. The selections cover six areas: History; Curriculum, Teaching, and Learning; Students; Faculty; Administration,, Leadership, and Governance; and Research.

Paperbound 658 pages ISBN 0–536–59003–6

COLLEGE STUDENTS: THE EVOLVING NATURE OF RESEARCH
Edited by Frances K. Stage, Guadalupe L. Anaya, John P. Bean, Don Hossler, and George D. Kuh

This reader highlights the latest in college student research which will inform and inspire both future researchers and administrators. The articles included are abstracted from a wide range of sources and reflect three perspectives: 1) summarizes of traditional college student research, 2) articles focusing on populations that are just now beginning to receive attention in college student research, and 3) critiques of the status quo in college student research which challenge the academic community to reexamine its way of viewing the research enterprise.

Paperbound 316 pages ISBN 0–536–59088–5

FACULTY AND FACULTY ISSUES IN COLLEGES AND UNIVERSITIES
Edited by Dorothy E. Finnegan, David Webster, and Zelda F. Gamson

This major revision provides students with articles about faculty issues that exhibit a wide range of subjects, philosophical perspectives, and methods. Beginning with a discussion of demographic trends, this reader addresses such topics as faculty roles, obligations, and career issues; the relation of the development of higher education as an institution to the development of the professional life of faculty; and how scholars approach research questions from diverse and emerging perspectives and with heterogeneous methodologies. Written for the faculty student, this reader concludes with issues that face faculty and institutions in the future.

Paperbound 650 pages ISBN 0–536–59295–0

To Order:

To order copies of these titles for your class, please contact your campus bookstore and provide them with the quantity and ISBN. You can receive a complimentary desk copy with an order of 10 or more copies.

To order copies for yourself, simply call Simon & Schuster Custom Publishing at 800-428-4466 (or 617-455-7000 in Massachusetts and Canada) from 8:30 to 5:00 EST.

PART I

FOUNDATIONS OF STUDENT
AFFAIRS ADMINISTRATION

*The first part of the Reader provides an overview of, and accul-
turation to, the past and present of college student affairs administration. Components of Part One include descriptions and
examinations of the history, philosophies, and purposes of college
student affairs administration. The development and evolution of
the field over time, implications of the past for the present and
future, and the place of student affairs in the development of U.S.
higher education are discussed.*

Reinventing Student Affairs: Something Old and Something New

Kathleen E. Allen and Elliott L. Garb (1993)

The authors question the current role of student affairs in higher education, offering a new vision and a new challenge for the profession.

Introduction

Higher education faces economic challenges unprecedented since World War II, as well as challenges to its institutional credibility unparalleled in history. This article questions the current role of student affairs in higher education. After a quick tour through higher education and the evolution of student affairs, it examines the dynamics and context for our professional development. It then draws on the historical relevance of the student affairs "points of view" and offers a new vision and new challenge for the profession.

The Evolution of Student Affairs

As a profession, we are confined and constrained by our history, our tradition, and our professional attitude and language. From early colonial days to the last half of the 19th century, classroom faculty throughout higher education were completely immersed in the process of educating their white male clientele. As institutions changed in the later part of the 19th century and the German model of higher education emerged, colleges and universities became more complex and classroom faculty shifted their focus from their students to their disciplines (Veysey, 1965). The first vestiges of bureaucracy also appeared at this time (Rudolph, 1962). Issues of control—both of students and of institutions—grew more prominent. The growth of bureaucracy continued into the 20th century and, with the introduction of vocational testing and counseling, expanded after World War I.

Universities responded to changes in faculty interests by appointing individuals to be responsible for student related issues. The Dean of Men and Dean of Women were forebears of today's student affairs administrators (Rudolph, 1962; Veysey, 1965). The post-World War II explosion of enrollments and the unprecedented investment in higher education by the federal government expanded the scope of what had now become student affairs responsibilities. The common thread throughout our history is the assumption of responsibility for the scraps and remnants of what were once classroom faculty duties. Our traditions grew out of being student-centered and service-oriented. Our initial attachment to the institutional organizational structure was through services not necessarily focused on learning.

The history and traditions of student affairs have also been affected by the larger organizational context in which the profession developed. Student affairs evolved within a hierarchical structure that, when combined with traditional management concepts of control, created a set of often unexamined assumptions about our work and our relationship with students. Hierarchy determined where we fit within higher education. Control and service, however, are rarely part of the institutional mission statements listed in the front pages of catalogs. The concept and practice of collegiality, an academic affairs cultural tradition, are strained and muted within a hierarchy, resulting in student affairs being separated from the primary delivery system—faculty.

Student affairs administrators carry the weight of second-class citizenship within higher education. The tradition of being responsible for classroom faculty leftovers and operating in a hierarchical manner within an organizational culture based on collegiality has created a professional psyche of second-class citizenship and victim mentality. We profess that something is being done to us by some all-powerful "they." Too often, we seem to accept conditions and circumstances as if we have no control over them and no responsibility for their presence.

Words are powerful shapers of perception and labels can become reality. The predominant words used within the higher education literature to label and describe student affairs work reflect service and support concepts. The language of higher education continually reinforces the belief that teaching and learning are confined to specific locations, essentially the classroom. Replication of this belief, aided by our victim mentality and history of faculty leftovers, feeds hidden assumptions about ourselves and our work.

Day-to-day conditions are at odds with the profession's philosophical tenets. The 1937 and 1949 *Student Personnel Point of View* statements (NASPA, 1989) define student affairs as educational and introduce a holistic approach to students that extends to all of higher education. These two *Points of View* clearly emphasize the belief that leaning is centered in the institution, not just in the classroom. Paradoxically, the two statements set in motion a fundamental conflict embedded in student affairs work: they proclaim student affairs staff are an important part of the educational process, yet that notion is frequently at odds with staff members' own perceptions (as well as the perceptions and expectations of others) that they are providers solely of support services.

These perceptions are reinforced by a variety of conditions. Our numbers are proportionally smaller than almost all other institutional constituencies. Thus, our representation on critical committees and our presence at important assemblies make it difficult to develop a shared perspective, a consensus on priorities, or a common vernacular that includes our experience and perceptions. There is even more confusion regarding our role. Many of our "colleagues" emphasize the heavy service orientation, with little acceptance or understanding of our role as educators, regarding us instead as control agents and social directors.

As a profession, we have gone through many phases in attempting to reconcile the philosophical underpinnings of student affairs work with the day-to-day realities of our responsibilities and expectations. Each of these phases reflects an attempt to gain acceptance within our institutions. To enhance our credibility we tried to prove we are good managers, quickly adopting efforts related to accountability (Harpel, 1976). The number of users, attendance, services provided—the thousand and one ways of counting we do—are all means of demonstrating the value of our work. This "Management-by-objectives" phase has continued into today's current focus on total quality management.

But once we found that being good managers was not sufficient for acceptance, we turned to the "in-search-of-discipline" phase. Student development theory became part of our professional repertoire (Knefelkamp, Widick, & Parker, 1978; Miller & Prince, 1976) not only because it is an important tool in our work, but also because it might make us more acceptable in a discipline-driven environment.

We continue to try to fit into our own institutional environments on terms other than our own. The current political phase is best illustrated by the 1987 publication *A Perspective on Student Affairs* (NASPA, 1989), more a political statement than a reaffirmation of the 1937 and 1949 *Point of View* statements. Its aim was to get the attention of movers and shakers in the higher education community. Developing political skills in student affairs staff is necessary for the profession's evolution (Moore, 1991). The use of power and influence in obtaining resources and achieving a hearing for issues and concerns must be acknowledged. This evolution has continued with the recognition of multiple and sometimes competing roles (Sandeen, 1991).

We in student affairs continually search for acceptance and recognition within academe. Unfortunately, we search for this acceptance from the wrong source. The profession's evolution has been necessary and brought us great gifts, including a set of professional behaviors, standards, and theoretical foundations. We do not need to look to our colleagues in other academic disciplines or professions for affirmation of our status within our institutions or within higher education in general. We have a rich history, an extensive tradition, a set of standards and ethical behaviors, and a growing body of literature based on sound scholarly practices. All of these confirm our status as a profession.

Positive Marginality

The historical context and dynamics outlined above have placed the practice and perspectives of student affairs professionals in the margins of higher education. Patterns of change and growth in the field have often been marked by the tensions surrounding this marginal existence and by the effort to "fit in."

Webster defines *marginal* as follows:

> 1: written or printed in the margin of a page or sheet such as a place to jot notes that may help clarify but are not included in the main text; 2: relating to or situated at a margin or border, for example, the border of a territory where outlier activities are not considered as central and therefore nothing to worry about; 3: characterized by the incorporation of habits and values from two divergent cultures and by incomplete assimilation in either; 4: located at the fringe of consciousness; 5: close to the lower limit of qualification, acceptability, or function.

Each of these definitions suggests different concerns about the experience of marginality and reflects strategies student affairs has used to alter its position within institutions.

The first suggests that student affairs exists in the margins of institutions and explains its strategies over the years to get written into the "main text" through inclusion in mission statements and strategic plans. The second definition reminds us of student affairs' identity as "fun and games," implying that it is involved with activities not central to institutional missions. Definition three describes the incomplete assimilation of student affairs' and academic affairs' cultural values. The fourth definition eloquently applies the notion of fringe consciousness to the perception of student affairs by the majority of people in institutions of higher education. And the fifth helps explain why so much energy has been expended on the preparation standards and credentials of student affairs professionals.

The consciousness of marginality, while often perceived as negative, has provided significant impetus in the evolution of student affairs. It has helped the profession focus on ways to fit in, upgrade credentials, increase institutional awareness, and be incorporated into strategic plans and mission statements. It has also, however, limited our own awareness of the positive aspects of marginality itself.

Some aspects of marginality, as practiced by student affairs, provide particular benefits for higher education. One such benefit is embedded in the field's philosophical underpinnings—as stated in the *Student Personnel Point of View* (1937, 1949)—which emphasize education and the place of student affairs within it. The 1937 version of the *Student Personnel Point of View* states that the enterprise of higher education is about learning in its fullest sense:

> This philosophy imposes upon educational institutions the obligation to consider the student as a whole—his intellectual capacity and achievement, his emotional make up, his physical condition, his social relationships, his vocational aptitudes and skills, his moral and religious values, his economic resources, and his aesthetic appreciations. It puts emphasis, in brief, upon the development of the student as a person rather than upon his intellectual training alone. (NASPA, 1989, p. 49)

The same philosophy of education appears in the 1949 version:

> The development of students as whole persons interacting in social institutions is the central concern of student personnel work and of other agencies of education. . . . The student personnel point of view encompasses the student as a whole. The concept of education is broadened to include attention to the student's well-rounded development—physically, socially, emotionally, and spiritually—as well as intellectually. (NASPA, 1989, pp. 21–22)

The *Student Personnel Point of View* implies that learning in all its forms is at the center of the educational enterprise. It is precisely this philosophy that has atrophied, however, in our efforts to "fit in." As we have tried to diminish our marginality, we have abdicated our role as active shapers of learning-centered education that includes character formation as well as the transmission of information. In times when education seems to be about knowing more and more about less and less, this abdication has had dire results for society and for the quality of higher education.

The second benefit student affairs' marginality brings to higher education is reflected in the academic backgrounds of its professionals. Students affairs is one of the few divisions employing people from a wide variety of disciplines. If academic training shapes one's world view and the questions one asks, then student affairs is one of the few areas in higher education that functions in a multidisciplinary manner. Multidisciplinary thinking allows us to see issues and concerns in richer terms; to be the individuals who connect issues, concerns, and concepts in a fragmented society; and to serve our institutions by helping to create meaning across disciplines.

The student affairs culture, with its multidisciplinary focus, suggests we have something significant to offer higher education. We must be true to ourselves and value our perspectives and philosophy. We must also think of ourselves as among the leaders in the institutional enterprise. In our efforts to fit into the academic culture we have abdicated our role and value as institutional leaders.

When we withdraw our voice and our perspective, the quality of the educational experience diminishes. Student affairs practitioners must see themselves as leaders in reshaping higher education as a learning-centered enterprise. In this role, our marginality helps us. Conceptually, leaders have always operated from the margins of organizations. Change comes in part from identifying what is missing in the present and from being able to see a different future (Bennis & Nanus, 1985; Burnes, 1978; Foster, 1988). Creating change, by definition, starts with a marginal perspective that requires an act of leadership to bring it into the central vision. As a profession we need to reengage as leaders so our institutions return to being learning—rather than information—centered.

Something Old

The *Student Personnel Points of View* from 1937 and 1949 (NASPA, 1989) impart wisdom still relevant to student affairs today. They include a holistic perspective of the individual, the institution, and society. In addition to focusing education on learning in its broadest sense, the statements reinforce what we know through experience and scholarship. The "separate container" model that segmented cognitive development from social-emotional and psychomotor development has not held up to the tests of time and diversity (Allen, 1992; Baruch, Barnett, & Rivers, 1983; Belenky, Clinchy, Goldberger, & Tarule, 1986; Josselson, 1987).

The 1937 and 1949 *Points of View* use the language of values and moral development significantly more than the 1987 *A Perspective on Student Affairs* (NASPA, 1989). Value inquiry (defined as the intentional teaching of how to inquire about and struggle with value conflicts) needs to be taught and practiced in student affairs, just as critical thinking is taught and practiced in the classroom.

Something New—Reinventing Student Affairs

As a profession, student affairs must build on the strength of its growing tradition and its repertoire of skills and competencies, while remaining true to its philosophical foundation. Built on this foundation is the evolving knowledge base on how students develop and on the changes in developmental theory driven by gender, age, sexual orientation, culture, and ethnicity (Belenky et al., 1986; Franz & White, 1985; Gilligan, 1982; Hanson, 1991; Keen, 1991; Kuh, Whitt, & Shedd, 1987; Thompson, 1991).

The new vision of student affairs includes an attitude of positive marginality, which entails valuing student affairs perspectives, acting as leaders within institutions, and articulating a vision of holistic development that includes a learning focus. To illustrate, we juxtapose below a statement from the 1987 *A Perspective on Student Affairs* (NASPA, 1989) with a statement reflecting a new vision of student affairs:

> **The Academic Mission of the Institution is Preeminent.** Colleges and universities organize their primary activities around the academic experience: the curriculum, the library, the classroom, and the laboratory. The work of student affairs should not compete with and cannot substitute for that academic experience. As a partner in the educational enterprise, student affairs enhances and supports the academic missions.

> Learning is the cardinal value of the institution. Colleges and universities organize their primary activities around learning. Within the educational mission of the institution, student affairs is integral to the learning enterprise.

The new vision of student affairs challenges us to reinstall learning, in its broadest sense, into the heart of our institutions. Learning then becomes the superordinate value that brings academic and student affairs into complementary balance. Placing the focus on learning reframes the issues and draws us away from schisms created by being either discipline-centered or student-centered. It forces us to be both, thereby drawing on the cultures of academic and student affairs. Such a vision demands that we reclaim our professional self-esteem. It also affirms our position within institutions, requiring us to think and act as leaders in higher education.

Conclusion

Student affairs professionals know how to lead, create change, and influence environments. Exercise of their leadership has centered primarily on students. This new vision of student affairs requires the application of these abilities to the larger culture of higher education. It is no longer sufficient to do excellent work within the boundaries of student affairs, as defined by organizational charts. Higher education needs the knowledge and perspective we have gained from the margins.

If we implement this new vision, how might our work change? First, practitioners would see themselves as people who nurture, applaud, and support a holistic perspective of students across the institution. They would find ways and means to develop a seamless educational experience. Student affairs would shift, but not abandon, its traditional emphasis from service and activity to shaping institutional culture. Services and programs would not disappear, but a meta-level of work would be introduced into student affairs professionals' lives. As a result, a learning focus and holistic thinking would be applied to higher education policies and practices.

This would entail a shift in our own approach to territoriality. When we shape culture we cannot be defined by hierarchy and confined by territory. The boundaries between student affairs and other areas of the institution become blurred. Under these circumstances, student affairs professionals' role is to lead—shaping culture and connecting activities with learning.

Finally, time for reflection is critical to the process of reinventing student affairs. We need time to observe and create meaning to avoid losing sight of our purpose. We (the authors) believe this vision of student affairs remains incomplete. It is an initial challenge to the way student affairs professionals perceive themselves and their relationship to the educational enterprise. We hope that our ideas will intrigue, anger, and excite readers. Any of these responses should trigger their own journeys toward invigorating the profession. Think of this as the beginning of a dialogue with an invitation to respond.

References

Allen, K. (1992, February). *A nonlinear model of student development*. Paper presented at the NASPA IV-E Conference, Minneapolis, MN.

Baruch, G., Barnett, R., & Rivers, C. (1983). *Life prints: New patterns of love and work for today's women*. New York: New American Library.

Belenky, M. F., Clinchy, B. M., Goldberger, N. R., & Tarule, J. M. (1986). *Women's ways of knowing*. New York: Basic Books.

Bennis, W., & Nanus, B. (1985). *Leaders: The strategies for taking charge*. New York: Harper & Row.

Burns, J. M. (1978). *Leadership*. New York: Harper & Row.

Foster, W. (1988). *Toward a critical practice of leadership*. Manuscript submitted for publication.

Franz, C. E., & White, K. M. (1995). Individuation and attachment in personality development: Extending Erikson's theory. *Journal of Personality*, 53(2), 224–255.

Gilligan, C. (1982). *In a different voice: Psychological theory and women's development*. Cambridge, MA: Harvard University Press.

Hanson, G. (1991). The call to assessment: What role for student affairs? In K. Beeler & D. Hunter (Eds.), *Puzzles and pieces in wonderland: The promise and practice of student affairs research* (pp. 80–105). Washington, D.C.: National Association of Student Personnel Administrators (NASPA).

Harpel, R. L. (1976). Planning, budgeting, and evaluation in student affairs programs: A manual for administrators [Special Insert]. *NASPA Journal*, 14(1), i–xx.

Josselson, R. (1987). *Finding herself: Pathways to identity development in women*. San Francisco: Jossey-Bass.

Keen, S. (1991). *Fire in the belly: On being a man*. New York: Bantam.

Knefelkamp, L., Widick, C., & Parker, C. A. (1978). Editors' notes: Why bother with theory? In L. Knefelkamp, C. Widick, & C. A. Parker (Eds.), *Applying new developmental findings (New Directions for Student Services*, No. 4, pp. vii–xvi). San Francisco: Jossey-Bass.

Kuh, G. D., Whitt, E. J., & Shedd, J. D. (1987). *Student affairs work, 2001: A paradigmatic odyssey* (ACPA Media Publication, No. 42). Alexandria, VA: American College Personnel Association (ACPA).

Miller, T. K., & Prince, J. S. (1976). *The future of student affairs*. San Francisco: Jossey-Bass.

Moore, P. L. (1991). Editors' notes. In P. L. Moore (Ed.), *Managing the political dimension of student affairs (New Directions for Student Services*, No. 55, pp. 1–4). San Francisco: Jossey-Bass.

National Association of Student Personnel Administrators (NASPA). (1989). *Points of view*. Washington, D.C.: Author.

Rudolph, F. (1962). *The American college and university*. New York: Knopf.

Sandeen, A. (1991). *The chief student affairs officer*. San Francisco: Jossey-Bass.

Thompson, K. (Ed.). (1991). *To be a man: In search of the deep masculine*. Los Angeles: Tarcher.

Veysey, L. R. (1965). *The emergence of the American university*. Chicago: University of Chicago Press.

Note

Kathleen E. Allen, Vice President for Student Development, College of Saint Benedict, St. Joseph, MN 56374. Elliot L. Garb, Assistant Chancellor for Student Affairs, University of Wisconsin–Eau Claire, WI 54702–4004. Accepted September 25, 1992.

A Student Development Model for Student Affairs in Tomorrow's Higher Education

AMERICAN COLLEGE PERSONNEL ASSOCIATION (1975)

Summary of the T.H.E. Project

The Tomorrow's Higher Education (T.H.E.) Project was conceived by the American College Personnel Association in 1968 as a planned response to the rapid and extensive changes expected in higher education in the years ahead. Phase I was implemented for purposes of defining the nature of learning and identifying the fundamental goals and premises of higher education. The Brown monograph entitled Student Development in Tomorrow's Higher Education: A Return to the Academy *was published to this end.*

Phase II was designed as the model building part of the T.H.E. Project for the purpose of developing a new operational model for student affairs professionals. While student development is viewed as being the responsibility of the full academic community, attention in the following statement is focused on the role of student affairs in tomorrow's higher education. This statement is an outgrowth of T.H.E. Phase II Model Building Conference held June 4–8, 1974, at the University of Georgia. Conference participants were: John Blackburn, University of Denver; Robert D. Brown, University of Nebraska; Richard B. Caple, University of Missouri; Everett M. Chandler, California Polytechnic State University; Don G. Creamer, El Centro College; Burns B. Crookston, University of Connecticut; K. Patricia Cross, Educational Testing Service; W. Harold Grant, Auburn University; Melvene D. Hardee, Florida State University; and Theodore K. Miller, University of Georgia, Chairperson. In addition, a process team of University of Georgia students and staff worked with the resource participants. They were Roger G. Bryant, Kenneth L. Ender, Barry L. Jackson, Martha C. McBride, Fred B. Newton, and Judith S. Prince, Process Team Chairperson.

Request for Reports of Model Programs

Outlines of specific programs which exemplify utilization of the rationale and competencies for student development presented in the T.H.E. Model are being solicited from student affairs practitioners and others. The programs selected from submitted outlines and the T.H.E. Model will be expanded into a working monograph for use by student affairs professionals for program planning in student development.

Outlines can be submitted for ongoing programs as well as for proposed programs. The outline should be no more than three double-spaced pages and should contain the following information arranged in approximately this order:

A. *Program title.*

B. *Rationale for the program.* In 100 words or less describe the core idea of the program including the student needs and developmental goals for which it is designed.

C. *Characteristics of the program.* Briefly describe the population toward which the program is directed (individuals, groups or organizations), time sequence, staffing needs, facilities used, limitations, etc.

D. *Collaborative efforts.* Specify the role faculty, staff, students and others played in both the development and implementation of the program.

E. *Goal setting process.* Describe the specific outcomes expected as a result of participation in the program.

F. *Assessment procedures.* Include a brief description of all assessment techniques used (i.e. instruments, behavioral observation, criteria, etc.)

G. *Strategies utilized.* Describe the change process used in the program, i.e. instruction (include brief course outline), consultation (techniques used), and/or milieu management (identify resources and outline procedures).

H. *Evaluation procedures.* Describe the ways in which the program is evaluated and in which students evaluate their progress toward attaining goals.

I. *Location and participants.* List the institution, subdivision, and staff members responsible for the program (names as well as positions).

J. *Contact person.* Name, address and phone number of the individual who may be contacted should clarification or more information be desired.

K. *Signed release.* Please include a short statement authorizing ACPA and the T.H.E. Phase II Chairperson to use part or all of the information submitted for the proposed monograph. Appropriate credit will, of course, be given for exemplary programs used.

Mail the original and two (2) copies of the double-spaced outline to:

Dr. Judith S. Prince
Chairperson, T.H.E. Phase II, ACPA
Wesleyan College
Macon, Georgia 31201

In addition to the outline, supportive descriptive materials are welcomed.

Introduction to the T.H.E. Philosophy

Higher education in America is a dynamic institution which, by its very nature, is constantly in a process of change as is the society from which it derives. As our nation has evolved for nearly two hundred years through the agrarian and industrial phases to the present technological era, our educational system has made steady progress from a predominantly elitist toward a predominantly egalitarian system aimed at the development of an educated and enlightened citizenry.

At the present time, we are experiencing the most rapid and dramatic changes in our history, which will demand an ever increasing tempo of activity and response from higher education. In recent years, post-secondary education's needs for renewal and reformation have generated universities without walls (campus free colleges), community colleges, cluster colleges, credit by examination, continuing education units, external degree programs, off-campus experiential semesters, study abroad programs, upward bound programs, and change in liberal arts education as well as an increasing concern for student development. The directions which current change in higher education will ultimately take, however, are not yet clear.

The traditional approach to student affairs has been generally reactive in nature, rather than proactive. If we are to influence the directions to be taken in the future, we must anticipate change and help individuals and groups shape change, not merely adjust to it, Therefore, a statement of our purpose and the creation of an operational model to achieve that purpose is imperative. Such a model, stated in meaningful terms, will facilitate the development of a "proactive" approach which will better direct the efficient use of our professional resources for promoting more fully developed persons within the context of higher education in a world of accelerating change.

The essence of the Tomorrow's Higher Education Project is an attempt to reconceptualize college student affairs work in a way that will serve to provide a measure of creative input from our profession toward the shaping of higher education for the future. By reconceptualization we mean systematic review, reconstruction, and change in the fundamental conceptions about the specific roles, functions, methods and procedures that will characterize our future professional practice.

The T.H.E. Project emphasizes student development. Our need as a profession is to continue developing skills, competencies and knowledge which, when joined in a collaborative effort with others in post-secondary education, can lead to the achievement of the goal of facilitating student development. The role of the student affairs staff is to initiate, facilitate, and encourage actions which will unite the community toward the accomplishment of student development goals.

The Rationale for Student Development

Student development, in the higher-education context, is the application of human development concepts in the post-secondary setting. Human development is a patterned, orderly, lifelong process leading to the growth of self-determination and self-direction, which results in more effective behavior.

The theoretical base of the Tomorrow's Higher Education model for student development can be described as eclectic. A synthesis of constructs from several hypotheses about the developmental process, including humanism, life stages and developmental tasks, and behaviorism, suggested the structure for the model and operational definitions for each function. Humanistic theories, such as those proposed by Maslow and Rogers, stress that each individual has within himself or herself the potential to become self-actualized or fully functioning and that growth will occur naturally toward that full potential in an environment conducive to such growth. Developmental-stage theories, such as those presented by Erikson, Havighurst, Blocher, Piaget, Kolberg, and Perry, divide growth into life stages for descriptive purposes. Each life stage is characterized by concurrent and interrelated developmental tasks, defined as the major learnings, adjustments, and achievements facing all individuals in a given society which must be mastered for the continuation of optimal development. Behaviorism attempts to describe human developmental processes by linking the response of organisms to stimuli in the environment; therefore, planning and programming with respect to the environmental conditions in which individuals behave and learn is emphasized. Because the functions identified as important for fostering student development are not tied to any one theory, they can be applied from various theoretical frameworks.

The concept of student development presented herein affirms that in post-secondary education cognitive mastery of knowledge should be integrated with the development of persons along such dimensions as cultural awareness, development of a value system, self-awareness, interpersonal skills, and community responsibility. Self-determination and self-direction can best result when both cognitive and affective development are considered essential to the educational missions of post-secondary institutions.

Student Development Dimensions:
Who, When and Where

While the concept of developmental tasks applies equally to infancy and old age, student development focuses upon the developmental tasks encountered by students in post-secondary educational settings, which now must be defined to include late adolescence through adulthood. The focus of student development programming is directed primarily toward students as individuals, in groups, and in organizations, who affiliate themselves as developing learners within any post-secondary institution, whether they be adolescents or mature adults.

If the focus is on students only, however, the goals of student development cannot be fully accomplished. Since every aspect of the higher education environment influences the developmental climate of students, it is imperative that the development of all individuals in the academic community be considered. Therefore, the view of student development in higher education must he broadened to accommodate students, faculty, and staff—all of whom are involved in the process of learning and in the resolution of developmental tasks covering all phases of development.

The developing person is limited neither to a given population nor to a given time frame. The viable student development program takes students wherever they are, developmentally, at the moment and facilitates growth for the future. Since human development is continuous and extends throughout life, institutional responsibilities to students do not end when the academic course of study has been completed. Rather, individuals must be prepared to continue their development in meaningful ways beyond the initial college experience.

Student development is incorporated into and throughout the total institution and, to the extent that students are involved, into the larger community, wherever students involve themselves and whatever they experience is appropriately the concern of the student development program. This implies that the student's milieu is a significant factor in development and includes both place and time not scheduled by the institution.

Student Development Functions and Staff Competencies in the Student Development Model

The T.H.E. Model calls for a move away from a status-based staffing approach toward a competency-based approach. Functions necessary to create a setting for optimal student and institutional growth are *goal setting, assessment,* and *strategies for student development,* three specific strategies being teaching, consultation, and milieu management. The contribution of the student affairs staff to the creation of an environment in which the student's development is facilitated will depend on the extent to which they systematically possess knowledge and expertise in these functions. The process of student development, therefore, as well as the content, represents a primary area of concern for the student affairs professional desiring to become a student development specialist.

I. Goal Setting

Goal setting involves collaboration between students, student affairs professionals, and faculty for determining the specific behaviors toward which the student wishes to strive. The first step in the setting of goals is to state the general outcome expected from the resolution of developmental tasks. The focus here is not on the developmental process but on the expected outcomes of that process. The second step is the determination of specific objectives consistent with the overall goal. Both goals and objectives are based on sound human development theory and value judgments.

For the student affairs professional, goal setting requires skill in teaching students how to establish general goals and write specific objectives. The prime skill is to focus attention on the student and to interact in ways which will assure that the student takes responsibility for the decisions involved in the goal-setting process.

The primary function served by goal setting within the student developmental process is to establish guidelines for planned development. Through self-determined goals, students are more likely to become responsible for their own learning. By establishing short, intermediate, and long-range goals, students can assess progress in development and student affairs professionals can assess the effectiveness of their approaches.

II. Assessment

Assessment is the determination of the student's present developmental level through techniques such as behavior observation, instrumentation, and self-report. Assessment should focus on academic accomplishments and the broad range of human development tasks and related behavior, including intellectual, personal-social, aesthetic, cultural, and even psychomotor dimensions.

For the student affairs professional, assessment requires skill in both test and non-test techniques as well as an understanding of the potentialities and limitations of any data collected. In the context of student development, assessment must be designed with students rather than for or about them; therefore, students should participate directly in the assessment process. Only data which can be of direct assistance in increasing student self-understanding should be collected. Although not all staff members will specialize in assessment activity, all need to be familiar with its importance to students and its place within the student development program.

As a result of the assessment process the student, in collaboration with student affairs staff and faculty, can better formulate specific personal objectives and identify appropriate behavioral change strategies to be utilized in attainment of those objectives. Likewise, through assessment procedures, the professional staff and faculty can better identify the strengths and weaknesses existent in programming and curricular endeavors.

III. Strategies for Student Development

The strategy or strategies for change selected for use by students must be based on goals which have been collaboratively determined and on the student's current level of development as assessed. The strategies include instruction, consultation, and milieu management.

Instruction refers to any interaction between student and teacher in which learning takes place and includes the more formalized teaching function applied to the achievement of a student's developmental objectives. This strategy combines knowledge and practice as the primary means to facilitate student development.

The teaching approach has potential to "academically legitimize" many valuable out-of-class developmental experiences by making them available to all students and by giving them academic recognition. Some developmental goals common to many students, such as learning how to make decisions, lend themselves very well to systematic teaching approaches. Instruction represents a way of accomplishing these legitimate learning goals via a more formalized teacher-learner relationship rather than indirectly. Integration of developmental goals with ongoing academic programs is desirable as well as the establishment of new curricula, when necessary, designed to give academic credit for structured and unstructured experiences that foster affective as well as cognitive growth.

Application of instructional strategies might include

1. Cooperation with or formulation of a department of human relations: student affairs professionals and academic faculty would teach classes concerned with developmental tasks related to human relations, value clarification, personal and group decision-making processes, and human sexuality.

2. Practicum experiences in human development: student affairs professionals would offer practical experience opportunities concerned with development of self-awareness, interpersonal relationships, effective leadership, and decision-making processes—all offered for academic credit.

3. Individual courses: student affairs professionals would offer individualized developmental courses, continuing orientation courses, weekend workshops, paraprofessional helper training, and career planning programs.

Any human developmental task which lends itself to a teaching approach would be considered appropriate for inclusion within the framework of the instruction strategy for student development.

Consultation represents the utilization of knowledge, technology, and expertise toward achieving a desired objective through counseling, modeling, and similar processes. Inherent in this strategy is the concept that the primary means to self-direction is the acceptance of personal responsibility for one's own development. The role of the student development consultant should include influencing program direction and facilitating action; but it must be remembered that the client, whether student or colleague, must control the decisions and be responsible for the consequences resulting from those decisions.

The consultant should be an expert in the process and content of human development to be sought out as a resource aid to facilitate the decision-making process. Advising, counseling, and collaborative skills are used by the consultant to provide direction for individuals, groups, and organizations in order to facilitate student self-responsibility and self-direction. Two types of consultation in creating an environment conducive to student growth and development are (1) consultation with resource persons, such as faculty, student affairs staff, or administrators and (2) direct consultation with individuals, groups, or organizations seeking help. Examples of consultation methods are

1. Consultation agency or student development center: staffed by experts in research, assessment, group behavior, human development, management, and counseling and others who make themselves available to consult with all members of the campus community.

2. Project teams: staff, faculty, and students with necessary competencies join together to complete a specified task such as planning a learning assistance program or a course for residence hall assistants.

3. Professional staff development: program for faculty and staff to increase their capacity to deal effectively with a wide range of students or to facilitate the introduction of developmental task goals into current curriculum offerings of student activities programs.

4. Direct consultation with students: assistance provided to a residence hall community when a hall council or floor government is being established.

In effect, the consultant facilitates development in others through both indirect and direct contact approaches.

Milieu management is a form of intervention that may be more complex than either instruction or consultation. This change strategy calls for marshalling all pertinent resources of the campus community in an attempt to shape the institutional environments in ways which will facilitate desired change and maximize student development. Solid understanding of campus ecology, management theory, social systems, and the behavioral sciences is basic to the implementation of milieu management programs. A major role of the student affairs professional is one of coordinating and integrating activities to establish a developmental milieu designed to facilitate change toward achieving the desired goals of student self-direction, community maintenance, and an enlightened, democratic citizenry. Understanding of human development processes and the influence of the environment upon those processes is essential as is collaboration among the various institutional constituencies if successful implementation is to be achieved. Examples of milieu management include

1. Development of residence community groups based on common interests or goals which the members wish to explore or achieve (e.g., establishment of an intentional democratic community).

2. Establishment of programs designed to offer students opportunity to meet, mingle, and work together with peers on selected campus or community projects.

3. Implementation of a tutorial program or other student self-help programs designed to involve students in the helping processes with others.

Since development is a function of the interaction processes between the individual and the environment, milieu management is an effective and productive way to change behavior through intervention with the total environment as well as directly with the student. The goal of milieu management is to coordinate all facets of an institution so that they contribute to student development.

Tomorrow's Higher Education in Action

Evaluating Student Development Processes and Outcomes

Constant and rigorous evaluation should be an integral part of the Tomorrow's Higher Education student development model. Collection and interpretation of information should be accomplished in two areas: individuals should be helped to monitor their progress toward achievement of personal goals; programs should be evaluated to determine the extent to which they optimize the opportunity for participants to achieve desired outcomes. If individuals systematically assess their movement toward specified goals and objectives, continued development is facilitated. The attainment of predetermined goals by individuals can be assessed for the purpose of evaluating a developmental program, with the quality of the program determined by its influence upon participant outcomes.

Evaluation should begin with an examination of how well the goals and objectives of programs relate to the participant's goals and objectives and how well these are being achieved. To be meaningful, evaluation must be based on preestablished criteria. It is essential, with few exceptions, that both process and outcome criteria be an integral part of the planned student development program. Only as the student and others involved in developmental planning objectively articulate the desired behavioral outcomes and procedures to achieve them can appropriate evaluative measures be employed.

Many suitable techniques (such as instrumentation, self-report, or behavioral observation) which can aid in determination of the degree of progress toward the goal(s), may be utilized. Objective quantitative research and subjective self-survey are acceptable forms of evaluation.

Evaluation offers the best means for clarifying both individual and program objectives and therefore provides a sound basis for modification and future planning. As accountability consciousness grows, the need for evaluating both student development processes and outcomes becomes imperative.

Establishment of Student Development Programs

Applying student development principles in practice does not necessarily call for a total reorganization of the student affairs structure within an institution, although application of the essential elements may lead to new and different associations and alliances within the academic community. There are at least four basic principles which need to be considered when establishing a student development program.

1. Collaboration, both formal and informal in nature, between student affairs staff and faculty, is essential to the success of the student development program.

The collaborative relationship may be quite simple and informal or it may be quite complex and formal. It may involve faculty in residence hall or orientation programs and student affairs professionals in teaching or co-teaching academic courses. Collaboration implies that all facets of the academic community work closely and cooperatively concerning the facilitation of student growth.

2. The degree of commitment of the institution to student development is in direct proportion to the number of collaborative relationships (links) established between the student affairs staff and the faculty.

The more interaction and collaborative planning and programming in existence at a given institution, the more likely the student is to be exposed to and have opportunity for development in a fuller sense. Institutions which are truly committed to the concept of student development will invariably exhibit a climate of mutual cooperation throughout.

3. The flexibility and efficiency of the student affairs staff is increased by the degree in which each staff member has minimal competency in all change processes and excellence in at least one.

Success in any program is largely dependent upon the ability of the individuals involved to implement the necessary means to the desired end. The greater the ability of the institution to mobilize staff and faculty possessing competencies and skills essential to achieving the task at hand, the greater the capacity of the institution to achieve its educational mission. Staff development programs designed to upgrade student development competencies are particularly desirable and necessary to continued success.

4. The success of a student development program is not necessarily dependent on the institution's formal structure. Informal linkages which cross formal structures to achieve common goals may be equally successful.

Freedom to cross over the imaginary lines of demarcation and develop new and different linkages within the academic community usually results in creative student development programming. Facilitating cooperative endeavors of an informal nature which may blossom into comprehensive programs or which can be withdrawn represents a most effective way to utilize human resources. This is not to say that support from the top administrative levels is not extremely important. It does suggest, however, that much of value can result from informal interactions within the institution.

Available institutional resources, then, rather than formal organizational structures, determine the most desirable framework with which to structure the student development program. As student affairs professionals, faculty, and students work in mutually cooperative ways; and as they develop skills in all the student development functions, the formal lines between members of the academic community begin to evaporate and more of a team approach tends to emerge wherein the full staff represent a resource pool for student development programming. As this begins to occur, a more fully coordinated and effective program for student development will result.

Summary

The goal of the Tomorrow's Higher Education Project is to reconceptualize student affairs work in a way that will provide a measure of creative input from the student affairs profession toward the shaping of post-secondary education for the future. Student development must be the keystone of future programs, and Phase II of T.H.E. presents a viable operational model to incorporate student development into and throughout the institution.

The competencies necessary to create a setting for optimal student growth are goal setting, assessment, and three strategies for student development—instruction, consultation, and milieu management. The success of the student development program is based on the extent to which there is collaboration, both formal and informal, between students, student affairs staff, and faculty.

As members of the academic community both learn to understand the stages of development and related developmental tasks through which those in post-secondary institutions are passing and develop competency in the functions necessary to implement the student development model, a learning environment which maximizes the integration of the student's cognitive development with the development of the whole personality can be created.

The Student Personnel Point of View

AMERICAN COUNCIL ON EDUCATION (1937)

Foreword

In January 1925 the Division of Anthropology of the National Research Council sponsored a meeting in Washington, D.C., of representatives of fourteen institutions of higher education to discuss the problems of vocational guidance in college. Out of this conference developed the Intercollegiate Council of Personnel Methods which undertook to investigate ways and means of making available to educational institutions knowledge concerning students as individuals. In 1926 this group requested the American Council on Education to sponsor a study of personnel practices in colleges and universities. As a result of this request the Council established the Committee on Personnel Methods with H. E. Hawkes as chairman.

The initial undertaking of the Committee on Personnel Methods was a survey by L. B. Hopkins to determine what a number of institutions were then doing to assist the students to develop as individuals. The publication of the Hopkins report in *The Educational Record* of October 1926 focused national attention upon the importance of this area and upon the need for further research. During the next several years, the Committee on Personnel Methods, working through a number of subcommittees, inaugurated studies on certain aspects of the total student personnel problem. As a result of these studies, certain tools were prepared including the cumulative record cards, personality rating scales, and comparable achievement tests, which have influenced the improvement of student personnel services.

The American Council on Education in 1936 received the report of the Committee on Review of the Testing Movement[1] which recommended the establishment of a Committee on Measurement and Guidance to coordinate activities of the Council in the preparation of measurement materials. As a result of this recommendation, the Council discharged the Committee on Personnel Methods and assigned its measurement functions to the new committee. The Council, however, recognized the need for further investigation of certain fundamental problems related to the clarification of so-called personnel work, the intelligent use of available tools, and the development of additional techniques and processes. Consequently, the Executive Committee authorized the calling of a conference to discuss the possible contribution of the Council in this area.

The following individuals met in Washington, D.C., on April 16 and 17, 1937, and unanimously adopted the following report. The group voted to refer the report to the Committee on Problems and Plans in Education of the American Council on Education.

Thyrsa Amos	Burton P. Fowler	D. G. Paterson
F. F. Bradshaw	D. H. Gardner	C. Gilbert Wrenn
D. S. Bridgman	H. E. Hawkes	
A. J. Brumbaugh	L. B. Hopkins	C. S. Marsh
W H. Cowley	F. J. Kelly	D. J. Shank
A. B. Crawford	Edwin A. Lee	G. F. Zook
Edward C. Elliott	Esther Lloyd-Jones	

The Committee on Problems and Plans in Education at its meeting on May 6, 1937, approved the report of the conference and recommended to the Executive Committee of the Council that a Committee on Student Personnel Work be established with instructions to propose a program of action in line with the general statement of the conference. The Executive Committee authorized the organization of the new committee at its last meeting.

George F. Zook
President

June 1937

Philosophy

One of the basic purposes of higher education is the preservation, transmission, and enrichment of the important elements of culture—the product of scholarship, research, creative imagination, and human experience. It is the task of colleges and universities so to vitalize this and other educational purposes as to assist the student in developing to the limits of his potentialities and in making his contribution to the betterment of society.

This philosophy imposes upon educational institutions the obligation to consider the student as a whole—his intellectual capacity and achievement, his emotional make-up, his physical condition, his social relationships, his vocational aptitudes and skills, his moral and religious values, his economic resources, his aesthetic appreciations. It puts emphasis, in brief, upon the development of the student as a person rather than upon his intellectual training alone.

A long and honorable history stands behind this point of view. Until the last three decades of the nineteenth century interest in the whole student dominated the thinking of the great majority of the leaders and faculty members of American colleges. The impact of a number of social forces upon American society following the Civil War, however, directed the interest of most of the strong personalities of our colleges and universities away from the needs of the individual student to an emphasis, through scientific research, upon the extension of the boundaries of knowledge. The pressures upon faculty members to contribute to this growth of knowledge shifted the direction of their thinking to a preoccupation with subject matter and to a neglect of the student as an individual. As a result of this change of emphasis, administrators recognized the need of appointing a new type of educational officer to take over the more intimate responsibilities which faculty members had originally included among their duties. At the same time a number of new educational functions arose as the result of the growing complexity of modern life, the development of scientific techniques, the expansion of the size of student bodies, and the extension of the range of educational objectives.

These officers were appointed first to relieve administrators and faculties of problems of discipline; but their responsibilities grew with considerable rapidity to include a large number of other duties: educational counseling, vocational counseling, the administration of loans and scholarship funds, part-time employment, graduate placement, student health, extra-curricular activities, social programs, and a number of others. The officers undertaking responsibility for these educational functions are known by many names, but during the past two decades they have come, as a group, to be called personnel officers.

A number of terms are in general use in colleges and universities related to the philosophy of education which we have outlined. Illustrative of these terms are "guidance," "counseling," "advisory," and "personnel." Of these, we believe the term "personnel"—prefaced by "student"—to be the least objectionable. Rather than attempt a specific definition of "student personnel" as it is combined with such nouns as "work," "service," "administration," "research," etc., we offer the term, "the student personnel point of view" as indicative of the total philosophy embodied in the foregoing discussion. The functions which implement this point of view—indicated in the next section—may be designated as "student personnel services." Similarly, the performance of these functions may be designated "student personnel work."

This background and discussion of terminology we believe to be important. Personnel work is not new. Personnel officers have been appointed throughout the colleges and universities of the country to undertake a number of educational responsibilities which were once entirely assumed by teaching members of faculty. They have also, because of the expansion of educational functions, developed a number of student personnel services which have but recently been stressed. The philosophy behind their work, however, is as old as education itself.

I. Student Personnel Services

This philosophy implies that in addition to instruction and business management adapted to the needs of the individual student, an effective educational program includes—in one form or another—the following services adapted to the specific aims and objectives of each college and university:

1. Interpreting institutional objectives and opportunities to prospective students and their parents and to workers in secondary education.

2. Selecting and admitting students, in cooperation with secondary schools.

3. Orienting the student to his educational environment.

4. Providing a diagnostic service to help the student discover his abilities, aptitudes, and objectives.

5. Assisting the student throughout his college residence to determine upon his courses of instruction in light of his past achievements, vocational and personal interests, and diagnostic findings.

6. Enlisting the active cooperation of the family of the student in the interest of his educational accomplishment.

7. Assisting the student to reach his maximum effectiveness through clarification of his purposes, improvement of study methods, speech habits, personal appearance, manners, etc., and through progression in religious, emotional, social development, and other non-academic personal and group relationships.

8. Assisting the student to clarify his occupational aims and his educational plans in relation to them.

9. Determining the physical and mental health status of the student, providing appropriate remedial health measures, supervising the health of students, and controlling environmental health factors.

10. Providing and supervising an adequate housing program for students.

11. Providing and supervising an adequate food service for students.

12. Supervising, evaluating, and developing the extra-curricular activities of students.

13. Supervising, evaluating, and developing the social life and interests of students.

14. Supervising, evaluating, and developing the religious life and interests of students.

15. Assembling and making available information to be used in improvement of instruction and in making the curriculum more flexible.

16. Coordinating the financial aid and part-time employment of students, and assisting the student who needs it to obtain such help.

17. Keeping a cumulative record of information about the student and making it available to the proper persons.

18. Administering student discipline to the end that the individual will be strengthened, and the welfare of the group preserved.

19. Maintaining student group morale by evaluating, understanding, and developing student mores.

20. Assisting the student to find appropriate employment when he leaves the institution.

21. Articulating college and vocational experience.

22. Keeping the student continuously and adequately informed of the educational opportunities and services available to him.

23. Carrying on studies designed to evaluate and improve these functions and services.

Coordination

The effective organization and functioning of student personnel work requires that the educational administrators at all times (1) regard student personnel work as a major concern, involving the cooperative effort of all members of the teaching and administrative staff and the student body; and (2) interpret student personnel work as dealing with the individual student's total characteristics and experiences rather than with separate and distinct aspects of his personality or performance.

It should be noted that effective personnel work may be formally organized or may exist without direction or organization, and that frequently the informal type evidences a personnel point of view in an institution. In either case the personnel point of view is most likely to permeate an entire staff when it is the result of an indigenous development in the institution. Imposition of personnel theories and practices from above or from outside is likely to result in pseudo-personnel work, with probable antagonism developing therefrom. However, it is obvious that coordination of student personnel work is urgently needed. We suggest several varieties of such needed coordination.

I. Coordination within Individual Institutions

The student personnel functions set forth earlier in this report should be coordinated within each educational institution. Existing conditions emphasize the need for such coordination. All personnel workers within an institution should cooperate with one another in order to avoid duplications of effort and in order to develop student personnel work evenly. The plan of coordination and its administration will, of course, vary with institutions of different types.

II. Coordination between Instruction and Student Personnel Work

Instruction is most effective when the instructor regards his classes both as separate individuals and as members of a group. Such instruction aims to achieve in every student a maximum performance in terms of that student's potentialities and the conditions under which he works. Ideally each instructor should possess all the information necessary for such individualization. Actually such ideal conditions do not exist. Therefore a program of coordination becomes necessary which provides for the instructor appropriate information whenever such information relates to effective instruction.

An instructor may perform functions in the realms both of instruction and student personnel work. Furthermore, instruction itself involves far more than the giving of information on the part of the teacher and its acceptance by the student. Instructors should be encouraged to contribute regularly to student personnel records such anecdotal information concerning students as is significant from the personnel point of view. Instructors should be encouraged to call to the attention of personnel workers any students in their courses who could profit by personnel services.

Certain problems involving research are common to instruction and student personnel work. Any investigation which has for its purpose the improvement of instruction is at the same time a research which improves personnel procedures. Similarly, the results of any studies, the aim of which is to improve personnel procedures, should be disseminated throughout the instructional staff. In both cases wherever possible such projects should be carried on as cooperative ventures.

III. Coordination between the Business Administration and Student Personnel Work

In all financial or business matters having to do with student activities or student problems, either in terms of individuals or groups of individuals, coordination and correlation must exist between business administration and student personnel work. Examples of such matters are:

Student loans
Dormitories
Dining halls
Scholarships
Student organizations
Athletic management
Deferred payments of fees
Student participation in business management of institution.

IV. Coordination of Personnel Work between Institutions of Secondary and Higher Education

There is a pressing need for further coordination between secondary schools and institutions of higher education. Since a special need exists for coordination between student personnel work in colleges and in secondary schools, copies of the data sent to the admissions department should be available to other college personnel officers. This would be a desirable place to begin coordination. The selection of students, where conditions will permit, should be based upon total personnel records as well as grades in courses. Examples of items in such a record are:

Ability in critical thinking
Ability to cooperate
Physical and mental health
Aesthetic appreciation
Test records such as aptitude tests, reading ability, etc.
Vocational objective
Summarized predictions of college performance.

Coordination should also result in more effective interchange of information, problems, and techniques between the personnel units of colleges and secondary schools. Competent individuals should be available whenever secondary schools desire a presentation, either to students or faculty, of college opportunities and requirements.

Problems of research which require coordination between secondary schools and colleges reside in such areas as:

a. Transfer from high school to college with particular reference to the last year in high school and the first year in college.

b. The basis upon which high schools guide toward college.

c. The basis upon which colleges select entrants.

d. Freshman failures.

e. Variations in the total requirements of different types of colleges; for example, engineering, dentistry, liberal arts, teacher training, etc.

f. Existing types of coordination between secondary schools and colleges; for example, high school visitors, examination systems, coordinating committees, experimental investigations, etc.

V. Coordination among National Personnel Associations

During the past two decades a number of associations of various types of student personnel workers have come into existence. These associations perform valuable services in furthering personnel work and in bringing workers in the field into closer professional and personal contact. We believe that the point of view for which all personnel people stand and the services which they render would be greatly enhanced were closer coordination developed between these associations. Hereinafter we propose that the American Council on Education establish or sponsor a committee on student personnel work in colleges and universities. We recommend that this committee, as one of its functions, undertake to bring about closer relationships between these associations.

VI. Coordination of Student Personnel Work with After-College Adjustment

Effective student personnel work should include as its culminating activity adequate provision for induction of students into after-college life.

The satisfactory adjustment of graduates to occupation life constitutes one important basis for evaluation of an institution's educational effectiveness, since it stimulates a continual re-examination of educational procedures and the effect of those procedures upon the men and women who make up the student body of the college. Moreover, coordination between college and occupational life rests essentially upon more complete information covering the various types of work into which college graduates go.

This conference also wishes to emphasize the necessity for conceiving of after-college adjustment as comprehending the total living of college graduates, including not only their occupational success but their active concern with the social, recreational, and cultural interests of the community. Such concern implies their willingness to assume those individual and social responsibilities which are essential to the common good.

Future Development

Student personnel work is developing with some rapidity throughout the country. Annually a large number of institutions undertake for the first time additional student personnel functions or they further develop services already established. At the same time new methods of organizing student personnel services are coming into prominence; the literature of the field is expanding voluminously; and problems in need of careful investigation become more numerous every year.

Because of these and other considerations a need for national leadership in student personnel work is becoming continuously more obvious. If the expansion and development that the colleges and universities of the country are experiencing in the student personnel field is to be as desirable and effective as it should be, some national agency needs to be available to assist administrators, faculty members, and student personnel officers in their developmental efforts. No such national agency now exists, and a careful canvassing of the student personnel associations which have grown up brings us to the unanimous conclusion that no one of them is able to become that national agency.

We, therefore, propose that the American Council on Education establish or sponsor a committee on student personnel work in American colleges and universities. This committee should, in our judgment, undertake the following activities:

I. National Survey of Student Personnel Work

This survey should be conducted throughout the country after the pattern of the one undertaken by L. B. Hopkins for the American Council on Education in 1926. Such a study would require the services of but one individual who would visit five or six institutions in each of half a dozen institutional categories. The undertaking would result in an overview rather than a detailed study, and its publication would satisfy the growing demand for current authoritative information about the student personnel field. It would be built around a check list of the functions we have listed. The Hopkins survey had such great influence that we believe an up-to-date and analogous study published in concise form would be of immediate interest and value to administrators and faculty members throughout the country.

II. Interpretation of the Problems of College Students

A short volume with some such title as "The College Student and His Problems" should be written and published. The purpose of this volume would be to inform administrators, faculty members, and the general public of the complex human problems that are involved in education. Stressing scholarship and intellectual development, educators frequently take for granted or actually over-look the philosophy which we have hereinbefore called the student personnel point of view. The preparation and publication of the volume which we propose would, we believe, do much to bring this philosophy to the attention of all individuals concerned with higher education. It would, moreover, bring this philosophy to their attention in terms of the actual experiences of students rather than through an abstract discussion.

III. Handbooks on Student Personnel Functions

A series of handbooks on particular student personnel functions should be written and published. The survey proposed above would provide a panoramic picture of the entire field. The handbooks that we are suggesting would furnish detailed information about specific personnel functions. Data for these handbooks would come from two general sources: first, from the information gathered by the surveyor on the detailed operation of specific personnel functions in the institutions he visits and, second, from the literature. Each handbook would stress the best practices developed in the handling of each function. The work of writing each handbook should be under the direction of a committee of three. This committee should include an active worker in the special field under discussion and a representative of the appropriate national personnel organization.

IV. Research

Obviously, student personnel services will never develop as they should unless extensive and careful research is undertaken. We, therefore, urge that the facilitation and direction of research be considered an essential responsibility of the committee. In this field we envisage the committee as important in two directions: first, in encouraging other agencies to undertake investigations, and, second, in carrying on several investigations on its own. We list below projects of both types.

Research by Other Agencies

We propose that the Committee on Measurement and Guidance of the American Council on Education be requested to consider the desirability of the following four investigations:

1. *Aptitude testing.* The investigation of aptitudes on a national scale comparable to the work undertaken by the Cooperative Test Service but in the field of differential vocational as well as educational aptitudes.

2. *Social development.* The development of instruments for measuring social adjust-ment and social maturity.

3. *Diagnostic techniques.* The study of the field of usefulness of existing diagnostic instruments and the development of new instruments.

4. *Scholastic aptitude test scale.* Bringing together on a comparable scale the norms of various widely-used scholastic aptitude tests.

We also propose that the National Occupational Conference be requested to consider the desirability of carrying forward the following work:

1. *Occupational information.* Gathering and publishing occupational information for college students with particular emphasis upon periodic census data and trends.

2. *Traits needed in occupations.* Working with the Committee on Measurement and Guidance in the study of human traits significant for various occupations, particularly those which college students enter.

Research by the Committee on Student Personnel Work

A number of research projects need to be undertaken in the immediate future, responsibility for which no existing agencies seem able to assume. We, therefore, propose that the committee secure support for the following four studies:

1. *Student out-of-class life.* College students spend the majority of their time outside the classrooms and laboratories. We have, however, no significant data as to the activities in which they engage. In order to understand the educational importance of their activities we propose that on a score of campuses throughout the country data be collected. Incidentally, this research would be relatively inexpensive since on every campus individuals may be found to do the work without compensation.

2. *Faculty-student out-of-class relationships.* Much is said frequently of the place that faculty members have in student personnel work. We have, however, few facts and we propose that data should be gathered from a number of institutions following much the same technique as proposed in study "1" above.

3. *Financial aid to students.* Large sums of money are available in many institutions for scholarships and loans. In addition the National Youth Administration has been spending many millions during the past three years to help students to stay in college. The problem of who should be helped and how much is growing more important every year. We propose that this problem in its wide ramifications might well be studied. Perhaps funds for much of this work could be secured from the National Youth Administration.

4. *Follow-up study of college students.* Every year over a hundred thousand students graduate from our colleges. What happens to them and what effect their college work has had upon their vocational and personal adjustments we can only guess. We, therefore, propose that the committee develop a method for making follow-up studies and that this method be made available to interested institutions.

V. Advisory Service to Colleges and Universities

An advisory service to colleges and universities interested in the improvement of student personnel work should be developed. While the proposed survey is being undertaken and while the suggested handbooks are being written, the committee will inevitably have addressed to it a number of inquiries about problems within its field of interest. These inquiries cannot be answered authoritatively until these two ventures are finished, but meanwhile the committee should assume responsibility for directing such correspondents to the individuals best qualified to assist them. When the survey is finished, and the handbooks available, however, we propose that the committee actively promote the best student personnel practices which its work has brought to light.

Note

1. *The Testing Movement,* American Council on Education Studies, Series I, Vol. I, No. 1 (February 1937).

The Student Personnel Point of View (1949)

E. G. Williamson, Chairman

Willard W. Blaesser

Helen D. Bragdon

William S. Carlson

W. H. Cowley

D. D. Feder

Helen G. Fisk

Forrest H. Kirkpatrick

Esther Lloyd-Jones

T. R. McConnell

Thornton W. Merriam

Donald J. Shank

I. Philosophy and Objectives

The central purpose of higher education is the preservation, transmittal, and enrichment of culture by means of instruction, scholarly work, and scientific research. During the past few decades experience has pointed up the desirability of broadening this purpose to embrace additional emphasis and objectives. Among these new goals, three stand out:

1. Education for a fuller realization of democracy in every phase of living;

2. Education directly and explicitly for international understanding and cooperation;

3. Education for the application of creative imagination and trained intelligence to the solution of social problems and to the administration of publications.[1]

Although these added goals aim essentially at societal growth, they affect positively the education and development of each individual student. The development of students as whole persons interacting in social situations is the central concern of student personnel work and of other agencies of education. This emphasis in contemporary education is the essential part of the student personnel point of view.

The student personnel point of view encompasses the student as a whole. The concept of education is broadened to include attention to the student's well rounded development—physically, socially, emotionally and spiritually, as well as intellectually. The student is thought of as a responsible participant in his own development and not as a passive recipient of an imprinted economic, political, or religious doctrine, or vocational skill. As a responsible participant in the societal processes of our American democracy, his full and balanced maturity is viewed as a major end goal of education as well, a necessary means to the fullest development of his fellow citizens. From the personnel point of view any lesser goal falls short of the desired objective of democratic educational processes, and is a real drain and strain upon the self-realization of other developing individuals in our society.

The realization of this objective—the full maturing of each student—cannot be attained without interest in and integrated efforts toward the development of each and every facet of his personality and potentialities. His deepening understanding of his world is not sacrificed to his emotional maturing. His physical well-being does not become a limited end in itself. His maturing sense of values, social and spiritual, is not sacrificed to his understanding of the world of man and nature. His need for developing a sound philosophy of life to serve as the norm for his actions now and in adult life is not neglected in the college's emphasis on his need for intellectual and professional competence. Rather are all known aspects of the personality of each student viewed by the educator and personnel worker as an integrated whole—as a human personality living, working, and growing in a democratic society of other human personalities.

A long and honorable history stands behind this point of view. From the Middle Ages until the beginning of the nineteenth century, European higher education and its American offshoots gave as much attention to the social, moral, and religious development of students as to their intellectual growth. But the rise of the modern research-centered German university early in the nineteenth century led to the abandonment of this personal concern for students and centered on an intellectualistic concern. Influenced by German models, American educators steered American higher education toward intellectualism.

Prosecution of scientific research and the stimulation of the intellectual development of students became the dominant emphases in American higher education. The earlier concern of Colonial educators for the spiritual, social, and personal development of students was shunted aside for more than a half century in most universities and in some colleges. At the turn of the present century certain great social forces matured and converged to shift attention back to the student's broad development in all aspects of his personality.

The student personnel movement developed during the early twentieth century in part as a protest against German-born intellectualism and also as the result of the findings of the psychology of individual differences during the second decade of the present century. Its evolution was stimulated by the huge growth of American colleges and universities following the First World War. With hordes invading institutions of higher education, colleges sought means to maintain some personal and individual relationship with students.

Present-Day Objectives

The student personnel movement constitutes one of the most important efforts of American educators to treat the college and university students as individuals, rather than as entries in an impersonal roster. The movement, at the same time, expresses awareness of the significance of student group life in its manifold expressions from student residence to student mores, from problems of admission to problems of job placement. It has developed as the division of college and university administration concerned with students individually and students as groups. In a real sense this part of modern higher education is an individualized application of the research and clinical findings of modern psychology, sociology, cultural anthropology, and education to the task of aiding students to develop fully in the college environment.

The specific aspects of the student personnel program stemming from the above point of view will be discussed in a later section. In addition, however, certain fundamental issues in education are affected by the application of the personnel point of view.

The optimum development of the individual necessitates the recognition by teachers and administrators, as well as by professional personnel workers, of individual differences in backgrounds, abilities, interests, and goals. In the light of such individual variations each institution should define its educational purposes and then select its students in terms of these purposes. This concept of development demands flexibility in methods of teaching and in the shaping of content to fit the individual differences found in students. It also requires integration of various aspects of the curriculum.

The individual's full and balanced development involves the acquisition of the pattern of knowledge, skills, and attitudes consistent with his abilities, aptitudes, and interests. The range of acquisition is a broad one. Through his college experiences he should acquire an appreciation of cultural values, the ability to adapt to changing social conditions, motivation to seek and to create desirable social changes, emotional control to direct his activities, moral and ethical values for himself and for his community, standards and habits of personal physical well-being, and the ability to choose a vocation which makes maximum use of his talents and enables him to make appropriate contributions to his society.

But such broad-gauge development of the individual should in no sense be considered as a sufficient and complete goal in itself. It is axiomatic today that no man lives in a social vacuum. Rather individual development is conditioned by the kind of society in which a person lives, and by the quality of interpersonal and group relationships which operate around him. He is constantly affecting society and society is constantly shaping him. These relationships constitute the cultural patterns with which higher education must be concerned in its efforts to stimulate and guide the development of each of its students.

The cultural patterns of America have been, and will continue to be, deeply affected by the emergence of the United States as a world power. With the nation's new status in world affairs, the preservation of basic freedoms and responsibilities at home becomes increasingly important. Our way of life depends upon a renewed faith in, and extensive use of, democratic methods, upon the development of more citizens able to assume responsibilities in matters of social concern, and upon the active participation of millions of men and women in the enterprise of social improvement.

Such a social philosophy as that outlined above thrust upon the college an urgent responsibility for providing experiences which develop in its students a firm and enlightened belief in democracy, a matured understanding of its problems and methods, and a deep sense of responsibility for individual and collective action to achieve its goals. Both classroom and out-of-class activities of the college should be related to these ends, and students' organizations should be incorporated in the institution's total educational program. In both the curricular and the co-curricular program of the college the dynamic forces of society should be skillfully organized for the use of their learning values in furthering the development of students.

As educators, our attention should be focused upon the social forces of the institution itself, which also provide learning experiences for the student. For example, the relationships among the various groups on the campus affect such social development. If faculty and students and faculty and administration work closely together in achieving common objectives, curricular and co-curricular, the learning of socially desirable processes is thereby enhanced.

The college or university which accepts these broad responsibilities for aiding in the optimum development of the individual in his relations to society will need to evaluate carefully and periodically its curricular offerings, its method of instruction, and all other resources for assisting the individual to reach his personal goals. Among its important resources, it also will need to provide and strengthen the type of services, as outlined in the next section, encompassed within the field of student personnel work.

II. Student Needs and Personnel Services

During their college years, students have opportunities for intensive classroom learning supplemented by many of the major elements of community living. Students live, work, make friends, have fun, make financial ends meet—all within the community of scholars. Since colleges seek to assist students to achieve optimum development of powers and usefulness, a comprehensive and explicit plan and program embracing many personnel services are necessary for this undertaking. The essential parts of such a plan and program are outlined in the following sections.

The student personnel point of view holds that the major responsibility for a student's growth in personal and social wisdom rests with the student himself. Necessarily, however, his development is conditioned by many factors. It is influenced by the background, the abilities, attitudes, and expectancies that he brings with him to college, by his college classroom experiences, and by his reactions to these experiences. A student's growth in personal and social wisdom will also be conditioned by the extent to which the following conditions are attained:

The student achieves orientation to his college environment. Individuals are freer to learn, are under less strain, suffer less confusion, and have more consistent and favorable self-concepts if they feel at home and oriented in relation to their environment. The personnel worker attempts to help students feel at home in their college environment through:

1. Interpreting institutional objectives and opportunities to prospective students, to their parents, and to high school faculties;

2. Selecting students who seem, after study, to be able to achieve in relation to the college offerings and requirements;

3. Orienting students to the many phases of their college lives through a carefully designed program that involves such methods and experiences as personnel records, tests, group instruction, counseling, and group life.

The student succeeds in his studies. The college or university has a primary responsibility in selecting for admission students who have the basic qualities of intelligence and aptitudes necessary for success in a given institution. However, many otherwise able students fail, or do not achieve up to maximum capacity, because they lack proficiency or personal motivation for the tasks set by the college, because of deficiency in reading or study skills, because they do not budget their time properly, have emotional conflicts resulting from family or other pressures, have generally immature attitudes, are not wisely counseled in relation to curricular choices, or because of a number of other factors. In order that each student may develop effective work habits and thereby achieve at his optimum potential, the college or university should provide services through which the student may acquire the skills and techniques for efficient utilization of his ability. In addition to the contribution of counseling in removing blockages from his path toward good achievement, the student may also need remedial reading and speech services, training in effective study habits, remediation of physical conditions, counseling concerning his personal motivations, and similar related services.

The student finds satisfactory living facilities. Comfortable and congenial living arrangements contribute to the peace of mind and efficiency of the student. If effectively organized and supervised, the facilities that provide for food and shelter can also contribute to his social development and to his adjustments to group opportunities and restraints.

The student achieves a sense of belonging to the college. To a large extent the social adjustment of an individual consists of finding a role in relation to others which will make him feel valued, will contribute to his feeling of self-worth, and will contribute to a feeling of kinship with an increasing number of persons. The student personnel program will help him achieve these goals through:

1. Stimulating the development of many small groups;

2. Fostering the development of a program of student-initiated activities;

3. Encouraging the development of a diversified social program;

4. Developing opportunities for participation in college-community cooperative activities;

5. Fostering teacher-student intellectual and social relationships outside of the classroom.

The student learns balanced use of his physical capacities. It is not enough to conceive of a health service as an agency only for the treatment of illness in order to keep the student operating in the classroom at regular maximum efficiency. To be broadly effective, the health program should also aggressively promote a program of health education designed to equip each student with self-understanding and self-acceptance at his optimum personal level of physical competence. The adjustment of the individual to his physical potentialities as well as to his irremediable limitations is a basic element in his full development of personality.

The student progressively understands himself. This is the process of self-discovery and rediscovery which, progressively over a period of time, must unfold for the student in terms of his individual readiness for it. Through a rich program of experiences and skillful counseling, the student may acquire an understanding of himself, his abilities, interests, motivations, and limitations. With such understanding the student becomes ready to make long-range life plans; he acquires the understandings and skills necessary to cope with life problems; he learns to face and solve his own personal problems; he grows personally and, in the process, makes constructive social contribution. To aid in this development, the college or university provides:

1. Adequate services for testing and appraisal;

2. Skilled counselors trained in the art of stimulating self-understanding without directing decisions;

3. Useful records available for study so that the student may inform himself of his present status and be apprised of whatever growth and development he has thus far achieved;

4. Other services which will help the student acquire such specialized knowledge as the individual should have concerning himself in order to make reasoned and reasonable choices and decisions.

The student understands and uses his emotions. As mainsprings of action, emotions either may lead to disorganized and random behavior or to concerted, directed, worthwhile accomplishment. Directed emotions may enrich and strengthen action which is otherwise sterile and terminal. A human being is a creature of emotions as well as intellect. Effective personal counseling will help the student to understand and use his emotional powers for maximum, directed action. Without such understanding and self-direction the student may soon find himself not only ineffective, but also socially inept and unacceptable. The counseling service, psychiatric services, and organized group activities are among the parts of the student personnel services which may assist the student in this area of achievement.

The student develops lively and significant interests. Many aspects of personality directly related to attractiveness, alertness, and forcefulness are conditioned by the number and depth of interests an individual is able to cultivate. The effective college will recognize this by:

1. Helping the student to discover his basic interests; and,

2. Fostering a program of recreational and discussional activities that is diversified.

The student achieves understanding and control of his financial resources. Learning how to live within his income, how to increase that income, how to find financial aids that are available are part of an understanding of the student's economic life. Such an understanding of money-values must be achieved in balanced relationships to physical energy, curricular, and social demands.

Counseling students on financial matters and administering financial aids in such a way as to help the most worthy and most needy are important parts of the student personnel program.

The student progresses toward appropriate vocational goals. Some students enroll in college with a definite plan of preparation for a career. Others will modify their plans as they acquire new interests or gain clearer understanding of their own capacities and of requirements for certain occupations in relation to the needs of society. But many men and women who come to college do so without any plans or understanding of themselves in relation to the world of work. The college has a responsibility to see that these students have access to accurate, usable information about opportunities, requirements, and training for various occupations appropriate to their possible levels of vocational preparation. Vocational counseling given on a basis of insight, information, and vision can help students to relate their future work to their life goals. When conducted with social imagination, such counseling can help to develop these leaders who will pioneer in new professions and in the extension of needed services for the country's welfare.

The student develops individuality and responsibility. Progressive emancipation from the restrictions of childhood is a major challenge to every adolescent. Reveling in his new found freedoms, for which he may not yet be prepared by adequate self-discipline, the college student may find himself in conflict with accepted social patterns and standards. Other students, whose domination by their families may extend to the college campus, may voice their rebellion in actions offensive to their fellow-students or embarrassing to the college family to which they now belong. In such situations, preventive therapy may be accomplished by enlisting parental cooperation in counseling in such personal problems when they are discovered and diagnosed. When the need for social discipline does arise, the college should approach the problem as a special phase of counseling in the development of self-responsibility for behavior rather than in a spirit of punishment of misbehavior.

The student discovers ethical and spiritual meaning in life. For many students the introduction to scientific understandings and meanings in the classroom may necessitate a drastic reorientation of religious ideology at a new level of objectivity. The time-honored teachings of organized religion may lose their effectiveness both as explanatory and guiding principles. The resultant disturbance may have deep and far-reaching ramifications into personal as well as family, and even broader social, conflicts. In his new search for values which are worthy of personal allegiance in a time of social conflict, the student needs mature guidance. The religious counselor and the religious-activities program with a broad social reference may assist the student in developing an understanding of proper concepts of behavior, ethical standards, and spiritual values consistent with his broadened horizons resulting from newly acquired scientific and technical knowledge.

The student learns to live with others. The maintenance of individual integrity within a framework of cooperative living and working with others in a spirit of mutual service is the highest expression of democracy. By intelligent followership as well as by permissive leadership the student prepares himself for his social obligations beyond the college. By means of special-interest groups, student government, dormitory and house councils, and other guided group activities, the student personnel program can provide opportunities for developing in the student his capacities for both leadership and followership. The counseling service will also use such activities as may be appropriate for individual therapy and development as the needs may be revealed through suitable diagnostic procedures.

The student progresses toward satisfying and socially acceptable sexual adjustments. During the years when young people are in college, they are normally deeply, although perhaps covertly, concerned with finding congenial marriage partners. This concern may produce anxieties which eventuate in behavior that may be either acceptable or unacceptable to society, and satisfying or unsatisfying to the individuals. Since marriage adjustment is basic to family stability, and since the family is our most important social institution, colleges should help students to effect satisfying, socially acceptable, and ethically sound sexual adjustments by (1) encouraging the development of a rich and diversified social and recreational program, (2) providing counseling on relationship and marriage problems.

The student prepares for satisfying, constructive post-college activity. For most students the activities of postcollege years will be a combination of the practice of a profession, progression in an occupation, marriage and family life, and service as a community and world citizen.

Personnel services of the college appropriate to these attainments may include job placement, information about jobs, internships, graduate training programs, or opportunities for volunteer service. Some colleges include also some periodic follow-up contacts to determine the success of their graduates.

Elements of a Student Personnel Program

The achievement of the foregoing objectives requires the cooperative and integrated functioning of classroom and extra-class activities with the growth and development of the student as the focal point of all that is implied in the educational process. To be sure, not every student will need or make use of all the student personnel services just as, by the same token, not every student studies courses in every academic department. But the college should make optimum provision for the development of the individual and his place in society through its provisions for:

1. The process of admissions, not as a credit-counting service, but rather as a first step in the counseling procedure designed to interpret the institution to the student, his family, and his high school teachers in terms of its requirements for success, its services, and its ability to satisfy his educational and personal needs.

2. The keeping of personnel records and their use in the improved understanding of, and service to, the individual student as he has contact not only with the classroom, but also in all phases of his college or university life.

3. The service to the student of trained, sympathetic counselors to assist him in thinking through his education, vocational, and personal adjustment problems. Such a service should be so designed as to be in effect a cohesive agency drawing together all the institution's resources in the process of facilitating the student's efforts to achieve the objectives of higher education. This service will have access, either through direct association or as a supplementary service, to psychological testing and other special diagnostic services as may be necessary to achieve better and more objective appraisal and understanding of the individual. Resources for adequate vocational information as may be needed by the student in the process of his orientation should be closely correlated with the counseling program. Special attention should be given to the educational importance of supplementing the efforts of counseling specialists by the use of carefully selected, specially trained faculty members serving as advisers and counselors.

4. Physical and mental health services whose orientation is not only the treatment of illness, but also, and even primarily, an educational program of preventive medicine and personal-hygiene counseling.

5. Remedial services in the areas of speech, reading, and study habits, recognizing that the presence of defects in these areas may seriously impede the functioning of many able students and also restrict the contributions which may be made by otherwise adequate personalities.

6. Supervision and integration of housing and food services to the end that they shall not only provide for the physical comforts of students, but also shall contribute positively to education in group living and social graces.

7. A program of activities designed to induct the student into his new life and environment as a member of the college or university family.

8. The encouragement and supervision of significant group activities arising from the natural interest of students.

9. A program of recreational activities designed to promote lifetime interests and skills appropriate to the individual student.

10. The treatment of discipline as an educational function designed to modify personal behavior patterns and to substitute socially acceptable attitudes for those which have precipitated unacceptable behavior.

11. Financial aid to worthy students, not as a dole, but as an educational experience in personal budgeting and responsibility.

12. Opportunities for self-help through part-time and summer employment, geared as nearly as possible to the defined vocational objectives of the student.

13. Assistance to the student in finding appropriate employment after leaving college and subsequently assisting alumni in further professional development.

14. The proper induction, orientation, and counseling of students from abroad.

15. The enrichment of college and postcollege life through a well-integrated program of religious activities, including interfaith programs and individual religious counseling.

16. Counseling for married students and for those contemplating marriage to prepare them for broadening family and social responsibilities.

17. A continuing program of evaluation of student personnel services and of the educational program to insure the achievement by students of the objectives for which this program is designed.

III. The Administration of Student Personnel Work

The administrative pattern of student personnel work in any one college or university will necessarily be adapted to the local resources and personnel. Although no definitive and evaluative studies of different types of administrative organization are available, yet in the last decade of student personnel work, the following generalizations have evolved.

Interrelation of Campus Resources

Everyone on a campus, from the students to the president, participates in some phase of the student personnel program. But certain personnel functions are usually the direct responsibility of designated staff members. Interested teachers devote time to counseling and the guidance of student organizations. Dormitory directors organize recreational and hobby activities. Such specialists as counselors, medical officers, psychiatrists, and psychometrists assist students in various ways. Many other examples of the range and types of personnel workers will be identified by the interested observer.

The nature of student personnel work is such that certain aspects of most activities may involve the interrelationship of a number of individuals in varying ways. For example, the operation of an effective orientation program for new students draws on many different persons. The teacher-counselor, the admissions officer, the doctor, other students, the administrative heads of the institution, the housing officer, recreational leaders, and others must contribute to an effective orientation program. Such interrelation of resources makes coordination necessary.

Administrative Structure

Experience indicates that specialized functions performed by trained personnel staff members should be organized with the customary definiteness found in instructional departments and colleges. For example, functions related to counseling need to be organized in a department, bureau, or center manned by the staff performing such functions. In similar manner, the functions of admissions, supervision of extracurricular activities, and many others of those discussed in the previous section need to be assigned to designated persons and departments.

This is not to say, however, that each personnel function needs to be organized in a separate bureau or assigned to a different individual or that each bureau or individual has a monopolistic control over its special functions. In smaller institutions, where the volume of work and the number of available staff members are limited, the form of organization can be simpler. But the principle of definiteness of assigned responsibility for each personnel function should be clearly established, even though only one member of a staff may be available to perform the function. In larger institutions, the volume of work permits, and sometimes compels, more formal organization and greater degrees of specialization.

As volume of services and size of staff increase, the necessity for centralization of administrative responsibility of an over-all nature becomes more readily apparent. The experience of the past decade indicates the desirability of assigning the responsibility for personnel work to an administrator. This generalization follows the pattern clearly established historically of designating instructional responsibility in the dean of a faculty or in the president in a small institution. When volume of work and other factors warrant it, a personnel administrator should be free from responsibility for any one personnel function or service in order that he may be able to deal effectively with over-all program development and coordination on a college-wide basis. As in the case of the instructional program of a college, the major personnel administrator, working with and through a staff council of personnel workers, should be held responsible for such administrative functions as budget-making and distribution; recruitment of staff; appointment and induction of staff members; stimulation of professional growth of personnel staff members; planning the continuous development of cooperation and coordination among the personnel specialists and between personnel work and the instructional program of the institution; and evaluation of the effectiveness of the total program.

The advocacy of a single administrative head for personnel work does not imply the assignment to such a person of complete and arbitrary authority. Instructional administrators have developed modifications of this centralization of authority in the form of program and policy committees composed of deans and faculty members and students. Indeed, the president of a college leans heavily upon his council of deans for aid in administration. In turn, each dean shares his administrative responsibilities with an executive committee of his faculty. In similar manner personnel administrators must enlist the help of specialists and of members of the instructional staff in determining policies and in planning personnel programs. Policy committees and coordinating councils should assist in administration and in continuous development of more effective services to education.

Decentralization of functions, as opposed to centralization in one person or one department, actually may increase the direct effectiveness of these services to students, provided that coordination produces the exchange of information and leads to the avoidance of conflict of services. Each institution must develop its own coordinating mechanisms for bringing together these decentralized services into a balanced, institution-wide program. Coordinating councils, informal meetings, exchange of memorandums, the maintenance of friendly working relationships—these and many other administrative devices need to be developed and maintained at a high level of effectiveness.

Process in Program Administration

Preoccupation with problems of administrative structure should not lead to neglect of process. Personnel literature to date is full of discussions of structure, of line and staff relationships, the points at which various responsibilities should rest, assignments of responsibility to various points of the structure, the ways in which parts should fit together, how they may be expected to work in relation to each other, and related topics.

Equal attention should be given to process. In a simple line and staff structure, for example, communication involves sharing information through organizational lines—down from the top in a relay pattern and sometimes up from the bottom along the established lines. Personnel administrators recognize that even two-way communication, however efficiently carried out, is not adequate for personnel work, and further experience is needed with respect to alternative forms of communication and administrative relationships. For example, personnel workers of all types need to meet regularly for discussions of common problems and for planning of interrelated programs of services. Experience indicates that not only information, but also feelings, always important in cooperative undertakings and other types of human relations, can best be transmitted in such face-to-face situations, and in well-planned and executed staff discussions of common problems and cooperative enterprises. Similarly, group planning of programs and discussions of issues and problems may produce better results than are obtained through the efforts of any single staff member. Furthermore, although each group will almost always create a leader role and ask someone to take this role, full participation of all members is best achieved when the role is passed from person to person within the group in terms of the differing competencies and experiences of the members in relation to the varying needs of the total program.

Participation in Institutional Administration

Personnel workers at all levels of specialization and administrative responsibility should be given appropriate opportunity and responsibility for participating in planning and policy-making for all phases of the institution's instructional and public-relations programs.

Students' Participation in Administration

Students can make significant contributions to the development and maintenance of effective personnel programs through contributing evaluations of the quality of the services, new ideas for changes in the services, and fresh impetus to staff members who may become immersed in techniques and the technicalities of the professional side of personnel work.

In addition to the use of advisory student councils and committees for reviewing programs and policies, personnel administrators and specialists should avail themselves frequently of opportunities for informal consultation with many individual students.

A Balanced Staff

Personnel specialists as well as personnel administrators should be chosen for their personal and professional competence to discharge their responsibilities. Personnel specialists and administrators, both men and women, should be available in all of the personnel departments. That is, competent men counselors should be available for those students who prefer to consult a man. In like manner, competent women counselors should be available for those men and women who prefer to consult a woman about scholastic or personal adjustments. Both men and women administrators should be members of top policy-making councils.

Special attention needs to be given to the maintenance of balance in another respect, namely, narrow specialization in one type of technique, adjustment problem, or school of thought. Each personnel staff should be maintained in a balanced manner with respect to desirably varied professional points of view and professional backgrounds of specialists.

Criteria for Evaluating Program

The principal responsibility of all personnel workers lies in the area of progressive program development. Essentially this means that each worker must devote a large part of his time to the formulation of new plans and to the continuous evaluation and improvement of current programs. The test of effectiveness of any personnel service lies in the differences it makes in the development of individual students, and every worker must develop his own workaday yardsticks for evaluation. The following suggest themselves as possible criteria for a continuing day-by-day appraisal of the program. No single criterion, alone and independent of others, would probably have much validity, but, taken together, they may provide an effective working relationship among staff members with respect to their program responsibilities.

These criteria are:

1. Students' expression of satisfaction and dissatisfaction with services received. These expressions may be informally collected or may be gathered systematically. Obviously such expressions need to be critically evaluated in terms of the total situation.

2. Expression of satisfaction and dissatisfaction with the program by members of the teaching staff. Again, such expressions need to be evaluated.

3. The extent of students' uses of the personnel services. Again, this criterion must be applied with full cognizance of the limitations of financial resources and other institutional factors balanced against the needs of the personnel departments.

4. The continuance of improvement in the professional training and professional status of members of the personnel staff through additional formal training, experiences, committee assignments, and other local, regional, and national recognition.

5. The quality of the interpersonal relationships and cooperation between personnel workers and members of the instructional and non-instructional staffs, and among personnel specialists themselves.

Institutional Mores and Policies

The effectiveness of a student personnel program is determined not solely by either its technical quality or its administrative and financial structure, but even more by its institutional setting. In an institution where conditions are favorable to the maintenance of friendly, informal working relationships between teachers and students, and where the institutional leaders explicitly support such relationships, effective counseling may be developed far more readily and effectively than would be the case in institutions burdened with an anti-faculty attitude established among student leaders.

Personnel workers of all types, particularly those involved in group-work functions, need to give continuous attention to the development of positive relationships in their work with student leaders. But, essentially, the institutional leader, the president, must set the standard of such mores. He can accomplish this by making clear his own basic attitudes toward students, teachers, and personnel workers, and the interrelated contributions of each group to the total institutional program of assistance to each student in his efforts to achieve full and broad development.

Note

1. Adapted from *Higher Education for American Democracy: The Report of the President's Commission on Higher Education, Establishing the Goals* (Washington, D.C.: Government Printing Office, 1947 New York: Harper & Bros., 1948).

The Student Learning Imperative: Implications for Student Affairs

AMERICAN COLLEGE PERSONNEL ASSOCIATION (1994)

Preamble

"The interval between the decay of the old and the formation and the establishment of the new, constitutes a period of transition which must always necessarily be one of uncertainty, confusion, error, and wild and fierce fanaticism."

John C. Calhoun

Higher education is in the throes of a major transformation. Forcing the transformation are economic conditions, eroding public confidence, accountability demands, and demographic shifts resulting in increased numbers of people from historically underrepresented groups going to college. More people are participating in higher education than ever before, yet the resources supporting the enterprise are not keeping pace with the demand. Because of these and other factors, legislators, parents, governing boards, and students want colleges and universities to re-emphasize student learning and personal development as the primary goals of undergraduate education. In short, people want to know that higher education is preparing students to lead productive lives after college including the ability to deal effectively with such major societal challenges as poverty, illiteracy, crime, and environmental exploitation.

Both students and institutional environments contribute to what students gain from college. Thus, the key to enhancing learning and personal development is not simply for faculty to teach more and better, but also to create conditions that motivate and inspire students to devote time and energy to educationally-purposeful activities, both in and outside the classroom. The recent focus on institutional productivity is a clarion call to re-examine the philosophical tenets that guide the professional practice of student affairs and to form partnerships with students, faculty, academic administrators, and others to help all students attain high levels of learning and personal development.

Purpose

This document is intended to stimulate discussion and debate on how student affairs professionals can intentionally create the conditions that enhance student learning and personal development. It is based on the following assumptions about higher education, student affairs, and student development:

- Hallmarks of a college-educated person include: (a) complex cognitive skills such as reflection and critical thinking; (b) an ability to apply knowledge to practical problems encountered in one's vocation, family, or other areas of life; (c) an understanding and appreciation of human differences; (d) practical competence skills (e.g., decision making, conflict resolution); and (e) a coherent integrated sense of identity, self-esteem, confidence, integrity, aesthetic sensibilities, and civic responsibility.

- The concepts of "learning," "personal development," and "student development" are inextricably intertwined and inseparable. Higher education traditionally has organized its activities into "academic affairs" (learning, curriculum, classrooms, cognitive development) and "student affairs" (co-curriculum, student activities, residential life, affective or personal development). However, this dichotomy has little relevance to post-college life, where the quality of one's job performance, family life, and community activities are all highly dependent on cognitive *and* affective skills. Indeed, it is difficult to classify many important adult skills (e.g., leadership, creativity, citizenship, ethical behavior, self-understanding, teaching, mentoring) as *either* cognitive or affective. And, recent research shows that the impact of an institution's "academic" program is mediated by what happens outside the classroom. Peer group relations, for example, appear to influence *both* affective and cognitive development. For these reasons, the terms learning, student development, and personal development are used interchangeably throughout this document.

- Experiences in various in-class and out-of-class settings, both on and off the campus, contribute to learning and personal development. Indeed, almost any educationally purposeful experience may be a precursor to desired outcomes. However, optimal benefits are more likely to be realized under certain conditions, such as active engagement and collaboration with others (faculty, peers, co-workers, and so on) on learning tasks.

- Learning and personal development occur through transactions between students and their environments broadly defined to include other people (faculty, student affairs staff, peers), physical spaces, and cultural milieus. Some settings tend to be associated with certain kinds of outcomes more than others. For example, classrooms and laboratories emphasize knowledge acquisition among other things while living in a campus residence, serving as an officer of a campus organization, or working offer opportunities to apply knowledge obtained in the classroom and to develop practical competencies. Environments can be intentionally designed to promote student learning. For example, students learn more when faculty use effective teaching techniques and arrange classroom space to promote interaction and collaboration; similarly, when student affairs staff discourage students from spending time and energy on non-productive pursuits, and encourage them to use institutional resources (e.g., libraries, student organizations, laboratories, studios), to employ effective learning strategies (e.g., study time, peer tutors), and to participate in community governance and other educationally-purposeful activities, students learn more. Institutional and student cultures also influence learning; they warrant attention even though they are difficult to modify intentionally.

- Knowledge and understanding are critical, not only to student success, but also to institutional improvement. To encourage student involvement in learning tasks, thereby improving institutional productivity, the outcomes associated with college attendance must be assessed systematically and the impact of various policies and programs on learning and personal development periodically evaluated.

- Student affairs professionals are educators who share responsibility with faculty, academic administrators, other staff, and students themselves for creating the conditions under which students are likely to expend time and energy in educationally-purposeful activities. They endorse talent development as the over-arching goal of undergraduate education; that is, the college experience should raise students' aspirations and contribute to the development of skills and competencies that enable them to live productive, satisfying lives after college. Thus, student affairs programs and services must be designed and managed with specific student learning and personal development outcomes in mind.

The Learning-Oriented Student Affairs Division

A student affairs division committed to student learning and personal development exhibits the following characteristics:

1. **The student affairs division mission complements the institution's mission, with the enhancement of student learning and personal development being the primary goal of student affairs programs and services.**

Student affairs professionals take seriously their responsibilities for fostering learning and personal development. Their efforts are guided by a holistic philosophy of learning that is congruent with their institution's mission and clearly distinguishes between the institution's commitment to process values (e.g., ethnic diversity, gender balance, equity, and justice) and desired outcomes (e.g., student learning and personal development). If learning is the primary measure of institutional productivity by which the quality of undergraduate education is determined, what and how much students learn also must be the criteria by which the value of student affairs is judged (as contrasted with numbers of programs offered or clients served).

Questions and challenges
- Does the division mission statement explicitly address student learning and personal development as the primary objectives of student affairs?
- Do staff understand, agree with, and perform in ways congruent with this mission?
- What must staff know to implement this mission?

2. **Resources are allocated to encourage student learning and personal development.**

The division reward structure values those processes and conditions that are associated with desired student outcomes. The orientation of many student affairs professionals, and the activities in which they engage, emphasize certain aspects of learning and personal development (e.g., psycho-social) over others (e.g., knowledge application or intellectual development). For this reason, student affairs divisions must attract and reward people who design programs, services, and settings that encourage student involvement in activities that have the potential to foster a wide range of learning and personal development outcomes. Staff themselves model such behaviors as collaboration and reflection that are likely to promote learning and participate in training and professional development opportunities that focus on talent development strategies.

Questions and challenges
- How can student affairs professionals be more intentional about promoting student learning while continuing to provide needed services to students and the institution?
- What is the role of professional associations in preparing student affairs staff to focus on student learning as a primary goal of student affairs?
- To what extent do student affairs staff attend institutes and programs that address the student learning imperative?

3. **Student affairs professionals collaborate with other institutional agents and agencies to promote student learning and personal development.**

As with other units in a college or university, student affairs divisions often are highly specialized, compartmentalized, fragmented units that operate as "functional silos"; that is, meaningful collaboration with other units is at best serendipitous. The learning-oriented student affairs division recognizes that students benefit from many and varied experiences during college and that learning and personal development are cumulative, mutually shaping processes that occur over an extended period of time in many different settings. The more students are involved in a variety of activities inside and outside the classroom, the more they gain. Student affairs professionals attempt to make "seamless" what are often perceived by students to be disjointed, unconnected experiences by bridging organizational boundaries and forging collaborative partnerships with faculty and others to enhance student learning. Examples of campus agencies that are potentially fruitful links include instructional design centers, academic enrichment programs, and faculty and staff development initiatives. Off-campus agencies (e.g., community service) and settings (e.g., work, church, museums) also offer rich opportunities for learning and students should be systematically encouraged to think about how their studies apply in those settings and vice versa.

Questions and challenges

- What are promising strategies for developing collaborative projects between student affairs and other campus and off-campus agencies committed to enhancing student learning and person development?
- How can student affairs professionals help students and faculty to intentionally connect academic work and out-of-class experiences?
- What is the role of professional associations in establishing linkages with other organizations with similar interests?

4. **The division of student affairs includes staff who are experts on students, their environments, and teaching and learning processes.**

Student affairs staff should know how students spend their time and whether students are using the institution's resources to educational advantage. They share responsibility for initiating conversations—with students and other institutional agents—about how students could make more effective use of their time and institutional resources. They monitor whether institutional policies and practices enhance or detract from learning and personal development. Moreover, they integrate data about student performance from faculty and others with their own observations of students' experiences and disseminate this information to stakeholders.

Questions and challenges

- How can student affairs staff obtain and synthesize information about student performance?
- What must student affairs staff know and be able to do to assist faculty in creating cooperative learning environments?
- What additional skills and knowledge are needed to successfully translate information about student behavior to faculty and others?

5. **Student affairs policies and programs are based on promising practices from the research on student learning and institution-specific assessment data.**

Certain conditions promote learning more than others. For example, learning and personal development are enhanced when students participate in groups organized around common intellectual, curricular, or career interests. Student affairs professionals should adapt to their institutional setting promising practices from those fields that contribute to the body of knowledge about student learning and personal development. They should routinely collect information to redesign institutional policies and practices and rigorously evaluate their programs and services to determine the extent to which they contribute to the desired outcomes of undergraduate education. Toward this end, student affairs staff should participate in institution-wide efforts to assess student learning and personal development and periodically audit institutional environments to reinforce those factors that enhance, and eliminate those that inhibit, student involvement in educationally-purposeful activities.

Questions and challenges

- Do student affairs have the knowledge and expertise in learning theory and student development research needed to shape policies and practices that will lead to increased levels of student learning, personal development, and institutional productivity?
- What must graduate programs do to prepare the next generation of student affairs professionals to base their work on theory and research on learning and intellectual as well as psycho-social development?

Conclusion

As with individuals, colleges and universities rely on experience to guide behavior. But when external forces (budget constraints, shifting demographics, accountability) produce radical changes, familiar, comfortable practices may no longer work. Change brings uncertainty as well as opportunity.

Student affairs professionals must seize the present moment by affirming student learning and personal development as the primary goals of undergraduate education. Redefining the role of student affairs to intentionally promote student learning and personal development will be dismissed by some as a restatement of the status quo ("old wine in new bottles") or an attempt to rekindle the momentum of a bygone era; others will interpret the message as forsaking the special humanizing role student affairs plays in the academy; others will conclude that to proceed as this document suggests will force student affairs to invade faculty territory; still others will be intimidated by the prospect of changing their behaviour. None of these views speaks to the concerns of students, parents, and other stakeholders who have high expectations for higher education. Student affairs must model what we wish for our students: an ever increasing capacity for learning and self-reflection. By redesigning its work with these aims in mind, student affairs will significantly contribute to realizing the institution's mission and students' educational and personal aspirations.

Contributors

The Student Learning Project was initiated by ACPA President Charles Shroeder in the fall of 1993 by convening a small group of higher education leaders to examine how student affairs educators could enhance student learning and personal development. The group included Alexander Astin, Helen Astin, Paul Bloland, K. Patricia Cross, James Hurst, George Kuh, Theodore Marchese, Elizabeth Nuss, Ernest Pascarella, Anne Pruitt, Michael Rooney, and Charles Schroeder. Following a three day retreat in Colorado, a version of this document was developed by George Kuh to spark discussion at the 1994 ACPA meeting in Indianapolis. This is a revised version of the original draft informed by comments and suggestions made at the Indianapolis meeting, and continuing dialogue since in various forms and forums.

Note

The Student Learning Imperative Project was sponsored by the American College Personnel Association. The mission of ACPA is to serve students by means of the Association's programs for educators who are committed to the overall development of students in post-secondary education.

A Corrective Look Back

JAMES R. APPLETON, CHANNING M. BRIGGS,
AND JAMES J. RHATIGAN (1978)

Few administrators see the relevance or importance of historical forces and issues to the present status of student affairs administration. This is a grievous miscalculation. History provides perspective and without an understanding of the role our predecessors played, the circumstances in which they worked, and the contributions they may have made to higher education in the United States, we have a truncated knowledge of our profession in particular and of campus development in general. In our field, the present is a dominant preoccupation. The price of this preoccupation is the diminution not only of our predecessors but also of ourselves.

With only a handful of people having an understanding of our history, it is not surprising to find a paucity of articles on the history of student personnel work. Of those who have commented on historical issues, few have been practicing administrators. This has resulted in a serious void; those who could provide a unique perspective have been unwilling or unable to do so. Perhaps they have been simply indifferent, failing to appreciate the value of historical writing to our field.

Some excellent documents that exist are seldom used. Some documentation has been lost, and of course it will never be recovered. But it is the history never recorded that might have been the most significant, involving the daily work of men and women who were too busy to consider writing, or who failed to leave ample records. History, as one writer put it, "is what evidence obliges us to believe," and our "evidence" has been insufficiently developed. *We must understand that, in substantial ways, professional identity is rooted in the past.* We cannot afford to continue a legacy of indifference.

Obviously, this chapter can do little justice to the history of our field. It may be useful, however, to review some issues that have contributed to the reputation accorded us by some writers (Penney, 1969; Brown, 1972; O'Banion and Thurston, 1972; Birenbaum, 1974) and to suggest that these views are rooted as much in stereotype as they are in scholarship. It is also hoped that as a result of this effort other persons in our field with an interest in history will find their appetites whetted, and that additional work in this area will receive attention.

A corrective look backward may seem unduly defensive. To those who feel good about their work, it may even seem irrelevant. Vermilye (1973) has aptly observed, "If we defined ourselves by our deeds and how well we perform them, we would need no other definitions." It is the view of this writer, however, that we cannot escape history, as enriching or as damaging as it might be. Because an understanding of our past is necessary, it deserves our thoughtful, continuing attention. Whether we like what we find or not, the understanding gained from historical examination should help us to move ahead with greater confidence and perspective.

This chapter finds its way into a book dealing with the role and style of administrators because present roles and styles are a function of history. Throughout the observations offered by the eight administrators, history is at work, whether they know it or not. Our work today is firmly tied to the past, in the most direct possible sense; this is quietly, often unrecognizably, but surely true.

41

Beginnings

Our work is largely a phenomenon of American higher education in the twentieth century, though its halting beginning is in evidence in the last quarter of the nineteenth century. Other writers have pointed to antecedents dating to the universities of the Middle Ages (Cowley, 1940) and to Athenian education (Bathurst, 1938).

The phenomenal growth and resilience of student personnel work are sources of constant amazement and its development vexing to many. Arguments abound as to whether it is a profession; some of its own practitioners show a lack of understanding about it; its future is frequently seen as tenuous; some prescient group or prophet is nearly always working at the task of reorganizing, reevaluating, reshaping, or renaming it. Some writers have suggested that the field came into existence because the president needed help in regulating student behavior. Clearly, a larger understanding is needed. Several factors influenced the development of this new field of work. The weighting these factors deserve, their interrelationships, and the way in which their individual impact varied from campus to campus are imprecisely understood.

Factors contributing to the origin of our profession would include: (1) the development of land-grant institutions and the rise of public colleges and universities; (2) increasing enrollments, and the accompanying increase in the heterogeneity of student populations; (3) social, political, and intellectual ferment in the nation; (4) the rise of co-education, and the increase in numbers of women entering institutions; (5) the introduction of the elective system in higher education; (6) an emphasis on vocationalism over the traditional liberal arts (or at least in growing competition with the liberal arts); (7) the impact of science and the scientific method; (8) the emerging signs of fundamental struggle between empiricism and humanism; (9) the apparent correlation between intellectualism and impersonalism on the part of faculty, notably those educated in German institutions; (10) expanding industrialization and urbanization, and the closing of the American "frontier"; (11) the view of higher education as a social status phenomenon, with less student commitment to "academic" subjects; (12) the establishment of a true "University" system; (13) the impact of liberal immigration laws in the United States; and (14) the changing roles of students in higher education. There were undoubtedly any number of other factors, but certainly all of those above are related to the changes that occurred, though one is not sure of the precise interplay.

For an understanding of the dramatic features of these changes, one must return to an earlier setting. The early American college was heavily value-oriented, with the president serving as the chief moral font. As Frederick Rudolph (1976) has observed, "moral purpose, values, and the reality of heaven," were dominant characteristics of those institutions and their prime administrators. College embraced the totality of the student but emphasized his spiritual needs. There were few public institutions, and the central religious emphasis did not erode until secular institutions gained a permanent foothold.

Nevertheless, it would be difficult to exaggerate the importance of public education. Because its value centers were not based in religion, its mission had to be developed differently. Some of the early public institutions were established to serve pragmatic needs (agriculture, technological subjects, home economics, etc.). The establishment of Johns Hopkins as the first legitimate American "university" had a dramatic and opposite effect. Institutions followed pell-mell in search of scholars interested in research; a growing number went to Germany for their training, returning to the United States with that model of education in mind. They showed little interest in student life outside the classroom. As the number of elective courses grew, so did the fragmentation of higher education, and the resulting fractionalization of learning still exists today in most institutions.

During this period the moral force of the president was greatly diminished. His efforts were diverted to the problems of finance, capital construction, faculty recruitment, the establishment of new programs, and the politics of growth stemming from legislative bodies and lay boards. Problems of accommodating increasing numbers of students, many of whom were not well prepared for higher education, were demanding. Rudolph notes that the senior course in moral philosophy, often taught by the president of the old-time college, was its "most effective and its most transparent repository of values. . . . Once that course died, as in time it did, there would really be no way to prevent the formation of the National Association of Student Personnel Administrators" (Rudolph, 1976).

Contending philosophies were vigorously present during the period 1870–1920, and students were no more immune to them than was the larger population. The impact of these several philosophies upon education, and through education to the student affairs field, needs more careful examination. (Three examples are considered later in this chapter.) One thing is clear: A rapidly growing and heterogeneous population of students entered higher education needing substantive assistance in other than curricular matters at approximately the time much of higher education was jettisoning that responsibility. The early efforts to restore the concern and effort to help students were principal conditions leading to the birth and early growth of the field of student personnel administration. No one knew for sure what needed to be accomplished, or how, but only that needs were there. We began by serving needs that had been pushed to the periphery, and some would argue that the field has remained there ever since. Our existence was predicated upon being out of the mainstream; how to become (or whether to become) a part of the mainstream is our continuing dilemma, complete with contradiction, contumely, and irony. Whether this is the glory or the burden of the field is the prevailing subject of concern and discussion among those in the profession today—in random rap sessions at professional meetings. The concerns of the early deans of men and deans of women were not always incidental to higher education, but *only incidental to that period*. Before that, much of what these deans worried about had been central issues in higher education. The early deans were humanists in a venture increasingly dominated by empiricists. It probably is helpful to consider that if faculty at the turn of the century had viewed what we did as important, we probably would not exist in the organizational form found today. If, as has been suggested, we are a constant reminder to faculty of their failure to cope with the lives of students, we must then realize also that we are a source of unconscious resentment. This is a legacy we are capable of overcoming, if it indeed is true.

The Dean and the Personnel Worker

While factors contributing to the emergence of the field may have been similar, they surfaced in different ways in different places. It is likely that few administrators understand that our work emerged from three separate sources: the dean of women, the dean of men, and the personnel worker. Their vestiges are still apparent in the existence of three major national organizations ([NAWE], NASPA, and ACPA). Anyone doubting the influence of history should be advised of the several efforts to merge these three organizations. The inability to accomplish any merger can be traced to various conditions, but a dominant reason surely is the function of history.

There is some disagreement as to who the first dean might have been, and while this is not especially critical, this writer relies on the work of W. H. Cowley, who believes that the dean of deans was LeBarron Russell Briggs of Harvard, who assumed his position in 1890. Blackburn (1969) reports "dean of women" appointments as early as 1890 (Swarthmore) and 1892 (University of Chicago). Thomas Arkle Clark (Illinois) claimed to be the first administrator to carry the title "dean of men," beginning in 1909, though he assumed the responsibilities earlier.

It is difficult to understand why the deans of men and deans of women have fared so poorly in the way they are remembered. A review of the *Proceedings* of the early meetings of deans of men and deans of women reveals a great majority of persons having high ideals, warmth, optimism, and genuineness. They appear to have enjoyed the respect of, and to have shown affection, compassion, and concern for, students. They evidenced strong qualities of leadership. Most of them were deeply religious; it is interesting to observe that most came from backgrounds in the liberal arts; our kinship with the liberal arts is a facet of our history that warrants more careful examination and articulation.

These men and women moved without the benefit of prior history, professional preparation, substantial financial support, clearly outlined duties, adequate communication across campuses, an agreed-upon sense of direction, or tools of any kind save their own values, skills, and leadership qualities. Nevertheless, they laid a foundation upon which a field of work could later be built. This was reflected in a growing professionalization, that developed with grudging but genuine recognition from other campus segments. This may not be a cheerful observation for those currently interested in "reconceptualizing" the field, but it is wholly supportable.

The early deans' positions emerged as they worked. As this writer has written elsewhere, the field developed from the campus up, not from the theory down (Rhatigan, 1975). Dean Stanley Coulter of Purdue observed: "When the Board of Trustees elected me Dean of Men I wrote them very respectfully and asked them to give me the duties of the Dean of Men. They wrote back that they did not know what they were but when I found out to let them know" (Secretarial Notes, 1928). Thomas Arkle Clark noted: "I had no specific duties, no specific authority, no precedents either to guide me or to handicap me. It was an untried sea upon which I was about to set sail. *My only chart was that the action of the Board of Trustees said I was to interest myself in the individual student*" (Secretarial Notes, 1924). Both of these early deans referred to trustees, causing one to wonder what role these Boards played in our history. Were trustees acknowledging requests from presidents, or was their role more active than that?

Definitions of the position of dean of men began to take shape as the deans examined their roles in the period roughly from 1910–1930. A typical definition was "that officer in the administration who undertakes to assist the men students (to) achieve the utmost of which they are individually capable, through personal effort in their behalf, and through mobilizing in their behalf all the forces within the University which can be made to serve this end" (Secretarial Notes, 1932). President Cloyd Heck Marvin of George Washington University observed, "The Dean of Men is most free to interpret his position in terms of modern University life because he is handling problems dealing with the adaptation of student life to the constantly changing social surroundings. . . . You are dealing in men, helping the student to get hold of life, to find the right environment in which he can develop himself to his fullest capacity" (Secretarial Notes, 1929).

The deans of men often commented about their basic roles but the illustrations above are typical of their views. It seems appropriate to suggest that their notion of "service" was quite different from that attributed to them by later writers (Brown, 1972; Crookston, 1972). Far from the analogy of "service station," the early deans' statements seem to stem in part from a religious orientation. It is also interesting to observe the frequency of their references to the "development of students," which some writers today see as unique to our own time. The early deans simply did not differentiate between "service" and "development," and one could take the view that the latter follows from the former. This is a matter of definition, but it is clear to this writer that the early deans of men and women (1) saw "service" as a much more fundamental phenomenon than have later writers, and also (2) that one aspect of the phenomenon was rooted in religion.

The issues facing the early deans of women overlapped those of their male counterparts, but had some understandably unique features. Many educators were unenthusiastic about the increasing enrollment of women students, feeling that they were physically and emotionally ill-equipped to cope with the rigors of higher education. As early as the mid-1800s we note the liberal Horace Mann, serving as president at co-educational Antioch College some years earlier, commenting on women's enrollment to the Regents of the University of Michigan, who were considering co-education: "The advantages of a joint education are great. The dangers of it are terrible" (Holmes, 1939). He argued that either the moral dangers facing women would have to be dealt with or he would prefer that "young women of that age" not have the advantages of an education. Deans of women were expected to deal with these issues. The deans undoubtedly privately despaired of their situation, yet they took advantage of the opportunity to participate.

Most of the early deans of women were nonconformists. They were a first-of-a-kind in institutions that were first-of-a-kind (co-educational). The frustrations they encountered were enormous, a product of working in an alien environment dominated by men. It seems clear that they were treated with respect in a personal sense, but their ambitions for young women were not always respected. They were particularly irritated about the expectations of student discipline thrust upon them. Many male counterparts saw this as the central role of deans of women, whose annoyance over this attitude is apparent in the literature.

The precarious position of the deans of women affected their language, which was circumspect in every respect, and their behavior, which was more formal than that of the deans of men. But their purpose was clear: to enlarge the possibilities and influence the potential of the young women they served in every possible way.

In spite of a clear recognition of their disadvantaged status, these women tended to think and write in broad terms. In the first text of its kind, Mathews wrote: "The major opportunities (of the dean of women) are . . . educational, involving the varying roles of vocational preparation appropriate to higher education" (Mathews, 1915). Urging that the proper role for a dean of women was to be as a specialist in women's education, Mathews believed the position to have a primary and unique responsibility for an entire generation of young women. This sense of destiny did much to overcome the deans of womens' continual frustration, a function of the slow progress apparent to them. Mathews noted that any woman considering being a dean must be prepared to "run a wide gamut of joy and sorrow." This admonition seems appropriate even now.

Like their male counterparts, the position of dean of women varied greatly from campus to campus. In an early history of the position, Holmes (1939) observed that the position was not standardized and probably should not be. Holmes outlined many of the obstacles, opportunities, and quality programs found in her study of various campuses. For those who might be guilty of seeing these women as gray-haired ladies looking after routine chores, Holmes reports that 60 percent had faculty rank and taught regularly. One would hypothesize that the early deans saw the recognition not only as earned, but essential to their reputations as deans. Fley (1963) has observed of these women that a remarkable breadth of interest, keen insight, and scholarship were evident from the beginning.

One is now left to inquire as to why only a stilted caricature remains as the legacy of these deans of women. Except for their own professional *Journal*, little attention has been paid to these remarkable women, except as "snooping battle-axes," as Fley puts it.

We have largely forgotten their essential courage in the face of formidable circumstances; their dedication in attempting to open new fields of study for women; their persistence even in failure; the stereotype they fought to overcome; the ethical standards evidenced in their work; the example they set for all who have followed. We have diminished them when they should stand as role models, rather a matter of ignorance than of malice, but the result is very nearly the same. In searching through a number of examples that might capture the views of these women, this writer selected a sentence by Kathryn Sisson Phillips, the first president of the National Association of Women Deans (NAWD), written shortly before her death: "Life can be good, but we must make it so, and we all have so much to give to each other along the way" (Cook, 1976). Romanticized pap? Probably the cynic will see it that way; but from any viewpoint, we have come a long way from the environment that spawned such feelings toward the role of women deans.

The third group comprising the field was the "personnel" worker. It should be pointed out, however, that no early dean of men or dean of women ever referred to the word "personnel."

In 1911, Walter Dill Scott, a psychologist at Northwestern University, published the first book known to apply principles of psychology to employees in industry. As World War I approached, Scott was asked to offer assistance to the U.S. Army to develop a classification system for the Army. In 1917, a Committee on Classification of Personnel was formed that, in retrospect, included a who's who of the emerging fields of psychology, measurement, and educational psychology. Among them were E. K. Strong, Jr., E. L. Thorndike, W. V. Bingham, John B. Watson, Louis M. Terman, Robert M. Yerkes, and J. K. Angell.

When Scott accepted the presidency of Northwestern in 1919, he did so with the understanding that he could develop a personnel program for the institution. In a meeting with the Northwestern Board of Trustees, Scott described his concept of personnel work:

> It is my belief that the emphasis should be on the individuality of the student and his present needs and interests. The student should be looked upon as more than a candidate for a degree, he is an individuality that must be developed and must be trained for a life of service . . . inadequate attention has been given to the fundamental problem of personnel. The great problem in our nation today is the problem of people. . . . (Blackburn, 1969).

The focus Scott chose was to guide students intelligently into the proper field of work, and vocational guidance was to be performed by the personnel administrator. Both the number of personnel workers and the variety of services they offered multiplied rapidly, but the emphasis on vocational guidance became such a dominant theme that, in time, for many, the terms "guidance" and "student personnel" were seen as nearly synonymous. One difficulty was apparent. The work Scott envisioned for the field entailed efforts already under way, having been organized by deans of men and deans of women. *On some campuses they coalesced immediately, but on others the groups worried about each other, and instances of hostility resulted.*

A number of events coincided with the work of Scott, involving the scholars engaged in the activities of the Army classification system. A discussion of this issue would require an historical outline of the study of psychology in the United States. This discussion is available elsewhere (Murphy, 1949; Boring, 1950), but the impact of these influences on the field of student personnel must be acknowledged.

The status of psychology in the United States was altered by John B. Watson. The introspective psychology which Wundt had formulated proved frustrating because it was found lacking in objectivity. Predictability was difficult and replication was nearly impossible. Lowe (1969) reports that disillusionment with introspection led to behaviorism, the application of the objective methods of animal psychologists to human beings. Watson wrote that "psychology as the behaviorist views it is a purely experimental branch of natural science" (Lowe quoting Watson, 1914). This opened a field of study that has been flourishing ever since. It is clear that the field of student personnel owes a debt to behaviorism, but as is characteristic of much of our dilemma, the weighting of that debt could be enhanced by historical analysis applied to our present status.

A second element in this time frame included a group of people interested in measurement. While Cattell has been credited with instituting the first American testing and data collection (at Columbia University), the work of Alfred Binet was of major influence. His tests were translated and produced in several versions, the most important of which was the Stanford-Binet, first produced by Lewis Terman in 1916. Thorndike and Strong, among others, turned their creative attention to the educational implications of psychological testing. The enthusiasm generated from developments in measurement was pronounced, but the field has had an uneven history. A reading of any issue of the *Personnel and Guidance Journal* today reveals the student personnel fascination with measurement, at a time when its tenets are under heavy attack elsewhere.

A third element in an understanding of the "personnel movement" concerns the social philosophy and hard work of Frank Parsons. Brewer (1942) summarized Parsons' work in thorough fashion, so it may be sufficient here merely to note that perhaps more than any one other individual, Parsons was responsible for bringing to public consciousness the concept of "vocational guidance." His response to the cruelties of industrialism was timely and thoughtful. While his interests were directed toward public school youths, higher education embraced the guidance concept, and in 1911 Harvard offered a short course on the subject. John Brewer was appointed as a full-time faculty member at Harvard in 1916, to teach courses in vocational guidance. The use of the analytical tools previously noted were ready-made for those attempting to embellish Parsons' ideas.

A final "personnel" element emerged from the field of mental health. "It came to be recognized that mental health really depended on the way people got along with each other on the college campus. Increasingly, it was seen that it was closely tied up with the morale of the college, with the presence or absence of conflicts in the environment or within the personality" (Brubacher and Rudy, 1968). The general American public seemed ready for the development, as Clifford Beers' *A Mind That Found Itself*, published in 1909, was already well known. Mental health came to be seen as more than an absence of illness, involving preventive devices that should certainly be employed on the campus.

The work of John Dewey has a place of its own but the voluminous nature of that work cannot be approached here except to alert the reader. The issues of educational sociology and educational philosophy which Dewey (and his followers) brought to the schools were clearly consistent with the soon-to-be introduced idea of a "student personnel point of view" in higher education.

There were other issues, and certainly those touched upon above were far more complex than reported here. The intent of these remarks is simply to emphasize the separate emergence of the personnel worker. From the beginning, these persons used the tools of science and humanistic learning to the extent that the tools were available, adapting them to the needs of the student.

The growth of services has continued nearly unabated; by 1977, the American Personnel and Guidance Association reported 11 divisions of professional interest and a membership exceeding 41,000. If one were to subtract one division from the total, those affiliated principally with the American College Personnel Association, few deans would be found in APGA. Other professional groups with a background related to the early days of student personnel have branched out into full-fledged national associations. Some of their numbers today report to a chief student personnel officer, but others do not. One sign of success, size, has inherent problems complete with diverse goals, practices, jargon, and specialized tools. *Some see this diversity as wholly understandable, a natural outcome of specialized interests, but others see it as evidence that the field has lost its compass.*

An entirely different story relates how the dean of students' position emerged as the principal personnel office on the American college campus. It is clear that the development of the new position was tied to campus territorial conflicts concerning the management of expanding services. In a general sense, the deans of women and deans of men were outflanked in these conflicts, because the broader services provided by the student personnel worker commanded more territory.

The deans of men and deans of women had relied heavily on the force of their personalities, and their reputations as effective teachers, in their work as deans. They held no special corner on administrative skills. The personnel workers tended to approach their work more scientifically and typically denied any administrative role. Nonetheless, they all sought to serve the same clientele. The inevitable conflict surfaced, resulting in some fundamental changes.

The dean of students' position was established to bring some order out of the substantial overlapping which resulted on some campuses. Persons with administrative skills were hired to direct the various staff and offices involved in working with students outside the classroom. Similarly, the notion of a campus "environment" began to emerge, resulting in organized planning and programs that were more comprehensive than the one-to-one delivery of services characteristic of the early period of our history.

The growth of the dean of students' position ushered in some subtle changes in the field. The leader was no longer (necessarily) an inspirational figure, but was more likely selected for his/her ability to develop or manage a variety of programs and services in behalf of students. *After losing the battle to the personnel worker, the dean of men frequently won the war by moving up to the dean of students' position.* This created additional problems, some of which are recognizable to the present time, as evidenced by the organizational arrangements of student personnel programs on individual campuses. The full impact of this benchmark change in our field, however, has yet to be explored.

Writers have been fond of referring to our role as disciplinarians and as paternalistic figures. These two labels have frequently resulted in unproductive embarrassment, chagrin, apology, and other responses. The observations seem as apt to come from those inside the field as outside, again suggesting limited historical understanding. It is not necessary to justify old behaviors as appropriate to the present, but it may be useful to consider the periods and circumstances in which these behaviors once had meaning. It may also be possible to show that the language we use to describe these old behaviors is one-dimensional, enhancing clarity but eroding accuracy. *A clearly understood distortion is a poor substitute for comprehending the complex circumstances that challenge our understanding. The choice seems fairly clear to this writer: Either we try to retreat from a past that we think we understand or we take a critical if uncomfortable look backward.* This will require a comprehensive approach on the part of future writers; the brief sections that follow are simply illustrative of the issues that should be resolved.

Discipline

The subject of discipline has been one of the most pervasive and painful topics in the history of student personnel administration. Where it exists as a function of a student affairs office today, it is likely that structure and procedure dominate philosophy as matters for attention. This is understandable in view of recent court decisions. It might have been avoidable, but for excessive concern over "image" on our part.

From the beginning of our history, discipline has had several connotations. Three definitions are offered here: (1) discipline as a virtue, in other words self-discipline, the essence of education; (2) discipline as a process, a form of reeducation or rehabilitation; (3) discipline as punishment, typically seen as having redemptive features even in this narrow construction. Fley (1963) has conducted an excellent, comprehensive analysis of these features of discipline, a model historical study.

The first two definitions occupied most of the time and attention of the early deans, yet they are largely remembered for the third definition. Whatever the facts, "dean and discipline" are an integrated historical legacy. Barry and Wolf (1963), who have developed one of the few excellent historical overviews of the field, say of discipline: *"Despite all their later disclaimers, most deans of men seem to have been appointed primarily to act as disciplinarians."* (They did not say "were appointed," but the qualifying feature of the sentence might well be missed.) Fley (1963) notes, "The denial of the disciplinary function in student personnel work has resulted not so much from solid educational theories, as from a belief on the part of the present-day personnel worker that his predecessors in the field were snooping, petty battle-axes who made it their business to ferret out wickedness and punish all offenders promptly." The power of accepted history prevails, even though it is demonstrably inadequate.

The deans of men and deans of women dealing with "discipline" had distinctly different problems, and they are treated separately here.

Marion Talbot, one of the most influential early deans, and a founder of the Association of Collegiate Alumnae (later to be known as the American Association of University Women) gave "discipline" a broad construction (1898):

> It must not be limited to the mental powers—accuracy, agility, firmness and clean-ness of mind and keenness of observation—it often does and always should include the training of the moral powers—truth, honor, justice, forbearance, self-control, patience, and reverence. Indeed, there can be no longer nor better aim for all educa-tional effort than such all-inclusive discipline, and I believe that it not only now exists, but is growing to be more and more the chief end of training during the years with which we are dealing.

Talbot's statement is representative of the broad view of discipline. She saw it as "unlocking the virtues found in every student," a humanist position discussed in a later section of this chapter. Many deans of women offered comments in this vein.

One must eventually move from statements of ideals, however, to the essentials of practice. The deans of women, of course, were faced with responding to the apprehensions of their male colleagues with respect to women students. They were seen by some as potentially corrupting or corruptible, and there was concern about their health, state of mind, and general ability to cope in the collegiate setting. It was impossible for the deans of women to ignore these concerns. One reality was clear, as indicated by an early dean. "Indiscretion and folly meant a far bitterer repentance for one sex than the other . . ." (Mathews, 1915). No doubt the deans of women were eager to avoid any problems that would give credence to the view that women did not belong in these institutions. If they took a no-nonsense approach, it was likely because they had high moral standards, and because diversions cost them time and energy best spent elsewhere.

Fley (1963) notes that the deans of women rarely referred to "discipline" in their proceedings, choosing instead words such as "character formation," "moral and ethical training," and "citizen-ship training." It was impossible for them to fend off the role of "discipline," but in accepting it they were able to attempt to cast this responsibility in ways they deemed appropriate. The issue was a difficult but not a central concern. Simply put, they sought to enlarge the career and leadership opportunities of women, and they recognized competence as crucial. Nowhere in the written word is punishment, the third view of discipline, found in the thinking of these women. Every cute story (e.g., the enforcement of a rule requiring a magazine be placed under any young woman sitting on someone's lap) cruelly discredits the remarkable work of a group of remarkable women.

Deans of men had their definitions, and faced their own set of conditions and expectations, and their struggle with the concept is duly recorded. The deans of women either suffered in silence or took an oblique view, but the deans of men were more verbal and more straightforward. Some of them accepted the responsibility, taking the view in behavior situations that positive relationships could grow out of negative beginnings. Others were not so sanguine. As one dean put it, "Discipline is about as welcome as a cow-bird in a cuckoo's nest."

The deans of men saw increasing discipline problems on the campus and pressed for the reasons. Many talked about the aftermath of war (World War I) and the general breakdown in values in the larger society following it. The representative of another group observed that it was more pressing, "in direct . . . proportion as the curriculum has become more illogical or superficial" (Secretarial Notes, 1927). They possessed the same high ideals and moral standards that characterized the early deans of women, and the crisis of values perceived in American society was profoundly disturbing to many of them.

The long-standing assumption that moralizing, exhortation, or threat were the principal tools of the deans of men could not be substantiated by this writer. Additionally, any joy in meting out punishment is totally absent in the *Proceedings* of either the deans of men or women in those times.

Some of the statements attributed to the deans could, on the one hand, be characterized as paternalistic; a broader view might favor a kind of *noblesse oblige* approach, wholly in keeping with their own high ideals. Dean Stanley Coulter of Purdue offered one perspective:

> Unless the Dean of Men . . . is something of a practical idealist of youth . . . unless he is all consumed with a passion of love for young people, his work is nothing. The biggest job I have is not the control of delinquents, it is not the control of ordinary misconduct, but in doing and living so well, showing the individual his powers and how with the right use of those powers he can live a life of honor or how he can waste all these inheritances. (Secretarial Notes, 1928)

Many of the deans of men were faced with enforcing rules established by the faculty, and it is clear that this was an odious assignment. If ample records were available, they might well show the dean of men as "subverter" rather than "enforcer." They were required to finesse their way through the turmoil created by rules that generally lagged behind the prevailing attitudes and behaviors of young people. This was an extraordinary task, requiring unique styles of response, but today many in the field underestimate these early challenges, or simply distort them through superficial attention.

Robert Reinow, the University of Iowa's first dean of men, was clearly angry about the situation he faced, as the following passage reveals:

> . . . it is plain to see that our worn-out system of traditional discipline, our enforcement of faculty-made regulations, are futile. They are not constructive; they are not inspiring; they are not educational. They were never intended as such. They are, and have been, a sort of protective measure established by the faculties to maintain a decent awe and respect in the number of students with a fear of the consequences that might follow violation of the same. (Secretarial Notes, 1929)

Yet he observed that somehow during college the ideals of life, of conduct, of behavior, and of self-discipline must be developed.

There are many additional aspects of the concept of "discipline" in this century. Some key people who initially felt it to be inimical to the field later changed their minds. Prominent among these were E. G. Williamson and Esther Lloyd-Jones. Fley believes that the statement on self-discipline by Lloyd-Jones and her colleague, Margaret Ruth Smith, to be one of the finest in the literature (Lloyd-Jones, 1938). Perhaps the most supportive analytical treatment of the subject was written by another early critic, E. G. Williamson, who collaborated with J. D. Foley in *Counseling and Discipline*, published in 1949. Fritz Redl introduced the idea of group work in discipline in 1947.

Carl Rogers had problems with the idea of discipline, making one of the strongest cases against it in noting, "Therapy and authority cannot be co-existent in the same relationship," but "yet . . . mere leniency is not the answer." (Rogers, 1942) He offered some alternatives, but his reservations have been persuasive to many in the field.

Why has this issue been of such importance to the field? The "control of behavior" theme has been a vocal interpretation of the question, but it is incomplete. The question is deeply philosophical; there are writers who have recognized it as such, but their numbers are small. The Athenians believed that values could be taught, and must be taught. Centuries later, John Dewey would write: "Restoring integration and cooperation between man's beliefs about the world in which he lives and his beliefs about the values and purposes that should direct his conduct is the deepest problem of human life."

Dewey's words may seem obscure today, but they reflect the attitudes of the early deans, who brought high ideals, well-defined values, and a strong moral sense to their work. These traits governed their work and were transmitted to their students. What was once a virtue has become the opposite, an observation not inconsistent with Eric Fromm's views in *The Sane Society* (1955). The prevailing judgment we have of these deans tends to be unsympathetic, but we may have it backward.

In Loco Parentis

The concept of *in loco parentis* is another educational household word glibly used but incompletely understood. It illustrates how events relevant at a given point in time can take on meanings later that are only loosely related to the origins from which they stemmed. Modern student personnel workers have cringed at the thought of being party to the concept of *in loco parentis*.

There are at least two ironies in the concept of *in loco parentis*. First, it is a legal doctrine not an educational statement, and its formalization into law occurred long after the original relationship was abandoned in practice. Second, it is a doctrine that has come to characterize much of student personnel work, but its legal application referred almost entirely to matters of student discipline, which at the time were generated by rules developed and enforced by faculty members. *Far from rebutting the issue, our profession meekly accepted its tenets and was apologetic thereafter. The price of neglecting a rebuttal has been so high that it appears beyond repair.*

The preponderance of writers describing the relationships between student and institution in colonial America refer to *in loco parentis*. (They also borrowed the term from the courts, applying the nomenclature retroactively.) The relationship, to the extent that it did exist, was understandable, given the age of students and the difficulties associated with travel and communication during the colonial period. *In loco parentis*, however, probably misstates the case. Certainly it is doubtful that colonial college faculty ever thought of the matter that way. This is a matter for other researchers, but this writer feels that the relationship was moral, in religious terms, a deeper concern than simply serving as surrogate parents, which the college also did. Rudolph (1976) leans this way in noting that *the souls of these students were what the college felt was at stake.* If this produces chuckles in our modern age, *we can be sobered in realizing that, in the view of Jacob (1957), institutions may be making few value-oriented contributions to their students.*

It is clear in any case that the relationship of student and institution changed with the rise of the public university. The institution might indeed have felt a relationship with students like that of the colonial college, but it simply did not exist. Thus, while the *facts* of this relationship changed, a strong residual tradition remained. In the last decades of the nineteenth century, the neglect of student life was a growing phenomenon, and any characterization of higher education having a parental relationship distorts the matter completely.

The approach to the relationship might well have been argued to be *educational*, entailing the view that an institution should have, within the bounds of fairness, the inherent power to establish regulations in its own behalf. The notion of inherent power did surface but never took hold. The case for an educational relationship had some spotted success, but its potential is fast disappearing.

It is regrettable that the Gott court (which introduced the language of in *loco parentis* in 1913) did not reach a decision on the basis of an earlier case, Hill vs. McCauley, recorded in 1887. Much of the "due process" frame of reference found in the landmark case of Dixon vs. Alabama State Board of Education (in 1961) rests in the decision rendered in Hill vs. McCauley. The Hill decision noted, "The dismissal of students from college should be in accordance with those principles of justice. . . which are recognized as controlling in the determination of the rights of men in every civilized nation on the globe" (Cazier, 1973). Certainly this is true, and we should be none the poorer for having to comply with the "due process" procedures outlined in Dixon vs. Alabama State Board of Education. None of these early cases, however, involved student personnel administrators. Yet from the specific case of discipline, which became a student personnel function, developed the notion of "parental" which spread across the profession in an interesting manifestation of guilt by inference. The fact that the "parental" case has never been made is an inconvenient irritation long since fallen by the wayside. Certainly we can take no pride in instances of capricious treatment on the part of student personnel officers, and just as certainly students do not give up their basic rights once they enter the campus. The growing body of law applied to higher education, however, relies on analogy, and every case provides a precedent for yet another case. This introduces the risk of administrators' dwelling on procedures rather than upon the substantive personal or educational issues they face with respect to problems of student behavior. A new surrogate parent is on the horizon, with muscle few parents ever had, and the "parent" is looking at higher educational institutions, not the student. This writer recalls the admonition of Learned Hand: "A society so driven that the spirit of moderation is gone, no court can save; . . . in a society which evades its responsibility by thrusting upon the courts the nurture of that spirit, that spirit will surely perish."

We have failed to address an inaccurate analogy applied to us unfairly. This has resulted in a one-dimensional view of discipline. Our chances of countering the view seem slim indeed.

One last lament will close this section. A parental relationship, if the analogy holds, could well involve love, mutual respect, and certainly a concern for a student's growth and development. This aspect of the argument must be absurd, for no one has given it any attention.

Values in Historical Perspective

The early deans in the field were deeply concerned about values, though they are remembered best as "moralizers" rather than as "moral." And yet, fifty years and more later, the APGA national award for outstanding research (1976) dealt with moral education. V. Lois Erickson, the winner of the award, notes: "There are many kinds of values, and moral values are only one of them . . . but moral development involves restructuring empathy and issues of justice to lead to a greater good for more people." This observation reflects the same kind of ideals espoused by our predecessors and bears upon the style they brought to their work.

Is it important at all for us to consider that we are still concerned about the basic human issues that were discussed by the early deans? It is at least an arguable point that the major difference between the field then and today, is the eighty or so years of experience that they lacked.

It is clear that in every age thoughtful men and women have pondered over value issues; that is evident in every enduring piece of literature written about human dilemmas. In the following paragraphs, this writer hopes to suggest some value issues outside the field of student personnel that have influenced our work, because their influence pervades our culture. They are suggestive of the ways we make choices, the ways our predecessors made choices, indeed the ways such choices were *allowed* to be made in the face of powerful cultural forces.

There are dozens of definitions of the word "value," some of them understandable and others less clear. The definition offered by W. H. Cowley (1966) is adequate for purposes of this chapter: "A value constitutes a subjective attitude of a human individual or group at a given point in time and space about the worth of any objective, projective, or subjective entity."

Note the notion of "subjective," as it can be argued that no entity has value in itself. Note also the reference to time and space, a critical flaw in the informal history we have come to accept in student personnel administration. Note also that values are not ideals, though there can be ideal values. This is not double-talk; it means that ideals are positive, while values can be positive or negative (or something else). It is recognized, of course, that, in combination, one acquires a set of values resulting in a personal value system. This is a crucial matter; through it one transcends momentary pain and pleasure, enabling one to coordinate a virtually unlimited number of experiences encompassing the whole of one's life.

Our interests are not only concerned with the content of values, but also the way in which they are acquired, and the way in which they are held, their *salience* with regard to self-appraisal and ultimate behavior; for values imply choices made or not made, deeds done or not done, enjoyments experienced or not experienced, etc., ad infinitum.

And of course we don't live alone. The way in which a society, or any segment of that society, behaves is a product of values. Culture, or society, can be seen as a system of consensually validated social expectations derived from the personal values of diverse individuals. Cultural sanctions and expectations take on "good" and "bad" connotations, then, which are frequently referred to as morals. It is hoped that this thin introduction to sociology is not new to the reader, but simply a reminder of the ways we have operated in the varying milieus of our time.

A glimpse of some of these historical forces is all that can be offered here. No special claim is made for them, except that they need more examination than they have received from other authors and more than they will receive here.

The first of these forces is *humanism*. Originating in the Renaissance and gaining its full stature during the European Age of Reason, its vital values are: (1) a belief in human rationality; (2) confidence in the possibility of human perfectibility; (3) a recognition of the importance of self-awareness. One will immediately recognize our debt to these concepts.

It should not be necessary to indicate the importance of humanism in American history, as the historical humanists were especially persuasive to Thomas Jefferson and James Madison, the principal architects of our system of government.

During the nineteenth century, humanism took on some decidedly American pragmatic qualities. Reason, it was averred, should result in action, and reason and achievement became joined in ways unique to the American nation. Its existence coincided with the growth of our industrial nation, and for a time the two continued side by side. As the American frontier closed and people were thrown into close contact in the country's growing cities, the unfettered enthusiasm for men's right to achieve began to wane. The exploitation of immigrant workers, women, and children began to cast doubt on the virtue of unbridled individualism; the humanists faced some problems that they are still pondering. They faced these problems in higher education toward the end of the nineteenth century.

The second humanist value is the actualization of one's inner potential. As Marshall Lowe (1969) puts it, "Humanists continue to emphasize individual initiative and to believe in progress and in man's ability to perfect his world." It is in this second humanistic value that the notion of achievement sets its deepest roots. As a matter of fact, human achievement yokes the idea of rationality with the concept of self, of self-awareness.

Attention to the third tenet of humanism, that of self-awareness, characterizes our field. As far back as William James, we are introduced to the concept of self in a specific psychological sense; even Emerson once said, "This thought which is called I."

The notion of a self-concept has broadened to the point that it has many variations in psychological usage. Perhaps the case is made best by Abraham Maslow, who gave us the concept of self-actualization, which the humanists would see as the highest good. Carl Rogers made this point in the 1950s. A positive regard for oneself is so important, according to Rogers, that he wrote an entire book, *Client-Centered Therapy*, about it in 1951. That title-phrase is certainly a household word for those in our profession who come from counseling backgrounds. The views he sets down are those of the classical humanist: failing in self-awareness, in a concept of self, individuals encounter deficiencies and difficult adjustments that must be corrected if they are to have a productive life.

The goal of therapy was to expand self-awareness. He saw this effort as a process, a direction, not a destination, but it was a *crucial* process.

Perhaps the most powerful and enduring American humanist is Erich Fromm. While arguing for the self in *Escape From Freedom* (1941), Fromm notes that the price of individual freedom may be too high for many, resulting in loneliness and isolation. He was deeply concerned with the persuasive reasons that could be developed for conforming to more dominant voices. This view was expanded six years later in *Man For Himself,* in which Fromm created the phrase "marketing orientation" as a fearful trend in American society. Here the self must conform and please in order to get along, a function, he thought, of the marketing orientation of an industrial society inappropriately applied to individuals. This assertion is still sound; a fear of group rejection is a *paramount* human concern, a pervasive anxiety of our time. In *The Sane Society*, perhaps Fromm's best work, written in 1955, he observed that our society is well on the path to replacing virtue with vice.

In summary, humanists are basically optimistic; they embrace reason, perfectibility, and self-awareness as their human imperatives. These values were the stock-in-trade of the early deans. A thoughtful writer needs to examine their status today.

In higher education, the humanistic orientation of higher education was weakened by an influx of teachers with an allegiance to science, an *empirically* schooled professoriate which embraced the principles of what has come to be called "the scientific method." In its human sense, it sought to measure experience through the senses. Because values cannot be perceived in this way, the empiricist is tempted to avoid the dilemma altogether, leaving the matter to indirection. The empiricists hoped to achieve through science an understanding of self that had failed in philosophy.

In psychology, Freud was the first dominant figure, the first to use a scientific medical model in examining human problems. Our field has fastened onto the tool of science now known as behaviorism. The prevailing view is that behaviorism is a rejection of humanism; having lost confidence in reason as a sufficient device, the behaviorist chose to encounter human problems through scientific observation and experimentation. Its building-block approach has achieved some spectacular results, but its basic weakness lies in the thorny questions of goals and purposes. One should be quick to point out that behaviorism is not "anti-human." Behaviorists simply hold the view that their work is a corrective to the failure they see in classical humanism.

The last historical force noted in this brief section is existentialism. Rollo May has observed that it is an attempt to resolve the "reason" and "science" cleavage that has characterized Western thought, moving away from a view of humans in the subject-object terms of humanism and behaviorism. The boundaries of existentialism are not yet fully understood, but Paul Tillich believed existentialism to be the prevailing intellectual force of our time. A complex phenomenon, it has been seen by Max Wise (1966) as having four characteristics that are helpful to understanding:

1. It is a protest against the assumption that reality can be grasped primarily or exclusively by intellectual means.

2. It is a protest against the view which regards men as "things," as assortments of functions and reactions. It stands against naturalism (of which behaviorism is a part) and mechanism.

3. It makes a drastic distinction between subjective and objective truth and gives priority to the subjective. This means, not the denial of objective truth, but a denial of its adequacy on matters of ultimate concern, which are always dealt with by the person.

4. It regards man as fundamentally ambiguous; he is free to act, yet he is enmeshed in the natural and social order. He is finite, yet he can on occasion rise above any situation. He is bounded by time, yet he has a kinship with eternity.

In the *Courage to Be* (1952), Paul Tillich identifies World War I as the crucial point for the onset of sustained existentialist thought, although it is a much older philosophy. During World War I, old beliefs in the inevitability of human progress and the rationality of human thought were shattered, particularly in Europe but with considerable force in this country as well. Rollo May describes the movement as a response to the increasing fragmentation and compartmentalization of personality, a function of industrialized society, factors sensed but not fully understood by the early deans.

Existentialism represents a search for new moral values; it is a quest for personal meaning. It has declared war on older, conventional values; certainly that is its hallmark. It has both theistic and atheistic features, but they are not differentiated in this brief discussion.

In many respects, existentialism is a philosophy of anxiety, though its American version is more optimistic than its European counterpart. It stresses the development of self through intense inwardness, our modern hope of keeping or regaining an individualism opposed by technological society. One will note the similarities here with humanism but the principal battle is not based primarily in reason; it is between being and non-being. Non-being, for purposes here, can be considered as the constant threat of personal and social annihilation, an unrelenting battle. The greatest fear is man as object, according to Sartre. While Sartre describes the necessity of the freedom to be (through negation), Tillich turns to the courage to be through the affirmation of self. Carl Roger's book, *On Becoming a Person* (1961), has a distinctive, American existential feeling to it.

It is no doubt true that these schools of thinking do not arrange themselves as neatly in our lives and work as they are set out here. But neither are they simply interesting abstractions. Indeed, they are forces that are influencing us whether we know it or not. But how? This writer has found few persons with the capacity or interest to adapt the thinking inherent in these philosophies (and no doubt other philosophies) to our work. An important contribution to the field can be made by persons willing to examine and present these issues.

It can be argued that the press for "student development" is grounded in one or more of these philosophies. The available literature, however, is strong in technique and weak in philosophy. It is clear that there is a "student personnel point of view." But the statements of philosophy that are affecting modern civilization and to which that "point of view" is tied are worthy of more thoughtful analysis.

This is a drama without end; but clearer perspectives are needed. If we understand the need for mutuality, affiliation, and community with other human beings, we at least have some things to talk about. If it seems depressing, we can take hope in noting that men and women have shown resilience in facing all of these problems, beyond that recognized by many writers. A central question is whether society needs a center of meaning to give it the coherence necessary for the quality of life its members are seeking, or whether a personal center of meaning is possible and then sufficient enough to provide the stability necessary for persons having broadly diverse goals and values. This is an on-going dilemma found on nearly every campus.

Historical Writing

Before closing this chapter, it would seem appropriate to note some issues that have a bearing on historical writing. These are not just abstractions; they influence the way we come to view ourselves.

In looking at the study of history, one may fail to note how complex and forbidding it tends to be. Lay persons typically see it as involving the location, digestion, and interpretation of sources found in places where historians ordinarily look. It may be surprising to those who have not had the opportunity, nor the interest in pursuing the matter, to learn that historians suffer many professional problems and divisions. This writer could not help but observe that many of these problems and divisions also mirror those in the field of student personnel administration.

Historians have been at their work longer, of course, but they are still arguing epistemological questions. They constantly haggle over terms and definitions and face astonishing semantic problems in general. The impact of the "scientific method" has troubled them throughout this century. They approach their work with a variety of prejudices and sentiments. They understand human behavior incompletely. They must rely heavily on fair-minded, professional judgments in order to draw conclusions. Some methods and formulations they desperately need are simply not available to them. Finally, as one historian put it, "Historians . . . have to accept much knowledge on trust" (Renier, 1965).

Historians are typically forced to confront the uncontrolled and merciless evidence of the written word. This presents for them the problem of *context*. To identify an isolated issue is not sufficient; only an understanding of the surrounding circumstances will yield the meaning sought. It can be argued that any "issue" that ignores a larger context of circumstances may well not be the "issue" but something else entirely, or partially, with critical shadings and nuances. To miss some of these, and perhaps to focus inappropriately on others, is to illustrate the difficult problems historians must resolve if they are to give their work value. It is the connectedness of the events that brings meaning to the best historical writing, an art of the highest order.

Even *words, terms, and/or phrases* understood when spoken or written in a given period may become misleading and/or useless as their meanings change over time. Certainly this is well understood in theory, but violations of the theory in practice are evident in the writing available to us. "Moral," "citizenship," "character development," "adjustment," and the "whole student" illustrate this point—words once understood may have had different connotations at that time than they now have.

Similarly, words used at any one point in time may take on different meanings. In our field, "discipline" would be one such word; the meaning of "discipline" has perhaps caused more consternation in our field than has any other single word, yet it has had concurrent meanings. "Student development" may be a phrase which future writers will find puzzling, frustrating.

Historical writing is a cumulative venture, like most other intellectual disciplines in which scholars rely heavily on the good work of their predecessors. It is obvious, of course, why this is so, lest every historical writer have to return to primary source material found all over the globe. *Accepted history* or *accepted sources*, then, are valuable tools for the historian. They emerge from the quality of care and scholarship which later writers see in a predecessor's efforts. The principal risk of accepted history is that it may become invulnerable to challenge. (It must be noted that this is not so much a problem for professional historians as it is for lay persons like ourselves, who are apt to assume that our accepted history must be accurate.) Student personnel administrators have failed to challenge the accepted history of the field, writing that for the most part was set out a quarter of a century or more ago, and which has been tested only indifferently, if at all, since. Certainly we do not want to create any new myths, but just as surely we must question many. We have dehumanized our predecessors through basic ignorance, writing them off as "paternalistic" or "disciplinarians" or suffering other unhappy fates, principally because we have been indifferent historians in our own field.

Consider the following example, an illustration of stereotyped thinking and writing; the authors' names are omitted to eliminate any possible embarrassment.

> One of the historical models for the student personnel worker is that of regulator or repressor. The student personnel profession came into being largely because the president needed help in regulating student behavior. In the early 1900s student personnel workers were given the titles of 'monitor' and 'warden.'

> In this model the student personnel regulator works on colonial campuses as a mercenary of the president at war with students. He is the president's *no-man*. He tends to behave in ways that regulate, repress, reject, reproof, reprimand, rebuff, rebuke, reserve, reduce, and even remove human potential. In this system all the negative aspects of *in loco parentis* are practiced as staff members attempt to maintain a strict supervision over the affairs of students.

If the profession deserves this bitter pill, then certainly it should work to recover from such a harmful, negative beginning. But the concern here is that the book from which this material is quoted, a book written principally for community college administrators, may become part of our accepted history. (This has already happened, in the judgment of this writer, though the severity of this material is unparalleled elsewhere.) As such, other writers may draw upon this reference as an accurate description. It may be useful to look more carefully at these two paragraphs, to ask some reasonable questions, and to make some general observations.

1. **What citations are provided to verify the several assertions of the writers?** None.

2. **Why are the references absent?** Because no primary materials exist that would support these views. Careful investigation will inevitably reach this conclusion.

3. **What evidence exists to indicate that the "president needed help" in regulating student behavior?** This is a partial truth, but void of any of the several nuances it deserves. If anything, this might have been more true of the role of deans of women, but even this statement by itself is inadequate. The best test of this statement is found in early *Proceedings* of the deans of men and of women. Their view of their responsibilities, and their behavior on the job, adequately rebuts the simplistic view of the authors. The authors' position is principally incorrect *by itself*, by what it ignores.

4. **"In the early 1900s student personnel workers were given the titles of 'monitor' and 'warden.'"** This is a factual misstatement, but even if it were not, one might say, "so what?" Today they are called vice presidents! A denigrating interpretation of the title monitor and warden in the 1970s is useless, aside from the fact that they had disappeared by the early 1900s.

5. **"In this model the student personnel regulator works on colonial campuses . . ."** The last referent was to the 1900s, so the reader is left with an abrupt and confusing transition. The colonial reference, of course, is ludicrous. There were no personnel workers on the colonial campus (Leonard, 1955). Any antecedent personnel services that existed in the colonial college were performed by the president and the teaching faculty. It seems unjustified that we would have to accept responsibility for the behavior of the faculty of the colonial college, even without conceding that the behavior of these colonial figures was inappropriate to their circumstances.

6. **The faculty of the colonial college had a clear frame of reference, highly moral, with a kinship to the Puritan views of the period, with all that implies.** The authors show no evidence of appreciating or understanding the differing motivations and values of historical periods. The sneering in the two quoted paragraphs obviously implies that we are in much better shape today. It is an arguable point; we aren't interested in souls any longer, because we aren't sure there is any such thing. It probably follows that we would not appreciate those for whom this was a preeminent concern.

7. **Note the reference to** *in loco parentis.* This is a legal term which did not find its way into higher education until the twentieth century. It was meant to apply to the entire collegiate system, not to student personnel work. One would suspect that the 14-year-old boys attending the colonial college probably did need some careful guidance. The important point here is that the college viewed itself as wholly responsible for these young boys (no girls, of course) and applying a twentieth century term to a complex set of concerns occurring a hundred years (and more) earlier is wholly unjustified.

8. **"He is the president's no-man."** One must glumly conclude here that the authors consulted none of the early deans' *Proceedings* readily available.

9. **In the period that spawned the creation and development of the field of student personnel administration, any number of factors existed, as indicated earlier in this chapter.** The authors have simply ignored them all.

10. **Perhaps the most revealing feature of the two paragraphs is the seventeen pejorative words contained therein, written no doubt for purposes of alliteration, but wholly void of fairness.** We find here that our predecessors sought even to "remove human potential." How believable is this assertion, even in common-sense terms?

It seems only fair to consider the authors' possible rebuttal to these comments, had they been given the opportunity. They might point out that the "model" does not necessarily refer to the later practices stemming from it. It seems clear, however, that the authors' views of the behavior of deans of the early 1900s were patterned on the model. This is an associationistic approach, and certainly the approach is valid. The argument, however, is one of content. Simply to note the "B" behavior follows from "A" behavior does not excuse the critical factor of evidence. (The laws of association date back to Aristotle!)

Why should time be spent in such an extensive rebuttal of two small paragraphs? It is important because one is not sure what impact these paragraphs will have as a written legacy. The rebuttal illustrates how difficult it would be for any of us to closely examine the written material to which we are exposed. Typically, we do not have the background, nor certainly the time, to scrutinize in depth all that we read. Although we read questioningly, we must depend upon the credibility of writers. We must be able to trust the *care* with which writers approach their work. Readers have to contend with errors of fact and problems of interpretation; it is hoped that they can avoid having to be suspicious of prejudicial work. Every writer must work to minimize this suspicion, moving the reader to the real issues under discussion.

A last example of the dilemma of historical writing is the phenomenon of *revision*. This is not a rewriting of the truth but an examination of what was genuinely thought to be true in the face of new evidence. Revision must always be held as a clear possibility in historical writing. Even long-standing assumptions should be vulnerable as new writing and thinking emerge. John Dewey once observed that as new material is developed, it will always be at the mercy of the discoveries which made it possible. Historically speaking, our field has no new materials; worse, we have not made good use of the material which already exists.

Without exception, historians must face all of the issues outlined here; they are as much a part of the discipline as are the tentative judgments that eventually find their way to the printed page. The struggle to overcome these limitations is the essence of historical writing. The accumulated successes of historians represent one major contribution to modern civilization. Our profession apparently has chosen to ignore the struggle. Our graduate schools, with some notable exceptions, have failed to prepare emerging student personnel professionals either with the tools of historical research or with an appreciation of the worth of historical understanding.

In Summary

Any number of topical issues could have been treated historically in this chapter—a practice not common in our literature. This writer has attempted to indicate a few of these issues that have had a particularly important impact on the profession, and to suggest that the myths which surround these issues have resulted in legacies which have been harmful in some instances to our self-perception and the views others have of us.

It will be necessary for future writers to research questions bearing upon the field, to see what kind of myths remain in our midst. Once new interpretations are made and reported, they will be used again, contributing to an *accepted history* that is different from present views. This may take much time, and many contributors, but until it is done the student affairs practitioner will remain cut off from the past, or will suffer from a past that never existed at all, but is believed, nonetheless.

References

Barry, R. and Wolf, B. *Modern Issues in Guidance-Personnel Work*. New York: Teachers College, Columbia University, 1963.

Bathurst, J. E. What is Student Personnel Work? *Educational Record*, 1938, 19, 502–515.

Birenbaum, W. M. The State of the Art. In T.F. Harrington, *Student Personnel Work in Urban Colleges*. New York: Intext Educational Publishers, 1974, 145–181.

Blackburn, J. L. Perceived Purposes of Student Personnel Programs by Chief Student Personnel Officers as a Function of Academic Preparation and Experience. Unpublished doctoral dissertation, Florida State University, 1969.

Blaesser, W. W. The Contributions of the American Council on Education to Student Personnel Work in Higher Education. Unpublished doctoral dissertation, George Washington University, 1953.

Boring, E. G. A *History of Experimental Psychology*. New York: Appleton, 1950.

Brewer, J. M. *History of Vocational Guidance*. New York: Harper and Brothers, 1942.

Brown, R. D. *Student Development in Tomorrow's Higher Education: A Return to the Academy*. Monograph No. 16, The American College Personnel Association, 1972.

Brubacher, J. S. and Rudy, W. *Higher Education in Transition*. New York: Harper and Row, 1968.

Callis, R. Educational Aspects of *In Loco Parentis*. *Journal of College Student Personnel*, 1967, 8, 231–234.

Cazier, S. *Student Discipline Systems in Higher Education*, (ERIC Higher Education Research Report no. 7). Washington, D.C.: American Association for Higher Education, 1973.

Cook, B. I. Sixty Years and Beyond. *Journal of the National Association for Women Deans, Administrators, and Counselors*, 1976, 39, 196–204.

Cowley, W. H. The History and Philosophy of Student Personnel Work. *Journal of the National Association of Deans of Women*, 1940, 3, 153–162.

Cowley, W. H. A Holistic Overview of American Colleges and Universities. Mimeographed, 1966, 69–86.

Crookston, B. B. An Organizational Model for Student Development. *Journal of the National Association of Student Personnel Administrators*, 1972, 10, 3–13.

Duricka, P. Moral Development: Restructuring Values. *APGA Guidepost*, May 13, 1976, 18 (1), 4.

Fley, J. Discipline in Student Personnel Work: The Changing Views of Deans and Personnel Workers. Unpublished doctoral dissertation, University of Illinois, 1963.

Fromm, E. *Escape from Freedom*. New York: Farrar and Rinehart, Inc., 1941.

Fromm, E. *Man for Himself*. Greenwich, Connecticut: Fawcett Publications, 1947.

Fromm, E. *The Sane Society*. New York: Rinehart, 1955.

Heath, K. G. Our Heritage Speaks. *Journal of the National Association for Women Deans, Administrators, and Counselors*, 1976, 39, 90–97.

Holmes, L. *A History of the Position of Dean of Women in a Selected Group of Co-educational Colleges and Universities in the United States*. New York: Teachers College, Columbia University, 1939.

Jacob, P. E. *Changing Values in College*. New York: Harper and Brothers, 1957.

Laudicina, R. and Tramutola, J. L. *A Legal Perspective for Student Personnel Administrators*. Springfield, Illinois: Charles C. Thomas, 1974.

Leonard, E. A. Origins of Personnel Services in American Higher Education. Minneapolis: University of Minnesota Press, 1956.

Lloyd-Jones, E. M. and Smith, M. R. *A Student Personnel Program for Higher Education*. New York and London: McGraw-Hill, 1938.

Lowe, C. M. *Value Orientations in Counseling and Psychotherapy*. San Francisco: Chandler Company, 1969.

Mathews, L. K. *The Dean of Women*. Boston: Houghton Mifflin Company, 1915.

Moore, P. An Analysis of the Position of Dean of Students in Selected Institutions of Higher Education. Unpublished Dissertation, The University of Southern California, 1977.

Murphy, G. *Historical Introduction to Modern Psychology*. New York: Harcourt, Brace, 1949.

Nunn, N. L. Student Personnel Work in American Higher Education: Its Evolution as an Organized Movement. Unpublished doctoral dissertation, Florida State University, 1964.

O'Banion, T. and Thurston A. (Eds.) *Student Development Programs in the Community Junior College.* Englewood Cliffs, N.J.: Prentice Hall, Inc., 1972.

Penney, J. F. Student Personnel Work: A Profession Stillborn. *Personnel and Guidance Journal,* June 1969, 47, (10), 958–962.

Phillips, K. S. *My Room in the World* (with Keith Jennison). New York, Abingdon, 1964.

Renier, G. J. *History: Its Purpose and Method.* New York: Harper and Row, 1965.

Rhatigan, J. J. History as a Potential Ally. *Journal of the National Association of Student Personnel Administrators,* 1974, 11, (3), 11–15.

Rhatigan, J. J. Student Services versus Student Development: Is There a Difference? *Journal of the National Association for Women Deans, Administrators, and Counselors,* 1975, 38 (2), 51–58.

Rogers, C. R. *Counseling and Psychotherapy.* New York: Houghton Mifflin Company, 1942.

Rogers, C. R. *Client-centered Therapy, Its Current Practice, Implications, and Theory.* Boston: Houghton Mifflin Company, 1951.

Rogers, C. R. *On Becoming a Person; a Therapist's View of Psychotherapy.* Boston: Houghton Mifflin, 1961.

Rudolph, F. The American College Student: From Theologian to Technocrat in 300 Years. Mimeographed. An address to the fifty-eighth annual conference of the National Association of Student Personnel Administrators, April, 1976.

Secretarial notes on the annual conferences of deans and advisers of men of midwestern institutions. 1921; 1923; 1924; 1927; 1928; 1929; 1932.

Talbot, M. *Journal of the Association of Collegiate Alumnae,* Series III, No. 1, 1898, 25.

Tillich, P. *The Courage To Be.* New Haven: Yale University Press, 1952.

Vermilye, D. W. Student Development in Tomorrow's Higher Education: The Beginning of a Dialogue. *Journal of College Student Personnel,* 1973, 14, (1), 77–87.

Watson, J. B. *Behaviorism.* Chicago: The University of Chicago Press, fourth impression, 1962.

Williamson, E. G. and Foley, J. D. *Counseling and Discipline.* 1st ed. New York: McGraw-Hill, 1949.

Wise, M. Existentialism and Guidance-Personnel Work. *Journal of the National Association for Women Deans, Administrators, and Counselors,* 1976, 39, 196–204.

Student Affairs and Liberal Education: Unrecognized (and Unappreciated) Common Law Partners

GEORGE D. KUH, JILL D. SHEDD, AND ELIZABETH J. WHITT (1987)

The goals of student affairs and liberal education are similar, yet in many institutions student affairs is considered ancillary to the primary purposes of the academy. The authors discuss some of the reasons for this anomaly.

The thesis of this essay is that student affairs work is undervalued in many institutions of higher education for the same reason that liberal education is not the central focus of the undergraduate curriculum of most colleges and universities. A pervasive belief system exists, particularly in large universities, that subordinates non-intellectual activities—including ways of knowing, such as intuition and esthetic appreciation—to rational, empirically based knowledge.

We provide a synopsis of the traditional roles and functions of student affairs and document the congruence between the stated purposes of liberal education and student affairs, which leads to a puzzling anomaly: If the purposes of liberal education and student affairs are similar, why are student affairs staff not usually considered equal participants in the academy? In this article we offer a partial explanation for this state of affairs and identify trends that promise some relief from the deeply embedded attitudes that fail to acknowledge contributions of student affairs to the central purposes of the academy.

Professional Heritage

Since 1870, when Harvard's president delegated to the dean responsibility for students' deportment and their spiritual and moral development, attention to the student as a "whole person" has been the raison d'être of student affairs work (Williamson, 1961). This role became even more pronounced early in the 20th century, when the rise of coeducation, coupled with a dramatic increase in the number of public colleges and universities, attracted students of more diverse backgrounds, interests, and needs to higher education (Appleton, Briggs & Rhatigan, 1978).

At approximately the same time, adaptations of the German model of higher education established research and scholarly activities as priorities at many institutions. The role expectations and responsibilities of faculty changed accordingly as increased emphasis on research and specialization began to overshadow the importance of personal growth, general studies, and ethical dimensions of higher education. "German-trained professors . . . abandoned the holistic conception of the student" (Cowley, 1983, p. 19) and emphasized the intellectual aspects of education (Williamson, 1961). The character-developing function of the professoriate all but disappeared at many institutions as teaching and research became two distinct activities (Fenske, 1980). Student affairs workers

60

willingly assumed more of the tasks that faculty had performed, including personal counseling, academic advising, recreation, vocational guidance, and student discipline—responsibilities that, if ignored, could interfere with the educational process (Appleton et al., 1978; Mueller, 1961; Williamson, 1961).

This phase in the evolution of student affairs work has been described as a protest "against the fragmentation of the individual into separable parts" (Williamson, 1961, p. 13), a reaction against rationalism and the singular emphasis on development of reason and intellect. By articulating an interest in the education of the "whole student," student affairs became the campus agency that emphasized both affective and intellectual development as important educational objectives (Appleton et al., 1978; Brown, 1972; Williamson, 1961).

Because student affairs workers performed tasks that many faculty members no longer considered integral to the academic enterprise, the faculty understandably came to regard student affairs functions as separate from the academic core of the institution. Hence, "we began by serving needs which had been pushed to the periphery . . . how to become (or whether to become) part of the mainstream is our continuing dilemma" (Appleton et al., 1978, p. 21).

In the 1970s, advocates of the student development movement claimed that an emphasis on student development would integrate out-of-classroom educational experiences into the core educational purposes of the institution (Crookston, 1976) and underscore the importance of the affective domain to the education of the "whole person" (Brown, 1972). It was presumed that, by collaborating with the faculty in interventions grounded in developmental theory, the comparability for student development principles and activities with the central teaching function of the university would become obvious. Student affairs workers would then be afforded academic credibility and respect. Credibility, however, remains an issue with which some remain concerned (Stamatakos, 1981a; Stamatakos & Rogers, 1984).

There are a number of possible explanations why faculty have had difficulty considering student affairs to be closely linked to the academic mission. A declining revenue base has made it more difficult than ever for institutions to address all desirable goals. Therefore, one can argue that activities considered by some to be tangential to the academic mission of the college, such as the extracurriculum, should be de-emphasized in times of fiscal austerity. Some of the paragons of institutional excellence, such as the Ivy League colleges and other elite liberal arts institutions, employ few professionally prepared student affairs staff members (Astin 1984), which implies that such staff may be unnecessary. Also, many institutions continue to fill student affairs positions with recent alumni whose credentials, in terms of academic or professional preparation, do not compare favorably with those presented by the faculty. Thus, in many institutions a negative role model may operate that detracts from the credibility and centrality of student affairs work.

For these reasons and others, many persons, including some who support the student affairs mission (Starnatakos & Rogers, 1984), continue to perceive the espoused goals of student affairs work (i.e., students' moral social, and physical development) to be superfluous when compared with the core activities (teaching, research, public service) of the academic enterprise (Fenske, 1980). This belief is puzzling because the aims of student affairs work seem quite compatible with the stated goals of liberal education, the alleged cornerstone of the undergraduate curriculum.

Student Affairs and Liberal Education

The objectives of a liberal education are consistent with a holistic approach to human growth and development (Berg, 1983). In ancient Greece, liberal education was a moral enterprise intended to liberate an individual from his or her limitations through mastery of fundamental concepts and principles. The "liberation" experience was thought to encourage the development of intellectual and moral autonomy and a sense of self-direction (Bailey, 1984).

In the United States, the goals of liberal education were typified by the 1828 Yale Report, which advocated development of the whole person, expanding—but keeping in balance—one's intellect and social character (Conrad & Wyer, 1980). Liberal education was considered necessary "to round out man physically and morally as well as intellectually; . . . to cultivate imagination, lengthen perspective, sober judgment, and refine taste at the same time it gave life direction and purpose" (Brubacher & Rudy, 1976, p. 280).

> No theme runs more consistently throughout the . . . literature. Education should be directed toward the growth of the whole person through the cultivation not only of the intellect and of practical competence but also of the affective dispositions, including the moral, religious, emotional, social, and esthetic aspects of the personality. (Bowen, 1977, p. 33)

Although liberal education was the foundation on which most colleges and universities established undergraduate curricula (Brubacher & Rudy, 1976), the emphasis given to liberal education has waxed and waned over the years. During the twentieth century, general education reform movements followed each of the world wars. The focus after World War I was the survey course designed to introduce undergraduates to principles and assumptions common to various disciplines. After World War II, a second revival of general education was fomented by the Harvard Report (Boyer, 1981), which recommended establishment of a core curriculum. Impetus for the current reform movement was summarized by the Carnegie Foundation for the Advancement of Teaching (1977), which described general education as a "disaster area" (p. 11). Since that time, several study commissions have condemned the specialization and vocationalism that typify undergraduate curricula, and they have challenged faculty to revise the undergraduate curriculum.

Contemporary advocates of liberal education argue that the curriculum should emphasize the incorporation of esthetic values and ethical reasoning in discussions and analyses of issues facing society (Gregory, 1982). Berkowitz's (1982) list of liberal education objectives included learning and thinking for oneself, communicating effectively, fostering intellectual curiosity and confidence, and encouraging responsibility. One-third of the institutions responding to an American Council of Education survey reported that changes in the undergraduate curriculum had recently been made (Evangelauf, 1986). These revisions have taken various forms, such as interdisciplinary courses, required or recommended distribution courses, "smorgasbord" (students select courses they deem most appealing) requirements, and models based on particular outcomes in which curriculum objectives and content are clearly explicated. Ironically, most of these reform proposals continue to underemphasize human factors such as faculty-student interaction, the ethical character of the educational enterprise, and the dynamic tradition of liberal education (Conrad & Wyer, 1980).

Comparison of Goals

In Appendix A the dimensions of student development as described in the student affairs literature are compared with the intended outcomes of liberal education. Except for two categories, interpersonal skills and physical well-being, the objectives of student affairs have obvious counterparts in the goals of liberal education.

Proponents of liberal education and champions of student affairs work seem to agree that higher education should address the development of students' personal identity, interpersonal skills, and esthetic sensibilities in addition to intellectual and academic skills (see Appendix A). "To educate liberally, learning experiences must be offered which facilitate the maturity of the whole person and enhance development of intellectual maturity. These are the goals of student development and clearly they are consistent with the mission and goals of liberal education" (Berg, 1983, p. 12).

The Anomaly

Considered together, the tradition of liberal education in American colleges and universities and the similarities between the objectives of student affairs work and liberal education present an anomaly: Given the similarities, why are student affairs staff not perceived by faculty and institutional leaders to be integral participants in the central mission of higher education? One explanation may be found in "the pervasive influence in all its myriad forms of positivist consciousness" (Lucas,

Appendix A
Comparison of Student Affairs and Liberal Education Objectives

Dimensions of Student Development	Goals and Presumed Effects of Liberal Education
Intellectual and Academic Skills	*Intellectual and Academic Skills*
• Increased complexity of thinking related to problem solving	• Independent thinking
• Enhanced capability to distill, analyze, and synthesize information	• Critical, analytical thinking
• Encouragement of lifelong learning	• Learning how to learn
Personal Identity Formation	*Personal Identity Formation*
• Sense of purpose, confidence, unified self-view	
• Empathy and trust	
• Group interaction skills	
Esthetic Development	*Esthetic Development*
• Enhanced sensitivity to and awareness of arts	• Participation in and enjoyment of cultural experience
Moral Reasoning	*Moral Reasoning*
• Integration of valid internal and external criteria	• Mature social and emotional judgment, personal integration
Physical Well-Being	*Physical Well-Being*
• Physical recreation skills	
• Personal responsibility for health	
Social Perspective	*Social Perspective*
• Ethnocentricity toward anthropocentric perspective	• Empathizing, seeing all sides of an issue

Editors Note: The Dimensions of Student Development used in the appendix were synthesized from Morrill and Hurst (1980) and Delworth and Hanson (1980). The Goals and Presumed Effects of Liberal Education used in the appendix were synthesized from Winter, McClelland, and Stewart (1981).

1984, p. 22). Positivists consciousness undergirds a more encompassing conventional paradigm, or world view, in which causal scientism is the only legitimate approach for examining events in what is believed to be a logically ordered world (Kuhn 1970; Schwartz & Ogilvy, 1979). Conrad and Wyer (1980) described a similar belief system, consisting of dualism and cognitive rationality, which is thought to be widely shared by faculties at colleges and universities.

In the positivist paradigm, dualism represents the belief that intellectual functioning is independent of affective functioning. The philosophical basis for dualism can be found in the Cartesian split between the mind and the physical realm—the bifurcation of human experience into (a) the internal and subject and (b) the object and natural (Lucas, 1985). In institutions of higher education, dualism is manifested in the distinctions drawn between intellectual functioning and personal development, the cognitive and the affective, fact and value, and the sciences and the humanities.

The companion to dualism in the positivist belief system is cognitive rationality, the method of inquiry used to achieve dualistic forms understanding. Cognitive rationality promotes a model of reason that is objective and value free. Excluded as legitimate means of understanding are morality, art, politics and religion—ways of knowing that have enriched inquiry into the human experience. "The holy triumvirate has been reason, fact and theory standing, if not opposition, certainly in superiority, to imagination, value and practice" (Conrad & Wyer, 1980, p. 54). These divisions are not value free they reflect institutionalized priorities, fueled in part by the federal government's willingness to support research in the natural sciences at a disproportionately high level, while providing less money than is needed for research in the social sciences and the humanities.

It is ironic that some theoretical scientists, especially those in physics and mathematics, have rejected the cognitive, rational model of inquiry because it is too narrow to describe adequately phenomena in the natural world (Capra, 1983; Gribbin, 1984; Kuhn, 1970). Most social scientists, however, remain devoted to the supposedly value-free objectivity of scientism and its concomitant technologies. The consequence is a sharply circumscribed conception of inquiry and understanding (Conrad & Wyer, 1980; Lincoln & Guba, 1985), which lacks a capacity to encourage interpretation and evaluation of the quality of the human experience and fails to acknowledge distinctions made possible by contributions from the affective domain.

Restraints imposed by cognitive rationality on the study of human behavior are corroborated by the lack of attention given to students' social-emotional development in the literature regarding higher education (Brown, 1972). Even in student affairs journals, personal growth is not discussed as frequently as is academic achievement and is often treated as a by-product of the educational experience or a function of the normal maturation process (Kuh, Bean, Bradley & Coomes, 1986).

Institutions of higher education have created separate but not quite equal structures to accommodate the pervasive notion of a dualistic education. The student affairs division is not engaged in curricular activities. The faculty is responsible for students' acquisition of cognitive skills and learning in the classroom. In the contrived division of labor the student is treated as a "storage tank" to be filled with facts, and, unfortunately, the integrative experiences required to apply knowledge to moral or social ends is undervalued (Cross, 1976).

An emphasis on intellectualism (manifested as dualism and cognitive rationality) has dominated American higher education since the nineteenth century and has worked against personal concern for students on the part of the faculty (American Council on Education, 1949). It is not surprising, given the pervasive influence of this positivist belief system, that students' intellectual and personal development are thought to be discrete, mutually exclusive domains and student affairs work is viewed as ancillary to the primary mission of the academy. To believe otherwise denies the existence of the positivist belief system. The power of this belief system to shape expectations for appropriate behavior and rewards in institutions of higher education should not be underestimated.

By asserting that intellectual activity is always superior to any non-intellectual or irrational behavior, the pervasive positivist belief system presents a formidable barrier to a central role for liberal education and student affairs. In contrast, advocates for student affairs and liberal education acknowledge the importance of values, emotions, and personal growth issues and argue for a holistic perspective of students' development in which the intellect and the affect are psychological domains of equal importance (Brown, 1972). Just as student affairs professional have sought recognition as full partners in the educational process, so have proponents of liberal education struggled to restore preeminence to the goal of liberal learning; that is, education of the whole person.

Cracks in the Positivist Paradigm

Challenges to the positivist belief system are being raised in many quarters. The wall dividing the scientific and human cultures in the academy

> is being continuously breached; the pattern of intellectual investigation is being rearranged . . . researchers feel the need to communicate with colleagues in other fields. This epistemological change may have a profound impact on the future of general education. Scholars . . . will, of necessity, make new connections between their own discipline and the disciplines of others. This more integrated view of knowledge and a focus on the larger questions will create . . . a climate favorable to [holistic] education. (Carnegie Foundation, 1981, p. 20)

In addition, there are stirrings beyond the academy that indicate a blurring of distinctions between the sciences and humanities, between facts and values (Ferguson, 1980; Lincoln & Guba, 1985; Schwartz & Ogilvy, 1979). A new order of things, or a new world view, is emerging to challenge many of the assumptions on which the positivist belief system is based. For example, economists once thought they could predict and influence business cycles, oil prices, exchange rates, and international competition. But the roller coaster economy of the 1970s ended such expectations (Samuelson, 1984). In a new journal, *Economics and Philosophy*, conventional, econometric models grounded in positivist assumptions are rejected and an interdisciplinary, humanistic approach to understanding human behavior in economic terms is advocated (Winkler, 1985).

Many "cutting edge" questions in physics today are not unlike those addressed by theologians and philosophers (Pagels, 1985). For decades, physicists studying quantum mechanics have observed paradoxical behavior of matter under certain conditions. Sometimes light takes on the characteristics of particles; at other times light seems wave-like (Capra, 1983). At the sub-atomic level, some experiments have suggested that particles can exist in two places at the same time (Jonas, 1982). In many other fields, such as psychology, economics, law, history, and literature (Schwartz & Ogilvy, 1979), theorists are pressing for a new synthesis that acknowledges the interrelatedness of all disciplines.

It is possible that as this synthesis or new world view evolves and positivist values of differentiation and separateness are replaced by expectations for connectedness and interrelatedness, distinctions such as "liberal education" and "student affairs" may become irrelevant. At such time, perhaps both liberal education and student affairs functions will be recognized by faculty members as central to the mission of higher education (Kuh, Whitt, & Shedd, 1987).

Coping During the Transition

Most articles in journals for practitioners close with implications and recommendations for practice. Such suggestions are often posited as an agenda of action steps that student affairs staff can follow to exert some control or influence in the college environment. One of the assertions of the emergent world view is that certainty about control or direct influence over the behavior of others is not possible because connections between causes and effects are indeterminate (Ferguson, 1980; Lincoln & Guba, 1985; Schwartz & Ogilvy, 1979). Whatever influence one has is only a small part of the numerous mutual shaping properties at work in a college or university. For example, policy enforcement and educational programming are only two of many influences on a student's use of alcohol. Just as the student affairs staff members attempt to affect students' behaviors, students are influencing the student affairs staff, other students, the faculty and parents' attitudes. The myriad reciprocal elements that constitute a campus ecology preclude prescriptions for practice.

This is not to say that student affairs staff cannot or should not act purposefully. Indeed, "the most rational response to an irrational, profoundly antihuman culture cannot be passivity or supine acquiescence but vigorous dissent, exposure, and protest" (Lucas, 1984, p. 25). Our response, however, must be deliberate and must accommodate Bullock's (1980) caveat that the emergence of a new world view and its implications for student affairs work cannot be systematically planned or manipulated like a political campaign or a religious movement. "A New Age cannot be summoned or engineered on demand" (Lucas, 1984, p. 25).

Perhaps the best a student affairs staff can do for the present is to anticipate some implications of the breakdown of the positivist belief system for student affairs. The work of Caple (1985, 1987a, 1987b) and Kuh et al. (1987) offers some suggestions in this regard. What student affairs staff should not expect is "full colleagueship" on the faculty's terms (Hurst, 1980, p. 322). Even if persuasive descriptions of the theoretical and philosophical foundations on which student affairs work is based are provided, it will be some time—if ever—before the higher education community in general is prepared to acknowledge the centrality of student affairs functions. If the past is prophetic, student affairs workers who continue to seek and perceive as valuable only one kind of recognition (i.e., the faculty's acceptance of student affairs workers as equals) will perpetuate the status quo: the primacy of the positivist belief system and (according to some) negative self-perceptions and wasted energy for student affairs workers (Stamatakos, 1981a).

We urge different tactics for the time being. First, what, if any, impact the positivist belief system has in one's institutional context must be determined by each student affairs staff member. In small liberal arts colleges, where liberal education is the institution's mission, the contributions of the student affairs staff may be considered by most faculty members to be integral to the college's mission.

Second, to cope effectively with the positivist belief system, members of the student affairs staff should hold fast to their shared purposes and more cogently articulate the contributions student affairs makes to the quality of life on college and university campuses. The current reform movement in liberal education provides what may be an unprecedented opportunity for student affairs staff to become advocates of the goals of liberal education and to exert leadership in promoting the importance of personal development and its relationship to the institution's mission (Berg, 1981). Strange (1983) recommended that student affairs staff "assume a more persuasive and knowledgeable posture in advocating *The Student Personnel Point of View*" (American Council on Education, 1949), and in nurturing a campus ethos congenial to education for the person as a whole. Advocacy of this nature must be done using language free from the jargon indigenous to the student affairs "rainforest" (Schroeder, Nicholls, & Kuh, 1983).

Third, student affairs professionals can build on the similarities between student affairs work and liberal education by continuing to collaborate with like-minded faculty members to create environments conducive to learning both inside and outside the classroom. Berte and Jackson (1985) recommended that colleges and universities adopt a systemic perspective when attempting to integrate liberal education objectives into the curriculum. That is, rather than concentrating on specific components of the curriculum, the total college environment must be considered, including departmental colloquia, institution-wide convocations, student life policies and programs, and the structure of majors. This action will require engendering a spirit of collaboration and establishing creative partnerships across campus units (academic departments, student affairs staff) to identify and articulate complementary goals of liberal education, academic majors, and student affairs programming and services. Ideas on how to establish different kinds of campus partnerships are present throughout the literature (e.g., Geller, 1982; Kuh, Schuh, & Thomas, 1985; McFarland & Meabon, 1980). One of the subthemes of the 1986 meeting of the American College Personnel Association (i.e., student affairs relationship with academic affairs) attracted 31 sessions that addressed some aspect of collaboration between student affairs professionals and the faculty (e.g., Hester, 1986; Hozman, 1986; Kim, 1986; Marrs, 1986).

Finally, the Carnegie Foundation (1985) indicated that the most common mechanism for identifying modifications for the curriculum was an all-college review committee. Representatives from the student affairs division must be involved in campus curriculum review processes to articulate curriculum revisions with student service efforts (Waters, 1985). At the least, collaboration by the student affairs staff can provide an important perspective on estimating the impact of curriculum modifications on students. Ideally, collaborative ventures are synergistic, mutually reinforcing, and self-affirming both for the faculty and the student affairs staff who are committed to the goals of liberal education.

Conclusion

As students and faculty become increasingly pluralistic, the capacity of student affairs professionals to recognize and to respond with sensitivity and creativity to individual differences will become increasingly valuable to both students and institutions (Kuh et al., 1987). In Peters and Waterman's (1982) terms, the student affairs staff members are encouraged to "stick to the knitting" (i.e., concentrate on what they do best) and not waiver from their responsibilities to promote high quality living and learning environments and help students negotiate obstacles to their education. In addition, professionals must continue to take advantage of opportunities to collaborate with faculty members in pursuing the liberating goals of the academy (Brown, 1972). But student affairs workers should evaluate their accomplishments and contributions within a humanistic frame of reference, not a positivist belief system in which the goals to which they are committed are devalued (Stamatakos, 1981b).

The emergent world view will evolve slowly. Considerable time will pass before the intellectual and affective domains are routinely viewed as inextricably intertwined rather than as mutually exclusive. Student affairs professionals must remain patient, ever vigilant to signposts of the rapprochement between the intellect and the affect, and ready to seize opportunities to demonstrate the symmetry between the holistic developmental goals of student affairs and the liberal education mission of the academy.

References

American Council on Education. (1949). *Student personnel point of view.* Washington, DC: Author.

Appleton, J., Briggs, C., & Rhatigan, J. (1978). *Pieces of eight.* Portland OR: National Association of Student Personnel Administrators.

Astin, A. W. (1984). *Achieving educational excellence.* San Francisco: Jossey-Bass.

Bailey, C. (1984). *Beyond the present and the particular: A theory of liberal education.* London: Routledge & Kegan Paul.

Berg, T. G. (1983). Student development and liberal arts education. *NASPA Journal, 21*(1), 9–16.

Berkowitz, L. J. (1982). Specifying the objectives of general education. *Journal of General Education, 34,* 210–223.

Berte, N. R., & Jackson, S. A. (1985). A system approach to a liberal arts college. *Liberal Education, 71,* 85–91.

Bowen, H. R. (1977). *Investment in learning.* San Francisco: Jossey-Bass.

Boyer, E. L. (1981). The quest for common learning. In *Common learning: A Carnegie colloquium on general education.* Washington, DC: Carnegie Foundation for the Advancement of Teaching.

Brown, R. D. (1972). *Student development in tomorrow's higher education: A return to the academy.* Washington, DC: American College Personnel Association.

Brubacker, J. S. & Rudy, W. (1976). *Higher education in transition.* New York: Harper & Row.

Bullock, A. (1980). The future of humanistic studies. *Teachers College Record, 82,* 170–172.

Caple, R. B. (1985). Counseling and the self-organization paradigm. *Journal of Counseling and Development, 64,* 173–178.

Caple, R. B. (1987a). The change process in developmental theory: A self-organization paradigm, part 1. *Journal of College Student Personnel, 28,* 4–11.

Caple, R. B. (1987b). The change process in developmental theory: A self-organization paradigm, part 2. *Journal of College Student Personnel, 28,* 100–104.

Capra, F. (1983). *The turning point: Science, society, and the rising culture.* New York: Basic Books.

Carnegie Foundation for the Advancement of Teaching. (1977). *Missions of the college curriculum. A contemporary review with suggestions.* San Francisco: Jossey-Bass.

Carnegie Foundation for the Advancement of Teaching. (1981). *Common learning: A Carnegie colloquium on general education.* Washington, DC: Author.

Carnegie Foundation for the Advancement of Teaching. (1985). General education: New support growing on campuses. *Change, 17,* 27–30.

Conrad, C. F., & Wyer, J. C. (1980). *Liberal education in transition.* Washington, DC: American Association for Higher Education.

Cowley, W. H. (1983). The nature of student personnel work. In G. Saddlemire & A. Rentz (Eds.), *Student affairs: A profession's heritage* (pp. 47–73). Carbondale: Southern Illinois University Press.

Crookston, B. B. (1976). Student personnel: All hail and farewell. *Personnel and Guidance Journal, 55,* 26–29.

Cross, K. P. (1976). *Accent on learning.* San Francisco: Jossey-Bass.

Delworth, U., & Hanson, G. R. (Eds.). *Student services: A handbook for the profession*. San Francisco: Jossey-Bass.

Evangelauf, J. (1986, July 30). *Chronicle of Higher Education*, pp. 1, 20–21.

Fenske, R. H. (1980). Current issues. In U. Delworth & G. R. Hanson (Eds.), *Student services: A handbook for the profession* (pp. 45–72). San Francisco: Jossey-Bass.

Ferguson, M. (1980). *The Aquarian conspiracy: Personal and social transformation in the 1980s*. Boston: Houghton Mifflin.

Geller, W. W. (1982). Strengthening the academic-student affairs relationship. *Journal of College Student Personnel, 23*, 355–357.

Gregory, M. W. (1982). Liberal education, human development, and social vision. *Journal of General Education, 34*, 143–158.

Gribbin, J. (1984). *In search of Schrodinger's cat*. New York: Bantam.

Hester, C. (1986, April). *Student affairs-academic affairs collaborative consultations: A review of two programs bridging the gaps*. Paper presented at the meeting of the American College Personnel Association, New Orleans.

Hozman, I. (1986, April). *Credibility, confidence, collaboration: Let's get it together with academics*. Paper presented at the meeting of the American College Personnel Association, New Orleans.

Hurst, J. C. (1980). Challenges for the future. In W. Morrill & J. Hurst (Eds.), *Dimensions of intervention for student development* (pp. 321–324). New York: Wiley.

Jonas, G. (1982, July). Reality anyone? *Science Digest*, p. 11.

Kim, J. (1986, April). *Our working relationship with academic affairs*. Paper presented at the meeting of the American College Personnel Association, New Orleans.

Kuh, G. D., Bean, J. P., Bradley, R. K., & Coomes, M. D. (1986). Contributions of student affairs journals to the college student research. *Journal of College Student Personnel, 27*, 292–304.

Kuh, G. D., Schuh, J. H. & Thomas, R. O. (1985). Suggestions for encouraging faculty-student interaction in a residence hall. *NASPA Journal, 22*(3), 29–37.

Kuh, G. D., Whitt, E. J. & Shedd, J. D. (1987). *Student affairs, 2001: A paradigmatic odyssey*. Alexandria, VA: American College Personnel Association.

Kuhn, T. S. (1970). *The structure of scientific revolutions* (2nd ed.). Chicago: University of Chicago Press.

Lincoln, Y. S. & Guba, E. (1985). *Naturalistic inquiry*. Beverly Hills, CA: Sage.

Lucas, C. J. (1984). Liberal learning and the humanities: A reaffirmation. *Journal of General Education, 36*, 20–31.

Lucas, C. J. (1985). Out at the edge: Notes on a paradigm shift. *Journal of Counseling and Development, 64*, 165–172.

Marrs, R. (1986, April). *The integration of student affairs and academics in the talent development approach*. Paper presented at the meeting of the American College Personnel Association, New Orleans.

McFarland, D. E. & Meabon, D. L. (1980). A renewed self-image for student affairs. *Journal of College Student Personnel, 21*, 280–281.

Morrill, W. H. & Hurst, J. C. (Eds.). (1980). *Dimensions for intervention for student development*. New York: Wiley.

Mueller, K. (1961). *Student personnel work in higher education*. Boston: Houghton Mifflin.

Pagels, H. R. (1985). *Perfect symmetry: The search for the beginning of time*. New York: Simon & Schuster.

Peters, T. J. & Waterman, R. H., Jr. (1982). *In search of excellence: Lessons from America's best run companies*. New York: Harper & Row.

Samuelson, R. J. (1984, April 2). The tranquility trap. *Newsweek*, p. 66.

Schroeder, C. C., Nicholls, G. E., & Kuh, G. D. (1983). Exploring the rain forest: Testing assumptions and taking risks. In G. D. Kuh (Ed.), *Understanding student affairs organizations* (New Directions for Student Services. No. 23, pp. 51–65). San Francisco: Jossey-Bass.

Schwartz, P., & Ogilvy, J. (1979). *The emergent paradigm: Changing patterns of thought and belief* (SRI International Analytical Report No. 7). Menlo Park, CA: Values and Lifestyles Program.

Stamatakos, L. C. (1981a). Student affairs progress toward professionalism: Recommendations for action, part I. *Journal of College Student Personnel, 22,* 105–113.

Stamatakos, L. C. (1981b). Student affairs progress toward professionalism: Recommendations for action, part 2. *Journal of College Student Personnel, 22,* 197–207.

Stamatakos, L. C. & Rogers, R. (1984). Student affairs: A profession in need of a philosophy. *Journal of College Student Personnel, 25,* 400–411.

Strange, C. C. (1983). Human development theory and administrative practice. Ships passing in the daylight? *NASPA Journal, 21*(1), 2–8.

Waters, G. I. (1985). Implementing general education. *Liberal Education, 71,* 335–339.

Williamson, E. G. (1961). *Student personnel services in colleges and universities.* New York: McGraw-Hill.

Winkler, K. J. (1985, June 26). Questioning the science in social science: Scholars signal a "turn to interpretation." *Chronicle of Higher Education,* pp. 5–6.

Winter, D. G., McClelland, D. C., & Stewart, A. J. (1981). *A new case for the liberal arts.* San Francisco: Jossey-Bass.

College Personnel Work as a Profession

KATE HEVNER MUELLER (1961)

The Nature of a Profession

Definition

Many definitions have been given to the word "profession," but essentially they all are in agreement. In 1936, Roscoe Pound identified a profession as "an *organized* calling in which men pursue some *learned* art and are *united* in pursuit of it as a *public service.*"[1] Earlier, Abraham Flexner had set forth six criteria to follow in determining professional status: (1) intellectual aspirations coupled with large individual responsibilities, (2) raw materials drawn from science and learning, (3) practical application, (4) educationally communicable techniques, (5) tendency toward self-organization, and (6) increasingly altruistic motivation.[2] These criteria have been modified and expanded but not substantially changed. One critic summarized his studies with the statement that there is no accepted definition of *profession* and that the interpretation of such a concept is a matter of personal temperament.[3]

The purpose of defining an organization, aside from the interests of the lexicographer, is to redirect the attitudes of both those inside the group and those outside it. Since any profession demands arduous training and a personal commitment to an exacting ethical code, individuals need a special kind of persuasion in order to enter it. If it is to make progress, the idealistic concepts of yesterday must become today's operating principles and tomorrow's action. Any profession which does not concern itself with its own history and its own problems may become unsure of its rights, privileges, and responsibilities; unaware of the creeping encroachment of other professions, or of the shifting currents of public attitudes. The American Association for the Advancement of Science asserts that its goals are to further the work of scientists, facilitate co-operation among scientists, improve the effectiveness of science in the promotion of human welfare, and increase public understanding and appreciation.[4] Membership in a professional organization is voluntary. The organization decides on its own existence and purpose, expresses the aspirations of its members, and is stable only so long as the need for it continues.[5]

The most significant role of any professional organization is to serve its individual members, for the members in turn serve society. Service to members is of three kinds: (1) clarifying the objectives and stimulating members to achieve them; (2) meeting the member's needs for knowledge, status, and security; and (3) recruiting new members. The first—the continuous forward-looking study and modification of objectives and issues—is the most difficult. It requires imagination, the broadest possible perspective, and diligent study on the part of many leaders. It is not easy to achieve the needed perspective by means of tracing the history, or more properly the evolution, of issues. Issues are not usually clearly stated in official reports or summaries, but are more often introduced obliquely in comments or criticisms which are sometimes buried in by-laws or resolutions, sometimes neglected and unpublished. Perhaps this situation is to be expected of a young and overgrown profession attempting to meet the exorbitant public demands made upon it.

The accumulated knowledge of the profession reaches its members through published journals, monographs, and books and, of course, meetings, conventions, and workshops. Status and security are offered by means of fellowship and enjoyment of personal relationships, pride in the central office and group achievements, identification with the ideologies and the individuals representing the best professional standards, placement opportunities, and the maintenance of the bulwarks of research.

The recruiting of new members and the building of good public relations are reciprocal functions, sustained by a continuous barrage of information, both formal and informal, and by individual example as well as planned group endeavor.

As a profession, college personnel work is only a few decades old. The first formal curriculum "for deans and advisers of women and girls" was offered in 1913.[6] Of all the professional organizations in this field, the National Vocational Guidance Association is the oldest and largest; as is implied in the name, it has been most concerned with vocational, less concerned with educational, guidance. The present National Association of Student Personnel Administrators had its origins in the former National Association of Deans of Men organized about 1919. The National Association of Women Deans and Counselors dates from 1916. The American College Personnel Association originated in the twenties, and was one of the associations which, in 1934, helped to establish a loose federation, the Council of Guidance and Personnel Associations, whose chief function lay in planning joint conventions. Not until 1952 did the Council members work toward one over-all, more unified and representative association, the present American Personnel and Guidance Association.

Since these associations are, for the most part, young as compared with most such affiliations, Caplow's delineation of the steps by which working groups achieve full recognition and status makes provocative reading for all personnel workers:

> The first step is the establishment of a professional association, with definite membership criteria designed to keep out the unqualified.

> The second step is the change of name, which serves the multiple function of reducing identification with the previous occupational status, asserting a technological monopoly, and providing a title which can be monopolized, the former one being usually in the public domain.

> The third step is the development or promulgation of a code of ethics which asserts the social utility of the occupation, sets up public welfare rationale, and develops rules which serve as further criteria to eliminate the unqualified and unscrupulous. The adoption of the code of ethics, despite certain hypocrisies, imposes a real and permanent limitation on internal competition.

> The fourth step is a prolonged political agitation, whose object is to obtain the support of the public power for the maintenance of the new occupational barriers. In practice this usually proceeds by stages from the limitation of a specialized title to those who have passed an examination (registered engineer, certified public accountant) to the final stage at which the mere doing of the acts reserved to the profession is a crime.

> Concurrently with this activity, which may extend over a very long period of time, goes the development of training facilities directly or indirectly controlled by the professional society, particularly with respect to admission and to final qualification; the establishment through legal action of certain privileges of confidence and inviolability, the elaboration of the rules of decorum found in the code, and the establishment—after conflict—of working relations with related professional groups.

> It is difficult to exaggerate the importance of this general phenomenon for the structure of the economy. So powerful are the motives conducive to professionalization that it may be observed underway in occupations once considered entirely commercial (banking, advertising), in occupations which never involve

independent work (drafting, photographic processing), and in those which used to be thought of as quite removed from the economic arena (philanthropy and the research sciences). Even pure management is perhaps in the process of being professionalized, and it is not farfetched to suppose that the professional society may eventually be counted among the major social institutions.[7]

Shartle's description of the rise and fall of organizations is not meant to be applied to professional associations, but, since cycles of some kind seem to be characteristic of human groups, his theory deserves some thought. Briefly, it is as follows. Groups are formed with high expectations, but the early difficulties are not correctly anticipated; the groups must be reorganized and revitalized, when they encounter reality. The reorganization is followed by a period of growing achievement which reaches and maintains a peak before the beginnings of decline are detected. Decline may be due to a lack of vitality within the group or to failure to keep step with the environment. Serious difficulties arise, one after another, and eventually a major deterioration is evident. Extinction follows, or sometimes absorption into another organization. The latter marks a rejuvenation, and the beginning of a new cycle.[8]

Wrenn and Darley agreed in 1947 that college personnel work was not yet fully a profession, although some of its members were professionals and some of its duties and levels met the criteria for professional status.[9] It is obvious that, to use Smith's term, different parts of a profession "metabolize" at different rates.[10] From Horton's criteria,[11] Wrenn and Darley chose eight which seemed applicable for judging personnel's claim to professionalization and appraised the progress as follows:

1. *Standards of selection and training.* Here they observed striking evidence of progress, although there was much variation within levels and specialties.

2. *Definition of jobs and titles.* There were few, if any, attempts at standardization in this area, although personnel was no worse than any other professions.

3. *The profession of specialized knowledge and skills.* For personnel work, there is not one unique skill, but the specialization takes the form of a pattern or combination of skills which have been developed or which have been borrowed from other disciplines.

4. *Development of professional consciousness and professional groups.* This process was still in the promotional stage but well begun.

5. *Self-imposition of standards of admission and performance.* Only the American Psychological Association and the Certification of Public School Guidance Workers could be cited as organizations which had fulfilled this criterion.

6. *Legal recognition of the vocation.* Here there was very little progress.

7. *Development of a code of ethics.* For personnel work good morale and personal integrity took the place of a more obvious formulation of a code.

8. *Performance of a socially needed function.* Whether personnel work met this criterion was difficult to appraise, but there was an abundance of pertinent evidence leading Wrenn and Darley to believe that the work was needed by society.

The characteristic problems of a profession identified by sociologists and other analysts can be readily observed in the histories of the various personnel associations. Membership, selection, and training present special dilemmas in the growing years of a profession. Most personnel associations, recognizing as of first importance the need to educate and inspire their practitioners to better work in whatever situation they are now, have admitted members on the basis of actual job responsibilities rather than on the basis of educational requirements or other standards. If an individual is holding a position in which counseling, advising, or personnel administration is a part of the assignment, and even if he is a mere beginner shifting into this field from some other, he is welcome to membership. Ordinarily a college degree is required.

Caplow explains that the supply of practitioners is, in the short run, unchangeable, and he has observed a general tendency for the supply of workers to decrease in periods of increased demand, for an increase in the demand for professional service tends to strengthen the entire system of professional controls by first eliminating substandard training centers and also by tightening eligibility requirements for candidates.[12] But this state of affairs would hardly apply to personnel work at present, for, as Hitchcock and others have pointed out, the shift from teaching to counseling is easily made.

The question whether highly selective recruitment is a guarantee of competent service to the client or a guarantee of economic protection to the successful candidate and an artificial restriction of vital public services has been answered by Caplow, who estimates that at both extremes of the business cycle, in economic depressions and in booms, "professional service will become flatly unavailable to large segments of the population."[13] In periods of depression clients cannot afford the services, and in good times the demand outstrips the supply. It is especially difficult for any group to maintain professionalism when both the state and the large corporations are demanding more workers than can readily be supplied. College personnel, like other academic groups, must always bewail the loss of its trained professional workers to industry. An individual member of any professional group may develop a personal problem and find it necessary to resign if he is dissatisfied with the prescribed ethical code, or with other restrictions, or if he finds that he can move into a neighboring profession which offers more prestige—for example, into a group who have higher membership standards or higher salaries.

Another recognized problem is the tendency of large and powerful subgroups within an overall parent association to dominate the interests or prestige or leadership of a profession. Sometimes the very existence of a small division—for example, the Esthetics Division of the American Psychological Association with only one hundred members—has been threatened with elimination unless more members were forthcoming and more interest demonstrated among the 16,000 members in the Association. Subgroups sometimes prefer the fellowship and social contacts made possible by maintaining the smaller group. Occasionally, a subdivision of a large organization—for example, the Teachers' College Section of the National Association of Women Deans and Counselors—has voluntarily voted itself out of existence when there developed too much overlapping of activities and interest. The typical tendency would have been to perpetuate the division even beyond its period of usefulness.

Other problems arise as a result of the inevitable discrepancy between ideal and practice. For example, the welfare of the members takes priority as an announced policy of the profession, but in actual practice the issues become confused. More widespread knowledge and insight are needed to clarify them. As Hilton observes, ideally the needs of women counselors and women students should be met when men and women work together in a joint association, but practically they are not. For the present at least, women will find it necessary to belong to both the general and the special group.[14]

Evaluating the Professional Status of College Personnel Work

To attempt to evaluate an abstract quality such as professional status is quite a different matter from the task of evaluating the workings of a machine or even of the human body. The latter can be determined by strictly empirical means, and it makes little difference (1) who is doing the evaluating, (2) what he is looking for, or (3) how the process of examination itself may affect the machine or body. Evaluation of a social institution, however, such as a personnel organization, which may be small and local or large and national, is a self-initiating process in which each of these three questions becomes of vital importance.

There seems to be no disagreement at the moment concerning the need or the authority for the evaluation of the profession of personnel work, for many individuals both inside and outside the profession are asking for it, raising questions, and seeking issues. The first question of who has the skills, the experience, the information, and the perspective for the job is spontaneously resolved whenever a scholar or reputable committee has the courage to undertake it. Anyone is welcome to the job, and much can be learned from the attempt, although the self-appointed or duly assigned evaluator has no authority over the profession, no privileges, and no contract. He is completely on his own; he may or may not exert some influence or produce an effect, but the exercise itself is satisfying and stimulating.

The examiner is looking for any possible sign of effective or defective functioning, as measured against (1) what he conceives to be the goals of the operation, (2) what rate of efficiency he accepts as standard, (3) how keenly he perceives the meanings of certain signs, and (4) how deeply he probes for the signs themselves. Obviously, any evaluator needs help on all four aspects of his inquiry. There seems to be no limit to the methods, ideas, and facts that he must borrow for his work, and likewise no limit to the improvement for the association if his work counteracts complacency, stimulates imagination, and widens perspectives.

The profession of college personnel work suffers and benefits from being allied with another profession, higher education, which has its own trouble with a precise definition of ends and means. One cannot even assume that the personnel movement's goals are accepted as a part of the goals of formal education, although the two must at least be superficially coordinated and reconciled. In the interest of efficiency and especially for the purpose of training its recruits, it seems wise to pose the question, What can personnel work offer today's youth which he patently needs but cannot receive from any other professional worker in the whole system of higher education?

In order to answer this question effectively, personnel work must take a good look at its history and present status and at the persons, groups, movements, philosophies, policies, and services with which the personnel worker and his professional organization are related. Earlier evaluators of older professions have described the points of reference which are useful for such a judgment. It will also be enlightening to compare personnel's patterns of growth with theirs as it repeats the same stages of development. These points of reference for evaluation, for encompassing the data, and for describing issues and prophesying the future include the following:

1. *History and perspective.* The evaluator should seek information about the origins of personnel activity, the trends it nurtured, the tools it devised, successes and failure it encountered, specialties it developed, and schisms it fostered from the early beginning through the years up to the present.

2. *Neighboring professions.* We need to know how and how much they overlap with personnel, their pressures and resistances, their attitude, the degree of their co-operation with personnel, current trends and basic philosophies.

3. *Objectives.* An evaluation of objectives must explore the number and variety of different points of view, how they relate to each other, to various philosophical systems, and to ethics, psychology, and the social sciences.

4. *Members.* It is important to know how many members there are; into what group, layers, and strata, levels of work, and fields of endeavor they are divided, who among them are leaders and followers, their geographical distribution, and their security and orientation.

5. *Required skills and training.* The evaluator must discover the variation in levels of work, learn the difference in degree between the most adequately and least adequately trained and the number in each category, determine a hard core of essential skills, and measure the average length of training of the generalists and the specialists.

6. *Public relations.* The evaluator must find out what the public's image of the profession is—the "professional fictions," the stereotypes, the public rewards and prestige and the degree of rapport and morale.

Since all modern complex professions have multiple relations with other groups and with the public, to say nothing of the multiple interrelations among the subgroups which they foster within themselves, the rate of growth and the professional health of each subgroup show great variations. Therefore, the major questions—What are the issues? Is the progress satisfactory? Are the goals appropriate and the skills adequate? Which philosophy is most acceptable?—can have only multiple answers, different ones for each subgroup and each relationship. The attempt to resolve any one issue of any one subgroup can elicit only a summary approximation; an "answer" for the whole profession would come only from some rash interloper who could take the next train out of town.

Can any critic hope to identify just those issues which are most significant for present needs, to omit no important or relevant fact or historical event in evaluating them, to purge any bias of his own which would vitiate his judgment? Yet this near-perfection is required for useful insights and profitable predictions; therefore, most critics are reluctant to add the role of prophesy to that of present appraisal, and long-term programs, though needed, are rare.

History and Perspective

The past history, or rather histories, of the personnel profession (before enough of the various movements had merged to give it a unified character) is devious and difficult to trace, because it is a composite of many diverse activities: the industrial and business personnel movements, at first quite separate from the educational streams, as well as the development of the techniques of testing and counseling, the fortuitous impetus to personnel growth granted by two world wars, and the needs growing out of the tremendous changes in society. There have been many criticisms to be absorbed and some unwelcome pretensions to be outgrown.

Many of the issues which the profession faces today are the result of historical accident; for example, the lack of numerical balance among the subgroups of the profession as well as the alienation of some of them.

The American Personnel and Guidance Association has about 11,000 members, owns a headquarters building in Washington with an executive secretary and staff, and includes the following divisions: The American College Personnel Association; the National Association of Guidance Supervisors and Counselor Trainers; the National Vocational Guidance Association; the Student Personnel Association for Teacher Education; the American School Counselors Association (for those in secondary schools) the Division of Rehabilitation Counseling. It publishes the *Personnel and Guidance Journal* with nine issues each year.

The National Association of Women Deans and Counselors numbers 2,000 members and employs an executive secretary and staff housed in the Washington headquarters of the National Education Association, of which this group is a department. Its sections include the College, the University, the Junior College, the High School, and the Junior High School. It publishes a quarterly journal.

The National Association of Student Personnel Administrators has only a small proportion of women members, and it encourages corporate memberships, i.e., with the institution, rather than the individual, paying the dues. It publishes its annual convention proceedings and a news sheet, both mimeographed.

The American Psychological Association includes a Division of Counseling Psychology which serves the needs of many personnel workers who are also psychologists.

Tradition has dictated more of the present alignments of personnel groups than either logic or a genuine sharing of goals and interests. This fact, of course, is true of the subgroups of many other professions, and, although it does not constitute a real threat, it may be a danger to organizational health. It is obvious that, in evaluating the profession, historical accident must always temper the critic's judgment. It is obvious, too, that the existence of specialties foster the formation of independent groups who cherish their exclusiveness, their practice of invited memberships.

Neighboring Professions

The neighboring professions have a strong and, in some but not all respects, a legitimate voice in determining the objectives and methods of any new profession. They are the most insistent in demanding to know why the new service is necessary and what demonstrated need of society it meets. For personnel workers some of the more obvious problems which demand professional attention are the undersupply and oversupply of trained workers in various occupations, the waste of high intellectual ability with the parallel waste of educational opportunity on the academically inadequate, and the burden of socialization placed on higher education by the increasing heterogeneity of student populations. As the new profession develops, it may attract recruits from contiguous professions, and it inevitably comes into some conflict with the closest ones. The conflict will be more or less serious depending on how much income or prestige or job satisfaction is involved.

The steps in the process of professionalization, Caplow claims, are quite definite.

> Even the sequence is explicit, so that we may illustrate it with equal facility from the example of newspaper reporters (journalists), real estate agents (realtors), undertakers (morticians), junk dealers (salvage consultants), or laboratory technicians (medical technologists).[15]

As the new profession emerges, it tries to take on the functions of the group just above it and slough off the unwanted tasks to those below. Members of contiguous groups are always caught in a crossfire when their directives are at variance. Thus, pathologists claim the right to see the patient at his bedside (a right resisted by physicians), and nurses assign certain jobs to nurses' aids.[16]

Darley's forthright description of the attitudes of the neighboring profession of teaching is fourfold. (1) Those in personnel work are seen as members of the administrative hierarchy; "the nicest thing they can say about administration is that it is a necessary evil, and they are sure that they could get along with much less of it." (2) Personnel workers represent ancillary services and if there is pressure to reduce expenditures faculty think that they can get rid of them. (3) The counselor coddles and salvages those who would otherwise flunk out and should flunk out. (4) The counselor's quasi-Freudian, quasi-psychometric jargon is pure nonsense, and his pretense of confidentialness merely a shield to hide behind when the welfare of the institution may be involved.[17]

All the mental therapists, psychiatrists, clinical psychologists, psychometrists, and especially counseling psychologists belong to important contiguous groups whose goals and methods overlap with those of personnel workers. The separation is clearly marked by medicine and psychology with their national boards of examiners and diplomates and by school psychologists and psychometrists with public school licensing; and the American Personnel and Guidance Association has recently established its own Board of Professional Standards.

The personnel worker is quite aware of his own limitations in counseling; therefore, he focuses his efforts quite properly on the normal, not the pathological, personality. Of course, in view of the extent of the public need, there is plenty of room for workers at all levels, for it has been repeatedly pointed out that an adequate program of mental health in any community would take *all* the man hours of time of *all* the physicians available. One critic has declared that it requires ten thousand dollars, three years, and an intelligent client to come to grips with the total personality in psychoanalysis and that it is even more difficult in working with an adolescent for whom the norm is much more difficult to determine; yet personnel workers with much less training show no hesitation in tackling the problem perhaps at the rate of an hour a month for one semester! The educators claim that by their teaching and their continuous process of grading, they are actually hastening the student's maturing fully as much as any personnel specialist.[18]

Management, whether college vice-presidents or secondary school principals, forms another contiguous group which may look askance at personnel work as a haven for "empire-building" and the fulfillment of Parkinson's Law, "Work expands so as to fill the time available for its completion."[19] The matter of budget is frequently a major point of conflict. Also, on occasion the genus "administrator" in a young profession has a pretentiousness which becomes most objectionable, for in the younger professions the aggressive personality sees its best chance for rapid rise. Many in the top echelons of personnel work are thoroughly modest and sensitive persons but one who is not, too easily becomes the stereotype. Administration and faculty, however, are very glad to have the personnel worker relieve them of the onerous duty of discipline, and they would also prefer not to return to the campus early in September to deal with orientation.

Objectives

Some evaluators have sought to relate the personnel profession to one or another current philosophical system and thereby to identify a "philosophy" of personnel work. "Objectives," however, seem to be a more meaningful concept than "philosophy" for the following reasons. From the most ancient times, philosophy has sought to explain the nature of knowledge by the armchair method using speculation and logic. But modern education is an applied social science and therefore seeks its theory and principles in the social sciences of psychology, sociology, anthropology, even perhaps in history and economics, relating its principles only remotely and much less profitably to the basic concepts of philosophy. The foundations of modern education are observation and experimentation, concerning the laws of learning, the nature of personality, and the behavior of man interacting with others.

> No philosophical concept or philosophy of education ever appears in actual existence as a pure form and no matter how hard an educator tries, he cannot build an educational institution upon conceptions which then reproduce themselves in reality.[20]

For example, the instrumentalist philosophy, which seems most compatible to personnel workers, depends for its usefulness to educators on a special interpretation: "not individualism as a doctrine of enlightened self interest, but individualism as the full development of the individual in the development of his society." [21]

In other words, the current philosophies which might be useful to education are themselves expressed in terms of the individual and his society, thus making it clear that it is to psychology and sociology that the educator must look to test his goals and methods. Whether these sciences have themselves absorbed the functions of philosophy for the educator or whether philosophy is expressing itself through these sciences is not of first importance to the personnel profession, which is primarily concerned with the soundness of its methods and objectives. "Philosophy" for our purposes is, therefore, a matter of establishing ends and means in current psychological and sociological systems and research. Thus the term "objectives" is perhaps more suitable to the subject at hand.

In 1947, student personnel work was defined as "actually a collective term for a number of specialized vocations having a common goal in the extra classroom adjustment of the student."[22] Today the "adjustment" concept is not so acceptable. Shoben describes the goal of personnel work in relation to one of the basic functions of higher education, that of being a socialization agent in order to facilitate the personal development of young people in the interest of enriching the human resources of American society. More particularly, he outlines college personnel functions as directed toward (a) helping students to gain greater personal maturity through reflected-upon experience; (b) increasing their interpersonal effectiveness; (c) deepening their sensitivity to human needs including their own; (d) clarifying their long-range objectives in both vocational and more personal terms; (e) assisting in their interpretation of education both in their active student careers and in their lives after graduation.

His point of view is further clarified by noting the means to these ends: (a) facilitating the formation of personal identifications, and burnishing one's ideas in social skills through personal relationships; (b) conceiving of the campus as a kind of social microcosm in which students may acquire knowledge, skills, motivations, values, and personal attributes, in which the programs of the counseling service, student government, residence halls, clubs, etc., are neither fundamentally rehabilitative nor basically recreational in any narrow sense, but rather (1) opportunities for the students to test and to modify their growing knowledge and experience in situations of immediate importance to them; (2) encouragement of contacts for students with staff and faculty and thereby exposing them to many models of educated adults.[23]

Shoben rightly observes that "there is no contradiction between the objectives of personnel officers and their instructional colleagues." Critics would point out, however, that neither is there any differentiation between the objectives, except perhaps a quantitative one, with the classroom teacher doing less work toward socialization and the counselor more. They would also further point out that all these objectives and methods are those of life itself. Other objections arise with such questions as: How much of all these high-sounding goals can or should be accomplished during the four campus years? How well can any *one* profession be prepared to carry out such an assignment?

In addition to Wrenn's definition, based on observation of the programs of the college personnel divisions, and Shoben's seemingly unlimited perspectives, the profession needs a more specific answer to our original question: What can personnel workers offer to youth which is needed, and which no other profession has the opportunity and skill to provide? Barry and Wolfle have set forth eight possible answers or approaches to personnel work gleaned from their study of the history of the guidance-personnel movement, each of them differentiated as clearly as possible.[24] Each of their central concepts is therefore a specific working theory for one aspect of the profession's total program, and is in some cases the only theory behind the individual program of one campus or public school system. These all-inclusive concepts would be more useful to the profession if the leaders in the field could determine which ones are waxing or waning in effectiveness and could embrace one or the other as the most fruitful or promising. The approaches are, (1) the educational-vocational view, (2) the services view, (3) the counseling view, (4) the adjustment view, (5) the problem-centered view, (6) the educative view, (7) the developmental view, and (8) the integrated view. The last, also called the eclectic view, is mainly in the theoretical stage and is the most radically different approach.

The educational-vocational view emphasizes the practical ends of education for the world of work, and therefore leans heavily on quantitative measurement and occupational research. It obviously requires special knowledge and methods which the classroom teacher cannot develop, and it is aimed at Shoben's "clarifying the student's long-range objectives in vocational terms."

The services view, commonly held in college personnel work and growing in emphasis in secondary-school work, is a justification, for the melange of personal responsibilities that college personnel workers had acquired by 1930. It views the student as a whole, but as a whole which is the sum of many parts, and provides services for those parts of the student personality which had been neglected by higher education's attention to the intellectual.

The counseling view emphasizes the developing personality by adapting the deeper therapy of the clinicians to the typical and normal problems of the adolescent as he is confronted with the complexities of campus life and educational choices.

The adjustment view extends the counseling view to include the development of the person in relation to all the problems of society as well as to his own self-integration. These two views have sometimes been combined to produce the problem-centered view.

The problem-centered view, in which the emphasis has shifted toward the diagnostic function rather than the therapeutic, is significant because present-day educational pressures have too often forced personnel workers to concentrate on the misfits and problem groups.

The educative view calls attention to the talents and opportunities of the classroom teacher in guidance work, and the unfortunate results when an amateur works "on" the student rather than "with" him.

The developmental view has the advantage of emphasizing the developmental tasks at each age level, and makes a nice compromise between the educative and services views by recognizing the inner life as a continuous unfolding which demands special services at strategic points.

The integrated view might also be called the ideal view. It is actually rooted in a reaction to all the other prevalent approaches. In this view, might not the profession recognize the first seven merely as historical incidents from which useful objectives and theory for the present might be constructed? This would call for a separation of the ideal not only from the impractical but also from the unsound. It is, for example, impractical to emphasize individual counseling when the rising tide of students calls for the extension of group techniques. It is impractical to expect the older generations of classroom teachers to embrace with enthusiasm the attitudes and methods for successful counseling. But it is unsound to accept the campus as a microcosm of the world outside, for this is not the case. The campus is a very specialized "slice of life" in its superficial characteristics as well as in all its deeper attitudes and motivations.

Members

In any evaluation and search for issues which need thought and planning, a study of the individual members provides important clues to the status of the profession. Within the subgroups—counselor trainers, deans of men and women, administrators, college and high school divisions—there are not only varieties of functions, levels, and training, but also different ages, ambitions, sexes, and personalities. Smith points out that the officers and leaders are usually selected from the avant-garde, those with higher-level jobs and long training. They are oriented to the future and, therefore, demand change, tending to ignore those whose training fitted them for their present functions only and whose wish is therefore to maintain the status quo.[25] Wrenn and Darley indeed question whether all divisions and members of a profession *should* be professionalized.[26] Quite obviously the divisions of guidance personnel work have tacitly operated on this principle, for they do not set up training criteria or levels of membership even though such steps have often been recommended and discussed.[27] Many members actually feel closer to neighboring professions—e.g., psychology or another social science, management, or even subject-matter fields, if they plan eventually to return to teaching. This may be true in other professions as well; some nurses may feel closer to administration than to nursing as such, some psychiatrists may feel closer to the social sciences than to medicine, etc.

The leadership which any professional organization always feels that it owes to its members may be regarded as service either to present constituencies or to future programs. The very planning of conventions and the publication of journals, handbooks and monographs provides the information and motivation necessary for the routine functioning of the members in their jobs; and, whenever leaders are forced to choose between these services and planning for the future, they can do no less than tip the balance in favor of the members' immediate needs. On the other hand, many of the individual leaders are active in neighboring professions or other groups whose functions are more clearly defined as future- or research-oriented. Thus outstanding scholars in personnel work have pioneered through membership on committees of the American Council on Education with funds which would have been unavailable in their own professional subgroups. Likewise, in the Division of Counseling Psychology of the American Psychological Association, research is undertaken as often as not by members who are primarily personnel workers. In the war years, well-trained personnel workers moved into Army, Navy, or Air Force research and the not-so-well trained moved along with them to complete their training, pushing their well-financed "leadership" far beyond the limits afforded by their previous academic and professional affiliations. The war service illustrates very clearly the outside pressures which mold the direction of leadership. Leaders are not free agents whose sole function is to think deeply and judge wisely, and the anticipated increases in campus populations can be expected to diminish quite considerably the time and energy available for research, as well as to determine to some extent the general direction.

Individuals within a profession also want the pride and security which come with such amenities as a central office for their organization, a placement service, eminent speakers, and travelling officers, but, often underpaid themselves, they complain about the increasing costs. They are especially reluctant to assume the expense of belonging to several subsections with financial dues to perhaps three different parent groups: the National Education Association, the American Psychological Association, and the American Personnel and Guidance Association.

It is said that a professional association should also offer its members leaders with whom they can find an identification which adds to their job satisfaction. Here, again, great differences in level, training, orientation, and function between the leader and the individual members may invite hostility rather than identification. Such a dichotomy exists in other educational associations where there are great differences in level and training. Obviously, those who have made it their business to train counselors, to write books, to carry on research, and supervise theses are better prepared for leadership than those who have not. In spite of sincere efforts to the contrary, their faces and names are prominent in conventions, publications, and projects, partly because they are likely to have personal funds or expense accounts to help finance them in such work. More subdivisions by level may dispel the problem which Hitchcock foresees: that guidance in the public schools will not get the understanding and qualitative emphasis of personnel work on the college level.[28]

The American College Personnel Association and others have studied the possibilities for holding a biennial national convention and regional meetings in alternate years—a pattern which has been found satisfactory in some other professions. Combinations of various subgroups and neighboring professions by means of councils at the local level could explore the declared need for better communications. Either plan might build up personal relationships which would in turn obviate the confusion and lack of warmth at the national conventions. However, such factors as specialty, sex, and level of education and responsibility affect the backgrounds, personal qualities, and interests of individuals attracted to the profession; therefore, attempts to "warm up" the professional ties at yearly meetings will inevitably strike some members as cheap and artificial.

Required Skills and Training

A young profession must always justify its claim to certain skills which other professions and the general public do not possess. As yet, however, college personnel has no convincing answers to the three searching questions: To what specific end are you helping your client? How do you know that he has been helped? How do you know that some other person or method might not have helped him?

The tools of the profession include tests of all kinds, interviewing and counseling, statistical processes, all the varieties of group dynamics and social interaction, the principles of management, and all the methods of teaching. All these, of course, have widely advertised inherent weaknesses; they are also often misapplied and go through cycles of waxing and waning popularity. After reviewing many of the texts and monographs on counseling, Shoben reported that

> with the public demand for service high, there is apparently a considerable interest in publications dealing with techniques, less in books seriously occupied with knowledge and understanding. There seems to be a tendency for practice to divorce itself from science.[29]

With a similar outlook Darley says that we have outrun our research substrates and traditions in our desire to be of help to individuals and that we too often retreat to doctrinaire or cook-book treatises.[30]

Borow explains this dilemma as follows:

> With the exception of the classical psychoanalysts, neo-analysts, and client centered counselors (and in the strict sense most student personnel workers are none of these), there are few who operate out of an established system. This is partly because the training of personnel workers is likely to be eclectic rather than doctrinal and partly because they perceive the practical and urgent demands of their jobs as unmet by current theoretical models of behavior. Thus, the attractiveness of theory among those who *write about* students is unmatched by those who *serve* students. . . . The serious question of the moment is whether or not current theory is sufficiently mature to generate the productive research hypotheses which are indispensable to the advancement of the field.[31]

Eli Ginzberg recently made some forthright statements characteristic of the economist's emphasis on vocational counseling. Effective guidance, he says, comes with the pressures of society and the shape of the economy, as well as from traits and interests within the family and the community culture. He and others in his field question the efficacy of formalized guidance programs since the best economic predictions cannot foretell conditions a decade in advance! Can guidance explain why, for those not going to college, there is no relation between the future occupation and the first job?

Criticisms of the methods of guidance are probably not so devastating as its enemies have suspected nor so inconsequential as the guidance enthusiasts have hoped. Perhaps the commonest error both inside and outside the profession, especially outside, is to take techniques designed and found fruitful in research and to use them too literally with clients. The amateur will always have difficulty in interpreting the knowledge gained in research. The important issue for the profession, then, probably lies not in the inadequacies in research and the use of method, but rather in the rank-and-file counselor's too great reliance on any and all techniques as straightforward means for achieving announced goals.

The loose and confusing use of the terms "counselor" and "counseling" is another source of criticism. A decade ago, Wrenn could say:

> Training for counseling has been more clearly formulated than that of any other function, with the exception, of course, of the health service function. This is as it should be, for counseling is basic to almost all types of personnel work. Such training can be considered as basic to the performance of specific personnel functions as general medical training is to its specialties.[32]

More recently, however, there seems to be little argument on this score. Perhaps the great advances in counseling theory and method have made the profession more self-conscious in its use of the term, underlining the vast difference between the experienced counselor and a 22-year-old graduate of a single two-hour course in counseling techniques. The word "counselor," however, is still widely used. Hitchcock, in his illuminating presentation of public school guidance problems to the Association for Higher Education, says that "education for most guidance positions is basically the education of the counselor and the counselor is the principal professional person in any guidance program."[33] Counselor is so evidently a more convenient word than the unglamorous circumlocutions of "guidance worker" or "personnel worker." A new nomenclature for personnel work is badly needed.

The knowledge and skills required for personnel work have been listed and classified by many individuals and by appointed committees of the professional associations, and hardly a year goes by without some published opinions or data on this subject. One writer specified the following: (1) skill in the use of personnel procedures, (2) skill in identifying needs and problems, and (3) skill in handling interviews and group leadership situations. Longer lists have included many more items, and there is no lack of curriculum specifications and other prerequisites. Wrenn suggested two years of graduate work as a minimum; he specified a genuine interest in people, an emotional detachment, and a personality fitted for a role at once subordinate and responsible. He also recommended the Ph.D. degree rather than the Ed.D. to "avoid real or imagined condescension."[34]

If a personnel division in some of our larger universities can offer graduate internships in personnel when not one counseling staff member meets the requirements of diplomate under the National Board of Examiners in Counseling, the students, both graduate and undergraduate, may not be well served. There is some sympathy with the faculty complaint that

> individual counseling . . . is too frequently hit or miss and haphazard in application, carried on by personnel of good intent but little training or natural aptitude for counseling, and brought into play only when a student's problem has reached the point where it may be too late for counseling.[35]

There have also been many studies of the functions performed by personnel workers and careful job analyses of a dozen or more college personnel assignments. Embree accounts for the confusion in training standards as a result of (1) lack of clear and universally understood concepts of what the counselor is and does, (2) the fact that institutions have been forced to train workers for a broad variety of jobs and levels (indicating a need for a basic core of training and experience for all counselors), and (3) the lack of regular evaluation and supervisory principles for it, such as would be provided by a licensing or certification agency on a national scale.[36] The American Psychological Association's Division of Counseling Psychology long ago (1947) set its own standards for Members, Fellows, and Diplomates, but its use of the term "counselor" does not coincide with the concept and use of the term by the public or the personnel worker. The functions of the college personnel worker (commonly called "counselor") are much broader than those of the psychological counselor.

The confusion surrounding terminology cannot be interpreted as a lack of quality in the training programs offered in the graduate schools. These curricula include courses in vocational information and theory, developmental psychology of learning and personality, the processes of individual and group counseling, trends in higher education, administrative theory, societal mores and pressures, and others. All the schools have the same standards for admission, but, although everyone agrees with Hoppock that maladjusted individuals should be barred from professional training, almost no one has done anything about it.[37] Or at least, we might venture to add, nothing to describe for publication. It is recognized also that there must be both generalists and specialists, and it is obvious that there will continue to be many part-time workers who also maintain their study and work in a subject-matter field for teaching.

Wrenn pointed out the most serious deterrent to training programs, namely, that college administrators can and do hire anyone who pleases their fancy for personnel work. He quotes an instance of a college president who offered his highest personnel position in turn to a superintendent of schools and to a high school principal, in spite of the fact that the worker would have been expected to supervise a staff of well-trained specialists.[38] Russell claims that the main source of personnel workers is the faculty.[39] Hitchcock explained to the Higher Education Association in 1958 the common pattern by which the public school counselor develops: The principal finds a teacher with the right personal qualifications and asks that he assume some counseling duties; the teacher, if he likes the assignment, can be approved by the state because he is not yet a full-time counselor, and then begin his training in summer-school study. He may escape the training, however, if he chooses to remain a part-time worker in the field.[40] As late as 1959, it was reported that one administrator, explaining the appointment of a physical education teacher to fill a new counselor's position, said: "He has been teaching a long time and he is tired; he wants to sit down."

Speculation about the objectives and the required training for personnel work, especially in view of the expected rise in the demand for services, may lead to varied solutions for its problems. It may be affected by the discernible trend toward greater breadth and flexibility in training based on the theory that a better knowledge of concepts of the behavioral sciences and a better grasp of educational and cultural theories would permit the essential specific methods to be assimilated more quickly and many other techniques and specialties to be learned on the job. Agreements in principle to such a revision could be easily obtained, but major difficulties would be encountered in attempting to differentiate theory from methods. In practice it is often apparent that the able student of personnel work is happy and successful with more emphasis on theory, but the weak student demands more attention to procedures and techniques.

Mayhew noted a new emphasis on general or liberal, or at least flexible, basic education to which any specialty can easily be grafted. Many employers are saying with industrialist Alfred P. Sloan, "Give us the educated man. We can train them ourselves, but we cannot educate them." Mayhew inquires, "Can we write the job description for a vice-president of X Company for 1965 or 1975? What new skills, what new sensitivity, will he have to possess to deal successfully with the new elements or the new combinations of old elements?"[41] Dael Wolfle points out that only 38 per cent of the employed college graduates work in the field of their major study, even including lawyers and physicians.[42] If this is true, the training of many classroom teachers for personnel work does not seem so fantastic. Perhaps the help of college administrators might be enlisted to give personnel training the same kind of prestige that management has given to the education of its promising young leaders through year-long study grants or extensive summer workshops. Members of the personnel profession might need such special training for new objectives if there were major changes in the admission policies, or if the function of the colleges were shifted to the graduate schools, or if a greater emphasis were given to liberal rather than to vocational education.

Recently, when it has been introduced as an economy measure, in-service training has been criticized as merely a continued practicing of mistakes; however, a new awareness of its weaknesses, new methods such as the technique of presenting and discussing case histories, and more substantial content can restore its usefulness.

Public Relations

One of the reasons for establishing a professional organization is the need of the profession for good public relations. To pursue its objectives, public understanding and appreciation must be cultivated. Furthermore, there is good evidence for the importance of adapting programs to the characteristics of American society and operating within the present framework of its ideologies. The College Personnel Association began its 1957 search for new programs by listing fourteen major trends in higher education and in society as a whole.[43] The "weight of the culture" plays a significant part in shaping purposes and objectives. The important issues for any profession lie in the selection of the pressures of society which may be successfully augmented or opposed and of the timing and method to be used in the process.

Every profession operates in terms of some stereotypes and fictions about itself which are at once a help and a hindrance—e.g., the absent-minded professor, the physician with his stethoscope, the chemist with his test tube, the "gloomy" dean lurking somewhere behind the title on his door. As Caplow has pointed out:

> Highly visible, moderately privileged, partially isolated and responsible in the exercise of their authority . . . professional men are logical targets for popular aggression. In the case of physicians an intensive propaganda has somewhat dissipated this sentiment, but no study of professional groups should overlook the fact . . . of the unfavorable stereotypes of shyster, quack, butcher, pedant, sissy and the like which . . . keep them slightly on the defensive.[44]

A small, impecunious, and new profession, personnel work cannot close its eyes to the need for propaganda in building its prestige, even though it may not be able to afford such an undertaking.

These stereotypes and "professional fictions" help the professional person to relate to the public in terms of mutual expectations, and are the primary focuses of recruitment. They also provide an image of massive unity for the public. The danger is that the profession may accept the fictions as accurate as well as useful. Obviously, one fiction may replace another; for example, psychological tests were first given an exaggerated importance by the public, and later suspected of gross fraud. The fictions also tend to concentrate the rewards of prestige on some of the more dramatic professional activities— e.g., murder trials, cancer research, the search for talent and genius, in contrast to corporation law, dermatology, or disciplinary counseling.

In summary, all the evaluations of a profession and the recommendations for future growth must be checked against these many dimensions; the entrenched traditions, the neighboring professional groups, the objectives, the individual members, the training, and the public relations. Issues and programs for the future must be defined in these terms. The demand for one consistent, all-purpose philosophy or objective is the most difficult to meet. The complexity of the educational programs taken in their entirety, together with the rapid changing of the society, render a general consensus or a stable agreement unprofitable as well as improbable. Different objectives are needed for different levels (elementary, secondary, higher education), different specialties (individual and group counseling, vocational or educational advising, housing, discipline, etc.), and different functions (research, teaching, administration). The needs of the profession must also be met on the local levels in relation to individual institutions, with another set of objectives tailored to each locale.

Earlier descriptions of objectives in terms of existing personnel programs are no longer satisfactory. Training formulas and membership standards for our rapidly growing profession require more systematic statements of goals, which will in turn allow for a more specific delineation of issues. Personnel workers played an important part in developing awareness of the *whole* person rather than merely the intellect, but this is past history. *Everybody* is now interested in the whole person—ministers, physicists, linguists, economists, columnists, parents and businessmen—but it takes nothing less than the whole world and a long lifetime to deal with one single whole person. For professional efficiency, security, and prestige, it seems necessary to revise the present broad statements of purpose in three directions: (1) to differentiate them from educational objectives in general; (2) to reduce their unjustifiable pretentiousness, and (3) to bring them into better alignment with the training and skills of the individual practitioners.

The general objectives which have served as the basis for the personnel functions described in the foregoing chapters, and which grew out of the parallel objectives for higher education, may be reviewed briefly:

1. To support, complement, strengthen academic learning.

2. To develop all other aspects of the personality as they are needed to sustain and enhance the intellectual: physical, emotional, social, etc.

3. To provide wide opportunity for the learning of leadership theories, skills, and values.

4. To continue the training in good citizenship begun in the elementary and secondary schools.

Essentials for Professional Progress

The activities essential to professional, institutional, and individual progress in college personnel work today fall into three classes: (1) those which involve theory and objectives, (2) those which have to do with techniques and procedures, and (3) those which maintain the health and growth of the profession as a whole.

Theory and Objectives

The theory—or as many might say, the "philosophy"—and the objectives for college personnel have already been laid before the profession in forthright terms by committees, by individuals, and from various points of view. It is inevitable that there will be several schools of thought and that general concepts will only gradually evolve and stabilize. In this process, the following questions arise.

1. *What objectives should obtain for the personnel profession as a whole?* How are they related to the objectives of higher education, and what is the order of their importance? If the profession's objectives are to be effectively integrated with those of higher education, it will be necessary to lead the way to a more realistic and fruitful distinction between vocational and liberal education. For the effectiveness of its own program the profession should also differentiate occupational theory from occupational information. New concepts in this field indicate a much greater emphasis for counselors and advisers on occupation as it affects the developing personality.

2. *Since theory is always modified by practice, under what conditions and to what extent may objectives be changed and still be counted as worthy professional goals?* In other words, how much deviation can be tolerated? The factors which tend to compromise or evade the professional objectives (each must be studied and evaluated separately) are: (a) the limited goals of each college as affected by its physical, educational, and financial facilities and by overzealous or unsympathetic administrators; (b) societal pressures such as demands of parents, resistance of students, expectations of alumni; and (c) inadequacies of the leaders on the personnel staff. Especially important among the societal pressures is the strong motivation of the student toward his future occupation as opposed to the determination of the college to develop his full capacities for all other aspects of life. Personnel could play a significant part in closing this gap.

Inadequacies of leaders may be due to a lack of balance in training with an overemphasis on one phase such as counseling, research, testing, or group dynamics; general intellectual deficiency; inadequate personality, immaturity, lack of force, laziness, or a lack of personal or professional integrity exhibited by sacrificing principles to expediency; the dearth of trained and competent workers; and academic tenure or vested interests which preclude the elimination of incompetent staff members.

Techniques and Procedures

There are far too many unsolved problems in this area. Here we can mention only four of the major areas of concern.

Counseling. First, there are those problems centering on the concept of counseling with its curious complexities and rich ramifications. The place of the different kinds of counseling in the personnel program is not clear, for, even if one takes the broadest view of counseling as any contact between a qualified professional and one or more amateurs who can profit from his services, it is not identical with personnel work, and perhaps is not even its major tool. Counseling must be evaluated in respect to its nature, function, strengths, limitations, efficiency, costs, etc. On the basis of such evaluations, choices must be made, a hierarchy of emphases established, and the appropriate training given. The types of counseling for which training might be provided are: (1) individual conferences for interviewing, clarifying, discussing, quite different from probing, diagnosis, and therapy; (2) group counseling, including teaching, discussing, organizing, group dynamics, role-playing, buzz sessions, etc.; and/or (3) a kind of group and individual advising which is more superficial, less time-consuming, and more information-giving and which can be conducted by part-time workers with less training in personnel— i.e., the faculty —to supplement the activities of the personnel worker. The indoctrination and training of such workers should be standardized by the profession and supported by college administrations.

The place of the generalist. A second and parallel issue in methods concerns the place of the generalist or the administrator in college personnel programs. How will his personality and training differ from that of the counselor?

> The professions must face the challenge presented to them by the Protean growth of the administrative function. . . . It challenges the independence and self-government of almost every professional man and woman. . . . Nor will it be sufficient to "expose" their students to a very few hours of humanities and the subject called "industrial administration" or "social administration" as the case maybe. What they have to rethink, in order to solve the administrative problem, is nothing less than the whole question of specialization. The dilemma confronting almost every profession is whether its members shall concentrate on "strictly professional" work and lose their power to direct it, or to learn administration so as to be able to remain in control of it, thus losing the time to practice it.[45]

Student-personnel worker relationship. A third issue in procedure is centered in the general attitude to be maintained by both students and personnel workers. It will be necessary to explore the nature and function of such relationships as they run the gamut from laissez-faire and permissiveness through guidance and teaching to authority and dominance. Again both the strengths and limitations of each approach must be better understood.

The role of research. A fourth issue involves the role of research for the personnel division. Not every personnel worker should carry on research, not every problem is appropriate for experimentation, and not every hypothesis need invoke the most refined and elaborate methods. Specialists in psychology and sociology—e.g., in counseling, personality, group process, and communications—accumulate mountains of research every year, and specialists are needed who will sift out just those facts and theories which will promote the profession's own practical interests and research programs.

Health and Growth of the Profession

So many issues are involved in the health and growth of the profession that only the more obvious can be mentioned.

Standards of membership. First in importance are those issues which involve the standards of membership, the professional education. The screening of all the graduate students in the accredited schools is already established on a sound basis. Any weakness in recruiting for college personnel would lie only in the general attractiveness of this profession in competition with all others, e.g., physics, medicine, law, management, college teaching, etc., which in turn depends on the rewards to be won (chiefly financial) and the years of training required.[46] Tests for intelligence are more easily administered than for personnel qualities, such as balanced temperament, stable values, and social skills. That more elusive but most important factor, "character," is probably screened most effectively not by test or interview but by observation on the job, both self-observation and professional appraisal. The two factors of greatest significance are (1) the satisfaction and pleasure derived (or not experienced) from the daily routines and (2) the presence of colleagues or students who are congenial, with whom the neophyte feels comfortable and can identify himself. It is a great change for the young apprentice to move away from the comfortable student goals—good grades, peer approval, conformity, popularity—and to embrace self-competition as the criterion of accomplishment, to hold both the self *and the student clients* to the objectives of higher education, and to accept professional over material and personal gain. These are nevertheless his developmental tasks.

The training and apprenticeship issues are simplified by good screening practices. There are many ideal models and many operating models of curricula in college personnel work, all of them honored more in the breach than in the observance. These issues cannot be resolved by any one school, no matter how excellent. Continuing and hard-working committees, surveys, job descriptions, research, and subsidies are needed to arrive at a solution.

Practical problems. The maintenance of effective personnel operation on the campus requires much more than ruthless screening and good training, and it involves some of the knottiest problems in professional history.

1. Licensing and certification should follow logically after screening and training, but resistance will be stubborn because the needs of society are overwhelming. These processes must go hand in hand with all the other methods of eliminating the incompetent workers, even some who stand high in professional hierarchies. Professionalization demands that we meet certain requirements, not all of which are agreed on by the professionals. Brown warns, for example, that "the boards and staff of some professional associations are composed so exclusively of practitioners who have had no training or experience in research that they are not aware of the degree of its utility," but she tempers this statement with heartening examples of professional endeavor.[47] Members of the profession of dentistry, for example, noted twenty-five years ago that a clinical study had found that disorders of the teeth produce serious systemic effects and that superficially perfect dental service judged by mechanical and aesthetic standards may hide or induce local pathological processes which have far-reaching consequences for general health. The implications for dentistry, which had been up to that time a restorative service, were profound. Committees, research, and practical and curricular studies were mobilized for the revision of the profession's educational requirements in relation to its service to society with the result that the curriculum was not only remodeled but extended by several years.[48]

2. Salaries and working conditions are continuing issues in all professions, and the National Education Association considers them its second largest area of research. Included in this category are tenure, retirement, sabbatical leaves, status of women (especially married women), selection and appointment, hours of work, etc.

3. Good working relations with colleagues within the profession and also with faculty members and administrators might have been classified as an issue within the area of education and training. There are, however, factors other than professional competence which may be involved; matters of administrative practice, general prestige, budget, and assigned status, and the business of educating—or, better, propagandizing—other professions and the public to a better understanding of personnel work.

4. Ethical considerations, both personal and professional, have had only sporadic attention. Indeed, it is doubtful whether the profession could attack more than the realm of professional ethics, which may be less significant than personal. A code of professional ethics would be more simple to establish, more welcome, and easier to follow. Personal ethics, or the everyday behavior of many professional persons, are today under frequent attack, and may actually be at a low ebb.

5. Other issues are concerned with the enlargement of professional services to society. It is naive to hold that professionalization is all to the good. One can argue only that the favorable aspects outweigh the unfavorable. As Lieberman says:

> The irresponsible exercise of professional autonomy is as great an evil as its absence; furthermore every failure on the part of teachers to fulfill their professional responsibilities weakens their claim to professional autonomy.[49]

An ominous phrase, "fulfill professional responsibilities"! For responsibilities to parents, faculty members, and administrators include teaching the student better values than he would absorb from the feeling-drenched, juvenile, materialistic, nonintellectual world from which the campus withdraws him. This is something more than "counseling" with individual misfits, jockeying for position with vested interest groups, containing the campus high jinks and maneuvering for a favorable press. Campus personnel workers, whatever their age or station, owe all their constituents, and most especially their reluctant youthful charges, a positive, unrelenting program (1) *for* self-understanding, ego-integration, and personal growth; (2) *against* cheating and slipshod intellectual work of any nature; and (3) *in support* of learning and enjoyment of all the arts. These programs must be successful and sophisticated; therefore, carefully studied, planned, and endorsed in a nationwide professional effort.

Undoubtedly, there are other activities and issues of perhaps equal importance, and it is the duty of each student, each member, and each subgroup to ferret them out. Those for the larger profession will serve to identify and illuminate those for the college and the individual. Self-criticism, harsh and audacious, is both the measure of stature and the prescription for growth.

Suggested Readings

Barry, Ruth, and Beverly Wolfe, *Modern Issues in Guidance-Personnel Work.* New York: Bureau of Publications, Teachers College, Columbia University, 1957.

Caplow, Theodore, *The Sociology of Work.* Minneapolis: University of Minnesota Press, 1954.

Lieberman, Myron, *Education as a Profession.* New York: Prentice-Hall, Inc., 1956.

Wolfle, Dael, *America's Resources of Specialized Talent.* New York: Harper & Brothers, 1955.

Notes

1. Roscoe Pound, "What is a Profession?" *Review of Reviews*, 94:84–85 (December, 1936).

2. Abraham Flexner, "Is Social Work a Profession?" *School and Society* (June 26, 1915).

3. Oliver Garceau, quoted by Morris Cogan, "The Problem of Defining a Profession," *The Annals*, 297:105–111 (January, 1955).

4. "Facts about the American Association for the Advancement of Science," 1957, p. 22. This pamphlet can be obtained by writing to the American Association for the Advancement of Science, 1515 Massachusetts Avenue, N.W., Washington 5, D.C.

5. Eunice Hilton, "The Professional Organization: Its Role in a Democratic Society," *Journal of the National Association of Women Deans and Counselors*, 20:139–146, (June, 1957).

6. Esther Lloyd-Jones, "The Beginnings of Our Profession," in *Trends in Student Personnel Work*, ed. E. G. Williamson, (Minneapolis: University of Minnesota Press, 1949), pp. 260–264.

7. Theodore Caplow, *The Sociology of Work* (Minneapolis: University of Minnesota Press, 1954), p. 139.

8. Carroll Shartle, *Executive Performance and Leadership* (Englewood Cliffs, N.J.: Prentice-Hall, 1956), p. 50.

9. C. Gilbert Wrenn and J. G. Darley, "An Appraisal of the Professional Status of Personnel Work," Parts I and II, in *Trends in Student Personnel Work*, ed. E. G. Williamson (Minneapolis: University of Minnesota Press, 1949), pp. 264–287.

10. Harvey L. Smith, "Contingencies of Professional Differentiation," *American Journal of Sociology*, 63: 410–414 (January, 1958).

11. B. J. Horton, "Ten Criteria of a Profession," *Science Monthly*, 50: 164 (February, 1944).

12. Caplow, *op. cit.*, pp. 170–171.

13. *Ibid.*, p. 171.

14. Hilton, *op. cit.*, p. 141.

15. Caplow, *op. cit.*, p. 139.

16. Smith, *op. cit.*, p. 412.

17. John G. Darley, "The Faculty Are Human Too," *Personnel and Guidance Journal*, 35:225–230 (December, 1956).

18. Eli Ginzberg, "Guidance and Manpower Policy," address to the American Personnel and Guidance Association, St. Louis, April, 1958.

19. C. Northcote Parkinson, *Parkinson's Law and Other Studies in Administration* (Boston: Houghton Mifflin, 1957), p. 113.

20. Harold Taylor, "The Philosophical Foundations of General Education," Fifty-first Yearbook of the National Society for the Study of Education (Chicago: University of Chicago Press, 1952), Part I, p. 22.

21. *Ibid.*, p. 42.

22. Wrenn and Darley, *op. cit.*, p. 279.

23. Edward J. Shoben, Jr., "A Rationale for Modern Student Personnel Work," *Personnel-O-Gram*, 12:9–12 (March, 1950).

24. Ruth Barry and Beverly Wolfe, *Modern Issues in Guidance-Personnel Work* (New York: Bureau of Publications, Teachers College, Columbia University, 1957), p. 234.

25. Harvey L. Smith, *op. cit.*, p. 414.

26. Wrenn and Darley, *op. cit.*, p. 285.

27. "Report of the 1956 Workshop," American College Personnel Association, *Personnel-O-Gram*, 11:6 (December, 1956).

28. Arthur A. Hitchcock, review of Barry and Wolfe, *Modern Issues in Guidance-Personnel Work, Personnel and Guidance Journal*, 36:647–648 (May, 1958).

29. Edward J. Shoben, Jr., "Special Review: Some Recent Books on Counseling and Adjustment," *Psychological Bulletin*, 52:262 (May, 1955).

30. Darley, "The Faculty Are Human Too," *op. cit.*, p. 227.

31. Henry Borow, "Frontiers of Personnel Research in Education—Modern Perspectives in Personnel Work," Fifty-eighth Yearbook of the National Society for the Study of Education (Chicago: University of Chicago Press, 1959), p. 216.

32. Wrenn and Darley, *op. cit.*, p. 271.

33. Arthur A. Hitchcock, "By What Means Can the Quality and Quantity of Guidance Services Be Increased?" Thirteenth National Conference on Higher Education (Chicago: Mimeographed, 1958).

34. Wrenn and Darley, *op. cit.*, p. 269.

35. Austin MacCormick, paper given for the 38th Anniversary Conference of the National Association of Student Personnel Administrators (Mimeographed, 1956), p. 12.

36. Royal B. Embree, "The Use of Practicing and Internship in Counselor Training," *Educational and Psychological Measurement*, 11:752–760 (Winter, 1951).

37. Robert Hoppock, "The Selection of Doctoral Candidates," *Occupations*, 29:420–422 (March, 1951).

38. Wrenn and Darley, *op. cit.*, p. 272.

39. John Dale Russell, "Changing Patterns of Administrative Organization in Education," *The Annals*, 301:23 (September, 1955).

40. Hitchcock, *op. cit.*, p. 6.

41. Lewis B. Mayhew, "Implications of Changed Institutional Responsibilities in American Society," Twelfth National Conference on Higher Education, March, 1957, mimeographed, p. 2.

42. Dael Wolfle, *America's Resources of Specialized Talent* (New York: Harper, 1955).

43. "Report of the 1956 Workshop," *op. cit.*, p. 2.

44. Caplow, *op. cit.*, p. 135.

45. Roy Lewis and Angus Maude, *Professional People in England* (Cambridge: Harvard University Press, 1953), pp. 7, 224–225.

46. W. H. Cowley, "Some History and a Venture into Prophecy," in *Trends in Personnel Work*, ed. E. G. Williamson (Minneapolis: University of Minnesota Press, 1949), p. 25.

47. Esther L. Brown, *The Use of Research by Professional Associations in Determining Program and Policy* (New York: Russell Sage Foundation, 1946), p. 9.

48. *Ibid.*, p. 20.

49. Myron Lieberman, *Education as a Profession* (New York: Prentice-Hall, 1956), p. 490.

Student Personnel Work:
A Profession Stillborn

JAMES F. PENNEY (1969) ·

In half a century, student personnel work has not achieved professional recognition on campuses. As evidence, basic literature is cited both quantitatively and qualitatively. Preoccupation with housekeeping functions remains a major reason for the field's low esteem. The personnel point of view provides an inadequate base for professional organization. Fragmentation into a growing number of specialities characterizes current developments. The early dreams of a profession of student personnel work cannot be realized.

Few occupational entities have devoted as much energy to self-examination and attempts at self-definition as has the amorphous body calling itself student personnel work. The specialty is roughly half a century old—surely time enough to achieve whatever degree of recognition and maturity the academic community is likely to allow. It is certainly time enough for it to establish itself as a profession among professions, if it is ever to do so. In that same half-century or less, a score or more new specialties have been born, matured, and become professionally established in the world of academe.

Student personnel work has not achieved professional recognition in the community of professionals operating on campuses. While it has sought to establish a position among the dominant power centers—faculty, administration, students—a realistic assessment of campuses in the 1960s can lead only to the conclusion that the effort has failed. Student personnel workers, their philosophy, and their goals are not among the major influences today in colleges and universities.

Basic Literature: Quantity

An attempt to identify causative factors may begin with an examination of the literature in the field. Analysis suggest several characteristics, each of which contributes to the conclusion that the occupation is not truly a profession and is not moving toward becoming one. Striking is the observation that there is a paucity of basic literature in the field. Though disconcerting to practitioners inundated by a plethora of journals, research reports, convention proceedings, position formulations, and policy statements, the observation remains supportable.

Where, for instance, are to be found basic writings that trace in their conceptualizations the development of a field of endeavor? Where are the rival statements of thesis, antithesis, and synthesis that have provided the crucial methodology through which knowledge has developed in the West? Where are the fundamental descriptions of the occupation and its practitioners that can serve to identify for it a place in the sun?

The student personnel specialty has produced surprisingly little of this sort of writing that endures. What are the basic textbooks in the field? Arbuckle (1953), Lloyd-Jones and Smith (1938), Mueller (1961), Williamson (1961), and Wrenn (1951) constitute the core. Included as historically significant might be the pamphlets in the American Council on Education Series on Personnel Work in Colleges and Universities, produced sequentially between 1939 and 1953. While each dealt with a specific topic, it is not unreasonable to consider the series as an entity that provided basic textual material representing the activities, rationales, and objectives of the field in an important period of its development. Altogether, the list is not quantitatively imposing as to represent a half-century of effort.

In contrast, problem-centered writings abound: Journals, abstracting services, and monographs multiply *ad infinitum*. Quantity, however, may be misleading. The fact of its timeliness implies that a journal article, research report, or monograph is likely to be of short-term value. Further, it has probably been developed upon already available principles and accepted concepts instead of having focused upon the production of original formulations. In this context, the problem-centered literature of a field, appearing in periodical publications, may not be a valid index of the field's strength, endurance, or professional status. Student personnel work has not historically produced, and is not currently producing, a large body of permanent, fundamental literature by means of which the specialty can be identified, evaluated, and its progressive development calculated.

Basic Literature: Quality

A qualitative assessment of the literature in student personnel work leads to other observations. The contents of the seminal books fall generally into three groupings. In the first is a large quantity of material taken over wholesale from the social sciences, chiefly psychology. Included is information on counseling, vocational development, group processes, the subculture of the campus, human development, and learning. The implication is that these materials have direct relevance to the activities of the student personnel worker. The inclusion of a major emphasis on counseling, for example, suggests that he is a psychological counselor. But is he also to be a test administrator-interpreter? A group dynamics leader-trainer? A manager of residences and food services? A manipulator of environments to enhance their contribution to learning? The student personnel worker, by implication, must be a multi-specialist. Can one individual be adequately prepared to do all the things that student personnel workers are supposedly competent to do? In an age of specialization and expertise, it seems unlikely. Perhaps, then, he should be considered not a specialist, but a generalist.

The value of the generalist and the point of view he can bring to administrative and managerial tasks is an important concept in the era of the specialist. Is there a place for the generalist in student personnel work? Can the student personnel worker, "broadly educated," expect to be accepted as competent when he performs tasks that overlap with the operations of more "specialty-educated" colleagues? The hope has historically been that generalist preparation plus good will and the "personnel point of view" will enable the student personnel worker to perform student-related tasks in ways that "experts" could or would not do. Three results may be discerned currently:

1. The student personnel worker has not been accepted by academicians as competent in some areas where recent developments have produced highly trained specialists with whom the student personnel worker competes. This is especially true in counseling, where the specialty of counseling psychology has developed; other areas where parallel trends are visible are housing administration, union programming and management, foreign student advisement, and financial aid administration.

2. Student personnel workers tend to be relegated to subordinate and peripheral positions as middle and lower-level administrators who are seen by academicians as essentially uninvolved in the real-life issues of campuses in the 1960s.

3. When given the option, students, having learned to value expertise, will turn to "fully qualified" specialists rather than to generalists whose role and qualifications are less clearly identified.

Personnel Work as Housekeeping

A second category of textual material is concerned with administrative, organizational, and coordinating matters that may appropriately be called housekeeping activities. To so designate them is not to deny their urgency, but to suggest that they are hardly matters about which a learned, academically based discipline or profession will be fundamentally concerned. Indeed, the student personnel specialty's long-time preoccupation with such how-to-do-it issues as admissions, orientation, housing, financial aid, student activities, and campus discipline has been a factor that has encouraged campus colleagues to denigrate the student personnel worker and to reject his aspiration to equality in a world dominated by teaching and research.

The fact that current thinking continues to focus on housekeeping and technique-centered matters is evidenced by the subject matter of the monographs in the Student Personnel Series of the American College Personnel Association. Eight booklets have appeared since 1960; included are considerations of financial aid, housing, health service, discipline, testing, and group activities. While in most cases the contents represent careful thinking about some functions of student personnel work, it is quite impossible to read the entire series without recognizing that the field under consideration is one that should, by its nature, be at the center of campus life and activity. Discussion of the matters with which students are centrally concerned in the 1960s is conspicuously absent in these publications. One wonders how the publication series of a major student personnel group could appear so irrelevant and prosaic in a decade of monumental change.

The Personnel Point of View

A third portion of the texts in the field is devoted to elaborations of the personnel point of view. The authors are unified in urging that not only workers in the specialty but all members of the academic community embrace what is essentially a value orientation. The personnel point of view may be characterized by three postulates: (a) Every student should be recognized as unique; (b) Every individual should be regarded as a total person; c) The current needs and interests of individual students are the most significant factors to be considered in developing a program of campus life. Concern with particular values, of course, is not uncommon among professions. Medicine, law, and the natural sciences—all, in their devotion to objectivity, are committed to humanly derived values. But in contrast to the established professions, student personnel work has developed primarily as an enterprise defined by a point of view rather than by its content or the services it provides. Indeed, as Shoben (1967) pointed out, most of the services that represent personnel functions are not distinctive to student personnel work, but fall also within the province of other professions and occupations. The things that make such activities part of a student personnel program are the outlook, the assumptions, and the general philosophy of those who participate in them. The concept of a single professional entity, student personnel work, is therefore abortive.

Emergence of the Council of Student Personnel Associations (COSPA)[1] in the 1960s indicates that in reality there are several readily identifiable specialties (together with organizations representing them). All of them may be seen as falling more or less within the province of student personnel work, while at the same time each provides a service reasonably distinct from the others. Are there, then, enough common interests, activities, and objectives to provide a base for any sort of shared professional identification?

Parker (1966) proposed that it should be possible to identify a student personnel worker as one whose occupational tasks enable him to find membership in one of the COSPA organizations. His approach rests on the assumption that counseling is the one common aspect of all student personnel jobs. It follows that each student personnel worker should be educated primarily as a counselor who includes in his preparation some peripheral study of other aspects of personnel work. Parker's rationale includes the observation that there are five critical skill areas possessed by the counselor that are basic to virtually all student personnel functions. They are: (a) the counselor's sensitivity to others, enabling him to develop effective working relationships; (b) the counselor's skill in objectively analyzing the strengths and weaknesses of individuals; c) the counselor's skill at interviewing; (d) the counselor's awareness of the nature and extent of individual differences in those with whom he works; (e) the counselor's ability to identify learning difficulties and his expertise in knowing how learning takes place.

No one is likely to disagree that these would be distinct assets for student personnel workers to possess. This is not to say, however, that they are *uniquely* valuable to student personnel workers. On the contrary; they would be invaluable to *anyone* who deals directly and professionally with human relationships. To conclude that education in counseling should be the basic preparation for student personnel work, therefore, is to say very little. The question is whether such preparation is enough to identify a professional group, or to serve as the foundation for membership in professional organizations. Obviously, it is not.

Organization Fragmentation

The COSPA phenomenon represents a proliferation of so-called professional organization. Several of these organizations are of quite recent origin: more than half the COSPA groups have been organized since approximately 1960. Examination of the literature, activities, and job titles represented suggest that several of the organizations have quite specific and unique interests that are shared only peripherally—if at all—by the others. For other members who attempt to be more general in their interests and global in their constituencies (i.e., ACPA and NAWDC), the literature suggests a major concern with unresolved matters of identity, purpose, and role. Such observations lead reasonably to the conclusion that the field of student personnel work is in the process of becoming increasingly fragmented and diversified as time goes on and new specializations develop. The longer this process continues, the less likely it will be that common interests, activities, and a universal core of training can be possible or relevant for all.

Conclusions

The issues raised here lead to a fundamental conclusion. No longer viable is the hypothesis under which the early writers of the 1930s and 1940s operated—namely, that there was an identifiable point of view and an occupational entity that might be recognized as the student personnel work profession. The field is now composed of a number of relatively separate and distinct specialties linked largely by organization contiguity (i.e., they all involve working with students out of classrooms) and, to a lesser extent, by the sharing of a common philosophical view of their tasks. The long-sought "profession" of student personnel work has not been, is not, and will not be recognized or accepted as a vital aspect of the academic world.

References

Arbuckle, D. S. *Student personnel services in higher education*. New York: McGraw-Hill, 1953.

Lloyd-Jones, E. M., & Smith, M. R. *A student personnel program for higher education*. New York: McGraw-Hill, 1938.

Mueller, K. H. *Student personnel work in higher education*. Boston: Houghton Mifflin, 1961.

Parker, C. A. The place of counseling in the preparation of student personnel workers. *Personnel and Guidance Journal*, 1966, *45*, 254–261.

Shoben, E. J. Psychology and student personnel work. *Journal of College Student Personnel*, 1967, *8*, 239–245.

Williamson, E. G. *Student personnel services in colleges and universities*. New York: McGraw-Hill, 1961.

Wrenn, C. G. *Student personnel work in college*. New York: Ronald Press, 1951.

Note

1. The Council of Student Personnel Associations includes the following organizational members: American College Personnel Association, Association of College Unions, American Association of Collegiate Registrars and Admissions Officers, Association of College and University Housing Officers, Association of College Admissions Counselors, Association for Coordination of University Religious Advisors, College Placement Council, Conference of Jesuit Student Personnel Administrators, National Association of Student Personnel Administrators, National Association of Women Deans and Counselors, National Association of Foreign Student Advisors.

PART II

Contexts of College Student Affairs Administration

Part Two focuses on the institutional and external contexts in which student affairs administration takes place. Topics addressed include the influence of external contexts and constituencies of higher education; descriptions of the institutional structures and cultures within which student affairs exists; and a general discussion of the characteristics and needs of undergraduate students.

Culture and Character:
The Historical Conversation

ROBERT N. BELLAH, RICHARD MADSEN, WILLIAM M. SULLIVAN,
ANN SWIDLER, AND STEEN M. TIPTON

To an American reader, the individualism that pervades the four lives described in chapter 1 may at first glance seem not to have anything to do with cultural tradition, but simply to express the way things are. Yet when we look more closely, we see that there are subtle differences among our four characters. There are different modes even within the vocabularies of each individual. Brian Palmer, for example, was at one time in his life single-mindedly devoted to career success, sacrificing everything to attainment of that goal. Later, he came to value quite different things—classical music, books, relationships, the immediate enjoyment of life—and left behind his total devotion to career. Both these modes are individualistic, but they are rooted in different traditions and have different implications. We propose to call the former mode "utilitarian individualism" and the latter "expressive individualism." Joe Gorman and Wayne Bauer combine their individualism with somewhat different languages of civic responsibility. Margaret Oldham holds a more sharply formulated version of Brian's individualism.

These differences derive from a historical past of which none of our characters is entirely aware. In our forward-facing society, however, we are more apt to talk about the future than the past and to imagine that the differences between us derive largely from a conflict of current interests. Yet even in the debate about our future, our cultural tradition, in its several strands, is still very much present, and our conversation would probably be more to the point if we were aware of that fact.

So long as it is vital, the cultural tradition of a people—its symbols, ideals, and ways of feeling—is always an argument about the meaning of the destiny its members share. Cultures are dramatic conversations about things that matter to their participants, and American culture is no exception. From its early days, some Americans have seen the purpose and goal of the nation as the effort to realize the ancient biblical hope of a just and compassionate society. Others have struggled to shape the spirit of their lives and the laws of the nation in accord with the ideals of republican citizenship and participation. Yet others have promoted dreams of manifest destiny and national glory. And always there have been the proponents, often passionate, of the notion that liberty means the spirit of enterprise and the right to amass wealth and power for oneself. The themes of success, freedom, and justice that we detected in chapter 1 are found in all three of the central strands of our culture—biblical, republican, and modern individualist—but they take on different meanings in each context. American culture remains alive so long as the conversation continues and the argument is intense.

The Biblical and Republican Strands

Most historians have recognized the importance of biblical religion in American culture from the earliest colonization to the present. Few have put greater emphasis on the religious "point of departure" of the American experiment than Alexis de Tocqueville, who went so far as to say, "I think I can see the whole destiny of America contained in the first Puritan who landed on those shores." Just as we have used several individuals to introduce aspects of contemporary American culture, we will look at several representative individuals to introduce earlier strands.

John Winthrop (1588–1649) was one of those "first Puritans" to land on our shores and has been taken as exemplary of our beginnings by commentators on American culture from Cotton Mather to Tocqueville to Perry Miller. Winthrop was elected first governor of the Massachusetts Bay Colony even before the colonists left England. Just over forty years of age, he was a well-educated man of good family and earnest religious convictions, determined to start life anew in the wilderness in company with those of like religious commitment. In the sermon "A Model of Christian Charity," which he delivered on board ship in Salem harbor just before landing in 1630, he described the "city set upon a hill" that he and his fellow Puritans intended to found. His words have remained archetypal, for one understanding of what life in America was to be: "We must delight in each other, make others conditions our own, rejoice together, mourn together, labor and suffer together, always having before our eyes our community as members of the same body." The Puritans were not uninterested in material prosperity and were prone when it came, unfortunately, to take it as a sign of God's approval. Yet their fundamental criterion of success was not material wealth but the creation of a community in which a genuinely ethical and spiritual life could be lived. During his twelve terms as governor, Winthrop, a relatively rich man for those days, devoted his life to the welfare of the colony, frequently using his own funds for public purposes. Near the end of his life, he had to step down from the governorship because his neglected estate was threatened with bankruptcy. The Puritan settlements in the seventeenth century can be seen as the first of many efforts to create utopian communities in America. They gave the American experiment as a whole a utopian touch that it has never lost, in spite of all our failings.

For Winthrop, success was much more explicitly tied to the creation of a certain kind of ethical community than it is for most Americans today. His idea of freedom differs from ours in a similar way. He decried what he called "natural liberty," which is the freedom to do whatever one wants, evil as well as good. True freedom—what he called "moral" freedom, "in reference to the covenant between God and man"—is a liberty "to that only which is good, just and honest." "This liberty," he said, "you are to stand for with the hazard of your lives." Any authority that violates this liberty is not true authority and must be resisted. Here again, Winthrop perceives an ethical content to the central idea of freedom that some other strands of the American tradition have not recognized.

In like manner, Winthrop saw justice as a matter more of substance than of procedure. Cotton Mather describes Winthrop's manner of governing as follows: "He was, indeed, a governor who had most exactly studied that book which, pretending to teach politics, did only contain three leaves, and but one word in each of those leaves, which word was 'Moderation.'" When it was reported to him during an especially long and hard winter that a poor man in his neighborhood was stealing from his woodpile, Winthrop called the man into his presence and told him that because of the severity of the winter and his need, he had permission to supply himself from Winthrop's woodpile for the rest of the cold season. Thus, he said to his friends, did he effectively cure the man from stealing.

The freemen of Massachusetts did not always appreciate Winthrop's leniency, for it made it seem that there was no law but the governor's will. He was voted out of office and quietly served in minor posts for several years before being recalled to leadership. Petty leaders in far-flung colonial outposts have not always taken demotion with such equanimity. Winthrop accepted the procedural principles of self-government enough to temper his own preference for magnanimous, if personal, substantive justice. If our "whole destiny" is not quite contained in Winthrop, as Tocqueville thought, something very important about our tradition nonetheless derives from him and from his fellow Puritans.

The founding generation of the American republic produced so many individuals exemplary of the republican tradition that it is hard to choose among them. George Washington seemed to his contemporaries like some figure out of the early Roman republic. Though he would have preferred to live quietly on his country estate, Washington responded to his country's call to be commander-in-chief of the revolutionary army and, later, first president of the United States. After graduating from Harvard College, John Adams of Massachusetts, a descendant of the Puritans, devoted his talents as a young lawyer to the constitutional defense of the rights of his fellow colonists, and subsequently to the revolutionary cause. Thomas Jefferson (1743–1826), however, as author of the Declaration of Independence and leader of the popular cause, stands out as a particularly appropriate example of republican thinking.

Jefferson came from the planter class of western Virginia. After graduating from William and Mary College, he early took an active part in the politics of the Virginia colony. At the age of thirty-three, he drafted the Declaration of Independence, and with the words "All men are created equal" gave enduring expression to his lifelong commitment to equality. Jefferson did not believe that human beings are equal in all respects. By equality, he meant fundamentally political equality. No man, he believed, is born with a saddle on his back for another man to ride. Therefore, however much he temporized on the practical issue of emancipation, Jefferson vigorously opposed slavery in principle.

Though he held that equality is a universal principle, true at all times and places, Jefferson was a genuine adherent of the republican tradition in believing that it is only effective politically at certain times and places where relatively rare conditions allow it to be operative. Political equality can only be effective in a republic where the citizens actually participate. "The further the departure from direct and constant control by the citizens," he said, "the less has the government of the ingredient of republicanism." Indeed, the ideal of a self-governing society of relative equals in which all participate is what guided Jefferson all his life. In comparison to Europe, he thought this ideal was realizable in the United States in large part because Americans, at least white Americans, were not divided into a few very rich aristocrats and a poverty-stricken mass. Jefferson's ideal was the independent farmer who could at the same time make his living and participate in the common life. Cities and manufacturing he feared precisely because they would bring great inequalities of class and corrupt the morals of a free people.

Late in life, he saw that manufactures were necessary if the nation itself was not to lose its liberty, but at the same time he more insistently than ever stressed the principle of citizen participation. He proposed to subdivide counties into "wards" of approximately 100 citizens that would be "small republics" in which every citizen could become "an acting member of the Common government, transacting in person a great portion of its rights and duties, subordinate indeed, yet important, and entirely within his own competence." Such small republics would help to guarantee the health of the large one. In such a society, Jefferson's injunction "Love your neighbor as yourself, and your country more than yourself" could have an immediate meaning to the citizens. But Jefferson feared that "our rulers will become corrupt, our people careless." If people forgot themselves "in the sole faculty of making money," he said, the future of the republic was bleak and tyranny would not be far away. Like Winthrop, Jefferson left office much poorer than he entered it and faced bankruptcy in his later years.

Freedom was not so tightly tied to substantive morality for Jefferson as it had been for Winthrop. Indeed, Jefferson's first freedom, freedom of religion, aimed at ensuring that people like Winthrop would not have legal power to force their views on others. In general, Jefferson favored freedom of the person from arbitrary state action and freedom of the press from any form of censorship. Yet he also believed that the best defense of freedom was an educated people actively participating in government. The notion of a formal freedom that would simply allow people to do what they pleased—for example, solely to make money—was as unpalatable to Jefferson as it had been to Winthrop. However important formal freedom was to either of them, freedom only took on its real meaning in a certain kind of society with a certain form of life. Without that, Jefferson saw freedom as quickly destroying itself and eventuating in tyranny.

Listing the essential principles of government in his first inaugural address, Jefferson began with: "Equal and exact justice to all men, of whatever state or persuasion, religious or political." While he certainly believed in the procedural justice of our legal system, he could not forget that there is a higher justice that sits in judgment over human justice: "the laws of nature and of nature's God." In considering the continued existence of slavery, Jefferson wrote, "Indeed I tremble for my country when I reflect that God is just; that his justice cannot sleep forever." The profound contradiction of a people fighting for its freedom while subjecting another to slavery was not lost on Jefferson and gave rise to anxiety for our future if this contradiction were not solved.

Utilitarian and Expressive Individualism

Benjamin Franklin (1706–1790) was long regarded at home and abroad as the quintessential American. Though uncomfortable with the Puritanism of his native Boston, Franklin learned much of practical use from Cotton Mather, whose life his own overlapped by twenty-two years. One of the founders of the American republic, Franklin often gave evidence of his republican convictions. And yet it is finally neither for his Christian beliefs, which he embraced rather rapidly and perhaps more for their social utility than for their ultimate truth, nor for his republicanism, which he more genuinely espoused, that he is best known. Rather he is the archetypal poor boy who made good. It is the *Autobiography* that recounts Franklin's worldly success and the maxims from *Poor Richard's Almanack* advising others how to attain the same that are most indelibly associated with him.

Born the son of a soap and candle maker, Franklin was largely self-educated, for he could not afford the college education that Adams and Jefferson took as their due. Seeking a respectable craft, he apprenticed himself to his older brother, a printer. So began the vicissitudes of a career too familiar to readers of the *Autobiography* to need summary here. Suffice it to say that by the age of forty-two Franklin was established in Philadelphia as a printer and publisher and had made a sufficient fortune to be able to retire from the active direction of his business to devote himself to his political, philanthropic, and scientific interests for the rest of his life.

The *Autobiography*, a secular version of John Bunyan's *Pilgrim's Progress*, which had much impressed Franklin in his youth, is the archetypal story of a young man who, though poor, attains success by dint of hard work and careful calculation. Both famous and revealing is Franklin's account of how he attempted to lead a virtuous life by making a "little book" in which he allotted a page to each of the virtues and marked his progress as in a ledger. The twelve virtues themselves, derived from classical and Christian tradition, undergo a subtle revision in the direction of utilitarianism. "Chastity," for instance, is given a somewhat novel meaning: "Rarely use Venery but for Health or Offspring, Never to Dulness, Weakness, or the Injury of your own or another's Peace or Reputation."

Even more influential than the *Autobiography* are the aphorisms in *Poor Richard's Almanack* which have passed into the common sense of Americans about the way to attain wealth: "Early to bed and early to rise, makes a man healthy, wealthy, and wise." "God helps those that help themselves." "Lost time is never found again." "Plough deep, while Sluggards sleep, and you shall have Corn to seed and to keep, says Poor Dick." In short, Franklin gave classic expression to what many felt in the eighteenth century—and many have felt ever since—to be the most important thing about America: the chance for the individual to get ahead on his own initiative. Franklin expressed it very clearly in his advice to Europeans considering immigration to America: "If they are poor, they begin first as Servants or Journeymen; and if they are sober, industrious, and frugal, they soon become Masters, establish themselves in Business, marry, raise Families, and become respectable Citizens."

What Franklin thought about freedom and justice followed pretty plainly from his understanding of success. Defending popular government in the Pennsylvania Colony in 1756, he wrote: "The people of this Province are generally of the middling sort, and at present pretty much upon a Level. They are chiefly industrious Farmers, Artificers, or Men in Trade; they enjoy and are fond of Freedom, *and the meanest among them* thinks he has a Right to Civility from the greatest." Franklin understood, with Jefferson, that it was only a certain kind of society that was likely to give such scope to ordinary citizens, to protect their rights, and to secure their equal treatment before the law. But for many of those influenced by Franklin, the focus was so exclusively on individual self-improvement that the larger social context hardly came into view. By the end of the eighteenth century, there would be those who would argue that in a society where each vigorously pursued his own interest, the social good would automatically emerge. That would be utilitarian individualism in pure form. Though Franklin never himself believed that, his image contributed much to this new model of human life. Along with biblical religion and republicanism, utilitarian individualism has been one of the strands of the American tradition since Franklin's time.

By the middle of the nineteenth century, utilitarian individualism had become so dominant in America that it set off a number of reactions. A life devoted to the calculating pursuit of one's own material interest came to seem problematic for many Americans, some of them women, some of them clergymen, and some of them poets and writers. The cramped self-control of Franklin's "virtues" seemed to leave too little room for love, human feeling, and a deeper expression of the self. The great writers of what F. O. Matthiessen has called the "American Renaissance" all reacted in one way or another against this older form of individualism. In 1855 Herman Melville published *Israel Potter*, a novel that subjected Franklin himself to bitter satire. Emerson, Thoreau, and Hawthorne put aside the search for wealth in favor of a deeper cultivation of the self. But it is perhaps Walt Whitman who represents what we may call "expressive individualism" in clearest form.

Walt Whitman (1819–1892), like Franklin, was the son of an artisan (in his case, a carpenter), was too poor to go to college, largely educated himself, and became a printer and journalist. But there the resemblance ends. At the age of thirty-six, Whitman brought out a slim volume of poems entitled *Leaves of Grass*, and he spent the rest of his life nurturing it through one edition after another, with little financial security. The first edition of *Leaves of Grass* begins with a poem he would later aptly call "Song of Myself," whose first line is "I celebrate myself." Franklin was not above celebrating himself, but he would not have put it so bluntly. The fourth line, however, is hardly one to which Franklin would have given assent: "I loaf and invite my soul."

For Whitman, success had little to do with material acquisition. A life rich in experience, open to all kinds of people, luxuriating in the sensual as well as the intellectual, above all a life of strong feeling, was what he perceived as a successful life. Whitman identified the self with other people, with places, with nature, ultimately with the universe. The expansive and deeply feeling self becomes the very source of life, as in "Passage to India":

> Passage indeed O soul to primal thought,
> Not lands and seas alone, thy own clear freshness,
> The young maturity of brood and bloom,
> To realms of budding bibles.
>
> O soul, repressless, I with thee and thou with me,
> Thy circumnavigation of the world begin,
> Of man, the voyage of his mind's return,
> To reason's early paradise,
> Back, back to wisdom's birth, to innocent intuitions,
> Again with fair creation.

Freedom to Whitman was above all the freedom to express oneself, against all constraints and conventions:

> Afoot and light-hearted I take to the open road,
> Healthy, free, the world before me,
> The long brown path before me, leading wherever I choose.

The frankness of Whitman's celebration of bodily life, including sexuality, was shocking to nineteenth-century Americans and led to more than a few difficulties, though he never compromised the integrity of his expression. His homosexuality, vaguely but unmistakably expressed in the poetry, was another way in which he rejected the narrow definition of the male ego dominant in his day.

For all his unconventionality, there was a strong element of the republican tradition in Whitman, particularly evident in *Democratic Vistas* (1871) and elsewhere in his prose writings. The self-sufficient farmer or artisan capable of participation in the common life was Whitman's ideal as well as Jefferson's and Franklin's. He would thus have shared their idea of justice. But for Whitman, the ultimate use of the American's independence was to cultivate and express the self and explore its vast social and cosmic identities.

Early Interpretation of American Culture

One of the first to speak of the specifically American character was J. Hector St. John de Crèvecoeur, a French settler who published his *Letters from an American Farmer* in 1782. He set the tone for many future discussions when he observed that Americans tended to act with far greater personal initiative and self-reliance than Europeans and that they tended to be unimpressed by social rank or long usage. He describes the transformation of the European immigrant into an American: "From nothing to start into being; from a servant to the rank of a master; from being the slave to some despotic prince, to become a free man, invested with lands, to which every municipal blessing is annexed! What a change indeed! It is in consequence of that change that he becomes an American."

Schooled by the *philosophes* of the eighteenth-century French Enlightenment, Crèvecoeur had no difficulty appraising the typical American as a kind of "new man," an emancipated, enlightened individual confidently directing his energies toward the environment, both natural and social, aiming to wring from it a comfortable happiness. The type of personality Crèvecoeur sketched approximated the rational individual concerned about his own welfare that had been the model character of Enlightenment thought and that was at that time receiving renewed emphasis in the writings of political economists such as Adam Smith. Crèvecoeur wrote of the American that, "Here the rewards of his industry follow with equal steps the progress of his labour; his labour is founded on the basis of nature, *self-interest*; can it want a stronger allurement?" The rational, self-interested individual had emerged as Economic Man and, as such, was conceived as living most naturally in the conditions of a competitive market in which trade and exchange would replace traditional ranks and loyalties as the coordinating mechanism of social life. As Crèvecoeur said, "We are all animated with the spirit of an industry which is unfettered and unrestrained, because each person works for himself."

Clearly, among our four exemplary Americans, it is Benjamin Franklin, at least the Franklin of legend, who comes closest to Crèvecoeur's ideal of American character. Indeed, Franklin was taken as both an ideal American and an ideal *philosophe* by many French intellectuals of the day, a number of whom created a virtual cult of Franklin during his years in Paris. But Crèvecoeur's exclusive emphasis on this aspect of American culture and character blinded him to other facets. He saw American religion as gradually fading away into bland tolerance or indifference—as, according to Enlightenment views, it should. Crèvecoeur did not understand the strand of American tradition represented by John Winthrop, and one would not know from his writings that a great series of religious revivals was about to begin around 1800. He ignored almost as completely the specifically republican political culture that was so much a part of the revolutionary generation. He did not see what many Americans of his generation did, that a purely economic man would be as unsuited to a self-governing society as would the rank-bound subject of traditional regimes. Fortunately, another Frenchman, Alexis de Tocqueville, who visited the United States in the 1830s, gave a much more adequate view. Nonetheless, Crèvecoeur's view as to the essential nature of American character and society has long been influential, appearing in recent times in the much-quoted books of Louis Hartz and Daniel Boorstin.

For Tocqueville, the optimism of the Enlightenment had been tempered by the experience of the French Revolution and its aftermath, and the prophecies of the early political economists were finding an alarmingly negative fulfillment in the industrial infernos of English mill towns. Tocqueville came to the United States as a sympathetic observer, eager to determine what lessons the first fifty years of the first truly modern nation might have to teach prudent and uncertain Europeans. He added to Crèvecoeur's earlier sketch a more penetrating and complex understanding of the new society, informed by republican convictions and a deep sensitivity to the place of religion in human life.

In *Democracy in America* (published in two parts, in 1835 and 1840), Tocqueville was concerned to understand the nature of the democratic society he saw everywhere coming into existence but most fully exemplified in the United States. In particular, he was attempting to assess whether such democratic societies would be able to maintain free political institutions or whether they might slip into some new kind of despotism. He appreciated the commercial and entrepreneurial spirit that Crèvecoeur had emphasized but saw it as having ambiguous and problematic implications for the future of American freedom.

Tocqueville argues that while the physical circumstances of the United States have contributed to the maintenance of a democratic republic, laws have contributed more than those circumstances and mores (*moeurs*) more than the laws. Indeed, he stresses throughout the book that their mores have been the key to the Americans' success in establishing and maintaining a free republic and that undermining American mores is the most certain road to undermining the free institutions of the United States. He speaks of mores somewhat loosely, defining them variously as "habits of the heart"; notions, opinions and ideas that "shape mental habits"; and "the sum of moral and intellectual dispositions of men in society." Mores seem to involve not only ideas and opinions but habitual practices with respect to such things as religion, political participation, and economic life.

In short, Tocqueville, unlike Crèvecoeur, saw the great importance, in the American mores of his day, of the continuing biblical and republican traditions—the traditions of Winthrop and Jefferson. He also saw very vividly the way in which Americans operated in the tradition of Benjamin Franklin, and to describe this, he helped to give currency to a new word. "'Individualism' is a word recently coined to express a new idea," he wrote. "Our fathers only knew about egoism." Individualism is more moderate and orderly than egoism, but in the end its results are much the same: "Individualism is a calm and considered feeling which disposes each citizen to isolate himself from the mass of his fellows and withdraw into the circle of family and friends; with this little society formed to his taste, he gladly leaves the greater society to look after itself." As democratic individualism grows, he wrote, "there are more and more people who, though neither rich nor powerful enough to have much hold over others, have gained or kept enough wealth and enough understanding to look after their own needs. Such folk owe no man anything and hardly expect anything from anybody. They form the habit of thinking of themselves in isolation and imagine that their whole destiny is in their hands." Finally, such people come to "forget their ancestors," but also their descendants, as well as isolating themselves from their contemporaries. "Each man is forever thrown back on himself alone, and there is danger that he may be shut up in the solitude of his own heart." Tocqueville mainly observed the utilitarian individualism we have associated with Franklin. He only in a few instances discerns something of the expressive individualism that Whitman would come to represent.

Tocqueville saw the isolation to which Americans are prone as ominous for the future of our freedom. It is just such isolation that is always encouraged by despotism. And so Tocqueville is particularly interested in all those countervailing tendencies that pull people back from their isolation into social communion. Immersion in private economic pursuits undermines the person as citizen. On the other hand, involvement in public affairs is the best antidote to the pernicious effects of individualistic isolation: "Citizens who are bound to take part in public affairs must turn from the private interest and occasionally take a look at something other than themselves." It is precisely in these respects that mores become important. The habits and practices of religion and democratic participation educate the citizen to a larger view than his purely private world would allow. These habits and practices rely to some extent on self-interest in their educational work, but it is only when self-interest has to some degree been transcended that they succeed.

In ways that Jefferson would have understood, Tocqueville argues that a variety of active civic organizations are the key to American democracy. Through active involvement in common concerns, the citizen can overcome the sense of relative isolation and powerlessness that results from the insecurity of life in an increasingly commercial society. Associations, along with decentralized, local administration, mediate between the individual and the centralized state, providing forums in which opinion can be publicly and intelligently shaped and the subtle habits of public initiative and responsibility learned and passed on. Associational life, in Tocqueville's thinking, is the best bulwark against the condition he feared most: the mass society of mutually antagonistic individuals, easy prey to despotism. These intermediate structures check, pressure, and restrain the tendencies of centralized government to assume more and more administrative control.

In Tocqueville's still-agrarian America, as indeed throughout the nineteenth century, the basic unit of association, and the practical foundation of both individual dignity and participation, was the local community. There a civic culture of individual initiative was nurtured through custom and personal ties inculcated by a widely shared Protestant Christianity. The mores Tocqueville emphasized were still strong. Concern for economic betterment was widespread, but it operated within the context of a still-functional covenant concern for the welfare of one's neighbor. In the towns, the competitive individualism stirred by commerce was balanced and humanized by the restraining influences of a fundamentally egalitarian ethic of community responsibility.

These autonomous small-scale communities in the mid-nineteenth century were dominated by the classic citizens of a free republic, men of middling condition who shared similar economic and social positions and whose ranks less affluent members of the population aspired to enter, often successfully. Most men were self-employed, and many who worked for another were saving capital to launch themselves on their own. Westward expansion, as Tocqueville noted, reproduced this pattern of a decentralized, egalitarian democracy across the continent. American citizenship was anchored in the ethos and institutions of the face-to-face community of the town.

The Independent Citizen

It was this Tocquevillean image of the American town that Joe Gorman evoked as his own vision when we met him in chapter 1. For American republicans of the nineteenth century, the town at its best was a moral grid that channeled the energies of its enterprising citizens and their families into collective well-being. The moral life of the community, it was believed, would simultaneously increase material welfare and nourish public spirit. The life of the towns was tightly bounded, however, and if it could yoke individual initiative for the common good, it could also exclude the different and suffocate the unconforming. The strictures of town morality were in part generated by the citizens' unease at trying to create community while navigating the flood of geographical, demographic, and economic expansion. For, as Tocqueville saw, the American, that new kind of person, was a tentative character type shaped by inherited values on the one hand and the challenges of the expanding frontier on the other.

A representative character is a kind of symbol. It is a way by which we can bring together in one concentrated image the way people in a given social environment organize and give meaning and direction to their lives. In fact, a representative character is more than a collection of individual traits or personalities. It is rather a public image that helps define, for a given group of people, just what kinds of personality traits it is good and legitimate to develop. A representative character provides an ideal, a point of reference and focus, that gives living expression to the vision of life, as in our society today sports figures legitimate the strivings of youth and the scientist represents objective competence.

Tocqueville's America can be viewed as an interlocking network of specific social roles: those of husband, wife, child, farmer, craftsman, clergyman, lawyer, merchant, township officer, and so on. But the distinctive quality of that society, its particular identity as a "world" different from other societies, was summed up in the spirit, the mores, that animated its members, and that spirit was symbolized in the representative character of what we can call the independent citizen, the new national type Tocqueville described. In many ways, the independent citizen continued the traditions of Winthrop and Jefferson. He held strongly to biblical religion, and he knew the duties as well as the rights of citizenship. But the model of Benjamin Franklin, the self-made man, loomed ever larger in his defining traits. Abraham Lincoln was perhaps the noblest example of the mid-nineteenth-century American independent citizen. In his language, he surpassed the biblical eloquence of John Winthrop and his understanding of democratic republicanism was even more profound than that of the man he always recognized as his teacher, Thomas Jefferson. And yet it was Lincoln the railsplitter who went from log cabin to White House rather than Lincoln the public theologian or Lincoln the democratic philosopher who captured the popular imagination.

In any case, representative characters are not abstract ideals or faceless social roles, but are realized in the lives of those individuals who succeed more or less well in fusing their individual personalities with the public requirements of those roles. It is this living reenactment that gives cultural ideals their power to organize life. Representative characters thus demarcate specific societies and historical eras. The new American republic of the nineteenth century was the era of the independent citizen as surely as it was defined by the town and national expansion.

Because representative characters are the focal point at which a society encounters its problems as interpreted through a specific set of cultural understandings, they have frequently been mainstays of myth and popular feeling. Certainly, powerful American myths have been built around the self-reliant, but righteous, individual whose social base is the life of the small farmer or independent craftsman and whose spirit is the idealized ethos of the township. These myths are important sources of meaning in the lives of a number of the characters we describe in this book, and they have lately come to play a large, if somewhat disingenuous, role in national political rhetoric. Myths often tell important truths about the tensions people experience and their hopes for resolving those tensions or somehow turning them to constructive use.

Tocqueville depicted the conflicts between the democratic citizen's concern for individual advancement and security on the one hand and religion and local political participation on the other. He traced privatizing tendencies to the new spirit of individualism attendant on nascent commercial capitalism and concern for community to the republican and biblical traditions.

The focus of the new democratic culture was on male roles. But the ethic of achievement articulated by men was sustained by a moral ecology shaped by women. Among artisans and farmers, the household unit played a vital economic role, within which men's and women's positions, though unequal in power and prestige, were largely complementary. In the larger towns and cities, however, and particularly among the professional and business classes, women were more and more deprived of an economic role and were expected to specialize in the expressive and nurturing roles of mother and beautifier of the home, itself viewed more as a retreat from the everyday world than as a part of it. As women reacted differently to these new pressures, the first consciousness of, and opposition to, the inequality of women came to be expressed in America. By the end of the nineteenth century, the fact that women were not "independent citizens" was experienced as a major social strain.

The relevance of Crèvecoeur and Tocqueville for orienting our understanding of the present is suggested by the echoes of their respective analyses in the characters of our study. Brian Palmer's relatively private and optimistic orientation rehearses Crèvecoeur, while Joe Gorman's anxiety and Margaret Oldham's sense of isolation seem to confirm some of Tocqueville's fears of privatism, an anticipation at least somewhat counterbalanced by the contemporary public passion of Wayne Bauer. To understand the representative characters of present-day America, we need to move beyond Tocqueville's era, but in Tocqueville's spirit, noting the evolution of new characters emerging in response to the transformation of the United States into an industrial world power.

The Entrepreneur

The citizen perceived by Tocqueville was indeed closer to being an individual "shut up in the solitude of his own heart" than earlier Americans of religious and republican stripe had been. Yet he was a considerably less isolated and self-regarding figure than the entrepreneurs of the Gilded Age of the late nineteenth century or the bureaucratic managers and therapists of the twentieth.

Tocqueville voiced great misgivings about two phenomena that he thought threatened the moral balance of Jacksonian democracy. One with the slave society of the South, which not only treated blacks inhumanely but, as Tocqueville, like Jefferson, noted, degraded whites as well. The second danger lay in the industrial system, which first made its appearance in the Northeast. Factories had concentrated great numbers of poor and dependent workers, often women and immigrants, into rapidly growing mill towns, and Tocqueville feared the rise of a new form of aristocracy that would make owners and managers into petty despots and reduce workers to mechanically organized, dependent operatives, a condition incompatible with full democratic citizenship. Just as the plantation system subordinated the yeoman farmer in the South, so the spread of industrial organization both concentrated economic control in the hands of relatively few owners and threatened to displace the independent artisans so central to nineteenth-century democratic life. Ironically, the traumatic Civil War that destroyed the slave civilization enormously furthered the growth of the industrial structures that would fatally unbalance the original American pattern of decentralized, self-governing communities.

Between the period of rapid westward expansion and industrial growth that followed the Civil War and the entry of the United States onto the world scene in World War I, American society passed through the most rapid and profound transformation in its history, not excluding our own time. Nothing less than a new national society came into being in those years, a society within whose structure we still live, and one markedly unlike that of most of the nineteenth century. By the end of that century, new technologies, particularly in transport, communications, and manufacturing, pulled the many semi-autonomous local societies into a vast national market. Though fostered in many ways by the federal government, the new expansion was largely carried out by private individuals and financial groups, who generated private wealth and control on a previously unheard-of-scale.

The new economically integrated society emerging at the turn of the century developed its own forms of social organization, political control, and culture, including new representative characters. The new social form, capable of extending the control of a group of investors over vast resources, huge numbers of employees and, often, great distances, was the business corporation. The Pennsylvania Railroad, with its tentacular reach, its supervised, graded, and uniformed army of workers, its mechanical precision of operation and monopolistic ambitions, became the model of a new institution destined eventually to affect the lives of almost all Americans. The steel, oil, banking and finance, and insurance industries rapidly adopted the new bureaucratic form of the corporation.

The old local governments and organizations lacked the capacity to deal with problems that were increasingly national in scope. Under these conditions, the traditional forms of social and economic life of the town lost their dominant position, in fact, if not in symbol, and the traditional idea of American citizenship was called into question. The new industrial order was focussed on large cities that seemed the antithesis of the order and decency of the town. Factories, slums, immigrants, and ward bosses seemed "foreign" and frightening. In those years, a new politics of interest developed, with the powerful national economic interests of the corporations, banks, and their investors, and, eventually, the labor movement, competing with the old regional, ethnic, and religious interests. These developments changed the workings of the political parties in the national government. By the early decades of the twentieth century, the Progressive movement was calling for a smoother partnership between large-scale economic organizations and government at all levels to "rationalize" the tumultuous process of social and political change. If all generations of Americans have had to confront "future shock," surely the turn-of-the-century generation faced the most severe challenge.

The eclipse of the old economic and social patterns brought stormy political conflicts and complex cultural changes in its wake. One was the acceleration of a possibility always available to some in American society, the emancipation of the successful entrepreneur from the confining ties of the old town morality. The Gilded Age was the era of the spectacular "self-made" economic success: captains of industry who could ignore the clamor of public opinion and rise to truly national power and prestige by economic means alone. In the predatory capitalists the age dubbed robber barons, some of the worst fears of earlier republican moralists seemed confirmed: that by releasing the untrammeled pursuit of wealth without regard to the demands of social justice, industrial capitalism was destroying the fabric of a democratic society, threatening social chaos by pitting class against class. Where, many wondered, could new limits and directions for individual initiative be found beyond the broken bounds of the local self-governing community? The inability of the old moral order effectively to encompass the new social developments set the terms of a cultural debate in which we as a nation are still engaged.

The most distinctive aspect of twentieth-century American society is the division of life into a number of separate functional sectors: home and workplace, work and leisure, white collar and blue collar, public and private. This division suited the needs of the bureaucratic industrial corporations that provided the model for our preferred means of organizing society by the balancing and linking of sectors as "departments" in the functional whole, as in a great business enterprise. Particularly powerful in molding our contemporary sense of things has been the division between the various "tracks" to achievement laid out in schools, corporation, government, and the professions, on the one hand, and the balancing life-sectors of home, personal ties, and "leisure," on the other. All this is in strong contrast to the widespread nineteenth-century pattern in which, as on the often-sentimentalized family farm, these functions had only indistinct boundaries. Domesticity, love, and intimacy increasingly became "havens" against the competitive culture of work.

With the industrialization of the economy, working life became more specialized and its organization tighter. Simultaneously, industrialization made functional sectors of the economy—various industries, whole geographical regions—more interdependent than before. Yet the sectoral form of organization and the competitive pressures of the national market made this interdependence difficult to perceive. While the pressures to compete and the network of private life were immediately perceptible, the interrelationships of society as a whole were largely abstractions. The sectoral pattern of modern American society has thus often been able to contain potential conflicts by separating those who are different without impairing the economic linkages of sectors within the larger economy.

Under such conditions, it is not surprising that the major problems of life appear to be essentially individual matters, a question of negotiating a reliable and harmonious balance among the various sectors of life to which an individual has access. As its points of reference contracted from an economically and occupationally diverse local community to the geographically spread, but functionally homogeneous, sector within which a person competes, success came to be defined in professional terms. The concept of one's "peers" concomitantly underwent a subtle, but important, shift of meaning. It came to signify those who share the same specific mix of activities, beginning with occupation and economic position, but increasingly implying the same attitudes, tastes, and style of life.

The responses to all this that were articulated around the turn of the century have continued to shape our ways of conceiving and relating to American society. Those responses have all along been closely interwoven with new character types that, like the earlier ones, have come to seem representative approaches to the common conditions of life, giving moral meaning and direction to the lives of individuals.

The Manager

The self-sufficient entrepreneur, competitive, tough, and freed by wealth from external constraints, was one new American character. Certainly much of the moral appeal of the self-made man is his apparent freedom, not only from traditional restraints, but from the tight organization, the drudgery and banality, of so much of modern industrial life. The irony, of course, is that the entrepreneur's major historical role has been to create the modern industrial context. Celebrating the economic struggle, the self-made man of means became the legitimizing symbol for some of the aspiring middle class. Yet in practice the recurrent American dream of success has often continued to approximate the old image of the businessman as family provider and citizen. The turn-of-the-century nabobs themselves frequently sought legitimation through public philanthropy and national service, drawing on models more deferential—their critics said "feudal"—than American republican tradition countenanced. But the activist individual entrepreneur, though a continuing feature of American life and still a powerful symbol, has not represented the dominant direction of economic and social development.

The bureaucratic organization of the business corporation has been the dominant force in this century. Within the corporation, the crucial character has been the professional manager. The competitive industrial order with its sectoral organization and its push toward profitability has been the indisputable reality of modern life for the manager, rather than the object of a passionate faith in "progress," as for the entrepreneur. Although the manager in effect builds upon the work of the entrepreneur and shares with him the drive to achieve and problem-solving activism that are old American traits, the social positions and outlooks of the two types differ importantly.

The essence of the manager's task is to organize the human and nonhuman resources available to the organization that employs him so as to improve its position in the marketplace. His role is to persuade, inspire, manipulate, cajole, and intimidate those he manages so that his organization measures up to criteria of effectiveness shaped ultimately by the market but specifically by the expectations of those in control of his organization—finally, its owners. The manager's view of things is akin to that of the technician of industrial society par excellence, the engineer, except that the manager must admit interpersonal responses and personalities, including his own, into the calculation of effectiveness.

Like the entrepreneur, the manager also has another life, divided among spouse, children, friends, community, and religious and other nonoccupational involvements. Here, in contrast to the manipulative, achievement-oriented practices of the workplace, another kind of personality is actualized, often within a social pattern that shows recognizable continuity with earlier American forms of family and community. But it is an outstanding feature of industrial life that these sectors have become radically discontinuous in the kinds of traits emphasized and the moral understandings that guide individuals within them. "Public" and "private" roles often contrast sharply, as symbolized by the daily commute from green suburban settings reminiscent of rural life to the industrial, technological ambience of the workplace.

The split between public and private life correlates with a split between utilitarian individualism, appropriate in the economic and occupational spheres, and expressive individualism, appropriate in private life. For a long time such a split was incipient in American life. Early in the nineteenth century, indeed already in the eighteenth century, an appeal to calculating utility was complemented by an appeal to sentiment or emotion. Jefferson, following the eighteenth-century Scottish philosophers, believed in an innate "moral sentiment" that impelled men toward benevolence. The Puritan theologian Jonathan Edwards (1703–58) had seen religion, too, as located in the "affections." When science seemed to have dominated the explanatory schemas of the external world, morality and religion took refuge in human subjectivity, in feeling and sentiment. Morality and religion were related to aesthetics, the realm of feeling par excellence, as we saw in the case of Whitman. When morality came to be associated with the role of women and the family, and religion to be largely a matter of revivalistic emotion, the split between the utilitarian and the expressive spheres in nineteenth-century America widened. Nonetheless, theologians and moralists believed feeling had some cognitive content, some access to the external world, and Whitman certainly believed his poetry was expressing the truth not only of himself but of the world. But with the emergence of psychology as an academic field—and, even more important, as a form of popular discourse—in the late nineteenth and early twentieth centuries, the purely subjective grounding of expressive individualism became complete.

The town had provided a metaphor of a moral ecology in which the polarities of public and private, masculine and feminine, were integrated by means of generally shared codes of behavior. Preindustrial American character surely oscillated between the instrumental orientation of the "masculine" world of work achievement and the values of the "feminine" spheres of nurturing domesticity. But the cultural framework made that oscillation, including its conflicts, intelligible.

With the coming of the managerial society, the organization of work, place of residence, and social status came to be decided by criteria of economic effectiveness. Those same economic criteria further facilitated the growth of national mass marketing and, with it, expanded consumer choice. The older social and moral standards became in many ways less relevant to the lives of those Americans most directly caught up in the new system. The manager could reorganize resources for greater effectiveness in economic life. Similarly, the relatively affluent twentieth-century American could reorganize habits and styles of life experimentally to achieve a more gratifying private life. In this process, Americans learned to become more efficient in adapting to new sets of expectations and styles of consumption.

The Therapist

Like the manager, the therapist is a specialist in mobilizing resources for effective action, only here the resources are largely internal to the individual and the measure of effectiveness is the elusive criterion of personal satisfaction. Also like the manager, the therapist takes the functional organization of industrial society for granted, as the unproblematical context of life. The goal of living is to achieve some combination of occupation and "lifestyle" that is economically possible and psychically tolerable, that "works." The therapist, like the manager, takes the ends as they are given; the focus is upon the effectiveness of the means.

Between them, the manager and the therapist largely define the outlines of twentieth-century American culture. The social basis of that culture is the world of bureaucratic consumer capitalism, which dominates, or has penetrated, most older, local economic forms. While the culture of manager and therapist does not speak in the language of traditional moralities, it nonetheless proffers a normative order of life, with character ideals, images of the good life, and methods of attaining it. Yet it is an understanding of life generally hostile to older ideas of moral order. Its center is the autonomous individual, presumed able to choose the roles he will play and the commitments he will make, not on the basis of higher truths but according to the criterion of life-effectiveness as the individual judges it.

The moral language and images of this culture of utilitarian and expressive individualism have influenced the lives of most of the characters in this book, and one of our chief tasks in the chapters that follow will be to delineate and understand its forms. As we shall see, the effects of this managerial and therapeutic understanding are not always benign; it does not always succeed, even by its own standards. Indeed, the very term *therapeutic* suggests a life focussed on the need for cure. But cure of what? In the final analysis, it is cure of the lack of fit between the present organization of the self and the available organization of work, intimacy, and meaning. And this cure is to take the form of enhancing and empowering the self to be able to relate successfully to others in society, achieving a kind of satisfaction without being overwhelmed by their demands. In its own understanding, the expressive aspect of our culture exists for the liberation and fulfillment of the individual. Its genius is that it enables the individual to think of commitments—from marriage and work to political and religious involvement—as enhancements of the sense of individual well-being rather than as moral imperatives.

The culture of the manager and the therapist is thus both recognizably continuous with earlier American cultural forms and yet different from them. The obvious point of similarity is the emphasis on the independence of the individual. As we have seen, self-reliance is an old American value, but only one strand of the complex cultural weft we have inherited. The expressive culture, now deeply allied with the utilitarian, reveals its difference from earlier patterns by its readiness to treat normative commitments as so many alternative strategies of self-fulfillment. What has dropped out are the old normative expectations of what makes life worth living. With the freedom to define oneself anew in a plethora of identities has also come an attenuation of those common understandings that enable us to recognize the virtues of the other.

In fact, the new culture is deeply ambiguous. It represents both the easing of constraints and dogmatic prejudices about what others should be and an idealization of the coolly manipulative style of management. In our society, with its sharply divided spheres, it provides a way for the beleaguered individual to develop techniques for coping with the often-contradictory pressures of public and private life. Yet it does so by extending the calculating managerial style into intimacy, home, and community, areas of life formerly governed by the norms of a moral ecology.

Some Recent Interpretations

Robert and Helen Lynd in *Middletown* (1929) and *Middletown in Transition* (1937) offered the most extensive sociological study hitherto undertaken of a single American community (Muncie, Indiana). The Lynds sought to show what was happening to America under the impact of industrialization and the social changes accompanying it. They took the year 1890 as a baseline with which to compare the America of the twenties and thirties that they studied firsthand. They saw the typical nineteenth-century town that Muncie had been in 1890 transformed into the rapidly changing industrial city of thirty or forty years later. In particular, they noted the split into a business class and a working class, with the former dominant and the latter in many ways excluded from full participation in community life. What becomes clear from the two Middletown books and from *Knowledge for What?* (1939), Robert Lund's more general book about American culture, is that the Lynds brought a rich harvest of sociological detail to document what was by then an old theme among social critics—namely, the decline of the culture of the independent citizen, with its strong biblical and republican elements, in the face of the rise of the business (managerial) class and its dominant ethos of utilitarian individualism. The Lynds viewed this change with foreboding, feeling that the future of American democracy lay in the balance.

Much of the public interpreted David Riesman's widely read *The Lonely Crowd* (1950) in the same way. The old independent "inner-directed" American was being replaced by new, "other-directed" corporate types, with lamentable results. Read carefully, Riesman's argument is considerably more complex, and his evaluations are rather different from the Lynds. Riesman actually proposes four character types, not two. Tradition-directed character is what most premodern societies produce. It is represented in America largely by immigrants from peasant societies. Riesman's inner-directed type characterizes old American culture and seems to be an amalgam of our biblical, republican, and utilitarian individualistic types. Perhaps the inner-directed person is the old independent citizen, more attuned to his own internal morality than to the cues of his neighbors. But Riesman is far from endorsing the inner-directed type, for the superego of the inner-directed person is itself an introject from social authority experienced in childhood. Like the other-directed person responding to the conformist pressures of the immediate social environment, the inner-directed person lacks genuine autonomy. The autonomous character is Riesman's fourth type and the only one he genuinely admires. Riesman's concept of the autonomous character is clearly related to some of the ideas of Erich Fromm and seems to be close to what we have called the expressive individualist type, especially in its relatively pure therapeutic form. Indeed, whatever its immediate reception, Riesman's book seems to herald an increasing importance of the expressive individualist style in postwar America, relative to which the other-directed, or conformist, character seems to have been a relatively transient type. That Riesman grew alarmed at some of the implications of his work, or some of the implications some readers drew from it, is documented in the prefaces he supplied in successive reprintings. But Riesman's later hesitations do not in the least detract from the value of *The Lonely Crowd* as a landmark study of the transformation of American character.

The only book that we would place together with those of the Lynds and Riesman as a major interpretive contribution to the understanding of twentieth-century American character and society is Hervé Varenne's *Americans Together* (1977). Varenne's classic study of a small town in southern Wisconsin is the subtlest depiction to date of how American culture and character interacted in recent times. Varenne clearly sees the dominance of utilitarian and expressive individualism as modes of character and cultural interaction, and especially the delicate balance between them and their mutual dependence. The drive toward independence and mastery only makes sense where the individual can also find a context to express the love and happiness that are his deepest feelings and desires. Fragile communities are put together to meet the utilitarian and expressive needs of individuals, with only a peripheral survival of older biblical and republican themes. For Varenne, this balance represents a successful cultural code containing and equilibrating its inner contradictions. While our reading of modern American history makes us more doubtful about the success of this equilibrium, we remain indebted to the brilliance of his insights, which, besides those of the towering figure of his fellow Frenchman, Tocqueville, have most influenced our study.

American Culture Today

Perhaps the crucial change in American life has been that we have moved from the local life of the nineteenth century—in which economic and social relationships were visible and, however imperfectly, morally interpreted as parts of a larger common life—to a society vastly more interrelated and integrated economically, technically, and functionally. Yet this is a society in which the individual can only rarely and with difficulty understand himself and his activities as interrelated in morally meaningful ways with those of other, different Americans. Instead of directing cultural and individual energies toward relating the self to its larger context, the culture of manager and therapist urges a strenuous effort to make of our particular segment of life a small world of its own.

However, the cultural hegemony of the managerial and therapeutic ethos is far from complete. It is rooted in the technological affluence of postwar society, a prosperity that has been neither equitably shared nor universally accepted. Challenges to that ethos have arisen from a variety of quarters, from those left out of that prosperity, as well as from those who, while its beneficiaries, criticize it for moral defects. Sometimes the criticism seems to be motivated by a desire to hold on to the last vestiges of the autonomous community and its ideal of the independent citizen. Sometimes it is motivated by a desire to transform the whole society, and particularly its economy, so that a more effectively functioning democracy may emerge. In either case, there is a powerful rejection of the managerial-therapeutic ethos, in which we can see not only the discontents of the present economic and social order, but also reminders of the continuing importance of the biblical and republican cultural traditions in American politics.

We see a number of surviving forms of the old ideal of the independent citizen in America today. In some cases, what we call the concerned citizen is devoted to defending the moral beliefs and practices of his or her community in the face of a permissive therapeutic culture and the decisions of administrators and managers that do not understand, and are not answerable to, local community feeling. We find what we call civic volunteers, often professionals, committed to helping their communities adjust to new challenges in a way that does not rupture tradition or destroy democratic participation. And we also find movement activists for whom the task of forming a new public, organized for discussion and action, is a major commitment. The activist works within the political order, but also hopes to influence understandings of society in the direction of significant change. None of these present-day representatives of the ideal of the independent citizen can avoid being influenced by utilitarian and expressive individualism, the pervasive world of the manager and the therapist. But they give evidence that the old cultural argument is not over, and that all strands of our tradition are still alive and still speak to our present need. Perhaps it is now clear that Brian Palmer, a manager; Margaret Oldham, a therapist; Joe Gorman, a concerned citizen; and Wayne Bauer, a movement activist, though all deeply individualist in their language, draw on a more complex tradition than any of them quite realizes.

The Campus: "An Island of Repression in a Sea of Freedom"

CHESTER E. FINN, JR.

Two weeks before the Supreme Court held that the First Amendment protects one's right to burn the flag, the regents of the University of Wisconsin decreed that students on their twelve campuses no longer possess the right to say anything ugly to or about another. Though depicted as an anti-discrimination measure, this revision of the student-conduct code declares that "certain types of expressive behavior directed at individuals and intended to demean and to create a hostile environment for education or other university-authorized activities would be prohibited and made subject to disciplinary sanctions." Penalties range from written warnings to expulsion.

Several months earlier, the University of Michigan adopted a six-page "anti-bias code" that provides for punishment of students who engage in conduct that "stigmatizes or victimizes an individual on the basis of race, ethnicity, religion, sex, sexual orientation, creed, national origin, ancestry, age, marital status, handicap, or Vietnam-era veteran status." (Presumably this last bizarre provision applies whether the "victim" is labeled a war hero or a draft dodger.)

Nor are Wisconsin and Michigan the only state universities to have gone this route. In June, the higher-education regents of Massachusetts prohibited "racism, anti-Semitism, ethnic, cultural, and religious intolerance" on their 27 campuses. A kindred regulation took effect on July 1 at the Chapel Hill campus of the University of North Carolina. And in place for some time at the law school of the State University of New York at Buffalo has been the practice of noting a student's use of racist language on his academic record and alerting prospective employers and the bar association.

Not to be outdone by the huge state schools, a number of private universities, like Emory in Atlanta and Stanford in California, have also made efforts to regulate unpleasant discourse and what the National Education Association terms "ethnoviolence," a comprehensive neologism that includes "acts of insensitivity."

Proponents of such measures are straightforward about their intentions. Says University of Wisconsin President Kenneth Shaw of the new rule: "It can particularly send a message to minority students that the board and its administration do care." Comments Emory's director of equal opportunity: "We just wanted to ensure that at a time when other universities were having problems that we made it clear that we wouldn't tolerate graffiti on walls or comments in classes." And in Massachusetts, the regents concluded that "There must be a unity and cohesion in the diversity which we seek to achieve, thereby creating an atmosphere of pluralism."

Not so for those running universities. "What we are proposing is not completely in line with the First Amendment," a leader of Stanford's student government has acknowledged to a reporter, but "I'm not sure it should be. We . . . are trying to set a standard different from what society at large is trying to accomplish." Explains the Emory official: "I don't believe freedom of speech on campus was designed to allow people to demean others on campus." And a Stanford law professor contends that "racial epithets and sexually haranguing speech silences rather than furthers discussion."

Disregard the hubris and the sanctimony. Academics and their youthful apprentices have long viewed their own institutions and causes as nobler than the workaday world and humdrum pursuits of ordinary mortals. Forget, too, the manifest evidence of what some of the nation's most esteemed universities are teaching their students about basic civics. Consider only the two large issues that these developments pose, each freighted with a hefty burden of irony.

The first can still evoke a wry smile. We are, after all, seeing students pleading for controls to be imposed on campus behavior in the name of decency and morality. Yet these same students would be outraged if their colleges and universities were once again to function *in loco parentis* by constraining personal liberty in any other way. What is more, faculties, administrators, and trustees are complying with the student demands; they are adopting and—one must assume—enforcing these behavior codes. By and large, these are the same campuses that have long since shrugged off any serious responsibility for student conduct with respect to alcohol, drugs, and promiscuity (indeed, have cheerily collaborated in making the last of these behaviors more heedless by installing condom dispensers in the dorms). These are colleges that do not oblige anyone to attend class regularly, to exercise in the gym, to drive safely, or to eat a balanced diet. A student may do anything he likes with or to his fellow students, it appears, including things that are indisputably illegal, unhealthy, and dangerous for everyone concerned, and the university turns a blind eye. But a student may not, under any circumstances, speak ill of another student's origin, inclinations, or appearance.

The larger—and not the least bit amusing—issue is, of course, the matter of freedom of expression and efforts to limit it. That the emotionally charged flag-burning decision emerged from the Supreme Court the same month as authorities in China shot hundreds of students (and others) demonstrating for democracy in the streets of Beijing is as stark an illustration as one will ever see of the gravity and passion embedded in every aspect of this question.

One might say that the precepts embodied in the First Amendment have applied there with exceptional clarity, and long before they were vouchsafed in other areas of society. For while private colleges are not formally bound by the Bill of Rights, they, like their public-sector counterparts, are heirs to an even older tradition. The campus was a sanctuary in which knowledge and truth might be pursued—and imparted—with impunity, no matter how unpopular, distasteful, or politically heterodox the process might sometimes be. That is the essence of academic freedom and it is the only truly significant distinction between the universities of the democracies and those operating under totalitarian regimes. Wretched though the food and lodging are for students on Chinese campuses, these were not the provocations that made martyrs in Tiananmen Square. It was the idea of freedom that stirred China's students and professors (and millions of others, as well). And it was the fear of allowing such ideas to take root that prompted the government's brutal response.

Having enjoyed almost untrammeled freedom of thought and expression for three and a half centuries, and having vigorously and, for the most part, successfully fended off efforts by outsiders (state legislators and congressional subcommittees, big donors, influential alumni, etc.) to constrain that freedom, American colleges and universities are now muzzling themselves. The anti-discrimination and anti-harassment rules being adopted will delimit what can be said and done on campus. Inevitably, this must govern what can be taught and written in lab, library, and lecture hall, as well as the sordid antics of fraternity houses and the crude nastiness of inebriated teenagers. ("The calls for a ban on 'harassment by vilification' reached a peak last fall" at Stanford, explained the New York *Times*, "after two drunken freshmen turned a symphony recruiting poster into a black-face caricature of Beethoven and posted it near a black student's room.")

Constraints on free expression and open inquiry do not, of course, depend on the adoption of a formal code of conduct. Guest speakers with controversial views have for some years now risked being harassed, heckled, even shouted down by hostile campus audiences, just as scholars engaging in certain forms of research, treading into sensitive topics, or reaching unwelcome conclusions have risked calumny from academic "colleagues." More recently, students have begun to monitor their professors and to take action if what is said in class irks or offends them.

Thus, at Harvard Law School this past spring, Bonnie Savage, the aptly-named leader of the Harvard Women's Law Association (HWLA), sent professor Ian Macneil a multicount allegation of sexism in his course on contracts. The first offense cited was Macneil's quoting (on page 963 of his textbook) Byron's well-known line, "And whispering, 'I will ne'er consent,'—consented." This, and much else that he had said and written, the HWLA found objectionable. "A professor in any position at any school," Savage pronounced, "has no right or privilege to use the classroom in such a way as to offend, at the very least, 40 percent of the students. . . ."

This was not private communication. Savage dispatched copies to sundry deans and the chairman of the faculty-appointments committee because, she later explained, "We thought he might be considered for tenure." The whole affair, Macneil responded in the *Harvard Law Record*, was "shoddy, unlawyerlike, reminiscent of Senator McCarthy, and entirely consistent with HWLA's prior conduct." As for the Byron passage, it "is in fact a perfect summary of what happens in the Battle of Forms" (a part of the contract-making process).

Macneil is not the only Harvard professor to have been given a hard time in recent years for writing or uttering words that upset students, however well-suited they might be to the lesson at hand. Not long ago, the historian Stephan Thernstrom was accused by a student vigilante of such classroom errors as "read[ing] aloud from white plantation owners' journals 'without also giving the slaves' point of view.'" Episodes of this kind, says Thernstrom, serve to discourage him and other scholars from even teaching courses on topics that bear on race and ethnicity.[1]

Nor is Harvard the only major university where student allegations, unremonstrated by the administration, have produced such a result. At Michigan last fall, the distinguished demographer, Reynolds Farley, was teaching an undergraduate course in "race and cultural contact," as he had done for the previous ten years, when a column appeared in the *Michigan Daily* alleging racial insensitivity on his part, citing—wholly out of context, of course—half a dozen so-called examples, and demanding that the sociology department make amends. Farley was not amused and, rather than invite more unjust attacks, is discontinuing the course. Consequently 50 to 125 Michigan students a year will be deprived of the opportunity to examine issues of ethnicity and the history of race relations in America under the tutelage of this world-class scholar. And to make matters even worse, Farley notes that several faculty colleagues have mentioned that they are dropping any discussion of various important race-related issues from their courses, lest similar treatment befall them.

This might seem perverse, not least from the standpoint of "aggrieved" students and their faculty mentors, because another of their major goals is to oblige everyone to take more courses on precisely these topics. "I would like to see colleges engage all incoming students in mandatory racial-education programs," William Damon, professor of psychology and chairman of the education department at Clark University, in the *Chronicle of Higher Education*. And his call is being answered on a growing number of campuses, including the state colleges of Massachusetts, the University of Wisconsin, and the University of California at Berkeley.

Ironies abound here, too, since the faculties and governing boards adopting these course requirements are generally the very bodies that resist any suggestion of a "core curriculum" or tight "distribution requirements" on the ground that diverse student preferences should be accommodated and that, in any case, there are no disciplines, writings, or ideas of such general importance that everyone should be obliged to study them. Curricular relativism can be suspended, though, when "pluralism" is itself the subject to be studied, "It is important to make such programs mandatory," Professor Damon explains, "so that they can reach students who otherwise might not be inclined to participate."

Save for the hypocrisy, this may appear at first glance to be part of an ancient and legitimate function of college faculties: deciding what subjects are of sufficient moment as to require students to examine them. If a particular university has its curricular priorities askew, requiring the study of racism rather than, say, mathematics, one can presumably enroll elsewhere (there being about 3,400 institutions to choose from).

A second glance is in order, however, before conceding legitimacy. What is commonly sought in these required courses, and the noncredit counterparts that abound on campuses where they have not yet entered the formal curriculum, is not open inquiry but, rather, a form of attitude adjustment, even ideological indoctrination. Thus Professor Damon:

Such programs should emphasize discussions in which trained instructors explore students' beliefs concerning racial diversity and its societal implications. . . . They should cover, and *provide clear justification for, any racially or ethnically sensitive admissions or hiring criteria* that students may see on campus. [Emphasis added]

Along similar lines, the Massachusetts regents insist that each campus provide "a program of educational activities designed to enlighten faculty, administrators, staff and students with regard to . . . ways in which the dominant society manifests and perpetuates racism." So, too, the Berkeley academic senate last year voted (227 to 194) to begin requiring all undergraduates to sign up for new courses in "American cultures" in which they will explore questions like, "How have power relations between groups been manifested in such matters as racism, economics, politics, environmental design, religion, education, law, business, and the arts in the United States?"

In response to Professor Damon's description of the instructional goals of the mandatory course he is urging, Harvard's Thernstrom wrote in a letter to the *Chronicle of Higher Education*:

Justification? Is that what educators are supposed to provide? For "any" criteria that omniscient administrators choose to adopt? . . . How about a mandatory course providing "a clear justification" for American foreign policy since 1945? Or one justifying the Reagan administration's domestic policies? . . . True, Professor Damon declares that such courses should "avoid preaching and indoctrination," but it seems to me that providing "justification" for highly controversial social programs cannot be anything but indoctrination.

Whether this bleak assessment will prove accurate hinges in large part on who ends up teaching these courses and the intellectual norms to which they hew. With scholars of the stature of Farley and Thernstrom already deterred—coerced into self-censorship—it is likely that colleges will enlist as instructors people who agree that the purpose of these "education" efforts is more political than intellectual. Such individuals are not hard to find in the curricular domain now known as "cultural studies." In this field, acknowledged Professor Donald Lazere at the 1988 conference of the Modern Language Association (MLA), "politics are obviously central." Indeed, the agenda of the field itself was defined by Richard Johnson, an Englishman who is one of its leading figures, as

a series of critiques of innocent-sounding categories or innocent-sounding practices, obviously culture, and art and literature, but also communication, and consumption, entertainment, education, leisure, style, the family, femininity and masculinity, and sexuality and pleasure, and, of course, the most objective-sounding, neutral-sounding categories of all, knowledge and science.

It is not far from MLA discussions to campus staffing decisions. Here is how the historian Alan C. Kors of the University of Pennsylvania describes the organization of a dorm-based program to educate students at his institution about "racism, sexism, and homophobia":

[W]hat the administration has done, in fact, is turn this education of the students over to ideologically-conscious groups with ideological and political agendas, namely, the "Women's Center" and the Office of Affirmative Action. . . . These are people who have been granted, in effect, to use a term they like, the "privileged ideological position" on campus. Now the notion that the Penn Women's Center speaks for Penn women is absurd, since it obviously doesn't speak for more than a very small minority of a diverse, individuated female population. . . . But the university's administration has an easy way of buying off certain pressure groups, and it consists of giving those in possession of privileged ideologies the responsibility for reeducating students and faculty with improper attitudes. As a result, you really have the foundations of a University of Beijing in Philadelphia.

These additions to the formal and informal curricula of American colleges and universities, like the behavior codes and anti-harassment policies the institutions are embracing, are invariably promulgated in the name of enhancing "diversity" on campus. That has become the chief purpose of present-day affirmative-action hiring and admissions policies, too. It has, after all, been a while since one could observe prospective students or instructors turned away in any numbers at the campus gates because they were women or minority-group members or because of their religion or handicap. The one exception in recent years has been Asian students, whose dazzling academic performance led some universities to impose admission quotas lest this group become "overrepresented" in the student body. Asians, in fact, recently won a victory at Berkeley, when the chancellor apologized for admissions policies that had held down their numbers and announced a new one. The changes include raising from 40 to 50 percent the fraction of Berkeley undergraduates who will be admitted on the basis of academic merit alone; the other half must be "underrepresented minorities." (The likely impact of this new policy will be to maintain the enrollment shares of black and Hispanic students, to boost the numbers of Asians admitted, and to cause a drop in white matriculants, who plainly will not make it as a minority and who may be trounced by the Asians in the merit competition.)

With these few exceptions, however, affirmative action in the late 80's has nothing to do with invidious discrimination on grounds of race, gender, etc. Most colleges and universities would kill for more blacks and Hispanics in their student bodies and for more of the same minorities, as well as more women, in their faculties. (The only reason they are not equally eager for additional female *students* is that women today constitute a clear majority of the nation's 12.8 million higher-education enrollees.) "Diversity," then, is now the goal.

That we have generally grown used to this in matters of campus admission and employment does not mean that the academy lacks the capacity to surprise and dismay. These days that capacity usually entails a faculty-hiring decision where the race or gender or ideology of the candidate is entangled with his academic specialty. In recent months, I have run into several outstanding young (white male) political scientists who are finding it impossible to land tenure-track teaching posts at medium- and high-status colleges because, as one of them wryly explained to me, their scholarly strengths lie in the study of "DWEMs." When I confessed ignorance of the acronym, he patiently explained that it stands for "Dead White European Males." Had they specialized in revolutionary ideologies, the politics of feminism and racism, or trendy quantitative social-science methodologies, they could perhaps have transcended their inconvenient gender and mundane color and have a reasonable shot at academic employment. But to spend one's hours with the likes of Aristotle, Machiavelli, Hobbes, and Burke is to have nothing very important to offer a political-science department today, whatever one's intellectual and pedagogical accomplishments.

One can, by contrast, get wooed by the largest and most prestigious of academic departments, no matter how repugnant one's own views, provided that one offers the right blend of personal traits and intellectual enthusiasms. Richard Abowitz recently recounted the efforts by the University of Wisconsin to attract June Jordan, a radical black activist (and poet), from Stony Brook to Madison.[2] After examining her writings and orations spanning the previous fifteen years, Abowitz concluded that, if Jordan remained true to form, "her courses at the University of Wisconsin would do nothing more than propagate the crudest forms of social, political, and economic prejudice," exactly the attitudes that the university has dedicated itself to wiping out through such measures as the new student conduct code. Yet with but a single abstention, Madison's English department voted unanimously to offer her a tenured position with a generous salary. (Berkeley's offer must have been even more attractive, for that is where Jordan now teaches.)

Esoteric forms of affirmative action are by no means confined to the professoriate. Last year the editors of the *Columbia Law Review* adopted a new "diversity" program that will reserve special slots on the editorial board for individuals who qualify by virtue of their race, physical handicap, or sexual orientation. Law-review boards, of course, have customarily been meritocracies, with membership gained through outstanding academic achievement. With Columbia in the lead, one must suppose this will no longer be the rule even though, the New York *Post* commented, "No one has yet stepped forward . . . to explain why sexual orientation, for instance, would keep a student from performing well enough in law school to compete for the law review on the same basis as everyone else."

Diversity and tolerance, evenhandedly applied, are estimable precepts. But that is not how they are construed in the academy today. Nor do the narrowing limits on free expression lead only to penalties for individuals who engage in "biased" talk or "hostile" behavior. They also leave little room for opinion that deviates from campus political norms or for grievances from unexpected directions. During Harvard's race-awareness week last spring, when a white student dared to complain that she had experienced "minority ethnocentrism" on campus—black and Hispanic students, it seems, often ignored her—she was given short shrift and no sympathy by the speaker (who had already suggested that Harvard and Dartmouth were "genocidal" institutions).

More commonly, however, it is rambunctious student newspapers and magazines that get into trouble with academic authorities for printing something that contravenes the conventional wisdom. Given the predominant campus climate, it is not surprising that these are often publications with a moderate or Right-of-Center orientation. Sometimes, clearly, they do mischievous, stupid, and offensive things, but for such things the degree of toleration in higher education seems to vary with the ideology of the perpetrator. (Acts of discrimination and oppression based on political views, it should be observed, are *not* among the categories proscribed in the new codes of behavior.) In addition to a much-reported sequence of events at Dartmouth, there have been recent efforts to censor or suppress student publications, and sometimes to discipline their staff members, at Brown, Berkeley, UCLA, Vassar, and California State University at Northridge.

The last of these prompted one of the most extraordinary media events of 1989, a joint press conference on May 16 featuring—no one could have made this up—former Attorney General Edwin Meese III and the director of the Washington office of the American Civil Liberties Union (ACLU), Morton Halperin. What brought them together was shared outrage over what Halperin termed the "double standard" on campus. "Our position," he reminded the attending journalists, "is that there is an absolute right to express views even if others find those views repugnant." He could cite numerous instances, he said, where campus authorities were making life difficult for outspoken conservative students, yet could find "no cases where universities discipline students for views or opinions on the Left, or for racist comments against non-minorities."

Meese, not surprisingly, concurred, as did James Taranto, the former Northridge student journalist whose lawsuit settlement afforded the specific occasion for the press conference. In 1987, Taranto, then news editor of his campus paper, had written a column faulting UCLA officials for suspending a student editor who had published a cartoon mocking affirmative action. Taranto reproduced the offending cartoon in the Northridge paper, whereupon its faculty adviser suspended *him* from his position for two weeks because he had printed "controversial" material without her permission. The ACLU agreed to represent him in a First Amendment suit—"We were as outraged as he was by the attempt to censor the press," Halperin recalled—and two years later a settlement was reached.

While we are accumulating ironies, let it be noted that the ACLU, the selfsame organization in which Michael Dukakis's "card-carrying membership" yielded George Bush considerable mileage in the 1988 election campaign, has been conspicuously more vigilant and outspoken about campus assaults on free expression in 1989 than has the Bush administration. The Secretary of Education, Lauro Cavazos (himself a former university president), has been silent. The White House has been mute. During an incident at Brown in May, when an art professor canceled a long-planned screening of the classic film, *Birth of a Nation*, because the Providence branch of the NAACP had denounced it, the local ACLU affiliate was the only voice raised in dismay. "University officials," declared its executive director, "have now opened the door to numerous pressure groups who may wish to ban from the campus other films that they too deem 'offensive.'" Indeed. A colleague of mine recently revived a long-lapsed membership in the ACLU on the straightforward ground that no other national entity is resisting the spread of attitude-adjustment, censorship, and behavior codes in higher education.

All this would be worrisome enough even if the academy were doing well with respect to actual education for the minority students whose numbers it is so keen to increase and whose sensibilities campus administrators are so touchy about. But that is simply not the case.

Black and Hispanic students are less likely to enroll in college to begin with. This is not because admission offices turn them away—to the contrary—and not because too little student aid is available to help them defray the costs. (In any event, 80 percent of all students attend state institutions, in which tuitions average about $1,200 per year.) The largest reason more minority students do not matriculate is that so many attended wretched elementary and secondary schools in which they took the wrong courses, were poorly taught, had little expected of them, skipped class a lot, never learned much, and may well have dropped out.

Minority youngsters are not, of course, the only victims of our foundering public-education system, but they are the ones whose life prospects are most blighted by it, the ones for whom a solid basic education can make the biggest difference. Academic leaders know this full well, just as they understand that shoddy schools are major producers of ill-prepared college students. Yet for all its protestations and pieties, and notwithstanding its ardor for enhancing "diversity" on campus, the higher-education system has done essentially nothing to strengthen the schools that serve as its feeder institutions. It has not even taken the straightforward steps that are well within its purview—such as a complete overhaul of the education of teachers and principals. It has not reached down into the schools to begin the "admissions-counseling" process with disadvantaged fifth- and sixth-graders. And it most certainly has not made the tough decisions that over time could have a profound influence on the standards of the entire elementary-secondary system, such as announcing well in advance that beginning in, say, 1998 no student will be admitted to college who has not actually attained a specified level of knowledge and skills.

Such strong medicine is resisted with the argument that it must surely be bad for minority youngsters. That has been precisely the response to the NCAA's attempts to curb exploitation of minority athletes by requiring them to meet minimum academic standards in order to play intercollegiate sports or receive athletic scholarships. Georgetown's basketball coach staged a well-publicized one-man "strike" to protest this, claiming that the rules are discriminatory. The NCAA is expected to recant, heedless of the warning by the black tennis champion Arthur Ashe that "Black America stands to lose another generation of our young men unless they are helped to learn as well as play ball."

Getting more adequately prepared students inside the campus gates might also help to boost the egregiously low proportion of minority matriculants who end up with a degree. The college dropout rate is a problem for everyone, and has been rising over the past decade, but it is manifestly worse for black and Hispanic students. According to the U.S. Department of Education, among the 1980 high-school graduates who immediately enrolled full-time in college, 50 percent of the Asians and 56 percent of the white students earned their bachelor's degrees within five-and-a-half years, but this was true for only 31 percent of black students, and for 33 percent of Hispanics. (For minority *athletes*, the dropout rate is higher still. "It's no secret," Ashe writes, "that 75 percent of black football and basketball players fail to graduate from college.")

One has got to conclude that if the colleges and universities put as much effort into high-quality instruction, vigorous advising, extra tutoring, summer sessions, and other supplementary academic services as they do to combating naughty campus behavior and unkind words—and maximizing fieldhouse revenues—they could make a big dent in these numbers. But, of course, it is easier to adopt a behavior code for students than to alter faculty-time allocations and administration priorities.

Completing the degree, regrettably, does not end the matter, either. While possessing a college diploma will indisputably help a person get ahead in life even if he is still ignorant and intellectually inept, for a variety of public and private reasons it is desirable that college graduates also be well-educated. For minority graduates, it may be especially important that any plausible grounds for doubt be erased from the minds of prospective employers, among others—as to the actual intellectual standards that their degrees represent.

Today, unfortunately, one cannot equate the acquisition of a bachelor's degree with possession of substantial knowledge and skills. When the Department of Education examined literacy levels among young adults in 1985, it accumulated data that enable us to glimpse the cognitive attainments of college graduates, as well as those with less schooling. The good news is that the former had generally attained a higher level than the latter. The bad news is that degree-holders did none too well.

Three scales were used, representing "prose literacy," "document literacy," and "quantitative literacy." At the highest level of the scales, white college graduates were to be found in proportions of 47, 52, and 48 percent, respectively—not really very laudable considering that the intellectual challenges to be mastered at those levels entailed such tasks as discerning the main point of a newspaper column, coping with a bus schedule, and calculating the change due and tip owed on a simple lunch. Among black college graduates, however, these levels were reached by only 18, 11, and 14 percent, respectively. (The number of Hispanic college graduates in the sample was too small for statistical reliability.)

The higher-education system, in short, is awarding a great many diplomas to individuals whose intellectual attainments are meager, even at the end of college, and for minority graduates this is happening so often that the academy may be faulted for massive deception. It is giving people degrees which imply that they have accomplished something they have not in fact achieved. Like driving a new car home from the dealer only to discover that it is a lemon, the owners of such degrees are likely one day to think themselves cheated rather than aided by the hypocrisy and erratic quality control of the academic enterprise. The taxpayers who now underwrite most of that enterprise are apt to feel much the same. Over time this can only diminish the support, the respect, and the allure of higher education itself, as well as further depleting its tiny residuum of moral capital.

Some academic leaders understand this. A few also have the gumption to say it. "The alternatives I see ahead for our higher-education system are reform from without or reform from within," Stephen J. Trachtenberg, the new president of George Washington University, predicted in a recent address to the American Association of University Administrators. "The present situation cannot hold because too many Americans are coming to regard it as incompatible with ethics, values, and moral imperatives."

Reform from within would surely be preferable. It nearly always is. But in 1989 the most prominent forms of spontaneous change on many of our high-status college and university campuses are apt instead to exacerbate the gravest problems the academy faces. Creating more complex and onerous rituals as they worship at the altar of "diversity," they concurrently provide the putative beneficiaries of their efforts so feeble an education as to suggest a cynical theology indeed. Meanwhile, in the realms of intellectual inquiry and expression, they permit ever less diversity, turning the campus (in the memorable phrase of civil-rights scholar Abigail Thernstrom) into "an island of repression in a sea of freedom."

Notes

Chester E. Finn, Jr., who served as Assistant Secretary of Education from 1985 to 1988, is professor of education and public policy at Vanderbilt University and director of the Educational Excellence Network.

1. See "A New Racism on Campus?" by Thomas Short, *Commentary*, August 1988.
2. See "Revolution by Search Committee," *The New Criterion*, April 1989.

Race and Fear:
The Real Hot Buttons Behind
the Diversity Debate

INTERVIEW WITH WILLIAM H. GRAY, III

*In the United Negro College Fund's new Fairfax, Virginia, offices, former House Major-
ity Whip and current UNCF President William H. Gray, III, recently spent a morning
with* Educational Record's *editor-in-chief. During this graciously afforded interview,
Gray contemplated the major challenges facing diversity, both on campus and throughout the larger society, shared his perspectives on the current debate around these challenges and offered his thoughts on potential remedies. The following are excerpts from his
comments.*

On the Major Challenges to Diversity . . .

A major challenge is fear—fear that with change, there are those who are going to lose—lose jobs,
lose contracts, lose status, lose seats in higher education and graduate schools, lose scholarships.
Those who exploit that fear, for whatever purposes, present the greatest challenge to diversity.
Another challenge to diversity is the lack of resources to achieve it. There are groups of citizens—
especially in higher education—who are highly qualified to excel but who don't have the resources
to participate. Thus, the ability to diversify often is limited by financial constraints.

On the Role of Economics . . .

I think economics plays a part in fear, especially during times of uncertainty. Even though there's
been a pretty strong economy for the last year or so, it's clear from all data that most Americans still
feel pretty uncertain about their economic future. And that uncertainty is brought on by a rash of
monumental changes taking place—changes in the economy, changes in the world economic
structure, changes in geopolitical structures that have an impact on Americans.

But, really, the fundamental question that we are facing in diversity issues in this country goes
beyond economic uncertainty; it goes to the bedrock of who we are. Probably the most emotional,
gut-wrenching issue of American history is race.

America has gone though a variety of economic changes; we've survived depression, recession,
ups and downs. But race is the one issue that we have never fundamentally been able to deal with.
It's the most volatile and most painful issue in our history. We fought America's greatest war not in
Vietnam, not in Korea, not in Word War II or World War I, not even in the American Revolution. It
was the Civil War, and it was fought over the issue of race. Yes, there were economic, political and
cultural consequences, but they weren't the causes; they were the effects. The real cause of that great

war was race. And then we ended up having American apartheid for another 100 years anyway. Today, we're only 30 years away from that climate of legally sanctioned racism.

Here's the problem: Diversity brings into focus all of that painful, 300-year history and all of its implications. The reason it does is because the diversity issues of the late 20th century all involve race. One hundred years ago, diversity was not race-based, it was ethnic—it was immigrants from Europe, it was the Irish, the Italians, the Jews. But now we are facing a diversity that is characterized to a great extent by significant differences of both color and culture; it is Afro-centered, Hispanic, Asian, and Native American. So when we talk about diversity in the twentieth and twenty-first centuries, who are we talking about? We're talking about people of color. Racism and fear are the major issues in this diversity—even more than economic uncertainty.

On Where the Debate Is Taking Place . . .

It's very interesting to note where the debate about diversity is taking place. It is taking place primarily in the political arena. Here at the College Fund, we have a lot of contact with top corporate leaders; none of them is talking about getting rid of those instruments that produce diversity. In fact, they say that if their companies are to compete in the global village and in the global marketplace, diversity is an imperative. They also say that the need for talented, skilled Americans means we have to expand the pool of potential employees. And in looking at where birth rates are growing and at where the population is shifting, corporate America understands that expanding the pool means promoting policies that empower and provide skills to more minorities, more women, and more immigrants. Corporate leaders know that if that doesn't occur in our society, they will not have the engineers, the scientists, the lawyers, the business managers, or the accountants they will need.

Likewise, I don't hear people in the academy saying, "Lets go backward. Let's go back to the good old days, when we had a meritocracy" (which was never true—we never had a meritocracy, although we've come closer to it in the last 30 years). I recently visited a great little college in upstate New York—Geneseo, part of the State University of New York system—where the campus has doubled its minority population in the last six years. I talked with an African American who has been a professor there for a long, long time, and she remembers that when she first joined that community, there were fewer than a handful of minorities on campus. Now all of us feel the university is better because of the diversity. So where we hear this debate is primarily in the political arena and in the media—not in corporate board rooms or on college campuses.

On the Realities Underlying the Debate . . .

When I hear the debate, it reminds me of what I learned growing up in the South: that when people prey on fear, there is no substance.

According to the Glass Ceiling Commission's recently released study, in the 25 years since the late President Nixon mandated affirmative action, progress has been minimal in the private sector. In the top 1,000 corporations in America, women and minorities account for only 3 percent of the executive leadership. When you stretch it to the top 2,000 corporations, it jumps an amazing 2.5 percent, to 5.5 percent. So who's taking whose jobs?

Where the commission reported more progress was in middle management, and there, the progress was made primarily by white women, who account for 40 percent of the managers. In contrast, black males account for just 4 percent, and others, for less than that. So the fear and debate that center around the argument that someone is taking some other, more qualified person's job because of affirmative action just aren't statistically supported. And neither are the fears and arguments about college admissions. The number of blacks at white colleges in America averages only 6 percent nationwide. If you add Hispanic and Asian Americans and Native Americans to the mix, minority presence on white campuses jumps up into the mid-teens. The numbers show that no one is taking anyone else's place.

There are the arguments about preferences and standards. I recently met with the president of an Ivy League institution who told me that the university had done a review of its minority students' SAT scores and had found that the average minority student scored at the 50th percentile of the white students. This flies in the face of those who argue that affirmative action is lowering entrance standards: If those minority students didn't deserve to be at that Ivy League institution, then about 40 percent of the school's white students also didn't deserve to be there.

Thus, the statistics prove that whether in the private sector or in the academy, the competition has increased only slightly and that increase primarily has come *not* from racial minorities, but from women. The confusion over increased competition from minorities versus increased competition from women was made evident by a recent *USA Today* poll, which asked, "Are you in favor of affirmative action for racial minorities?" More than two-thirds of the respondents said "No." But when asked if they were in favor of affirmative action for women, two-thirds of the respondents said "Yes." Therefore, I believe the issue here tends to be one of perception: it's emotional, and it tends to focus on that hot button of American history: race.

On "Self-separation" on Campus . . .

The so-called self-separation issue is again one that applies only to racial minorities. No one ever says a word about ten Catholic kids having lunch together. No one ever questions why several Jewish student sit together at a table in the cafeteria. No one raises a fuss about Hillel House, Newman House, Presbyterian Synod House, or Methodist House. Why is it that if ten black kids want to room together in a dorm, it becomes "self-separation" or "separatism?" Why is it that if a bunch of black kids sit down together at a lunch table, it becomes such a threat that we have to give it a label and question why our black college students are separating themselves? The reason, once again, is race. We create special standards for black kids, and we label them in dehumanizing, patronizing ways. We don't do that to other ethnic groups.

When I was a student at Franklin & Marshall University there were 12 fraternities. There were five black students on the entire campus, and we could join only one fraternity—a Jewish fraternity that was willing to accept blacks. The rest of the fraternities were all white, but nobody made anything of that.

Now, all of a sudden, in the last few years, people have become terribly concerned and have begun to say how un-American it is for black students to want to room together or to want to sit together. At the University of Pennsylvania, there is a residence hall called the Du Bois House, named after W. E. B. Du Bois (who, by the way, graduated from the University of Pennsylvania but was not allowed to be a professor there). Du Bois House wasn't intended to be black, but black students, attracted by the name, started to bid for that dormitory. Before long, the dorm was 90 percent black, and people started saying, "This is segregation." The black students who lived in the dorm accounted for less than 10 percent of all the black students on campus; the other 90 percent were living in integrated dorms with white students.

My point is simply the focus on perception: Why are people so threatened by Du Bois House? I'm not threatened every time I see a group of whites sitting together with no blacks. Why do we expect kids—white or black—who grow up in a largely segregated America, live in largely segregated neighborhoods, go to largely segregated churches, and belong to largely segregated clubs to suddenly want to live with one another the second they arrive on campus? What is amazing is how *little* conflict we have when these youngsters, the vast majority of whom have lived segregated existences, come together at universities.

I find that at most institutions, integration *has* taken place. Are there some students who prefer the company of other African American students because they perceive the university as a hostile environment (and sometimes it is), because words like "nigger" are scrawled in the bathrooms and terrible things are written in the newspapers about them? Yes. But the fact of the matter is that they're very small in number. Why do we apply a double standard? Why don't we say anything about white kids who cling to ethnicity or religious heritage to define who they are on campus? We don't. So why do so for blacks?

On the Language Used to Define Diversity Issues . . .

I do have a problem with the language, a lot of which is cryptic jargon used by those pro and con. For example, we call the debate over affirmative action a "liberal" versus "conservative" debate. Richard Nixon was not, I think, a liberal. But he was the one who instituted specific goals and timetables back in 1970. That's where affirmative action originated.

The issue of "race-based scholarships" also seems to be about language, but really, it's about race. In America today, race-based scholarships, where race is the sole determining factor, account for less than 1 percent of all graduate and undergraduate scholarships, and about 5 percent of all scholarships exclusively at the undergraduate level. Scholarships that include race as a component account for less than 5 percent of all scholarships in America. Yet 9 percent of all scholarships in America are based on religion. There are scholarships for descendants of Confederate soldiers. I don't think too many blacks would be eligible. There are Daughters of Norway scholarships, I don't think too many Hispanic women would be able to apply. Why is it that we worry only about race-based scholarships?

And what is political correctness? What is political incorrectness? The words have no meaning for me. *People* define who they are. We once thought of America as a "melting pot." Later, we thought about America as a "pluralistic society." Now people talk about "multiculturalism." And those people who don't want to face up to the demographic changes in America are talking about going back to the "values of the past."

But the values of the past kept me out of Duke and Arkansas and 80 percent of America's other universities. So when I hear talk show hosts and politicians urging us to "get back to good old American values," I ask, "What values are you talking about?" Segregation and sexism are not good values. Do you want to go back to the values Elizabeth Dole talked about in her autobiography, when the first day she went to work at a law firm, a male turned to her and said, "You're taking up the space of a qualified man"? Are those the values we're talking about? I don't want those values. I don't want the old America under any circumstances.

The old America was not the best America. This is a better America, where we have more opportunity for more people, and where our institutions and our marketplaces are reflecting a little bit more—a very little bit more—of what America is really about. I heard one famous reporter who happened to have a severe physical disability talking about going back to an America that values merit, and I thought to myself, "Do you realize what you're saying? Twenty-five years ago, society would have barred you from becoming a syndicated columnist because of your disability. The reason you are a syndicated columnist is that we got rid of the false value that said, "If you are disabled, you can't possibly think, speak, or write." Yet here was a person leading the charge in the name of conservative politics and a conservative agenda that attacks diversity and calling multiculturalism a politically correct phenomenon that has killed American values and merits. What people really are fighting about is, at its core, a significant change in American society that involves the issue of race.

Why are we having this argument? The real issue ought not to be about language, but about our future: If America is going to be greater in the twenty-first century than it has been the twentieth century, all of us have to develop skills to be included in this society. It's as simple as that.

On What Higher Education Leaders Can Do . . .

I think they've got to help the people of the academy understand the needs for inclusiveness, and that being inclusive does not mean lowering standards. Instead, it means looking for qualified people who can contribute to the community and to society, and it means recognizing that *how* we judge those people is an ever-evolving process. Higher education leaders must constantly assess their financial assistance programs to make sure they are providing financial aid to those who most need it. And they've got to explain how those aid systems work. They've also got to explain to the student body and to the faculty the institution's mission and how it works—that even though the campus may be located in some isolated spot, it's going to reflect the population that makes up the nation. And that's essentially what they have to do.

In Summing Up . . .

The real question is: In 30 years, have we made so much progress that we no longer need special efforts to redress past and present discrimination based on race and gender? I would say, clearly and unequivocally, "No." And I think most Americans, when pushed, will admit that. The question then becomes: What are the appropriate remedies? You can't apply an economic class remedy to what is a race problem (even though it is reflected in class). That's like treating people who have cancer for pneumonia. Now, they may have pneumonia as a side effect of the cancer, but if you treat only the pneumonia, and not the cancer, they will not be cured.

And that's one of the confusions behind the current debate. Many people say, "Look, we've made enough progress in the past 30 years that really, the problems, the behaviors, and the dysfunctionality that we see are class oriented. They're class oriented, nor race-oriented, not gender-oriented." But they fail to reveal the cancer, and they fail to acknowledge that the remedy to cure the cancer is a medicine called affirmative action. And, further, they fail to tell people the truth about the medicine: that historically, statistically, and any other way you want to look at it, the medicine does *not* create reverse discrimination.

The real bottom line, though, is that we ought to be looking at this issue from the other side. Diversity should not be seen as a problem with which we have to deal. Diversity is really or greatest opportunity. It's how we make America stronger, not weaker. It only takes a quick look at the world—through the prism of reality—to see that.

In the next ten years, more than half of all new entrants into the American work force will be minorities. Another 35 percent will be women and new immigrants. If we don't educate *all* Americans to world class standards, we simply will not be able to compete in the global market. Corporate America has recognized this essential fact. As recently as May 1995, Proctor & Gamble Chairman and CEO Ed Artzt said in a major speech,

> Diversity is an integral part of the character of our company. It is very real to us. It gives us unity. It gives us strength. And it gives us talent—the richness of talent that we need to successfully sell our products to people of all cultures in every market of the world.

We all need to learn this lesson.

The Invisible Tapestry: Culture in American Colleges and Universities
Culture Defined and Described

GEORGE D. KUH AND ELIZABETH J. WHITT

If there were any word to serve the purpose as well, I would unhesitatingly use it in preference to one that seems at times downright slippery and at other times impossibly vague and all-embracing. But although "culture" has uncomfortably many denotations, it is the only term that seems satisfactorily to combine the notions . . . of a shared way of thinking and a collective way of behaving (Becher 1984, p. 166).

Certain ideas burst upon the intellectual landscape with such a force that they seem to have the potential to resolve all fundamental problems and clarify all obscure issues facing a field (Langer, cited in Geertz 1973). Cultural perspectives have been widely used in a general, all-encompassing manner to subsume almost every concept, event, or activity that might occur in an organized setting (Deal and Kennedy 1982; Schwartz and Davis 1981). Some (see, for example, Morgan 1986) have suggested that culture is a metaphor for organizations. Because culture lacks conceptual clarity, however, its utility as a metaphor for colleges and universities seems limited, perhaps even confusing. Indeed, unless more precision is achieved, cultural perspectives may obscure more than they reveal. That is, if cultural elements are not more clearly explicated, the insights into college and university life promised by cultural views will be blurred, thus reducing their power and utility (Trice and Beyer 1984).

Risks are inherent, however, in attempting to flesh out or specify the elements of culture. For example, thinking about cultural properties as distinct institutional attributes (e.g., beliefs, stories, norms, and so on) that can be separated and independently analyzed is compatible with conventional assumptions undergirding organizational rationality. The perception that culture can be intentionally controlled does violence to some important properties of culture, such as its complex, holistic character (Geertz 1973), an entity greater than the sum of its parts (Morgan 1986). Nevertheless, when talking about and studying culture, we do separate properties, such as language, from rituals, stories, belief systems, and values. In doing so, however, we must acknowledge the contradiction inherent between analysis and holistic perception and the distortion that results whenever a single element is isolated in the complex web of history, traditions, and patterns of behaviors that have developed in a college or university (Taylor 1984).

Toward a Definition of Culture

> [We] have been entrusted with the difficult task of speaking about culture. But there is nothing in the world more elusive. One cannot analyze it, for its components are infinite. One cannot describe it, for it is Protean in shape. An attempt to encompass its meaning in words is like trying to seize the air in the hand when one finds that it is everywhere except within one's grasp (Lowell, cited in Kroeber and Kluckhohn 1952, p. 7).

Asked to define the institution's culture, an MIT student, "without batting an eye, . . . responded by saying: 'It's everything we aren't tested on in the classroom'" (Van Maanen 1987, p. 5). Although most social scientists would not be satisfied with this level of precision, her response is consistent with the myriad meanings and connotations of culture reported in the literature. Indeed, culture cannot be succinctly defined because it is an inferential concept (Cusick 1987), "something that is perceived, something felt" (Handy 1976, p. 185).

Culture is described as a social or normative glue (Smircich 1983)—based on shared values and beliefs (see Pascale and Athos 1981)—that holds organizations together and serves four general purposes: (1) it conveys a sense of identity; (2) it facilitates commitment to an entity, such as the college or peer group, other than self; (3) it enhances the stability of a group's social system; and (4) it is a sense-making device that guides and shapes behavior. In addition, the culture of a college or university defines, identifies, and legitimates authority in educational settings (Gage 1978; Goodlad 1984). Therefore, studies of institutional culture have implications for policy and strategies for institutional change (Elmore 1987).

Most definitions of culture convey one or more of the following properties (Schein 1985): (1) observed behavioral regularities (Goffman 1959, 1961; Van Maanen 1979), such as the hours faculty spend in the office; (2) norms (Homans 1950) or specific guides to conduct, some of which (e.g., mores) are more salient than others (Broom and Selznick 1973); (3) dominant values espoused by the organization (Deal and Kennedy 1982), such as the importance of inquiry in research universities and the commitment to undergraduate teaching in liberal arts colleges; (4) the philosophy that guides an organization's attitudes and actions toward employees or clients (Ouchi 1981; Pascale and Athos 1981); (5) rules for getting along in the organization (Schein 1968; Van Maanen 1979); and (6) the feeling or organizational climate and the manner in which members of the culture interact with those outside the culture (Tagiuri and Litwin 1968).

Behavioral regularities should not be overemphasized as a manifestation of culture (Schein 1985). Who talks with whom may be more a function of environmental contingencies, such as physical proximity, rather than a behavioral manifestation of deeper assumptions and beliefs at the "core" of culture. For example, inferring cultural groupings based on the location of faculty offices may or may not be appropriate. Faculty with adjoining offices could share cultural bonds—or the arrangement might merely reflect a confluence of factors, such as random space assignment following renovation of the physical plant or historical accident.

The "small homogenous society" analogue used in anthropological studies of culture (discussed later) is sorely strained when applied to many contemporary institutions of higher education. Large public, multipurpose universities are comprised of many different groups whose members may or may not share or abide by all of the institution's norms, values, practices, beliefs, and meanings. Instead of viewing colleges and universities as monolithic entities (Martin and Siehl 1983), it is more realistic to analyze them as multicultural contexts (March and Simon 1958; Van Maanen and Barley 1984) that are host to numerous subgroups with different priorities, traditions, and values (Gregory 1983).

Culture is potentially divisive. If routine patterns of behavior within one group are considered normal, different activities performed by another subgroup may be judged abnormal (Morgan 1986, p. 120). Such ethnocentric behavior may be a form of cultural nearsightedness (Broom and Selznick 1973) or socialized differences that increase the possibility that misunderstandings and conflicts will occur (Gregory 1983).

Faculty in the humanities are socialized into "a structure of values, attitudes, and ways of thinking and feeling" (Clark and Corcoran 1986, p. 30) quite different from the structure to which physicists and chemists are socialized. Career path patterns of faculty in "pure" disciplines (e.g., biology, history) and "applied" fields (e.g., engineering, education) are different. Faculty in the former group learn how to behave by working side by side with senior professors in the laboratory as postdoctoral research associates. Faculty in the latter group are more likely to learn about the academic profession "on the job" during the first years of a professorial appointment after postdoctoral experience as a practicing professional in private industry, government, medicine, law, or education (Becher 1984). These and other differences (epistemological and ideological views, for example) encourage the formation of separate academic clans or subcultures, a topic examined in more depth later.

So how, then, does one define culture? Three and one-half decades ago, Kroeber and Knuckhohn (1952) reported 164 different definitions of culture. Given the myriad qualities contained in the concept of culture, it is not surprising that a common definition remains elusive (Smircich 1983), but it has been defined, for example, as:

> The core set of assumptions, understandings, and implicit rules that govern day-to-day behavior in the workplace (Deal and Kennedy 1983, p. 498);

> The shared philosophies, ideologies, values, assumptions, beliefs, expectations, attitudes, and norms that knit a community together (Kilman et al. 1985, p. 5);

> The traditional and social heritage of a people; their customs and practices; their transmitted knowledge, beliefs, law, and morals; their linguistic and symbolic forms of communication, and the meanings they share (Becher 1984, p. 167);

> An interpretive paradigm . . . both a product and process, the shaper of human interaction and the outcome of it, continually created and recreated by people's ongoing interactions (Jelinek, Smircich, and Hirsch 1983, p. 331).

Based on a review of the literature, another definition of culture is "the shared values, assumptions, beliefs, or ideologies that participants have about their organization (colleges and universities)" (Peterson et al. 1986, p. 81). While this definition is parsimonious, it does not explicitly acknowledge the influence culture has on the behavior of faculty and students, the holistic, evolutionary qualities of culture, and the influence of the external environment on institutional culture.

For the purposes of this report, then, culture in higher education is defined as *the collective, mutually shaping patterns of norms, values, practices, beliefs, and assumptions that guide the behavior of individuals and groups in an institute of higher education and provide a frame of reference within which to interpret the meaning of events and actions on and off campus.* This definition emphasizes normative influences on behavior as well as the underlying system of assumptions and beliefs shared by culture bearers.

Properties of Culture

This section describes many of the subtle aspects of experience subsumed under the concept of culture as a complex whole, paying particular attention to artifactual manifestations of culture as they can be observed and providing clues to hidden properties (e.g., values and assumptions).

Culture and meaning are inextricably intertwined (Hall 1976).

> The more we have learned about colleges, the more we have been struck by their uniqueness. True, colleges run to "types," and types ultimately converge on a national academic model. One might therefore lump together the Universities of Massachusetts and Connecticut, or Harvard and Yale, or Boston College and Fordham, or San Francisco State and San Diego. But on closer inspection these colleges appear to draw on quite different publics and to have quite different flavors (Riesman and Jencks 1962, p. 132).

Because culture is bound to a context, every institution's culture is different. Therefore, the meaning of behavior can be interpreted only through a real-life situation within a specific college's cultural milieu (Hall 1976). To attempt to divorce an interpretation of behavior "from what happens—at this time or in that place, what specific people say, what they do, what is done to them, from the whole vast business of the world—is to divorce it from its applications and render it vacant" (Geertz 1973, p. 18). Thus, descriptions and interpretations of events and actions from one institution are not generalizable to other institutions. "The essential task [is] not to generalize across cases but to generalize within them" (Geertz 1973, p. 20).

The manner in which culture is transmitted and through which individuals derive meaning from their experiences within the cultural milieu are essentially tacit (Geertz 1973; Hall 1976; Schein 1985). In this sense, culture is an "unconscious infrastructure" (Smircich 1983), a paradigm for understanding nuances of behavior shaped by shared understandings, assumptions, and beliefs. The cultural paradigm serves as an organizing framework within which to determine rewards and punishments, what is valued and what is not, and moral imperatives (see, for example, Gardner 1986; Schein 1985) that bond individuals and groups and order behavior. Culture provides contextual clues (Hall 1976) necessary to interpret behaviors, words, and acts and gives these actions and events meaning within the culture bearers' frame of reference (Corbett, Firestone, and Rossman 1987). Culture also enhances stability in a college or university through the socialization of new members (Van Maanen and Barley 1984). Because culture exists largely below the level of conscious thought and because culture bearers may themselves disagree on the meaning of artifacts and other properties of culture, describing the culture of a college or university in a way that all faculty and students find satisfactory may not be possible (Allaire and Firsirotu 1984).

> [Culture is] a process of reality construction that allows people to see and understand particular events, actions, objects, utterances, or situations in distinctive ways. These patterns of understanding also provide a basis for making one's own behavior sensible and meaningful . . . [Culture is] an active living phenomenon through which people create and recreate the worlds in which they live (Morgan 1986, pp. 128, 131).

Thus, although culture is fairly stable, it is always evolving, continually created and recreated by ongoing patterns of interactions between individuals, groups, and an institution's internal and external environments. Although these patterns of interaction may change over time to reflect changing assumptions, values, and preferences, they are stable enough to define and shape what is acknowledged to be appropriate behavior in a particular setting. Thus, the dominant constellation of assumptions, values, and preferences introduces and socializes new members into the accepted patterns of behavior, thereby perpetuating—for all practical purposes—many of the dominant assumptions and beliefs of the culture. In this sense, culture provides stability for a college during turbulent periods and also contributes to the general effectiveness of the institution (Smircich 1983) by reminding students and faculty of what the institution values and by punishing undesirable behavior.

The press toward behaving in culturally acceptable ways, which is invariably an outcome of a strong culture (Deal and Kennedy 1982; Gregory 1983), may constrain innovation or attempts to do things differently. A dominant culture presents difficulties to newcomers or members of underrepresented groups when trying to understand and appreciate the nuances of behavior. At worst, culture can be an alienating, ethnocentric force that goads members of a group, sometimes out of fear and sometimes out of ignorance, to reinforce their own beliefs while rejecting those of other groups (Gregory 1983).

The relative strength of a culture or subculture is impossible to determine (Van Maanen and Barley 1984). While this question begs for an empirical answer, the weight of the argument seems to be on the side of those who claim that cultures do vary in the degree to which they influence members' behavior and guide institutional responses in times of crisis (Deal and Kennedy 1982; Peters and Waterman 1982).

Some writers have developed typologies or inventories of organizational characteristics based on their observations of what seem to be "healthy" cultures (see, for example, Peters and Waterman

1982; Peterson et al. 1986). Given the context-bound, perspectival qualities of culture, however, attempts to determine whether one institutional culture is better than another seem wrongheaded. Some institutional cultures clearly support research activity over undergraduate instruction and vice versa (Riesman and Jancks 1962). University trustees, state legislators, and students will continue to be wary of prevailing norms that encourage faculty to cloister themselves in library carrels or in the research laboratory rather than increase the number of office hours to meet with students. Standards for academic productivity, such as papers published or number of courses and students taught, are different in a church-related liberal arts college, a state-supported university whose mission is teacher education, and a research-oriented university (Austin and Gamson 1983; Baldridge et al. 1977).

Any culture has two basic components; (1) "substance, or the networks of meanings contained in its ideologies, norms, and values; and (2) forms, or the practices whereby these meanings are expressed, affirmed, and communicated to members" (Trice and Beyer 1984, p. 654). In this sense, culture is both a product and a process.

Culture has been discussed as both an independent and a dependent variable (Ouchi and Wilkins 1985; Peterson et al. 1986). Culture, when viewed as an independent variable, is a complex, continually evolving web of assumptions, beliefs, symbols, and interactions carried by faculty, students, and other culture bearers (Smircich 1983) that cannot be directly purposefully controlled by any person or group. Culture as a dependent variable is the constellation of shared values and beliefs manifested through patterns of behavior like rituals, ideologies, and patterns of interactions. An administrator may attempt to change seemingly dysfunctional aspects of a culture by encouraging different behaviors on the part of faculty and students, and suggestions have been offered about how one might attempt to manipulate organizational culture (Kilmann et al. 1985; Ouchi 1981; Peters and Waterman 1982). The culture of a college or university—as substance and form, as process and product, and as independent and dependent variables—shapes human interactions and reflects the outcomes of mutually shaping interactions (Louis 1980; Siehl and Martin 1982; Smircich 1983).

Levels of Culture

Some find the essence of culture to be the tacit assumptions and beliefs that influence the way a group of people think and behave (Schein 1985). These guiding assumptions and beliefs, which are below the surface of conscious thought, are manifested in observable forms or artifacts. In an effort to increase analytical precision and avoid unnecessary confusion, Schein (1985) divided culture into a conceptual hierarchy comprised of three levels: artifacts, values, and basic assumptions and beliefs.

Artifacts

"Meanings are 'stored' in symbols" (Geertz 1973, p. 127). Because artifacts are largely symbols of culture, they represent a multitude of meanings and emotions. Evidence of an institution's culture may be found in norms, mores, formal and informal rules, routine procedures, behaviors that are rewarded or punished, customs, folkways, myths, daily and periodic rituals, ceremonies, interaction patterns, signs, and a language system common to the culture bearers (Broom and Selznick 1973; Morgan 1986; Schein 1985; Tierney 1985, 1987; Van Maanen and Barley 1984). A rite combines discrete cultural forms into an integrated, unified public performance. A ceremonial is the linking of several rites into a single occasion or event (Chapple and Coon 1942). For example, most commencement ceremonies are made up of discrete rites: the formation of candidates for degrees into one or more lines, the procession of faculty and students, the commencement address, the conferral of honorary degrees, the conferral of various degrees (baccalaureate, master's, professional school, Ph.D.), the hooding of doctoral degree recipients, the alumni association's welcome to those receiving degrees, the tossing of mortarboards into the air at the conclusion of the formal event, and the recession from the site of commencement.

Table 1 defines other frequently mentioned cultural forms (see also Boje, Fedor, and Rowland 1982). To underscore the connectedness and cumulative contributions of what appear to be discrete artifacts to the "whole" of culture, ritual, language, stories, and myths are discussed in some detail.

Rituals communicate meaning within a college community by calling attention to and transmitting important values, welcoming and initiating new members (Gardner 1986), and celebrating members' accomplishments. Essentially a social construction, rituals—such as convocations, graduations, presidential inaugurations, activities of secret societies, and dedications (Bushnell 1962)—help to create, maintain, and invent "patterns of collective action and social structure" (Burns 1978, p. 265; see also Turner and Turner 1985). "Above all, rituals are dramas of persuasion. They are didactic, enacted pronouncements concerning the meaning of an occasion and the nature and worth of the people involved in the occasion" (Myerhoff 1977, p. 22). Thus, rituals make statements about the quality of life within the community and set standards against which people are asked to compare and modify behavior, values, activities, and relationships (Manning 1987).

Table 1
Definitions of Frequently Studied Cultural Forms

Rite	Relatively elaborate, dramatic, planned sets of activities that consolidate various forms of cultural expressions into one event (e.g., dissertation defense meeting); carried out through social interactions, usually for the benefit of an audience.
Ceremonial	A system of several rites connected with a single occasion or event (e.g., commencement, orientation).
Ritual	A standardized, detailed set of techniques and behaviors that manage anxieties but seldom produce intended technical consequences of practical importance (e.g., freshman induction convocation, required chapel).
Myth	A dramatic narrative of imagined events, usually used to explain origins or transformations of something; also, an unquestioned belief about the practical benefits of certain techniques and behaviors that is not supported by demonstrated facts.
Saga	A historical narrative describing the unique accomplishments of a group and its leaders, usually in heroic terms (see Clark 1972).
Legend	A handed-down narrative of some wonderful event that is based in history but has been embellished with fictional details.
Story	A narrative based on true events, often a combination of truth and fiction.
Folktale	A completely fictional narrative.
Symbol	Any object, act, event, quality, or relation that serves as a vehicle for conveying meaning, usually by representing another thing (e.g., school mascot, campus statues, or other objects, such as the axe that symbolizes rivalry between the University of California at Berkeley and Stanford—Basu 1984).
Language	A particular form or manner in which members of a group use vocal sounds and written signs to convey meanings to each other (e.g., an institution's fight song or Alma Mater).
Gesture	Movements of parts of the body used to express meanings.
Physical setting	Those things that surround people physically and provide them with immediate sensory stimuli as they carry out culturally expressive activities.
Artifact	Material objects manufactured by people to facilitate culturally expressive activities.

Source: Adapted from Trice (1984) and Trice and Beyer (1984).

Rituals are staged, public, and stylized versions of how things should be and beliefs about how things are that eloquently describe and shape cultural patterns (Goody 1977). Although the possibilities for expression are endless, similar patterns are repeated over time and become part of, as well as reflect, a group's history. These patterns teach cooperation, the importance of tradition, social relations and solidarity, tasks and goals of the group, and the place of authority (Burns and Laughlin 1979; Moore and Myerhoff 1977).

Rituals have certain properties:

1. A collective dimension in which the social meaning inherent in the community is expressed

2. Repetition in content, form, and occasion

3. Self-conscious or deliberate action by the participants as part of the special behavior or stylized performance

4. Orderly action achieved through exaggerated precision and

5. Evocative style of presentation and staging to engage and focus the attention of the audience (Manning 1987; Myerhoff 1977).

Rituals depend on a system of *language* to communicate important ideas and feelings (Gordon 1969). Language is more than an inventory of words and expressions to describe objects and behaviors; it is a guide to social reality that typifies, stabilizes, and integrates experience into a meaningful whole (Pettigrew 1979). All cultures have a language that links "the collective, cultural, and cognitive domains" of everyday living (Forgas 1985, p. 252). Language systems are based on symbols and metaphors and serve as analogues of life that convey thoughts, perceptions, and feelings associated with experiences in a particular social context (Bredeson 1987; Langer 1953). "Language is not (as commonly thought) a system for transferring thoughts or meaning . . . but a system for organizing information and releasing thoughts and responses in other organisms" (Hall 1976, p. 49). Thus, symbols and metaphors do not so much reflect reality as translate it in a form that can be shared and understood by others (Morgan, Frost, and Pondy 1983). Because colleges and universities are rich in symbolism and ceremony, an awareness of the systems of symbols that mediate meaning between individuals and their cultures is important to understanding events and actions (Kuh, Whitt, and Shedd 1987; Masland 1985).

Symbols, such as organizational signs, communicate the value placed on time, space, and communication, different modes by which institutional agents express their feelings about others, and the activities of a college.

> Signs exist as fluid examples of how people define and give meaning to organizational culture. Thus, signs change over time and acquire and lose power due to the constantly shifting nature of the organization and its participants (Tierney 1987, pp. 20–21).

The significance of analyzing how leaders spend their time, where they spend it, and how they communicate (writing, speaking from written notes) leads to different understandings about how people within a college may influence organizational leadership and decision making. For example, how faculty members or administrators spend time can be effective at one university and inefficient elsewhere because of the cultural meaning given to time in their institutional context (Tierney 1985). Organizational time has three different dimensions: formal/informal, historical, and seasonal/ceremonial (Tierney 1985). The formal and informal use of time refers to how individuals structure their own time, such as appointments and meetings, versus dropping in for a visit (Deal and Kennedy 1982; Peters and Waterman 1982).

Historical time refers to the manner in which individuals and organizations use the experience of the past in responding to current challenges (Gadamer 1979), while seasonal or ceremonial time refers to the institutional events with which people attempt to synchronize their own activities. Seasonal festivals, the beginning and ending of academic years, the informal coffee hour, the preregistration period, the change in athletic seasons, the movement from outdoors to indoors in the winter and vice versa in the spring all impart organizational meaning and have an influence on how faculty and students perceive and act in a college or university. Problems can arise when administrators rely on a functional interpretation of time that violates the institution's conception of ceremonial time.

> At one institution, . . . Honors Day and Founders Day traditionally were in the fall. A new president and a new academic vice president decided to delay the ceremonies until springtime. They had proposed a massive overhaul of the academic and fiscal sides of the institution, and they did not believe they had time to spend on Honors Day or Founders Day. . . .
>
> The community decried the move. One observer noted, "It's kind of chintzy if you ask me. It used to be really special and everything." Another person said, "Those days stand for what we're about. Everybody got involved, and in one fell swoop they just decided to get rid of them, tell us that we've got to stick to our desks" (Tierney 1985, p. 17).

How time is used influences sense making. What is appropriate use of time in one institutional culture may be inappropriate at another (Tierney 1985).

Stories are narratives—complete with plots, protagonists, antagonists, and action—that shape other aspects of the institutional culture, such as behavioral norms. Stories serve at least five functions: (1) providing information about rules in the institution or subculture: (2) reflecting the beliefs that faculty, students, and alumni have about how past events occurred, thereby keeping the institutional memory sharp (Wilkins 1983); (3) increasing commitment and loyalty to the institution; (4) undergirding and reinforcing other artifacts of culture; and (5) connecting current faculty and students with the institution's past and present (Brown, cited in Kelly 1985). Although stories provide distinctive information about a college, certain characteristics of stories are similar at many institutions (Martin et al. 1983). For example, written histories of colleges often describe the founders of the institution as heroes and depict, in sagalike language, the trials and travails endured in establishing the college (Clark 1970, 1972).

As stories are passed from one student generation to another (Trippet 1982), the stories sometimes take on legendary proportions and become tightly woven into the fabric of the institutional culture. Stories are told at Wabash College in Indiana about the founders of the college kneeling in the snow watching the burning of South Hall, the marching off to war of the "entire" student body in the 1860s, and the bloody class fights on Washington's birthday. Such stories, perpetuated by faculty members and administrators alike, sometimes have more influence on decisions and institutional commitments than policies or data from management information systems (Martin and Powers 1983).

Myths are substantially fictional narratives of events, usually expressed in symbolic terms and often endowed with an almost sacred quality (Allaire and Firsirotu 1984; Cohen 1969). Myths develop over time "to mediate and otherwise 'manage' basic organizational dilemmas," such as ambiguity and uncertainty (Boje, Fedor, and Rowland 1982, p. 27). Myths perform five functions: (1) legitimizing and rationalizing intended or completed actions and consequences; (2) mediating between political interests and competing values; (3) explaining or creating causal relationships; (4) dealing with turbulence in the external environment through rationalization; and (5) enriching the life of the institution or group (Boje, Fedor, and Rowland 1982). An innovative campus, the University of California—Santa Cruz attracted students with liberal social attitudes and developed the reputation for being "flaky" and "touchy-feely." A mythical tale about the origins of the school circulated among students during the 1960s:

> Like other conspiracy theories of the sixties, the myth was laced with paranoia and hysteria. The central administration of the University of California, the story went, had planned the Santa Cruz campus as a home for radical students. Like some enormous Venus's fly trap, innovation would attract the unorthodox. But the rural setting, decentralized structure, and close student-faculty contact envisioned for Santa Cruz would effectively disarm radical criticism of the university, turning potentially angry humanists into compliant and hard-working students (Adams 1984, pp. 21–22).

As with many myths, a kernel of truth was imbedded in this example. In the 1950s, predating student activism by about a decade, Clark Kerr, then president of the University of California system, and Dean McHenry, Kerr's assistant for academic planning (who later became chancellor of the Santa Cruz campus), envisioned the need for a campus that would be committed to innovative undergraduate education (Grant and Riesman 1978). Kerr and McHenry had no interest in isolating radicals; they were, however, committed to minimizing the bureaucracy of the research-oriented university in an effort to personalize the experience at Santa Cruz (Adams 1984).

Sometimes additional insights into culture can be gleaned from an analysis of organizational structure (Clark and Trow 1966) and substantive products like policy statements and standard operating procedures. Structure, as represented by an organizational chart, provides a point of reference for the way people think about and make sense of the contexts in which they work (Deal and Kennedy 1982). Written statements of institutional philosophy, mission, and purpose may communicate important messages to faculty, students, and others about what is valued in the institution. Artifacts also may take the form of technologies, such as ways of organizing work, how decisions are made, and course reservation and registration procedures for students (Kuh, Whitt, and Shedd 1987).

Identifying artifacts is relatively easy. It is much more difficult to determine how the nested patterns of assumptions and beliefs represented by artifacts influence the behavior of individuals and groups across time (Schein 1985). Slogans, symbols, language patterns, stories, myths, ceremonials, and rituals provide clues to a deeper, pervasive system of meaning. To understand the culture of a college or university is "to understand how this system, in its mundane as well as its more dramatic aspects, is created and sustained" (Morgan 1986, p. 133). Such understanding can be acquired by linking or contrasting artifacts with the values used in decision making (Schein 1985).

Values

The second level of culture (Schein 1985) is made up of values—widely held beliefs or sentiments about the importance of certain goals, activities, relationships, and feelings. Four values influence the academic enterprise: justice, competence, liberty, and loyalty (Clark 1984). Some institutional values are conscious and explicitly articulated; they serve a normative or moral function by guiding member's responses to situations. Most institutional values, however, are unconsciously expressed as themes (e.g., academic freedom, tradition of collegial governance) or are symbolic interpretations of reality that give meaning to social actions and establish standards for social behavior (Clark and Trow 1966). They often take the form of context-bound values that are related directly to a college's vitality and well-being (Clark 1970; Riesman and Jencks 1962; Sanford 1967).

In *The Small Room* (Sarton 1961), the faculty of a selective Eastern liberal arts college face a dilemma: The institution's literary journal published a promising student's paper that contained plagiarized material. The appropriate institutional response is problematic because the faculty feel they may have placed an undue amount of pressure on the student to perform brilliantly. The discussion among several faculty directly involved in the matter reveals the tension between the values of academic integrity, honesty, intellectual achievement, and the student's social-emotional well-being:

> "Well," Lucy swallowed and paused, then began in a rather stiff cold voice, "I think I am clear that Jane was put under more stress than she could stand. It looks to me as if she broke down not after the affair exploded, but that the real breakdown was clear in the act itself of stealing the Weil essay, and that she did it as a way out of unbearable pressure." . . .
>
> "You suggest that Professor Cope asked too much out of Jane?" . . .
>
> "Do you feel that there is an overemphasis on intellectual achievement in the college as a whole? Is that the essence?"

"... If Lucy is right ... then a serious attack is being made on the values of this college. We are going to have to do some hard thinking." ...

"... With your permission, I am going to call the faculty [together] and present Jane's case in light of all we have been saying. I shall try to move away from the passions all this has aroused to the big questions that confront us. ... " (pp. 179–81).

Cultural values are likely to be tightly linked to, or at least congruent with, basic beliefs and assumptions (the deepest level of culture, to be discussed next) and are embodied in the institution's philosophy or ideology, a "relatively coherent set of beliefs that bind some people together and that explain their worlds [to them] in terms of cause-and-effect relations" (Beyer 1981, p. 166). In this sense, values provide the basis for a system of beliefs (Allaire and Firsirotu 1984).

An illustration of using institutional values to work through dilemmas is provided in a description of Ryke College (a pseudonym), an urban, midwestern Protestant liberal arts college (1,635 full-time equivalent students) founded in 1874 that—like many institutions in the 1970s—was confronted with financial troubles precipitated by declining enrollments (Chaffee 1983). Three major traditions characterized Ryke's history: (1) a mutually supportive relationship with and commitment to its urban setting, (2) an openness to international perspectives, and (3) involvement in social causes. Although Ryke's faculty were receptive to new curricular ideas, any changes were cautiously integrated into the existing classical liberal arts curriculum. The strategy Ryke College followed was to hold fast to the image of "a small, fine liberal arts college" (Chaffee 1983, p. 182).

Ryke's values served as a bridge between artifacts and basic assumptions and beliefs. Ryke's new president attempted to make the college visible again within the urban community. The faculty renewed their commitment to a core liberal arts curriculum consistent with the institution's original mission. The college also made certain its mission statement and recruitment and socialization practices for faculty and students were consistent with the guiding values of the institution. Apparently, the key to the survival of this institution was "being true to its historical liberal arts mission ..." (Chaffee 1983, p. 183).

Values sometimes surface as exhortations about what is right or wrong, what is encouraged or discouraged—what "ought" to be. For example, statements by the chief academic officer about the importance of teaching or by the chief student life officer about the debilitating consequences of the inappropriate use of alcohol can, under certain circumstances (e.g., when the statements are repeated often and are accompanied by behavior suggesting the authenticity of the statements), communicate the institution's values. Of course, some values are merely espoused (Argyris and Schon 1978) and predict what people will say in certain situations but may not represent what they do. Espoused values are more like aspirations or rationalizations (Schein 1985). Examples of espoused values abound in many colleges and universities: commitment to increasing minority representation in the student body and faculty, assertions about the importance of undergraduate instruction in research universities, and mission statements underscoring an institution's commitment to students' holistic development.

Basic Assumptions and Beliefs

The third level, believed to be the core of culture, consists of basic but often unstated assumptions that undergird artifacts and values (Schein 1985). These assumptions and beliefs are learned responses to threats to institutional survival and exert a powerful influence over what people think about, what they perceive to be important, how they feel about things, and what they do (Schein 1985). Indeed, assumptions and beliefs determine the way reality is perceived and (albeit unconsciously) guide behavior. These conceptions are so deeply ingrained that they are by definition taken for granted, "not confrontable or debatable" (Schein 1985, p. 18); thus, such assumptions are difficult to identify.

The difficulty in identifying assumptions and beliefs is acknowledged in the advocacy of the use of a culture audit to systematically review aspects of an organization that reflect culture (Wilkins 1983). Tacit assumptions and beliefs are not possible to articulate. Assumptions may be implied, however, through concrete examples. ("I can't explain it in so many words, but I can give you a lot of examples"—Wilkins 1983, p. 27). Thus, to discover distinctive patterns of beliefs and assumptions, one must sift through numerous, diverse artifacts and talk with students and faculty at great length.

The existence of subcultures also adds to the challenge of mapping core assumptions. Clashes of subcultures may point to conflicting core assumptions (Wilkins 1983), such as students' expectation that the institution should prepare them for a vocation, while faculty assume the institution should provide adequate resources for them to pursue scholarly interests. Faculty expect that collegial governance structures can and should be used to guide the direction of the institution, while administrators, under pressure to make decisions and allocate resources, behave in what may appear to faculty to be a unilateral, rigidly bureaucratic manner.

Summary

Culture is a complex set of context-bound, continually evolving properties that potentially includes anything influencing events and actions in a college or university (Tierney 1988). As a result, precise definitions of culture remain elusive. Rituals, stories, language, and other artifacts are observable manifestations of culture that reflect deeper values and help faculty, students, staff, alumni, and others understand what is appropriate and important under certain situations. The core of culture is comprised of assumptions and beliefs shared—to some degree—by members of the institution that guide decision making and shape major events and activities.

The Importance of Institutional Mission

James W. Lyons

Emerson cautions us that "the one thing not to be forgiven to intellectual persons is, not to know their own tasks" (as quoted in Barzun, 1968, p. 207). As student affairs administrators, we must know our tasks, which flow from many sources, including both our students and our institutions. Other chapters in this volume will concentrate on student characteristics, needs, and differences; administrative processes and procedures; and the knowledge and skills essential to the creation of strong student affairs programs. This chapter, however, focuses on one essential element that shapes our work as student affairs professionals: the institutional mission.

There is great diversity in American higher education. "Together, over 3,000 colleges and universities serve about 13 million students" (National Association of Student Personnel Administrators [1987] 1989, p. 9). Beyond these numbers, however, the astute observer will see a rich landscape filled with differences between institutions of higher education. Each college or university is unique, and that uniqueness derives from a distinctive mission. For student affairs programs to be successful, a clear understanding of that mission is a necessary first step.

This chapter will first briefly discuss the history of American higher education from its beginnings in the colonial colleges to the present day. Second, attention will be given to the traditional missions and purposes of higher education, Third, illustrations will be provided of how several factors influence the character and mission of particular institutions and student affairs practice.

A Brief Historical Overview

Knock describes three philosophic orientations to higher education that have influenced its growth and development in the United States; education for the aristocracy, educational opportunities earned through merit, and an open, egalitarian system (1985). "Oxford and Cambridge furnished the original model which the colonial colleges sought to copy" (Brubacher and Rudy, 1976, p. 3). It became evident, however, that transplanting the traditional English model of higher education to the New World would require modification and adjustments. Among the changes were the establishment of collegiate boards of control that were either interdenominational in makeup or in "one case completely secular" (Brubacher and Rudy, 1976, p. 4). In addition, the colonial colleges were influenced by Scottish models and by continental universities and were modified to meet the needs of an expanding colonial population.

The goals of the early colonial colleges were well defined.

> The Christian tradition was the foundation stone of the whole intellectual structure which was brought to the New World. It is equally important, however, to keep in mind that the early colleges were not set up solely to train ministers; their charters make it amply clear that from the very beginning it was intended that they also educate professional men in fields other than the ministry and public officials of various kinds. The civil society would thus get educated orthodox laymen as its leaders; the church would get educated orthodox clergymen as its ministers. This

was the ideal that the colonial higher education hoped to attain [Brubacher and Rudy, 1976, p. 6].

Of course, times and purposes changed. In the period intervening between the establishment of the early colonial colleges to the present, a number of forces shaped higher education in the United States. The growing heterogeneity of the colonial population forced some institutions, supported by colonial legislatures, to modify their curricula beyond narrow sectarian ideas. "The nineteenth century witnessed a gradual decline in governmental involvement with sectarian schools. As states began to establish their own institutions, the public-private dichotomy emerged" in American higher education (Kaplin, 1985, pp. 16–17). "The first truly public institution of higher education was founded by Jefferson and became the University of Virginia" (Knock, 1985, p. 19). The Supreme Court case of *Trustees of Dartmouth College* v. *Woodward* (1819) ensured the existence of both public and private universities and colleges in the United States, because it ruled that the government could not alter the perpetual charter of a private institution.

During this time period, increased calls for curriculum reform and expanded opportunities could be heard across the country. The first non-military technical school, Rensselaer Polytechnic Institute, was established in 1824. Women's colleges first arose in the South: Wesleyan Female College in Macon, Georgia, in 1836, Judson College in 1838, and Mary Sharp College in 1852 (Brubacher and Rudy, 1976). (It was not until after the Civil War that many of the famous women's colleges (Smith, Vassar, Radcliffe) were established in the North.)

Oberlin established coeducation before 1860, an example that was followed by many institutions in the West. Denominational colleges continued to flourish during the nineteenth century, although there was a distinct separation of church and state. The period of growth for colleges for African Americans occurred in the thirty years after the Civil War (Brubacher and Rudy, 1976, p. 75). Concurrently, other educational models were introduced successfully. The German approach, with its focus on the expansion of knowledge (research), began to be perceived as a legitimate one and still can be found in major research institutions across the country, such as Johns Hopkins, the University of Chicago, and the University of Michigan. Science and mathematics were introduced as respectable subjects in the curriculum, laboratories were developed, and in some institutions a primary emphasis on graduate or professional education became the norm.

The Morrill Land Grant Act of 1862 was a landmark in the expansion of American higher education. Through the Morrill Act, the federal government set aside public lands to finance agricultural and mechanical schools in response to the needs of society. Three models emerged from the Morrill Act: (1) special institutions specifically geared to land-grant objectives in many states; (2) already-established institutions that received money to support new curricular objectives (the University of California, Berkeley, and the University of Minnesota); or (3) a blend of private and public institutions (Cornell) to meet land-grant objectives.

Although the intensive period for establishing colleges occurred from 1790 to 1859, 134 more colleges were founded in the years 1860 to 1890 and another 135 between 1890 and 1929 (Millett, 1952). And all of this growth in number and kind predated the massive community or junior college movement. In 1947, the President's Commission on Higher Education recommended that two more years of study be provided for about the 50 percent of young people who could benefit from formal study beyond high school (President's Commission on Higher Education, 1947). In 1947 there were a total of 650 public and private community or junior colleges, and by 1987 that number grew to 1,224 (Cohen and Brawer, 1989).

Other factors also influenced the history and growth of American higher education. For example, the G.I. Bill (1944 Veterans Readjustment Act) made it possible for veterans to attend institutions of higher education. Desegregation provided a second large wave of new students following the decision of *Brown* v. *Board of Education* (1954). The civil rights movement increased the expectation of minority group members for the right for higher education. The Higher Education Act of 1965 created Basic Educational Opportunity Grants, later renamed Pell Grants, and financial aid increased the opportunity and choice of higher education for financially needy students. The political activism of the 1960s and 1970s caused many institution to reassess both purpose and governance. Finally, the rise of the adult and part-time learner forever changed the characteristics of American higher education. Consequently, it is a diverse and complicated enterprise.

As described by Balderston (1974), the three traditional missions of higher education are teaching, research, and public service. Others have characterized its traditional purposes as "to preserve, transmit and create knowledge, to encourage personal development and to serve society" (National Association of Student Personnel Administrators, [1987] 1989; p. 9). What creates variation among institutions of higher education is the emphasis placed on each of these three objectives and the type of institution involved. The scope of institutions of higher education in the United States is enormous. Their enrollments range from fewer than five hundred to over fifty thousand. They are located in rural and small towns and in major cities. They may be independent, church-related, church-controlled, or publicly supported. Some are purely undergraduate institutions grounded in the liberal arts tradition. Some, most notably community colleges, are degree-granting institutions with a strong component of public service and public access to non-degree offerings. "Others have multiple purposes and include undergraduate, graduate, professional and technical education and serve students from around the world. Still others are community oriented, and their offerings reflect local or regional needs" (National Association of Student Personnel Administrators [1987] 1989, p. 9).

Although it would sometimes seem that most institutional mission statements "are remarkable more for their sameness than their distinctiveness and give little symbolic focus for collective action" (Alfred and Weissman, 1987, p. 34), the written and "living mission" statement of any institution can shape the collaborative learning processes within the academic community. Kuh, Schuh, and Whitt (1990) indicate that "the mission provides the rationale for what a college or university is and aspires to be and the yardstick used by students, faculty and others to determine if their institutional policies and practices are educationally purposeful" (p. 4).

The *Involving Colleges* (Kuh, Schuh, Whitt, and Associates, 1991) study concentrated on what made institutions successful in encouraging the achievement of students and a sense of community. Although the missions and philosophies of the institutions studied in *Involving Colleges* are many, all have clarity and coherence.

Discovering the Institutional Mission

Virtually all institutions have a mission statement that sets forth what they do, how they go about it, for whom it is done, and in some cases, the larger social, ethical, and educational world view that enlivens them. There is usually more to an institution's mission than a descriptive page or paragraph in the front of a catalogue. The heritage of an institution can be one of the building blocks of its mission. It is *always* worthwhile to ask who founded the institution? When? For whom? And to do what? No two institutions have evolved in the same way, and their history often accounts for their distinctiveness. Yet this history, important as it always is, may be only one of *many* portals that can lead to understanding the full meaning and texture of an institution's mission.

How does one learn what the mission of a college or university really is, especially when it is rarely spelled out? Much of the answer can be found in how those in the institution view what they do, how they live, how they relate to each other and to educational goals, and what they value. As Kuh and Schuh observe, "The 'living mission' of a college is how students, faculty, administrators, graduates, and others describe what the college is and is trying to accomplish" (1991, p. 12). To what extent is the institution residential? Are there educational purposes embedded in its residential programs and arrangements? Is "community" an important concept, and how is it encouraged? Why do students come? What kind of students attend? What are the key criteria for faculty selection, advancement, and retention? Are there significant organizing principles, such as religious, social, or special educational beliefs? Certainly one way to understand the mission of the institution is to ask what it *does not do*.

Terminology

The meaning of even common terms like *liberal arts* may vary according to the institution. At Allegheny College in Pennsylvania, for example, a liberal arts college, the core of its program is in liberal studies; however, students can major in communication arts, physical education, environmental science, and education and international studies, along with the more classic liberal arts fields (classics, physics, chemistry, history, humanities, and philosophy). Allegheny's idea of the liberal arts has evolved over time in much the same ways as has that of many other liberal arts colleges.

Reed College, also a liberal arts institution embraces a far more traditional and restrictive view of the liberal arts. Any subject matter that appears to be applied may have great difficulty finding its way into Reed's curriculum.

Moreover, the understanding and practice of student affairs are quite different on the two campuses. At Allegheny, the education of the whole person is valued. Attention is paid to students' affective, as well as cognitive, development. Reed, by contrast, focuses almost exclusively on the intellectual development of students. More than other institutions, the college tends to assume that students' social development matters less.

Heritage

Earlham, Haverford, and Guilford colleges are located in widely different parts of the country. They are private, residential, small liberal arts colleges, like many hundred others. They are distinctive, however, in that all were founded by Quakers (Society of Friends). Though Quakers constitute a very small portion of their student bodies, governing boards, and administrations, the Quaker tradition continues to play a significant role in determining how things get done, how members of the campus community relate to each other, and how policy is conceived and implemented. The work of the community (faculty meetings, residence meetings, and student government) is done by consensus, a way of doing business that is characteristically Quaker. Relationships among members of the communities are cemented by a deliberately nourished environment of trust and respect and forthrightness. All of these institutions are influenced by a strong peace testimony. All tend to avoid pretense in its many forms. For example, titles are used infrequently, if at all. The schools' architecture and furnishings are usually elegant in their simplicity. Learning viewed as a means to search for the truth in its many forms creates strong bonds to scholarship. To be effective, a professional in student affairs would have to learn, respect, and work within a cultural context of each college's Quaker tradition. Calling for a vote to decide disputed matters, seeking ROTC (or for that matter military) recruiters on campus, and creating prescriptive rules are not part of procedural or programmatic approaches on these campuses, although they are common elsewhere. The mission of these colleges cannot be understood fully without an appreciation of their heritage.

Geography, history, and tradition have thus shaped each of these colleges in a distinctive way.

Distinctive Systems

The University of California is a multi-campus system governed by a common board of regents. Its faculty has a governance system that transcends the boundaries of any given campus: a central administration sits at the head of its system. Yet the institutions within the University of California are quite different.

Every institution in the system has its own traditions, culture, distinctive geographical setting, and ways of approaching academics. Although all University of California (UC) institutions emphasize research, two of the older campuses, Berkeley and the University of California, Los Angeles (UCLA), are preeminent in that regard. UC Santa Cruz, founded in the 1960s, reflects many of the educational ideals that so characterized that decade. It has both academic departments and residential colleges with interdisciplinary themes and tends to emphasize teaching and undergraduate education. UC San Diego also has residential colleges with interdisciplinary themes. In addition, however, it has professional schools and an ambitious research agenda, especially in science and technology. UC Davis is different in other ways. While stressing teaching and research, it is heavily influenced by its agricultural heritage, including a tradition of everyone (as on a farm) pitching in at certain points for the good of the whole, regardless of role and specialty. It is therefore not surprising that UC Davis students take substantial responsibility for governing the institution and, as peer departmental advisers, their home departments.

A student affairs professional should understand these differences, even in a university system characterized by considerable centralized control. Standardization within student affairs might occur in admissions, conduct policies, financial aid processes, certain governance requirements, methods of allocating resources, and other common services. But building an organization to serve the *special* mission of each institution must be done very differently at UC Santa Cruz, UC Berkeley, UCLA, UC Davis, and UC San Diego. Creating and maintaining a high quality of student life will be achieved in distinctive ways on each campus. The skills that work on one campus are not easily transferable to another within the system.

Geography

What effect does geography have on the educational programs of the institution? It can range from subtle to dramatic. For example, it is not surprising that the educational priorities of the University of Alaska in Fairbanks include the education of rural Alaskan natives, fisheries research, and the study of Arctic phenomena. Student affairs staff members know the importance of hockey and cross-country skiing to the well-being of students in the long, dark winters. They also know that orientation activities must include lessons on how to dress for and cope with long periods of intense cold and how to handle the mental health issues that accompany the winters.

At the University of Arizona, Arizona State University, and the University of New Mexico, considerable attention in the curriculum and in campus life is devoted to the education of Native Americans and to the general cultural understanding of Hopi, Navajo, and Pueblo tribal cultures.

Many institutions on the ethnically rich West Coast have long faced the challenge of enriching students' understanding of the ethnic and racial diversity that characterizes their campus and their region. Student affairs professionals are called upon regularly to articulate and help create the ideal of multicultural communities marked by respect, trust, and the comfort needed by students to optimize their academic priorities. This process, of course, happens in many other parts of the country, but it is a regular and obvious feature of many West Coast schools.

An institution's history and location often work together to give it a distinctive mission. Xavier University in New Orleans was founded as a Catholic institution "to serve blacks and persons of color who were denied educational opportunities" (Kuh, Schuh, Whitt, and Associates, 1991, p. 74). The approaches and organization of student affairs are influenced heavily by Xavier's setting in an ethnically rich city and by the guidance of the Catholic faith. These act in concert to produce distinctive ways to recognize, reward, and encourage students to achieve, as well as to foster a special sense of community of family rarely found on campuses.

Geography, then, can have a profound affect on the mission of an institution. Looking at an institution through the lens of its geographical setting is thus another way to understand what it seeks to do and why.

Social Organization of Students

The social organization of students, or the lack of it, may also help one understand an institution's mission and the ways in which it is carried out. An urban institution such as Temple University cannot be evaluated by using criteria appropriate to a residential setting. At such institutions, the social organization and relationships of students may be relatively unimportant when compared with those at residential institutions. If the social organization of students has importance in such urban settings, it will more often than not be realized in the ways schools and departments work to build social structures for their students. The relationship between the institution and the community is also a significant factor in determining the social structures that benefit students. In the case of Wichita State University, one must understand the community in order to comprehend how the community serves as a surprising source of social support and organization for students attending the university.

The social structures of student life at residential institutions may look more alike than they really are and lead to erroneous conclusions about the mission of the institution. Cornell, Miami University (Ohio), and the University of Virginia are schools with fraternities and sororities that affect the social and organizational lives of many students on each campus. Each of the schools depends on residential fraternities and sororities to provide housing for students. Fraternal organizations have a recognizable presence on the campus. Beyond these facts, similarities are less obvious. The relationship between the institution and the Greek organizations—and its support for these groups—varies considerably.

It is fair to observe that Cornell and the University of Virginia tolerate their residential fraternities, though they are often troubled by them. Fraternal organizations have long histories at both schools, are seen by some as anachronisms or antithetical to education or both, and are a frequent source of conduct problems. The relationship between the institution and Greek organizations is sometimes marked by mistrust and suspicion. And the resulting town-and-gown dynamics can be volatile.

Though Miami also has a long history of fraternal organizations, its history is rooted in an early belief in the founding ideals of many fraternities and sororities. Three of the oldest national fraternities were founded there. Hence, Miami's history has been marked by good relationships with its Greek organizations. They are seen as important partners in the creation of a healthy organizational, residential, and university life.

Differences such as these are found throughout higher education and are an area in which student affairs professionals have a special interest and responsibility.

Somewhere in the living mission of each college and university are the expectations, behavioral customs, policies, and ways of relating that will shape the work of students affairs. The success or failure of student affairs may depend, in some measure, on the compatibility of the views of student affairs professionals and the mission of their institution. If they are highly congruent, student affairs work is more likely to be effective.

Institutions with Broad and Far-Reaching Missions

Some institutions, either by design or inadvertently, are many things to many people. It would be difficult to find much overall focus in a sprawling state university with large residential graduate and undergraduate student populations, several branch campuses, several professional schools, and many centers for research and service. The missions of such a mega-university may be little more than to provide an environment in which research, general and professional education and training, and service to the state will flourish. Distinctive purposes *do* exist within the components of such institutions, and it is to them that the student affairs staff should look. The missions of an adult education division are likely to be quite different from those of a school of law or a college of liberal studies. Each of these units will probably have its own student affairs organization and services within the larger whole.

Many student services and programs will be decentralized by necessity and occur within subcommunities such as residences or colleges and schools. Even some central services like unions or intercollegiate sports also have distinctive missions that give definition and substance to the more vague and overarching objectives of the university.

Community Colleges

Community colleges have widely varying missions. They usually exist to respond to the training and educational needs of a specific community or region; the curriculum may therefore be heavily influenced by local social and economic patterns. A community college in a manufacturing town will offer a curriculum that will reflect that industrial focus, whereas a community college in Reno, Nevada, may offer courses to run casino games and operations. A community college will also organize teaching and curriculum to respond to the special requirements and characteristics of the area's residents. Thus, understanding the mission of a community college will be easier to the extent that one understands its location. Nearly all community colleges offer a means of transfer to four-year institutions and provide a place to prove one's scholastic mettle and prepare for the academic specialization that awaits one in the university.

The subtleties of many community colleges' missions can also be understood by identifying what motivates students to attend in the first place. The wise and experienced student affairs vice president of a community college urges that we acknowledge some compelling motivations for attendance that will never be found in the mission statement: "To get out of the house; to feel better or get well; to get out of prison sooner; to please parents; to play basketball; to have status; to escape from _____; to learn English; to get promoted . . . " (Golseth, 1992, p. 20).

Institutions with Focused Missions

American higher education abounds with colleges and universities with specialized goals. Technical institutes like the Massachusetts Institute of Technology, California Polytechnic Institute, Virginia Polytechnic Institute and State University, Harvey Mudd College, and Rochester Institute of Technology are examples of institutions with missions focused on science and technology. Though all have these at their core, they are nevertheless quite different from each other. They are affected variously by geography, size, the relative importance placed on teaching and research and on graduate and undergraduate education, institutional age, sources of funding, admission standards, the degree to which their students reside on campus, and their public and private status.

Moreover, an institution's religious affiliation may account for some distinctive missions that may have a profound impact on the work and approaches of the student affairs staff. Georgetown University painfully labored in the full glare of the national press in deciding how it would recognize a gay and lesbian organization. Should a Catholic university condone, or appear to condone, an organization that appeared to flout an important tenet of its faith? Our higher educational landscape is full of examples, both visible and subtle, of how an institution's religious affiliation can affect its mission and therefore the work of student affairs.

The Evergreen State College in Olympia, Washington, is a wonderful instance of how influential a focused mission can be. Founded in 1967, its doors opening in 1971, Evergreen was conceived with the objective of providing a sound liberal arts education through nontraditional means. From that founding mission, a most imaginative, successful, and effective educational program has evolved. Traditional (or at least common) approaches to student affairs would thus be out of place and counterproductive at Evergreen.

Berea College is another institution with an unusual purpose. It is a liberal arts college founded to educate able but poor children in Appalachia. Among its several objectives is to demonstrate that labor, mental and manual, has dignity as well as utility. To achieve these aspects of its mission, its student body is limited to those who can pay little or no tuition, and all students must work for the institution for approximately fifteen hours per week. The work of student affairs at Berea will be as distinctive as it is at Evergreen. At both colleges, expectations for student life must be well understood if the professional student affairs staff is to succeed here.

Institution Missions That Predetermine How Student Services Will Be Organized

The same model of residential colleges found at the University of California campuses at Santa Cruz and San Diego can be found at other institutions as diverse as Yale, the University of Redlands (Johnston College), Western Washington University (Fairhaven College), and Harvard. These universities are organized into residential (except Fairhaven) colleges that have many things in common besides their relatively small size. These include affiliated faculty members who serve as advisers, mentors, and deans to furnish academic advising and help with personal problems. In addition, such faculty members monitor student academic standing, nurture students' self-governance, handle conflicts, and organize rituals such as orientation and graduation. Each residential college will generate its own leisure and extracurricular activities. The colleges usually have distinct personalities—cultures, traditions, rules, norms, and practices that set them apart from each other and from the larger institution and that persist over many generations of students (Jencks and Riesman, 1962). Many institutions have variations of the college or house system. Versions of one sort or another can also be found at Stanford, Bucknell, Cornell, and Princeton.

Professionals in the field working in more traditional settings often wonder just how student affairs activities are organized in such residential colleges. Most of the typical services and responsibilities are found there, but they are often labeled and organized differently. The boundaries between academic and nonacademic are quite permeable because faculty members assume general duties assigned to administrative professionals on other campuses. The line between students and administrators is also vague because students in such settings tend to assume significant responsibility for each other and their community. Highly technical services like financial aid, psychological counseling, career planning, and medical care are provided on a more centralized basis. Even then, these might be supplied in the residential college setting as well. Students routinely take charge of programs like orientation, campus communications, colloquia, admissions recruiting, the community paper or newsletter, or the campus (college) directory. The living mission almost always can be understood more clearly by looking at what students do to maintain their community and how they do it. To illustrate, at Fairhaven College at Western Washington University, a lively and immensely successful 1960s alternative learning community, the campus directory has no separate categories for students, faculty, and staff and is alphabetized by the person's first name.

As illustrated by these examples, the university's goals cannot be well understood without a knowledge of the special missions of its member residential colleges. In addition, the structure of the educational activities and the services of student affairs will be dramatically different in a university organized into colleges.

Summary

We have observed that the role of student affairs will nearly always differ from one institution to another. How the work of student affairs is structured, how its responsibilities are defined, how it is valued, and how it relates to the work and culture of an institution can vary greatly from one university to another and even within an institution.

The most important factor that determines the shape and substance of student affairs is the mission of the institution. There are other factors, of course, but none is as important or compelling. Terminology, heritage, academic focus, geography, and faculty involvement all reflect institutional objectives and the place of student affairs. Understanding this mission requires more than merely reading a statement. Homework must be done and understanding achieved. Institutional "fit" between student affairs staff members and their colleges and universities is very important to the success of each. Acceptance of and support for the institutional mission, then, seems a prerequisite to success in the student affairs profession.

References

Alfred, R., and Weissman, J. *Higher Education and the Public Trust*, ASHE-ERIC Higher Education Report, no. 6. Washington, D.C.: Association for the Study of Higher Education, 1987.

Balderston, E. F. *Managing Today's University*. San Francisco: Jossey-Bass, 1974.

Barzun, J. *The American University*. New York: HarperCollins, 1968.

Brubacher, J., and Rudy, W. P. *Higher Education in Transition*. (3rd ed.) New York: HarperCollins, 1976.

Cohen, A. M., and Brawer, F. B. *The American Community College*. (2nd ed.) San Francisco: Jossey-Bass, 1989.

Golseth, A. "Diversity—Beyond Celebration." In J. W. Lyons (ed.), *Student Affairs 1992: How Things Are and Are Becoming: A Collection of Essays*. A collection of essays prepared for the National Association of Student Personnel Administrators Western Regional Conference, 1992.

Jencks, C., and Riesman, D. "Patterns of Residential Education: A Case Study of Harvard." In N. Sanford (ed.) *The American College*. New York: Wiley, 1962.

Kaplin, W. *The Law of Higher Education*. (2nd ed.) San Francisco: Jossey-Bass, 1985.

Knock, G. "Development of Student Services in Higher Education." In M. J. Barr, L. A. Keating, and Associates, *Developing Effective Student Services Programs: Systematic Approaches for Practitioners*. San Francisco: Jossey-Bass, 1985.

Kuh, G., and Schuh, J. *The Role and Contribution of Student Affairs in Involving Colleges*. Washington, D. C.: National Association of Student Personnel Administrators, 1991.

Kuh, G. D., Schuh, J. H., and Whitt, E. J. "Involving Colleges: Characteristics of Colleges and Universities That Promote Involvement in Out-of-Class Learning." Unpublished manuscript, June 1990.

Kuh, G. D., Schuh, J. H., Whitt, E. J., and Associates. *Involving Colleges: Successful Approaches to Fostering Student Learning and Development Outside the Classroom*. San Francisco: Jossey-Bass, 1991.

Millett, J. D. *Financing Higher Education in the United States*. New York: Columbia University Press, 1952.

National Association of Student Personnel Administrators. "A Perspective on Student Affairs." In *Points of View*. Washington, D.C.: National Association of Student Personnel Administrators, 1989. (Originally published 1987.)

President's Commission on Higher Education. *Higher Education for American Democracy*. Washington, D.C.: U.S. Government Printing Office, 1947.

Legal Cases

Brown v. *Board of Education*, 347 U.S. 483 (1954).

Trustees of Dartmouth College v. *Woodward*, 17 U.S. 518 (1819).

College Life: Undergraduate Culture and Higher Education

MICHAEL MOFFATT

College in the United States is an odd mixture of higher learning and youth culture for its students, and it has been for over a hundred years. In the late nineteenth century American undergraduates themselves invented the youth culture of outside-the-classroom-college, naming it "college life" and passing it down to future student generations. What has happened to this same youth culture among the students in the 1980s?

In an effort to find out, I used anthropological methods, including two years of participant-observation in the residence halls of a state university, Rutgers, in New Brunswick, New Jersey, a college of eighty-five hundred undergraduates embedded in a much larger, fairly typical state university.[1] And the first thing I encountered in the Rutgers dorms was an elaborate, vigorous form of modern college life—not the "student life" of college catalogues, but an earthier set of mentalities and behaviors. Now as in the past, college life as the students understand it is one of the principal reasons they come to college, and it is what they often remember most fondly after they have left.

Why should we care about anything as nonintellectual and low-minded as college life often turns out to be? Because, though contemporary outside-the-classroom college is often the focus of popular fantasy,[2] it is almost entirely ignored in serious research on American colleges and universities. And because when we grasp its shape more accurately, we can understand certain higher aspects of American higher education more realistically.

In the absence of similar ethnographic studies done elsewhere, there is no way of knowing for certain how typical material from a single institution is likely to be. Rutgers student culture is unlikely to be entirely atypical, however. For as will be suggested below, the cultural worlds of the undergraduates are only occasionally formed from idiosyncratic local sources. Much more of what is important in them is shaped by the institutional structure of American higher education, by general American culture, and especially by nationally defined, media-born, youth culture. Similar mixes are likely to exist in other contemporary American colleges and universities.

What, then, are the outlines of modern college life as I was able to comprehend them through research in the Rutgers dormitories, by observing and listening in on the students in their informal moods and behaviors?

College Life in the 1980s

For reasons of perspective—differences of age, generation, and institutional location and agenda—college is never the same for the adults who run it as for the late-adolescents who typically make up most of its residential undergraduates. The purpose of a college education in the assumptions of most professors and educators tends to be what goes on in the classroom: learning critical thinking, how to read a text, mathematical and scientific skills, expert appreciation and technique in the arts, and so on. Some bigger thinkers propose broader, more humanistic goals for college, especially for the liberal arts: to produce "more competent, more concerned, more complete human being[s]"

[2, p. 1]; to give students a "hope of a higher life . . . civilization. " [1, p. 336]. And, almost all college authorities assume, whatever is valuable about college for the undergraduates is or ought to be the result of the deliberate impact, direct or indirect, of college adults such as themselves on the students.

The students agree that classroom learning is an important part of their college educations. College would not be college, after all, without "academics": professors, grades, requirements, and a bachelor's degree after four years. Most students also agree that college should be a broadening experience, that it should make you into a better, more open, more liberal, more knowledgeable person.

But, in the students' view, not all this broadening happens through the formal curriculum. College is also about what goes on outside the classroom, among the students with no adults around. College is about being on your own, about autonomy, about freedom from the authority of adults, however benign their intentions. And last but far from least, college is about fun, about unique forms of peer-group fun before, in student conceptions, the grayer actualities of adult life in the real world begin to close in on you.

Contemporary college life—the pleasurable, autonomous side of outside-the-classroom college as the students experience it—comes into clearer focus when we compare it to past forms of the same uniquely American undergraduate culture.

Work and Play

American college life has always rested on an understanding among the students about the proper relationship between formal academic work and other activities in college, about the relative value of inside-the-classroom education versus extracurricular experiences. A century ago the evaluation was a simple one. Extracurricular fun and games and the lessons learned in the vigorous student-to-student competitions that "made men"—athletics, class warfare, fraternity rushing, and so on— were obviously much more important than anything that happened to you in the classroom, most of the students maintained [5, pp. 23–55; 8].

The students cannot make the same aggressive anti-academic judgments in the late-twentieth century, however. For as Helen Horowitz has pointed out in a recent history of American under-graduate culture, once there were several routes to comfortable upper-middle class status in the United States, and college could be a lazy affair. In the increasingly bureaucratic, impersonal twentieth-century American economy, however, a college baccalaureate—and a good one with good grades—has become the indispensable initial qualification leading to the choicest occupations and professions, via law school, business school, medical school, graduate school, and other types of professional postgraduate education. Therefore, as Horowitz notes, despite periodic crises of confidence in higher education in the United States, American parents have sent higher proportions of their children to college every decade since 1890, and the trend apparently continues in the 1990s [5, pp. 3–22].

Contrary to Horowitz, however, this trend has not resulted in a grim, unrelieved work ethic among contemporary students.[3] For the students *are* still youths; and adolescents, especially as encouraged by late twentieth-century American consumer culture, are also expected to have fun. How much fun, and what kind in college?

Consider a crucial set of actions, the students' use of time in college. According to hundreds of 24-hour time reports made out for my Rutgers research, for ordinary days mid-week, mid-semester, 60 to 70 percent of the undergraduates studied about two hours a day. Another ten to fifteen percent indicated harder academic work, up six or seven hours a day, usually but not always students in the more difficult majors; and the remainder, about a quarter of those who filled out the time reports, hardly studied at all day-to-day, but relied on frenetic cramming around exams.

The students slept a surprising amount, an average of a little over eight hours a day, making up for late nights with later mornings and afternoon naps. They spent about four hours a day in classes, on buses or dealing with university bureaucracy. A quarter of them devoted small amounts of their remaining free time, one or two hours a day, to organized extracurricular activities, mostly to fraternities or sororities, less often to other student groups. An eighth worked at jobs between one and four hours a day (more worked on weekends). A tenth engaged in intramural or personal athletics. And two-fifths mentioned small amounts of TV watching, less than the average for American children or adults.

The students' remaining free time in college was given over to friendly fun with peers, the bread-and-butter of college life as the undergraduates enjoy it in the 1980s. Friendly fun consists almost entirely of spur-of-the-moment pleasures; with the exception of the fraternities and sororities (see below), very little of it has to do with the older college extracurriculum. It includes such easy pleasures as hanging out in a dorm lounge or elsewhere, gossiping, wrestling and fooling around, thinking up the odd sophomoric prank, going to dinner or having a light or serious discussion with friends, ordering out for pizza, visiting other dorms, going out to a bar, flirting and other erotic activities, and so forth.

The average time the undergraduates reported for this informal sociability across the entire sample of time-reports was a little over four hours a day. On the face of it, then, the students were enjoying themselves about twice as much as they were studying in college. But this is a deceptive conclusion, for from their point of view "college work" also includes going to classes, and the total of their classroom time plus their study time was about six hours a day. They also almost all studied harder and played less around exams or when big papers or other projects were due.

It is fairer to generalize that, in student assumptions, academic work and friendly fun ought to be equally important activities during one's undergraduate years. And so the students also say in various ways. Incoming freshmen usually have two goals for their first year in college, "to do well in classes" and "to have fun" (or "to make friends," or "to have a good social life"). Older students look back on college as an even or shifting mixture of work and play. And students in college who are deviating from the ideal balance almost always know that they are and often sound defensive about it. Here, for instance, is a contemporary "grind" confessing to her excessive scholarliness almost as if it were a personality defect:

> I am a little too serious about my studies. . . . I often give up extracurricular activities
> to stay home and study. This is not to say that I am a "nerd" . . . I have a variety of
> good friends, and I party as much as is feasible. . . . [But] I am the type of person who
> *has* to study. . . . This inner force or drive has been contained in me since childhood.[4]

"Blow-it-offs," on the other hand, overly lazy students, tend to be equally defensive in opposite directions.

What is the sane middle-of-the-roader, then? Obviously someone who maintains a healthy balance between academics and college life. The two halves of college ought to be *complementary* ones in student opinion, You come to college for the challenge, for the work, and to do your best in classes in order to qualify for a good career later in life—and possibly to make yourself into a broader, more liberally educated person. College life is the play that makes the work possible and that makes college personally memorable.

Autonomy

College life is also about the freedom to enjoy your adolescent pleasures in college independent of adult supervision. On first impressions in the dorms, contemporary students appear to be almost entirely free to do whatever they like, but they actually live in three different zones of relative autonomy and control in college. They are freest in their private lives. Rutgers, like other American colleges, officially renounced *in loco parentis* authority over the personal conduct and moral behavior of its students in the late 1960s. Many other reforms which the protesting students of the '60s tried to make in higher education have long since been rolled back. But this fundamental shift in college authority has endured for a generation.

The students are least free, on the other hand, when it comes to their formal educations. Here they have to submit to adult authority in certain ways—to professors, who give them grades, their fundamental institutional reward. They have to sit passively through scheduled classes. They have to learn the material the professors think is important. They often feel that they have to think like their professors to get good grades, whether they agree with them or not. They have to meet "requirements."

Between their private lives and "academics" lies a third intermediate zone, where the authority of the dean of students is still intact after the liberalization of the late '60s. Residential students literally walk into this area of deanly authority whenever they leave the privacy of their dorm rooms. At Rutgers, their dorm floors are supervised by undergraduate preceptors, at the bottom of the chain of command. The dorm as a whole belongs to graduate student residence counselors, one link up the chain. Sets of dorms have full-time area coordinators looking after them. Extracurricular organizations are similarly monitored. And so on up to the dean of students himself, behind whom stands the university police, wielding physical force.

How does the average student experience the power of the deans in the 1980s? Most of the time, not at all. At Rutgers, about seven thousand residential students are ultimately held in check by an adult staff that numbers twenty-seven individuals, a typical ratio for state institutions. The students rarely see a dean in the flesh outside of orientation and the odd official function. The deans do have their more numerous undergraduate preceptors and other student agents, of course, whose "personal development" they are "fostering" by co-opting them to their purposes. But they are never completely sure just how loyal these agents of theirs are being. And, in fact, the average preceptor functions best by exerting as little authority and as much "friendliness" as possible among her or his peers.

Consequently, the students live most of their daily lives in college without being aware of or thinking about the authority of the deans much at all. But they do know the deans are there, and the deans' authority can effectively penetrate even the often tight solidarity of undergraduate collectivities such as coed dorm floor groups. During one research year in the dorms, for example, responding to the legal restoration of the 21-year-old minimum drinking age, the deans effectively pushed drinking out of dorm lounges, into private rooms or off-campus, and they also successfully "cracked down" on one particular do-it-yourself student festivity which offended their sensibilities, "Secret Santa."[5]

The students usually resent the deans' power when it is brought to bear on them directly, often rapidly shifting from ignoring deans to imagining them as far more powerful personages than they actually are—stereotypically as small-minded, power-hungry, dictatorial autocrats. Images of adult authority drawn from popular culture seem to shape the students' thinking as much as any other cultural influences. One year in the dorms, for instance, when the deans were insisting that some particularly rundown Rutgers fraternities upgrade their facilities, I listened as three fraternity brothers compared the dean of students of Rutgers College directly to "Dean Wormer, "villainous college authority in that modern college-life classic, *Animal House*.

National traumas can also influence student notions of local authority—Watergate, for instance. Later that same year, as another student confessed to me that for some months she had wrongly believed I was a spy for the deans, she added, in self-defense: "But when you think about it, they *could* do anything they wanted to here. I mean, they could have all these rooms wired for sound. They could be listening in on us all the time!"

Private Pleasures and Extracurriculum

Late nineteenth century college life was a vigorous organizational culture entirely of the students' own creation: college class organizations, fraternities, glee clubs, campus newspapers, yearbooks, intramural and intercollegiate sports teams, and other student collectivities. Not one college authority had anything to do with these extracurricular student organizations for many years.

In the early twentieth century, however, American social psychologists invented the modern concept of adolescence [4, pp. 133–183; 6, pp. 215–244], and burgeoning American college administrations invented specialists in college adolescence, deans of students. These deans borrowed the notion that college was about late-adolescent development from late nineteenth-century undergraduates, making the older students' "college life" their own new professional specialty, "student life." And from now on, down to the present, the peculiarly American notion that higher education is as much about adolescence as it is about formal learning has been institutionalized; it has been inscribed in the bureaucratic organization of most residential colleges and universities in the United States.

Early twentieth-century deans moved the undergraduates into dormitories under their control on the expanding campuses, and the colleges added new layers of staff to deal with the extracurricular undergraduate: directors of residence life, directors of student activities, athletic directors and coaches, musical directors, health specialists, psychological counselors, career counselors, and so on. As they did so, however, the students— faithful to the older student concept that college was, among other things, fundamentally about adolescent autonomy—progressively revised their own notions of college life so that it still belonged to them, moving its essential pleasures closer and closer to their private lives. The end of *in loco parentis* in the '60s was a key victory in this progressive privatization of college life by the students, at Rutgers and elsewhere.

Hence the dominance of informal, *ad hoc*, forms of student fun in the 1980s. There are over a hundred and fifty duly constituted student groups at Rutgers at present, not counting the fraternities and the sororities. Most undergraduates probably are affiliated with one or two of them. But according to time-reports, dorm observations, and the estimates of knowledgeable undergraduates, no more than one in ten of the undergraduates is extracurricularly active.[6]

Contemporary students do make distinctions among extracurricular groups. The radio station is so focal to the interests of current youth culture that it is a prestigious involvement even if the deans ultimately oversee its operations. So too are the Concerts Committee of the Program Council, and the campus newspaper (which the deans do not oversee at Rutgers). Student government, on the other hand, is a joke in the opinion of most students, and they vote for its representatives in the tiniest of turnouts. The only reason to become a student leader, many students assume, is to get to know some dean for reasons of your own.

The undergraduates also invented intercollegiate athletics in the late nineteenth century, but in the twentieth century, following nationwide trends, the alumni and a growing professional coaching staff took sports out of the hands of the students. At present in the 1980s, most Rutgers students in the dorms do not know any major varsity athletes personally. Some students enjoy intramural athletics, or jog, or work out. Most are as likely to be fans of nearby professional teams as of any college teams.

The one exception to the students' generally casual interest in the organized extracurriculum at present, the fraternity and sorority system, proves the rule. Given the defenses the fraternities and sororities have been able to mount through their secret ritual constitutions, their intense peer solidarity, and their private ownership, the deans have not really succeeded in penetrating and controlling them despite almost a century of trying. Thus the fraternities and sororities still provide undergraduates with a zone of real autonomy in a group setting of a sort that has not been available elsewhere in undergraduate culture since the early twentieth century. Therefore they are still going strong, joined by about a quarter of the students at Rutgers, utilized by at least as many more for their wild partying.

Friends and Lovers

The predominantly private pleasures of contemporary college life are those of friendship and sexuality. Intense friendship has been the staple of American college life for two centuries, its central social relationship. It may be culturally even more salient in the 1980s. For like other middle-class Americans, contemporary undergraduates tend to be "privatized individualists" in their most general cultural orientations, seeking "meaningful relationships" in personal worlds of their own construction, in worlds divorced as much as possible from the constraints of the "real world."

According to the assumptions of American individualism in the 1980s, most other social connections, relationships of family, class, race, and ethnicity, impose themselves upon the self from without (they are "ascriptive": you do not choose them; they choose you). Even sexual love and lust can "overwhelm you" according to American folk psychology [3]. Your friends, on the other hand, are the perfect alters for the modern privatized ego—freely and mutually chosen other selves with often mysterious natural affinities for your own self.

As it is elsewhere in American middle-class culture, *friendliness* is the central code of etiquette in student culture, the expected code of conduct in student collectivities such as dorm-floor groups and fraternities, the one taken-for-granted politesse whose systematic breach almost always generates anger and even outrage in students. To act friendly is to give regular abbreviated performances of the behaviors of "real" friendship: to look pleased and happy when you meet someone, to put on the American friendly smile, to acknowledge the person you are meeting by name (first name, shortened, among the students: "Mike" rather than "Michael"), to make casual bodily contact, to greet with one of two or three conventional queries about the "whole self" of the other ("How are you?"; "how's it goin?"; "what's new?"). But the students, like other Americans and unlike most foreigners, also know the subtle differences between friendliness and "really being friends," and real friendships are crucial to their happiness and their senses of self.

The social structure of the students' college life consists of the thousands of ever-changing ego-centered friendship networks which each of them constructs. After a month at Rutgers, the average residential freshman already considers five to six new college acquaintances to be friends or close friends, and more than half say they would take an intensely confidential problem to one of their new college friends rather than calling home with it. Within two months, first-year students on three different dorm floors named almost one-third of the sixty odd female and male residents of the same floor as friends or as close friends. In one longitudinal sample, freshmen and sophomores indicated that a little less than half of their five best friends in the world were already friends they had made since coming to college, and the percentage of best college friends then rose to about three in five for juniors and seniors.

Sexual relationships are even more focal to the private lives of most students. Space prohibits more than roughest indication of their contemporary complexities [see 10, pp. 181–270]. One complication is the widespread existence of genuine cross-sex friendships in the 1980s. As late as 1970, a sociologist could still generalize, probably hyperbolically, that male and female college students were "not expected to form friendships with one another; . . . thus the assertion that 'men and women can be lovers but never friends'" [7, p. 145]. But such friendships are now common in the intimate environments created by the historically recent "coed dorms," women and men living side-by-side in "alternating rooms." About one-third of the hundreds of reciprocated close friendships reported in my research were between women and men.[7] Most students carefully distinguish cross-sex friendships from erotic or "romantic" attachments, suggesting that they value their cross-sex friends for the perceived closeness of their true selves rather than for their sexual attributes. Such connections also can and often do include erotic interests as well, the students admit, usually undeclared ones, usually unilaterally. But eroticism is not an invariant component, and if lust is all that is going on, then a given friendship is "false" rather than "true."

Rutgers women and men have not somehow lost erotic interest in one another because of these recent moves in the direction of gender-free friendship between the sexes, however; quite the contrary. If relaxed, friendly fun is the private pleasure to which the students devote most of their free time in college, sexual and erotic fun are the even-more-private pleasures they find most intensely exciting. And by all indicators, at Rutgers and nationwide, contemporary students seek and partake of much more "real sex" than undergraduates did a generation or two ago.

Although various forms of the sexual double standard still persist among the undergraduates, women students nevertheless have access to about as much sexual pleasure as men. Most women apparently assume that there are a few "natural" differences between the sexes: "naturally" women have to guard their reputations more carefully than men, "naturally" women have to worry more about sexual danger than men, "naturally" women have a more direct investment in birth control than men, and so on. But, when asked about their political attitudes toward sex and gender, most undergraduate women seem to feel that these natural differences are "no big deal" compared to the real sexual autonomy they now enjoy, and compared to their general equality with undergraduate men in most other aspects of their daily lives in college.

Students "party" for the pure fun of it, but they also go to parties—scheduled or *ad hoc* events centering on loud music and alcoholic consumption, conducted in dorm rooms, fraternities, off-campus bars and apartments—to meet new sexual partners or to get in the mood for erotic pleasures with those they already know. Liquor lubricates undergraduate partying, and the reinstatement of the 21-year-old minimum drinking age has not done much to alter this fact at Rutgers.

Erotically, the college and the larger university in which it is embedded present themselves to the undergraduate as places of opportunity for exactly the same reasons that the institution is often criticized by the students in other contexts—for being a big impersonal place where "no one really knows who you are." There are no adults supervising their behavior and thousands of other players in the game of undergraduate sex on campus. They will never be known by everyone; they do not need to be labeled indefinitely as having any one sexual reputation or orientation. And, after all, as the deans exhort new students during orientation lectures, the whole point of a liberal education is to broaden oneself by seeking out new and different experiences during one's college years.

Not every student does so sexually in college, however, and the sexual behaviors reported in anonymous self-reports by the undergraduates are exceptionally diverse and idiosyncratic. Some students report "going wild" when they first encounter the sexual smorgasbord of college life; many others find sex in college a simple, progressive development of what they were already doing in high school. Some women and men describe years of sexual experience before arriving in college; others are still virgins as college seniors. A majority of the sexually active students restrict themselves most of the time to sex with established "girlfriends" or "boyfriends" and to conventional heterosexual practices.[9] A minority sample every sexual elective in the modern erotic curriculum.

AIDS, sexual diseases, assault, abuse, and violence are only occasionally mentioned in these student sexual self-reports, which center, as do most of the students' evident mentalities in the dorms, on sexual pleasure and adventure rather than on sexual danger. Homoeroticism is disliked by most of the students, and gay and lesbian students, about five percent of my samples, report living happily only off-campus.

College life is not an arena of unrestricted sexual freedom for the students, however. There are many cultural and behavioral constraints for the students as well, most of them self-imposed. Considering the potential, the late-adolescent women and men who live together on most coed dorm floors maintain remarkably discrete, self-monitored sexual codes among themselves without adult supervision, generally but not invariably relating within a given dorm floor group as friends or friendly acquaintances rather than as erotic partners. Among the students more widely, a significant minority of both sexes is probably sexually inactive at any given time, either out of choice, lack of opportunity, or ineptitude.

Most of the students who are not inactive are guided by the same range of sexual moralities that most middle-class Americans under the age of forty-five follow or espouse in the 1980s. Regardless of their own choices about what kind of sex to engage in, for instance, all but very few of the undergraduates believe that long-term sexual relationships with love or commitment or emotional involvement are more rewarding than casual sex.

Youth Culture and College Culture

From its nineteenth-century origins until the 1960s, American college life was an exclusively collegiate culture, one that also marked an elite among the students. For as Horowitz points out, not just non-college youths were excluded from college life; so too were many of the less affluent or more declassé undergraduates—from the "best" fraternities, and so forth. These students were often "grinds" who were working hard in college in order to elevate themselves to the economic level the college life elitists took for granted.

In the '60s, however, the students thoroughly and deliberately stripped themselves of most of their older collegiate symbolism. Between 1964 and 1968, casually well dressed college men and women were replaced on most campuses by bluejean-clad, bearded or longhaired undergraduates, who were making very different sartorial identifications—with a classless, internationally defined youth culture. Similarly radical transformations occurred in the students' musical tastes during these same years; from "cool jazz" and collegiate-looking groups such as Peter, Paul and Mary to hard rock and other new genres shared with most youths.

American undergraduates at present no longer look like students from the late '60s. But in the way in which general youth culture rather than a specifically collegiate culture dominates their lives—a youth culture available to everyone and not just a student elite—they are still very much the children of the '60s. The closest style to the older collegiate look in the mid-80s, for instance, was "preppie," named with obvious irony for prep school students rather than for college students. Other '80s clothing fashions at Rutgers and elsewhere —punk," "gay," "GQ," (a layered, somewhat European look characteristic of the male fashion magazine *Gentleman's Quarterly*), "jock"—have had nothing to do with specifically collegiate identity. The students' contemporary musical tastes also come to them directly out of popular culture, and they recognize the '60s, whose music they now revere as "classical rock," as the *fons et origio* of music as they know it.

Similar arguments can be made about what one sees and hears in the dorms. Some of it originates very locally and particularly in the students' experiences outside college or in their knowledge of small groups of friends and acquaintances in college. As much of it comes to them from mass culture, however. Widely marketed images of near-nude young adults of the opposite sex or pictures of celebrities are much more likely to adorn the walls of the students' rooms than college symbolism. References to the culture of adolescent-market TV, music, or cinema are far more common in student talk than references to literate culture or anything that appears in *The Chronicle of Higher Education.*

Though specifically collegiate "traditions" may have been handed down from undergraduate generation to generation in the past, such traditions are no longer particularly important among the students at present.[9] Most undergraduates at Rutgers and elsewhere, for instance, probably know only a few things about older college cultures. They know that college is about adolescent autonomy. They know that it is about fun and games: elaborate college pranks, and so forth. They know that they will find such typical college institutions as dormitories and fraternities on most campuses. Since the '60s, they have also expected to find political protesters and cultural radicals of a particular type in college.

Otherwise, almost everything in the college lives of students in the 1980s is less a product of the collegiate past than a projection of contemporary late-adolescent mass culture into the particular institutions of youth which colleges now represent—places where everyone else is fairly intelligent, places where students are on their own with large numbers of their age-mates and with considerable amounts of free time, and places where adult authorities have minimum knowledge of and impact on their private lives.

Implications

Why do American college professors tolerate the comparatively modest commitments implied by the current student belief that college should consist of at least as much of late-adolescent play as of academic work? Because, given student vocationalism, and the competition for enrollments built into much of American higher education, it is in the best interests of many of the faculty to do so.

Thus in most colleges and universities, because department resources (numbers of faculty positions, staff support, and so on) are at least partially tied to enrollments, a department in one of the sciences or in economics whose subject is perceived as vocationally valuable by the undergraduates can afford to run tough courses and "maintain standards" if it wishes and still have plenty of students. The putatively less lucrative social sciences and humanities, on the other hand, must attract students to themselves with particularly lively and interesting courses—and, it turns out, with somewhat easier courses.

At Rutgers, for instance, a generally inverse correlation exists between perceived vocational necessity and the percentage of A's and B's a particular department gives out on the average (10, pp. 276–82). Since the academic marketplace operates similarly elsewhere, a similar grading economy is likely to obtain more widely. Thus there is probably always a good supply of relatively non-demanding college courses available to undergraduates throughout American higher education.

To ask a bigger question, why are most American undergraduates generally satisfied with their college educations[10] at a time when most experts and pundits agree that American colleges and universities are serving the interests of their students rather poorly (due to an unclear sense of mission, lack of community, the indifferent teaching of increasingly research-obsessed professors, and so on)?

One answer lies outside the present analysis. When thinking about contemporary higher education, the students do not usually compare it to idealized alternatives, as adult critics and commentators conventionally do—to a smaller, early twentieth-century liberal arts ideal, to a "never-never land" of great men and great books, and so on. They compare it to what they have already known in their young lives to date. And viewed against the life of the mind as they have experienced it in their suburban hometowns and high schools and in modern American popular culture, college still looks good to them by contrast, uniquely intellectually impressive in many cases, in fact.

Another reason for generally high levels of student satisfaction, however, is college life as the students experience it at present. For in ways I have tried to suggest above, when the undergraduates think about college, they think about it as much as an institution for their late-adolescent pleasure and development as they do as a place for the formal education purveyed by their professors. And as such, it apparently pleases them well.

Nor are they necessarily always thinking strictly about college fun when they pursue this line of evaluation. For closely related to college life in their students' view of the actualities of college is "outside-the-classroom" learning. There are many kinds of outside-the-classroom learning according to student notions. Some are linked to formal learning or to other officially sponsored college cultural activities, to high culture as it filters down to the undergraduates—browsing through the books in the library for a few student scholars, doing "homework" in subjects particular students enjoy, attending the occasional concert or poetry reading or evening lecture, having one of the intense philosophical arguments in which most students still engage but which they no longer call "bull sessions" at Rutgers.

Other types of informal college learning have to do with important "life experiences" which prepare the students for adulthood in the real world as the students think of it: learning to take responsibility for their own actions in a big institution where nobody monitors them closely, learning to cope with university bureaucracy, and learning from their successes and failures in college life—from what they sometimes call "social learning." Most of them are hoping to improve their ability to present themselves well and to influence others during their college years. To learn to do such things in the extracurricular college is not to approach all of college life strictly as fun-and-games.

When students are asked to rate these two sides of the college, inside-the-classroom versus outside-the-classroom learning, they produce responses similar to their evaluations of academics versus college life—they are about equally important, the students say, with some tilt in this case toward informal learning as the more important of the two activities.

Different institutional priorities might result in different balances within undergraduate culture. But the present shape of American college life and undergraduate culture also helps us to understand how contemporary American higher education functions as a largely unplanned trade-off of interests between the undergraduates who attend college and the faculty who teach them. Given student priorities, the professors can concentrate on what matters most to their careers and to the most prestigious, grant-producing university agendas—research and publication—devoting no more than half their time to the undergraduates. The students, reciprocally, can devote their energy to the pleasures and challenges of college life and to as much extracurricular learning as they desire, while attending classes at whatever rate suits them to learn what their professors, most of whom are otherwise complete strangers to them, are up to at the moment.

This quiet accommodation will not make many professional educators happy. But professors, the usual critics of American undergraduates, are creatures of the same system. American college and university professors have been drawing away from the undergraduates through increasing professionalization and specialization for at least a century. If they do not like the result, the simplest solution is to deprofessionalize as researchers and get back to teaching and closer contact with the undergraduates.

To put an even finer point on it, if American colleges and universities had not made their odd historical link between higher education and late-adolescence in the early twentieth century—if American undergraduate populations were now limited to youths who "really belonged in college" (that is, who were in college just for the formal education)—then American college-going populations would arguably be considerably smaller. American higher education would then be less expansive and less well funded than it is, and there would be fewer academic jobs and fewer critics in employment to deplore the fact that American colleges *are* in fact two very different kinds of institution.

References

1. Bloom, A. *The Closing of the American Mind: How Higher Education Has Failed Democracy and Impoverished the Souls of Today's Students.* New York: Simon and Schuster, 1987.

2. Boyer, E. *College: The Undergraduate Experience in America.* New York: Harper and Row, 1987.

3. D'Andrade, R. "A Folk Model of the Mind," in *Cultural Models in Language and Thought,* edited by Dorothy Holland and Naomi Quinn, Cambridge: Cambridge University Press, 1987, 112–148.

4. Gillis, J. *Youth and History: Tradition and Change in European Age Relations 1700–Present.* New York: Academic Press, 1974.

5. Horowitz, H. L. *Campus Life: Undergraduate Cultures from the End of the Eighteenth Century to the Present.* New York: Basic Books, 1987.

6. Kett, J. F. *Rites of Passage: Adolescence in America 1790 to the Present.* New York: Basic Books, 1977.

7. Kurth, S. B. "Friendships and Friendly Relations," in *Social Relationships,* edited by George J. McCall, Michal M. McCall, Norman K. Denzin, Gerald D. Suttles, and Suzanne B. Kurth, Chicago: Aldine, 1970, 136–170.

8. Moffatt, M. "Inventing the 'Time-Honored Traditions' of 'Old Rutgers': Rutgers Student Culture, 1859–1900." *Journal of the Rutgers University Libraries* 41(1985), 1–11.

9. ____. "How Meatballs Became Nerds" [review of reference 5], *The Sunday New York Times Book Review,* 9 August 1987, p. 16.

10. ____. *Coming of Age in New Jersey: College and American Culture.* New Brunswick: Rutgers University Press, 1989.

Notes

Michael Moffatt is associate professor in the Department of Anthropology at Rutgers University.

1. Participatory research was done in 1978–1979 and 1984–1985, and further research through student self-reports between 1986 and 1988. See reference 10 for more on research methods (pp. 1–23, 187–193, 327–330) and on the probable typicality of these data (pp. 331–339). The present article brings together points made at greater length in reference 10, and draws some new conclusions from them.

2. See, for instance, such apparently endlessly self-replicating films as *Animal House, Fraternity Vacation, Spring Break, The Sure Thing, Revenge of the Nerds, Real Genius, Soul Man, Back to School,* and so on.

3. Horowitz's interview method probably encouraged the contemporary students who were her subjects to respond to her research questions in their most serious, adult-like voices. Apparently due to her lack of participatory knowledge of the students, Horowitz almost entirely missed the pleasure-centered, adolescent side of American undergraduate life in the 1980s. See also reference 9.

4. From an intellectual self-report written for a class at Rutgers in 1987.

5. Gift exchanges before Christmas, linked to challenges to perform embarrassing stunts, usually sexually embarrassing stunts. See reference 10, pp. 104–111.

6. Boyer reports similar indifference to most of the older extracurricular organizations nationwide; see reference 2, pp. 177–195. His assumption that student enthusiasm for these organizations can be reestablished by college authorities, however, is naive, in my judgment.

7. This new gender egalitarianism also has its limits, however. Women have to play more by men's older rules in the dorms than vice versa, and between a quarter and a third of the male undergraduates do not go along with the new egalitarianism. Many of these rules move as quickly as possible into their more natural habitats, into the fraternities.

8. Foreplay including mutual oral sex; heterosexual intercourse preferably to mutual orgasm; an interest in technique and variety—of positions, times of day, locations, and so on.

9. Here I disagree with Horowitz, who bases much of her argument about the shape of contemporary American student culture on the assumption of strong patterns of cultural transmission of undergraduate tradition for two centuries, down to the present (5, pp. 263–288). Such intramural historical forces were undoubtedly important among the undergraduates at one time, especially in the late nineteenth and early twentieth centuries. But after the 1960s, once there was no longer a strongly marked, highly valued, specifically collegiate subculture to transmit (older, elite versions of "college life"), these forces became far less significant. The growing scale and diversity of most institutions of American higher education, especially at big public schools such as Rutgers, has also increasingly mitigated against such internal inheritance of student culture.

10. During the period of my research, returns on a survey administered by the Office of Institutional Research at Rutgers indicated that 90 percent of the undergraduates were "generally satisfied" with their college educations. And between 1983 and 1985, according to "Student Opinion Survey Normative Data" collected nationwide by the American College Testing Service, 79 percent of all students were "satisfied" with their particular colleges, and 83 percent were satisfied at universities of over ten thousand students (various documents distributed to subscribers by the American College Testing Service, Iowa City, Iowa).

Adapting to New Student Needs and Characteristics

BLANDINA C. RAMIREZ

Several years ago, I witnessed a hit-and-run accident in which a young Mexican-American woman was run over by a speeding car as she walked from her residence hall to the campus library. After calling 911, we university officials proceeded to ascertain as much about the victim as we could. She was one of two sisters attending the university as the result of intensified efforts to recruit minority students. Her parents were non-English-speaking farmers living outside the city. After talking to the other sister, I concluded that the family was a very traditional one that had managed to educate their daughters by living simply on a farm, working hard, and adhering to strong religious values.

The president, the university's only high-ranking, Spanish-speaking administrator, turned to me and asked if I would call the girl's family. For the twenty-two minutes it took the emergency medical services vehicle to arrive, I watched in anguish, attempting to frame what I would say to the parents according to what I would learn from the medics. As my usual response to any crisis involving bodily danger is to sink into a deep, frightened silence, I feared that I would not be able to say anything at all. I called up the image of my elementary school principal, Mrs. Cardwell. Speaking with great authority and greater sensitivity, she could always get exactly the reaction she desired from the parents of Mexican-American students with whom I grew up. As the ambulance transported the young woman to a local hospital, I was grateful that I would not have to tell the parents that their daughter was in danger of dying.

Her mother answered the phone with a voice that conveyed greater strength and clarity of thought than I felt. I was very formal and used my doctoral title. I explained the situation and suggested that it would be important for her and her husband to come to the hospital. I asked if they had a car. When she said no, I offered to drive the thirty miles to get them. She explained that a neighbor could drive them more quickly. She told me that her husband was in the fields and that she needed to tell him what had happened. I requested her to leave the phone line open and said that I would wait to talk to him. He came on the line and in very formal Spanish thanked me for calling. He asked me to make sure that the doctors treated his daughter immediately upon arrival; he assured me that he would get the money to pay the hospital. I explained that the insurance that the university required would apply. He then said that he would call his son to transport them to the hospital, and that his son knew English. After giving him directions to the hospital, using the landmarks that I thought he would easily recognize, I told him that I would stay by the phone until I knew that they had reached the hospital and that they should call me collect if they had any difficulties. Before too long, we got word that our student (their daughter) was going to be all right.

As I talk to student affairs professionals today, I am often reminded of the many skills and sensitivities required by that situation; the institution was called upon to respond to the needs of a student's family that was quite different from what we have considered typical in the past. Language, cultural nuances, and economic considerations came into play creating a relationship of trust and respect between the institution and the family. More importantly, the institution had the opportunity to see beyond the stereotype of "disadvantaged minority student" and encounter familial strength and dignity that would make many affluent and more "typical" students appear truly disadvantaged. But the challenge facing higher education in general and in the student services profession in particular is far more complex than increasing an institution's capacity to deal with any one cultural group.

Over the course of the next several decades, higher education will be transformed by the effects of two powerful trends in American society. The first is the continuing struggle in the institutions that shape the society to embrace populations that have experienced historical exclusion based on gender, race, culture, national origin, age, disability, and sexual orientation. Though the pace will vary for each group, the incompatibility of exclusion with the shared values, ideals, and needs of this country makes eventual inclusion inevitable. The second trend is the dramatic demographic shifts within the country; these include a rapid growth in the proportion of the population that lives into old age, an even greater increase in the number of children who grow up in poverty, an increase in students who are members of what we call historical United States minority groups, and the immigration to the United States of new groups of people from highly populated areas of the world.

In short, America will become one of the most open, longest lived, and culturally and racially complex societies in the history of humankind. College and university campuses will face the turbulence and the promise of that diversity first and most intensely as traditional structural barriers to higher education are dismantled. Student affairs professionals will be required to respond to these changes at the human level and with increasing understanding, sensitivity, courage, creativity, and competence.

This chapter will discuss the need for a different paradigm in higher education and the evolving needs and characteristics that student affairs must confront. Finally, the implications of these changes will be discussed in detail. In a real sense, we have no models for creating campus communities in this new context, for the paradigm that defines equality and inclusion in this country, and perhaps around the world, has shifted markedly. That shift is a triumph for American values, not a repudiation.

Understanding the Paradigm Shift

History would indicate that issues of race, gender, and cultural equality and inclusion may well represent the most difficult challenges in human experience. Human beings of all cultures and all races tend to form a view of their world early in life, and some elements of that world view continue to influence their thinking and actions in spite of conscientious efforts to assimilate new information and experiences. The separateness of society in the United States is so powerful a reference that it continues to dominate and is reinforced by popular media, patterns and places of worship, and family and leisure activities. And that separateness is not limited to the many kinds of segregation experienced by Hispanics, African Americans, Asian Americans, and Native Americans.

Until very recently, for example, specialized institutional facilities for persons with one or more disabilities created a situation in which most Americans acquired neither the sensitivity, comfort, or competence needed for their interaction with persons with disabilities. Persons with disabilities were literally removed from the broader society's presence and consciousness.

Fortunately, that situation is changing. To illustrate, at the Dallas-Fort Worth airport recently, I waited at a gate while a team of basketball players in wheelchairs came off their flight. The manner in which the airline staff met the physical needs of these passengers was almost as inspirational as the strength, independence, and joy with which the basketball players assisted the airline staff in getting the job done. Then, as I stood there reflecting on this remarkable change in human behavior after centuries of devaluing and disregarding the disabled, a group of men and women traveling home after participating in the Senior Olympics came up behind me. Among them was a tall, strong woman—She could have been seventy or eighty—who wore several medals won in running events. She told me that she had always been "the best runner" until forced by her parents to stop when she reached her teens. She had resumed running three years before, when she joined the senior citizens group after her husband died. Now she was winning all the time. Although her manner was matter of fact, she spoke as if a great hunger had finally been satisfied.

Coming to understand this kind of change, both intellectually and through personal experience, is essential to student services professionals. It is certainly imperative in developing a conceptual framework for student affairs programs, minimizing dysfunctional responses to students, and building the institutional and individual strength for coping with both the turbulence and the promise of diversity. Most importantly, it is crucial to enabling student affairs professionals to make sense of their work and to derive from it the intellectual and personal satisfaction that is the hallmark of the profession.

The struggle for equality in American society is as old as the republic. From the moment that this nation based its right to exist on the premise that all men are created equal, it invited the agitation of thinking men and women who would resist laws and practices that belied the premise. Because we see ourselves as a nation ruled by law, rather than ruled by the personal whim or belief of those who have secured power, that struggle has affected government social policy, which eventually is translated into institutional policy.

Successive groups within society have confronted their discrimination and exclusion from its full benefits. Most have been able to overcome exclusion and discrimination within two generations by coming to understand and make use of the regular institutional processes. Incorporating each successive group has pretty much been a process of "seeing them like us, accepting them like us, and making them like us." But for women, racial and national origin minority groups, and the disabled—groups whose exclusion has been sanctioned in law, broadly institutionalized, and culturally and socially accepted—it has been necessary to change laws, reverse institutional practices and their persistent effects, and replace deeply held cultural biases, attitudes, and social behaviors.

Although the experience and development of both individuals and groups have differed in significant ways, the same remedies to discrimination and exclusion have been applied to all groups with minimal variation. As groups have succeeded in gaining political attention to their plight, they have become part of the "protected" classes and have been able to gain access to those remedies that would supposedly enable them to become one with the dominant group.

Like that traditional thinking in linear physics, both the history and the substance of social policy on equity have been additive, linear and based on the existence of a mythical "typical" dominant standard and the relative deviation of each group from that standard. Like the 1950s fifth-grade science book picture of the solar system showing one sun and nine planets in a straight line, the old paradigm framed the equitable treatment of excluded groups solely in relation to their relative distance from white, mostly male, "American" whole.

The old paradigm allowed those at the margin to approach the center only to the extent that they were willing or able to become like the group at the center. Responsibility for adaptation rested wholly on the formerly excluded and on those with the least resources to adapt. For European immigrants, this meant relinquishing languages, culture, and to a great extent identity, including the Anglicizing of family names. The old paradigm viewed equality as a finite resource and assumed that equity for one group necessarily resulted in loss for the others. Competition and domination were the primary forces upholding the old paradigm and were highly valued because they had always been the basis of success in the past.

It is new thinking that the universe itself is a nonlinear, chaotic balancing of overlapping energies in which, as Marilyn French says, "Nothing rules, yet there is peace as each segment follows its own course and exists in cooperative relation with everything else" (1985, p. 498). These attitudes provide the analogy for the paradigm and the challenge of serving students and creating campus communities in the midst of dynamic and accelerating diversity.

The paradigm shift, of course, requires a mind shift. Minorities in the United States are not only a majority in the world but may increasingly represent the majority population in certain parts of this country. We can no longer speak in a general way of minorities as a group or of any one minority group. We must instead seek to understand the immense diversity within as well as between groups. For example, though women wish to be accorded the same equality of being, they are (as they have always been) different in race, culture, sexual orientation, socioeconomic condition, age, and ability. The other characteristics of a disabled person outweigh any handicap. One ages but may not be "old" until the onset of a terminal illness.

Understanding Changing Student Needs and Characteristics

The extent and rate of change in the population of college and university campuses, though far from adequate, are still nothing short of revolutionary. It is important to understand the depth and extent of the change that has already occurred, even as we challenge ourselves to accelerate the pace of inclusion.

As Boyer tells us (Carnegie Foundation for the Advancement of Teaching, 1990), America's first colleges were guided by the vision of coherence. For the first two hundred years, college students were socially and economically very much alike. Campuses were populated by men, drawn primarily from the privileged class. Virtually no black students were enrolled in college until the appearance of the traditionally black institutions. When a few Native Americans were provided higher education opportunities, these were also in segregated settings, and too often the consequences of isolation from home and culture were tragic. The number of Asian-American and Hispanic students in higher education was minuscule.

Although the benefits of the GI Bill following World War II increased the presence of working-class white and minority men in higher education, gender- and race-specific institutions provided the bulk of college opportunities for women and minorities. The postwar era did, however, begin to focus the value of a higher education for a more varied population. In 1950, 5 percent of women and 27 percent of men aged twenty-five to thirty-four had completed four or more years of college. By 1987, the comparable figures were 23 percent for women and 25 percent for men (Touchton and Davis, 1991).

At the same time, the traditions of higher education institutions, particularly those within the purview of student services professionals, continued to be firmly set in a distant era of homogeneity and privilege. It is a wonder that this institution designed by males for their male, privileged children functions as well as it does in the face of an exploding market with vastly different needs and characteristics.

Approximately 1.3 million (or 10.5 percent) of the 12.5 million students now enrolled in the nation's postsecondary institutions are students with at least one disability. They represent 10.8 percent of the undergraduate, 8.4 percent of the graduate, and 7.3 percent of the first-professional (medicine, business, and law) students (American Council on Education, 1991b). These percentages almost doubled in the period between 1978 and 1988. The disabilities most frequently reported by postsecondary students relate to vision, health, and hearing; however, improved early medical treatment, more equitable elementary and secondary educational opportunities, and increased legal protections will lead to greater participation of students with a broader spectrum of disabilities, including psychiatric and emotional disabilities (Unger, 1991).

The *Fact Book on Women in Higher Education* (Touchton and Davis, 1991) offers a fascinating account of the ways in which women's drive to empower their lives is affecting higher education institutions and will continue to alter the characteristics of student bodies. Since 1979, women have constituted a majority of students in higher education. In 1987, women were 53 percent of the 12.6 million students enrolled in higher education (6.7 million women; 5.9 million men). The substantial increase in part-time enrollment over the past two decades appears to be more significant for women, with almost one-half (47 percent) of women enrolled on a part-time basis, compared to 39 percent of men. Minority women have also experienced formidable increases in college attendance; in 1986, women constituted 60 percent of the African American students, 56 percent of the Native American students, 53 percent of the Hispanic students, and 47 percent of the Asian students.

Enrollment of women aged twenty-five and older has increased by more than one million in the past fifteen years. Today more than 40 percent of women college students (approximately 2.7 million) are age twenty-five or more. Men in this age group increased by .2 million, from 1.2 million in 1972 to 1.4 million in 1987. Between 1972 and 1987, the fastest-growing group of college students was made up of women over age thirty-five. Approximately 1.2 million women over age thirty-five are now in higher education—triple the number in 1972. Men over age thirty-five have doubled their presence in higher education since 1972, from slightly more than .3 million to .6 million (Touchton and Davis, 1991).

It is in the area of defining institutional responses to an aging society that we are least prepared. This is the first generation that will see massive numbers of individuals living into advanced age in relatively good health and having experienced the enriching value of education. The expectations of this population with regard to using continuing education for a variety of purposes are now barely beginning to surface. By the same token, we are only now starting to understand the physical, intellectual, and emotional passages encountered by these individuals and the ways in which we can more fully influence those passages. The exceptional older individual who completes a new venture in formal schooling later in life is becoming less exceptional all the time. Nonetheless, it is important that we understand that we can stereotype the older population, both negatively and positively, as easily as we stereotype minority groups, women, and the disabled. The fact is that in a society that continues to adulate youth, coping with the aging process is too often a confusing, lonely experience perhaps most popularly understood in relation to the "midlife crisis." As more than one wise woman has said, "Growing old ain't for sissies."

The number of Native American, Hispanic, African-American, and Asian-American students on campuses is increasing rapidly (in spite of a percentage-rate decline in the college participation of Hispanics and African Americans). Native American, Hispanic, African-American, and Asian-American students will represent one-third of the school- and college-age population by the beginning of the next century. Still grossly under-represented on predominately white campuses, approximately 56 percent of Hispanic students, 46 percent of African-American students, 52 percent of Native American students, and 38 percent of Asian-American students in higher education attend two-year institutions, and fewer than one fifth transfer to four-year campuses. Approximately 20 percent of African-American students and 30 percent of Hispanics attend historically black institutions or Hispanic-serving institutions. In spite of these current patterns of institutional attendance, the rapid growth in the size of these populations will spur rapid increase in their presence on all college campuses (Carter and Wilson, 1992).

As we stated earlier, the most grievous and common mistake in assessing the needs and characteristics of members of minority groups is to generalize. This population will vary significantly in terms of socioeconomic circumstances, group identity, educational preparation, group and family experience with the educational system, articulation and influence of traditional culture, and family circumstances.

More than 40 percent of Native Americans, African Americans, Hispanics, some Asian-Americans groups, Native Hawaiians, and Alaskans come from homes where the income is below the poverty line. This is two and three times the rate for white non-Hispanic Americans, and that figure has increased in the last decade, not decreased. There is evidence that structural forces in the American economy are pushing greater numbers of the working middle class (and disproportionate numbers of middle-class minorities) into the low-income category (U.S. Census Bureau, 1992). The low rates of participation in higher education of these groups clearly show that most minority students who attend college will be among the first of their families to do so. Indeed, the data for Hispanics and Native Americans indicate that students from these groups are highly likely to be the first in their family to complete high school. Serving a population characterized by poverty or near poverty, little experience with higher education institutions, and often differing language capabilities, implies that all the assumptions about the students' ability to understand and comply with the fiscal, social and academic demands of college must be reexamined. What are the information needs of students in these circumstances? What are the information needs of their families? How does one respond to those requirements in a manner that recognizes and builds on the strengths of these students, even as appropriate support systems are designed? Most importantly, how does the institution develop a capacity to recognize and appreciate those cultural and social elements within the family that can strengthen the students' college experience?

The experience of some historically black colleges and universities, some of the institutions now represented among the Hispanic Association of Colleges and Universities, the American-Indian Higher Education Consortium, as well as research analyzing the success of Asian-American groups indicates that incorporating the students' culture in the creation of both the social and academic climates of institutions is an important element in their relative success. It is important, however, to understand that this approach does not merely entail the celebration of formal or superficial cultural manifestations; also required are deeper cultural forms of nurturing, relating, interacting, reflecting, and affirming, occurring in an manner that communicates to students an institution's expectation of and commitment to their success. Consistently and repeatedly, students sum up this experience (as well as successful experiences on predominantly white campuses) by explaining "[Someone] believed I had it in me!"

Of course, a growing number (if not proportion) of minority group students come from homes where income levels and educational experience are rising. These students may or may not know the language of their group, may have grown up in neighborhoods populated mostly by white, non-Hispanic families, and may be supported by parents with high expectations of both their children and the institutions that serve them. These students, no less than their less privileged peers, face a unique developmental task for minorities in our society: to arrive at a sense of their own identity and to make choices about their identification with their own group and the larger society. What often makes the task more difficult for minority students of privilege is that college often represents their first day-to-day visceral encounter with the divisions of our society.

Understanding the Implications

For the student services professional, the implications of this exploding diversity in the student body are all-encompassing. There is a need to understand the many ways in which students are unique—and yet the same. The diversity we confront grows exponentially as we learn to see each new element. It is as if we are looking at our campus communities through a kaleidoscope and every movement to improve the whole picture changes the design. But it is the student affairs professional who has the most accurate lens on the campus community and on the individual students within it. It is student affairs that has the responsibility to lead the campus community to an understanding of the implications of diversity. And it is our profession that must assess the institution's capacity to fulfill its mission and lead, cajole, and assist the institution in developing the ability to meet its emerging challenges. In short, the student affairs professional must be prepared to assume leadership at the institutional, programmatic, and individual level.

Leadership

The exercise of leadership is a significant area of study; empirical research is now attempting to identify those elements of leadership that are art and those that are science (Gardner, 1990). It may be quite useful for the student affairs professional to engage in the examination of both writing and research and the training in the area of leadership. Ultimately, of course, those who would exert influence over others are alone with their own understanding of the skills, resources, and gifts available to them. Whether individuals rely on science or art, they are still required to know themselves; to have complete, specific, and accurate information; to develop consensus within diverse constituencies; to manage what is attempted well enough to enable it to succeed or fail on its own merits; to have some way of testing whether they are doing the right thing well enough and whether it continues to be appropriate to the context that they originally wished to change.

Planning

Neither professionals nor the institution can fully and accurately envision the changes that will occur in the student body over the next several decades. The only thing we can be sure of is that change will occur and at an ever-accelerating pace. The American Council on Education (ACE) has developed an approach to comprehensive institutional planning that is contained in *Minorities on Campus: A Handbook for Enhancing Diversity* (Green, 1989). Although minorities are the focal point of this guide, the assessment, consensus-building, and implementation processes that are suggested can be adapted to include other groups. *Focus on Adults: A Self-Study Guide for Postsecondary Educational Institutions* (American Council on Education, 1991a) is helpful in developing programs and services for adult students. ACE's National Clearinghouse on Postsecondary Education for Individuals with Disabilities (telephone 800-544-3284) can be a source of assistance in understanding and responding to the needs of persons with disabilities (American Council on Education, 1991b), and perspective on the needs of women are contained in *Educating the Majority: Women Challenge Tradition in Higher Education* (Pearson, Shavlick, and Touchton, 1989).

Information Gathering

The sources just listed can also be helpful to the student services professional as programmatic innovations are developed. Just as at the institutional level there is a need for accurate, timely, and relevant information, it is also necessary that such information be systematically examined at the program level. Quantitative and qualitative strategies must be created to gather information about the well-being of each identifiable group, as well as the perceptions, attitudes, and behaviors of all students. Too many of the problems faced by student affairs professionals with regard to diversity are the product of "squeaky wheel" program development and management. When only the squeaky wheel secures a response, being noisy is the most intelligent course of action.

Teamwork

Student affairs professionals, more than any other group in the institution must develop a team that reflects the varied nature of the population. Not only does this variety improve the probability that the information used for program design and management will be more accurate and relevant, but that information will also have more meaning and importance for the team. Achieving a team commitment to the whole of the many different parts of a student body is vital, if not easy. The student services leader will need to be concerned about more than recruiting and hiring diverse staff: staff training and development and the creation of a consensus on shared goals are imperative.

Student affairs professionals working with a heterogeneous student population must arrive at a commonly held philosophy or guiding principles of student development programming. Basic understanding of what constitutes equitable treatment of all groups should be achieved. Student affairs staff members must appreciate that treating everyone equally does not always mean treating everyone the same. Differences exist and must be recognized. Guiding principles should be examined regularly and should evolve as greater understanding about diversity is gained.

Support

Programmatic development in an institution characterized by changing student populations ultimately comes down to choosing from an array of activities that will require fiscal and staff support. At the point of decision making at the budgetary level, the tension between supporting things as they have always been and changing them becomes most difficult. Again, it becomes necessary to rely on information to provide a rationale for the choices that will be made. What are the guiding principles for student affairs programming? What are the assumptions about students that shape the design of the student affairs program? How relevant and inclusive are current programmatic activities? What are needs that are not met by current programmatic activities? What are the views of students? How do the activities under consideration support the building of community on campus?

Summary

Examining the assumptions that we make about atypical students is essential to planning responsible student services activities. I remember the rage that I felt while visiting an institution that had become a predominantly minority institution after an early history as a somewhat elitist single-sex institution. When I asked why nearly all of the early cultural traditions of the institution had been abandoned, I was told that it was unlikely that low-income minority students would want to see a play or go to the symphony. What is even more tragic is that little cultural activity of any kind had replaced the traditional program. Two Christmas events at the institution proved that the institution's current students were eager to participate in these activities, both new and familiar. One was a songfest in the early English minstrel tradition; the second was a Mexican posada in which carolers recreated Mary and Joseph's search for lodging.

The most exciting challenges and implications for the student affairs professional, who faces ever-increasing diversity in the student body, are those that require the enhancement of individual understanding, perspective, skills, and gifts for living and serving in a varied society. Diversity requires that individuals take risks in challenging their view of their work, creating relationships with people whose differences may make them feel less competent than they would like, accepting the opinions and views of a broad range of individuals, and examining long-held values and beliefs. There is risk involved in attempting new ways of accomplishing objectives in the development of students, and there is risk in discarding the traditional. Only the certainty that things will never be the same again can sustain the quest for new answers.

References

American Council on Education, Center for Adult Learning and Educational Credentials. *Focus for Postsecondary Educational Institutions*. Washington, D.C.: American Council on Education, 1991a.

American Council on Education, National Clearinghouse on Postsecondary Education for Individuals with Disabilities. "Facts You Can Use." In *Focus on Adults: A Self-Study Guide for Postsecondary Educational Institutions*. Washington, D.C.: American Council on Education, 1991b.

Carnegie Foundation for the Advancement of Teaching. *Campus Life: In Search of Community*. Princeton, N.J.: Carnegie Foundation for the Advancement of Teaching, 1990.

Carter, D. J., and Wilson, R. *Tenth Annual Status Report on Minorities in Higher Education*. Washington, D.C.: American Council on Education, 1992.

French, M. *Beyond Power*. New York: Summit Books, 1985.

Gardner, J. *On Leadership*. New York: Free Press, 1990.

Green M. F. (ed.) *Minorities on Campus: A Handbook for Enhancing Diversity*. Washington, D.C.: American Council on Education, 1989.

Pearson, C. S., Shavlick, D. L., and Touchton, J. G. (eds.) *Educating the Majority: Women Challenge Tradition in Higher Education*. New York: Macmillan, 1989.

Touchton, J. G., and Davis, L. *Fact Book on Women in Higher Education*. Washington, D.C.: American Council on Education, Macmillan, 1991.

Unger, K. "Servicing Students with Psychiatric Disabilities on Campus: Clarifying the DDS Counselor's Role." *Journal of Postsecondary Education and Disability*, Fall 1991, pp. 21–28.

U.S. Census Bureau. *Trends in Relative Income: 1964 to 1989*. Washington, D.C.: U.S. Census Bureau, 1992.

Academic Life:
Some Virtues, Some Vices

HENRY ROSOVSKY

For a large segment of the population, going to work in the morning is a chore. Jobs are monotonous; discipline is imposed by machines, time clocks, and authoritarian superiors. In factories, the physical setting is unattractive and noisy. Work that is physically punishing is not confined to blue-collar occupations. As a young man some forty years ago, I spent a few months selling toys at Macy's in New York City. Twice a week, the store was open from 9:00 A.M. to 9:00 P.M., and standing behind the counter on those long days was sheer torture.

At executive levels, one encounters different forms of pain: implicit dress codes, implicit political codes, a controlled lifestyle. And people have to be concerned about layoffs, discharges later in their working life, or hopeless unemployment in obsolescent industries.

These are not, of course, universally the conditions of work. Many workers are happy in their jobs, and alienation is a tired, overused concept. Nevertheless, many go to work without joy, primarily to earn a living. It is my observation supported by some evidence that professors at good universities have a much more positive attitude toward their work.[1]

One reason may be that most of our colleges and universities are physically attractive. The very notion of campus evokes in our minds a picture of trees, lawns, and imposing structures. Campuses contain a significant proportion of the best examples of American architecture. I have spent a considerable number of years at each of three institutions—William and Mary, Berkeley, and Harvard—and I have visited many more. William and Mary is the site of the only building in this country "perhaps" designed by Sir Christopher Wren. It is a lovely, modest brick structure, housing chapel, hall, and classrooms, and overlooking an impressive sunken garden. Everything at William and Mary also harmonizes elegantly with Colonial Williamsburg; it is one of the most beautiful locations on the East Coast.

Berkeley is a campus of the University of California; state bureaucracy combined with post-World War II expansion have done much to obliterate what once was an Eden. Nevertheless, there are few more gorgeous sites anywhere. From many of its parts the great reaches of San Francisco Bay are visible; the fog can lend its own special magic to Berkeley; and many of the older buildings represent the best of late nineteenth-century California creativity.

Harvard Yard—elsewhere it would be called a campus—and its surroundings are a history of American and European architecture in three dimensions. Harvard Hall and Massachusetts Hall, built before the Revolutionary War, are still in daily use. The finest building in the Yard, the gray stone University Hall erected in the early nineteenth century and designed by Charles Bullfinch, shelters the dean of the Faculty of Arts and Sciences. In front is Daniel Chester French's idealized statue of John Harvard, in all seasons the object of tourist attention. And I could go on to the Yard dormitories, Widener Library, Memorial Church, the Carpenter Center for the Visual Arts designed by Le Corbusier (his only building in North America).

I return to urge my point: the physical setting in which we labor matters enormously. Of this I am aware every morning as I cross the ever-changing urban squalor of Harvard Square and enter the Yard. It is an oasis; it pleases the eye and the mind in all seasons; it is a refreshing start to any working day. I think with pity of my neighbors arriving in downtown Boston to inhabit all day the synthetic atmosphere of yet another glass-lined tower.

The attraction of a campus goes well beyond architect and landscape. People like to be around universities—they enjoy the ambience. Boston, with its many colleges, has been called the youth capital of America. Psychiatrists and successful businessmen—who else can afford to pay the real estate prices?—live in Cambridge because of Harvard's presence. For them, the campus is a circus with many free side shows: museums, libraries, lectures, entertainment. Students are part of the spectacle—they set or reflect the latest in dress, music, movies, and food. To be near students—near and yet far enough away to permit occasional withdrawal—is to feel young and alive well into late middle age. It is why Palo Alto, Durham-Chapel Hill, Ann Arbor, as also Cambridge and Berkeley, have all become favored places of residence for the non-academic upper middle class.

The major aspect of the professor's work is not however the setting but the content, and here again the virtues of academic life become apparent. A friend of my father's, a tutor at St. John's College in Annapolis, when asked about his choice of occupation, said that he loved reading more than anything else; college teaching was the only profession that paid a salary for doing that. The essence of academic life is the opportunity—indeed, the demand—for continual investment in oneself. It is a unique chance for a lifetime of building and renewing intellectual capital. For many, teaching provides the greatest satisfaction.[2] For others, research is the key: it satisfies intellectual curiosity and nourishes the joys and glories of discovery.

You ask: is this not true of all occupations that exercise the mind? Is it not true of teachers at all educational levels? This is a matter of degree, but the differences are significant. In universities that emphasize research—and this is my main topic—keeping up to date can be extremely demanding and time-consuming. Modern biology, for example, has been exploding with new knowledge ever since the cracking of the genetic code by James Watson and Francis Crick in the 1950s. Its practitioners tell me that to remain abreast of current findings even in their own narrowly defined fields is almost a full-time occupation. They regularly follow these assertions with requests for reduced teaching loads—"we really do not have the time!" While thus arousing the suspicions of a dean, I know that they have a case.

Modern biology may be the most extreme example of such pressure and strain, although computer sciences and some branches of physics cannot be far behind. Nor is the phenomenon confined to the natural sciences. I completed the formal part of graduate studies in economics in the early 1950s. At that time, a knowledge of mathematics was not considered an absolutely necessary part of an economist's toolkit. By the end of the decade it was; without training in econometrics and mathematical economics, it had become impossible to read much of the professional literature. What happened in economics is now occurring in political science with the increasing use of quantitative models. Even the humanities are not immune to these revolutions, although scholars here resist change with more energy. The last twenty years have witnessed the growing influence of literary theory, semiotics, new historicism, bringing with them new constructs, a different vocabulary, and non-traditional philosophical assumptions. So for the individual humanist it has become necessary to acquire new skills, to learn a new and difficult language.

These are only random examples of the pressure on academic life of research. A complementary pressure comes from graduate students. young scholars have their eyes exclusively on the future. The "leading edge" is their ticket to success. Adherence to tradition may be dangerous. Since professors are in large measure judged by the size and quality of their graduate student followings, the incentives to be *au courant* with the latest fashion are again considerable.

Thus academic life is a world in motion. Some changes revolutionize fields of study; occasionally new subjects are born; some innovations are ephemeral and quickly forgotten. New ideas can make life miserable for the many who have a stake in the old ways, generating conflict between the adherents of the old and the new. Every scholar has to face these fundamental challenges during his or her lifetime. It is at once a burden, a challenge, and one of the attractions of academic life.

Intellectual investment is not entirely a response to challenges from others. Many scholars pursue their own ideas with little reference to peer groups. Whatever the motive, the act of research is a form of mental renewal and a great potential benefit to the individual. These challenges and opportunities can be present in some degree in other occupations, but not so often, I suspect, and I would argue that the combination of research and new ways of looking at things is a special characteristic of the university. The share of routine is smaller than in any other occupation.

Another critical virtue of academic life—I am thinking of tenured professors at, say, America's top fifty to one hundred institutions—is the absence of a boss. A boss is someone who can tell you what to do, and requires you to do it—an impairment of freedom. As a dean—i.e., as an administrator—my boss was the president. I served at his pleasure; he could and did give me orders. But as a professor, I recognized no master save peer pressure, no threat except, perhaps, an unlikely charge of moral turpitude. No profession guarantees its practitioners such a combination of independence and security as university research and teaching. Let me amplify this point.

In the early 1950s, the University of California was plunged into grave controversy by the state's insistence that all its employees sign an anti-Communist loyalty oath. Those were the days of McCarthy and the red scares. State and federal committees on un-American activities stalked the land. There was opposition to the loyalty oaths inside and outside the university, although in the end nearly everyone signed. A few professors refused and were dismissed.

The most interesting refusal was tendered by Professor E. K. Kantorowicz, a famous medieval historian and refugee from Hitler's Germany. He did not particularly object to a loyalty oath requirement—I am not suggesting that he approved it. Rather, he had a deeper objection: he did not wish under any circumstances to be classified as an employee of the state of California. Kantorowicz believed professors were not university employees subject to the usual job discipline. To be a professor was to be of a different calling. Employees work specified hours and may be paid overtime; they are given specific tasks; in most cases there is a sharp separation between work and leisure; frequently the service performed is impersonal. Does it really matter who sells you a pair of shoes?

In Kantorowicz's own words:

> There are three professions which are entitled to wear the gown: the judge, the priest and the scholar. This garment stands for its bearer's maturity of mind, his independence of judgement, and his direct responsibility to his conscience and his god.

> It signifies the inner sovereignty of those three interrelated professions: they should be the very last to allow themselves to act under duress and yield to pressure.

> Why is it so absurd to visualize the Supreme Court Justices picketing their court, bishops picketing their churches and professors picketing their universities? The answer is very simple: because the judges *are* the court, the ministers together with the faithful *are* the church, and the professors together with the students *are* the university . . . they are those institutions themselves, and therefore have prerogative rights to and within their institution which ushers, sextons and beadles, and janitors do not have.[3]

The distinction held by Kantorowicz is most valuable. We professors have the income of civil servants but the freedom of artists. This imposes certain obligations. The formal duties imposed by our institutions are minimal, anywhere between six and twelve hours in the classroom per week during eight months of the year.[4] Yet most of us work long hours and spend many evenings at our desks or in our laboratories. We do not tell students that this is our day off, that they must seek someone else with whom to discuss their problems. We do practice our profession as a calling, considering ourselves not employees but shareholders of the university: a group of owners. "Share values" are determined by the quality of management and the product. We seek to keep those values as high as possible. None of this is to deny that we very much enjoy the calling, and believe that we are engaged in activities of high social value.

I must mention Professor Kantorowicz again, for on his death in 1963 there was an ironic twist to what I have just written. He was then a professor at the Institute for Advanced Studies in Princeton, New Jersey. The San Francisco *Chronicle* took note of the passing away of a distinguished former Californian. Besides misspelling his name (Catorowicz), an indignity that some of us get used to, the obituary said: "He was *employed* at the University of California at Berkeley from 1939 to 1950."[5]

There are yet other rewards that apply particularly to tenured members of the faculty. Sabbatical leaves are an especially agreeable custom. A university professor so favored is relieved of teaching duties every seventh year in order to allow mental refreshment. This year of refreshment is accompanied by a reduction in salary, but research or other grants on many occasions make up the shortfall. Faculty members love sabbaticals. Projects can be completed, sites visited, colleagues in distant places consulted. Professors tend to be enthusiastic travelers and their way of life encourages this natural proclivity. For the best among them, the reference groups are thoroughly international. In addition, a significant proportion of research topics require travel and foreign residence.

My own case may be only slightly untypical. I lived in Japan for nearly five years as a soldier, graduate student, teacher, and researcher. I spent fairly long periods lecturing, researching, and consulting in the United Kingdom, Indonesia, and Israel. And I have lost count of the foreign countries in which I have attended conferences. Since these activities combine business and pleasure, they can be viewed as fringe benefits. University professors at major institutions are among the leading "frequent travelers" in this country—I should think immediately behind pilots, flight attendants, professional athletes, and on a par with salesmen. Abuses do exist, and some of my friends, with heavy sarcasm, have been referred to as the "Pan American Airways Professor of Biology," the "Swissair Professor of Physics," or the "El Al Professor of Sociology."

In a recent study of academic mores, the novelist David Lodge—who first noted that the three things that have revolutionized academic life in the last twenty years were jet travel, direct-dialing telephones, and the Xerox machine—describes our periodic gatherings this way:

> The modern conference resembles the pilgrimage of medieval Christendom in that it allows the participants to indulge themselves in all the pleasures and diversions of travel while appearing to be austerely bent on self-improvement. To be sure, there are certain penitential exercises to be performed—the presentation of a paper, perhaps, and certainly listening to the papers of others. But with this excuse you journey to new and interesting places, meet new and interesting people, and form new and interesting relationships with them; exchange gossip and confidences (for your well-worn stories are fresh to them, and vice versa); eat, drink and make merry in their company every evening; and yet, at the end of it all, return home with an enhanced reputation for seriousness of mind. Today's conferees have an additional advantage over the pilgrims of old in that their expenses are usually paid, or at least subsidized, by the institution to which they belong, be it a government department, a commercial firm, or, most commonly perhaps, a university.[6]

The alleged abuses can be more apparent than real. In 1984, my former colleague Carlo M. Rubbia won the Nobel Prize in Physics. A Harvard professor and high-energy physicist in search of new particles, he required the services of a large accelerator. None was available in Cambridge, Massachusetts. Other sites in the United States proved unsuitable, and so Rubbia shifted his activities to the European Center for Nuclear Research in Geneva, Switzerland. Every two weeks or so he traveled abroad to carry out experiments, spending many days away from Cambridge. A clever individual, Rubbia purchased a string of the cheapest APEX tickets every seven days or so and used them on a staggered basis, thereby circumventing the requirement that the user remain abroad more than fifteen days. I am told that the people at Swissair got to know him so well that an upgrade to first class virtually became automatic—long before the Nobel award. On my own rather frequent trips to the West Coast I usually spot a colleague or two on their way to SLAC—the Stanford linear accelerator.

Closely connected with sabbaticals and travel is another generally positive feature of academic life—at least from the point of view of the faculty. Along with professional independence, the absence of bosses and the light nature of formal obligations have been mentioned. (Informal obligations when taken seriously, and that is the normal case, are demanding and time-consuming.) The professor controls his or her time to an unusual degree, and it is generally accepted that some time can be used for "outside work." The long vacations are available for that purpose. In addition, at Harvard and elsewhere a professor is permitted to spend one day a week on non-university activities.[7]

"Outside work" can take many forms and at the margins is extremely difficult to define. Public service is generally encouraged, although with disagreement as to what fits under that rubric. There is an evident difference between campaigning for a political candidate and testifying as an expert before a congressional committee. Still, public service—for example, unpaid leave from the university for one year or more to take an assignment in Washington—is favorably viewed.[8]

For some, though by no means the preponderance of the faculty, there is also the opportunity of earning additional money from extramural activities. In one highly unusual case at Harvard, a professor became a part-time salesman in Filene's basement. Consulting for private industry is a more common and remunerative activity. Some have successfully started companies. My late colleague, the distinguished economist Otto Eckstein, founded DRI, a highly successful economic forecasting enterprise. At least five biogenetic firms have been started by Harvard professors. Many professors go on lecture tours and a few have the skills to give concerts. In certain faculties, notably at the Business School, corporate board memberships are readily available. It is even possible to make a fortune by writing, and Professor *emeritus* J. K. Galbraith has been the outstanding example at Harvard during the last three decades.

There are significant negatives associated with outside activities to which I will return, but a word is needed now. The ability to sell our services beyond the walls of the academy is closely correlated with the institutional label we are able to use. It helps to be at a famous university: economists would say that we derive a rent from such association. Since outsiders have some difficulty in making independent judgments as to talent, they, sometimes unwisely, put much faith in labels—a Harvard professor. The individual sells his institution at least in part. Also, only a relatively small proportion of a faculty possess skills that are readily marketable on the outside. Leaving aside the professional schools as belonging to a different universe, sizable extra earnings come primarily to scientists, economists, and a few other social scientists. A successful history or English text will earn money, but such opportunity is far less available than imagined. I am aware of no reliable figures on this entire topic, but my guess is that in Harvard's Faculty of Arts and Sciences, only about one third of the members earn 20 percent or more of their salaries on the outside. Many fewer will exceed that 20 percent by a large margin. In considering the financial aspects of university life, for most people the salary must be thought controlling.

The View from Below

Some of my colleagues—especially those on probationary appointments without the boon of tenure —may take a different view of our profession and its pleasures. They will consider my words to be smug and self-satisfied, written in praise of those who have "made it," and out of touch with younger scholars still climbing the ladder or with those who may never reach the top. These feelings are understandable, even though no one starts out as a tenured professor, and all of us have experienced some of the same agonies. What does change from time to time is the state of the academic market during the early years of a career. For example, the 1950s were a mediocre decade from job seekers; good positions were hard to find. I easily recall my last year as a research student in Japan (1957–58). Having already acquired a wife and child, I desperately awaited a job offer from home. Berkeley finally came through in the late spring—it was my only offer. By way of contrast, the 1960s were absolutely outstanding, as universities in all parts of the country expanded in the wake of Sputnik and the Great Society. Demand was so strong that standards for appointment probably declined. Government cutbacks in education and general stagflation created disastrous job markets for academics during nearly all of the 1970s and the first half of the 1980s. Many of the finest young scholars had difficulties in being placed. Currently the situation is getting better as the postwar generation of professors reaches the age of seventy and as institutions of higher learning benefit from a general improvement in the economy. Obviously the mood of young faculty members competing for positions and promotions is closely related to their own opportunities in the academic marketplace. A few geniuses or near geniuses will always be in demand, but the mood of individuals even with outstanding talents will be greatly affected by the number of vacancies at the top.

Strengths and weaknesses of market forces are not the whole story. As a consequence of an "up or out" or probationary system, the environment will always appear cruel to the "junior faculty." The very use of that term creates a condescending atmosphere. Those so-called juniors all hold the Ph.D. or similar advanced degrees. They are adults, mostly in their thirties, and not infrequently internationally recognized authorities in their subjects. Their technical competence and command of the latest research tools is often superior to that of their senior colleagues—largely a result of having been trained more recently. In terms of teaching, research, advising, or committee assignments, they perform exactly the same duties as their elders; in truth, junior professors are routinely given the least desirable assignments. They are assigned unpopular required courses, equally unpopular student advising, and classes that meet at eight in the morning or late Friday afternoon. And finally we come to the basic oddity of the non-tenured faculty's position: they do exactly what the senior faculty does, only for half the pay, less status, fewer amenities, and an uncertain future. It is a most unusual and alienating situation.

In an army—to cite the example of another hierarchical organization—the officer corps is divided into company grade, field grade, and general officers, all with different pay and privileges. These reflect seniority, duties, and responsibilities. Commanding a platoon and commanding an army are not the same thing. To do the job properly, a general needs more staff than a lieutenant. A law firm comes closer to a university department, with its division between associates and partners. Even here the academic situation remains unusual, because associates in law firms often assist or work under the supervision of partners. That is not at all the situation in a university. An assistant professor does not assist anyone; an associate professor is not anybody's associate. These are merely designations for independent scholars who receive low pay and little secretarial help, while performing the same tasks as full professors. To outsiders—as well as many insiders—all this has to appear quite exploitative.[9]

As if all of this were not sufficient, we add one more blow that creates the deepest of all psychological wounds: explicit rejection frequently occurring at the end of a six- to eight-year term. At Harvard, in the Arts and Sciences, rejection happens in approximately eight out of ten cases. Proportions will vary, but in institutions that are included in "Two Thirds of the Best," retention is never routine. Furthermore, failure to be promoted to tenure is not the consequence of a casual act. It does not come about because some faceless authority forgets to renew a contract or cites plausible reasons of, say, economic hardship. On the contrary, rejection is carefully calculated, determined by close associates, and it is even public. From that point on, the scholar is marked with a scarlet letter, always having to explain the basis of a presumably mistaken negative judgment. In every case with which I am familiar, the result is a scar that may not be wiped out by the award of the highest professional honors.

Why would anybody, apparently so smart, be dumb enough to permit him- or herself to be placed in the situation of a junior faculty member? Are they masochists? Not at all: theirs is a reasonable choice because the pain of the early years is outweighed by the rewards of a tenured career. What economists call "revealed preference" tells the story; non-tenured faculty members want most of all to be professors at good universities; other attractive alternatives are clearly second choices. These so-called victims of exploitation are strong believers in the virtues of academic life as revealed by their attitude and, above all, actions.

Although based on impressionistic evidence, I believe that observers of the university scene will agree that the very best graduate students and junior professors want to remain in the academy. This is certainly true in arts and sciences; to a lesser degree it applies also to professional schools. Economics can serve as an excellent example because it is a field whose skills are used inside and outside of the university.

A number of Harvard graduates in economics have made distinguished careers in banking or government, or perhaps international organizations. Some have made large fortunes. When their names and achievements arise in conversation, there is likely to be an undertone of sorrow: "Rubinstein owns a quarter of Manhattan, and is regularly consulted by the President of the United States. I remember him as a pretty bright young fellow. Too bad he wasn't quite good enough to become a professor at Berkeley." Rubinstein may not share these feelings, but I think they fairly represent academic attitudes of all ranks. I have also known a number of students who—during the lean years of the 1970s and early 1980s—took lucrative posts in business. At the first good opportunity they were happy to resume academic careers.

In fact, most non-tenured professors eventually receive permanent posts somewhere, but not necessarily at the institution of initial appointment. When the academic market is strong, it is still not possible for a few top schools to provide posts for all talented scholars. At those times, however, a junior appointment at—for example—Harvard, Standford, or Chicago pretty much guarantees an excellent post at some reasonable university in the United States. At other times, tenure at a good place can be a more elusive goal. During the 1970s there developed a class of academic journeymen whose members never climbed "up" and were always shown the way "out." They became permanent visitors, and without a doubt some left the professoriate for other more welcoming occupations. I do not know of any firm estimates concerning the size of this unhappy cohort. Personal observation leads me to believe that the number is not large. Achieving tenure is not an unrealistic expectation, although many younger scholars at the most highly ranked universities may have to move down a notch in order to gain security. That improves quality on a national basis and is one reason for the growing number of centers of academic excellence in our country.

An additional refinement is useful. The supply of academic talent can be—in my view—divided into two broad categories: those with great comparative advantage for teaching and research (sometimes manifestly unfit for other types of work), and those possessing more general talents (individuals who can do a variety of other things just as well). The first group is easily seduced by the attraction of university life. They love knowledge in depth and playing with ideas; they hate the time clock and want to be their own bosses; they may prefer books and ideas to human beings. They may be repelled by what the *Harvard Crimson* calls "The Real World." All of us have known many examples of this type; it is almost the accepted caricature of a professor and does contain a few grains of truth. The second group will join the pool of academic talent only when the financial sacrifice is not too great. When the market is strong, they are pleased to be part of our company; when it is weak, and professional alternatives exist, they will look far beyond ivy-colored walls. Relying only on people whose "fire in the belly" is exclusively academic may not lead to a sufficiently large pool of talent. It is one important reason for us always to remain concerned about the attractiveness of our working conditions.

"Up or out" is a brutal slogan and the root cause of non-tenured misery. While a necessary and entirely defensible practice, it is not an especially friendly sign of welcome. Where tenure track is practiced and where social Darwinism is slightly more muted, there may be less anxiety among the probationary ranks, but probation is a trial and, by definition, the outcome is uncertain. All true, but surely there is no need to glory in the suffering that is inflicted on our younger colleagues. A university term appointment need not be the moral equivalent of a fraternity initiation in which most pledges are rejected. "Up or out" can only be justified as a way to raise the quality of tenured appointments, and a gauntlet of putdowns and petty humiliations administered to prospective candidates does not improve performance.

For those of us who are permanent shareholders in the university, there are two duties *vis-à-vis* our non-tenured co-workers that are only rarely performed adequately or gracefully. First, we have to be able—at all times—to put on their shoes. Where they pinch should enable us to understand the anxieties, pains, and occasional neuroses that afflict this group. Looking at the world from their perspective will encourage more thoughtful, supportive, and sympathetic attitudes. It should also greatly diminish petty annoyances. The other duty—and this is a matter of plain self-interest—is to create circumstances that will allow these scholars to attain maximum possible intellectual growth during their term. Needs will vary with the times in which we live, with our fields, and various other special circumstances. In my experience, our best universities do not always fulfill this duty at a high level of excellence. I would like to make a few modest suggestions.

Some things are now being addressed: improving the circumstances of two-career couples by providing day care and job-placement assistance for spouses. In some areas of the country, housing subsidies are crucial. All these are expensive and obvious steps.

Far less well understood and only rarely put into practice is the principle that *professional fringe benefits should be independent of professorial rank*. As I have already pointed out, the unusual aspect of our hierarchy is that members perform essentially the same tasks without regard to rank. Then why should full professors be advantaged in terms of secretarial assistance or research help? Or laboratory equipment? Or money for travel to conferences?[10] A greater stress on equality for these benefits—a redistribution of resources—would help younger colleagues reach their potential and improve the chances for internal promotion. In turn, that would raise morale and cost efficiency: internal promotion is far cheaper than bringing in a "star" from outside.[11]

My last suggestion is the most difficult to put into practice; perhaps it is also the most important. Academic departments need to provide young scholars with a sense of community, with mentors—with seniors who take the role of colleague seriously. Although assistant and associate professors are not anyone's assistants, they can at least be treated as associates, and not as transients. A good academic department should resemble a family: supportive, guiding, and nurturing. At its best, the department can become a partner in the progress of its younger members, helping each one to attain their capabilities.

None of this will eliminate the pain of eventual rejection. The chances remain very high that it will occur. But surely the pain is lessened and can gradually be transformed into pleasant memories. These memories will positively affect future generations of students who may be tempted by academic careers. To transform a vicious into a virtuous circle is possible.

This introduction to university life from the professorial point of view has already referred to tenure a number of times. Academic security of employment is an important and frequently misunderstood subject. An elaboration of this topic is my next entry.

Notes

1. "American academics are generally happy with their choice of careers. Eighty-eight percent of them, for example, maintain that, were they to begin anew, they would still want to be college professors." E. C. Ladd, Jr., and S. M. Lipset, *The Chronicle of Higher Education*, May 3, 1976.

2. Only 25% of American professors indicate a strong interest in research. The remainder indicate a stronger commitment to teaching. These results are reported in the Ladd-Lipset surveys. See *The Chronicle of Higher Education*, March 29, 1976. Obviously the proportion of committed researchers will be larger in the better universities.

3. Grover Sale, Jr., "The Scholar and the Loyalty Oath," San Francisco *Chronicle*, December 8, 1963.

4. Another California story seems appropriate. A professor was testifying before a state committee in Sacramento. The chairman asked: "How many hours do you teach, doctor?" Reply: "Eight hours." The chairman then said: "That is excellent. I have always been a strong supporter of the eight-hour day."

5. San Francisco *Chronicle*, September 13, 1963.

6. David Lodge, *Small World* (New York: The Macmillan Company, 1984), prologue.

7. To enforce this rule is impossible: try to define "one day a week." Surely vacations are not included. How about weekends? In any event, surveillance is impractical and objectionable. As usual, one has to rely on the sense of obligation of the individual.

8. The Harvard rule permits no more than one year of leave under ordinary circumstances. Public service is the only exception, when a two-year leave is permitted. These rules differ significantly from place to place.

9. Some of my colleagues may object to this description. They will claim that tenured professors have more burdensome administrative duties inside and outside of the university. Many serve on national committees and are active in a variety of academies and professional societies. Senior professors will also point to their heavier load in guiding Ph.D. theses. Although individual situations differ, I reject the average validity of these claims. Administrative duties are benefits as well as costs, and one is rarely forced into these tasks. The same is true of national service. Furthermore, not all professors have many Ph.D. students, and when they are numerous, their

presence is certainly taken as a sign of one's own intellectual excellence. The one clear difference is that the non-tenured members do not participate in the labor-intensive work connected with promotion to tenure. Surely that is not a sufficient discrepancy to account entirely for the cleavage between the two groups.

10. To make my meaning clear, I have no problem whatever with allocating offices on the basis of seniority. That is a matter of cosmetics: the quality and quantity of work is relatively unaffected. (That is not true of studies in libraries; these could affect quality and quantity of research.) Secretarial or research assistance has a much more direct bearing on professional activities.

11. An internal promotion always applies to a relatively young scholar who shows promise. The bargaining power of that individual is bound to be lower than that of an established star at a rival institution.

Living with Myths: Undergraduate Education in America

PATRICK T. TERENZINI AND ERNEST T. PASCARELLA

In early civilizations, myths played important roles in people's lives, bringing order to what would otherwise have been a chaotic and uninterpretable world. The Greeks *had* to have *some* plausible explanation for the passage of the sun across the heavens. But when myths continue to guide thought and action, despite evidence that they are without empirical foundation, they become dysfunctional and counterproductive. Persistence in the belief that the sun is actually Apollo's chariot passing across the heavens forecloses geocentric and heliocentric explanations of the movements of the sun and other heavenly bodies.

Does higher education have its own dysfunctional myths? From 1985 to 1990, we reviewed some 2,600 books, book chapters, monographs, journal articles, technical reports, conference papers, and research reports produced over the past two decades describing the effects of college on students (Pascarella and Terenzini, 1991). Based on that literature, we can identify at least five myths about undergraduate education in America. Faculty members and administrators alike embrace these myths, which structure how we think about and design undergraduate educational programs. The evidence also suggests these myths may impede the improvement of teaching and learning in our colleges and universities.

Myth Number 1: Institutional Prestige and Reputation Reflect Educational Quality

Most people believe that, for any given student, going to an institution with all (or most) of the conventionally accepted earmarks of "quality" will lead to greater learning and development. The fact of the matter is that it probably won't.

The evidence on this point is strikingly clear and cuts across a wide array of educational outcomes, including gains in verbal, quantitative, and subject-matter competence; growth in cognitive complexity and the development of intellectual skills; educationally desirable changes in a wide range of psychosocial traits, attitudes, and values; and the emergence of principled moral reasoning. Across all these outcomes, the net impact of attending (versus not attending) college tends to be substantially more pronounced than the impact attributed to attending one kind of institution rather than another.

After taking into account the characteristics, abilities, and backgrounds students bring with them to college, we found that how much students grow or change has only inconsistent and, perhaps in a practical sense, trivial relationships with such traditional measures of institutional "quality" as educational expenditures per student, student/faculty ratios, faculty salaries, percentage of faculty with the highest degree in their field, faculty research productivity, size of the library, admissions selectivity, or prestige rankings. Even when taking into account several methodological considerations that might partially explain this finding, the evidence is still persuasive: similarities across kinds of colleges substantially outnumber and outweigh their differences in terms of their effects on student learning and other educational outcomes.

It is important to be clear about two things we are *not* saying. First, we are not suggesting that graduates of all colleges have reached the same level of academic achievement or psychosocial development. The evidence suggests nothing of the kind. Indeed, after four years, the graduates of some colleges reach a level of achievement or development approximately equal to that of freshmen entering some other institutions. The point to remember is that differences across institutions in levels of student performance on outcomes measures (e.g., Graduate Record Examination scores) are attributable not so much to the institutions attended as to the kinds of students who enroll at those institutions in the first place. Most schools that *graduate* high-performing students also *admit* high-performing students.

Second, we are not saying that *any given institution* has no greater educational impact that any other. Indeed, certain individual institutions probably combine many or most of the things that *are* related to student learning and development (see below) into particularly potent educational programs and environments. Our point is that it is hardly possible to identify the most education-ally effective institutions by relying simply on the resource dimensions traditionally used to judge or rank institutions for "educational quality." These widely used indicators of college quality are, more appropriately, measures of institutional advantage. They may look good and have intuitive appeal, but they reveal little of substance in terms of educational impact.

The evidence we reviewed strongly suggests that *real* quality in undergraduate education resides more in an institution's educational climate and in what it does programmatically than in its stock of human, financial, and educational resources. That is not to say that resources are irrelevant, but that to understand educational quality one must look beyond the obvious and easy measures of institutional wealth, resource availability, and advantage. One must look at factors such as

1. the nature and cohesiveness of students' curricular experiences;
2. their course-taking patterns;
3. the quality of teaching they receive and the extent to which faculty members involve students actively in the teaching-learning process;
4. the frequency, purpose, and quality of students' non-classroom interactions with faculty members;
5. the nature of their peer group interactions and extracurricular activities; and
6. the extent to which institutional structures promote cohesive environments that value the life of the mind and high degrees of student academic and social involvement.

What happens to a student *after* arrival on campus makes a markedly greater difference in what and how much students learn than the prestige, reputations, or resources of the institution. The questionable relevance of the characteristics we conventionally use to differentiate among institu-tions leads us to ask more about what our colleges do that *does* make a difference. That brings us to a second myth.

Myth Number 2: Traditional Methods of Instruction Provide Proven, Effective Ways of Teaching Undergraduate Students

Lecturing is the overwhelming method of choice for teaching undergraduates in most institutions. One study (Pollio, 1984), for example, found that teachers in the typical classroom spent about 80 percent of their time lecturing to students who were attentive to what was being said about 50 percent of the time. The evidence we reviewed is clear that the lecture/discussion mode of instruc-tion is not *in*effective (indeed, we estimate average freshman-senior gains of 20–35 percentile points across a range of content and academic/cognitive skill areas). But the evidence is equally clear that these conventional methods are *not* as effective as some other, far less frequently used methods.

Long trails of research suggest that certain individualized instructional approaches are consis-tently more effective in enhancing subject-matter learning than are the more traditional approaches.

These more effective approaches emphasize small, modularized units of content, student mastery of one unit before moving to the next, immediate and frequent feedback to students on their progress, and active student involvement in the learning process.

Of the five individualized instructional approaches we reviewed, four of them (audio-tutorial, computer-based, programmed, and visual-based instruction) showed statistically significant learning advantages of 6–10 percentile points over traditional approaches. The fifth method, the Personalized System of Instruction (PSI, or "Keller Plan") approach, produced an average learning advantage of 19 percentile points, approximately twice as large as any of the other forms of individualized instruction. (PSI involves small, modularized units of instruction, study guides, mastery orientation and immediate feedback on unit tests, self-pacing through the material, student proctors to help with individual problems, and occasional lectures for motivation.)

The differences in effectiveness between individualized and conventional methods of instruction probably have multiple sources, but two are prominent. First, the lecture/discussion format rests on several assumptions:

1. that all students are equally prepared for the course;

2. that all students learn at the same rate;

3. that all students learn in the same way and through the same set of activities; and

4. that differences in performance are more likely due to differences in student effort or ability than to the faultiness of any of the foregoing assumptions.

If these assumptions are valid, why *not* deliver course material at the same pace and in the same fashion to all students?

Despite the fact that the research evidence, personal experience, and common sense all suggest these assumptions are untenable, most faculty members persist in teaching (and academic administrators encourage it) as if they were true. Individualized and collaborative approaches to instruction are more effective because they respond better to differences in students' levels of preparation, learning styles, and rates.

Second, in contrast to the passive roles students are encouraged to play in most lecture/discussion classes, individualized and collaborative teaching approaches require active student involvement and participation in the teaching-learning process. Such methods encourage students to take greater responsibility for their own learning; they learn from one another, as well as from the instructor. The research literature indicates active learning produces greater gains in academic content and skills; it clearly supports efforts to employ various forms of "collaborative learning."

Myth Number 3: The Good Teachers Are Good Researchers

One of the most frequent criticisms of undergraduate education today is that faculty members spend too much time on research at the expense of their teaching. The typical defense against this charge is that faculty members must do research in order to be good teachers. Faculty members who are researchers, so the argument goes, are more likely to be "on the cutting edge" in their disciplines; they pass their enthusiasm for learning on to their students. This faith in the instructional benefits of research is, of course, reflected in our faculty reward structures.

Proponents of the good-researchers-make-good-teachers point of view usually argue by anecdote; they cite faculty members who are noted scholars and who bring their research to the classroom, there (presumably) intellectually energizing their students. We do not doubt the existence of such faculty members. Indeed, most of us can think of individuals who are both outstanding scholars and extraordinary teachers. But such people are probably outstanding in most every academic thing they do, and the reason they come to mind is precisely because they *are* extraordinary. And one wonders: is exposure to these exceptional individuals a part of the experience of most undergraduates in today's universities?

The available empirical evidence calls the "good-researcher = good-teacher" argument sharply into question. Our review indicates that, at best, the association between ratings of undergraduate instruction and scholarly productivity is a small, positive one, with correlations in the .10 to .16 range.

In the most comprehensive literature review on this issue, Feldman (1987) reviewed more than 40 studies of the relation between faculty productivity or scholarly accomplishment and instructional effectiveness (as perceived by students). He found the average correlation between scholarly productivity or accomplishment and instructional effectiveness to be +.12. Put another way, scholarly productivity and instructional effectiveness have less than 2 percent of their variance in common. That means that about 98 percent of the variability in measures of instructional effectiveness is due to something *other* than research productivity or accomplishment. Feldman concluded that "in general, the likelihood that research productivity actually benefits teaching is extremely small or [alternatively] that the two, for all practical purposes, are essentially unrelated." It is worth noting, however, as Feldman points out, that if the evidence does not support the good-researcher = good-teacher argument, neither does it support claims that doing research *detracts* from being an effective teacher.

So long as the myth that research and teaching are closely and positively related persists, promotion and tenure decisions will continue to be made on the presumption that an institution can have the best of both worlds by allowing research productivity to dominate the faculty reward structure. Why bother to scrutinize *both* the teaching and research abilities of candidates for appointment, promotion, and tenure if looking mostly at the one will do? Find and reward good researchers, the logic goes, and chances are high you'll find and reward a good teacher.

Where the belief persists that research and teaching effectiveness are opposed to one another, proposed "reforms" of teaching will focus on quantitative solutions, on how *much* faculty members are required to teach rather than on how *well* they do it. Many statehouses and coordinating agencies are busy passing faculty workload policies that will require all full-time faculty members to teach a minimum number of credit hours. Such policies are likely to be counterproductive. There's no reason to believe that teaching more courses will result in better instruction. Moreover, since time is a finite commodity, such policies are likely to reduce the amount of research being done, in many cases by the country's best researchers.

In neither case is the teaching of undergraduates likely to improve. Teaching and research appear to be more or less independent activities. Each is essential to the mission of most of our colleges and universities, and each deserves recognition and reward. Until the good-researcher = good-teacher myth is put to rest, however, the research on effective teaching methods will continue to be ignored, reward structures will continue to go unexamined, good researchers will be excused for marginally competent teaching, and good teachers who do not publish will continue to be denied tenure. As for undergraduate instruction, it will be business as usual.

Somehow, as college and university faculty and academic administrators, we must get beyond the smoke of this long-standing myth and turn our energies to what *really* makes a difference in helping students learn. That leads to a fourth myth.

Myth Number 4: Faculty Members Influence Student Learning Only in the Classroom

Many faculty members and more than a few administrators appear to believe that faculty obligations to contribute to the education of undergraduate students begin and end at the classroom or laboratory door. If these obligations extend beyond the classroom at all, it is only to the faculty member's office, to class-related questions or academic advising. Faculty workload policies and reward systems implicitly support this narrow conception of the faculty member's sphere of influence. The research literature does not.

What a host of studies demonstrate is that faculty exert much influence in their out-of-class (as well as in-class) contacts with students. "Instruction," therefore, must be understood more broadly to include the important teaching that faculty members do both inside and outside their classroom.

As a backdrop, remember that as much as 85 percent of a student's waking hours are spent *outside* a classroom. Common sense should tell us that educational programs and activities that address only 15 percent of students' time are needlessly myopic. What the research tells us is that a large part of the impact of college is determined by the extent and content of students' interactions with the major agents of socialization on campus: faculty members and student peers. Further, faculty members' educational influence appears to be significantly enhanced when their contacts with students extend *beyond* the formal classroom to informal non-classroom settings.

More particularly, controlling for student background characteristics, the extent of students' informal contact with faculty is positively linked with a wide array of outcomes. These include perceptions of intellectual growth during college, increases in intellectual orientation and curiosity, liberalization of social and political values, growth in autonomy and independence, increases in interpersonal skills, gains in general maturity and personal development, orientation toward a scholarly career, educational aspirations, persistence, educational attainment, and women's interest in, and choice of, a sex-atypical (male-dominated) career field. It also appears that the impact of student-faculty informal contact is determined by its content as well as by its frequency; the most influential forms of interaction appear to be those that focus on ideas or intellectual matters, thereby extending and reinforcing academic goals.

Some faculty members consider informal, out-of-class contact with students to be "coddling" or (worse) irrelevant or inappropriate to the role of a faculty member. Such views reflect, at best, little knowledge of effective educational practices and of how students learn, and, at worst, a callous disregard. "Talk with students as persons outside of class? That's the dean of students' job": behind this attitude lies still another myth.

Myth Number 5: Students' Academic and Non-academic Experiences are Separate and Unrelated Areas of Influence on Learning

Most theoretical models of student learning and development in no way suggest, much less guarantee, that any *single* experience—or class of experiences—will be a crucial determinant of change for students. Our review of the evidence indicates that the impact of particular within-college experiences (e.g., academic major, interactions with faculty, living on- or off-campus, interactions with peers) tends to be smaller than the overall net effect of attending (versus not attending) college. That same evidence suggests that a majority of the important changes that occur during college are probably the *cumulative* result of a set of interrelated and mutually supporting experiences, in class and out, sustained over an extended period of time.

To break this out further, the evidence shows that, compared to freshmen, seniors have a greater capacity for abstract or symbolic reasoning, solving puzzles within a scientific paradigm, intellectual flexibility, organizing and manipulating cognitive complexity, and using reason and evidence to address issues for which there are no verifiably correct answers (e.g., dealing with toxic waste, capital punishment, abortion, or even buying a used car). Students, however, not only become more cognitively advanced (i.e., become better learners), they also demonstrate *concurrent* changes in values, attitudes, and psychosocial development that are consistent with and probably reciprocally related to cognitive change. While there is insufficient evidence to conclude that changes in some areas actually *cause* changes in other areas, it is nonetheless abundantly clear that documented change in nearly every outcome area appears to be embedded within an interconnected and perhaps mutually reinforcing network of cognitive, value, attitudinal, and psychosocial changes—all of which develop during the student's college experience. In short, the student changes as a *whole, integrated* person during college. (All these changes *may* be independent of one another, but we doubt it.)

Moreover, while intellectual growth may be primarily a function of the student's academic involvement and effort, the content and focus of that same student's interpersonal and extracurricular involvements can have a mediating influence on that growth, either promoting or inhibiting it. In some areas of intellectual development (such as critical thinking), for example, the evidence suggests it is the *breadth* of student involvement in the intellectual *and* social experiences of college, and not any particular type of involvement, that counts most. Thus, although the weight of evidence indicates that the links between involvement and change tend to be specific, the greatest impact may stem from the student's *total* level of campus engagement, particularly when academic, interpersonal, and extracurricular involvements are mutually supported and relevant to a particular educational outcome.

The Campus' Role

What we've just said stresses the importance of individual student effort and involvement as a determinant of college impact, but it in *no* way means that particular campus policies or programs are unimportant. Quite the contrary. If individual effort or involvement is the linchpin for college impact, then a key matter becomes how a campus can shape its intellectual and interpersonal environments in ways that do indeed encourage student involvement.

The research on within-college effects suggest programmatic and policy levers. For example, we have long known that students living on-campus enjoy larger and more varied benefits of college attendance than do commuting students. A college might usefully ask, how can the most educationally potent characteristics of the residential experience (e.g., frequent academic and social interaction among students, contact with faculty members, more opportunities for academic and social involvement with the institution) be made more readily available to students who commute?

Research on the impacts of student residence offers more clues. Considerable evidence suggests discernible differences in the social and intellectual climates of different residence halls on the same campus; halls with the strongest impacts on cognitive development and persistence are typically the result of *purposeful, programmatic* efforts to integrate students' intellectual and social lives during college—living-learning centers are not only a neat idea, they actually work! On relatively few campuses, however, are such programs available to students today.

Plenty of other ways exist for integrating students' classroom and non-classroom experiences in ways that reasonably reflect how students learn. While a discussion of those ways is beyond the scope of this article, it is useful here to return to our first finding, that the impact of college is more general than specific, more cumulative than catalytic. *Real* college impact is likely to come not from pulling any grand, specific (and probably expensive) policy or programmatic lever, but rather from pulling a number of smaller, *interrelated* academic and social levers more often. If a college's effects are varied and cumulative, then its approaches to enhancing those effects must be varied and cumulative, too, and coordinated.

Academic Affairs/Student Affairs

There is an organizational analog to Myth Number 5, that students' academic and non-academic experiences are separate and independent sources of influence on student learning. Since 1870, when Harvard's Charles William Eliot appointed Ephraim Gurney "to take the burden of discipline off President Eliot's shoulders" (Brubacher and Rudy, 1968), the academic affairs and student affairs functions of most institutions have been running essentially on parallel but separate tracks: academic affairs tends to students' cognitive development while student affairs minister to their affective growth.

This bureaucratization of collegiate structures is a creature of administrative convenience and budgetary expedience. It surely has not evolved from any conception of how students learn, nor is it supported by research evidence. Organizationally and operationally, we've lost sight of the forest. If undergraduate education is to be enhanced, faculty members, joined by academic and student affairs administrators, must devise ways to deliver undergraduate education that are as comprehensive and integrated as the ways students actually learn. A whole new mindset is needed to capitalize on the interrelatedness of the in- and out-of-class influences on student learning and the functional interconnectedness of academic and student affairs divisions.

In describing her efforts to bring together the activities of inner-city schools, social agencies, and neighborhoods to meet the basic physical, developmental, and educational needs of inner-city children, Cicely Tyson cites a suggestive African proverb: "It takes a whole village to raise a child."

John F. Kennedy stated that "the great enemy of truth is very often not the lie—deliberate, contrived and dishonest—but the myth, persistent, persuasive and unrealistic" (Schlesinger, 1965). It is time we put to use what we know with some confidence about what constitutes effective teaching and learning and put to rest educational myths that have outlived their usefulness.

References

Brubacher, J. S., and W. Rudy. *Higher Education in Transition: A History of American Colleges and Universities, 1636–1968* (Rev. Ed.), New York: Harper & Row, 1968.

Feldman, K. A. "Research Productivity and Scholarly Accomplishment of College Teachers as Related to Their Instructional Effectiveness: A Review and Exploration," *Research in Higher Education,* Vol. 27, 1987, pages 227–298.

Pascarella, Ernest T. and Patrick T. Terenzini. *How College Affects Students: Findings and Insights from Twenty Years of Research,* San Francisco: Jossey-Bass, 1991.

Pollio, H. *What Students Think About and Do in College Lecture Classes,* Teaching-Learning Issues, No. 53, Knoxville, TN: University of Tennessee, Learning Research Center, 1984.

Schlesinger, A. M., Jr. *A Thousand Days: John F. Kennedy in the White House,* Boston: Houghton Mifflin, 1965.

Notes

Patrick T. Terenzini is Professor, Senior Scientist, and Associate Director of the National Center on Postsecondary Teaching, Learning, and Assessment in the Center for the Study of Higher Education at The Pennsylvania State University.

Ernest T. Pascarella is University of Illinois Foundation James T. Towey Scholar and Professor of Policy Studies at the National Center of Postsecondary Teaching, Learning, and Assessment in the College of Education at the University of Illinois-Chicago. An earlier version of this article was presented as an address to the Council on Academic Affairs and the Council on Student Affairs of the National Association of State Universities and Land Grant College, New Orleans, November 9, 1992.

An American Imperative: Higher Expectations for Higher Education

WINGSPREAD GROUP ON HIGHER EDUCATION
AN OPEN LETTER TO THOSE CONCERNED ABOUT THE AMERICAN FUTURE

Everything has changed but our ways of thinking, and if these do not change we drift toward unparalleled catastrophe.

Albert Einstein

A disturbing and dangerous mismatch exists between what American society needs of higher education and what it is receiving. Nowhere is the mismatch more dangerous than in the quality of undergraduate preparation provided on many campuses. The American imperative for the 21st century is that society must hold higher education to much higher expectations or risk national decline.

Establishing higher expectations, however, will require that students and parents rethink what too many seem to want from education: the credential without the content, the degree without the knowledge and effort it implies.

In the past, our industrial economy produced many new and low-skill jobs and provided stable employment, often at high wages, for all. Now the nation faces an entirely different economic scenario: a knowledge-based economy with a shortage of highly skilled workers at all levels and a surplus of unskilled applicants scrambling to earn a precarious living. Many of those unskilled applicants are college graduates, not high school dropouts.

Like much of the rest of American education, the nation's colleges and universities appear to live by an unconscious educational rule of thumb that their function is to weed out, not to cultivate, students for whom they have accepted responsibility. An unacceptably high percentage of students leaks out of the system at each juncture in the education pipeline. This hemorrhaging of our human resources occurs despite the low standards prevalent in American education and the existence of a wide diversity of institutions offering many options for students. It is almost as though educators take failure for granted.

Education is in trouble, and with it our nation's hopes for the future. America's ability to compete in a global economy is threatened. The American people's hopes for a civil, humane society ride on the outcome. The capacity of the United States to shoulder its responsibilities on the world stage is at risk. We understand the explanations offered when criticisms are leveled at higher education: entrants are inadequately prepared; institutional missions vary; we are required by law to accept all high school graduates; students change their minds frequently and drop out of school;

controlling costs is difficult in the labor-intensive academy; cutting-edge research consumes the time of senior faculty. All of these things are true.

But the larger truth is that the explanations, no matter how persuasive they once were, no longer add up to a compelling whole. The simple fact is that some faculties and institutions certify for graduation too many students who cannot read and write very well, too many whose intellectual depth and breadth are unimpressive, and too many whose skills are inadequate in the face of the demands of contemporary life.

These conclusions point to the possibilities for institutional decline given that an increasingly skeptical public expresses the same sense of sticker shock about college costs that is now driving health care reform. The withdrawal of public support for higher education can only accelerate as students, parents, and taxpayers come to understand that they paid for an expensive education without receiving fair value in return.

The seeds for national disaster are also there: the needs of an information- and technology-based global economy, the complexities of modern life, the accelerated pace of change and the growing demands for competent, high-skill performance in the workplace require that we produce much higher numbers of individuals—whether high school, community college or four-year graduates—prepared to learn their way through life. Most Americans and their policymakers, concerned about the quality of pre-collegiate education, take heart in the large numbers of Americans who receive associate's and bachelor's degrees every year. The harsh truth is that a significant minority of these graduates enter or reenter the world with little more than the knowledge, competence, and skill we would have expected in a high school graduate scarcely a generation ago.

What does our society *need* from higher education? It needs stronger, more vital forms of community. It needs an informed and involved citizenry. It needs graduates able to assume leadership roles in American life. It needs a competent and adaptable workforce. It needs very high quality undergraduate education producing graduates who can sustain each of these goals. It needs more first-rate research pushing back the important boundaries of human knowledge and less research designed to lengthen academic résumés. It needs an affordable, cost-effective educational enterprise offering lifelong learning. Above all, it needs a commitment to the American promise— the idea that all Americans have the opportunity to develop their talents to the fullest. Higher education is not meeting these imperatives.

A Changing America and a Changing World

American society has never been static, but now change is accelerating. The United States is becoming more diverse: by the year 2020, about one-third of Americans will be members of minority groups, traditionally poorly served by education at all levels. New information and technologies are accelerating change: with a half life of less than five years, they are reshaping the way the world lives, works, and plays. Our society is aging: in 1933, 17 Americans were employed for every Social Security recipient; by 2020, the ratio will have dropped from 17-to-1 to 3-to-1. in 1950, the Ford Motor Company employed 62 active workers for every retiree; by 1993, the ratio dropped to 1.2-to-1. These statistics are a stark reminder of our need to assure that American workers are educated to levels that maximize their productivity and, hence, our collective economic well-being.

A generation ago, Americans were confident that the core values which had served our nation well in the past could guide it into the future. These values were expressed in homey statements such as: "Honesty is the best policy"; "Serve your country"; "Be a good neighbor." Today we worry that the core values may be shifting and that the sentiments expressed are different: "Don't get involved"; "I gave at the office"; "It's cheating only if you get caught." Too many of us today worry about "me" at the expense of "we."

A generation ago, our society and its institutions were overseen by white males. Immigration policy favored peoples from Northern Europe. The television images of "Ozzie and Harriet" were thought to reflect the middle-class American family. Almost all of that has changed as women and members of minority groups increasingly have assumed their place at the table, and immigrants and refugees from once-distant lands have remade the face of the United States.

A generation ago, computers took up entire rooms; punch cards for data processing were the cutting edge of technology; operators stood by to help with transatlantic calls; many families watched the clock each afternoon until local television stations began their evening broadcasts. Today, microprocessors, miniaturization, and fiber optics have made information from the four corners of the world instantaneously available to anyone with a computer, transforming the way we manage our institutions, the way we entertain ourselves, and the way we do our business.

A generation ago, our society was affluent, richer than it had ever been, with the prospect that its wealth would be more widely and deeply shared than ever before. The American economy—our assembly lines, our banks and farms, our workers and managers—dominated the global economy. Ours was the only major economy to emerge intact from World War II. Trade barriers limited global competition. Our industrial plant and national infrastructure were the envy of the world. As a people, we believed we could afford practically anything, and we undertook practically everything.

Those days are behind us. Global competition is transforming the economic landscape. Fierce competitors from abroad have entered domestic markets, and one great American industry after another has felt the effects. We have watched with growing concern as our great national strengths have been challenged, as the gap between rich and poor has widened, and as the nation's economic energy has been sapped by budget and trade deficits. We have struggled—so far unsuccessfully—to set the country back on the confident, spirited course we took for granted a generation ago.

We can regain that course only if Americans work smarter. Otherwise, our standard of living will continue the enervating erosion that began two decades ago. Individual economic security in the future will depend not on job or career stability, but on employability, which itself will be a function of adaptability and the willingness to learn, grow, and change throughout a lifetime.

Americans may be aware of all of this, but we are prisoners of our past. Our thinking and many of our institutions, including our educational institutions, are still organized as though none of these changes had occurred.

The 3,400 institutions of higher learning in America come in all shapes and sizes, public and private. They include small liberal arts institutions, two-year community colleges, and technical institutions, state colleges and universities, and flagship research universities. In each of these categories, models of both excellence and mediocrity exist. Despite this diversity, most operate as though their focus were still the traditional student of days gone by: a white, male, recent high school graduate, who attended classes full-time at a four-year institution and lived on campus. Yesterday's traditional student is, in fact, today's exception.

There are more women than men among the 13.5 million students on today's campuses. Forty-three percent of today's students are over the age of 25, including 300,000 over the age of 50. Minority Americans now make up about 20 percent of enrollments in higher education. Almost as many students attend part-time and intermittently as attend full-time and without interruption. More college students are enrolled in community colleges than in four-year institutions. And there are more students living at home or off-campus than there are in dormitories. Fixed in our mind's eye, however, the image of the traditional student blocks effective responses to these new realities.

These demographic, economic, and technological changes underscore the mismatch between what is needed of higher education and what it provides. Because we are now a more diverse people, society needs a much better sense of the things that unite us. Because the global economy has had such a profound effect on American standards of living, individuals in our society and the economy as a whole need to be much better prepared for the world of work.

In short, we need to educate more people, educate them to far higher standards, and do it as effectively and efficiently as possible.

Warning Signs

Institutions, like organisms, must respond to changes in their environment if they are to survive. Not surprisingly, given higher education's slow adaptation, real problems shadow the real successes of the nation's colleges and universities.

Crisis of Values. The nation's colleges and universities are enmeshed in, and in some ways contributing to, society's larger crisis of values. Intolerance on campus is on the rise; half of big-time college sports programs have been caught cheating in the last decade; reports of ethical lapses by administrators, faculty members and trustees, and of cheating and plagiarism by students are given wide-spread credence.

From the founding of the first American colleges 300 years ago, higher education viewed the development of student character and the transmission of the values supporting that character as an essential responsibility of faculty and administration. The importance of higher education's role in the transmission of values is, if anything, even greater today than it was 300 or even 50 years ago. The weakening of the role of family and religious institutions in the lives of young people, the increase in the number of people seeking the benefits of higher education, and what appears to be the larger erosion of core values in our society make this traditional role all the more important.

In this context, it is fair to ask how well our educational institutions are transmitting an understanding of good and bad, right and wrong, and the compelling core of values any society needs to sustain itself. While there is a paucity of concrete data, enough anecdotal evidence exists to suggest that there is too little concerted attention, on too many campuses, to this responsibility.

In the final analysis, a society is not simply something in which we find ourselves. Society is "we." It is our individual and collective integrity, our commitment to each other and to the dignity of all. All of the other accomplishments of higher education will be degraded if our colleges and universities lose their moral compass and moral vocation,

The Costs of "Weeding." Few thoughtful observers believe that our K–12 schools are adequate for today's needs. About half our high school students are enrolled in dead-end curricula that prepare them poorly for work life, or additional learning. Too many of the rest are bored and unchallenged. Too few are performing to standards that make them competitive with peers in other industrialized countries. Half of those entering college full-time do not have a degree within five years. Half of all students entering Ph.D. programs never obtain the degree. In short, our education system is better organized to discourage students—to weed them out—than it is to cultivate and support our most important national resource, our people.

The Uneducated Graduate. The failure to cultivate our students is evident in a 1992 analysis of college transcripts by the U.S. Department of Education, which reveals that 26.2 percent of recent bachelor's degree recipients earned not a single undergraduate credit in history; 30.8 percent did not study mathematics of any kind; 39.6 percent earned no credits in either English or American literature; and 58.4 percent left college without any exposure to a foreign language. Much too frequently, American higher education now offers a smorgasbord of fanciful courses in a fragmented curriculum that accords as much credit for "Introduction to Tennis" and for courses in pop culture as it does for "Principles of English Composition," history, or physics, thereby trivializing education—indeed, misleading students by implying that they are receiving the education they need for life when they are not.

The original purpose of an undergraduate education, the development of a broadly educated human being, prepared, in the words of Englishman John Henry Cardinal Newman, "to fill any post with credit", has been pushed to the periphery. That purpose, restated, was the essential message of a commission convened by President Harry S Truman 45 years ago. According to the Truman Commission, higher education should help students acquire the knowledge, skills, and attitudes to enable them "to live rightly and well in a free society." The 1992 transcript analysis cited above suggests that educators need to ask themselves how well their current graduates measure up to the standards of Newman and the Truman Commission, and to the needs of American society for thoughtful citizens, workers, and potential leaders.

For without a broad liberal education, students are denied the opportunity to engage with the principal ideas and events that are the source of any civilization. How then are they to understand the values that sustain community and society, much less their own values? Educators know better, but stand silent.

There is further disturbing evidence that graduates are unprepared for the requirements of daily life. According to the 1993 National Adult Literacy Survey (NALS), surprisingly large numbers of two- and four-year college graduates are unable, in everyday situations, to use basic skills involving reading, writing, computation, and elementary problem-solving.[1]

The NALS tasks required participants to do three things: read and interpret prose, such as newspaper articles, work with documents like bus schedules and tables and charts, and use elementary arithmetic to solve problems involving, for example, the costs of restaurant meals or mortgages. The NALS findings were presented on a scale from low (Level 1) to high (Level 5) in each of the three areas. The performance of college graduates on these scales is distressing:

- in working with documents, only eight percent of all four-year college graduates reach the highest level;

- in terms of their ability to work with prose, only 10 percent of four-year graduates are found in Level 5; and

- with respect to quantitative skills, only 12 percent of four-year graduates reach the highest level.

In fact, only about one-half of four-year graduates are able to demonstrate intermediate levels of competence in each of the three areas. In the area of quantitative skills, for example, 56.3 percent of American-born, four-year college graduates are unable *consistently* to perform simple tasks, such as calculating the change from $3 after buying a 60 cent bowl of soup and a $1.95 sandwich. Tasks such as these should not be insuperable for people with 16 years of education.

Growing Public Concern. Opinion polls leave no doubt that Americans have a profound respect for higher education. They consider it essential to the nation's civility and economic progress, and to advances in science, technology, and medicine. Americans are convinced that an undergraduate degree is as important to success in today's world as a high school diploma was in yesterday's.

But, simultaneously, the polls reveal deep public concern about higher education. The public is overwhelmed by sticker shock when it considers college costs. According to the polls, the overwhelming majority of the American people believes that colleges and universities—both public and private—are overpriced and lie increasingly beyond the reach of all but the wealthy. Public confidence in the "people running higher education" has declined as dramatically with respect to education leaders as it has with respect to the leadership of medicine, government, and business.

While the public is most interested in achievement, costs, and management, it believes that the academy focuses instead on advanced study and research. Several of the essays written for our study echo a number of the conclusions of the 1992 report of the President's Advisory Council on Science and Technology. Both remind us that the academic culture and rewards system too frequently encourages graduate education and research at the expense of undergraduate education. What emerges is a picture of academic life which only grudgingly attends to undergraduate learning, and to the advice, counseling, and other support services students need. The dominant academic attitude, particularly on large campuses enrolling most American students, is that research deserves pride of place over teaching and public service, in part because many senior faculty prefer specialized research to teaching, and in part because institutions derive much of their prestige from faculty research. Indeed, the ideal model in the minds of faculty members on campuses of all kinds is defined by what they perceive to be the culture and aspirations of flagship research universities.

Three Central Issues

It is hard not to conclude that too much undergraduate education is little more than secondary school material—warmed over and reoffered at much higher expense, but not at correspondingly higher levels of effectiveness. The United States can no longer afford the inefficiencies, or the waste of talent, time, and money, revealed by these warning signs. Indeed, the nation that responds best and most rapidly to the educational demands of the Age of the Learner will enjoy a commanding international advantage in the pursuit of both domestic tranquillity and economic prosperity. To achieve these goals for our country, we must educate more people, and educate them far better. That will require new ways of thinking.

Given the diversity of American higher education, there can be no single formula for change common to all, but we do believe that there are at least three fundamental issues common to all 3,400 colleges and universities:

- **taking values seriously;**
- **putting student learning first;**
- **creating a nation of learners.**

The nation's colleges and universities can respond to the agenda defined in this open letter. They can do so by reaffirming their conviction that the moral purpose of knowledge is at least as important as its utility. They can do so by placing student learning at the heart of their concerns. They can do so by working toward what educator John Goodlad has called "a simultaneous renewal" of higher education and the nation's K–12 schools as one continuous learning system.

To focus what we hope will be a vigorous, widespread national debate we have distilled the results of six-months' work and discussion into a compact document designed to make our line of reasoning as clear as possible. Our purpose is not so much to provide answers. Rather, we hope to raise some of the right questions and thus encourage Americans and their colleges and universities to consider and adopt a new direction. That is why we close this document not with a set of recommendations, but with a set of challenges for American higher education, for the public, and for its representatives.

We begin our discussion in the pages that follow with an argument for putting first things first: the need for a rigorous liberal education that takes values seriously and acknowledges that value-free education has proven a costly blind alley for society.

Taking Values Seriously

The Holocaust reminds us forever that knowledge divorced from values can only serve to deepen the human nightmare that a head without a heart is not humanity.

President Bill Clinton

Democratic societies need a common ground, a shared frame of reference within which to encourage both diversity and constructive debate about the common good. A free people cannot enjoy the fruits of its liberty without collaborative efforts in behalf of community. Higher education has a central obligation to develop these abilities.

There are some values, rooted in national experience, even defined in the Constitution, that Americans share. These "constitutional" values have evolved into a set of civic virtues:

- respect for the individual and commitment to equal opportunity;
- the belief that our common interests exceed our individual differences;
- concern for those who come after us;
- support for the freedoms enunciated in the Bill of Rights, including freedom of religion, of the press, of speech, and of the right to assemble;
- the belief that individual rights and privileges are to be exercised responsibly;
- respect for the views of others; and
- the conviction that no one is above the law.

If values are to be taken seriously, the place to start is by reaffirming the primacy of the visions of Newman and the Truman Commission: liberal education is central to living "rightly and well in a free society." We do not believe that a history major needs to know as much chemistry as a forest management major, that an engineering major needs to know as much literature as an English major. But every student needs the knowledge and understanding that can come only from the rigors of a liberal education. Such an education lies at the heart of developing both social and personal values. If the center of American society is to hold, a liberal education must be central to the undergraduate experience of all students. The essentials of a liberal education should be contained in a rigorous, required curriculum defined on each campus.

We believe, too, that every institution of higher education should ask itself—*now*—what it proposes to do to assure that next year's entering students will graduate as individuals of character more sensitive to the needs of community, more competent in their ability to contribute to society, and more civil in their habits of thought, speech, and action.

We are also convinced that each educational institution must, openly and directly, begin the kinds of discussions that promise to build campus consensus on the civic virtues it most treasures. The questions concluding this section, and repeated in Appendix A, define some of the issues that need to be addressed.

What do these issues mean in practice? Several implications appear obvious: campuses must model the values they espouse; they must help students experience society and reflect on it as an integral part of their education; they must act on their understanding that matters of the spirit reflect such a profound aspect of the human condition that they cannot be ignored on any campus.

With respect to modeling values, a former president of Yale University, A. Bartlett Giamatti, once said: "[A]n educational institution teaches far, far more, and more profoundly, by how it acts than by anything anyone within it ever says." Mr. Giamatti was echoed by one of our essayists, Robert Rosenzweig, who wrote, "American society needs colleges and universities to be active exemplars of the values they have always professed. . . . In both statements, the critical emphasis is on *acting* and *exemplifying*, not simply proclaiming. On campus, as elsewhere, the dictum "Do as I say, not as I do" is an invitation to cynicism among our citizens, particularly students.

We want also to stress that society's needs will be well served if colleges and universities wholeheartedly commit themselves to providing students with opportunities to experience and reflect on the world beyond the campus. Books and lectures provide an intellectual grounding in the realities of the marketplace and of the nation's social dilemmas. But there is no substitute for experience. Academic work should be complemented by the kinds of knowledge derived from first-hand experience, such as contributing to the well-being of others, participating in political campaigns, and working with the enterprises that create wealth in our society.

Last but not least, we want to suggest that matters of the spirit have a far more important role to play in institutions of higher education than has been encouraged in recent years. We do not argue for one system of belief or another, one denomination or another, or for compulsory religious observance of any kind. Certainly we understand that campuses must be dedicated to free inquiry, ungoverned by either faddish orthodoxy or intolerant ideology. But we do argue that faith and deep moral conviction matter in human affairs. Because they do, they must matter on campus.

We believe that the concept of a value-free education is a profoundly misleading contradiction in terms, a blind alley with very high costs to personal life, community, and even workplace. A campus community whose members cannot readily give answers to the following questions is a campus without a purpose:

- What kind of people do we want our children and grandchildren to be?
- What kind of society do we want them to live in?
- How can we best shape our institution to nurture those kinds of people and that kind of society?[2]

Initiating and sustaining discussions and initiatives of the sort suggested above will be difficult on large campuses, but not impossible. Organizing and sustaining community service programs for large numbers of students both inside and outside the classroom is difficult, but not impossible. Encouraging collaborative learning is perhaps more difficult than grading on the curve, but it is not impossible. Yet activities such as these both model and teach the skills of community.

The questions raised in the realm of values may, on occasion, be deeply troubling. In our view that is all to the good. If the journey is too comfortable, the right questions are probably not being asked, and asking the right questions is essential if higher education is to rise to Pericles' standards:

> Pericles knew that any successful society must be an educational institution. However great its commitment to individual freedom and diversity, it needs a code of civic virtue and a general devotion to the common enterprise without which it cannot flourish or survive.

> It must transmit its understanding of good and bad and a sense of pride, admiration, and love for its institutions and values to its citizens, especially the young.[3]

It is fashionable to decry the quality of American leadership, public and private. Yet virtually all our leadership emerges from one institution of higher education or another. As students are groomed on campus, so shall they live and lead. Pericles understood. Do we?

Taking Values Seriously

- How does our educational program match the claims of our recruiting brochures, and where is it falling short?

- How does our core curriculum of required courses respond to the needs of our students for a rigorous liberal education enabling them to "live rightly and well in a free society?" Where does it fall short?

- In what ways does our institution model the values and skills expected in our community? Where and how are we falling short?

- What steps might we take to improve the general climate of civility on our campus?

- How comprehensive and effective is the code of professional conduct and ethics for our faculty and staff? When was it last reviewed?

- In what ways does our institution and its educational program promote the development of shared values, specifically the civic virtues listed below, among our students?

- respect for the individual and commitment to equal opportunity in a diverse society;

- the belief that our common interests exceed our individual differences;

- support for the freedoms enunciated in the Bill of Rights, including freedom of religion, of the press, of speech, and of the right to assemble;

- the belief that individual rights and privileges are accompanied by responsibilities to others;

- respect for the views of others; and

- the conviction that no one is above the law.

- What moral and ethical questions should we be putting to the student groups and organizations we sanction on campus? What standards of conduct do we expect of these groups? How have we made these standards clear?

- How do the activities of our athletic programs square with our institution's stated values, and where do they fall short?

- What steps will we take to assure that next year's entering students will graduate as individuals of character more sensitive to the needs of community, more competent to contribute to society, more civil in their habits of thought, speech, and action?

- What other related questions should we address at our institutions?

Putting Student Learning First

The future now belongs to societies that organize themselves for learning.

Ray Marshall and Marc Tucker

If it is time to take values seriously on campus, it is also time to redress the imbalance that has led to the decline of undergraduate education. To do so, the nation's colleges and universities must for the foreseeable future focus overwhelmingly on what their students learn and achieve. Too much of education at every level seems to be organized for the convenience of educators and the institution's interests, procedures and prestige, and too little focused on the needs of students.

Putting students at the heart of the educational enterprise requires that we face a difficult truth: academic expectations and standards on many campuses are too low, and it shows. Institutions that start with learning will set higher expectations for all students, then do a much more effective job of helping them meet those expectations, points to which we return below.

Putting learning at the heart of the enterprise means campuses must:

- understand their mission clearly and define the kinds of students they can serve best;
- define exactly what their entering students need to succeed;
- start from where the students begin and help them achieve explicitly stated institutional standards for high achievement;
- tailor their programs—curriculum, schedules, support services, office hours—to meet the needs of the students they admit, not the convenience of staff and faculty;
- systematically apply the very best of what is known about learning and teaching on their campuses;
- rigorously assess what their students know and are able to do in order to improve both student and institutional performance; and
- develop and publish explicit exit standards for graduates, and grant degrees only to students who meet them.

Interestingly, steps such as these are among the recommendations recently advanced by some of this nation's most distinguished African-American leaders.[4] As they note, their recommendations for improving the learning environment for minorities will inevitably work to the advantage of all students, including disadvantaged *majority* learners. We were struck by how congruent their analysis and recommendations are to our own.

Putting learning at the heart of the academic enterprise will mean overhauling the conceptual, procedural, curricular, and other architecture of postsecondary education on most campuses. For some students this will mean greater independence. For others, the academic experience may change little outwardly; internally, it will be far more challenging and exciting. For many others— particularly those whose learning needs are being served poorly now—academic life will be more directive, more supportive, and more demanding. It will be more directive on the assumption that institutions are responsible for evaluating and responding to the learning needs of students. It will be more supportive because it will be focused on what students need in order to succeed. It will be far more demanding because it will be aimed at producing graduates who demonstrate much higher levels of knowledge and skills.

Skills. Traditionally, the acquisition of skills essential to life and work has been considered a by-product of study, not something requiring explicit attention on campus. We know of only a handful of the nation's colleges and universities that have developed curricular approaches similar to, for example, the list of critical skills developed by the Secretary of Labor's Commission on Achieving Necessary Skills (SCANS). But skills such as these—written and oral communication, critical analysis, interpersonal competence, the ability to obtain and use data, the capacity to make informed judgments, and the skills required in community life—are essential attributes of a liberal education when they are accompanied by discipline-based knowledge. These skills can be learned. If they are to be learned, however, they must be taught and practiced, not merely absorbed as a result of unplanned academic experience. We believe that the modern world requires both knowledge and such skills and competencies. Neither is adequate without the other.

Student Achievement. There is growing research evidence that all students can learn to much higher standards than we now require. When they do not, the flaw is most likely to be in the system, not the individual. We agree with those who make the important point that the truly outstanding educational institution graduates students who achieve more than would have been predicted on entry. (This is a standard, incidentally, that challenges even the most prestigious of our great universities and small liberal arts colleges, the institutions routinely enrolling the best secondary school graduates.)

There is a growing body of knowledge about learning and the implications of that knowledge for teaching. What is known, however, is rarely applied by individual teachers, much less in concert by entire faculties. We know that teaching is more than lecturing. We know that active engagement in learning is more productive than passive listening. We know that experiential learning can be even more so. We know we should evaluate institutional performance against student outcomes. We know all of this, but appear unable to act on it. It is time to explore the reasons for our failure to act.

No group has a greater stake in the new evidence relative to student achievement than socially and economically disadvantaged students, particularly disadvantaged minority Americans. At the elementary and secondary levels, the achievement gap separating minority and majority students is slowly closing. These results appear to reflect a combination of factors including minimum competency standards, on-going assessment, and programs to provide the special support many of these young Americans need. These were vitally important steps, but we share the distress of many Americans, including educators, that they have not gone far enough; minimum competency is not enough. Many minority Americans are still being left behind by an education system that is not serving their needs.

We also know that support services work. From a host of small experiments it is clear that when students—particularly those less advantaged in life—know their institution is unambiguously committed to their success, performance rises dramatically. Yet too few campuses have done much more than offer perfunctory, often inconvenient, student-support services. Too few have created one-stop "success centers" where students can find assistance with the full range of their concerns when they most need help—which is frequently before 9 a.m. and after 5 p.m. In the most impressive of these centers, a student enters into a relationship with a single individual who becomes an advocate for the student, responsible for marshaling all of the institution's assets and focusing them on the student's success.

Assessment. Finally, our vision calls for new ways of thinking about assessing what students know and are able to do. In medicine, testing and assessment are used to define the best course for future action. They provide data for both doctor (the teacher) and patient (the student) as to what steps to take to improve the individual's health (learning). In contemporary colleges and universities, however, such use of assessment is rare.

Examinations in educational institutions (including elementary and secondary schools) normally establish competitive rankings and sort students. They rarely diagnose strengths and weaknesses, examine needs, or suggest what steps to take next. In almost no institution are a student's skills systematically assessed, developed, and then certified. This assessment issue transcends the needs of learners. In an institution focused on learning, assessment feedback becomes central to the institution's ability to improve its own performance, enhancing student learning in turn.

New forms of assessment should focus on establishing what college and university graduates have learned—the knowledge and skill levels they have achieved and their potential for further independent learning. Only a few scattered institutions have instituted exit assessments.

The sad fact is that campuses spend far more time and money establishing the credentials of applicants than they do assessing the knowledge, skills, and competencies of their graduates.

Indeed, the entire system is skewed in favor of the input side of the learning equation: credit hours, library collections, percentage of faculty with terminal degrees, and the like. The output side of the equation—student achievement—requires much greater attention than it now receives. That attention should begin by establishing improved measures of student achievement, measures that are credible and valued by the friends and supporters of education, by testing and accrediting bodies, and by educational institutions themselves.

We understand that the changes we suggest will be difficult and demanding. We recognize that they will require new attitudes on the part of faculty and institutions and, most critically, new skills and ways of doing business. There will be costs associated with these changes—though relatively modest costs in the context of overall institutional budgets—notably for staff development and student support services. We believe it reasonable to suggest that campuses devote a greater percentage of revenues to these needs.

Finally, we want to stress that responsibility in a learning institution is a two-way street. Students, at any level of education, are the workers in the educational process. They have a major obligation for their own success. Too many students do not behave as though that were the case, apparently believing (as do many parents) that grades are more important for success in life than acquired knowledge, the ability to learn throughout a lifetime, and hard work on campus. Educational institutions, having accepted students and their tuition, have a positive obligation to help these students acquire the knowledge, skills, competencies, and habits of intellectual self-discipline requisite to becoming productive citizens and employees. Students, parents, and community leaders will have to be willing to support the high expectations and hard work that superior student achievement will require.

Too many campuses have become co-conspirators in the game of "credentialism." Many campuses still do not offer the guidance and support all students require to reach the higher levels of achievement contemporary life requires. Too few are sufficiently engaged in effective collaboration with other learning institutions, notably K–12 schools, to assure that students arriving on campus are prepared intellectually and are received in ways which enhance their prospects for success. Institutions of higher education must reach out much more effectively to colleagues elsewhere to help create a nation of learners and reduce the barriers to their learning.

Putting Student Learning First

- How recently have we reviewed our program offerings to assure that they match our mission and the needs and goals of the students we admit?

- In what ways could we do a better job of helping our students to attain higher levels of both knowledge and skills?

- What steps should we take to establish or improve a rigorous curriculum requiring core knowledge and competencies of our students?

- How have we tried to integrate curricular offerings for the benefit of students and faculty? Is "course sprawl" contributing to our budgetary problems and making it more difficult for students to register in courses required for graduation? What might be done?

- To what extent are our educational programs, class schedules, registration, and other administrative and support services organized around the needs of learners rather than the convenience of the institution? What improvements can we make?

- How do we encourage and assist students to develop the basic values required for learning, e.g., self-discipline, perseverance, responsibility, hard work, intellectual openness?

- In what ways are we assessing learning to diagnose needs and accomplishments? How could we improve feedback to students and faculty on student performance in order to enhance both teaching and learning?

- How does our institution assure that students have demonstrated a high level of achievement, consistent with our published standards for acquiring both knowledge and skills, as a basis for receiving our degrees or certificates? Can we raise our standards?

- In what ways are we applying what is known about learning to the teaching practices of our faculty and graduate students? How do our pedagogical approaches enhance learning, and where do they fall short?

- How do we support faculty initiatives to improve learning and teaching? In particular, is our faculty well grounded in the available research concerning adult learning? If not, what will we do to improve our record?

- How could we do a better job of helping students learn at lower overall cost to our institution? How would we reinvest the savings?

- What other related questions should we address at our institution to improve the quality of learning?

Creating a Nation of Learners

The fixed person for the fixed duties, who in older societies was a blessing, in the future will be a public danger.

Alfred North Whitehead

We must redesign all of our learning systems to align our entire education enterprise with the personal, civic, and workplace needs of the twenty-first century.

In the last generation, higher education has been swept up in the tide of social and economic change. The horizons and aspirations of women and members of minority groups have expanded. Older students have arrived on campus, many for the first time, seeking help to improve their skills, develop career prospects, and respond to new developments in technology. Family mobility is on the rise, and with it mobility from campus to campus. The modern workplace, open to global competition, requires levels of knowledge and skills beyond anything we have aspired to in the past, and well beyond what our schools and universities are now producing.

These changes demand that American education transform itself into a seamless system that can produce and support a nation of learners, providing access to educational services for learners as they need them, when they need them, and wherever they need them.

This is not an argument for merger or homogeneity. But colleges and universities need to understand that their business is *all* of education—learning. They can no longer afford to concern themselves exclusively with *higher* education. They must address themselves much more effectively to the other key pieces of the education enterprise. Americans and their educators are now handicapped by an education legacy from the past when what they need is a solution for the future. Our current educational institutions worked reasonably well in a society that had little need for large numbers of educated adults. Why question that structure when 90 percent of the population left school after 8th grade (the turn of the century); when only 50 percent of the population graduated from high school (1940); or even when only one-third of high school graduates enrolled in higher education (1950)? Now the need has changed. There can be no justification for such a system in today's world with its growing demand for better-educated people.

In this new environment many more educators must be prepared to say: "All of us, from pre-school to post-graduate, are in this together. It is not enough to complain about each other's failings. It is time to stop addressing the problem piecemeal. We must begin to work collaboratively on the system as a whole." It is no longer tolerable for so many in higher education to complain about the quality of those they admit, but do nothing to set higher standards and work with colleagues in K–12 schools to help students attain those standards. Our education system is in crisis; business-as-usual is a formula for national disaster.

Assessment and achievement are critical components of an enhanced education system. Experts today are thinking about the need for summary educational documents, not just grades, attendance records, and test scores, but data representing genuine learning achievements across a lifetime of educational and training experiences. The Educational Testing Service, the American College Testing program, and the American Council on Education are already piloting initiatives of this kind—Work Link, Work Keys, and the External Diploma Program respectively—which aim to revise quite radically how we think about and use assessment. These efforts deserve encouragement from everyone interested in improving the quality of learning, and in particular from the American business community. They will increasingly assure that learning, wherever it occurs, is valued and given credit; they will, in and of themselves, help to create a national culture encouraging lifelong formal and informal learning,

We are aware that a number of, institutions work with local schools, and that some are very serious and effective in these efforts. But as one of our essayists put it, "the sum of it all adds up to considerably less than a response to an urgent need that is grounded in both self-interest and national interest."

We join others in calling for a simultaneous renewal of both higher education and the nation's K–12 schools. A serious, sustained dialogue should start by identifying shared needs and problems:

- a clear public definition of what students should know and be able to do at each educational level;
- standards of entry *and exit* for higher education;
- increasing the use of assessment to diagnose learning needs and enhance student achievement;
- improving both the theory and practice of teaching and learning;
- recruiting and educating more effective teachers at all levels;
- bringing education's resources to bear on issues of character and its development;
- reducing the barriers to inter-institutional transfer among institutions of higher education; and
- exploring the implications for college admissions practices of the six National Education Goals established in 1989, and the potential for collaboration with K–12 schools.

The entire education establishment has a self-evident interest in this kind of collaborative dialogue and action. If a community college has developed an outstanding student support system, even the most prestigious research university should consider it as a benchmark. If a public school system has created a successful school-within-a-school to relieve the negative impact of size on students, public mega-universities should consider the possibility that they have something to learn from it. Any educational institution should want to practice existing, innovative, research-based approaches for applying to teaching what is known about learning. Where innovations in self-paced and distance learning are succeeding, any institution concerned about productivity and cost containment should examine them carefully as potential contributors to its own efficiency and effectiveness. Every campus has an interest in emulating those colleges and universities that have extended a collaborative hand to elementary and secondary education. Such collaboration can enhance course content and standards across the board, and raise the motivation and confidence of students who might otherwise not be considering postsecondary education.

Nor is the opportunity to learn from others restricted to the traditional world of education. Where a corporation has developed effective educational innovations, campuses should investigate the implications for their own work. Many museums are currently developing innovative and effective approaches to teaching and learning about science, history, and art. But all of these advances—and many others—are taking place independently of each other at a time when America needs a more collaborative, cost-effective and better-articulated way of responding to the lifelong learning needs of growing numbers of its citizens.

Creating a Nation of Learners

- In what ways have we organized our programs to develop and support a capacity for lifelong learning among our students?
- How might we provide the same level of service and support to "non-traditional" students, and students in non-traditional learning programs, as we do for traditional full-time students? Within our mission, when have we examined alternative, more flexible, and student-oriented ways to provide for student learning?
- How often do we survey employers of our recent graduates—and the graduates themselves—to discover how and under what circumstances graduates succeed or fall short? How can that process be improved?

- In what ways do we work with K–12 systems to enlarge our understanding of their difficulties, encourage teachers and administrators to see us as resources, and enlarge our own competencies? In what ways have we relegated this effort to our school of education? How have we tried to involve the entire campus?

- How are we working with high schools and other educational institutions both to communicate to them the knowledge and skills that students will need to be successful in higher education and to help students meet those requirements?

- How do our departments provide graduate students and professors with training in how people learn and what that means for teaching? What needs to be done to make this institution-wide and to set institution-wide standards?

- How is our campus working with local schools and other colleges and universities to bring teaching and learning to state-of-the-art standards from kindergarten through the undergraduate years? What more can we do?

- How might we bring our teacher recruitment and teacher education programs into better alignment with the real needs of both society and students? What are our benchmarks?

- What provisions might a statewide compact contain if we wished to ease student transfer between institutions?

- In what ways are we organized to make use of educational achievements from non-traditional organizations and settings?

- What other related questions should we address in an effort to reduce the institutional barriers to learning and to make our institution more responsive to the needs of others, e.g., K–12 education, employers, and other institutions of higher education?

First Steps: Challenges for Higher Education

For every right that you cherish, you have a duty which you must fulfill. For every hope that you entertain, you have a task that you must perform. For every good that you wish to preserve, you will have to sacrifice your comfort and your ease. There is nothing for nothing any longer.

Walter Lippmann

Our wake-up call places a heavy burden on the shoulders of the men and women in higher education. It will require rethinking the assumptions of the education enterprise and reinventing many of its ways of doing business. Educators, particularly faculty members, must demonstrate that they have noted the warning signs, understand the potential for institutional and national decline and are ready to act.

Solutions for the problems we have described will require vigorous, creativity and persistent leadership on campus, in the community, in state capitols, and in Washington. On the other hand, the problems of undergraduate education cannot effectively be addressed by bold strokes of state or national public policy. They can best be solved campus by campus with the active involvement of faculty, staff, students, trustees, and their friends and supporters off campus including, notably, state legislators. Hence, our solutions are cast not as recommendations for policymakers to impose from on high, but as challenges to be taken up on each of the nation's 3,400 campuses. Diversity and autonomy are among the great strengths of American higher education, as they are of American society itself. They are strengths to be respected and drawn upon as each institution decides itself how it will respond.

As first steps in what will be a long journey, we issue five challenges.

For colleges and universities:

- **We challenge** you to evaluate yourselves against the questions in the attached "Self-Assessment Checklist," and to commit yourself publicly to an institutional plan that builds on the strengths and remedies the deficiencies you identify.

- **We challenge** you to define and publicly state your standards of entry and exit in terms of the knowledge, skills, and abilities you expect from both applicants and graduates, and to put in place measures to assure student and institutional attainment of those standards by a fixed date.

- **We challenge** you to develop a curriculum that will assure all graduates—our future citizens, employees, and leaders—the benefits of a liberal education.

- **We challenge** you to assure that next year's entering students will graduate as individuals of character more sensitive to the needs of community, more competent to contribute to society, and more civil in habits of thought, speech, and action.

For trustees, regents, legislators, alumni, and funders in particular:

- **We challenge** you to respond to institutions that take up the first four challenges by giving them the regulatory and financial flexibility they need to get the job done. Institutional creativity, not micro-management, is the essential precondition to change. But we do urge you to urge them on. One of the best ways to do so is to insist that the campuses for which you have stewardship responsibility undertake the attached self-assessment.

We understand that some institutions will believe it unnecessary to respond to the challenges above. Perhaps they are correct, although we suggest that even the best can be better. Institutions hesitant to undertake a comprehensive self-assessment might consider administering the National Adult Literacy Survey instrument to a representative sample of graduating seniors. By permitting comparison of institutional performance with a nationwide sample of graduates of either two or four-year institutions, the NALS instrument can provide a minimally acceptable performance benchmark for any institution. No campus has anything to lose by turning to NALS, and it is difficult to imagine that most would not want to know where they stand. Some may be satisfied with the results, but many will be surprised.

Finally, we issue a challenge to the broader public, specifically to students, parents, employers, and citizens. This agenda for higher education is ambitious. It will not be accomplished easily or soon; nor can it bear fruit without your participation and support. All of us have contributed to the situation in which higher education today finds itself; we too must play our part in responding to the imperatives of the future. Every American must accept the fact that in an open, global economy, education is a critical national resource.

A generation ago, we told educators we wanted more people with a college credential and more research-based knowledge. Educators responded accordingly. Now we need to ask for different things. Students must value achievement, not simply seek a credential. Students (and parents) should look to the value added to their lives, not simply to the prestige of the institutions they attend. Employers must make clear to educators what they value in new employees. Without new public attitudes, higher education will find it difficult to persevere in the task ahead.

One of these difficulties is financial. Higher education's claim on public and private funds increasingly competes with a growing list of other compelling claims. One consequence is that after rising every year since the end of World War II, total state support for public higher education declined for two successive years as the 1990s began, and there is little reason to expect net new resources for the foreseeable future.

Since at least World War II, higher education's growth has been made possible by an expanding national economy. However, the post-World War II surge in productivity which fueled remarkable growth in our national wealth will not repeat itself unless educational institutions make a determined, successful effort to enhance the knowledge and skills Americans bring to the workplace. Thus, higher education's best financial hope rests on helping itself by helping expand the nation's wealth, by providing the knowledgeable and highly skilled workforce that can enhance our productivity, revitalize our communities, and rebuild our sense of "we."

We are convinced that those colleges and universities that demonstrate that they are doing more with what they have—those doing the best job of preserving strong, core programs and eliminating the less essential—will find not only that they have freed up resources to reinvest in themselves, but they will also have made a compelling case for additional external support. We also believe that institutions that defer change until new resources are available will find themselves waiting for a very long time. Financial salvation will begin on the campus or it will probably not begin at all. But as campuses begin to respond to the kind of challenges we issue, there must be solid public and financial support for higher education. It *is* a critical national resource.

Finally . . .

Higher education and the society it serves face a fork in the road. Either educators and other Americans raise their sights and take the difficult steps described in this open letter, or we all face the certain and unpleasant prospect of national decline. No one can look squarely at the quality of our undergraduate education, and its graduates, and come to a more optimistic conclusion.

We are guardedly hopeful that higher education will respond positively to the kinds of change we believe essential to our national well-being. That hope rests in the active participation of faculty members, administrators, and the public, many of whom understand the need for change and are working to effect it.

That hope rests on the fact that so many Americans understand how critical a productive and affordable system of higher education is to the American future. Even the most severe critic of higher education understands its importance and wishes it well.

Most significantly, there is hope, because when the nation has called on its colleges and universities to adapt in the past, higher education has always responded.

We cannot believe it will hesitate now.

Notes

1. Results of the NALS survey, conducted by the Educational Testing Service for the U.S. Department of Education, were released in September 1993. The largest effort of its type ever attempted, the survey offers a comprehensive analysis of the competence of American adults (both college- and non-college-educated) based on face-to-face interviews with 26,000 people. We note with concern that the 1993 survey findings reflect a statistically significant decline from those of an earlier survey conducted in 1985.

2. Questions taken from Howard Bowen, *The State of The Nation and the Agenda for Higher Education.* San Francisco: Jossey-Bass, 1982.

3. Donald Kagan, *Pericles of Athens and the Birth of Democracy.* New York: Simon & Schuster, 1991.

4. John Hope Franklin, et al., *The Inclusive University: A New Environment for Higher Education.* Washington: Joint Center for Political and Economic Studies, 1993.

PART III

THE EDUCATIONAL PRACTICE OF COLLEGE STUDENT AFFAIRS ADMINISTRATION

Because the functions and tasks of student affairs professionals vary with institutional size, type, cultures, and structures, the purpose of Part Three is to examine areas of responsibility and concerns that tend to be common regardless of specific job descriptions. These areas are (1) student learning and development, (2) community development, (3) reflective practice, and (4) research and assessment.

Student Involvement: A Developmental Theory for Higher Education

ALEXANDER W. ASTIN

A student development theory based on student involvement is presented and described, and the implications for practice and research are discussed.

Even a casual reading of the extensive literature on student development in higher education can create confusion and perplexity. One finds not only that the problems being studied are highly diverse but also that investigators who claim to be studying the same problem frequently do not look at the same variables or employ the same methodologies. And even when they are investigating the same variables, different investigators may use completely different terms to describe and discuss these variables.

My own interest in articulating a theory of student development is partly practical—I would like to bring some order into the chaos of the literature—and partly self-protective. I am increasingly bewildered by the muddle of findings that have emerged from my own research in student development, research that I have been engaged in for more than 20 years.

The theory of student involvement that I describe in this article appeals to me for several reasons. First, it is simple: I have not needed to draw a maze consisting of dozens of boxes interconnected by two-headed arrows to explain the basic elements of the theory to others. Second, the theory can explain most of the empirical knowledge about environmental influences on student development that researchers have gained over the years. Third, it is capable of embracing principles from such widely divergent sources as psychoanalysis and classical learning theory. Finally, this theory of student involvement can be used both by researchers—to guide their investigation of student development—and by college administrators and faculty—to help them design more effective learning environments.

Basic Elements of the Theory

Let me first explain what I mean by *involvement*, a construct that should not be either mysterious or esoteric. Quite simply, student involvement refers to the amount of physical and psychological energy that the student devotes to the academic experience. Thus, a highly involved student is one who, for example, devotes considerable energy to studying, spends much time on campus, participates actively in student organizations, and interacts frequently with faculty members and other students. Conversely, a typical uninvolved student neglects studies, spends little time on campus, abstains from extracurricular activities, and has infrequent contact with faculty members or other students. These hypothetical examples are only intended to be illustrative; there are many other possible forms of involvement, which are discussed in detail below.

In certain respects the concept of involvement closely resembles the Freudian concept of *cathexis*, which I learned about in my former career as a clinical psychologist. Freud believed that people invest psychological energy in objects and persons outside of themselves. In other words, people can *cathect* on their friends, families, schoolwork, and jobs. The involvement concept also resembles closely what the learning theorists have traditionally referred to as *vigilance* or *time-on-task*. The concept of *effort*, although much narrower, has much in common with the concept of involvement.

To give a better sense of what I mean by the term *involvement*, I have listed below the results of several hours that I spent recently looking in dictionaries and a thesaurus for words or phrases that capture some of the intended meaning. Because involvement is, to me, an active term, the list uses verb forms.

> attach oneself to
> commit oneself to
> devote oneself to
> engage in
> go in for
> incline toward
> join in
> partake of
> participate in
> plunge into
> show enthusiasm for
> tackle
> take a fancy to
> take an interest in
> take on
> take part in
> take to
> take up
> undertake

Most of these terms are behavioral in meaning. I could have also included words and phrases that are more "interior" in nature, such as *value, care for, stress, accentuate,* and *emphasize*. But in the sense that I am using the term, involvement implies a behavioral component. I am not denying that motivation is an important aspect of involvement, but rather I am emphasizing that the behavioral aspects, in my judgment, are critical: It is not so much what the individual thinks or feels, but what the individual does, how he or she behaves, that defines and identifies involvement.

At this stage in its development, the involvement theory has five basic postulates:

1. Involvement refers to the investment of physical and psychological energy in various objects. The objects may be highly generalized (the student experience) or highly specific (preparing for a chemistry examination).

2. Regardless of its object, involvement occurs along a continuum; that is, different students manifest different degrees of involvement in a given object, and the same student manifests different degrees of involvement in different objects at different times.

3. Involvement has both quantitative and qualitative features. The extent of a student's involvement in academic work, for instance, can be measured quantitatively (how many hours the student spends studying) and qualitatively (whether the student reviews and comprehends reading assignments or simply stares at the textbook and daydreams).

4. The amount of student learning and personal development associated with any educational program is directly proportional to the quality and quantity of student involvement in that program.

5. The effectiveness of any educational policy or practice is directly related to the capacity of that policy or practice to increase student involvement.

These last two propositions are, of course, the key educational postulates, because they provide clues for designing more effective educational programs for students. Strictly speaking, they do not really qualify as postulates, because they are subject to empirical proof. Indeed, much of the recommended research on involvement (discussed below) would be designed to test these two propositions.

Traditional Pedagogical Theories

A major impetus for the development of the student involvement theory was my exasperation at the tendency of many academicians to treat the student as a kind of "black box." On the input end of this black box are the various policies and programs of a college or university; on the output end are various types of achievement measures such as the GPA or scores on standardized tests. It seemed that something was missing: some mediating mechanism that would explain how these educational programs and policies are translated into student achievement and development.

I am not implying that the actions and policies of most faculty members and administrators are not guided by some kind of educational theory. But usually any such theory is only implicit in their actions; it is seldom stated formally or examined critically. Even when college personnel are aware of the theories that guide their actions, they seem to accept them as gospel rather than as testable propositions. In any event, it may be useful to examine these implicit pedagogical theories and to show how the theory of student involvement can help tie them more directly to student developmental outcomes. I have identified three implicit pedagogical theories, labeled for simplicity the *subject-matter*, the *resource*, and the *individualized* (or eclectic) theories.

The Subject-Matter Theory

The subject-matter theory of pedagogy, which could also be labeled the *content theory*, is popular among college professors. According to this theory, student learning and development depend primarily on exposure to the right subject matter. Thus, a "liberal education" consists of an assortment of "worthwhile" courses. Individual courses, in turn, are evaluated in terms of the content reflected, for example, in course syllabi. Indeed, in most colleges and universities teaching performance is evaluated by inspecting the professor's course syllabi. Given this strong emphasis on course content, it is not surprising that proponents of this theory tend to believe that students learn by attending lectures, doing the reading assignments, and working in the library. To the extent that written and oral presentations by the student are used as learning tools, they generally focus on the content of the reading or the lecture.

In the subject-matter approach to learning, those professors with the greatest knowledge of a particular subject matter have the highest prestige. Indeed, because of this emphasis on specialized knowledge, this approach seems to encourage the fragmentation and specialization of faculty interests and to equate scholarly expertise with pedagogical ability.

But perhaps the most serious limitation of the subject-matter theory is that it assigns students a passive role in the learning process: The "knowledgeable" professor lectures to the "ignorant" student so that the student can acquire the same knowledge. Such an approach clearly favors highly motivated students and those who tend to be avid readers and good listeners. Students who are slow readers or who have no intrinsic interest in the subject matter of a particular course are not well served by this approach. In fact, recent attempts to expand educational opportunities for underprepared students have probably been hindered by the continued adherence of most faculty members to the subject-matter theory of learning (Astin, 1982).

The Resource Theory

The resource theory of pedagogy is a favorite among administrators and policymakers. Used here, the term *resources* includes a wide range of ingredients believed to enhance student learning: physical facilities (laboratories, libraries, and audiovisual aids), human resources (well-trained faculty members, counselors, and support personnel), and fiscal resources (financial aid, endowments, and extramural research funds). In effect, the resource theory maintains that if adequate resources are brought together in one place, student learning and development will occur. Many college administrators believe that the acquisition of resources is their most important duty.

One resource measure that is particularly popular is the student-faculty ratio. Many administrators believe that the lower the ratio, the greater the learning and personal development that will occur. But the resource theory has qualitative as well as quantitative aspects, such as the belief that increasing the proportion of "high-quality" professors on the faculty (*quality* in this instance is defined primarily in terms of scholarly productivity and national visibility) will strengthen the educational environment. Actually, many research-oriented institutions could probably afford to hire more faculty members if they were less committed to recruiting and retaining faculty members who are highly visible in their disciplines. In short, such policies involve a trade-off between quantity and quality.

The resource theory of pedagogy also tends to include the belief that high-achieving students are a resource, that large numbers of such students on the campus enhance the quality of the learning environment for all students. Acting on this belief, many institutions invest substantial financial resources in the recruitment of high-achieving students.

The resource theory has two principal limitations. First, certain resources, such as bright students and prestigious faculty, are finite. As a result, the institutional energies expended in recruiting high-achieving students and prestigious faculty serve merely to redistribute these finite resources rather than to add to the total pool of such resources. In other words, a successful faculty or student recruitment program may benefit a particular institution, but the benefit comes at the expense of other institutions. As a consequence, widespread acceptance of the resource theory as it applies to faculty and students tends, paradoxically, to reduce the total resources available to the entire higher education community.

The second problem with this approach is its focus on the mere accumulation of resources with little attention given to the use or deployment of such resources. For instance, having established a multimillion-volume library, the administration may neglect to find out whether students are making effective use of that library. Similarly, having successfully recruited a faculty "star," the college may pay little attention to whether the new faculty member works effectively with students.

The Individualized (Eclectic) Theory

The individualized theory—a favorite of many developmental and learning psychologists (Chickering & Associates, 1981)—assumes that no single approach to subject matter, teaching, or resource allocation is adequate for all students. Rather, it attempts to identify the curricular content and instructional methods that best meet the needs of the individual student. With its emphasis on borrowing what is most useful from other pedagogical approaches, this flexible approach could also be termed *eclectic*.

In contrast to the subject-matter approach, which generally results in a fixed set of curricular requirements (i.e., courses that all students must take), the individualized approach emphasizes electives. Most college curricula represent a mixture of the subject-matter and individualized theories; that is, students must take certain required courses or satisfy certain distributional requirements but also have the option of taking a certain number of elective courses.

But the individualized theory goes far beyond curriculum. It emphasizes, for instance, the importance to the student of advising and counseling and of independent study. The philosophy underlying most student personnel work (guidance, counseling, selective placement, and student support services) implicitly incorporates the individualized or eclectic theory of student development.

The individualized approach is also associated with particular instructional techniques such as self-paced instruction. This theory has led some educators to espouse the "competency-based" learning model (Grant et al., 1979), whereby common learning objectives is highly variable and the instructional techniques used are highly individualized.

The most obvious limitation of the individualized theory is that it can be extremely expensive to implement, because each student normally requires considerable individualized attention. In addition, because there are virtually no limitations to the possible variations in subject matter and pedagogical approach, the individualized theory is difficult to define with precision. Furthermore, given the state of research on learning, it is currently impossible to specify which types of educational programs or teaching techniques are most effective with which types of learners. In other words, although the theory is appealing in the abstract, it is extremely difficult to put into practice.

The Place of the Theory of Student Involvement

In what way does the theory of student involvement relate to these traditional pedagogical theories? I believe that it can provide a link between the variables emphasized in these theories (subject matter, resources, and individualization of approach) and the learning outcomes desired by the student and the professor. In other words, the theory of student involvement argues that a particular curriculum, to achieve the effects intended, must elicit sufficient student effort and investment of energy to bring about the desired learning and development. Simply exposing the student to a particular set of courses may or may not work. The theory of involvement, in other words, provides a conceptual substitute for the black box that is implicit in the three traditional pedagogical theories.

The content theory, in particular, tends to place students in a passive role as recipients of information. The theory of involvement, on the other hand, emphasizes active participation of the student in the learning process. Recent research at the precollegiate level (Rosenshine, 1982) has suggested that learning will be greatest when the learning environment is structured to encourage active participation by the student.

On a more subtle level, the theory of student involvement encourages educators to focus less on what they do and more on what the student does: how motivated the student is and how much time and energy the student devotes to the learning process. The theory assumes that student learning and development will not be impressive if educators focus most of their attention on course content, teaching techniques, laboratories, books, and other resources. With this approach, student involvement—rather than the resources or techniques typically used by educators—becomes the focus of concern.

Thus, the construct of student involvement in certain respects resembles a more common construct in psychology: *motivation*. I personally prefer the term involvement, however, because it implies more than just a psychological state; it connotes the behavioral manifestation of that state. Involvement, in other words, is more susceptible to direct observation and measurement than is the more abstract psychological construct of motivation. Moreover, involvement seems to be a more useful construct for educational practitioners. "How do you motivate students?" is probably a more difficult question to answer than "How do you get students involved?"

The theory of student involvement is qualitatively different from the developmental theories that have received so much attention in the literature of higher education during the past few years. These theories are of at least two types: those that postulate a series of hierarchically arranged developmental stages (e.g., Heath, 1968; Kohlberg, 1971; Loevinger, 1966; Perry, 1970) and those that view student development in multidimensional terms (e.g., Brown & DeCoster, 1982; Chickering, 1969). (For recent, comprehensive summaries of these theories see Chickering & Associates, 1981; Hanson, 1982.)

Whereas these theories focus primarily on developmental outcomes (the *what* of student development), the theory of student involvement is more concerned with the behavioral mechanisms or processes that facilitate student development (the *how* of student development). These two types of theories can be studied simultaneously (see "Research Possibilities" section below).

Student Time as a Resource

College administrators are constantly preoccupied with the accumulation and allocation of fiscal resources; the theory of student involvement, however, suggests that the most precious institutional resource may be student time. According to the theory, the extent to which students can achieve particular developmental goals is a direct function of the time and effort they devote to activities designed to produce these gains. For example, if increased knowledge and understanding of history is an important goal for history majors, the extent to which students reach this goal is a direct function of the time they spend at such activities as listening to professors talk about history, reading books about history, and discussing history with other students. Generally, the more time students spend in these activities, the more history they learn.

The theory of student involvement explicitly acknowledges that the psychic and physical time and energy of students are finite. Thus, educators are competing with other forces in the student's life for a share of that finite time and energy. Here are the basic ingredients of a so-called "zero-sum" game, in which the time and energy that the student invests in family, friends, job, and other outside activities represent a reduction in the time and energy the student has to devote to educational development.

Administrators and faculty members must recognize that virtually every institutional policy and practice (e.g., class schedules; regulation on class attendance, academic probation, and participation in honors courses; policies on office hours for faculty, student orientation, and advising) can affect the way students spend their time and the amount of effort they devote to academic pursuits. Moreover, administrative decisions about many nonacademic issues (e.g., the location of new buildings such as dormitories and student unions; rules governing residency; the design of recreational and living facilities; on-campus employment opportunities; number and type of extracurricular activities and regulations regarding participation; the frequency, type, and cost of cultural events; roommate assignments; financial aid policies; the relative attractiveness of eating facilities on and off campus; parking regulations) can significantly affect how students spend their time and energy.

Relevant Research

The theory of student involvement has its roots in a longitudinal study of college dropouts (Astin, 1975) that endeavored to identify factors in the college environment that significantly affect the student's persistence in college. It turned out that virtually every significant effect could be rationalized in terms of the involvement concept; that is, every positive factor was likely to increase student involvement in the undergraduate experience, whereas every negative factor was likely to reduce involvement. In other words, the factors that contributed to the student's remaining in college suggested involvement, whereas those that contributed to the student's dropping out implied a lack of involvement.

What were these significant environmental factors? Probably the most important and pervasive was the student's residence. Living in a campus residence was positively related to retention, and this positive effect occurred in all types of institutions and among all types of students regardless of sex, race, ability, or family background. Similar results had been obtained in earlier studies (Astin, 1973; Chickering, 1974) and have been subsequently replicated (Astin, 1977, 1982). It is obvious that students who live in residence halls have more time and opportunity to get involved in all aspects of campus life. Indeed, simply by eating, sleeping, and spending their waking hours on the college campus, residential students have a better chance than do commuter students of developing a strong identification and attachment to undergraduate life.

The longitudinal study also showed that students who join social fraternities or sororities or participate in extracurricular activities of almost any type are less likely to drop out. Participation in sports, particularly intercollegiate sports, has an especially pronounced, positive effect on persistence. Other activities that enhance retention include enrollment in honors programs, involvement in ROTC, and participation in professors' undergraduate research project.

One of the most interesting environmental factors that affected retention was holding a part-time job on campus. Although it might seem that working while attending college takes time and energy away from academic pursuits, part-time employment in an on-campus job actually facilitates retention. Apparently such work, which also includes work-study combinations, operates in much the same way as residential living: The student is spending time on the campus, thus increasing the likelihood that he or she will come into contact with other students, professors, and college staff. On a more subtle psychological level, relying on the college as a source of income can result in a greater sense of attachment to the college.

Retention suffers, however, if the student works off campus at a full-time job. Because the student is spending considerable time and energy on nonacademic activities that are usually unrelated to student life, full-time work off campus decreases the time and energy that the student can devote to studies and other campus activities.

Findings concerning the effects of different types of colleges are also relevant to the theory of involvement. Thus, the most consistent finding—reported in almost every longitudinal study of student development—is that the student's chances of dropping out are substantially greater at a 2-year college than at a 4-year college. The negative effects of attending a community college are observed even after the variables of entering student characteristics and lack of residence and work are considered (Astin, 1975, 1977). Community colleges are places where the involvement of both faculty and students seems to be minimal. Most (if not all) students are commuters, and a large proportion attend college on a part-time basis (thus, they presumably manifest less involvement simply because of their part-time status). Similarly, a large proportion of faculty members are employed on a part-time basis.

The 1975 study of dropouts also produced some interesting findings regarding the "fit" between student and college: Students are more likely to persist at religious colleges if their own religious backgrounds are similar; Blacks are more likely to persist at Black colleges than at White colleges; and students from small towns are more likely to persist in small than in large colleges. The origin of such effects probably lies in the student's ability to identify with the institution. It is easier to become involved when one can identify with the college environment.

Further support for the involvement theory can be found by examining the reasons that students give for dropping out of college. For men the most common reason is boredom with courses, clearly implying a lack of involvement. The most common reason for women is marriage, pregnancy, or other responsibilities, a set of competing objects that drain away the time and energy that women could otherwise devote to being students.

The persister-dropout phenomenon provides an ideal paradigm for studying student involvement. Thus, if we conceive of involvement as occurring along a continuum, the act of dropping out can be viewed as the ultimate form of noninvolvement, and dropping out anchors the involvement continuum at the lowest end.

Because of the apparent usefulness of the involvement theory as it applied to the earlier research on dropping out, I decided to investigate the involvement phenomenon more intensively by studying the impact of college on a wide range of other outcomes (Astin, 1977). This study, which used longitudinal data on several samples totaling more than 200,000 students and examined more than 80 different student outcomes, focused on the effects of several different types of involvement: place of residence, honors programs, undergraduate research participation, social fraternities and sororities, academic involvement, student-faculty interaction, athletic involvement, and involvement in student government. In understanding the effects of these various forms of involvement it is important to keep in mind the overall results of this study: College attendance in general seems to strengthen student's competency, self-esteem, artistic interests, liberalism, hedonism, and religious apostasy and to weaken their business interests.

Perhaps the most important general conclusion I reached from this elaborate analysis was that nearly all forms of student involvement are associated with greater than average changes in entering freshman characteristics. And for certain student outcomes involvement is more strongly associated with change than either entering freshman characteristics or institutional characteristics. The following is a summary of the results for specific forms of involvement.

Place of Residence

Leaving home to attend college has significant effects on most college outcomes. Students who live in campus residences are much more likely than commuter students to become less religious and more hedonistic. Residents also show greater gains than commuters in artistic interests, liberalism, and interpersonal self-esteem. Living in a dormitory is positively associated with several other forms of involvement: interaction with faculty, involvement in student government, and participation in social fraternities or sororities.

Living on campus substantially increases the student's chances of persisting and of aspiring to a graduate or professional degree. Residents are more likely than commuters to achieve in such extracurricular areas as leadership and athletics and to express satisfaction with their undergraduate experience, particularly in the areas of student friendships, faculty-student relations, institutional reputation, and social life.

Honors Programs

Students who participate in honors programs gain substantially in interpersonal self-esteem, intellectual self-esteem, and artistic interests. They are more likely than other students to persist in college and to aspire to graduate and professional degrees. Honors participation is positively related to student satisfaction in three areas—quality of the science program, closeness to faculty, and quality of instruction—and negatively related to satisfaction with friendships and with the institution's academic reputation. These findings suggest that honors participation enhances faculty-student relationships but may isolate students from their peers.

Academic Involvement

Defined as a complex of self-reported traits and behaviors (e.g., the extent to which students work hard at their studies, the number of hours they spend studying, the degree of interest in their courses, good study habits), academic involvement produces an unusual pattern of effects. Intense academic involvement tends to retard those changes in personality and behavior that normally result from college attendance. Thus, students who are deeply involved academically are less likely than average students to show increases in liberalism, hedonism, artistic interests, and religious apostasy or decreases in business interests. The only personality change accentuated by academic involvement is need for status, which is strengthened. Being academically involved is strongly related to satisfaction with all aspects of college life except friendships with other students.

This pattern reinforces the hypothesis that students who become intensely involved in their college studies tend to become isolated from their peers and, consequently, are less susceptible to the peer group influences that seem critical to the development of political liberalism, hedonism, and religious apostasy. On the other hand, they experience considerable satisfaction, perhaps because of the many institutional rewards for good academic performance.

Student-Faculty Interaction

Frequent interaction with faculty is more strongly related to satisfaction with college than any other type of involvement or, indeed, any other student or institutional characteristic. Students who interact frequently with faculty members are more likely than other students to express satisfaction with all aspects of their institutional experience, including student friendships, variety of courses, intellectual environment, and even the administration of the institution. Thus, finding ways to encourage greater student involvement with faculty (and vice versa) could be a highly productive activity on most college campuses.

Athletic Involvement

The pattern of effects associated with involvement in athletic activities closely parallels the pattern associated with academic involvement; that is, students who become intensely involved in athletic activities show smaller than average increases in political liberalism, religious apostasy, and artistic interests and a smaller than average decrease in business interests. Athletic involvement is also associated with satisfaction in four areas: the institution's academic reputation, the intellectual environment, student friendships, and institutional administration. These results suggest that athletic involvement, like academic involvement, tends to isolate students from the peer group effects that normally accompany college attendance. For the studious person, this isolation results from the time and effort devoted to studying. For the athlete, the isolation probably results from long practice hours, travel to athletic competitions, and special living quarters.

Involvement in Student Government

Involvement in student government is associated with greater than average increases in political liberalism, hedonism, artistic interests, and status needs as well as greater than average satisfaction with student friendships. This pattern of relationships supports the hypothesis that the changes in attitudes and behavior that usually accompany college attendance are attributable to peer-group effects. That is, students who become actively involved in student government interact frequently with their peers, and this interaction seems to accentuate the changes normally resulting from the college experience.

Research on Cognitive Development

Although most research on classroom learning has been carried out at the precollegiate level, most of the evidence from this research strongly supports the concept of involvement as a critical element in the learning process. The concepts of time-on-task and effort, for example, appear frequently in the literature as key determinants of a wide range of cognitive learning outcomes (Bloom, 1974; Fisher et al., 1980; Gagne, 1977).

Practical Applications

There are several implications of the theory of involvement for practitioners in higher education. Some of the possible uses that could be made of the theory by faculty, administrators, and student personnel workers are briefly described below.

Faculty and Administrators

As already suggested, the content and resource approaches to pedagogy tend to favor the well-prepared, assertive student. In contrast, the concept of student involvement emphasizes giving greater attention to the passive, reticent, or unprepared student. Of course, not all passive students are uninvolved in their academic work, nor are they necessarily experiencing academic difficulties. But passivity is an important warning sign that may reflect a lack of involvement.

Perhaps the most important application of the student involvement theory to teaching is that it encourages the instructor to focus less on content and teaching techniques and more on what students are actually doing—how motivated they are and how much time and energy they are devoting to the learning process. Teaching is a complex art. And, like other art forms, it may suffer if the artist focuses exclusively on technique. Instructors can be more effective if they focus on the intended outcomes of their pedagogical efforts: achieving maximum student involvement and learning. (Final examinations monitor learning, but they come too late in the learning process to have much value for the individual student.)

The art-form analogy can perhaps be better illustrated with an example from sports. Any professional baseball player will confirm that the best way to develop skill in pitching is to focus not on the mechanics but on the intended results: getting the ball over the plate. If the player overemphasizes such techniques as the grip, the stance, the windup, and the kick without attending to where the ball goes, he will probably never learn to pitch well. In fact, the technique involved in pitching a baseball, shooting a basketball, or hitting a golf ball is really unimportant as long as the ball goes where the player wants it to. If the ball fails to behave as intended, then the player begins to worry about adjusting his or her technique.

In education, teachers and administrators often concentrate on their own techniques or processes and thus ignore or overlook what is going on with the student. I believe that the involvement approach has the advantage of encouraging educators to focus more on what the student is actually doing.

Counselors and Student Personnel Workers

If an institution commits itself to achieving maximum student involvement, counselors and other student personnel workers will probably occupy a more important role in institutional operations. Because student personnel workers frequently operate on a one-to-one basis with students, they are in a unique position to monitor the involvement of their clients in the academic process and to work with individual clients in an attempt to increase that involvement. One of the challenges confronting student personnel workers these days is to find a "hook" that will stimulate students to get more involved in the college experience: taking a different array of courses, changing residential situations, joining student organizations, participating in various kinds of extracurricular activities, or finding new peer groups.

The theory of involvement also provides a useful frame of reference for working with students who are having academic difficulties. Perhaps the first task in working with such students is to understand the principal objects on which their energies are focused. It might be helpful, for example, to ask the student to keep a detailed diary, showing the time spent in various activities such as studying, sleeping, socializing, daydreaming, working, and commuting. From such a diary the counselor can identify the principal activities in which the student is currently involved and the objects of cathexis and can then determine if the academic difficulties stem from competing involvements, poor study habits, lack of motivation, or some combination of these factors.

In short, the theory of student involvement provides a unifying construct that can help to focus the energies of all institutional personnel on a common objective.

Research Possibilities

My research over the past several years, applying the theory of student involvement, has generated many ideas for further research. There are possibilities not only for testing the theory itself but also for exploring educational ideas that grow out of the theory. The following are just a few examples of the kinds of research that could be undertaken.

Assessing Different Forms of Involvement

Clearly, one of the most important next steps in developing and testing the involvement theory is to explore ways of assessing different forms of involvement. As already suggested, a time diary could be valuable in determining the relative importance of various objects and activities to the student. Judging from my first attempt to develop time diaries (Astin, 1968), students vary considerably in the amount of time they spend on such diverse activities as studying, socializing, sleeping, daydreaming, and traveling. It would also be useful to assess how frequently students interact with each other, with faculty members and other institutional personnel, and with people outside the institution. In addition, it is important not only to identify the extracurricular activities in which the student participates but also to assess the time and energy that the student devotes to each activity.

Quality Versus Quantity

My colleague, C. Robert Pace, has developed an extensive battery of devices to assess the quality of effort that students devote to various activities (Pace, 1982). A number of research questions arise in connection with the quality versus quantity issue: To what extent can high-quality involvement compensate for lack of quantity? Can students be encouraged to use time more wisely? To what extent does low-quality involvement reflect such obstacles as lack of motivation and personal problems?

Involvement and Developmental Outcomes

The research reviewed earlier (Astin, 1977) suggests that different forms of involvement lead to different developmental outcomes. The connection between particular forms of involvement and particular outcomes is an important question that should be addressed in future research. For example, do particular forms of involvement facilitate student development along the various dimensions postulated by theorists such as Chickering (1969), Loevinger (1966), Heath (1968), Perry (1970), and Kohlberg (1971)? It would also be useful to determine whether particular student characteristics (e.g., socioeconomic status, academic preparation, sex) are significantly related to different forms of involvement and whether a given form of involvement produces different outcomes for different types of students.

The Role of Peer Groups

Considerable research at the precollegiate level suggests that the student's commitment of time and energy to academic work can be strongly influenced by student peers (Coleman, 1961; McDill & Rigsby, 1973). It would be useful to determine whether similar relationships exist at the postsecondary level and, in particular, whether different types of student peer groups can be consciously used to enhance student involvement in the learning process.

Attribution and Locus of Control

In recent years learning and developmental theorists have shown an increasing interest in the concepts of *locus of control* (Rotter, 1966) and *attribution* (Weiner, 1979). Considerable research, for example, suggests that students' degree of involvement in learning tasks can be influenced by whether they believe that their behavior is controlled by internal or by external factors. Weiner (1979) argued that even if students tend to view their locus of control as internal, involvement may be further contingent on whether the internal factors are controllable (e.g., dependent on effort) or uncontrollable (e.g., dependent on ability). It seems clear that the effectiveness of any attempt to increase student involvement is highly contingent on the student's perceived locus of control and attributional inclinations.

Other Questions

Other questions that could be explored in future research on the involvement theory include the following:

Exceptions to the rule. What are the characteristics of highly involved students who drop out? What are the characteristics of uninvolved students who nonetheless manage to persist in college? Are there particular developmental outcomes for which a high degree of involvement is contraindicated?

Temporal patterns of involvement. Two students may devote the same total amount of time and energy to a task but may distribute their time in very different ways. For example, one student preparing a term paper may work for 1 hour each night over a period of 2 weeks; another may stay up all night to do the paper. What are the developmental consequences of these different patterns?

Combining different forms of involvement. How do different forms of involvement interact? Does one form of involvement (e.g., in extracurricular activities) enhance or diminish the effects of another form (e.g., in academic work)? What are the ideal combinations that facilitate maximum learning and personal development?

Desirable limits to involvement. Although the theory of involvement generally holds that "more is better," there are probably limits beyond which increasing involvement ceases to produce desirable results and can even become counter-productive. Examples of excessive involvement are the "workaholic," the academic "grind," and others who manifest obsessive-compulsive behavior. What are the ideal upper limits for various forms of involvement? Are problems more likely to develop if the student is excessively involved in a single object (e.g., academic work) rather than in a variety of objects (e.g., academic work, part-time job, extracurricular activities, social activities, and political activities)?

Epidemiology of involvement. Can student involvement be increased if professors interact more with students? Can administrators bring about greater faculty-student interaction by setting an example themselves? Does focusing on student involvement as a common institutional goal tend to break down traditional status barriers between faculty and student personnel workers?

Summary

I have presented a theory of student development, labeled the *student involvement theory*, which I believe is both simple and comprehensive. This theory not only elucidates the considerable findings that have emerged from decades of research on student development; it also offers educators a tool for designing more effective learning environments.

Student involvement refers to the quantity and quality of the physical and psychological energy that students invest in the college experience. Such involvement takes many forms, such as absorption in academic work, participation in extracurricular activities, and interaction with faculty and other institutional personnel. According to the theory, the greater the student's involvement in college, the greater will be the amount of student learning and personal development. From the standpoint of the educator, the most important hypothesis in the theory is that the effectiveness of any educational policy or practice is directly related to the capacity of that policy or practice to increase student involvement.

The principal advantage of the student involvement theory over traditional pedagogical approaches (including the subject-matter, the resource, and the individualized or eclectic theories) is that it directs attention away from subject matter and technique and toward the motivation and behavior of the student. It views student time and energy as institutional resources, albeit finite resources. Thus, all institutional policies and practices—those relating to nonacademic as well as academic matters—can be evaluated in terms of the degree to which they increase or reduce student involvement. Similarly, all college personnel—counselors and student personnel workers as well as faculty and administrators—can assess their own activities in terms of their success in encouraging students to become more involved in the college experience.

References

Astin, A. W. (1968). *The college environment,* Washington, DC. American Council on Education.

Astin, A. W. (1973). The impact of dormitory living on students. *Educational Record, 54,* 204–210.

Astin, A. W. (1975). *Preventing students from dropping out.* San Francisco; Jossey-Bass.

Astin, A. W. (1977). *Four critical years.* San Francisco: Jossey-Bass.

Astin, A. W. (1982). *Minorities in American higher education.* San Francisco; Jossey-Bass.

Bloom, B. (1974). Time and learning. *American Psychologist, 29,* 682–688.

Brown, R. D., & DeCoster, D. A. (Eds.). (1982). *Mentoring-transcript systems for promoting student growth: New directions for student services no. 19.* San Francisco: Jossey-Bass.

Chickering, A. W. (1969). *Education and identity.* San Francisco: Jossey-Bass.

Chickering, A. W. (1974). *Commuters versus residents.* San Francisco: Jossey-Bass.

Chickering, A. W., & Associates. (1981). *The modern American college*. San Francisco: Jossey-Bass.

Coleman, J. S. (1961). *The adolescent society*. New York: Free Press.

Fisher, C. W., Berliner, D., Filby, N., Marliave, R. Cahen, L., & Dishaw, M. (1980). Teaching behaviors, academic learning time and student achievement. In D. Denham & A. Lieberman (Eds.), *Time to learn*. Washington, DC: National Institute of Education.

Gagne, R. M. (1977). *The conditions of learning*. (3rd ed.). New York: Holt, Rinehart and Winston.

Grant, G., Elbow, P., Ewens, T., Gamson, Z., Kohli, W., Neumann, W., Olesen, V., & Riesman, D. (1979). *On competence*. San Francisco: Jossey-Bass.

Hanson, G. R. (Ed.). (1982). *Measuring student development: New directions for student services no. 20*. San Francisco: Jossey-Bass.

Heath, D. (1968). *Growing up in college*. San Francisco: Jossey-Bass.

Kohlberg, L. (1971). Stages of moral development. In C. M. Beck, B. S. Crittenden, & E. V. Sullivan (Eds.), *Moral education*. Toronto: University of Toronto Press.

Loevinger, J. (1966). The meaning and measure of ego development. *American Psychologist*, 21, 195–206.

McDill, E. L., & Rigsby, L. C. (1973). *Structure and process in secondary schools: The academic impact of educational climates*. Baltimore: Johns Hopkins University Press.

Pace, C. R. (1982). *Achievement and the quality of student effort: Report prepared for the National Commission on Excellence in Education*. Los Angeles: Higher Education Research Institute, University of California at Lost Angeles.

Perry, W. G. (1970). *Forms of intellectual and ethical development in the college years*. New York: Holt, Rinehart and Winston.

Rosenshine, B. (1982). *Teaching functions in instructional programs*. Paper presented at the National Institute of Education's National Invitational Conference on Research on Teaching: Implications for Practice, Washington, DC.

Rotter, J. (1966). Generalized expectations for internal versus external control of reinforcement. *Psychological Monographs*, (Whole No. 609).

Weiner, B. A. (1979). Theory of motivation for some classroom experiences. *Journal of Educational Psychology*, 71, 3–25.

The Integration of Relational and Impersonal Knowing in Young Adults' Epistemological Development

Marcia B. Baxter Magolda

Data from the postcollege phase of a 7-year longitudinal study of college students' epistemological development—or their assumptions about the limits, certainty, and criteria for knowing—were analyzed. The data revealed that gender-related patterns these students demonstrated during college were integrated in the postcollege experience in work, advanced educational, and personal environments. Participants' stories illustrate how relational knowing, characterized by attachment and connection, and impersonal knowing, marked by separation and abstraction, were used dialectically as young adults adopted complex assumptions about knowing. Their stories are translated into implications for student affairs practice that promotes the integration of relational and impersonal knowing.

Modes of knowing and the nature of knowledge are topics of considerable debate in higher education and human development. Student development is no exception. The foundational theories used to understand students' intellectual (Perry, 1970), psychosocial (Chickering, 1969), and moral (Kohlberg, 1969) development all focus on development as an autonomous, rational process. Later student development theories added a relational dimension to intellectual (Belenky, Clinchy, Goldberger, & Tarule, 1986), psychosocial (Josselson, 1987; Straub, 1987), and moral (Gilligan, 1982) development. Many theorists are now advocating an integrated view of development that relies on both relational and rational modes of knowing. Chickering and Reisser's (1993) revision of psychosocial theory incorporates both autonomous (or separate) and relational (or connected) dimensions, as does recent work in moral development (Gilligan & Attanucci, 1988; Lyons, 1983). The current research demonstrated that these two dimensions are integrated in young adults' intellectual, or epistemological, development. I use the term *impersonal* to refer to the autonomous, objective, rational mode of knowing and the term *relational* to refer to the connected, subjective mode of knowing.

When originally describing college students' intellectual development Perry (1970) identified assumptions about the nature, limits, and certainty of knowledge—assumptions that Kitchener (1983) calls epistemic assumptions. Perry traced students' movement from dualistic epistemic assumptions—namely that knowledge was certain and was known to authorities—to relativistic epistemic assumptions—namely that knowledge was uncertain and was evaluated using evidence in a particular context. Perry's participants focused throughout this journey on the objective process for arriving at the truth. Belenky, Clinchy, Goldberger and Tarule (1986) offered a complementary but different picture of epistemological development based on their study of women. Although these participants followed the same overall trajectory, they often focused on understanding and connecting to others' thoughts, in a sense getting inside the knowing process rather than standing outside of it. Some participants did take the objective approach, leading Belenky et al. to articulate the concepts of separate and connected knowing. They argued that these two modes of knowing converged in what they called constructed knowing.

Because Perry's work was based on a predominantly male group and Belenky et al.'s work was based on women, the relationship between impersonal and relational modes of knowing remained unclear. Although King and Kitchener (1994) included both genders in their extensive longitudinal work on reflective judgment, they focused on the role of judgment in the face of ill-structured problems rather than on the two modes of knowing. I conducted a longitudinal study of college students' epistemological development that included both genders to explore the evolution of impersonal and relational modes of knowing (Baxter Magolda, 1992). The college phase of the project revealed that (a) the evolution of epistemic assumptions was similar to that described by Perry and Belenky et al.; (b) both relational and rational modes existed within the first three sets of epistemic assumptions, suggesting that they were equally complex modes of knowing; and (c) relational and impersonal modes of knowing seemed to converge in the fourth set of epistemic assumptions. The postcollege phase of the project, the focus of this article, involved the questions of how complex ways of knowing developed and how relational and impersonal modes of knowing evolved after college.

Modes of Knowing in College: Phase 1

Because the study is longitudinal, the college phase is briefly described next to serve as a backdrop for the post-college phase. The research methods used for both the college and postcollege phases have been described fully in previous publications and pertinent aspects are discussed here.

Method for the College Phase

The original longitudinal college study involved random selection of 101 first-year students (50 men and 51 women) attending a Midwestern, public, 4-year institution. They came from a variety of majors within all six divisions of the university, which has a liberal arts focus. Admission is competitive, and these students' entering class had a mean ACT score of 25.8; 70 percent had ranked in the top 20% of their high school class. The campus culture encouraged high involvement in campus activities, with one third of the student body involved in Greek organizations. Of these 101 students, 80 participated in all 4 years of the study.

In annual interviews, I invited students to talk freely about their role as learners, the role of instructors and peers in learning, their perception of evaluation of their work, the nature of knowledge, and educational decision making. These six areas revealed epistemic assumptions, as well as experiences that affected those assumptions. The question in each area introduced the topic but did nothing beyond that to frame the response. For example, I introduced the nature of knowledge with, "Have you ever encountered a situation in which you heard two explanations for the same idea?" When students said yes, I invited them to describe the experience, their reaction to it, and the way they decided what to believe.

Follow-up questions clarified each student's responses, and I routinely summarized the responses to make sure I understood the perspective. The interviews were tape recorded and transcribed verbatim. I used the same procedures for analyzing data in both the college and postcollege studies (described next).

Findings for the College Phase

Three sets of epistemic assumptions, or ways of knowing, were prevalent in college: (a) *absolute knowing*, characterized by viewing knowledge as certain; (b) *transitional knowing*, characterized by a growing awareness of uncertainty in some areas of knowledge; and (c) *independent knowing*, a perspective in which most knowledge was viewed as uncertain. In each way of knowing, two gender-related patterns appeared. I use the term *gender-related* to convey that patterns were used more often, but not exclusively, by one gender than by the other. These patterns revealed that some students approached knowing primarily through a *relational* mode characterized by attachment and connection, whereas others used an *impersonal* approach marked by separation and abstraction.

In absolute knowing, I labeled the patterns *receiving* (relational) and *mastery* (impersonal). Receiving-pattern students used an approach centered around listening and recording information. For example, Toni explained: "I like to listen—just sit and take notes from an overhead. The material is right there. And if you have a problem, you can ask him, and he can explain it to you. You hear it, you see it, and then you write it down." Receiving-pattern students relied on an authority for answers and relied on peers only for making the learning environment more supportive. Mastery-pattern students asked and answered questions to gain knowledge. Tim explained this approach: "I like getting involved with the class. Just by answering questions, asking questions. Even if you think you know everything, there're still questions you can ask. When he [the instructor] asks questions, you can try to answer them to your best ability. Don't just let the teacher talk but have him present questions to you." Mastery pattern students depended on authority for answers but viewed their own and their peers' involvement as a useful tool to master the material. Toni and Tim both endorsed the core belief of absolute knowing—the notion that knowledge is certain.

In transitional knowing the two patterns were characterized as *interpersonal* and *impersonal*. Interpersonal-pattern students addressed uncertainty by incorporating their own and others' experiences, whereas impersonal-pattern students relied on objective use of an individually focused process of knowing. A comparison of Kris's and Scott's approaches clarifies this distinction. Kris said: "Classroom discussions are better for me to learn. You have an opening lecture, where you have the professor discuss. Then students can contribute. Listening to other students contribute their ideas and putting in my own inputs—that makes learning better for me because it makes me think more and try to come up with more generative ideas as to what I would do in a situation." Scott offered: "The debate-and-discussion process for me is really interesting. I learn a lot more because I remember questions. And I guess I learn the most when I sit and I'm actually forced to raise my hand and then I have to talk. I have to sit there and think on the spot." Kris focused on connection and thought more effectively when she put her ideas together with others' ideas. Scott learned through thinking individually, focusing on the value of the discussion process to force him to think rather than to hear other perspectives. Both students are transitional knowers because they realize that some knowledge is uncertain and requires thinking rather than memorizing.

As students moved to independent knowing, the relational and impersonal patterns took the form of *interindividual* and *individual* patterns. Interindividual-pattern students focused primarily on others' perspectives whereas individual pattern students focused primarily on their own perspectives. For example, Alex described the interindividual approach:

> I listen to their arguments for it [one position]; then I listen to other people's arguments against it. And then it's just my own personal view, really, . . . I listen to both sides. I usually throw some of my own views into it as well. So I'm influenced by other people—like each member of the group should be influenced by each other. But when the final vote comes in, you should go with what you believe.

Alexis flipped back and forth between her views and others' and struggled to include her own in the final decision.

Lowell's comments show the contrast of the individual approach:

> He looked at it in this way, and I looked at it in another way . . . [You had] to try to get your point across without sounding too dominating—I'm searching for words and not finding them—to try to listen to theirs, to really listen, not to just hear it and let it go through, and then to try to take that into account and reach a compromise. . . . But I don't think the attempt was to try to change each other's mind. It was just, "Your point is all right, but you've got to look at this part, too, because this is as relevant."

Lowell had no problem keeping his own view in the forefront; his struggle was instead "really listening" to others' views. Alexis and Lowell share the core belief of independent knowing—that various arguments exist, and one decides what to believe by comparing ones' opinions to those of others.

The receiving, interpersonal, and interindividual patterns illustrate relational knowing due to their connection with others and what is to be known. Knowledge acquired via abstract modes does not connect with self for these knowers. Thus, they try to build belief systems through connection to others and their own experiences, often struggling to connect fully with themselves. In this study, women used these patterns more frequently than did men. The mastery, impersonal, and individual patterns reflect impersonal knowing in their focus on objectivity and separation of knower and known. These knowers build belief systems via abstract processing of information and others' perspectives. The men in this study used these patterns more often than the women did. No pattern was used exclusively by one gender. Perhaps the most important finding of the college phase was that these patterns existed within the same sets of epistemological assumptions, providing important evidence that the relational and impersonal patterns are equally complex approaches to knowing. Said another way, the pair of patterns in each way of knowing shared the same basic assumption about the nature of knowledge, despite students' different approaches to coming to know. A fourth way of knowing, in which the two patterns converged, appeared for a few students during college. This perspective was explored more fully in the postcollege years.

Method: Postcollege Study

Of the 70 participants in the postcollege study, 59 graduated with 4 years and the remaining 11 in 5 years. Only two were members of ethnic/racial minorities. The group remained fairly evenly balanced by gender, with 37 women and 33 men in the 5th year, 29 women and 22 men in the 6th year, and 27 women and 21 men in the 7th year. The occupational fields of the postcollege participants included insurance, sales, accounting, computing, teaching, mental health, advertising, communications, business, banking, real estate, retail management, airline services, and government services. Twelve were in advanced academic settings full time (three of these graduated from these settings in the 6th year), and 13 pursued a formal advanced education while holding full-time jobs. Nine were married, two had children, and one was divorced. Fourteen had left their original postgraduation job due to conflicts with their values (4), lack of fit (5), transfers due to marriage (3), transfer within a company (1) and pregnancy (1). Two of these individuals changed jobs three times between graduation and the 7th year.

I used qualitative interviews similar to those used in the college phase to keep the focus on learners' stories. The fact that few researchers have explored epistemological development after college increased the importance of allowing insights to emerge from the learners' experiences, prompting the use of an informal conversational interview (Patton, 1990). I began the annual interview with a summary of the project focus, reiterating my interest in exploring how participants learned and decided what to believe. The participant was then asked to think about important learning experiences that had taken place since the previous interview 1 year ago. The participant volunteered those experiences, described them, and described their impact on her or his thinking. I asked questions to pursue why these experiences were important, which factors influenced the experiences, and how the learner was affected. The interview addressed learning experiences in work life, everyday life, and academic life, if applicable. Work experiences invariably involved discussion about the workers' role, relationships with coworkers, supervision issues, and daily work decisions. Academic experiences involved discussion of the learning environment; the role learners, teachers, and peers played; and how work was evaluated. Discussions about everyday life revolved around insights that participants gained from interpersonal relationships and everyday living. I conducted all interviews by telephone, and they ranged from 60 to 90 minutes. All interviews were tape recorded and transcribed verbatim.

I analyzed interview responses using Glaser and Strauss's (1967) constant comparative method for processing naturalistic data. I reviewed transcription of the taped interviews, dividing them into units or sections that represented one idea. I then sorted the units into categories that fit together, and developed a classification system based on those categories (Patton, 1990). The quality of the classification system is determined by judging whether the units in a category fit together in a meaningful way and whether the distinctions between categories are clear (Patton, 1990). I adjusted the categories until they accounted for the units accurately. The analysis met Lincoln and Guba's (1985) recommendation that an accurate classification system should contain no more than 5% miscellaneous items. The theme of integration of relational and impersonal patterns of knowing, the focus of this article, emerged from this classification system. Themes about epistemic assumptions and experiences that promoted complex epistemological development also emerged and are reported elsewhere (Baxter Magolda, 1994).

Use of this systematic process heightened the credibility of my interpretations. Although the subjectivity I bring to the data analysis is valuable in gaining an in-depth understanding of the participants' thinking, it is equally important to insure that my interpretations are grounded in the data. The constant comparative method allows for revisiting interpretations to keep them consistent with the data. Because naturalistic data analysis is an inherently subjective process, I also used some of Lincoln and Guba's (1985) recommendations for enhancing credibility. I routinely sent summaries of my interpretations to participants and solicited their feedback during interviews. This member checking technique served as a test of the accuracy of my interpretations. Prolonged engagement over 7 years allowed me to build trust and rapport with the participants, increasing the likelihood of my obtaining their genuine perspectives. This enhanced the trustworthiness of the students' responses to the interviews and to my interpretations. The thick description of the participants and the detailed stories that follow are offered to help the reader judge transferability to contexts beyond the one in which the study was conducted.

Contextual Knowing in the Postcollege Years

One primary finding to emerge from the post-college phase was the integration of relational and impersonal patterns within a set of epistemic assumptions I called contextual knowing. Contextual knowers viewed themselves as capable of constructing knowledge. They did so by looking at all aspects of a situation or issue, seeking out expert advice in that particular context, and integrating their own and others' views in deciding what to think. The relational pattern is evident in their emphasis on using their own experience and perspectives, accessing others' perspectives, and getting inside the issue. The impersonal pattern is evident in contextual knowers' simultaneous emphasis on standing apart from the situation, abstractly processing experience and information. Participants' discussions about how they came to know and decide during their initial years after college illustrate the variations of how the relational and impersonal threads intertwine in their experience. I have chosen a few stories to describe this integration.

Integrating Relational and Impersonal Modes in Deciding What to Believe. Reginald's struggle to establish his perspective and simultaneously remain open to new ideas illustrates how the relational and impersonal patterns came together for him. As Reginald introduced important learning experiences he had encountered in seminary, he brought up his struggle to sort out the meaning of intellect and emotion during his second year:

> I think what I struggle with . . . is to claim the experience. . . . I have to have that identity of what I do believe . . . along with the open mind and the openness to other views and respecting that. Because if not I'm just sort of wishy-washy, flimsying around, . . . [claiming your experience] is part of what makes you who you are. That's perhaps the intellect and then when you live it that's the emotion or the passion perhaps that you bring to what you do. . . . The belief is sort of a clay that is not hardened, that is always being molded. It can shift; it can take new forms. But it's still the same, still a belief system within your self-identity, within your experience that won't deny your experience. It won't completely just blow away like sand, but it will form and it will be consistent—it has some weight to it.

Reginald struggled to claim what he believed, not wanting it to restrict his openness to others' ideas. Yet he was aware that he had to have some "form" for his perspective so it would not "blow away like sand." Reginald chose the word intellect to capture the experience he claimed, the basis of what he believed. This formed an identity that helped him balance accessing others' thoughts and acknowledging his experience.

He explained this notion further through the idea of boundaries:

> In defining that self, identifying that self, is the creation of boundaries in what we do personally and publicly. . . . If I didn't have that boundary, I might not bring out what it is that I need, what it is that I do believe. . . . If I disregard the boundary, I can be overwhelmed . . . I always considered the word *boundary* as a barrier. And so if I created these [barriers] I would be . . . a closed-minded person; . . . there wasn't a meeting place because there was this wall in the way. The other person would come to one side of the wall, I'd come to the other side of the wall, and we'd look at brick. And there wouldn't be a place where I could meet them. . . . But also, if I don't have anything, if I don't have boundaries, I lose the sense of who I am and I can't learn.

The boundaries of Reginald's identity keep him from being consumed as he meets others in dialogue. His thoughts suggest that learning through the dialogue requires both connection (to himself and to others' ideas) and separation (maintaining his boundaries to avoid complete connection). He argued that one cannot effectively "meet" others or learn without a self-identity.

The self-identity Reginald struggled to claim includes relational and impersonal dimensions. Reginald recognized the role emotion plays in what he claims as knowledge and in the "passion perhaps that you bring to what you do." He explored this topic further in a paper on Christian theology in which he struggled to explain how intellect, emotion, and action meshed. The following year he introduced the topic again, offering a more decisive statement:

> In the dialogue process there is emotion and intellect happening . . . because you can sense the passion sometimes behind someone's belief. I think from what I've heard from those who don't like that to be the case, . . . [the] fear is that in a setting of rationality one has to keep that intellect, [that] barrier strong against the tides of emotion. [If] the mere sweeping of one wave of emotion gets over the barrier, the whole area will be drowned. And intellect cannot stand against emotion. I don't think that's on the ball or that's where it's at. Emotion and intellect are always intertwined. You can't escape that. . . . They bounce off one another. An emotional experience may spark the intellect, and the intellect may spark an emotional experience. Those two are entwined quite nicely.

Following Reginald's thinking during these years shows that he initially had trouble avoiding being overwhelmed by his connection to others. He resolved this issue by connecting to himself (claiming his experience and defining his self-identity), something that allowed him to separate to an extent from others. Perhaps connecting to himself is what allowed Reginald to recognize that intellect is not separate from emotion, that his passion about something is part of the experience he has claimed.

Unlike Reginald, Sandra established a boundary in her college years. Describing herself early in college, Sandra said: "I think at the beginning of college it was more like, 'Could you prove it?' If it seemed really logical and it could be proven and it made a lot of sense to me, then I would probably take it in." Comparing this to the end of college, she added, "Whereas later in college, I had that basic framework laid down and I kind of thought, "Well, does this match or at least come close?" Talking about how she decided what to believe in the postcollege years, she said:

> I like to hear, especially, people with business backgrounds. . . . I like to hear their viewpoints because they're a lot of times very different from mine. How do I decide what I agree with? I guess I already have—especially from experience—. . . a pretty solid idea of how I think it should be. And if they say something that basically goes along with that, I'm willing to listen and hear what they have to say, but if it doesn't feel comfortable, I guess, sort of at a gut level, then I just figure, "Well, I'll stick with

what I've got." I think I've got a pretty good base and some experience in the different areas already. But, yeah, I guess I kind of go with a gut feeling. I don't know if that's a good way to do it or not.

Logic was largely sufficient for Sandra to believe something early in college. Later in college and in her professional work she began to consider how it matched with her knowledge base and particularly whether it felt comfortable or not. She did not recount a struggle claiming her knowledge base and clearly used it as a benchmark against which to consider others' claims, claims she was interested in hearing because they differed from hers. Because it was my impression based on her comments that she operated solely on a "gut feeling," I asked if proof was no longer needed. She replied:

> Well, I still have to prove it . . . oh, definitely. If there is no proof—forget it. I won't take it in. But I guess that you really, really have to work harder if it felt uncomfortable to me or if it was different from a basic knowledge that I had or a basic foundation for what I believed in. . . . I suppose I could be swayed, but you have to work 75% harder to do that if it doesn't kind of go along with what I already thought.

These comments make clear that Sandra still values the rational dimension; if there is no proof, there is no point in considering the idea. Yet, if the proof is inconsistent with her basic knowledge or foundation, it is going to be difficult to convince her to alter her perspective. Having connected with her own experience and beliefs, she was no longer willing to judge solely on logic.

Integrating Relational and Impersonal Modes in Career and Personal Decisions. Mark experienced integrating relational and impersonal modes of knowing in his decisions about his law career and personal life. Being a proponent of logic throughout his undergraduate career, Mark went to law school with a logical plan for his future. Much to his surprise, law school was not as stimulating as he had expected, and his first internship in a law firm was less than appealing. At the same time he was entertaining thoughts of marriage to a woman he had dated for years. His thought process still contained a strong logical component but it had an added dimension:

> As far as firm and personal life, I sit down and I write down things I know, pro and con, "Go into a relationship," "Don't go into a relationship," cost-benefit kind of analysis. Like I said, I don't leave my rationality behind because I think that's really an effective tool. And then I think about all my options, and there's something about it. It carries on its own momentum. . . . So I listen to those feelings, and I come to my room and I sit down and I push all my books away. I grab a sheet of paper or whatever and start writing things down, how I feel. And then when I feel like I've got a handle on those feelings and options, then I talk to the people affected. . . . When you bring other people into it, you push your feelings down just a touch because then you want to be open minded again at that point. And then you talk to people unaffected by it, too, because obviously when people are affected by it they're invested in it. . . . I don't let my feelings rush me into anything because . . . you're dealing with personal life more—if you do something rash, it can cost you a lot.

Mark clearly viewed logic and feelings as important factors in deciding. He used logic to check emotions, because he preferred to avoid doing anything rash on the basis of feelings. However, he had also discovered that the logical approach did not always lead to happiness. Summarizing how he felt about rationality and feelings, he said: "Rational thinking as best I can really gets me there. And then I get there and I see, 'Okay, here's the set of facts. What do I feel?' And then that carries me the rest of the way." These comments imply that Mark relied most on rationality, tried to approach his feelings from an objective stance, and acknowledged that feelings had to be included in the process.

A year later, still in law school and engaged to be married, he described writing down his feelings about being unhappy in a law firm so that he could look at them objectively. At this point I asked Mark to clarify whether the pro and con started out as objective but came to include feeling. He replied:

> Yes. Definitely. [My list of thoughts is] infused with feelings. But when I sit back and look at the list I try to look at it objectively. I try to sit back and weigh them. . . . Every term is loaded with feelings and emotions, and even in a secondary way—for instance, feelings and emotions as far as how the quota for billable hours will impact on my love relationship with my wife and my family. So there's all kinds of emotions in there. So they definitely get weighed objectively along with everything else. They're part of the mix. They're inseparable.

Although his thought process was still characterized by logic and a rational approach. Mark stated more definitively that feelings and logic are inseparable. The emptiness he experienced doing some of the things he thought were logically right during law school convinced him that happiness had to be a central criteria in his decisions. His logical approach up to this point was separate from self. Realizing his unhappiness. Mark connected with himself through acknowledging his feelings and their relevance in his decision making.

In contrast to Mark, Sheila was a strong relational knower throughout college. After college she advanced the notion that logic and intuition, or impersonal and relational dimensions, were equally intelligent. Marrying a man who used a strong logical approach led her to talk about how each affected the other. She commented: "[He] is learning to go forward with his heart a little bit more, and I'm working more with my mind a little bit. But . . . everyone regresses to what they are most comfortable with." Previous comments Sheila had made led me to ask whether she perceived both approaches as equally intelligent. She replied:

> Yes, I do, although it leads us to two different types of knowledge. . . . Whereas [he] is leading to a knowledge outside himself, . . . which is important, but he needs to be more in touch with himself, spiritually, emotionally. . . . I need to be a little bit more logical. So I can say I have a basis for my feeling on this situation. I think it's intelligent in both ways, but I've come to see how important it is to have both things. I think if you are self-absorbed, you turn into somebody who is selfish and rather out of touch. But at the same time, if you just do everything logically, sooner or later you are going to have a heart attack, because it's not logic that rules the world. The world keeps going logically, yes, but everybody's got their own heartbeat and their own speed of doing things and their own rationale. And if you run around and do things logically, that's not necessarily the pace or the rhythm of your own heart. . . . I waffle in between the two. I think it's a yin and yang situation. Each person needs to find that happy medium. Unfortunately, it's very difficult, because I think people tend to be one or the other. And you have to work at it just like learning to write or ride your bicycle.

Through interacting with her husband, Sheila decided that she could benefit from using logic a little more to back up her feelings. She also believed that her husband could benefit from adding a relational dimension to his way of knowing. Sheila emphasized the importance of working to find the balance. Sheila seemed to be saying that connection to self (relational knowing) is crucial, but total immersion in self is not healthy. The latter can be avoided by separating from self and using logic (impersonal knowing) in balance with connection. She also judged her husband's reliance on impersonal knowing as important, but unhealthy as the sole mode of thinking.

The Dilemma of Imbalance of Relational and Impersonal Modes. Sheila's caution about too much reliance on one mode of knowing was confirmed by other participants who described from their experiences the dangers of the two being out of balance. The primary theme here was that relying too heavily on one dimension results in being blinded, in being unable to know as accurately as possible. Mark's previous comments revealed the dangers of overlooking the relational dimension in decision making. Mark described this in more detail as he discussed the conflict he faced in law school. Describing his ability to be successful as an undergraduate because it did not conflict with who he was, he commented on the difference at law school:

> To do everything I thought was successful here but not buy into its values—it wouldn't have worked. Even when I came to law school with that plan in mind, the

ultimate plan was still, Do what's successful. But after my [envisioned U. S.] Supreme Court clerkship, what would I do? I thought . . . I would be in the *ultimate* position to do whatever I want to do because I will have done *everything* possible, and then I'd be in a position to make a choice that reflected exactly who I was, or at least more clearly. . . . I never *dreamed* that I would be unhappy working on the law journal. I didn't think it would be as tedious and boring as I found it. That never figured in. There was no way law school and its classes could be as big a turnoff as they were. I was like "this isn't going to be too bad." I had false expectations.

Mark's logical plan to obtain the ultimate freedom was sabotaged by his dissatisfaction with some aspects of law school. He clearly never expected feelings to get in his way and had not planned to deal with them until his plan had been implemented.

There are numerous examples of the dangers of overlooking the logical dimension as well. Lowell discovered this through the breakup of his marriage. Describing himself for not using his rationality earlier in the relationship:

Another flag that I think I should have seen: She basically went home every weekend—a half-hour drive away. I look back and say, " . . . How could you be so stupid?" You know. Hindsight is 20/20. Those are the type of flags that I keep thinking in my mind. . . . They're just popping up all over the place; the landscape is just littered with them. But you know, it is really easy to see once you step aside and take a look back. . . . And all those flags I talk about—they were logical things that if I had thought about them logically would have . . . I mean, I am still a human being, and I have emotional feelings . . . I don't disregard that. . . . I was blind to a lot of things. I don't think that it was that I chose not to see; it's that I was just blinded by it.

Lowell essentially was blinded by his feelings. Despite his ready use of logic at work and the flags he can now identify that signaled trouble, he could not see those flags or process them logically from his vantage point in the relationship. As he processed the experience of divorce, he emphasized the importance of balancing feelings and logic, or impersonal and relational patterns of knowing.

Sandra, though unwilling to describe the experience that led her to this view, concurred with the idea of balancing feelings and logic. She said that her emotional response to a bad experience prompted her to withdraw and mistrust everyone. Only later, when logic reentered her processing of the experience, did she distinguish between the person who betrayed her trust and others. Thus impersonal knowing helped her put the experience in perspective as well as think about how to approach people in the future. These stories reveal the necessity of connection to one's emotions and experiences balanced with abstract reflection on one's experience. Lowell and Sandra were initially too connected to their own experience and emotions; Mark was initially too disconnected from his emotions.

The Complex Interplay of Relational and Impersonal Modes. These stories revealed that contextual knowing was a matter not just of using both relational and impersonal modes of knowing but of integrating them. Reginald and Sandra both developed boundaries by connecting to their own experience. They then used those boundaries both to connect to others in dialogue and to maintain a necessary separateness from others in that dialogue. The participants recognized that connecting to their emotions was essential in deciding what to believe, yet they were aware that this had to be balanced with rational reflection. Contextual knowers emphasized that dialogue, or access to others' perspectives and experiences, was required for developing beliefs.

This process is relational in the individual's connection with her own basic belief system and with the experience of others; it is impersonal when the individual then stands apart to process abstractly others' contributions to the dialogue to determine whether they connect with that basic belief system. This integration is what Labouvie-Vief (1990) calls dialectic, and she argues for the mutually enriching dialogue between the two modes of knowing. According to Labouvie-Vief: "One mode provides precision, the other richness. One performs analysis, the other gives direction and significance. Without one, the dialogue would be without rule and form; without the other, it would not matter to anybody—it would not stir our fancy, capture our interest, incite our feelings" (p. 50). Labouvie-Vief suggested that developmental theory would be enhanced by adopting this dialectical view. The stories here confirm her emphasis on the value of dialogue.

Implications for Student Affairs Practice

The Student Learning Imperative: Implications for Student Affairs (American College Personnel Association, 1994) contains a description of a college-educated person as possessing complex cognitive skills and a coherent, integrated sense of identity, among other characteristics. The contextual knowers' experiences recounted here indicate that developing these characteristics involved recognizing the importance of the knower, or self, in what is known; the value of accessing and processing one's own and others' perspectives; and direct encounters and practice with relational and impersonal modes of knowing. Although some (e.g., Reginald) encountered these experiences in academic studies, many encountered them through relationships (e.g., Sheila and Lowell), work (e.g., Sandra), and career or personal decisions (e.g., Mark). Thus, their experiences seem to confirm a point made in *The Student Learning Imperative* that student affairs can be centrally involved in promoting student learning.

The contextual knowers' stories illustrate that the development of self-identity is necessary for contextual knowing. Balancing one's own and others' perspectives required a self-identity as a foundation (e.g., Reginald's boundary, Sandra's foundation of what she believed). Numerous student affairs arenas offer opportunities for developing identity. Peer interactions offer students opportunities to explore their values, compare them with other ideas, and make decisions about values to adopt as their own. When student affairs staff are involved in these interactions, students are more likely to construct their own belief systems rather than bow to peer pressure. Campus living environments and student groups can offer opportunities to evaluate various perspectives and make decisions about community rules. Leadership experiences can help students solidify their beliefs and build confidence in themselves as knowledge constructors. The collective group of longitudinal study participants reported that experiences such as these helped them view themselves as capable of knowledge construction (Baxter Magolda, 1992).

While developing self-identity, the contextual knowers needed help in learning to dialogue with others without losing their sometimes-fragile identity. Student affairs professionals who mediate roommate conflicts have a direct opportunity to teach students how to express their own needs and simultaneously respect those of others. Working with students who are struggling with relationship issues is another avenue for promoting this type of learning. Advisors to student organizations and student leaders can directly teach students how to learn about each others' perspectives and how to exchange, process, and decide about these perspectives in the course of their group's work. Programming aimed at seeing the world through the eyes of others—a prevalent focus of most student affairs divisions—has the potential to help students balance their own and others' perspectives. All of these avenues offer the direct practice of assessing one's own beliefs, analyzing other perspectives, and weighing both in deciding what to believe or how to act.

Integration of relational and impersonal patterns of knowing involved learning to value both in deciding what to believe and in making decisions about career and personal life. When young adults in this study faced the limitations of their pattern of knowing, they learned how to use the alternative and then integrate the two. Johnston (1985) reported that adolescents preferred either the care (relational) orientation or the justice (impersonal) orientation in solving moral problems, but they could articulate the alternative orientation when asked to consider another way to look at the situation. This finding suggests that college students, despite a preference for one mode of knowing, could use another mode if encouraged to do so. The avenues just described to help students balance their own and others' perspectives could intentionally focus on the value of both rational and impersonal patterns of knowing. Perhaps some students (e.g., Lowell) would gain valuable relational skills that would help them face relational dilemmas, whereas others (e.g., Sheila) would gain valuable objective skills that they might not otherwise recognize.

Career advising and academic advising are also areas in which the two modes of knowing could be introduced. For example, Mark was a highly successful undergraduate student but had no direct experiences in college that provided even a glimmer of the pending conflict between his values and his career plans. The conflict erupted when the direct experience of an internship in a law firm revealed that to be successful, he would have to stifle himself in many ways. Effective career planning and academic advising services could help students like Mark be more aware of the need to consider self and values in career decisions. Such services would engage students in actively constructing a career decision rather than adopting one without serious investigation and reflection. This requires helping students use both modes of knowing in thinking about career decisions, and helping them connect with themselves and others in order to process such decisions fully. Providing students with direct internship opportunities during college to experience the reality of their future work is one way to spark these connections.

Palmer (1990) proposed that educators must acknowledge the interplay of knower and known in teaching. He argued that the rational, objective approach distances students from knowing and hinders their use of the relational mode. He advocated the use of objective modes "in creative tension with their relational counterparts" (Palmer, 1987, p. 24). Student affairs has a long tradition of attending to the relational mode. Because the cocurriculum is characterized by direct involvement by students, it is perhaps the ideal context for teaching students to balance modes of knowing. As teachers in the cocurriculum, student affairs professionals can draw students into the process of knowing by emphasizing students' role in actively constructing knowledge in all areas of their lives and engaging them in exploring both impersonal and relational modes of knowing. In doing so, student affairs professionals will contribute markedly to promoting contextual knowing during college.

Correspondence concerning this article should be addressed to Marcia B. Baxter Magolda, EDL-350 McGuffey Hall, Miami University, Oxford, OH 45056.

References

American College Personnel Association. (1994). *The student learning imperative: Implications for student affairs*. Washington, DC: Author.

Baxter Magolda, M. B. (1992). *Knowing and reasoning in college: Gender-related patterns in students' intellectual development*. San Francisco: Jossey-Bass.

Baxter Magolda, M. B. (1994). Post-college experiences and epistemology. *Review of Higher Education, 18* (1), 25–44.

Belenky, M. F., Clinchy, B. M., Goldberger, N. R., & Tarule, J. M. (1986). *Women's ways of knowing*. New York: Basic Books.

Chickering, A. W. (1969). *Education and identity*. San Francisco: Jossey-Bass.

Chickering, A. W., & Reisser, L. (1993). *Education and identity* (2nd ed.). San Francisco: Jossey-Bass.

Gilligan, C. (1982). *In a different voice*. Cambridge, MA: Harvard University Press.

Gilligan, C., & Attanucci, J. (1988). Two moral orientations: Gender differences and similarities. *Merrill-Palmer Quarterly, 34*, 223–237.

Glaser, B. G., & Strauss, A. L. (1967). *The discovery of grounded theory*. Chicago: Aldine.

Johnston, D. K. (1985). *Two moral orientations, two problem-solving strategies: Adolescents' solutions to dilemmas in fables*. Unpublished doctoral dissertation, Harvard Graduate School of Education, Cambridge, MA.

Josselson, R. (1987). *Finding herself: Pathways to identity development in women*. San Francisco: Jossey-Bass.

King, P. M., & Kitchener, K. S. (1994). *Developing reflective judgment*. San Francisco: Jossey-Bass.

Kitchener, K. S. (1983). Cognition, metacognition, and epistemic cognition. *Human Development, 26,* 222–232.

Kohlberg, L. (1969). Stage and sequence: The cognitive developmental approach to socialization. In D. A. Goslin (Ed.), *Handbook of socialization theory and research* (pp. 347–480). Chicago: Rand McNally.

Labouvie-Vief, G. (1990). Modes of knowledge and the organization of development. In M. L. Commons, C. Armon, L. Kohlberg, F. Richards, T. Grotzer, & J. Sinnott (Eds.), *Adult development: Vol. 2. Models and methods in the study of adolescent and adult thought* (pp. 43–62). New York: Praeger.

Lincoln, Y., & Guba, E. (1985). *Naturalistic inquiry.* Beverly Hills, CA: Sage.

Lyons, N. P. (1983). Two perspectives: On self, relationships, and morality. *Harvard Educational Review, 53,* 125–145.

Palmer, P. J. (1987, September/October). Community, conflict, and ways of knowing. *Change, 19*(5), 20–25.

Palmer, P. J. (1990, January/February). Good teaching: A matter of living the mystery. *Change, 22*(1), 11–16.

Patton, M. Q. (1990). *Qualitative evaluation and research methods.* Newbury Park, CA: Sage.

Perry, W. G. (1970). *Forms of intellectual and ethical development in the college years: A scheme.* New York: Holt, Rinehart, & Winston.

Straub, C. (1987). Women's development of autonomy and Chickering's theory. *Journal of College Student Personnel, 28,* 198–204.

Listening to Voices We Have Not Heard: Emma Willard Girls' Ideas about Self, Relationships, and Morality

Nona P. Lyons

Responding to an interview question asking how she might like to see herself in the future, the young woman, a high school junior, acknowledges she would like to "improve or expand on my compassion." She explains:

> With compassion, I'm sometimes not very understanding. I have a habit of putting myself in [another] person's place, which I found is not fair because I would do things differently and I think in a different way. And if they get angry, I would say, All right, how can I understand that? I will put myself in her place. But then I say, I wouldn't get angry at that! That doesn't help very much. [So] I would like to have more compassion toward them, to accept the way they feel really, and respect that.

Having discovered that an old way of understanding others, by putting herself in their place, was not "fair," the young woman holds up for herself a new measure of her development: "To improve or expand on my compassion . . . to accept the way they feel really, and respect that." But in so characterizing her future change, this adolescent girl points to a set of ideas and activities only now being elaborated in the psychological literature on adolescence.

For example, psychologist James Marcia has enunciated a classic formulation of the adolescent transition. Studying identity in adolescence, Marcia construes "identity," following Erikson, as an "internal, self-constructed, dynamic organization of drives, abilities, beliefs and individual history." Marcia sees identity undergoing changes over time, some of which are crucial: "Adolescence seems to be one of these. It is a period of transition in approach to moral issues—from law-and-order ["duty"] reasoning to transcendent human values; in approach to psychosocial concerns—from others' expectations and directives to one's own unique organization of one's history, skills, short-comings and goals" (Marcia 1980, 190). But in trying to fit this formulation of the adolescent transition and its cognitive, moral, and psychosocial agenda with an adolescent girl's aspirations for herself in the future, a set of differences and discrepancies emerges.

Taking what traditionally has been defined as the essence of fairness—the capacity to put yourself in another's place—the student labels it "unfair." While it could be questioned if this young woman somehow misunderstands the Golden Rule, it seems rather that she has a different standard for evaluating its usefulness: that is, whether it helps very much. In substituting that pragmatic reality for an abstract principle, "fairness," she holds up not a "transcendent human value" but an empirical one: how to see and respect difference. With a self-chosen goal—to expand compassion and accept the way others feel and respect that—the young woman turns toward a new level of engagement with others, attentive not just to her own but to the unique organization, history, skills, shortcomings and goals of others. Thus, with an ethical standard born of observation, experience, and judgment, this adolescent girl sees and holds for herself a new way of being in relation to others.

224

The significance of growth in human attachments to an understanding of adolescent development is the subject of this chapter. Through listening to the voices of adolescent girls at Emma Willard School and attending to the way they see themselves and experience their relations to others, there emerges a new way to think about a set of ideas centrally related to development: that is, ideas about self and morality.

For relationships are linked to moral imperatives, to concerns about good and evil, right and wrong. Piaget reminds us that "Apart from our relations with others, there can be no moral necessity" (Piaget [1932] 1965). Questions of value are implied in human relationships. But if morality arises in the relations between people, it most centrally implies a self and involves a question of interpretation: How do individuals see and construct their own understanding of relational problems? What are the moral concerns that emerge in their relationships with others—the questions of right or good?

This chapter describes and explores the connections Emma Willard girls find between their relationships to others and morality. Using data from in-depth interviews during which these high school students were asked to speak about themselves and about moral conflicts they see and try to resolve, this chapter first identifies and shows how a characteristic way of dealing with moral choice is related to a girl's way of considering her relations to others and to a way of describing herself. Two distinct orientations to morality are presented: a morality of justice and a morality of care. Each moral voice implies or articulates a particular conception of relationships—relationships of equality and fairness, or relationships of responsiveness and interdependence. The logic of each is defined. In a clearly speculative way, the second part of this chapter explores how these ideas of self, relationships, and morality may change over time and become significant issues in a girl's development. Finally, in the last part of this chapter, the implications of this work are discussed, especially for considering the education of girls.

Two lines of research converge here to provide a context: research on psychological theory and women's development focusing on self, relationships, and morality; and new work on adolescent psychology. Research in developmental psychology first identified a "different voice" in women's conceptions of self and morality and challenged the field to expand beyond the traditional conception of the self as separate and of morality as justice in order to include both experiences of separation and connection and the values of justice and care (Gilligan 1977, 1982; Gilligan et al. 1982; Lyons 1982, 1983, 1987; see also Chodorow 1978; Miller 1976, 1986; Belenky et al. 1986). New directions in the study of adolescent development call for and urge new research on adolescent girls (Adelson and Doehrman 1980; Adelson 1986; see also Douvan and Adelson 1966). The stark assessment of Adelson in 1980 that "adolescent girls have simply not been much studied" called attention to the "masculine bias" in such accepted psychological categories as "identity" and "morality" and to the fact that girls' experience had not been considered when these categories were created. Adelson suggests that the exclusion of girls from theory-building research may account for the previous lack of serious investigation of such important concepts as relationships, intimacy, and so forth. Recently other researchers have argued that any conception of adolescent development must include not only individuation but connectedness to others as well (Grotevant and Cooper 1983; Youniss 1980; Gilligan 1987). And in 1986 Hartup and Hinde underscored the significance of relationships in psychological development by calling for systematic study of relationships, beginning with simple descriptive data, if a needed science of relationships were to be developed (Hartup and Rubin 1986; Hinde 1979; Hinde and Stevenson-Hinde 1986). This chapter focuses on the presentation of a set of ideas and descriptions about how relationships are implicated in identity and moral development of adolescent girls. Using data from the Dodge Study at Emma Willard, this chapter, while not offering a systematic representation of findings, does suggest new hypotheses for future research.

For example, in distinguishing two voices in girls' narratives of moral conflict—the voices of justice and of care—it is important to note that girls who focus on justice and girls who focus on care do not differ in their academic achievement as measured by grades or standardized scores (Hanmer 1987). Yet the different logics of the two moral orientations suggest an interpretation of differences in girls' day-to-day behaviors and their ways of interacting with others. Further, girls' methods of posing and solving moral problems suggest a more general model of problem solving; and how relationships enter into girls' development, as revealed in the two characteristic patterns presented in this work, offers the outline of a new relational model of adolescent development.

This present work, then, makes available needed descriptive data of adolescent girls' perceptions, thoughts, and feelings about relationships and promising hypotheses; it also suggests an interpretation of girls' behaviors, including a way of understanding why a high school junior can say that her development is best measured in terms of expanding her compassion and why she calls that an "ethical" and moral concern.

Two Emma Willard high school students exemplify the contrast between an orientation to justice and one to care as manifest in the thinking of Emma Willard students who took part in this study. The two students reflect as well a larger sample of people, male and female, who have similarly been found to use predominantly justice or care thinking when making moral choices (Gilligan et al. 1982; Lyons 1982, 1983; Johnston 1985; Gilligan and Attanucci 1988). Although it has also been found that there can be a third pattern in the use of justice and care reasoning, that is, a roughly equal use of both justice and care considerations, here the contrast between justice and care predominance is explored.

Two Perspectives: In Self, Relationships, and Morality

Responding to the question, what does morality mean to you?, two Emma Willard high school students give different definitions, elaborating in their respons?es how they think about morality and responsibility. Rebecca, a sophomore, says:

> Morality? Wow. If I just use the noun 'morals,' I guess . . . I guess just a code of beliefs, you know, a code of honor, that one person would follow that's not necessarily anyone else's beliefs. I think morality maybe is a level . . . of personal integrity someone has. . . . Personal integrity, I think, is also a level of following rules. It is a level of following rules so that you can function, because if I had no personal integrity . . . I would be amoral. . . . So I think also a level of personal integrity also establishes a basis for judging whether something is right or wrong.

The second girl, Beth, a freshman, replies:

> I see a moral question as like, say, Is it better to drop a bomb, would that save more lives than it would be to fight? Moral questions are like that, they have drastic effects on life, I think. . . . Should I go out and fight along with my friends, or should I go to Canada and watch my friends die? Or something like that . . . I'm not totally sure that [this situation] is a question of morality. It is a question of responsibility, I think. . . . (*What does responsibility mean to you?*) Something that if I don't do, other people will suffer. . . . My homework is my responsibility because I should, I have to, do it because, if I don't, that will bog other people down and then the class has to go over it again and I wouldn't be helping people and I don't want to hinder people. I don't think that is right.

For Rebecca, morality is a code of beliefs, a measure of personal integrity that is tied to abiding by rules, which can in turn become the basis for judging whether something is right or wrong. Her code is personal, not necessarily anyone else's. For Beth, morality is something that has to do with questions that can have drastic effects on life—like the dropping of a bomb—and yet is tied to ideas about responsibility, which in turn have to do with everyday things like failing to do one's homework because that might bog other people down and wouldn't be helping them. For Rebecca, morality has to do with following one's code; for Beth, it has to do with helping people, being sure to do something so that others will not be hurt or hindered.

While at first glance the contrast between these two responses may not appear especially striking, it does suggest that different kinds of issues can become moral concerns and have implications not just for how a girl constructs the meaning of morality, but for how she might act. Given these different perspectives, it is possible to ask: What are likely moral problems for these young women? In an examination of the conflict they report, the logic and consistency of two moral orientations—what are called here a morality of justice and a morality of care or response—are revealed. And two ways of being in relation to others are revealed as well.

For Rebecca, who defines morality as a code that gives her a way of judging what to do, an actual moral conflict emerged in trying to determine if she should follow school rules. The situation occurred when she was sitting as an active member of a school disciplinary committee, the Faculty Student Judiciary Committee (FSJ), which determined what to do with students who broke school rules.

> I remember when I was confronted with a situation where I could go out and get drunk with some friends who were on the FSJ. . . . This was at the time when I was saying, Well, if this rule really isn't ethical or moral, then to hell with it and, They don't really expect us to follow these rules, they just don't want us to get caught. But a little voice in me was yelling, It's wrong, it's wrong. And I think of all those people whose cases I sat on, where people were caught drinking . . . [but] I think I turned the girl down more from an extreme fear of getting caught. It wasn't any great moral realization . . . I thought about it and we are not dealing with, Oh, come back to me in an hour. This was minutes, seconds. I said, 'No, thanks. I've got to go.' But through my mind in those few seconds flashed, you know, stuff that I was breaking a rule.
>
> Out of that, I think . . . it forced me, I said . . . it's wrong to break a rule and if you go here, you abide by the rules . . . if you don't like them, leave. So this is another one of my great theories.

In recounting this situation, Rebecca reveals a complex and changing way of thinking about rules and why she will obey them. Forced to respond to the friend who invites her to break a rule, she judges it is wrong and suggests the grounds on which she makes that judgment. Thinking first of all of the cases she herself has witnessed and judged as a member of the FSJ, she goes on to acknowledge as well that it was really no great moral realization, just a fear of getting caught that made her say, No. The implications of not obeying rules have consequences. Seeing that she would be breaking a rule if she went out drinking, she simultaneously reasons that if you go to school here, you abide by school rules. Thus, she judges her own behavior with a standard she uses for others as well. Rules, applied universally across situations, mediate her relationships and her moral decision making, in this instance.

For Beth, who is concerned not to hinder others, moral conflict arises from a situation in her relationship with her mother:

> I was in a situation where my parents are divorced, and I wanted to go to boarding school because I didn't want to live with my parents at that point. And my mother didn't want me to go. I have a younger sister by her second marriage, and she said that I should stay home with my sister and take care of my sister and help the family in that sense. . . .
>
> So I thought about it [and] decided to come back [here]. . . . I guess I took an objective viewpoint . . . and decided that I love my sister and I love my family and I love my mother, but staying there and doing what she wanted me to do wasn't healthy for our relationship. . . . I did have a responsibility toward my family, but that was not to take care of my sister but to make myself a person that wasn't going to be dependent on my family constantly and the only way to do that was to go [here] and . . . make something of myself. And then I could help my family.

In a dilemma caused by the special request of her mother, to come home from school to take care of a younger sister, Beth considers both what is healthy for their relationship and how she can help her family. Asked to comment if she thought her decision was the right thing to do, she goes on to say:

> I felt very guilty. I almost changed my mind . . . but I walked away and tried to think about what I was doing, and I realized that I was right and—for me, I was right—I

don't think you could be totally right in that situation because there are different parts, different amounts of being right. And [I] could have done one thing and I could have stayed with my mother and that would have been partially right; or I could have come here and that would have been partially right. But each way I am cheating someone. But I have to work for myself. I have to do things for myself because if I can't do them now, how will I be able to do them when I become an adult and am supposed to?

Concerned then that "each way I am cheating someone," Beth sees no one right way, only different amounts of right. She resolves her conflict by seeing that "making something of myself" is necessary in order to be able sometime "to help my family." From a way of thinking about morality that is constructed as not hindering others, to a definition, resolution, and evaluation of a moral problem, a logic is revealed in this young woman's thinking: Individuals in relation must each be considered in their own contexts and needs.

In contrast, Rebecca, also responding to the question, Do you think it was the right thing to do?, says:

Definitely. . . . I think it is not fair for this school to ask you to live under some sort of rule, and to break those rules and then sit in on a case where you are judging someone else for doing the very same thing that you did. That is why it seemed like a contradiction to me because you are creating the wrongness the FSJ deals with, and I don't think [it is fair] for someone to sit there and talk about punishing someone else if they had been drinking themselves last night.

Embedded in the two kinds of conflicts these students present are what may be called two kinds of logic, two different ways of thinking about the relationships between people that give rise to different moral considerations. For Rebecca, relationships are construed as if through some kind of contract with an underlying conception of fairness and equality between individuals. All individuals should be, and are, considered in fairness.

Beth looks at the situation from the point of view of each person, including herself, not in strict equality but in each person's terms and contexts. She acts to do what is right for herself and her family—considering their long-term relationship. Here the underlying value is interdependence and responsiveness, responsiveness implying an acknowledgment of the reality of the situation as well as an understanding of each person's particularity and need.

From perspectives of fairness and "reciprocity" or of "response" and interdependence, these young women see and seek to resolve conflicts they term moral conflicts. Other examples from the experiences of Emma Willard students similarly reveal the two orientations to self in relationship or morality (see table 1 on following page).

Table 1

Moral Conflicts Emma Willard Girls Report Framed with Justice and Care Considerations

1. Justice Focus*: Considerations of Self: Respecting and Upholding Rights, Contract or Fairness in Relationships.

I didn't get my math homework done. . . . We had to hand in computer tapes and my friend had an extra computer tape, and I knew that the teacher was absolutely going to freak out and scream at me and I would get into trouble if I didn't hand in a tape. And my friend had an extra one she was offering me, but I couldn't do it. I couldn't take it. . . . Sort of like the principle, damn it, I didn't do the computer tape . . . I couldn't hand it in when I didn't do it. It would have been like cheating.

I don't go to chapel anymore because I find that offensive and I guess that's moral. We have required chapel once a week and I don't like the idea of being required to go, of being forced into religion. I go to church on my own sometimes. I think that's enough for me and I don't feel that I need to go to these required services. It was a big decision.

2. Care Focus: Considerations of Self: Creating and Maintaining Interdependence and Response in Relationships.

I lied to my parents about my grades. I told them that my biology grade was going to be marvelous, and it is not going to be marvelous. . . . Suddenly, my sister who has always been national honor society and all those wonderful things, has gotten horrible grades this past month, and [my parents] called me up and told me this and then wanted to know how mine were. And it was the difference between, knowing my parents, they would go to the ends of the earth if they know both their children were doing horribly in school—my parents are educational fanatics—and so I've told them that my grades are fine, and there was almost a sigh of relief from my father. And I think that outweighed the idea that I was lying to them. . . . I couldn't bring myself on the phone to say, Well, Dad, you are looking at two academic failures for the term. And I think that's a moral dilemma.

My roommate and I were in the same class and I lost my book, and she lost her book. And then I lost my book and she found hers and I borrowed her book one night to do my homework. And I noticed my name in it, and I realized that she had taken my book and erased my name and wrote hers over it. And I had to decide whether I should save embarrassing her by confronting her with the problem and just go out and get another book, or whether I should say, Hey, did you take my book? I know this is my book, and give it back.

I had a problem with a . . . girl whom I [as editor] would tell that I needed her to get something done and I would tell her weeks ahead of time . . . and then when I needed whatever she was supposed to have done, she hadn't done it. And this went on for a long time. . . . And I felt like I needed someone else to be doing the job, and yet whenever I would talk to her, she would say, 'Yah, I really do want to do it and I want to be able to help.' . . . I didn't really want to confront her and I knew I had to. . . . I didn't know if I was being unreasonable in things I was asking her to do—maybe I didn't make it clear to her the things I needed [her] to do.

3. Mixed Considerations of Care and Justice.

Last year some friends and I went out and we were having a little celebration. . . . One girl met a friend of hers and she wanted to stay longer and talk. . . . The next morning we realized that our friend had gotten busted. . . . I didn't know if I should turn myself in or what. In the end, I really had a hard time deciding what to do because I felt it was really unfair . . . she had gotten busted and we hadn't. And the problem was if I turned myself in I would have been responsible for the four other people. . . .

Focus is a term used to indicate a primary or predominant way of framing conflict. For example, if seventy-five percent of all ideas—called considerations—are of one orientation, justice or care, that determines a focus.

Similar Issues—Different Moral Conflicts; Different Issues—Similar Moral Concerns

Two Perspectives: Equality and Rights or Interdependence and Responsiveness in Relationships

In these examples what is first apparent is not just that different issues can become salient moral conflicts for students, but that the same issue can be construed with different meanings. Lying is a case in point. The student who talks about lying to her parents about her grades is seeing a different problem than the student who cannot lie about the computer tapes. For the girl concerned about the tapes, to hand in as hers her friend's homework would have been cheating and, for her, would have involved violating a principle of fairness. She says, "I didn't do the tape. . . . I couldn't hand it in." Applying a general principle to her situation, she declares it not right to hand in her friend's tape. But a different kind of issue concerns the student who lies to her parents about her grades: that is, the direct effect on her parents of the bad news of her failing grades. It is, as she says, knowing her parents in their particularity—the intense value they place on their children's education—that makes her tell them that her grades will be good when they will not. In an instant, as she not only calls up the values of her parents but also enters into their world, she acts to hold off their disappointment for at least a short period of time. In these two constructions, different considerations frame and shape conflict—conflicts that both girls label as "moral."

Similarly, it is possible to examine the underlying perspectives of different conflicts presented and to see a similar logic at work across different situations. For example, the girl who found a moral conflict in deciding not to go to required chapel acts out of her principles and standards in much the same way as Rebecca, who decided it was wrong to break the school rule when she was sitting on the Judiciary Committee. Both act to apply a set of standards they hold about what is the right thing to do in a particular situation. The underlying values are equality and reciprocity, or, fairness. This way of thinking about real-life moral conflict is termed here a morality of justice.

So also, the editor who does not know whether to tell a fellow student that she must get her work in on time acts to respond to the girl in much the same way as the girl who does not tell her parents she will have a failing grade. The logic that shapes their behavior is a logic that acts in response to knowledge of people, considering the pragmatic situation of the individuals involved as well as what constitutes care. This way of thinking about moral conflict is termed here a morality of response, or, care. And this orientation to morality can create a particular set of conflicts for women surrounding care of self and when to respond to self as well as others. For example, the girl who acts to retrieve her textbook from her roommate casts the problem in a particular and familiar form: whether she should embarrass her roommate or sacrifice her own needs and desire to have her book. This issue, which can be central to the development of girls and women (Gilligan 1977, 1982), is discussed later in this chapter.

While it is clear that girls can act out of either of these two moral orientations—and usually the conflicts they report have elements of both—girls also present both modes equally in their thinking. For example, the girl who did not know if she should turn herself in when a friend she had been with was caught outside of school grounds, when she herself had been breaking the school rule as well, presented the conflict as one embodying two terms: What was fair—"it really was unfair"—and what was responsible—"I would have been responsible for the four other people" who would have been implicated as well. Thus her dilemma pits the principle of fairness directly against responsibility for the weal and woe of others.

It seems important to emphasize again that in these examples Emma Willard girls present moral conflicts that include both justice (rights) and care (response) considerations. Here, however, we have been looking at "justice" or "response" to illuminate the characteristic features if one kind of moral consideration predominates in a girl's thinking. For a summary of the central moral issues and logic of the two moral orientations, see table 2.

Table 2

An Overview of the Central Moral Issues and Logic of Care and Justice in the Construction, Resolution, and Evaluation of the Resolution of Moral Dilemmas (Lyons 1982).

A Morality of Care/Response

A. *In What Becomes a Moral Problem*

A morality of "care" rests on an understanding of relationships that entails response to another in that person's terms and contexts. Therefore, what becomes a moral problem has to do with relationships or the activities of care.

The conflicts of relationships are raised as issues surrounding the potential fractures between people, that is, not with the breaking of trusts or obligations but with the severing of ties between people; or conversely, with restoring or maintaining relationships.

The conflicts surrounding the activities of care have to do with response itself, that is, how to respond (or the capacity or ability to respond) to another within the particular situation one encounters and how to promote the welfare or well-being of another or to relieve the individual's burdens, hurt, or suffering—physical or psychological. Included in this construction can be particular concerns about care of self and how to care for self especially in considering care of others.

B. *In the Resolution of Moral Conflict*

In a morality of care resolutions to moral conflict are sought: (1) in restoring relationships or the connections between people and (2) in carrying through the activities of care, ensuring that good will come to others or that hurt/suffering will be stopped for others or oneself.

C. *In the Evaluation of the Resolution*

In a morality of care the evaluation of moral choice is made considering: (1) whether relationships were restored/or maintained and (2) how things worked out or will work out; in some instances there is only the acknowledgment that no way to know or to evaluate resolution is possible. Whether relationships were restored can be measured in several ways: simply if people talk to one another, or if everyone is comfortable with the solution. If people talk and everyone agrees with the solution, one knows relationships are maintained.

How things work out is a measure of resolution in that in seeing what happens to people over time, one then knows if the resolution worked. This marker also carries the notion that *only* over time can one know results, that is, know in the sense of seeing what actually happens.

A Morality of Justice/Rights

A. *In What Becomes a Moral Problem*

A morality of justice or fairness rests on an understanding of relationships as reciprocity between separate individuals. Therefore, what becomes a moral problem has to do either with mediating issues of conflicting claims in the relationships between people; or with how one is to decide conflicts or how one can justify one's decision and actions, considering fairness as a goal between individuals.

The moral dilemmas of conflicting claims have to do with the conflicts of obligation, duty, or commitment stemming from the different role-relationships one may have: between self and others, self and society, or to one's own values/principles. The conflicts with respect to how one is to decide come from the need to have some impartial, objective measure of choice that ensures fairness in arriving at a decision.

B. *In the Resolution of Moral Conflict*

In a morality of justice resolutions to moral conflicts are sought considering (1) meeting one's obligations or commitments or performing one's duties and (2) in holding to or not violating one's standards and principles, especially fairness.

C. *In the Evaluation of the Resolution*

> In a morality of justice, the evaluation of moral choice is made considering (1) how the decision was justified, thought about and/or (2) whether values, standards, or principles were maintained, especially fairness.

How the decision was justified or thought about is an important measure to make of living up to one's obligations (duty or commitments) or of fairness. Whether values, standards, or principles were maintained is a measure of the self's ability to live up to one's obligations or principles; it is a measure, too, of the standards used in decision making.

This construction of morality as involving at least two voices, justice and care, expands the construction of morality described in the dominant model or moral psychology, notably in the work of Kohlberg (1969, 1984). In Kohlberg's model morality is defined as justice, and moral problems are seen to emerge from the conflicting claims of individuals and to be resolved through objectivity and the application of principles of justice as fairness. Fair treatment and broadly contractual rules and individual rights provide a set of related ideas within this orientation to morality. But a second construction offers another definition of morality: that is, morality as responsiveness to another. This ethic is called the ethic of care, or, response (Gilligan 1977, 1982; Lyons 1982, 1983). In this conceptualization of morality as care, moral problems are likely to emerge from the recognition of actual or potential fractures in the relationships between people or from concerns that someone has been excluded or not taken care of. Thus conceived, moral problems are resolved by stepping into— not back from—the situation and by acting to restore relationships or to address needs, including those of oneself.

For an expanded logic of the two moral perspectives with a related set of ideas, see table 3. While these summaries were prepared and developed from previous studies of people's use of the justice and care reasoning as well as from the Emma Willard study, it is useful here to identify a set of ideas—of self, relationships, and characteristic features of ways of thinking—that are interconnected to ideas about morality (Lyons 1983, 1987). It is important to restate, too, that most people (including the students presented here) show evidence of both kinds of considerations in their thinking about moral conflict. Yet it is the patterning of these responses so that one mode predominates, shaping the way issues are constructed and resolved, and the logic that this implies that are of interest (see table 3 on page 234).

How these ideas of self, relationships, and morality may change over time and become issues in girls' development is taken up next. Through case materials examining the moral conflict of two girls—girls introduced in the preceding pages—it is possible to suggest different pathways of girls' development in the adolescent years.

Themes of Development: Trying to Be Generous and Not Selfish

Asked to talk about herself, to describe herself to herself, the young woman, Anne, a high school sophomore, hesitates at first because "It's really hard to do this" but begins a response. As she does, she lays out a set of interconnected ideas.

> Describe myself? Um . . . I guess I'm a pretty outgoing person, likes people. Um . . . I'm a pretty intelligent person when I put my mind to it. It's really hard to do [this] . . . I know what I'm like but it's . . . Describe myself, like to me? . . . I try to be generous to people. It is very important to me not to be selfish. Um . . . Have very high standards for myself and for others, and that's not always good, but I have them.

Two themes that appear in this response may not at first glance seem critical. Yet they become central to Anne's growth and the focus of her conflicts in subsequent years. The themes are "selfishness" ("It is very important to me not to be selfish"); and "being generous" ("I try to be generous to people"). As Anne elaborates a context of values, however, she begins to reveal why "being generous" and "not selfish" will become issues in her relation to others. Before examining these, it seems useful to look at the values she identifies as important to her, seeing how they are revealed in and are part of her everyday life and why.

Answering the interviewer's question, Why is it not good to have high standards for yourself and others? Anne explains:

> Sometimes people are the way they are, and you have to accept them the way they are. And you can't say that this person is not good enough for me. . . . Somebody who maybe is an alcoholic or maybe . . . they are on drugs or something like that, I sometimes look at and say, That person isn't, you know, blah, something like that. But I shouldn't do that because that is the way they are and I think that . . . that is one of the bad things about having such high standards. And, I like a lot of people around me.

Anne's conflicts about "standards" arise from the concern about accepting people "the way they are." As part of an effort to see others in their own terms, Anne "tries to be generous."

> I like to do things for other people . . . to give somebody something that they don't have, or help with work or even if they need money. . . . I like to know, it is a matter . . . I go down and buy a flower for my mother or something. I like to do things like that. In that way I take after my mother, but it kind of runs in me now, too, . . . it is really important for me to see other people happy.

Thus, for Anne, connection to others is a central value, a way of being toward others that is part of the way she thinks about herself. Its importance lies not only in "just liking people around me," but also in "the feeling you can give each other." Interdependence is the underlying assumption. Anne describes one way these values emerge in her everyday affairs as she introduces her concern about competition in school.

Academic competition bothers Anne. She muses, "If you get a grade on a test and somebody else gets one lower than you, they are jealous of you, and they have to flaunt it, and that makes you feel bad because you got a high grade. Or like if somebody gets a higher grade than me, I get jealous. . . . I mean I never try to show it, but I still tend to feel jealous." Declaring that there is "no reason why people should be unhappy because you did well," she continues: "I don't think you should be feeling jealous. . . . When people do it to me, it wrecks the whole pleasure . . . and I know they feel bad. And that really bothers me a lot."

When asked to say if she is changing, Anne identifies the emerging issues that will challenge some of her values: "New things are becoming important to me. It's like trying to become on an adult level . . . presenting my ideas and trying to make myself be as well as I possibly can, on an adult level, trying to get them up to standard, up to a point where they are not childlike."

Commenting on this difference, between what is adult and what is childlike, she says:

> A child doesn't really take the world seriously; he doesn't see all the aspects of the world. And as an adult, you do. You see, you grasp, you grasp what your world is about and what . . . you take things seriously and start to bring them into reality. Whereas as a child it is kind of like a fairy world. I mean you have your family and that's kind of all you ever go outside of, whereas as an adult you are brought into contact every day to the different aspects of the world, be it starvation or poorness or the reality of having to get a job and have responsibility. Whereas as a child you don't have any responsibilities really. Other people take care of those for you so that when you grow to start to become an adult, you start to take on more responsibilities.

Table 3
The Logic of Two Moral Perspectives*

	Perspective toward others	Conception of self in relation to others
The perspective of response in relationships	See others in their own terms; contexts	Interdependent in relation to others
The perspective of rights in relationships	See others as one would like to be seen; in equality and reciprocity	Autonomous/equal/ independent in relation to others

To this interviewer's question, Such as? she says:

> Such as . . . supporting a family . . . I mean . . . taking care of yourself. When you are a little kid your mother dresses you, and you go to the stage where you dress yourself. And then you get to the stage where maybe you start to pick out your own clothes and just um, yah, you go from the stage where your mother takes care of you, where you start to get some type of individualism, and then you want more independence. And then finally you are independent and you have to support yourself and take care of yourself and see that you are, because otherwise you won't survive.

> I look outside my little own world here and when I was little, I never did. I always looked . . . I relied on my mother and my father and my relatives, my friends, just the people that I was in daily contact with, to keep me informed on what was going on, that is important to me, that is going to affect me. And now I've gotten to the point where I look outside myself, my little world. And I look for things, even if it doesn't affect me directly. I look to see what's going on and what's happening and try to get some individualism, too. . . .

It could be argued that these concerns for independence and "individualism" are classic statements of concern for autonomy and independence—ideals traditionally identified with the adolescent experience. Yet becoming independent to Anne means not only increasing her autonomy but also her capacity to see others in their reality. It is becoming responsible for "taking care of your world." For Anne becoming independent is joined with being interdependent in a new way.

When Anne describes a conflict, one that seems an everyday happening to adolescents, the values she holds come into conflict with one another: her concern about "selfishness," "being generous," and her emerging "individualism." She identifies the situation as occurring when a friend, a "really good friend," wanted her to go to her house after school, but Anne couldn't reach her mother: "I think she wanted me to stay overnight or something because she had had problems, and I couldn't get ahold of my mother, so I didn't know whether to go or not."

Ideas and images of relationships	Ways of thinking/knowing	Interpersonal ideas and processes
Attachment through response; interdependence of people in relationships; concern with responsiveness, isolation of people; relationships as webs	Particularistic; contextual; question posing; suspended judgment; use of dialogue, discussion; goal is understanding; thinking and feeling held together	Interdependent; emphasis on discussion and listening in order to understand others in own contexts
Attachment through roles, obligation, duty; concern with equality and fairness in relationships; relationships as hierarchies	Objective; generalizing; abstract; ruleseeking; goal is to critique, to analyze, to answer question, to prove; thinking and feeling seen as needing to be separated	Objective; role-related; in order to maintain fairness and equality in dealing with others

*From Lyons, N. *Visions and Competencies: Men and Women as Decision-Makers and Conflict Managers*, Harvard University, 1985.

In that situation, her concerns were: "My feeling of what I should do. And what my mother would want me to do. I didn't want to get in trouble." She elaborates what getting in trouble means:

> I get yelled at and then I feel bad because . . . I don't know . . . because it hurts, I guess. I mean it always hurts if you get in trouble. Nobody likes, I know I don't like for my mother to get mad at me because I don't think . . . I hate to have my mother upset with me for something. . . . It hurts both of us I think, you know, I don't think she likes to get mad at me either.

"Trouble" is not just an effect to Anne, some punishment, but involves hurt: hurt, both to her mother and herself. "Besides," she adds, "your parents run your life up until a certain point, and when I was at that point I was at that point where I am sure it was a struggle for independence and relying on other people to run my world, so it was kind of, I should let her decide because she runs my world."

Asked what she considered when she was trying to think about what to do, Anne responds, introducing a new concern:

> Well . . . it was something like I want to go for my own selfish reasons because I like to visit with my friend, and I think she needs me there for her, too. I don't think it is just my own selfish reasons, but I think it would be good for my friend to have me there when she needs somebody to talk to or something. And then the other side is I just don't want to do something without Mom's permission. I don't want to get in trouble . . . and that my friend wanted me to come, that also helped affect me and my decision. But the other side was very strong—I mean my mother's feelings on the subject—was very strong. Is she didn't like it, then I wouldn't do it, of course. . . .

In the end, Anne reveals, "I decided to go to my friend's, which was fine, because my mother wasn't mad anyway. She didn't mind at all." And that, to Anne, was the right thing to do. "Because she would have let me do it, and I wanted to do it, and it was important to my friend that I do it. So three ways in one direction is fine."

In the situation presented here, Anne grapples with the inherent conflict of "trying to be generous" to all the people around her—not wanting to hurt her mother, being there for her friend, as well as doing what she wants for her own "selfish reasons." She struggles to make her own decision, to be independent, and to consider, too, what she would like to do. But unable to grant her own view a place of parity with concern for her mother and concern for her friend, she marks it as "selfish." While Anne does, in fact, go to her friend's—she does do what she wants to do—she does not find a way to deal with or legitimize her own point of view.

Marking her own wishes in a self-evaluating way as "selfish," the task for her—and the difficulty—seems to be in finding a way to hold both self and other together. Individuation while maintaining connections to others is what she grapples with, and her relations to others complicate her task. Thus she juggles her knowledge of her mother with her understanding of her friend's need. But where can her own needs fit? Three years later she describes a different situation.

Anne as a Senior

During the interview in her final year of high school Anne comments, "Probably a lot of changes in your life throughout the years caused you to grow, and people you interact with grow around you. So you grow with them." Reflecting on her own change over the three years of school, Anne, a senior now, sums up, "I can look back on myself and . . . think about the decision which I made, or think about the way I felt about myself and when I felt really responsible or really mature. And now it's not a question of, Oh, I feel mature. Because I am. It is there and I know it." Calling herself "hard-working," "personable," "goal-oriented," and "pretty well put together," Anne states, "I enjoy interacting with people, getting to know them, seeing what they think about things." Then in discussing a real-life conflict she faced as a senior, Anne identifies continuities and change, sounding again the theme of "selfishness," but this time, two years later, it emerges in a different way.

Reflecting on the moral conflict she faced recently when she had to choose which colleges to apply to, Anne discloses that she wanted to apply to a certain school but her father could have gotten a tuition break if she attended another college. "Not that he doesn't have the money, but he just doesn't really want to go out and spend fourteen thousand dollars a year to send me to the first school—as opposed to sending me to the just-as-good school." She describes feeling "torn between doing what I felt I needed to do, which was to apply to the school which, for some reason, had really appealed to me, or applying to one that I knew would be best for my father and wouldn't be bad for me either."

In trying to decide what to do, Anne talks about the considerations she pondered: "I considered my father's feelings on the subject [because] it is really important to me to be able to get along, to do what is going to be best for everybody involved." But she goes on, "You know, it was more a question of whether or not I was being selfish in deciding to go where I wanted to apply, or whether I should be realistic almost in a sense, which isn't necessarily realistic, and apply to the place which is going to be best for all of us."

Not abandoning her old concern that "it is really important to me to get along, to do what is best for everybody involved," she now puts that alongside of another: "I considered my own feelings . . . a lot." Still unable to cast aside the issue of "selfishness," it appears now in a new way: that is, whether she is being realistic—in this case, to apply to the school that might be "best for all of us," for everybody. Thus she aligns her interests with the reality factors of her life and the lives of others— whether her father could, in fact, afford the school of her choice. Yet she acknowledges and gives a place to her priorities.

Talking about whether or not that was the right thing to do, Anne summarizes:

> I came to realize that you can't please everybody else all of the time, and if you are working on something that is that important to your life . . . going to school, gaining an education, then you should choose what you really want to do and go after it. If I hadn't, I would have been kind of abating myself, because I would have been saying, Oh yes, you really do want to go too, you really do. But somewhere deep inside me, and it would have come up to consciousness at some point or another, I would really

want to do something else. And so I thought that it was best that I do what I really wanted to do. And I think that my father feels that way now, too.

In identifying that "you can't please everybody all of the time" and that if something is important to you, "you should choose what you really want to do" because, as in her case, if she had not she "would have been abating" herself, Anne seems to shift to a new place, reorganizing both her way of being in relation to others and her way of thinking about herself. Her new perspective allows her a way to respond to herself as well as to others.

In this reorganization, what is interesting is that old elements of her thinking are transformed. Issues she identifies in her early years of high school—"being generous to people" and "selfishness"—carry new meanings. "Selfishness" is now acknowledged alongside of what is "realistic" given a situation, as well as "what is important to me." Not that acting in a selfish way is suddenly inconceivable; rather, the confusion of labeling what is important to her as "selfish" is being clarified and her wishes given legitimacy. Similarly, being generous to people is mitigated by her concerns and desires; and her desires are tempered by the "reality" of the situations. Thus a new way of thinking about herself cannot be disassociated from her new way of being and acting in relation with others.

What Brings About Change

Because the assurance and confidence of this young woman in her own point of view are clear and strong, unlike the faltering voice of her sophomore year, it seems fair to suggest that some change in her thinking has occurred. How this has come about is the question of interest. Turning again to examine the conflicts of her life, we look at the middle year of her schooling and speculate that the conflict she describes there may offer an explanation of change. The situation occurred when her father decided to get remarried, and she had to decide whether to tell her mother. She relates that "it was really a hard decision on my part as to whether and when to tell my mother that, because on the one hand, I knew that it was really going to kill her to find that out, and on the other hand, I thought I had na obligation to tell her." What made the situation a conflict for her was that while her mother and father were divorced, she knew, "my mother still loved my father a great deal."

Asked by the interviewer to say why this was a moral problem, Anne says moral problems usually occur for her when "I am struggling against myself to come to a solution to the problem." In her situation, the values that were conflicting were:

> The fact that I had always been brought up to care a tremendous amount about my parents' feelings and the way they feel. On the one hand, that conflicted with itself because my mother's feelings were going to be really upset and my father's feelings were good. So that conflicted with itself, and um, my [long pause] trying to figure out, I guess you would have to weigh the love that I have for my mother, which is in effect my morals, against if I love my mother enough to tell her something [so] that she won't hear [it] from other places and get upset. But then again, that's against mainly the feeling that I've been brought up with that I hate to see any member of my family hurt and that would conflict against that, so the two.

Thus caught in a dilemma of telling her mother what she knew and risking her hurt, or not telling her and risking the pain her mother would inevitably feel when she did learn of the remarriage, Anne decided to tell. But she did so knowing that she and her sister, who joined in the telling, could give their mother "our personal support so she could handle it." If we speculate what this young woman learned from this dilemma, we might say that she confronted the impossible situation—the inability not to hurt another or prevent hurt—and yet saw a way to deal with it.

Two issues emerge in Anne's story. Connection—attachment—is to be maintained as is a growing "independence." But independence comes within attachment to others and transforms both, leading to a new way of being and a new way of interacting with others.

Similarly, Anne says that morality is the "love" she has for her mother and her father. Thus, issues of morality, as she defines them, are not solely issues of fairness or rights as previous formulations suggest (Kohlberg 1969, 1984), nor are they the creation of agreements between people (Haan 1977 and Youniss 1983). Her concerns are for sustaining connections with others, not by a utilitarian calculus of "the greatest good for the greatest number of people," but rather by weighing the love that is her "morals"—responding to others in their own terms and contexts: Do "I love my mother enough to tell her something [so] that she won't hear [it] from other places and get upset?"

While one cannot speak about girls in general without studying girls in other situations, cultures, and social class, it is possible to summarize some issues central to the development of girls we characterize as "connected," or, "interdependent in relation to others." This connected mode of experiencing self and defining morality is more frequently found within the Emma Willard sample of students who revealed a certain set of characteristics:

At adolescence, issues of attachment for girls who were characterized as "interdependent in their relations to others" are the focus of attention in at least two ways: (1) maintaining connections with others, either in renegotiating old attachments or in forming new ones, personal or professional, and (2) how ideas and issues of caring for the self while maintaining connections are dealt with and negotiated within relationships.

The issue of holding together self and other—what has been called here caring for the self as well as caring for others—may be a special issue of development during adolescence for some girls. The special vulnerability may be in finding a way of caring for the self while maintaining connections with others.

Issues and conflicts of what girls label moral as well as issues of "identity" formation take place within relationships.

Before elaborating on some of the implications of this work we turn next to examine another, characteristically different, mode of response found in the answers of Emma Willard students.

Themes of Development: Choosing between Doing That the Rules Dictated and Maintaining My Friendship

In contrast to those adolescent girls whose high school years seem to be a time to work on a new capacity to care for others and oneself, a similar yet different configuration of these issues seems equally salient for other students, students characterized here as "autonomous in relation to others." While issues of attachment, of self, and relationships emerge in their development, there are differences. For these girls relationship concerns seem joined to issues of integrity and one's standards. To see this process at work, we turn now to a young sophomore, Rebecca, whom we have met before and who found as a member of the Faculty Student Judiciary Committee that she had to confront her own desires and standards. Listening first to how she describes herself and then contrasting the conflicts she experienced over her three years of high school, it is possible to examine how her relations to others and her ideas about her integrity and "standards" enter into her thinking.

Responding to the question, How would you describe yourself to yourself? the young woman, Rebecca, begins:

> Oh dear. I was thinking about that as I was getting dressed this morning. Um . . . to myself. I don't know, sometimes we have to do creative writing exercises; and Who am I? I think of myself as a person who gets involved. I am doing a lot this year. In fact, I overextended myself this year, but no problem. I like to get involved in things. I think I am well known by a large part of the student body only because I am always sticking my fingers in a lot of business and stuff like that. My personality, I don't know. I have certain aspects of me, like I think I am a very warm person. I think I am very good at articulating how I feel, identifying parts of my life, like I've just done. But that's about it. I can't think of anything right now that I would describe myself as. I'd describe myself as a changed person, definitely.

> I think I have changed a lot. I used to think when I was in the 7th and 8th grade that I was a liberated woman . . . but I don't know. I am at the stage now where I don't know if I'm liberated in the purest sense simply because, when in doubt, I always slip back into old traditions and old ways. If I go to a mixer at a boys' school, I don't ask guys to dance simply because I'm afraid of what kind of reaction I'll get. So I don't know if I am liberated, if I'm completely, totally free about, you know, about being liberated in front of men because a lot of people . . . This girl was extremely, extremely liberated or whatever, and she went to [x] boys' school during exchange time and she got nicknames like Amazon, and these guys thought . . .—this school is like the way the world was in 1950, to give you a little background—but they called her the Amazon, Gloria Steinem, . . . and they saw her as some female castrating bitch. They just couldn't handle [it], they didn't understand what she was doing so they tended to reject what she was saying. And I don't want to be rejected like that, and I don't want people talking about me like that. So I don't know how liberated I am. So I think I am a changed person is all I can say right now.

Characterizing herself with some ambiguity, as "good at articulating how I feel, identifying parts of my life" and "I can't think of anything right now that I would describe myself as," Rebecca, in part, characterizes herself in her differences from others. In spite of her tentativeness, she does identify that she is changed. She sees herself as "changed" in relation to a marker—how "liberated" she is. In a discussion of a moral conflict she faced, she picks up the theme of "difference" and identifies as well the issues she will continue to deal with for the next three years: her integrity and the integrity of her standards, her relation to them, and how they mediate her relations to others.

In her sophomore year of school, Rebecca talked about a conflict—one already presented here. "When I was confronted with a situation where I could go out and get drunk with some friends who were on the Faculty Student Judiciary Committee . . . this was at the time when I was saying, Well . . . if this rule really isn't ethical, or moral, then to hell with it. . . ."

Reflecting on that situation, she elaborates how her thinking was changing:

> That was one of my extremist theories . . . I just thought, I just went through a stage where I thought that anyone who came here and violated a rule should be kicked out of school because they couldn't handle it. They couldn't come here and totally stay within the rules, you know. And then I went through the thing: Is it possible to go through here four years without breaking a fundamental rule? And I asked someone, who said, I don't think so. So that is something I am going to have to deal with in the future.

In her construction of conflict and choice, Rebecca articulates a complex way of thinking about rules and their meaning in her life and in her relations with others. But as she sees the limits of the new place that she is at—that, indeed, she may not be able to avoid breaking a rule—her thinking is focused not on the situation and the others involved but rather on the values she holds and her integrity in maintaining them in dealing with others. Three years later she describes a different conflict and reveals how some old issues are reconstructed.

Rebecca as a Senior

Describing herself as "independent and very outgoing," "involved more in trying to change this environment," three years later Rebecca sees herself as "concerned" with getting things changed. Because she believes "this school has done a lot for me," she wants to help mold the environment so that it is best for "my needs, not only my needs personally, but for the students." Emphasizing why it is important to be concerned and give—"because the less control you have over your own environment, the more other people will control it for you and then you end up feeling helpless. And I don't want to feel helpless . . . small and alone"—Rebecca sees that for her it is necessary "to try to take control of my life." She tries to do that in school. While these words carry a new meaning, surely signaling a new place for this young woman, old themes reappear.

Focusing on a conflict she faced as a school leader, a proctor on a hall, she describes a situation in which she had to report students who did not follow school rules. Recounting a specific time where a friend of hers asked if she could sleep through morning reports, she says "that was hard" to decide because, "I was caught between choosing between a friend and what was right." Detailing an element of this conflict she says:

> It was a difference between choosing doing what the rule said, what the rules dictated, and maintaining my friendship with this girl, at least as I saw it, maintaining my relationship with this girl.

Asked to describe what she considered in trying to decide what to do, Rebecca goes on:

> I considered, okay, I mean, is this going to be, I mean it finally occurred to me that she knew my job, she knew that was my job, and she knew what kind of pressure I was under. And if she was going to sit there and pressure me, what kind of a friend was she? And if I said No to her over morning reports, and she decided this was the end of our friendship, maybe we didn't have that much of a friendship in the first place.

Although seeing her conflict as "choosing doing what the rule said, what the rules dictated, and maintaining my friendship with this girl," Rebecca identifies something new in her thinking as she works out a solution: "I realized that I can do what's right and at the same time not sacrifice relationships. That can work." She elaborates:

> And I realized that you can do what's right. This is something that has become new, too. I realize that I can do what's right and at the same time not sacrifice relationships. And as my friends have gotten older, they have an ability to do that, too. Like, you know, my friend the vice president of [x] and I have all sorts of arguments over what's wrong. It gets to the point where it is more than abstractions, but damn it, I believe this is right and the world is going to die unless this happens. And she believes something else very strongly, and we are able to argue about that. In fact, we are able to fight a lot, and we still get along, and our friendship still works. And that can work. I have discovered that you can do the "right" thing and not sacrifice a relationship. And I don't think that is something I would have learned if I had gone to a co-ed school, because I would have been a lot more desperate about relationships I think.

Rebecca describes her reflections, that her choice was the right thing to do:

> At that point in time, I was at the point that I needed to assert my authority as a leader, and she needed some limits set for her, too, because she was at the period where she was testing me out to see what I would do.

> Because it was new in the year, she had known me as somebody who kind of fooled around the year before. I mean by being late to study hall and not regarding the rules as a sacred cow and saying, That is a stupid rule and I am going to violate it because I don't feel it has a lot of merit. And so she was testing me out to see what kind of an authority figure I would be, and I needed to say to her, Hey, you are not going to be able to use our friendship as a tool to push me around with.

While it would be simple to suggest that perhaps this conception of friendship is instrumental, it is more complex. Elaborating on her reasons why this situation presented a moral conflict for her, Rebecca suggests a different way of seeing friendships as she discusses the question of what morality means to her.

> What does morality [mean to me]? Oh boy, such big questions, morality? I used to say every year when I did this, oh, it is a system of ethics that you live by. I think it basically comes down to whether you want to do what makes yourself more comfortable or whether you want to try to please other people. And I substitute the

phrase what is more comfortable for you, I substitute that in lieu of what's right. Because who's to say what's right. Usually when you do something 'right,' you feel good about it and you know, you know. And it's not that easy. Doing what's right I have discovered is not, you know, it's not some nebulous principle that's impossible to figure out and you feel good about what's right, *and what you do for other people is a sacrifice of what's right* [emphasis added]. Sometimes they don't conflict. But you usually know when you have done something that violates yourself, your concept of what's right, when you feel cruddy about it. And you feel really bad. So to me, that is what morality is.

Thus, identifying morality as a changing conception in her thinking, one more consistent with her own integral sense of "what is more comfortable" for her, Rebecca also seems to identify a point of tension—what you do for other people may be a sacrifice of what's right. Thus the very question of friendship can seem a threat to Rebecca's sense of self.

Change

If we look at the conflicts Rebecca reports at her first and last year of school, we see that "rules" and standards are part of a central set of ideas about herself and her relations to others that change over time. The dramatic shift occurs, however, from year one, when the people involved in breaking a rule were only shadowy figures. In contrast is the problem she constructs as a senior: "choosing between what the rule said and a friendship." Others it seems are now more centrally coming into focus. But what is at stake now is how to maintain what's right with friendship.

Talking about herself in her middle year of school, Rebecca articulates a set of ideas about her relations to others important to her own self-definition. Describing how she thought about herself in the past, she says:

> In the past I really had no notion of myself, of just me and not me in relation to my friends or me in relation to my parents or anything. I see myself. I have a better notion of what I am and who I am and everything. And I didn't before, because I was never, I never felt that I was really separate from my family or my friends so that was a different behavior, a different person.

> (*And now*?) Now, well, in friendships before, I felt like I was just part of the group and I would mold myself to a group, and what that group needed I would be. I would change or act a certain way. If they needed an airhead, I would be an airhead. If they needed a jock, I would act like a jock, or whatever. And now I know that this is what I am like and the friendships that I find now, those are going to be people who are going to have to deal with me as I am and like me as I am.

Identifying her separateness as giving her a "better notion of . . . who I am," Rebecca seeks to maintain that identity, to hold on to it even in friendships. People—friends—will have to deal with her as she "is." When asked about change—in particular, things about herself that she would not want to change—Rebecca says:

> Wouldn't want to change? I don't think I would like to change the way I look at life now and the way I see things. I don't really ever want to lose my perspective, from the way I see things now.

> It's a perspective in that I don't totally divorce myself from the world, but I am not totally wrapped up in the midst of. If somebody has a problem, usually before I'd get wrapped up in their problem and their problems would become my problem, you know, and I suppose that goes along with like molding into a group, you know.

> Now I think the perspective I have now is I can set myself apart from situations, and I can see situations. I can see the humor and I don't get too wrapped up, and I don't take everything too seriously and go overboard, which is what I used to do before.

Now celebrating her perspective that sets her apart from situations and people, that makes it possible that she will not find herself again lost or "molded into a group," Rebecca emphasizes her autonomy and sense of self in relation to others. This theme—consistent across three years of her high school—seems part of a central issue of her development. Manifested not only in her personal relationships, but found too in her schoolwide role as proctor, the themes of separateness, of maintaining her standards or her perspective can be traced across an evolution of a way-of-being in relation to others that has been modified over three years.

In a conflict she faced in her second year of school, a new element emerges in her thinking that perhaps accounts for change. The situation arose for her when her sister was planning to visit her at school at Thanksgiving, anticipating coming herself to Emma Willard. Rebecca wanted to go home for the holiday. Knowing that "the money for her to come here would be my money to go back home," Rebecca tells how she thought about it:

> I remember talking to my sister on the phone saying, "you don't really want to come out here now, your grades are so bad." And it was pretty selfish and pretty low of me and so . . . I said to my mom: 'I don't think she should come; her grades are bad.' So she [did not come] but I felt so guilty, I couldn't let myself go home.

Asked what the conflicts were, she says:

> The right side was she has been talking, she has been planning on coming out here for a long time and she wants to come. She should come. I promised that to her. My parents have made the arrangements she should come. Then, the other side was, I have never really gone home for Thanksgiving for several years. . . . I'd really like to see my friends.

Reflecting that "I think I hurt her feelings . . . I was willing to walk all over her to get what I wanted. So I guess that's what I mean by hurtful," Rebecca wrestles with a new element in her moral code—not hurting somebody. Framing the conflict in terms of issues of fairness—of what was promised to her sister, what was right—she reflects on it both from the perspective of fairness and that of not hurting someone. Thus over three years, while rules and integrity—the salient themes of Rebecca's development—have undergone change from things outside the self (school rules) to internal self-chosen ideals, the new edge of her growth is seeing the other more clearly. Seeing that another person has a context, goals, aspirations of his or her own, her standards and integrity give way to create a new way to maintain friendships.

Although these issues need more systematic attention with diverse samples of adolescent girls, some features of this way of being in relation to others can be identified:

That issues of a way of being in relation to others characterized as "autonomous in relation to others" seem to center around concern for autonomy, separateness—but only in relation to others.

That one feature of the developmental dynamic of this mode seems to be finding ways to hold on to one's integrity while dealing with one's relations to others. This can be seen in issues of identity and morality.

That seeing others in their own terms and contexts may be the cutting edge of growth and change.

The conflicts that Emma Willard girls reported at grade 10 and then at grade 12 changed (see table 4). In brief this comparison makes it possible to see in relief some elements of the issues discussed.

Themes of Change

In examining the conflicts Anne and Rebecca and other Emma Willard girls report, it is possible to see that a transformation in thinking has occurred. From ways of thinking about self in relation to others, nuances can be perceived suggesting the outline of themes of change over time along the following lines.

Table 4
Nature of Moral Conflicts Girls Report

At 10th grade	At 12th grade
Response mode	
1. Coming to school here: I didn't want to have my parents separated from me; decide between mother and father and school; should I help myself or my aunt (whom I was living with); I wanted to come here but if I went to public school I would be with my friends; will they want me next year [as friends].	1. Whether I should follow my own instinct and go tell the teacher what I think, whether or not to speak to the head of humanities about the teacher, or whether it would be selfish of me not to go?
2. Whether to go with a friend, stay out late when I could not get ahold of my mother.	2. I wanted to apply to a college but my father gets a tuition break at another.
3. What to do with sister who tells me things in confidence.	3. Whether to talk to my friend or not—we are not communicating.
Rights mode	
1. Whether to go out drinking with friends when I sit on the FSJ (Faculty Student Judiciary Committee).	1. Choosing between what the rules said or maintaining my friendship with this girl.
2. Not going to required chapel. I don't like the idea of being required to go.	2. Deciding to begin Stop Nuclear War. How far to stretch myself.

Response/Interdependent Mode: Themes of Change

Entering oneself in the dialogue. From thinking about simply one's concerns for others, what seems at stake at grade 12 is honoring one's own thinking: for example, "Should I follow my own instincts?" or "But I had to decide." Subtly there is a recognition of self, not simply a self-reflective self, but one engaged in the issue of choice.

Naming the psychological realities of self and others that one knows. One now needs to consider in the choices one makes what the realities of others and self are. "My father gets a tuition break at another college." That needs to be considered if I am to honor the particularity of others. But I will also honor my own self. "She was not doing her work—but I had to decide." "We are not communicating."

Speaking out about what one knows. Now the concerns about selfishness that seem to carry over across the years of girls' high school experience enter in the name of speaking out. "Whether it would be selfish of me not to go, not to speak out." One must act—speak—if one knows.

Autonomous/Independent Mode: Themes of Change

Bringing others into the dialogue with the self. Here the task is to acknowledge others, their contexts and needs.

Balancing the standards one holds with the needs of friendship, or against other values. For example, "Choosing between what the rules said or maintaining my friendship with this girl."

In each of the two modes—the interdependent or the autonomous—developmental issues involve both tasks of autonomy and tasks of attachment (see table 5).

Table 5

Developmental Tasks Related to Modes of Self Defined in Relation to Others

Relational modes	Developmental tasks of autonomy	Developmental tasks of attachment/connection
Interdependent in relation to others	Developmental tasks center on issues of caring for self; extricating self from others, but not at expense of connection to others. Inclusion of self—meets self's needs.	Growth continues in understanding others; attachment to others remains as issue of development.
Autonomous in relation to others	Growth continues around issues of separation/ autonomy in relation to others; idea is to maintain integrity of self, not compromise self's relationships, include others but not at expense of self.	Developmental tasks center around issues of seeing others in their own terms and contexts.

Implications

To gain perspective on the implications of this work, it is useful to consider the responses of some of the teachers of Emma Willard School and the implications they find in this work. Their comments provide one way to consider the validity of this research, that is, its usefulness to the people who work daily with Emma Willard girls.

For example, this research provided the dean of students with a new way to interpret behaviors he found disturbing. Noting that sometimes after "lights out," girls would be found rushing off to another girl's room, and when caught would argue that "I needed to see my friend. She is in a kind of bad way, and I wanted to talk with her." Thinking that this was just an excuse, and not a very compelling one, the dean discovered that the girls really were responding to needs they identified, and that school rules did not come first in the set of values they held about the importance of relationships in their lives. Similarly, a faculty member who had been the adviser to an editor of the school yearbook reported that although he was aware of a conflict the editor reported in trying to get another student to do her yearbook assignments, he had no idea how long it had gone on. He was unaware of how significant it was to the editor and how she had wrestled with the other student's desires to stay on the yearbook staff even though she had not done her assignment.

Similarly, teachers seeing the two moral orientations as embodying two logics now look at discipline issues differently. The recognize that girls may want to be involved in the school judiciary procedures for very different reasons—reasons that will shape their behavior: some to help prevent student troubles; others to have a chance to be in charge of the procedures that will guarantee fairness in deliberations. These views may be compatible. But they are subtly different, suggesting different values that, in turn, lead to different ways of interacting.

Probably the area of most significance to teachers comes in the ways teachers now think about the education of girls. Not only did Emma Willard faculty review and "balance" their curriculum to respond to the inclusion of women within it, that is, to guarantee that women were included (for example, in the novels assigned in reading, in the examination in history of the social features of people's lives as well as the political features), but teachers also became more attentive to their practices in support of student learning: in listening to questions students ask and in reflecting on their own responses; and in trying out diverse approaches, such as cooperative learning, in math classes and on the playing fields (McIntosh 1983). It is possible to show a hypothesized mode of the characteristic features of two approaches to learning implied in the two moral and self orientations: the justice and care modes with their related self-conceptions—the self as autonomous, or separate; and the self as interdependent, or connected (see table 6). This model is adapted from recent work of Belenky et al. (1986) and of Bruner (1986). The terminology of "connected" or "separate" knower is the one used by Belenky et al. adopted from my work (Lyons 1982, 1983) and that of Gilligan (1977, 1982, 1987). Here the emphasis is on different features of the learner's goals and interests, which reflect different approaches to learning.

While the two approaches to learning are thought of as clearly complementary although significantly different, understanding and articulating these differences is an important agenda for the future. Most schools tend to foster rule-oriented, abstract thinking, whether in mathematics and science or history and social studies: Less attention is given to features we identify here as associated with a response "connected" learner. Emma Willard teachers, for example, found themselves

Table 6

Learners and Learning Contexts: The Relationship of Mode of Self to Learner's Interests, Goals, and Mode of Thinking*

Mode of self / knower	Learner's interests and goals	Learner as thinker and knower
Autonomous (separate in relation to others) "paradigmatic" knower	To question, to prove, to find answers to questions, to solve problems To convince by argument, logic Know how to know truth	Analytical, procedural, truth seeking, rule seeking and using Test for truth: consistency, logic, reasoned hypothesis Transcend time and space and particulars; imagination: to see before proving; thought and feeling held apart
Interdependent (connected in relation to others), "narrative" knower	To question; to find understanding of situations, people, and their contexts; narrative-seeking; to convince by motives, particulars of lives	Tentative and questioning, judgment suspended, fact gathering, synthesizer Test for truth: believability; concern for understanding of human motivation, intention Imagination used to enter into situations, contexts; locate in time and place Thought and feeling held together

*Adapted from Belenky et al. 1986, Bruner 1986, Gilligan 1982, Lyons 1982, 1987.

thinking about student hesitancy and questioning in a different way once they had some familiarity with the two orientations. One recently hired Emma Willard teacher of history, for example, shared an incident with colleagues that he at first found perplexing. He was nearing the end of a class in which he had been emphasizing how the American political system worked in one presidential election during which a deal had been struck between Northern and Southern Democrats and Republicans. One girl raised her hand to ask what grounds the people involved had to trust one another. The teacher, feeling as if the question came from "left field" since it had nothing to do with a systems approach he was emphasizing, was puzzled at his failure to be clear. But in sharing this situation with colleagues he was offered a different interpretation: The girl was more interested as a learner in understanding the motives of those involved. She heard the event as a narrative, a story of an encounter in the relationships between individuals. The logic she sought was not the logic of a system. Rather she sought the logic of understanding, what Bruner calls "believability" (Bruner 1986). Unlike the teacher who sought to transcend time, she was rooted in it—in the particulars of the situation and in the relationship between people. It is this approach to learning, with its different concerns and interests, that educators need to understand better and for which they must listen. They also need to make opportunities for this voice to be expressed and heard. If this is a mode of learning more frequently found in the thinking of girls—although we know it is available to both sexes—we need to be attentive to that. Adolescent girls remind us of the centrality of Piaget's ([1932] 1965) insight that "apart from our relations to other people, there can be no moral necessity." Their thinking about what is morally necessary illuminates and helps us understand how morality, mind, self, and relationships are intricately linked in everyday ways of knowing and learning.

References

Adelson, J. 1980. *Handbook of Adolescent Psychology*. New York: John Wiley.

_____. 1986. *Inventing Adolescence: The Political Psychology of Everyday Schooling*. New Brunswick, N.J.: Transaction Books.

Adelson, J., and M. J. Doehrman. 1980. "The Psychodynamic Approach to Adolescence." In *Handbook of Adolescent Psychology*, edited by J. Adelson, New York: John Wiley.

Belenky, M. F., B. Clinchy, N. Goldberger, and J. Tarule. 1986. *Women's Ways of Knowing: The Development of Self, Voice, and Mind*. New York: Basic Books.

Bruner, J. 1986. *Actual Minds, Possible Worlds*. Cambridge, Mass: Harvard University Press.

Chodorow, N. 1978. *The Reproduction of Mothering: Psychoanalysis and the Sociology of Mothering*. Berkeley, Calif.: University of California Press.

Douvan, E., and J. Adelson. 1966. *The Adolescent Experience*. New York: John Wiley.

Erikson, E. 1968. *Identity: Youth and Crisis*. New York: W. W. Norton.

Gilligan, C. 1977. In a different voice: Women's conceptions of the self and morality. *Harvard Educational Review* 47:481–517.

_____. 1982. *In a Different Voice*. Cambridge, Mass..: Harvard University Press.

_____. 1987. Female development in adolescence: Implications for theory. Unpublished manuscript, Harvard University.

Gilligan, C., S. Langdale, N. Lyons, and M. Murphy. 1982. The contribution of women's thought to developmental theory: an interim report to the National Institute of Education. Unpublished manuscript, Harvard University.

Gilligan, C., and J. Attanucci. 1988. Two moral orientations: Gender differences and similarities. *Merrill-Palmer Quarterly*.

Grotevant, H. D. and C. R. Cooper, eds. 1983. *Adolescent Development in the Family: New Directions for Child Development*. San Francisco: Jossey-Bass.

Haan, N. 1977. *A Manual for Interpersonal Morality*. Berkeley, Calif.: University of California, Institute for Human Development.

Hanmer, T. 1987. Personal correspondence to N. Lyons.

Harre, R., and R. Lamb, eds. 1986. *The Dictionary of Personality and Social Psychology*. Cambridge, Mass.: MIT Press.

Hartup, W. W., and Z. Rubin, eds. 1986. *Relationships and Development*. Hillsdale, N.J.: L. Erlbaum Associates.

Hinde, R. A. 1979. *Towards Understanding Relationships*. London and New York: Academic Press.

Hinde, R. A., and J. Stevenson-Hinde. 1986. "Relating Childhood Relationships to Individual Characteristics." In *Relationships and Development*, edited by W. Hartup and Z. Rubin. Hillsdale, N.J.: L. Erlbaum Associates.

Johnston, D. K. 1985. Two moral orientations—two problem-solving strategies: Adolescents' solutions to dilemmas in fables. Ph.D. diss., Harvard University.

Kohlberg, L. 1969. "Stage and Sequence: The Cognitive Developmental Approach to Socialization." In *The Handbook of Socialization Theory and Research*, edited by D. Goslin. Chicago: Rand McNally.

_____. 1984. *The Psychology of Moral Development: Essays on Moral Development*. San Francisco: Harper and Row.

Lyons, N. 1982. Conceptions of self and morality and modes of moral choice. Ph.D. diss. Harvard University.

_____. 1983. Two perspectives: On self, relationships and morality. *Harvard Educational Review* 53:125–145.

_____. Forthcoming. "Visions and Competencies: Men and Women as Decision-Makers and Conflict Managers." In *Educating Women*, edited by J. Antler and S. Bicklen. Albany, N.Y.: SUNY Press.

_____. 1987. Ways of knowing, learning and making moral choices. *Journal of Moral Education* 16, no. 3.

Marcia, J. 1980. "Identity in Adolescence." In *Handbook of Adolescent Psychology*, edited by J. Adelson. New York: John Wiley.

May, R. 1980. *Sex and Fantasy: Patterns of Male and Female Development*. New York: W. W. Norton & Co.

McIntosh, P. 1983. Interactive phases of curricular re-vision: A feminist perspective. Working Paper. Wellesley College, Center for Research on Women.

Miller, J. B. 1976, 1986. *Towards a New Psychology of Women*. Boston: Beacon Press.

Piaget, J. 1965. *The Moral Judgment of the Child*. Glencoe, Ill.: Free Press. (Originally pub. 1932.)

Youniss, J. 1980. *Parents and Peers in Social Development: A Sullivan-Piaget Perspective*. Chicago: University of Chicago Press.

Incorporating the Development of African-American Students into Psychosocial Theories of Student Development

Marylu K. McEwen, Larry D. Roper,
Deborah R. Bryant, and Miriam J. Langa

Nine dimensions that address the development of African-American students are proposed for inclusion in psychosocial theories of college student development.

Colleges and universities in the United States have a tradition and mission of transforming and enriching the lives of students (Boyer, 1987). This mission is consistent with the goals of preserving, enriching, and transmitting culture, as was identified by the Student Personnel Point of View (SPPV) (American Council on Education [ACE], 1937, 1949). The SPPV suggests that college personnel, especially student affairs professionals, should fulfill their mission by responding to the whole person, acknowledging individual differences, and meeting students at their level of development (Saddlemire & Rentz, 1986). In addition, college and university programs help students to make "significant life transitions" (National Association of Student Personnel Administrators [NASPA], 1987). Implied in all three of these statements (ACE, 1937, 1949; NASPA, 1987) is that student affairs professionals also have a responsibility of responding to all students, which includes both majority and racial and ethnic minority students.

For much of history, however, higher education in the United States was racially segregated. Beginning in the 1960s, large numbers of Black students began attending predominantly White institutions (Fleming, 1984). The sudden influx of Black students created an educational dilemma for college and university professionals—how could they respond to the educational needs of students for whom their institutions were not designed? Predominantly White institutions (PWIs) were founded for the intention of educating the White middle class (Kovel, 1970). These institutions, based on Anglo-Saxon, Euro-American values, are like all social institutions; they survive because they are symbolically related to the cultural values of the broader American society.

The cultural values of PWIs also influence how students are viewed and how education is approached. The cultural values of institutions affect what students are taught, how they are taught, and how student learning is evaluated. Most important, cultural values influence the direction that educators attempt to move students, how student behavior is evaluated, and what knowledge base is used to explain student (human) development. Because educators at PWIs have historically relied upon a body of knowledge that supports and reinforces Euro-American values, they often prove unsuccessful in responding to the educational and cultural needs of African-American students (Bulhan, 1985). Black students at PWIs are taught and evaluated from an Anglo-Saxon perspective.

Those responsible for teaching and helping Black students must create models of human and student development that take into account the unique needs and experiences that Black students bring to the college campus. Issues specific to African-American students that are not accounted for in the traditional theories of human development are (a) the unique psycho-history of Blacks in this country and the adaptations that Blacks must make (Essien-Udom, 1971); (b) the "colonized" nature of Black existence in this country (Fanon, 1967); (c) the extended nature of the Black family and Black homelife (Willie, 1976); (d) the unique educational/socialization role of the Black family (Willie, 1976); (e) the oral tradition within the Black community (Hall & Freedle, 1975); (f) the impact of racial hostility and environmental press (Ogbu, 1981); (g) the unique character of Black Americans (Essien-Udom, 1971); (h) the psychological dynamics that accompany being "a caste-like minority" (Ogbu, 1981), representing a "rejected strain" in society (Cruse, 1967), being "codified" (Scruggs, 1971), and attempting to reconcile two identities (DuBois, 1953); and (i) the philosophical connections to African tradition, such as oral tradition, action/belief connection, elastic concept of time, kinship tradition/group consciousness, survival focus (collective versus individual), spiritual disposition, and view of people as an integrated whole (Baldwin, 1981; Nobles, 1980). Among other issues to be considered are the limitations of Euro-American definitions of normalcy (Bulhan, 1985) for African-American students.

Black scholars suggest that the Black experience in American society requires that Blacks interact with and participate in White institutions. This participation results in *oppression, dehumanization,* and *deracialization.* Deracialization occurs through a process by which people are required/ forced to abandon "cultural forms, . . . [one's] language, . . . [one's] food habits, . . . [one's] sexual behavior, . . . [one's] way of sitting down, of resting, of laughing, of enjoying [oneself]" (Fanon, 1972, pp. 20–21). Student affairs professionals must concern themselves with whether or not, through the use of traditional theories and practices, they are participating in the dehumanization of African-American students. One way of responding is by expanding psychosocial theories of college student development to address the experience of African-American students.

Psychosocial theories, one of five clusters of student development theories (Knefelkamp, Widick, & Parker, 1978, p. xi), are those based directly or indirectly on Erikson's (1968) theory of human development. Examples of psychosocial theories/models include those of Chickering (1969), Sanford (1962), Keniston (1971), Coons (1970), and King (1973). Roy Heath's (1964) typology model and Douglas Heath's (1968) maturity model can also be included in the psychosocial framework.

The purpose of this discussion is to offer ways in which proponents of psychosocial theories of student development can incorporate more effectively the developmental issues of African-American students. A number of different dimensions must be added to extend the boundaries of student development theories. Nine such dimensions for inclusion in psychosocial theories are proposed below. These issues have been identified both through theoretical literature and essays on the Black experience and through quantitative and qualitative research conducted with African-American students in higher education.

Developmental Issues

Nine factors relate to developmental tasks of African-American students. These issues, which either have not been addressed adequately in the psychosocial theories or need to be considered in more complex ways for African-American students, include developing ethnic and racial identity, interacting with the dominant culture, developing cultural aesthetics and awareness, developing identity, developing interdependence, fulfilling affiliation needs, surviving intellectually, developing spiritually, and developing social responsibility.

Developing Ethnic and Racial Identity

A number of authors have cited the need to expand the notion of identity development to include attitudes about the race to which one belongs, that is, the role of racial or ethnic identity (Baldwin, 1981, 1984; Baldwin & Bell, 1985; Baldwin, Duncan, & Bell, 1987; Cross, 1971, 1978; Fleming, 1984; Helms, 1981; Parham, 1989; Parham & Helms, 1981, 1985a, 1985b; Pounds, 1987). Fleming (1984) indicated that Black students may hold doubts about their ethnic identity and that they must put psychological energy into protecting themselves against identity loss. Helms (1984) contrasted this issue for Black students with that of Whites, in which many Whites do not see themselves as White and thus may not hold a set of attitudes about the racial group to which they belong.

Cross (1971, 1978) offered a useful model from which to consider the development of racial identity. He proposed five stages, namely, (a) Preencounter, in which the Black student has not yet encountered the issue of one's own racial identity; (b) Encounter, in which one has a significant experience and begins to develop a Black identity; (c) Immersion-Emersion, in which one becomes intensely focused upon one's new Black identity; (d) Internalization, in which one resolves the conflicts between the old and new worldviews; and (e) Internalization-Commitment, encompassing the previous stage but adding commitment to resolution of problems shared by one's racial group. In discussing cycles of psychological Nigrescence, Parham (1989) suggested that the racial identity of a Black person is "potentially influenced by his or her life stage and the developmental tasks associated with that period of life" (p. 196). Parham (1989) also described "how the stages of racial identity may be manifested at three phases of life (late adolescence/early adulthood, middle adulthood, and late adulthood)" (p. 197).

Parham and Helms (1981, 1985a, 1985b) have extended Cross's (1971, 1978) model by developing the Racial Identity Attitude Scale (Parham & Helms, 1981) and by conducting research with Black college students on the relationship between racial identity and self-esteem (1985a), self-actualization (1985b), and counselor preference (1981). In Parham and Helm's study of counselor preference, preencounter attitudes were negatively related and encounter attitudes positively related to preference for Black counselors; furthermore, preencounter attitudes were positively related to preference for White counselors (Parham & Helms, 1981). Parham and Helms (1981) summarized that (a) the preencounter stage is characterized by pro-White-anti-Black counselor preferences, (b) the encounter stage is characterized by pro-Black–anti-White counselor preferences, and (c) the immersion-emersion and internalization stages are similar in pro-Black attitudes but are not as anti-White as is the encounter stage (p. 254). In two studies, Parham and Helms found that both preencounter and immersion attitudes were significantly related to low self-esteem (1985a) and less self-actualization (1985b), whereas encounter attitudes were associated with positive self-esteem and greater self-actualization.

In both cases, the variance explained by a combination of the racial identity attitudes was between 15% and 18%. Parham and Helms (1985b) concluded that (a) the racial identity process may be more complex than is expected and (b) both professionals and Black students should be aware that some of the feelings associated with particular racial identity attitudes may be unpleasant and require resolution, but may be a natural part of the Nigrescence process. Parham and Helms (1985a) also concluded that "self-concept may be governed by the way the student handles the conditions of the Black experience" (p. 145). In a later study, Carter and Helms (1988) found that socioeconomic status variables were not significant predictors of racial identity attitudes.

Baldwin (1981, 1984), Baldwin and Bell (1985), and Baldwin et al. (1987) discussed the concept of African self-consciousness as "central to normal and healthy Black personality functioning" (Baldwin et al., 1987, p. 28). According to their theory, African self-consciousness involves (a) the recognition of oneself as "African" and what being "African means," (b) the recognition of African survival and proactive development as one's first priority value, (c) respect for and active perpetuation of all things African, and (d) having a standard of conduct toward all things "non-African" and "anti-African" (Baldwin et al., 1987, p. 29). Baldwin and Bell (1985) have developed the African Self-Consciousness (ASC) Scale that measures competency in the four areas of African self-consciousness identified previously. In a study of the relationship of background characteristics and social cultural setting to African self-consciousness, Baldwin et al. (1987) found that Black students at a predominantly Black college had significantly higher ASC scale scores than did Black students attending a predominantly White institution.

They also found that older students and upperclass students had higher ASC scores than did younger students and underclass students, with the class difference being more pronounced for students in the predominantly Black college. Baldwin et al. (1987) concluded that a predominantly Black academic setting may have a more positive influence on the development of African self-consciousness than will a predominantly White academic setting.

Interacting with the Dominant Culture

Another aspect of culture is the role that assimilation and acculturation play in the development of racial and ethnic minority students. Because White students are part of the majority and dominant culture, this issue of assimilation/acculturation does not emerge for students of the dominant culture. For African-American students, however, the task of "adjusting to living/learning in a campus environment that varies from the accustomed cultural frame of reference" (Wright, 1987, p. 11) is a most important issue.

Gibbs (1974) cited numerous studies in which Black students suffer from a series of identity problems resulting from culture conflict. Through clinical experience with Black students experiencing ethnic or cultural conflicts, Gibbs identified four modes of adaptation to the college and university environment. These four modes are withdrawal, described as movement away from the dominant culture and is characterized by apathy and depression; separation, described as movement against the dominant culture and is characterized by anger, hostility, and conflicts with the dominant culture; assimilation, described as movement toward the dominant culture and is characterized by social anxiety and desire for acceptance; and affirmation, described as movement with the dominant culture and is characterized by self-acceptance, high achievement, and a positive ethnic identity. Three of these modes of adaptation are similar to Pettigrew's (1964) three major modes of response to oppression. Among the 41 students in Gibb's study, withdrawal was the most frequent response mode. Gibbs found that 70% of those students who described themselves as feeling adequate were in the affirmation category, and 61% of those who felt inadequate were in the withdrawal category.

In examining four different categories of socioeconomic class, class differences were found among three of the four response categories. For students of the two highest socioeconomic classes, affirmation and assimilation were the second and third most frequent response modes. There were no students in the separation category among the highest class, and none in the assimilation or affirmation categories among the lowest class. Among working-class students (third lowest class), there were "fewer in the affirmation category and more in the separation and assimilation categories" (p. 738) than there were students in the top two socioeconomic classes.

Developing Cultural Aesthetics and Awareness

Developing cultural aesthetics and awareness is an additional developmental issue for African-American students (Jones, 1987; Stikes, 1984; Wright, 1987). This relates to an appreciation of one's own culture, and of other cultures, especially in addition to the dominant culture, and also developing ways in which African-American students can express and celebrate their own cultures.

Developing Identity

The general concept of identity must also be expanded and viewed from a different perspective for African-American students. Sedlacek (1987) addressed this in terms of the importance of self-concept and self-appraisal. Erikson (1968) noted the message of lost, confused and "surrendered identity" contained in the writings of revolutionary Black authors. These same authors speak of inaudibility, namelessness, facelessness, and invisibility that Blacks have been made to experience.

Knefelkamp and Golec (1985) echoed the invisibility that certain persons in American society have had to face. Others (Anson, 1987; DuBois, 1953; Wright, 1987) addressed the duality or even multiplicity with which Black students must struggle, an identity consideration not typically faced by majority students. As Wright (1987) indicated, many minority students live and learn in bicultural/biracial/bilingual environments, which are different from and frequently in conflict with those experienced at college. According to Bradley and Stewart (1982), Blacks experience depersonalization, which brings with it a loss of one's sense of identity, pride, and accomplishment. Cummins (1986) talked about bicultural ambivalence. Brown-Collins and Sussewell (1986) raised the issue of multiple self-referents for African-American students, especially Black women, and suggested at least three self-referents, that of the psychophysiological (Gilligan, 1982), the African American, and oneself (self-knowledge). All of these authors suggest the multiplicity of roles or identities, the implication of contextual identities for students of nondominant cultures, and the intense struggle for African-American students at PWIs to develop identity when the environment seems to work at cross-purposes to such development.

Furthermore, identity development, according to Erikson (1968), relates both to a developmental stage in the life of an individual and to a period in history. Thus, his statement provides strong support for DeVos's (1980) notion of the importance of considering the current social environment. Gurin and Epps (1975), in a series of studies conducted in several historically Black colleges between 1964 and 1970, found that the Black student's sense of identity involves both uniquely personal and collective elements that result from social interaction and group identifications and demonstrated that the students used being Black as the basis for collective elements of identity.

Developing Interdependence

For African-American students, developing independence and autonomy seems to occur within the context of interdependence and relationships, contrasted with the developmental issue of separating oneself from family and significant others as suggested by the literature (Chickering, 1969; Erikson, 1968). Hughes (1987), based on her qualitative research with 79 Black students, found patterns of individuation unique to Black students resulting from the close relationship that Black students maintain with their families. She highlighted the importance of interdependence in individuation and suggested that "it is likely that Black individuation helps to integrate Afrocentric culture values, commonly referred to as the 'extended family'" (p. 540). Hughes's findings are supported by the literature on the extended nature of the Black family and Black homelife (Willie, 1976) and the unique educational/socialization role of the Black family (Willie, 1976). The roles of family and community are also strongly tied to philosophical connections with the African tradition, such as kinship tradition/group consciousness, survival focus (collective versus individual) and view of people as an integrated whole (Baldwin, 1981; Nobles, 1980).

Fulfilling Affiliation Needs

The role of affiliation needs is also highlighted by Hughes (1987). Affiliation opportunities play a significant role in the survival, success, and development of African-American students, at PWIs. On predominantly White campuses, affiliations can counter the social isolation experienced by Black students. In Hughes's (1987) study, Black students' needs were fulfilled external to the university campus, through the Black community, Black churches, and the extended family. DeVos (1980) also addressed the importance of peers or a reference group in the development of Black students, especially in the development of ethnic identity.

Surviving Intellectually

The intellectual survival of African-American students on predominantly White campuses must also be addressed. Fleming (1984) eloquently discussed, based on her research, the impoverished environment for Black students in terms of their cognitive development and the intense struggle that many Black students face in developing the most basic intellectual competence, which is necessary for survival on the college campus. Others (DeVos, 1980; Hughes, 1987) also provide evidence in support of this issue. Hughes goes even further when she indicates that many Black students realize that development in other areas will be delayed or postponed because of their preoccupation with intellectual survival.

Developing Spiritually

The role of religion and spiritual development are two related dimensions that are frequently important to African-American students but that have not been accounted for adequately in most student development theories. Religion not only remains an important activity for African-American students throughout the college years (Wright, 1987) but the church is often an important support for African-American students (Erikson, 1968; Hughes, 1987). Similarly, spiritual development needs to be incorporated in student development theories for a better understanding of African-American students. As additional support reported by Black students in Hughes's (1987) study was reliance on spiritual strength, with spirituality being a deeply rooted aspect of Afrocentric culture (Hughs, 1987). Baldwin (1981) and Nobles (1980) also address the spiritual disposition of African Americans.

Developing Social Responsibility

Wright (1987) suggested that the development of social responsibility is a special psychosocial issue for racial and ethnic minority students. Because of their ethnic status and their exposure to real and perceived social injustice, African-American students frequently assume major responsibility for social advocacy roles on campus. Wright suggests that the greatest dilemma for racial/ethnic minority students in relation to social responsibility is not whether to assume it, but rather how it relates to other multiple responsibilities they hold.

Summary

The following recommendations are offered:

1. Student affairs professionals must develop out of the experiences of African Americans workable theories of student development. When traditional theories are used in working with Black students, conclusions are often reached that are not accurate. Traditional theories are based on the values, philosophical assumptions, and experiences of European Americans.

2. The philosophical connections to Africa have created a distinct African-American ethos. There are many additional factors that contribute to the unique experience and psychological disposition of African Americans. These issues must be taken into account if there is to be created an accurate working model to understand the attitudes, behaviors, feelings, and development of African-American students.

3. Because of the diversity in the Black community, there is no such thing as a "typical Black person." The shared experience of being Black in American society, however, provides a link in the experiences of all African Americans. The link consists of a core of behavioral/dispositional variables upon which theories of the development of African-American students may be developed.

4. Student affairs professionals can work with Black students neither meaningfully nor successfully without understanding their philosophical assumptions and their life experiences.

5. Black student development must not be viewed/approached as "deficit development." There are at least two approaches that may be taken to look at Black student

developmental issues. One approach focuses on the negative experiences that African Americans have in American society and at PWIs; the other approach focuses on the positive traits that connection to the African tradition brings to Black students and their efforts to succeed in an Anglo-Saxon social structure. Focus on the former causes a person to view the Black student from a deficit-deficiency perspective. By focusing on the latter, African-American students are approached based on the positive skills and personal characteristics that they bring to the campus community, and subsequent programs will build on those values, traditions, and attitudes.

6. One way of creating a workable theory of college student development is to incorporate the nine issues identified above into an existing psychosocial theory. Chickering's (1969) theory, as one of the most comprehensive of the psychosocial theories and also as one of the best known and most frequently applied theories, offers a good possibility. Some of the nine developmental issues discussed earlier, such as developing identity in multicultural environments, developing cultural aesthetics and awareness, and fulfilling affiliation needs, could be incorporated into a more comprehensive understanding of Chickering's seven vectors. One example would be expanding Chickering's conceptualization of developing identity with the notions of invisibility (Erikson, 1968; Knefelkamp & Golec, 1985), multiple identities (Anson, 1987; Cummins, 1986; DuBois, 1953; Wright, 1987), and African-American psychohistory (Essien-Udom, 1971). Other issues, such as developing racial and ethnic identity, interacting with the dominant culture, and developing spiritually, could become additional vectors in Chickering's theory. With such an approach, an empirical base would need to be developed to determine the appropriateness of such a rationally derived theory.

A real danger, however, is involved in taking an existing theory, such as Chickering's theory, which is based upon the values and philosophical assumptions of European Americans and upon research with predominantly Caucasian samples. The problem in revising an existing theory is making the assumption that the theory, such as Chickering's, is indeed appropriate for African-American students, although not sufficient. Straub and Rodgers (1986) and Taub (1989) have already raised questions about the applicability of the order of Chickering's vectors to female students. Taub (1989) also has reported findings that challenge the appropriateness of Chickering's theory for Black female students. Thus, as student affairs professionals attempt to make theories of human and student development more inclusive of other populations, it seems more important to create new theories rather than to modify or revise existing ones.

In conclusion, if colleges and universities are to achieve the lofty ideals that they have set forth in their various mission statements, they must begin to approach the education of African-American students in a more positive manner. This approach must include seeing the strengths that African-American students bring to the campus, understanding the influence of various life situations on the educational/developmental process, and treating the campus environment as the deficit in the deficit-deficiency model.

References

American Council on Education. (1937). *The student personnel point of view*. Washington, DC: Author.

American Council on Education. (1949). *The student personnel point of view* (rev. ed.). Washington, DC: Author.

Anson, R. S. (1987). *Best intentions: The education and killing of Edmund Perry*. New York: Vintage Books.

Baldwin, J. A. (1981) Notes on an Afrocentric theory of personality. *The Western Journal of Black Studies, 5*, 172–179.

Baldwin, J. A. (1984). African self-consciousness and the mental health of African-Americans. *Journal of Black Studies, 15,* 174–194.

Baldwin, J. A., & Bell, Y. (1985). The African self-consciousness scale: An Africentric personality questionnaire. *The Western Journal of Black Studies, 9,* 61–68.

Baldwin, J. A., Duncan, J. A., & Bell, Y. (1987). Assessment of African self-consciousness among Black students from two college environments. *The Journal of Black Psychology, 13,* 27–41.

Boyer, E. L. (1987). *College: The undergraduate experience in America.* New York: Harper & Row.

Bradley, L. R., & Stewart, M. A. (1982). The relationship between self-concept and personality development in Black college students: A developmental approach. *Journal of Non-White Concerns, 10,* 114–125.

Brown-Collins, A. R., & Sussewell, D. R. (1986). The Afro-American woman's emerging selves. *The Journal of Black Psychology, 13,* 1–11.

Bulhan, H. A. (1985). *Frantz Fanon and the psychology of oppression.* New York: Plenum Press.

Carter, R. T., & Helms, J. E. (1988). The relationship between racial identity attitudes and social class. *Journal of Negro Education, 57,* 22–30.

Chickering, A. W. (1969). *Education and identity.* San Francisco: Jossey-Bass.

Coons, F. (1970). The resolution of adolescence in college. *The Personnel and Guidance Journal, 48,* 533–541.

Cross, W. E., Jr. (1971). The Negro-to-Black conversion experience: Toward a psychology of Black liberation. *Black World, 20*(9), 13–27.

Cross, W. E., Jr. (1978). The Thomas and Cross models of psychological Nigrescence: A review. *The Journal of Black Psychology, 5,* 13–31.

Cruse, H. (1967). *The crisis of the Negro intellectual.* New York: Morrow.

Cummins, J. (1986). Empowering minority students: A framework for intervention. *Harvard Educational Review, 56,* 18–36.

DeVos, G. A. (1980). Ethnic adaptation and minority status. *Journal of Cross-Cultural Psychology, 11,* 101–124.

DuBois, W. E. B. (1953). *The souls of Black folks.* Greenwich, CT: Fawcett Publications, Inc.

Erikson, E. H. (1968). *Identity: Youth and crisis.* New York: Norton.

Essien-Udom, E. U. (1971). Black identity in the international context. In N. I. Huggins, M. Kilson, & D. M. Fox (Eds.), *Key issues in the Afro-American experience* (Volume 2, pp. 233–258). New York: Harcourt Brace Jovanovich.

Fanon, F. (1967). *Black skin, White masks.* New York: Grove Press.

Fanon, F. (1972). Racism and culture. In W. King & E. Anthony (Eds.), *Black poets and prophets: The theory, practice, and esthetics of the Pan-Africanist revolution* (pp. 13–25). New York: Mentor Books.

Fleming, J. (1984). *Blacks in college.* San Francisco: Jossey-Bass.

Gibbs, J. T. (1974). Patterns of adaptation among Black students at a predominantly white university: Selected case studies. *American Journal of Orthopsychiatry, 44,* 728–740.

Gilligan, C. (1982). *In a different voice.* Boston: Harvard University Press.

Gurin, P., & Epps, E. (1975). *Black consciousness, identity, and achievement.* New York: Wiley.

Hall, W. S., & Freedle, R. O. (1975). *Culture and language: The Black American experience.* Washington, DC: Hemisphere Publishing.

Heath, D. H. (1968). *Growing up in college: Liberal education and maturity.* San Francisco: Jossey-Bass.

Heath, R. (1964). *The reasonable adventurer.* Pittsburgh: University of Pittsburgh Press.

Helms, J. E. (1984). Toward a theoretical explanation of the effects of race on counseling: A Black and White model. *The Counseling Psychologist, 12*(4), 153–165.

Hughes, M. S. (1987). Black students' participation in higher education. *Journal of College Student Personnel, 28,* 532–545.

Jones, W. T. (1987). Enhancing minority-white peer interactions. In D. J. Wright (Ed.), *Responding to the needs of today's minority students* (pp. 81–94). San Francisco: Jossey-Bass.

Keniston, K. (1971). *Youth and dissent.* New York: Harcourt Brace Jovanovich.

King, S. H. (1973). *Five lives at Harvard: Personality change during college.* Cambridge: Harvard University Press.

Knefelkamp, L. L., & Golec, R. R. (1985). *A workbook for using the P-T-P model.* College Park, MD: University Book Store.

Knefelkamp, L., Widick, C., & Parker, C. A. (Eds.). (1978). *Applying new developmental findings.* San Francisco: Jossey-Bass.

Kovel, J. (1970). *White racism: A psychohistory.* New York: Vintage Books.

National Association of Student Personnel Administrators. (1987). *Perspective on student affairs.* Washington, DC: Author.

Nobles, W. W. (1980). African philosophy: Foundations for Black psychology. In R. L. Jones (Ed.), *Black psychology* (pp. 23–36). New York: Harper & Row.

Ogbu, J. U. (1981). Black education. In H. P. McAdoo (Ed.), *Black families* (pp. 139–153). Beverly Hills: Sage.

Parham, T. A. (1989). Cycles of psychological Nigrescence. *The Counseling Psychologist, 17,* 187–226.

Parham, T. A., & Helms, J. E. (1981). The influence of Black students' racial identity attitudes on preferences for counselor's race. *Journal of Counseling Psychology, 28,* 250–257.

Parham, T. A., & Helms, J. E. (1985a). Attitudes of racial identity and self-esteem of Black students: An exploratory investigation. *Journal of College Student Personnel, 26,* 143–147.

Parham, T. A., & Helms, J. E. (1985b). Relation of racial identity attitudes to self-actualization and affective states of Black students. *Journal of Counseling Psychology, 32,* 431–440.

Pettigrew, T. F. (1964). *A profile of the Negro American.* Princeton: Van Nostrand.

Pounds, A. W. (1987). Black students' needs on predominantly white campuses. In D. J. Wright (Ed.), *Responding to the needs of today's minority students* (pp. 23–38). San Francisco: Jossey-Bass.

Saddlemire, G. L., & Rentz, A. L. (Eds.). (1986). The student personnel point of view. In *Student affairs: A profession's heritage* (rev. ed., pp. 122–140). Alexandria, VA: American College Personnel Association.

Sanford, N. (1962). Developmental status of the entering freshman. In N. Sanford (Ed.), *The American college* (pp. 253–282). New York: Wiley.

Scruggs, O. M. (1971). The economic and racial components of Jim Crow. In N. I. Huggins, M. Kilson, & D. M. Fox (Eds.), *Key issues in the Afro-American experience* (Volume 2, pp. 70–87). New York: Harcourt Brace Jovanovich.

Sedlacek, W. E. (1987). Black students on White campuses: 20 years of research. *Journal of College Student Personnel, 28,* 484–495.

Stikes, C. S. (1984). *Black students in higher education.* Carbondale, IL: Southern Illinois University Press.

Straub, C., & Rodgers, R. F. (1986). An exploration of Chickering's theory and women's development. *Journal of College Student Personnel, 27,* 216–224.

Taub, D. G. (1989). *The patterns of development of autonomy and mature interpersonal relationships in Black and White undergraduate women.* Unpublished master's thesis, University of Maryland, College Park.

Willie, C. V. (1976). *A new look at Black families.* New York: General Hall Inc.

Wright, D. J. (1987). Minority students: Developmental beginnings. In D. J. Wright (Ed.), *Responding to the needs of today's minority students* (pp. 5–22). San Francisco: Jossey-Bass.

Note

Marylu K. McEwen is an assistant professor and coordinator of the College Student Personnel Program and can be contacted at the Department of Counseling and Personnel Services, College of Education, University of Maryland, College Park, MD 20742. Larry D. Roper is vice president and dean of students and can be contacted at St. John Fisher College, 3690 East Avenue, Rochester, NY 14618. Deborah R. Bryant is associate director for the Career Development Center and can be contacted at 3121 Hornbake Library, University of Maryland, College Park, MD 20742. Miriam J. Langa is academic adviser for the Center for Minorities and can be contacted at the College of Behavioral and Social Sciences, LeFrak Hall, University of Maryland, College Park, MD 20742.

How College Makes a Difference:
A Summary

Ernest T. Pascarella and Patrick T. Terenzini

How *does* college affect students? In responding to this question, we are reminded of a wonderful story told about Bernard Berelson (Menges, 1988). Berelson had published (with Gary Steiner) *Human Behavior: An Inventory of Scientific Findings* (1964) in which they synthesized over a thousand "verified generalizations" about human behavior. In reflecting on his work, Berelson is said to have offered three general conclusions (Menges suggests these were Berelson's "meta-findings"). Our conclusions about how college students change are the same as Berelson's about human change: "(1) some do, some don't; (2) the differences aren't very great; and (3) it's more complicated than that" (Menges, 1988, p. 259).

In the preceding ten chapters we have reviewed the evidence on a wide range of specific college outcomes. This chapter is our summary or, if you will, our own "meta-findings." It attempts a comprehensive synthesis of what we know about the impact of college on students; in short, it seeks to provide a general answer to this question: In what areas and through what kinds of conditions, activities, and experiences does college affect students?

In shaping this global synthesis we employ a somewhat different organizational framework than that used in Chapters Three through Twelve. In each of those chapters the evidence pertaining to a specific category of outcome (for example, learning, moral development, psychosocial development) was, where appropriate, summarized across six fundamental questions: (1) Do students change during the college years, and if so, how much and in what directions? (this is the "change" question); (2) To what extent are these changes attributable to college attendance as distinct from other sources, such as normal maturation or noncollege experiences? (the "net effects" question); (3) Are these changes differentially related to the kind of institution attended? (the "between-college effects" question) (4) Are these changes related to differences in students' experiences on any given campus? (the "within-college effects" question); (5) Are these changes differentially related to students' characteristics? (the "conditional effects" question); and (6) Is college's influence durable? (the "long-term effects" question).

In the present chapter, this organizational framework is inverted. Here we synthesize the evidence that addresses each of the six fundamental questions posed by the book across the various outcome categories. This will provide a somewhat different perspective than preceding chapters have given in that the focal emphasis will be on the various impacts of college on a broad spectrum of outcomes rather than on how a specific category of outcome may be influenced by various elements of the college experience.

In addition to the main objective of providing a comprehensive summary of major conclusions, this chapter also does some other things. First, it attempts, where possible, to draw comparisons between our conclusions and the major conclusions of previous comprehensive syntheses of the impact of college on students, primarily the work of Feldman and Newcomb (1969) and Bowen (1977). Second, where possible, it tries to articulate the extent to which the evidence is supportive of the major theses or models of student development and the impact of college. Finally, the chapter suggests important areas for future research and comments on methods of inquiry that may be most useful in increasing our understanding of the impact of college.

Change During College

Consistent with the composite findings of Feldman and Newcomb (1969) and Bowen (1977), our synthesis of the evidence indicates that the college years are a time of student change on a broad front. A number of the shifts we observed appear to be fairly substantial in magnitude. Indeed, the changes that occur during college from freshman to senior year are generally the largest "effects" we noted in our synthesis. It is the breadth of change and development, however, that is perhaps the most striking characteristic of the evidence. Students not only make statistically significant gains in factual knowledge and in a range of general cognitive and intellectual skills; they also change on a broad array of value, attitudinal, psychosocial, and moral dimensions. There is some modest tendency for changes in intellectual skills to be larger in magnitude than changes in other areas, but the evidence is quite consistent in indicating that the changes coincident with the college years extend substantially beyond cognitive growth. Thus, the change that occurs during the college years does not appear to be concentrated in a few isolated areas. Rather, the research portrays the college student as changing in an integrated way, with change in any one area appearing to be part of a mutually reinforcing network or pattern of change in other areas. Such a tendency in the evidence is generally consistent with the theoretical models of Chickering (1969) and Heath (1968), both of whom envision maturation during college as holistic in nature and embracing many facets of individual change.

There are some very clear directions to this overall pattern of change in college. The nature of the changes that occur and our best estimates of their average magnitude are shown in Tables 13.1 through 13.4. We turn now to a brief summary of those changes.

Learning and Cognitive Change

As shown in Table 1, students make gains from freshman to senior year on a variety of different dimensions of learning and cognition. Modest advances are evidenced in general verbal and quantitative skills, and fairly substantial advances are demonstrated in knowledge of the specific subject matter related to one's major field of study. These conclusions, particularly the latter, are not very surprising. Indeed, more surprising would be the discovery that such changes did *not* occur during college. Less intuitively obvious, perhaps, are the gains that students make on a range of general intellectual competencies and skills that may be less directly or explicitly tied to a college's formal academic program. Compared to freshmen, seniors are not only more effective speakers and writers, they are also more intellectually advanced. This intellectual change includes an improved ability to reason abstractly or symbolically and to solve problems or puzzles within a scientific paradigm, an enhanced skill in using reason and evidence to address issues and problems for which there are no verifiably correct answers, an increased intellectual flexibility that permits one to see both the strengths and weaknesses in different sides of a complex issue, and an increased capacity for cognitively organizing and manipulating conceptual complexity.

It is likely that gains in college on such dimensions as abstract reasoning, critical thinking, reflective judgment, and intellectual and conceptual complexity also make the student more func-tionally adaptive. That is, other things being equal, this enhanced repertoire of intellectual resources permits the individual to adapt more rapidly and efficiently to changing cognitive and noncognitive environments. Put another way, the individual be comes a better learner. It is in this area, we believe, that the intellectual development coincident with college has its most important and enduring implications for the student's postcollege life.

Attitudes and Values

Table 2 shows our estimates of the typical freshman-to-senior changes during college in the general area of values and attitudes. A number of these changes are quite consistent with the changes noted in the area of learning and cognitive development. Students not only become more cognitively advanced and resourceful, but they also make gains in their aesthetic, cultural, and intellectual sophistication, gains that are complemented by increased interests and activities in such areas as art, classical music, reading, and creative writing; discussion of philosophical and historical issues; and the humanities and performing arts. Similarly, there are clear gains in the importance students attach to liberal education and exposure to new ideas. In short, the enhancement of cognitive skills during college appears to be concurrent with an increased valuing of and interest in art, culture, and ideas.

If one theme underlying changes in values and attitudes during college is that they tend to be supportive of or at least consistent with observed changes in cognitive growth, a second theme is that the changes also coalesce around a general trend toward liberalization. Considering consistent changes in the areas of sociopolitical, religious, and gender role attitudes and values, it would appear that there are unmistakable and sometimes substantial freshman-to-senior shifts toward openness and a tolerance for diversity, a stronger "other-person orientation," and concern for individual rights and human welfare. These shifts are combined with an increase in liberal political and social values and a decline in both doctrinaire religious beliefs and traditional attitudes about gender roles. The clear movement in this liberalization of attitudes and values is away from a personal perspective characterized by constraint, narrowness, exclusiveness, simplicity, and intolerance and toward a perspective with an emphasis on greater individual freedom, breadth, inclusiveness, complexity, and tolerance.

A third unifying thread that characterizes attitude and values change during college is a shift away from the instrumental or extrinsic values of education and occupation toward a higher valuing of intrinsic rewards. Compared to freshmen, seniors attach greater importance to the value of a liberal education and less importance to the value of a college education as vocational preparation. Consistently, seniors (as compared to freshmen) also place greater value on the intrinsic characteristics of a job (intellectual challenge, autonomy, and so forth) and less value on extrinsic rewards (salary, job security, and the like).

At first glance such changes may seem inconsistent with what was clearly an increasing trend between 1970 and 1985 toward vocationalism or materialism in the reasons underlying an individual's decision to attend college (Astin, Green, & Korn, 1987). The motivation for attending college and the changes that occur during college, however, may be largely independent of each other. Thus, even if succeeding cohorts of recent freshmen have increasingly chosen to attend college for its instrumental or extrinsic returns, it would still appear that the freshman-to-senior changes that occur during college lead to an increased value being placed on the nonvocational aspects of one's educational experience and the intrinsic rewards of one's prospective work.

Psychosocial Changes

The motif noted earlier of the interrelatedness of student change during the college years is apparent in the several areas of student psychosocial change summarized in Table 3. While the changes in these areas are, on the whole, more modest than those relating to learning and cognitive development, they are approximately the same size as the shifts in attitudes and values. Moreover, their general character and direction are clearly consistent with those of the other two areas. Gains in various kinds of substantive knowledge and in cognitive competence may provide both a basis and the intellectual tools for students to examine their own identities, self-concepts, and the nature of their interactions with their external world.

Thus, perhaps as a partial consequence of their cognitive gains, students appear to move toward greater self-understanding, self-definition, and personal commitment, as well as toward more refined ego functioning. Similarly, students' academic and social self-images, as well as their self-esteem, while perhaps somewhat bruised initially, not only recover but become more positive over the college years.

The psychosocial changes experienced during the college years extend beyond the inner world of the self to include the relational aspects of students' lives: the manner in which they engage and respond to other people and to other aspects of their external world. As students become better learners, they also appear to become increasingly independent of parents (but not necessarily of peers), gain in their sense that they are in control of their world and what happens to them, and become somewhat more mature in their interpersonal relations, both in general and in their intimate relations with others, whether of the same or opposite sex. They also show modest gains in their general personal adjustment, sense of psychological well-being, and general personal development and maturity. Moreover, consistent with the observed shifts toward greater openness in attitudes and values, the evidence quite consistently indicates that students gain in their general intellectual disposition or orientation toward their world, their willingness to challenge authority, their tolerance of other people and their views, their openness to new ideas, and their ability to think in nonstereotypic ways about others who are socially, culturally, racially, or ethnically different from them.

Moral Development

As suggested in Table 4, there is clear and consistent evidence that students make statistically significant gains during college in the use of principled reasoning to judge moral issues. This finding holds across different measurement instruments and even different cultures. The absence of descriptive statistics in much of the evidence, however, makes it difficult if not impossible to estimate with confidence the magnitude of the freshman-to-senior change in the same way that we have done for other outcomes. As we have stressed in Chapter Eight on moral development, the magnitude of the freshman-to-senior gain may not be as important as the fact that the major shift during college is from conventional to postconventional or principled judgment. (The former is based strongly on morality as obedience to rules and meeting the expectations of those in authority, while the latter is based strongly on a view of morality as a set of universal principles of social justice existing independently of societal codification.) This shift in and of itself represents a major event in moral development.

The freshman-to-senior changes in moral judgment noted in our synthesis are perhaps another example of how change during college on one dimension is typically consistent with change in other areas. Measures of moral reasoning are themselves positively correlated not only with areas of general cognitive development that increase during college (such as abstract reasoning, critical thinking, and reflective judgment) but also with the general liberalization of personality and value structures coinciding with college attendance (for example, decreases in authoritarianism or dogmatism; increases in autonomy, tolerance, and interpersonal sensitivity; increased concern for the rights and welfare of others). Thus, the enhancement of principled moral judgment during college is embedded within an interconnected and perhaps mutually reinforcing network of cognitive, value, and psychosocial changes that occur at approximately the same time.

Some Final Thoughts on Change During College

Our conclusions about the changes that occur during college differ in only minor ways from those of Feldman and Newcomb (1969) and Bowen (1977). Indeed, taken as a total body of evidence, all three syntheses suggest that a reasonably consistent set of cognitive, attitudinal, value, and psychosocial changes have occurred among college students over the last four or five decades. Students learn to think in more abstract, critical, complex, and reflective ways; there is a general liberalization of values and attitudes combined with an increase in cultural and artistic interests and activities; progress is made toward the development of personal identities and more positive self-concepts; and there is an expansion and extension of interpersonal horizons, intellectual interests, individual autonomy, and general psychological maturity and well-being. Thus, it can be said that the nature and direction of freshman-to-senior changes appear to be reasonably stable and to some extent predictable.

In some instances our estimate of the *magnitude* of freshman-to-senior changes differs from estimates of previous syntheses, particularly Bowen's (1977). Since the differences are quite modest, however, we are inclined to attribute them to chance variations in the bodies of literature reviewed and perhaps even different typologies or operational definitions of outcomes. At any rate, it would seem that the consistency in the nature and direction of changes across syntheses is a much more salient and noteworthy characteristic of the evidence than are small differences in estimates of the magnitude of the changes across the same syntheses.

It may also be the case that the absolute magnitude of freshman-to-senior changes is not as educationally important as either the qualitative nature or the breadth and scope of the changes. One danger in focusing on quantitative estimates of change such as effect size is that one tends to consider change as happening on a continuum where all change is smoothly continuous and equally important. Many developmental theorists would argue that development does not always happen in such even and equivalent fashion (for example, Kitchener & King, 1990; Kohlberg, 1969; Perry, 1970; Rest, 1986b). Moreover, not all changes are equivalent in size or importance. Some shifts are particularly critical to development irrespective of whether or not they are reflected in a large quantitative change on some continuous scale. For example, the qualitative shift during college from a style of reasoning based on beliefs to one relying on evidence in making judgments represents a key prerequisite to rational problem solving. Similarly, the shift from conventional to principled reasoning during college represents a major qualitative advance in moral development. On both of these dimensions of development, the qualitative nature of the change is likely to be of greater consequence than the magnitude of the change.

We would also suggest that the magnitude of change on any particular dimension or set of dimensions during college may not be as significant as the pronounced breadth of interconnected changes we noted in our synthesis. As posited by major models of student development (for example, Chickering, 1969; Heath, 1968), the evidence indicates not only that individuals change on a broad developmental front during college but also that the changes are of a mutually consistent and supporting nature. Although there may be insufficient empirical grounds to speak of changes in one area causing or permitting changes in other areas, it is clear from the body of evidence we reviewed that the changes coincident with college attendance involve the whole person and proceed in a largely integrated manner. Certainly the notion of broad-based integrative change during college is not a new finding, but the evidence we reviewed was sufficiently compelling to warrant its reaffirmation.

There are, of course, at least three nontrivial problems endemic to the study of freshman-to-senior change. The first stems from the fact that the evidence is based largely on studies measuring typical or average change in some sample (longitudinal studies) or typical or average differences between samples (cross-sectional studies). By focusing on average group shifts or differences, the findings of such studies tend to mask individual differences in patterns of change. Some students may change substantially during college, some may change little or not at all, and some may actually shift in a direction counter to the typical movement of the group. Moreover, some students may change in one way on certain variables and in opposite ways on other variables. Thus, although the average change may be our best estimate of the dominant shift or development occurring in a group, it is not without limitations.

A second problem, one that we have emphasized throughout the book, is that freshman-to-senior change during college does not necessarily reflect the impact of college. Many of the dimensions on which change occurs during college may have a developmental base. If so, this means that individuals tend to exhibit more sophisticated levels of development through the process of maturation or simply growing older. Consequently, similar individuals not attending college might well change in essentially the same ways as college students over the same time period. In the absence of a control group of noncollege attenders (a typical weakness in most studies of change during college), it is essentially impossible to separate the changes due to college attendance from those attributable to natural maturation.

The focus on change during college as an indication of college impact can also be misleading in another way. Just as the presence of change does not necessarily indicate the impact of college, so too the absence of change does not necessarily indicate the absence of college impact. One important consequence of college attendance may be to fix development at a certain level and prevent reversion or regression (Feldman & Newcomb, 1969). If such were the case on a specific trait, little or no freshman-to-senior change would be noted. Those not attending college, however, might well regress or change in a negative direction. We will see an example of this as we turn to a summary of the net effects of college.

Finally, it is important to differentiate change from development. Whereas *change* simply means that some fact or condition at Time$_2$ is different from what it was at Time$_1$, *development* implies ordered, predictable, even hierarchical shifts or evolution have taken place in fundamental, intra-individual structures or processes. In many areas of observed change during college, it is tempting simply to conclude that observed change reflects some form of internal growth or development in the individual, that an inner restructuring has taken place, and that the senior is functioning with an advanced set of inner rules or perspectives not present in the typical freshman. This is a particular temptation when the changes that occur are consistent with those posited by developmental models or theories. The danger inherent in this assumption is that what we commonly refer to as development may in large measure be the result of an individual's response to the anticipated norms of new social settings or social roles. Different categories of people may be socialized to think and behave differently in society, and a substantial part of this categorization may have its basis in educational level. Thus, for example, college-educated men and women may have certain psychosocial traits and values and may think about controversial issues in certain ways not necessarily because of some inner developmental restructuring but because they have been socialized to behave and think in ways consistent with dominant cultural norms for educated adults.

This is not to say that the changes that occur during college merely represent the learning of social or cultural norms instead of important developmental steps. Rather, it is to suggest that we need to be wary of the tendency to equate the learning of social or cultural norms with development. It behooves us to bear in mind that change during the college years is produced by multiple influences, some internal (and perhaps ontogenetic) and others external to the individual. Theories can overly restrict as well as focus vision.

Net Effects of College

Because self-selection, as opposed to random assignment, determines who attends and who does not attend college, studies that seek to estimate the unique or net impact of college (as distinct from normal maturation, mere aging, or other noncollege sources of change) employ some rather creative research designs or, more typically, statistical controls. Although the causal inferences one can make from such studies are not of the same order of certitude as those made from randomized experiments, we can nevertheless arrive at a reasonably valid set of tentative conclusions about the changes or outcomes observed that are attributable to college attendance and not to rival explanations. It is worth recalling, however, that change during the college years involves a complex, weblike network. Change in one area may cause or be accompanied by change in other areas as well. Given this interrelatedness, estimates of change and of college's net effect in each discrete area no doubt understate college's overall, cumulative impact.

Tables 5 through 8 array those dimensions on which the weight of evidence offers support for claims about college's unique or net impact. (When we use the term *unclear* in the column reporting the magnitude of net effects in this and all subsequent tables in the chapter, we are acknowledging that the studies do not allow such estimates or that the evidence, though generally consistent, is still sufficiently complex to make an estimate of effect size hazardous.) As Tables 5 through 8 show, we judge the evidence on net impact to be more compelling for some outcomes than for others. Specifically, there is more extensive and consistent evidence to support the net impact of college on learning and cognition, moral reasoning, and career and economic returns than in the areas of attitudes, values, and psychosocial characteristics. This does not necessarily mean that college has a stronger impact on the former outcomes than on the latter ones. Indeed, we had a difficult time estimating the magnitude of the net impact of college in nearly all areas of our synthesis. Some of these differences could be more a reflection of variations in the extent and quality of the available evidence across different areas of inquiry than of major differences in the actual impact of college. More likely, they are real. It would probably be unreasonable to expect uniform changes across substantive areas. Students vary considerably in the characteristics they bring with them to college, not only in a wide variety of personal, educational, and family background traits but also in their readiness and capacity for change. Moreover, higher educational institutions do not invest their energies and resources equally across areas of change.

Learning and Cognitive Changes

Table 5 shows those learning and cognitive development outcomes that the weight of evidence suggests are significantly influenced by college attendance. Perhaps the clearest generalization to be made from this evidence is that on nearly all of the dimensions on which we find freshman-to-senior change, a statistically significant part of that change is attributable to college attendance, not to rival explanations. College not only appears to enhance general verbal and quantitative skills as well as oral and written communication, but it also has a statistically significant positive net effect on general intellectual and analytical skills, critical thinking, the use of reason and evidence in addressing ill-structured problems, and intellectual flexibility. These effects cannot be explained away by maturation or differences between those who attend and those who do not attend college in intelligence, academic ability, or other precollege characteristics.

These conclusions about the net effects of college on learning and cognitive development are limited by those dimensions that individual scholars have chosen to investigate. It is perhaps useful to think of these dimensions of net college effects as analogous to geological probes designed to define the nature and extent of mineral or oil deposits. They sample and begin to define the boundaries, but they may not capture the fullness of the phenomenon being measured. From this perspective, it is reasonable to conclude that college attendance positively influences a wide range of cognitive skills and intellectual functioning. The existing research, however, probably provides only a rough outline of the types of learning and cognitive development enhanced by college without necessarily tapping the full range or richness of effects.

As briefly alluded to in the previous section on change during college, research on college's net effects illustrates the potentially misleading nature of change. The net positive effect of college on general quantitative skills, for example, occurred not because students who attended college made greater gains than those who did not attend. Instead, the effect was largely attributable to the fact that college attendance tended to anchor quantitative skills at precollege levels while those not attending college actually regressed. Thus, an important net effect of college may be to stabilize an individual's development on certain dimensions and to prevent the regressions that might occur in the absence of college attendance.

Attitudes and Values

Evidence concerning the net impact of college on attitudes and values is summarized in Table 6. Although the weight of this evidence is not totally consistent and certainly not without rival explanations, it nevertheless suggests that a statistically significant, if modest, part of the broad-based attitudinal and value changes that occur during college can be attributed to the college experience. Perhaps of equal importance, the net effects of college, particularly in the areas of social, political, and sex role values, appear not to be simple reflections of trends in the larger society across the last two decades. Rather, college attendance seems to have an impact on attitudes and values in these areas, an impact that is generally consistent both within and across age cohorts.

This is not to say that what occurs during college happens in total isolation from cultural and social forces. Clearly, student values are significantly affected by those dominant in society, and general societal changes make unambiguous attributions of change to college more difficult. Nevertheless, college attendance would appear to influence political, social, and gender role attitudes and values in consistent ways regardless of cultural and societal trends.

A note of caution needs to be made with respect to this conclusion, because there is some evidence to suggest that recent college effects on social and political values may be less pronounced than earlier studies have indicated. Whether this is a chance fluctuation or the precursor of an important generational effect, however, awaits replication of the findings on future samples.

Psychosocial Changes

Table 7 summarizes the evidence relating to college's psychosocial net effects. As can be seen there, virtually nothing can be said with confidence about the net effects of college on changes in students' identity statuses or their stages of ego development. The research literature simply does not deal with the effects of college in these areas in any methodologically rigorous or generalizable way. The vast majority of studies are concerned with structural rather than process questions, with whether hypothesized statuses or stages exist and the characteristics of the individuals at any given stage rather than with the variables (including education) that influence status or stage change. Where change is examined, educational and age or maturational effects remain confounded.

Persuasive evidence exists to indicate that college attendance is reliably and positively related to increases in students' academic and social-self concepts, as well as their self-esteem. After holding constant a variety of relevant precollege characteristics, educational attainment is consistently and positively related to increases in students' perceptions of themselves relative to their peers in both academic areas (for example, writing and mathematical abilities, general academic abilities, intellectual self-confidence) and social areas (leadership abilities, popularity in general and with the opposite sex, general social self-confidence, and the like). Net college effects are also apparent in the increases students experience in their self-esteem: the general regard in which they hold themselves and their abilities, the extent to which they consider themselves to be capable, significant, worthy, or of value. After precollege self-concepts or self-esteem and other background characteristics have been controlled, however, college's effects in each of these areas appear to be small. Moreover, college's influence on students' self concepts appears to be *indirect* rather than direct, being mediated through certain characteristics students bring with them to college and through the kinds of academic and interpersonal experiences they have once on campus.

The net effects of college on changes in the ways students relate to people, institutions, and conditions in their external world are somewhat less limited. Consistent with the net gains made in cognitive areas, we can attribute to college (with moderate to considerable confidence) declines in authoritarianism and dogmatism and increases in students' internal sense (locus) of control, intellectual orientation, personal adjustment, and general psychological well-being. College's contributions to the declines in authoritarianism and dogmatism appear to be strong, but its effects in the other areas are much more modest, even small. Because of methodological limitations, however, few claims (if any) can be made with confidence about college's net effects on changes in students' levels of autonomy or independence, the maturity of their interpersonal relations, or their overall maturity and personal development.

Moral Development

Table 8 reveals that college has a net positive effect on the use of principled reasoning in judging moral issues. This effect holds even when controls are made for maturation and for differences between those who attend and those who do not attend college in level of precollege moral reasoning, intelligence, and socioeconomic status. The net impact of college on actual moral behavior is less clear. On the basis of a synthesis of two separate bodies of research, however, we hypothesize a positive indirect effect. College enhances the use of principled moral reasoning, which in turn is positively linked to a variety of principled actions. These include resistance to cheating, social activism, keeping contractual promises, and helping behavior. The acceptance of this hypothesis is tentative, however, and awaits fuller empirical support.

Long-Term Effects of College

Nearly all of the considerable body of research on the long-term effects of college is concerned with estimating the enduring impact of attending versus not attending college. Consequently, it has much in common, both conceptually and methodologically, with research that attempts to estimate the net effects of college. Indeed, one could reasonably regard evidence on the enduring impact of college attendance essentially as an estimate of the net effects of college extended over time. For this reason we depart from the typical pattern of most chapters and summarize the evidence on the long-term effects of college here rather than near the end of this chapter.

Our synthesis of the evidence suggests that college has a rather broad range of enduring or long-term impacts. These include not only the more obvious impacts on occupation and earnings but also influences on cognitive, moral, and psychosocial characteristics, as well as on values and attitudes and various quality of life indexes (for example, family, marriage, consumer behavior). Moreover, it would also appear that the impacts extend beyond the individuals who attend college to the kinds of lives their sons and daughters can expect.

It is clear that part of the long-term impact of college (for example, on job status and income) can be traced directly back to college attendance or degree attainment. Another part of this impact, however, may be an indirect result of the socioeconomic positioning and kinds of life interests, experiences, and opportunities made more likely by being a college graduate. As suggested by Withey (1971) and Bowen (1977), part of the impact of college arises out of the distinctive kinds of lives led by the people who attend and graduate from college. Such indirect routes of influence are a major consideration in understanding the long-term and full impact of college. In short, our conclusion about the nature of the long-term effects of college is generally consistent with that of Feldman and Newcomb (1969). The distinctive effects of college tend to persist in large measure as a result of living in postcollege environments that support those effects.

Socioeconomic Outcomes

The impact of college on socioeconomic outcomes (occupation and earnings) is a function not only of what happens during college but also of how college graduates are themselves regarded by employers. It is difficult to separate these two influences, but it is quite clear that obtaining a bachelor's degree has a strong net influence on one's socioeconomic attainments. We should perhaps avoid the temptation to make too much of these influences. Most prediction models of status attainment explain somewhat less than 50 percent of the individual differences in occupational status or earnings. Nevertheless, as summarized in Table 9, the evidence we reviewed is consistent in indicating that a bachelor's degree remains a major, if not *the* major, prerequisite for entrée into relatively high status and high paying technical, managerial, and professional jobs.

The socioeconomic impact of being a college graduate is not realized exclusively at the early stages in one's career, however. A college degree continues to provide advantages throughout one's working life. These are manifest as enhanced earnings, an increased likelihood of stable employment, and generally higher levels of career mobility and attainment. More over, despite periodic fluctuations, the private economic rate of return on investment in a bachelor's degree compares favorably to benchmark rates for alternative ways of investing one's money. In short, our reading of the body of evidence is quite consistent with that of Bowen (1977): A bachelor's degree continues to be a primary vehicle by means of which one gains an advantaged socioeconomic position in American society.

With respect to the importance of college graduation on other major indexes of socioeconomic attainment, such as occupational status and income, two additional observations are relevant. First, there is replicated evidence to suggest that in terms of the relative incremental advantage it confers, a bachelor's degree is typically the single most important educational rung on the socioeconomic attainment ladder. Second, although there are discernible between- and within-college effects, the occupational and economic impacts of completing one's bachelor's degree are typically more pronounced than the impacts due either to where one completes it or to the nature of one's educational experiences while doing so (for example, major field of study, academic achievement, extracurricular involvement).

The way in which a bachelor's degree positions one occupationally and economically represents an important long-term impact of college in and of itself. But this socioeconomic positioning effect has additional implications for other long-term impacts. One stems from the simple fact that the jobs that college graduates typically hold are characterized by a relatively high level of earnings. This permits the acquisition of a variety of material and nonmaterial resources and opportunities (including books, travel, cultural experiences, household maintenance, medical care, and additional education) that have potential impact on other long-term outcomes. A second implication stems from the fact that college graduates tend to be employed in jobs characterized by relatively high levels of social interaction and self-direction. Such job traits may provide an important continuing influence on trends in cognitive and psychosocial changes partially shaped during the college experience.

Learning and Cognitive Development

As indicated in Table 10, the body of evidence on the long-term impact of college on indexes of learning and cognitive characteristics is not without methodological problems. Nevertheless, there is clear evidence from extensive national samples to indicate that college graduates have a substantially larger general knowledge base across a wide range of topics than do individuals whose education ends with high school. Similarly, in an impressive set of national surveys, alumni were consistent in reporting that college had a major positive influence both on their specific and their general knowledge base and on their ability to think critically, analytically, and clearly.

As suggested by the retrospective perceptions of graduates, part of this enduring impact can probably be traced directly to what transpires in college. A substantial amount of factual learning and general intellectual development obviously occurs during that time. Yet it is likely that what happens during college represents only part of the story. Another part is probably the result of differences in the kinds of posteducation lives that college and high school graduates lead. The former are more likely to engage in intellectually challenging activities (serious reading, attending cultural events, participating in continuing education, and the like), and to be employed in the kinds of intellectually challenging jobs that further enlarge their knowledge base and continue to enhance their intellectual development. Moreover, even if college crystallizes one's interest in lifelong learning, the economic advantages linked to a college degree contribute in part by increasing one's ability to purchase the goods and services required. It is probably this complex interplay of mutually supporting direct and indirect influences (that is, what happens during college, postcollege experiences, and the ability to acquire material and nonmaterial opportunities) that most fully accounts for the long-term impact of college on knowledge acquisition and more general cognitive advances.

Attitudes and Values

The most notable conclusion from the body of research on the long term effects of college on attitudes and values, summarized in Table 11, is that nearly all of the trends that occur during college tend either to persist or to stabilize in the years following college. Certainly there are exceptions to this conclusion. Intervening experiences in such areas as work, marriage and family, military service, and graduate education are potentially profound influences on one's attitudes and values. Nevertheless, for college students as a group, the intellectual, aesthetic, social, political, religious, educational, and occupational attitudes and values one holds as a graduating senior appear to be an important determinant of the attitudes and values one holds throughout the adult years.

Part of this long-term impact may be directly traceable to the college experience. College may, in fact, function to influence a broad range of attitudes and values in directions that may be relatively impervious to subsequent influence and thus tend to persist throughout adult life. It is unlikely, however, that the total enduring impact of college on attitudes or values is confined to the college years. Perhaps more important is the fact that college tends to channel graduates into postcollege lives that often reinforce trends shaped by the college experience. This indirect impact on attitudes and values may manifest itself in a variety of ways. For example, one's attitudes and values may be influenced by the type of job one holds, by the attitudes and values of a spouse, professional acquaintances, and friends with a similar level of education; or by the nature of one's leisure time interests and activities (cultural opportunities, travel, civic involvement, reading, and so on), which is often shaped by interests and available financial resources. In short, the kinds of postcollege lives college graduates lead may transmit an important indirect long-term impact of college on attitudes and values.

The long-term effect of college on attitudes and values may also involve an intergenerational legacy; the attitudes and values that students develop at least partially as a consequence of their college experiences are passed on to their children. For example, a small body of evidence has found a positive link between a mother's education and nontraditional gender role attitudes in children, particularly daughters. This may be a less obvious part of the indirect impact of a mother's education on her daughter's conceptions of herself and on the likelihood of her entering a tradition- ally male-dominated occupation.

Psychosocial Changes

The nature and extent of college's long-term effects on students' psychosocial characteristics are summarized in Table 12. As can be seen there, the research literature is silent on the extent to which college has any identifiable long-term effect on identity status or ego stage development. While there is ample evidence that identity and ego development do not end with the college years, education's role in those changes remains virtually unexamined and thus unknown. Even though the research base is small, however, it is methodologically strong and consistent in indicating that college does have a positive and unique effect on students' academic and social concepts, as well as on their self-esteem. These effects are discernible up to a decade after matriculation, although they appear to be small and largely indirect, mediated through the higher-status jobs college graduates tend to obtain compared to those held by people with less education. Moreover, college's long-term effects on self-concepts appear to be greater among white students than among black students. Nine years after entry, college attendance appears to have no measurable effects—positive or negative, direct or indirect—on the self-concepts of black males.

With a few exceptions, the research base exploring long-term changes in the several facets of students' relational systems is severely constrained either by idiosyncratic samples or by designs that do not control plausible rival hypotheses (sometimes by both). Limited but sound nationally based evidence indicates that educational attainment is positively related to increases in individu- als' internal locus of control seven and nine years after high school graduation, but occupational effects were left uncontrolled, leaving claims of college's long-term effects open to challenge. The evidence in the other areas of relational change is explored by single-institution studies with only marginal generalizability. What evidence exists suggests little postcollege change in level of authoritarianism or in intellectual orientation, slight declines in anxiety and the willingness to express impulses, and gains in personal integration, psychological well-being, and general matu- rity. Thus, although the evidence is limited, there is some basis for believing that education at least has no deleterious effects on overall psychosocial status and probably has some decidedly benefi- cial ones, even though they may be slight and indirect.

Moral Development

As indicated in Table 13, there is strong evidence for an enduring impact of college on the use of principled moral reasoning, at least through the first six years after graduation. Students attending college not only make greater gains in the use of principled reasoning during college than individu- als whose formal education ends with high school, but the gap between the two groups continues to widen in the years subsequent to college. These different patterns of change cannot be accounted for by initial differences in moral development or differential regression effects. Again, we see evidence that part of this long-term impact is directly attributable to trends shaped by the college experience. Another part, however, is indirectly attributable to college through differences between high school and college graduates in posteducational environments, particularly in the area of continuing intellectual stimulation (reading, cultural events, travel, job demands, and so on). There is clear evidence that the level of continuing intellectual stimulation in one's posteducational life has a strong positive impact on further advances in principled moral reasoning.

Quality of Life Indexes

Problems in research design and the inability to control important confounding influences make causal attributions about the long-term impact of college on various quality of life indexes somewhat tenuous. As shown in Table 14, the overall quality of evidence is not particularly strong. Consequently, we consider the findings as more suggestive than conclusive.

Having said this, it nevertheless remains true that college-educated individuals consistently rank higher than those with less education on a clear majority of the quality of life indexes considered. Compared to those with less education, the college educated tend to have better overall health and a lower mortality rate, have smaller families and be more successful in achieving desired family size through informed and effective use of contraceptive devices, and spend a greater portion of time in child care, particularly in activities of a developmentally enriching nature (such as teaching, reading, and talking). They also tend to be more efficient in making consumer choices, save a greater percentage of their income, make more effective long-term investment of discretionary resources, and spend a greater proportion of discretionary resources and leisure time on developmentally enriching activities (reading, participation in arts and cultural events, involvement in civic affairs, and so forth).

It is likely that at least part of the impact of college on these indexes of life quality is indirect, being mediated through the socioeconomic advantages that tend to accrue to the college educated. Having the economic resources to pay for desired goods and services is not without important consequences for the quality of one's life. At the same time, the positive link between educational level and many quality of life indexes remains even after economic resources are held constant. This suggests the possibility at least that college may also have a direct impact on quality of life by enhancing such characteristics as the ability to acquire new information and process it effectively, the ability to evaluate new ideas and technologies, the capacity to plan rationally and with a long-term perspective, the willingness to accept reasonable risk, and the developmental and cultural level of one's leisure interests and tastes. It should be pointed out, however, that with some exceptions, such as health status, the absence of controls for initial traits makes it difficult to separate the direct impact of college from the confounding influence of preexisting differences between those who attend and those who do not attend college.

It is interesting that even though college-educated individuals clearly rank higher on a broad array of quality of life indicators, they do not, on the average, express appreciably greater satisfaction with their lives than do those with less education. We would suggest that this does not signify the absence of impact but rather reflects the fact that the impact of college has dimensions that function both to increase and to diminish expressions of satisfaction with one's life. On the one hand, the clear job status and economic returns to college are likely to have a positive impact on some dimensions of life satisfaction, particularly the intrinsic (for example, autonomy, challenge) and extrinsic (for example, earnings) aspects of one's work. This probably explains a major part of the modest direct impact of college on job satisfaction. On the other hand, one probable impact of college is that it tends to foster a more critical perspective in individuals. Consequently, as compared to those with less education, college-educated men and women may be more sophisticated, skeptical, analytical, and critical in their judgments of some facets of job satisfaction, marital satisfaction, and overall sense of well-being.

Intergenerational Effects

An often overlooked element of the long-term impact of college is the intergenerational transmission of benefits. Indeed, there is evidence to support the expectation that the net benefits of a college education are not restricted to the individual who receives them but are passed along to his or her sons and daughters. Most of the evidence on intergenerational effects concerns the socioeconomic achievements of offspring. These are summarized in Table 15. Having college-educated parents modestly enhances one's educational attainment, job status, early career earnings, and, if one is a woman, the likelihood of entering a male-dominated occupation. The last of these has consequences for gender equality in the work force in that male-dominated occupations are traditionally linked with relatively high status and earnings.

What is perhaps most notable about these intergenerational impacts, however, is that with the possible exception of offsprings' educational attainment, they manifest themselves essentially through indirect routes. Having college-educated parents positively affects the socioeconomic achievement of sons and daughters largely by influencing important intervening variables in the status attainment process. Such variables include family income, career aspirations, the type of college attended, and in some instances educational attainment. Through this complex matrix of indirect influences, a college education is likely to make nontrivial contributions to the socio-economic positioning of one's children.

Although the causal linkage is less clearly established, it is also likely that having college-educated parents may enhance the cognitive development of young children through the indirect route of the home environment. Compared to those with less education, college-educated parents, particularly mothers, spend more time with their children in developmentally enriching activities such as reading and teaching. Differences in such home activities may at least partially account for the positive link found between parental and, in particular, mother's education and the cognitive development of preschool children.

There is also reason to believe that the long-term effects of college via the intergenerational legacy also extend to the attitudes and values parents pass along to their children. Ample evidence indicates that successive generations and cohorts of students are increasingly more liberal in their social, political, religious, and sexual attitudes and values. These generational shifts are, of course, highly correlated with increases in average educational attainment levels over the past half-century. Thus, it would appear that as children are raised by successively better educated generations of parents who have themselves increased to varying degrees in social and political tolerance, humanitarianism, and sense of civic responsibility, the children's attendance at college leads to even greater differences relative to grandparents and great-grandparents. The long-term trend of these inter-generational legacies appears to be not only toward greater socioeconomic security and well-being but also toward greater cognitive growth and openness, tolerance, and concern for human rights and liberties.

Between-College Effects

Our interpretation of the body of evidence across all outcomes is that the net impact of attending (versus not attending) college tends to be substantially more pronounced than any differential impact attributable to attending different kinds of colleges. This conclusion is generally consistent with that of Bowen (1977), and several factors may contribute to such a conclusion.

First, estimates of between-college effects are based on much more selective and homogeneous samples than estimates of the net effect of attending college. The former are based only on college students, while the latter typically also include those who do not attend college. Restriction in the variability of a sample can attenuate the magnitude of associations among variables. This might naturally lead to smaller effects in between-college studies than in studies that assess the net effect of college.

A second possibility, similar to the first, is that the statistical procedures commonly used to analyze net college effects are essentially conservative ones. When institutional differences are under study, researchers typically control students' background characteristics by means of regression, covariance analysis, or partial regression techniques before estimating the amount of residual variance that can be explained by differences in institutional characteristics. With such procedures, however, any variance *jointly* due to the effects of students' backgrounds and institutional characteristics is attributed entirely to student differences. Consequently, institutional effects may be underestimated to some unknown degree. Thus, the failure to find differential institutional effects may to some extent be an artifact of the analytical procedures used.

Third, it is entirely possible (perhaps probable) that more variability exists *within* institutional classifications than across them. Categories that appear to be homogeneous (for instance, private four-year colleges) may very well be far more heterogeneous than they seem (see, for example, Astin & Lee, 1972). Under such conditions, detection of statistically significant differences becomes more unlikely.

Fourth, and perhaps most likely, the weight of evidence may well reflect the fact that the dimensions along which American colleges are typically categorized, ranked, and studied (such as size, type of control, curricular emphasis, and selectivity) are simply not linked with major differences in *net* impacts on students. To be sure, there are clear and unmistakable differences among postsecondary institutions in a wide variety of areas, including size and complexity, control, mission, financial and educational resources, the scholarly productivity of faculty, reputation and prestige, and the characteristics of the students enrolled. At the same time, however, American colleges and universities also resemble one another in a number of important respects. It may be that despite their structural and organizational differences, their similarities in curricular content, structures, and sequencing; instructional practices; overall educational goals; faculty values; out-of-class experiences; and other areas do in fact produce essentially similar effects on students, although the "start" and "end" points may be very different across institutions.

Finally, some of the conventional institutional characteristics may combine to produce measurable differences in institutional environments. There is evidence in several areas that institutional context—a college or university's educational and interpersonal climate (and subclimates)—may more powerfully differentiate among institutions in the extent of their influence on student change than do the typical descriptors. Different conceptualizations of institutional "environments" and analyses of subenvironments may reveal greater between-institution differences than are now apparent in the research literature (see Baird, 1988).

Yet overall, the body of evidence reviewed casts considerable doubt on the premise that the conventional, if substantial, structural, resource, and qualitative differences among schools are translated into correspondingly large differences in average educational effects. In short, similarities in between-college effects would appear to vastly outweigh the differences.

Of course, this is a general conclusion based on the total body of evidence. Although no specific institutional characteristic or set of characteristics appears to have a consistent impact across outcomes, there are, in fact, some modest between-college effects in certain areas. We turn now to a brief summary of these effects, which are shown in Tables 13.16 through 13.23.

Two-Year Versus Four-Year Colleges

It is clear that the two-year community college has played a major positive role in the social mobility of many individuals. This is particularly apparent when the socioeconomic attainments of community college students are compared to those of people whose education ends with high school. Nevertheless, there is reasonably strong evidence in support of Clark's (1960) argument that community colleges can also function to "cool out" students' educational aspirations. As indicated in Table 16, compared to similar students who begin in four-year institutions, community college students are significantly less likely to complete a bachelor's degree. This may be traceable in part to the social-psychological climate of community colleges, but it is probably also partially attributable to the structural obstacles and educational discontinuities involved in transferring to four-year institutions.

Because initial attendance at a two-year college is linked with a lower likelihood of completing a bachelor's degree, such attendance may have an indirect negative impact on occupational status and perhaps earnings. Such occupational and economic disadvantages are not inevitable, however. For those who can complete their bachelor's degree in the same period of time as similar students in four-year colleges, any negative impact of two-year college attendance on occupational status or earnings is quite small and perhaps trivial. Similarly, when individuals of equal educational attainment are compared, there is little to indicate that those starting out at two-year colleges are penalized in terms of job stability, unemployment rate, or job satisfaction.

College Quality

The educational impact of various measures of college quality has clearly dominated the research on between-college effects. Perhaps this is due to the expectation that those highly interrelated resource dimensions along which college quality has traditionally been defined (student body selectivity, prestige, or reputation; financial expenditures per student; library size; and the like) should be significant determinants of impact. Thus, those institutions with the most selective student bodies, the highest prestige, the most money, and the best facilities might reasonably be expected to provide the best education.

In considering the net impact of college quality, it is perhaps useful to divide outcomes into two broad categories that we might term developmentally oriented outcomes (learning, cognitive development, values, psychosocial change, and so on) and socioeconomic-oriented outcomes (career aspirations, educational attainment, occupational status, career mobility, and earnings, for example). What is clear from Table 17 is that college quality dimensions (most typically defined in terms of selectivity and prestige) have less extensive impacts on developmentally oriented outcomes than on socioeconomic-oriented ones.

In the category of developmentally oriented outcomes there is some weak to moderately consistent evidence that college selectivity has a small positive impact on aesthetic, cultural, and intellectual values; political and social liberalism; and secularism. In addition, selectivity may be inversely related to academic self-concept, but the effect is small and indirect, being mediated by grade performance. Beyond these small effects, however, there is little consistent evidence to indicate that college selectivity, prestige, or educational resources have any important net impact on students in such areas as learning, cognitive and intellectual development, other psychosocial changes, the development of principled moral reasoning, or shifts in other attitudes and values. Nearly all of the variance in learning and cognitive outcomes is attributable to individual aptitude differences among students attending different colleges. Only a small and perhaps trivial part is uniquely due to the quality of the college attended.

In various preceding chapters and earlier in this chapter, we described several possible methodological explanations for this rather counterintuitive conclusion. There are also explanations of a more substantive nature. For example, some evidence indicates wide variability in the cognitive effects of different departments within colleges at any particular level of student body selectivity. This suggests the possibility of considerably greater variability in cognitive impacts *within* colleges of similar selectivity than *between* colleges of different selectivity. Thus, differences in students' individual experiences within a particular college may be a more salient influence on learning and cognitive gains than any global or average measure of college quality.

Related to the preceding point, it may simply be that traditional definitions of college quality focus more on resource wealth than on those aspects of student life and experience that have important effects on learning and cognitive outcomes. There is at least some indication that certain aspects of college environments (for example, curricular flexibility, informal interaction with faculty and peers, a general education emphasis in the curriculum) have consistent though small net positive effects on learning and cognition, as well as on psychosocial and attitudinal change. This suggests that to understand between-college impacts on cognitive growth, we need to focus less on a college's resources and more on such factors as curricular experiences and course work patterns, the quality of teaching, the frequency and focus of student-faculty nonclassroom interaction, the nature of peer group and extracurricular activities, and the extent to which institutional structures and policies facilitate student academic and social involvement. It is likely that colleges of equal selectivity, prestige, and financial resources may differ substantially in these more proximal influences on student development.

Finally, factors such as student body selectivity may have a latent impact on cognitive and psychosocial change that is activated only when embedded in a supportive social-psychological context. Feldman and Newcomb (1969), Chickering (1969), and Heath (1968) have suggested that a social-psychological context maximizing impact would be characterized by factors such as small size, a cohesive peer environment, and frequent informal contact with faculty (presumed to be found most often in small, selective liberal arts colleges). To these factors we would add a common or shared intellectual experience in the college's curriculum and a common valuing of the life of the mind.

If college quality does not play a major role in influencing developmentally oriented outcomes, particularly those in cognitive areas, it would nevertheless appear to have a more extensive set of impacts on an individual's career. Part of this impact begins during college. Students who enroll in elite institutions tend to begin college with relatively high educational and occupational status aspirations. The overall net effect of attendance at such institutions is to maintain or modestly accentuate initial aspirations. For example, attending a selective or prestigious college has small positive net impacts on educational aspirations, plans for graduate or professional school, and choice of an academic career, particularly in high-status disciplines, and choice of sex-atypical majors and careers among women Thus, elite colleges not only recruit ambition, but they tend to nurture it, at least to a modest extent.

In addition to influencing aspirations and plans, attendance at an elite institution modestly enhances a range of actual socioeconomic attainments. These include bachelor's degree completion, attending graduate or professional school (particularly a school with high prestige), entering sex-atypical careers if one is a woman, level of managerial attainment, occupational status (at least in professional careers such as law and medicine), and earnings. It is tempting from such evidence to conclude, as did Wolfe (1971), that if one's goal is "success" then it matters much where one goes to college. This needs to tempered, however, by two facts. First, a substantial portion of the evidence is inconsistent. Second, the magnitude of the effect that can actually be attributed to college quality and not other influences is quite small, a good deal smaller than is commonly believed.

For example, in the area of earnings, where the evidence is perhaps the most extensive and the impact the largest, even our most liberal estimate is that less than 2 percent of the differences in earnings is attributable to college quality. This means that in excess of 98 percent of the differences in individual earnings is due to influences other than where one goes to college.

Thus, while a selective or prestigious college can modestly enhance one's chances of success, the preponderance of any socioeconomic advantage popularly attributed to attending the "best" colleges is more likely due to the kinds of students those colleges enroll. From the standpoint of *incremental improvements* in one's chances for success, it probably matters much more on the average that one *completes* a bachelor's degree than where one attends college.

College Type

Estimating the net impact of different college types is complicated by the fact that type itself is often confounded with other institutional characteristics. Indeed, the evidence that major research universities and selective liberal arts colleges have a positive impact on earnings is quite likely confounded by the fact that these institutions also tend to have academically selective student bodies. As shown in Table 18, there is modest evidence to suggest that even when student body selectivity is held constant, private colleges tend to have small positive effects on educational aspirations and educational attainment, and liberal arts colleges tend to enhance the likelihood that women will choose sex-atypical majors and careers. Similarly and not surprisingly, church-related colleges tend to have a negative influence on the development of secular values and attitudes and smaller-than-average effects on certain kinds of psychosocial changes (for example, authoritarianism) during college.

Beyond these few small impacts, however, institutional categorizations such as the Carnegie classification appear to tell us little about differences in between-college impacts. Perhaps even more than indexes of college quality, classifications such as research university, comprehensive private university, and liberal arts college may, as suggested, simply conceal so much between-college variability within each classification that consistent impacts on students cannot be found.

College Size

The impact of institutional size (that is, enrollment) varies with the outcome considered, as shown in Table 19. On the one hand, attending a large institution tends to have small positive direct impacts on both occupational status and income, impacts that remain even when college selectivity is held constant. Conversely, institutional size appears to have small negative impacts on bachelor's degree completion, educational attainment, and the development of social self-image during college. These impacts also hold irrespective of student body selectivity but tend to be manifest through indirect routes. Other factors being equal, attending a large institution tends to inhibit a student's level of social involvement (extracurricular activities, interaction with faculty, and the like) during college, and social involvement is a nontrivial determinant of such outcomes as educational attainment and self-concept.

College Racial and Gender Composition

Although the total body of evidence on standardized test performance (for example, Graduate Record Examination, National Teacher Examinations) is as yet inconclusive, attending a predominantly black (versus a predominantly white) college appears to have a modest positive impact on cognitive development and educational attainment for black students and a small positive effect on occupational status and on both academic and social self-image among black women (see Table 20). It is somewhat difficult to identify the causal mechanism underlying these findings. It has been hypothesized, however, that black colleges provide a social-psychological environment more conducive to black students' social integration and personal development than do predominantly white colleges.

Similarly, as further indicated in Table 20, there is also evidence to suggest that single-sex colleges tend to enhance students' socioeconomic aspirations and career attainments. This is particularly true for women. Net of college selectivity and individual factors, attending a women's college appears to enhance educational aspirations and attainment, choice of sex atypical (male-dominated) careers, and the achievement of prominence in a field. Although there is little support for impacts on occupational status and earnings generally, graduates of women's colleges are strongly overrepresented in the high-status, male-dominated occupations of medicine, scientific research, and engineering.

As with college racial composition, it is difficult to identify the causal mechanism that underlies such results. However, there is at least some support for the hypothesis that the critical factor is the presence in women's colleges of large numbers of female teachers as role models. The presence in large numbers of successful same-sex role models may be especially important to college women in overcoming sex-stereotypic attitudes in career aspirations and attainment.

College Environments

In our discussion of the apparent absence of impact of college quality on learning and cognitive development, we reviewed evidence suggesting that more proximal aspects of the college environment (for example, student-faculty interaction, curricular emphasis) may account for a large part of any between-college effects. As shown in Table 21, there is also reasonably consistent evidence to indicate that college environmental factors may influence both educational attainment and career choice and possibly aesthetic and cultural values and levels of authoritarianism, internal locus of control, and general psychosocial adjustment. The environmental factors that maximize persistence and educational attainment include a peer culture in which students develop close on-campus friendships, participate frequently in college-sponsored activities, and perceive their college to be highly concerned about the individual student, as well as a college emphasis on supportive services (including advising, orientation, and individualized general education courses that develop academic survival skills). It is possible, of course, that these environmental characteristics may be at least partially determined by other institutional traits, such as enrollment or the academic preparation of the student body. Nevertheless, it is worth noting that some of these environmental influences on educational attainment persist even after college size and student body selectivity are taken into account.

The most consistent college environmental impact on career choice is that of "progressive conformity." Progressive conformity holds that career choice will be influenced in the direction of the dominant peer groups in a college. The weight of evidence we reviewed tends to support this hypothesis. Irrespective of initial career choice, there is a small but persistent tendency for seniors to plan and subsequently enter careers consistent with the most typical academic majors at their institution.

Environmental effects are also evident in certain areas of psychosocial change. For example, decreases in authoritarianism and increases in general psychosocial adjustment and maturity appear to be greater on campuses where there is an emphasis on intrinsic motivations, student involvement in classroom discussions and course decision making, and general involvement with faculty in an academic community.

Geographical and Social Proximity

Between-college effects on socioeconomic outcomes may depend as much, if not more, on how individual institutions are regarded by employers as on any distinctive cognitive and noncognitive skills they impart to students. This may in part explain the modest occupational and economic advantages enjoyed by graduates of elite schools. In addition to the status allocating power of public reputation, another way in which a college may confer an occupational advantage on a graduate is through its geographical and social proximity to a prospective employer. (See Table 22.) A college that is geographically close to a company, that has frequent professional and consultative interactions with the company, and whose graduates are represented in the company's management tends to confer on its graduates employed by that company an advantage in initial job level and promotion rate. This advantage, moreover, appears to function independently of the selectivity of the college.

Thus, the occupational impact of where one attends college may not be independent of one's employment context. Indeed, the career mobility of graduates of certain colleges may be at least partially influenced by the dominant managerial culture of an employing organization.

Transfer Between Four-Year Institutions

Educational attainment is not only influenced by the type of institution in which one enrolls; it is also affected by the continuity of one's experience in that institution. An interruption in this continuity in the form of transfer from one four-year institution to another tends to inhibit degree attainment (see Table 23). This holds irrespective of race and gender but is particularly pronounced for black men. Not surprisingly, the inhibiting influence of transfer on degree attainment leads to a consistent set of negative indirect effects on occupational status and a less consistent set of negative impacts on earnings. Thus, institutional continuity in one's post-secondary educational experience not only enhances degree attainment but also has additional positive implications for early occupational and economic attainments. This suggests the potential importance of one's fit with the initial college of enrollment.

Within-College Effects

As evidenced in Chapters Three through Twelve, an extensive variety of within-college effects on students have been examined. Although a substantial number of individual studies have proceeded from a theoretical base, the evidence as a whole is not founded on a common set of conceptual or theoretical themes. Consequently, we organize the synthesis of this large body of research around our own understanding of the common threads running through the evidence. First, we offer several conclusions about the evidence as a whole. Second, we offer our conclusions about the major determinants of within-college effects, as organized under the categories of residence, major field of study, the academic experience, interpersonal involvement, extracurricular involvement, and academic achievement.

General Conclusions

The types of within-college experiences that maximize impact are not independent of the kind of college attended. Certain experiences that maximize change are more likely at some institutions than at others. For example, a social context that enhances frequent student-faculty informal interaction is more likely at small, primarily residential colleges than at large universities with a mix of residential and commuter students. Nevertheless, nearly all of the important within-college impacts persist irrespective of the institutional context in which they occur.

Similarly, many of the experiences that maximize impact are not independent of the kinds of students who engage in them. For example, students who are most likely to develop close informal relationships with faculty members are also likely to aspire to graduate or professional school when they enter college. The net impact of their informal interaction with faculty would be to even further strengthen their plans. Thus, consistent with Feldman and Newcomb's (1969) conclusion, we found many within college effects to be essentially the accentuation of initial student characteristics. Certain experiences tend to attract students with certain traits or dispositions and, in turn, tend to accentuate the traits or dispositions that drew those students to the experiences in the first place.

A third generalization is that within-college effects, like between-college effects, tend to be substantially smaller in magnitude than the overall net effect of college attendance. As with the research on between-college effects, there are several possible methodological reasons for this. Substantive explanations, however, are perhaps more valid. Most theoretical models of development in no way guarantee that any single experience will be an important determinant of change for all students. A majority of important changes that occur during college are probably the cumulative result of a set of interrelated experiences sustained over an extended period of time. Consequently, research that focuses on the impact of a single or isolated experience, a characteristic of most investigations of within-college influences, is unlikely to yield strong effects.

A final generalization concerns empirical support for theoretical models of college impact. In Chapter Two we briefly summarized the major elements of several such theories. On the basis of the extensive body of evidence reviewed, much of which would confirm expectations based on those theories, one of the most inescapable and unequivocal conclusions we can make is that the impact of college is largely determined by the individual's quality of effort and level of involvement in both academic and nonacademic activities. This is not particularly surprising; indeed, the positive effects of both the quality and extent of involvement have been repeatedly stressed by Astin (1984) and Pace (1984, 1987).

Such a conclusion suggests that the impact of college is not simply the result of what a college does for or to a student. Rather, the impact is a result of the extent to which an individual student exploits the people, programs, facilities, opportunities, and experiences that the college makes available. Students are not simply the recipients of institutional effects. They themselves bear a major responsibility for the impact of their own college experience. From this perspective it is the individual student who perhaps most determines the extent to which college makes a difference.

Although this conclusion stresses the salience of individual student involvement, it in no way means that individual campus policies and programs are unimportant. Indeed, we would strongly argue the contrary. If individual effort or involvement is the critical determinant of college impact, then a key question focuses on the ways in which a campus can shape its intellectual and interpersonal environments to invite increased student involvement. In the next sections we summarize salient within-college influences, some of which may provide colleges with programmatic or policy levers by which student involvement can be maximized.

Residence

Living on campus (versus commuting to college) is perhaps the single most consistent within-college determinant of impact (see Table 24). This is not particularly surprising because residential living creates a social-psychological context for students that is markedly different from that experienced by those who live at home or elsewhere off campus and commute to college. Simply put, living on campus maximizes opportunities for social, cultural, and extracurricular involvement; and it is this involvement that largely accounts for residential living's impact on student change. To be sure, those who live on campus may, as a group, be psychologically more open to many of the impacts of college to begin with than are their commuting counterparts. Even with this initial difference held constant, however, residential living is positively, if modestly, linked to increases in aesthetic, cultural, and intellectual values; a liberalizing of social, political, and religious values and attitudes; increases in self-concept, intellectual orientation, autonomy, and independence; gains in tolerance, empathy, and ability to relate to others; persistence in college; and bachelor's degree attainment.

Since the facilitation of campus social involvement or participation is the probable causal mechanism underlying the impact of living on campus, it is not surprising that the majority of the demonstrated effects of living on campus are in the areas of student values, attitudes, and psychosocial development. There is little compelling evidence to suggest that the knowledge acquisition or general cognitive effects of college are significantly related to living on campus compared with commuting to college. Indeed, there is at least a modicum of evidence to suggest that a high level of involvement in dormitory life and activities can actually function to isolate an individual from the intellectual life of a college and inhibit some aspects of cognitive growth.

It is likely that the impact of living on campus is not monolithic. Considerable evidence suggests discernible differences in the social and intellectual climate of different residences on the same campus. With a few exceptions (such as college grades), unfortunately, there is little consistent evidence linking differences in the climate of residences to various college outcomes. Not surprisingly, what evidence we do have suggests that those residence climates with the strongest impacts on cognitive development and persistence are typically the result of purposeful programmatic efforts to integrate the student's intellectual and social life during college. Moreover, as will be discussed in greater detail below, residential effects may well be indirect ones, mediated through the interpersonal experiences students have with peers and faculty members that are shaped by the residential setting.

It is important to be aware of two limitations if one is to place the impact of living on campus in its proper perspective. First, it is quite clear that over half of all students in American postsecondary education commute to college and if current trends continue that proportion is likely to increase. Similarly, fully a third of the nation's colleges and universities have no residential facilities, and given financial and student demographic exigencies, they are unlikely to ever have them. For this major group of students and institutions the potential educational benefits of living on campus are largely moot. Developing programs and policies that approximate the student involvement facilitated by residential living is a major challenge for those who educate commuter students or who administer commuter campuses.

A second limitation involves the somewhat narrow view many scholars have taken in assessing the impact of place of residence during college. The focus has been largely on outcomes traditionally valued by the academic community (intellectual values, tolerance, liberalization of social attitudes, and the like). Less sensitivity has been shown to the types of learning and maturing that may occur when the individual must successfully attend to work and family as well as to educational responsibilities. A far larger percentage of commuter students than of resident students are confronted with these additional responsibilities. As a result, the challenges that they face but that their resident counterparts are less likely to confront may lead to comparatively greater growth in areas not now explored by studies of traditional residential students.

Major Field of Study

One's major field of study creates a potentially important subenvironment during college. It not only focuses one's intellectual efforts in a particular direction, but it also has an influence on the kinds of students and faculty with whom one interacts. Consequently, it might be expected that in addition to what one learns, academic major would also have a significant impact on such outcomes as values, attitudes, and psychosocial change. The total body of evidence, however, suggests that the impacts of academic major are markedly stronger and more consistent in cognitive areas than in noncognitive ones.

As might be expected, and as indicated in Table 25, the cognitive impact of major field of study is selective. Students tend to demonstrate the highest levels of learning on subject matter tests most congruent with their academic major. Similarly, they tend to demonstrate the greatest proficiency on measures of general cognitive development when the content of problems is most consistent with their academic major or the disciplinary emphasis of their course work. Thus, for example, social science majors outperform others on tests of social science content and on measures of abstract reasoning and critical thinking applied to social science tasks and problems. The same tendencies hold for science and humanities majors. Beyond these selective impacts, however, we found little consistent evidence that one's major has more than a trivial net impact on one's general level of intellectual or cognitive outcomes.

In contrast, the impact of major field of study on noncognitive outcomes is substantially less apparent or consistent. The effects of major field on changes in students' identity status or ego development stage remain unexamined. Students majoring in the natural or physical sciences, mathematics, or technical fields appear to enjoy slightly greater gains in developing a positive academic self-concept, but major field is unrelated to changes in social self-concept. Similarly, the weight of evidence consistently indicates that few if any differential changes in any of the facets of students' relational systems or in attitudinal and value areas are attributable to academic major. As with the research on the effects of residence in these areas, however, there is some evidence to suggest that departmental environment, whatever the department, may be more important than the characteristics of the discipline in shaping psychosocial and attitudinal changes among students. The interpersonal climate and value homogeneity and consensus within a department appear to be particularly important. The salience of interpersonal relations is discussed at greater length below.

Major field of study does have a number of statistically significant links to the occupational structure in American society. Consequently, what one majors in during college has potentially important implications for the occupation one enters and the economic rewards one receives from his or her work. For example, majors in such areas as business, engineering, some preprofessional programs, and some natural sciences increase the likelihood that one will enter a job with skill requirements consistent with one's academic training, that women will enter relatively high status, male-dominated occupations, and that one will enjoy advantages in early career earnings. These major field impacts tend to persist above and beyond differences in student background traits linked to different majors, as well as level of academic achievement during college.

The occupational impacts of one's academic major, however, appear to be strongest in the earliest stages of one's career. As an individual's career matures, the impact of undergraduate field of study decreases in importance. For example, the specific skills learned in one's major are most important for productivity in the first job after graduation. Thereafter, they diminish in importance and are replaced in importance by general intellectual skills and the ability to learn on the job. Similarly, over the long term, career mobility and occupational attainment levels of liberal arts majors in the private business sector appear to equal (though not excel) those of business or engineering majors. While the existing evidence on earnings is less extensive, it suggests the same trend.

The Academic Experience

Although the body of research on the impacts of the college academic experience is extensive, it clearly does not match the large volume of research conducted with elementary and secondary school students. Nevertheless, we believe that the former permits four general conclusions (see Table 26).

Perhaps the strongest conclusion that can be made is the least surprising. Simply put, the greater the student's involvement or engagement in academic work or in the academic experience of college, the greater his or her level of knowledge acquisition and general cognitive development. Though less extensive, evidence also suggests that academic involvement enhances declines in authoritarianism and dogmatism and increases in autonomy and independence, intellectual orientation, and the use of principled moral reasoning.

If level of involvement were totally determined by individual student motivation, interest, and ability, the above conclusion would be uninteresting as well as unsurprising. However, a substantial amount of evidence indicates that there are instructional and programmatic interventions that not only increase a student's active engagement in learning and academic work but also enhance knowledge acquisition and some dimensions of both cognitive and psychosocial change. Instructional strategies such as note taking, peer teaching, and various individualized learning approaches (for example, personalized system of instruction, audio-tutorial instruction, computer-based instruction) are based to a large extent on increasing students' active engagement in learning. Each has been shown to enhance knowledge acquisition under experimental conditions. The evidence on interventions that influence cognitive development is less extensive. Nevertheless, the learning-cycle or inquiry approach, which stresses inductive learning based on concrete activities, shows evidence of enhancing the development of abstract reasoning and perhaps cognitive complexity. Similarly, there is at least modest evidence to suggest that critical thinking and the use of principled moral reasoning may be enhanced by instruction that stresses active student discussion at a relatively high cognitive level and instruction that engages students in problem solving.

A second general conclusion is that change in a wide variety of areas is stimulated by academic experiences that purposefully provide for challenge and/or integration. For example, cognitive-developmental instruction, which presents the student with cognitive conflict and forces the altering of previously held values and constructs for reasoning, shows evidence of uniquely stimulating growth in postformal reasoning abilities. Similarly, a curricular experience in which students are required to integrate learning from separate courses around a central theme appears to elicit greater growth in critical thinking than does the same curricular experience without the integrative requirement.

A third conclusion is that student learning is unambiguously linked to effective teaching, and we know much about what effective teachers do and how they behave in the classroom. Although a number of teacher behaviors are positively associated with student learning (rapport with students, interpersonal accessibility to students, feedback to students, and the like), two stand out as being particularly salient. These are instructor skill (particularly clarity of presentation) and structuring of the course (for example, class time is structured and organized efficiently). What is perhaps most important is that many of the elements of both dimensions of effective teaching can themselves be learned.

Finally, there is evidence in support of differential course work impacts. This conclusion is perhaps the most tentative in that the research is in its initial stages and the mapping of consistent and replicable patterns of results is still somewhat unclear. Nevertheless, it is quite possible that, irrespective of academic ability, the pattern and sequence of courses taken as an undergraduate may influence not only the subject matter content of what is learned but also more general cognitive abilities. To the extent that replicable findings are derived from this inquiry, it may be possible to plan one's academic program in ways that are most likely to maximize cognitive impact. While the effects of different course work patterns and sequences on psychosocial changes have not been examined, a number of studies indicate that course work in certain areas (the social sciences, for instance) may have a positive influence on increases in political liberalism and in other social attitudes and values (such as sex roles). And a substantial body of research points to course-related or special-program-related effects on a number of psychosocial characteristics. Studies in this research area are highly heterogeneous in focus and methodological rigor, however, making summary conclusions difficult.

Interpersonal Involvement

A large part of the impact of college is determined by the extent and content of one's interactions with major agents of socialization on campus, namely, faculty members and student peers. The influence of interpersonal interaction with these groups is manifest in intellectual outcomes as well as in changes in attitudes, values, aspirations, and a number of psychosocial characteristics (see Table 27).

The educational impact of a college's faculty is enhanced when their contacts with students extend beyond the formal classroom to informal nonclassroom settings. Net of student background characteristics, extent of informal contact with faculty is positively linked with a wide range of outcomes. These include perceptions of intellectual growth during college, increases in intellectual orientation, liberalization of social and political values, growth in autonomy and independence, increases in interpersonal skills, gains in general maturity and personal development, educational aspirations and attainment, orientation toward scholarly careers, and women's interest in and choice of sex-atypical (male-dominated) careers.

With some exceptions, much of the research on which these conclusions are based uses rather distal and often surface measures of student faculty interaction. Nevertheless, we do know that the impact of student faculty informal contact is determined by its content as well as by its frequency. The most influential interactions appear to be those that focus on ideas or intellectual matters, thereby extending and reinforcing the intellectual goals of the academic program.

Just as the impact of student-faculty informal contact is not independent of its content or focus, so too it is not independent of the characteristics of the individuals involved. The students most likely to engage in non-classroom interaction with faculty appear to be those most open to the influence of faculty to begin with. Thus, their ensuing interactions with faculty would tend to accentuate existing interests, aspirations, and values. Similarly, certain types of faculty may be more accessible or influential than others. There is clear evidence, for example, that faculty members who frequently meet with students outside of class give cues about their accessibility through their classroom behaviors. Somewhat less consistent evidence suggests that female faculty may be more influential than male faculty as role models for female students.

Consistent with evidence on the impact of student-faculty interaction, students' interactions with their peers also have a strong influence on many aspects of change during college. Included are such areas as intellectual development and orientation; political, social, and religious values, academic and social self-concept; intellectual orientation; interpersonal skills; moral development; general maturity and personal development; and educational aspirations and educational attainment. As one might expect, the degree of peer influence varies across outcomes, with some evidence suggesting that fellow students exert greater influence on change in attitudinal and psychosocial areas than in learning or cognitive ones, where the weight of faculty influence appears greater.

The direction of this impact appears to depend largely on the characteristics of the peers with whom students interact. For example, shifts in students' identities appear to follow from exposure to a wide diversity of other students who presumably challenge currently held beliefs and self-conceptions and who force introspection and reflection, leading perhaps to alterations in identity status or ego development state. In contrast, principled moral reasoning and more general cognitive complexity are enhanced through interactions with peers who are themselves functioning at more sophisticated levels of moral reasoning and intellectual complexity. Similarly, declines in authoritarianism and dogmatism are greatest among students on campuses with large numbers of nonconforming students. Findings consistent with these are reported in other psychosocial areas. The homogeneity of the peer group may not invariably be an asset, however. Like-mindedness is a distinguishing characteristic of peer groups, and a small body of evidence (dealing primarily with residence groups) suggests that the peer group can insulate against change in certain areas even as it stimulates change in others.

Details about the causal mechanisms behind the influence of these interpersonal interactions remain unclear, however. For example, little can be said with confidence about whether interpersonal effects are more closely related to the frequency of students' contact with peers and faculty members or to the nature of the contact. The influence may also originate in the more generalized context and climate created by the presence of individuals who possess knowledge, skills, psychosocial characteristics, and attitudes and values that differ to varying degrees from those of the student and toward or away from which the student may shift. Moreover, the causal direction of the influence remains uncertain. We do not yet know, for example, whether the manifest associations between student-faculty contact and various kinds of change are a function of faculty influence on students or of certain student characteristics (for example, eagerness to learn) that predispose them to seek out certain kinds of faculty members who rather than initiating change accentuate or reinforce changes already under way. In all likelihood, the causal flow is reciprocal, but at present that proposition remains more a belief than an empirically substantiated fact.

Extracurricular Involvement

From one perspective extracurricular involvement may be seen as a more formalized manifestation of one's interpersonal involvement during college. Thus, part of its impact may stem from an individual's participation in an influential peer culture. This may explain why extracurricular involvement has a positive impact on educational attainment (see Table 28). As a group, students who frequently participate in extracurricular activities tend to enter college with relatively high educational aspirations. Consequently, they may constitute a peer culture within the institution, a culture whose group norms tend to accentuate the educational aspirations of participating members.

Interestingly, we found little additional consistent evidence to suggest that extracurricular involvement per se has a broad-based impact on student development or change. To a great extent, however, this probably reflects the fact that the vast majority of studies make no clear distinction between peer involvement and extracurricular involvement. Indeed, the terms are often conceptually interchangeable in the body of evidence. Even though it may not be captured in the designs of the studies reviewed, it is quite likely that a major portion of the influential interactions that students have with peers takes place in the multifaceted extracurriculum.

From another perspective, extracurricular involvement, particularly in leadership positions, has at least modest implications for one's career. This may stem from the fact that such involvements enhance self-confidence along with interpersonal and leadership skills. Thus, net of background characteristics, holding extracurricular leadership positions during college increases the likelihood that women will enter male-dominated occupations. Similarly, alumni are reasonably consistent in reporting that involvement in extracurricular activities, particularly in leadership roles, significantly enhanced interpersonal and leadership skills important to job success. We found no consistent evidence, however, that extracurricular accomplishment has an independent influence on job status, career mobility, or earnings.

Academic Achievement

Although grades are limited as a reliable and valid measure of what is learned during college, they nevertheless reflect a number of personal traits that have implications for job productivity and success. These include requisite intellectual skills, personal motivation and effort, and the willingness and ability to meet organizational norms. The independent impact of undergraduate grades on various indexes of occupational success is small, but it is persistent. Net of individual background characteristics, as well as college selectivity and major field of study, undergraduate grades have a positive influence on the status or prestige of the job entered, career mobility, and earnings (see Table 29) Part of this effect is direct, but part is also indirect, being transmitted through the strong impact of grades on educational attainment. Thus, good undergraduate grades do give an individual a modest career advantage, at least in the early stages.

In some areas, such as entrance into the relatively high status professions of medicine and law, good grades appear to count more if they are earned at a selective undergraduate college. In terms of income, however, grades appear to count the same irrespective of college selectivity or even major field of study.

Selective or General Involvement?

It seems clear that involvement tends to be selective in its influence on change during college. By this we mean that there is some tendency for college impact to be commensurate with involvement in activities that are consistent with and support specific outcomes. Thus, intellectual development is most clearly influenced by classroom involvement or the quality of effort put forth in one's academic work. Conversely, changes in attitudes, values, and psychosocial dimensions may, on the whole, be more a function of one's interpersonal involvement.

Despite this clear tendency, there is also evidence to suggest a certain wholeness to the college experience, particularly in its impacts on intellectual development. Intellectual growth may be primarily a function of one's academic involvement and effort, but the content and focus of one's interpersonal and extracurricular involvements can have a moderating influence on that growth. Indeed, in some areas of intellectual development, such as critical thinking, there is evidence to suggest that it is the student's breadth of involvement in the intellectual and social experience of college, not any particular type of involvement, that counts most. Thus, although the weight of evidence indicates that the links between involvement and change tend to be specific, the greatest impact may stem from the student's total level of campus engagement, particularly when academic, interpersonal, and extracurricular involvements are mutually supporting and relevant to a particular educational outcome.

Conditional Effects of College

Despite many undoubtedly sincere statements in the postsecondary education literature about the need to respect individual student differences, relatively little attention has been paid to the assessment of conditional effects—changes that are differentially related to the interaction of students' characteristics and either the duration or nature of the collegiate experience. To be sure, there are isolated exceptions to this conclusion, for example, in research on instructional methods. By and large, however, the research has been more interested in assessing the average impact of various college experiences on all students than in determining whether different college environments or experiences have different effects on different kinds of students.

The presence of conditional effects is most pronounced in two areas of research on college impact: learning and cognitive development and the socioeconomic outcomes of college. (See Table 30.) In the area of learning and cognitive development there is reasonably strong evidence that certain kinds of students benefit more from one instructional approach than another. For example, instructional approach may interact with student personality traits. Students high in need for independent achievement or internal locus of control appear to learn more when instruction stresses independence, self-direction. and participation. Conversely, students high in the need for conforming or dependent achievement to external locus of control appear to benefit more from more highly structured, teacher directed instructional formats.

It seems reasonable that other types of instruction may also interact with individual student personality traits. Here the emerging work of Perry and colleagues with remedial instructional interventions, such as attributional retraining, shows considerable promise (Perry & Dickens, 1984; Perry & Magnusson, 1987; Perry & Penner, 1984; Perry & Tunna, 1988).

There is additional evidence to suggest that instruction interacts not only with personality but also with the student's level of cognitive development. For example, instruction stressing inductive learning based on concrete activities (learning-cycle or inquiry approach) appears to have its most pronounced benefits on the development of abstract reasoning for students functioning at initially lower (concrete) levels of reasoning.

What may be most important is not the findings we have to date but rather what they suggest. We should fully expect that individual student differences will moderate the effects of college instruction. Not all students will benefit equally from the same classroom settings and instructional approaches. A more comprehensive mapping of these interactions between student traits and the instructional process may allow for a more precise and effective application of different instructional approaches.

In terms of socioeconomic outcomes, perhaps the clearest set of conditional effects concerns race. Unfortunately, the analyses are largely limited to male samples, but it would appear that in terms of occupational status, nonwhite or black men derive somewhat greater relative benefits from a bachelor's degree than do white men. The evidence on earnings is less consistent but suggests that since about 1970 nonwhite or black men may also be receiving somewhat greater relative benefits from a bachelor's degree than are their white counterparts.

Gender effects are less clear and for private economic rate of return may depend on race. Of all groups, nonwhite women appear to receive the greatest economic return on investment from a bachelor's degree. In terms of incremental effects on earnings, a bachelor's degree is probably more valuable to a woman than to a man. What men and women major in during college can also have a differential impact on early occupational status. For example, women are less likely than men to major in the natural sciences or technical fields (for example, engineering), but they receive incrementally greater occupational status benefits from doing so than do their male counterparts.

What is perhaps most seductive about the conditional effects of college based on race and gender is that college appears to function in a compensatory manner. That is, it confers incrementally different socioeconomic benefits in a manner that should produce greater racial and gender equality. What should be kept in mind, however, is that the groups who would benefit most from obtaining a bachelor's degree (racial and ethnic minorities) or from majoring in scientific or technical fields (women) are at a distinct disadvantage when it comes to doing either. Thus, while the benefits may be greater, the chances of obtaining them are smaller.

A note of caution is in order here. As indicated by the above conclusions, our reading of the evidence suggests that replicable conditional effects involving gender and race are largely limited to socioeconomic outcomes. This in no way precludes the possibility, even the likelihood, that there may be significant gender or racial differences in the processes of intellectual and personal maturation. Our synthesis, however, was concerned with a different question: specifically, whether or not the magnitude of the impact of college on intellectual and personal maturation varies for gender or racial groups. We found little in the way of replicable evidence to indicate that this is the case.

A final set of conditional effects concerns the influence of college selectivity on various indexes of career attainment. Although the general effect of college selectivity on occupational status is quite small and perhaps trivial, there is reasonably consistent evidence that selectivity matters for occupational status in professional careers but may be of questionable value for business or managerial careers. Consistent with this evidence is the finding that good undergraduate grades have a more positive impact on entry into professional careers (for example, medicine and law) if they were earned at selective rather than at less selective institutions. Thus, part of the explanation for why college selectivity has trivial or at best small effects on overall occupational prestige and career mobility is that its impact is of greater consequence in some career paths than in others.

A similar conditional effect is that the positive net impact of college selectivity on earnings is stronger for men from relatively high family socioeconomic backgrounds (managerial, professional) than for men from lower socioeconomic origins (blue-collar). Such a finding suggests that attendance at a selective college may be part of the process of cumulative advantage in American society. Students from advantaged social backgrounds are not only more likely to attend elite undergraduate colleges than their counterparts from less advantaged social origins; they may also be more likely to convert the status conferred by such an institution into greater economic success.

Some Final Thoughts

When asked why he robbed banks, Willie Sutton, the notorious bank robber, is reputed to have replied: "Because that's where the money is." In developing this synthesis we have gone "where the evidence is," and that evidence is not without some bias. It is based almost exclusively on samples of traditional college students who are age eighteen to twenty-two, who attend four-year institutions full-time, and who live on campus. It has also tended to focus on nonminority students, although there have been some recent major exceptions to this. The research methodologies have almost exclusively been quantitative and positivistic in their orientation.

If there is a major future direction for research on the impact of college, it will be to focus on that growing proportion of students whom we have typically classified as nontraditional, although they are rapidly becoming the majority participants in the American postsecondary system. These include minority and older students, those who commute to college and quite likely work part- or full-time, and those who attend college part-time. Some of our most cherished notions about the determinants of impact may have little relevance to these students. Indeed, we may need to revise our traditional ideas about what the impact of college really means for nontraditional students. Specifying the effects of college for the vast numbers of nontraditional students who now populate American postsecondary education may be the single most important area of research on college impacts in the next decade. In mounting such a research effort, it may be necessary to be particularly sensitive to the impressive diversity of students classified as nontraditional. For example, in a national study of older students, Lenning and Hanson (1977) found that the category "older student" masks great variability in many individual traits and motivations that might well determine in what ways and to what extent postsecondary education will exert an influence on these students. Failure to take such diversity into account when studying the impact of college on nontraditional students could easily produce trivial or inconsistent general effects that mask important conditional effects.

The positivistic, quantitative paradigm has served us well. The vast preponderance of what we know about the impact of college has been learned from this approach to inquiry. Yet although the broad framework is in place, there is still much important fine-grained work to be done. We suspect that the most informative future research on the impact of college must take a number of directions.

First, greater attention needs to be given to the *rigorous* examination of net college effects. The drop in the volume of relevant research when one moves from studies of change *during* college to studies of change *due to* college is striking and a source of some concern. Current claims about the benefits of college attendance frequently extend well beyond the empirical evidence to support them. Controlling the numerous alternative, noncollege sources of influence can be a daunting undertaking. It will require greater use of noncollege control groups, more specific theories, and more extensive use of relevant theories in the design of studies. Such careful theoretical preparation and grounding is not one of the distinctive characteristics of most of the research done over the past two decades, but higher education as a field of inquiry has clearly started down that road, and we wish to encourage its continuation. Theory-based research will not only be more sharply focused and parsimonious but is also likely to reflect more fully the complexity of college impacts.

Second and relatedly, researchers need to make greater efforts to estimate the *magnitudes* of college's net effects. While it may be meaningful to report simply whether an independent variable is related to a dependent variable at some level of statistical significance, it is much more meaningful, as well as theoretically and practically more informative, also to estimate the strength of that relation. Many of the studies we reviewed failed to report even the most basic information (for example, means *and* standard deviations) that might be used to estimate effect sizes. Reporting estimated effect size can reasonably be expected to lead to theories that are more parsimonious and better reflect the reality of college impact, and to substantially improve the effective allocation of scarce resources to programs intended to enhance desired institutional impacts on student outcomes.

Third, greater attention in the preparation of research studies needs to be given to bodies of theory and evidence in fields not always reflected in past and present studies. This need is particularly acute in studies of students' noncognitive, psychosocial changes. Psychological paradigms have dominated this area of study over the past twenty years, although important inroads and contributions have been made by scholars trained as sociologists and anthropologists. An alarming number of studies reflect little familiarity with the knowledge base outside the author's main disciplinary paradigm. Whether many of the observed changes are due to developmental, psychosocial restructuring within students or to the learning, through the socialization process, of competencies, attitudes, values, and behaviors valued by important others remains very much an open and vital question.

Fourth, future theory-based research should consider indirect as well as direct effects. As much of the evidence we have reviewed suggests, it is entirely possible that we may be underestimating or even misrepresenting the impact of many college influences by failing to consider their indirect effects. Because some source of influence in the causal chain is one step removed from having a direct effect on a given outcome makes it no less theoretically or practically important. Indeed, its consideration may add substantially to our knowledge of educational effects. Of course, any consideration of indirect effects means that one must typically conceptualize research questions in terms of theoretical models; but such a process is likely to reflect the complexity of college impacts more fully.

A fifth direction for future research is to focus on conditional effects. We found few replicable conditional effects in the body of evidence. This is probably because such effects have not been assessed either routinely or consistently rather than because they do not exist. We still strongly suspect that students' individual characteristics frequently mediate the impact of college; not all students benefit equally from the same experience. If certain experiences are indeed shown to be especially beneficial for particular kinds of students, it may be possible to craft more developmentally specific and effective programs and policies.

Sixth, more attention needs to be given to the analysis of the *timing* of change during the college experience. Most studies of change focus on the freshman year or on freshman-senior differences. Only a handful of studies have monitored change on an annual, sequential basis. Thus, we know little about whether change is mostly linear and monotonic or primarily episodic and discontinuous over the college years. Moreover, it seems reasonable to suggest (and there is some basis for believing) that the pacing of change varies across outcomes areas. Designing maximally effective educational interventions requires knowing *when* an intervention will make a difference and when it will not.

A seventh important direction of future research on college impact should be a greater dependence on naturalistic and qualitative methodologies. When employed judiciously, such approaches are capable of providing greater sensitivity to many of the subtle and fine-grained complexities of college impact than more traditional quantitative approaches. Naturalistic inquiries may be particularly sensitive to the detection of the kinds of indirect and conditional effects just discussed. We anticipate that in the next decade important contributions to our understanding of college impact will be yielded by naturalistic investigations.

While there are a number of topics on which important research remains to be done, one in particular stands out as a significant focus for future inquiry. This is the impact of the academic program and the teaching-learning process. How do different teaching and instructional approaches influence not only how much content is learned but also what higher-order thinking skills are developed? How and in what ways does the academic program influence values and personal change? Are there particular teaching or instructional approaches that are differentially effective for different kinds of students? What is the connection between the intellectual competencies acquired through the academic experience and those required in one's career? Answers to these and similar questions would constitute a major contribution to our understanding of the impact of college.

Table 1

Summary of Estimated Freshman-to-Senior Changes: *Learning and Cognitive Development*

Outcome	Estimated Magnitude of Change	
	Effect Size[a]	Percentile Point Difference[b]
General verbal skills	.56	21
General quantitative skills	.24	10
Specific subject matter knowledge	.84	31
Oral communication skills	.60	22
Written communication skills	.50	19
Piagetian (formal) reasoning	.33	13
Critical thinking	1.00	34
Use of reason and evidence to address ill-structured problems (reflective judgment, informal reasoning)	1.00	34
Ability to deal with conceptual complexity	1.20	38

[a]Effect size = (senior mean minus freshman mean) divided by freshman standard deviation.
[b]Effect size converted to the equivalent percentile point under the normal curve. This is the percentile point difference between the freshman- and senior-year means when the freshman mean is set at the 50th percentile.

Table 2

Summary of Estimated Freshman-to-Senior Changes: *Attitudes and Values*

Outcome	Estimated Magnitude of Change		
	Effect Size[a]	Percentile Point Difference[b]	Percentage Point Difference Between Freshmen & Seniors[c]
Aesthetic, cultural, and intellectual values	.25–.40	10–15	
Value placed on liberal education			+20 to +30%
Value placed on education as vocational preparation			−10 to −30%
Value placed on intrinsic occupational rewards			+12%
Value placed on extrinsic occupational rewards			−10 to −15%
Altruism, social and civic conscience, humanitarianism	.10–.50	4–19	+ 2 to + 8%
Political and social liberalism	.20	8	+15 to +25%
Civil rights and liberties			+ 5 to +25%
Religiosity, religious affiliation	−.49	19 (in religiosity)	Up to −11% in conventional religious preferences
Traditional views of gender roles			−10 to −25%

[a]Effect size = (senior mean minus freshman) divided by freshman mean) standard deviation.
[b]Effect size converted to the equivalent percentile point under the normal curve. This is the percentile point difference between the freshman- and senior-year means when the freshman mean is set at the 50th percentile.
[c]Percentage point increase or decrease of seniors (versus freshmen) holding particular view or position.

Table 3

Summary of Estimated Freshman-to-Senior Changes: *Systems in Psychosocial Development*

| | Estimated Magnitude of Change | | |
Outcome	Effect Size[a]	Percentile Point Difference[b]	Percentage Point Difference Between Freshmen & Seniors[c]
Self Systems			
Identity status			+15 to +25% (in reaching identity achievement status)
Ego development	.50	19	
Self-concept			
Academic			+4 to +14% (rating self "above avg.")
Social			+7% (rating self "above avg.")
Self-esteem	.60	23	
Relational Systems			
Autonomy, independence, and locus of control	.36	14	
Authoritarianism	−.81	29	
Ethnocentrism	−.45	17	
Intellectual orientation	.30	12	
Interpersonal relations	.16	6	
Personal adjustment and psychological well-being	.40	16	
Maturity and general personal development	Not available		

[a]Effect size = (senior mean minus freshman mean) divided by freshman standard deviation.
[b]Effect size converted to the equivalent percentile point under the normal curve. This is the percentile point difference between the freshman- and senior-year means when the freshman mean is set at the 50th percentile.
[c]Percentage point increase or decrease of seniors (versus freshmen) holding a particular view or position.

Table 4

Summary of Estimated Freshman-to-Senior Changes: *Moral Development*

| | Estimated Magnitude of Change | | |
Outcome	Effect Size[a]	Percentile Point Difference[b]	Percentage Point Difference Between Freshmen & Seniors[c]
Use of principled reasoning in judging moral issues	Difficult to estimate magnitude of effect, but major change during college is from the use of "conventional" to "postconventional" or "principled" reasoning		

[a]Effect size = (senior mean minus freshman mean) divided by freshman standard deviation.
[b]Effect size converted to the equivalent percentile point under the normal curve. This is the percentile point difference between the freshman- and senior-year means when the freshman mean is set at the 50th percentile.
[c]Percentage point increase or decrease of seniors (versus freshmen) holding a particular view or position.

Table 5

Summary of Estimated Net Effects of College: *Learning and Cognitive Development*

Outcome	Strength of Evidence	Direction of Effect	Major Rival Explanations Controlled	Magnitude of Net Effect
General verbal skills	Strong	Positive	Precollege verbal skills, race, socio-economic status	.26 to .32 SD (10 to 13 percentile point advantage)
General quantitative skills	Strong	Positive	Precollege quantitative skills, race, socioeconomic status	.29 to .32 SD (11 to 13 percentile point advantage)
Oral communication skills	Moderate	Positive	Age, academic ability	Unclear[a]
Written communication skills	Moderate	Positive	Age, academic ability	Unclear
General intellectual and analytical skill development	Moderate	Positive	Age, verbal ability, quantitative ability	Community college graduates higher than incoming freshmen; magnitude of effect unclear
Critical thinking	Strong	Positive	Precollege critical thinking, academic aptitude, socioeconomic status, educational aspirations	Freshman-year net effect, .44 SD (17 percentile point advantage); magnitude of net four-year effect unclear
Use of reason and evidence to address ill-structured problems (reflective judgment, informal reasoning)	Moderate to strong	Positive	Age, academic ability	Unclear
Intellectual flexibility	Moderate to strong	Positive	Age, intelligence, aptitude	Unclear

[a]"Unclear," as used in this table, means we are acknowledging that the studies do not allow such estimates or that the evidence, though generally consistent, is still sufficiently complex to make an estimate of effect size hazardous.

Table 6

Summary of Estimated Net Effects on College: Attitudes and Values

Outcome	Strength of Evidence	Direction of Effect	Major Rival Explanations Controlled	Magnitude of Net Effect[a]
Aesthetic, cultural, and intellectual values	Moderate	Positive	Age, gender, religion, socioeconomic status, residential origin	Unclear[a]
Value placed on liberal education	Strong	Positive	Aptitude, race, gender, family socioeconomic status, precollege values	Graduates two to three times more likely to value education than are people with less education
Value placed on education as vocational preparation	Moderate	Negative	Aptitude, occupation, interaction thereof	Unclear
Value placed on intrinsic occupational rewards	Strong	Positive	Gender, race, socioeconomic status, job characteristics	Unclear, probably small
Value placed on extrinsic occupational rewards	Strong	Negative	Gender, race, socioeconomic status, job characteristics	Small
Social liberalism	Weak	Positive	Gender, race, age, religion, socioeconomic status, residential origin, cohort, aging and period effects	Unclear
Political liberalism	Strong	Positive	Gender, race, age, religion, socioeconomic status, residential origin, cohort, aging and period effects	Unclear
Civil rights and liberties	Mixed	Positive	Age, income, socioeconomic status, religion	Unclear, probably small
Secularism	Weak	Positive	Gender, race, initial religious attitudes	Unclear
Gender roles (toward the "modern")	Strong	Positive	Initial gender role values, gender, age, race, income, religion, marital status, work history, number of children, period and cohort effects	Unclear

[a]"Unclear," as used in this table, means we are acknowledging that the studies do not allow such estimates or that the evidence, though generally consistent, is still sufficiently complex to make an estimate of effect size hazardous.

Table 7

Summary of Estimated Net Effects of College: *Psychosocial Development*

Outcome	Strength of Evidence	Direction of Effect	Major Rival Explanations Controlled	Magnitude of Net Effect
Identity and ego development	Very weak	Positive	Few	Unknown
Self-concept: Academic	Strong	Positive	Gender, race, prior achievement, socioeconomic status, degree aspirations	Small, indirect
Self-concept: Social	Strong	Positive	Gender, race, prior achievement, socioeconomic status, degree aspirations	Small, indirect
Self-concept: Self-esteem	Strong	Positive	Ability, achievement, socio-economic status, race, precollege self-esteem	Small
Autonomy, independence, and internal locus of control	Weak to moderate (strong for locus of control)	Positive	Ability, socioeconomic status, precollege locus of control	Unclear[a] (small for locus of control)
Authoritarianism, dogmatism, and ethnocentrism	Moderate	Negative	Gender, ability, socioeconomic status	Unclear
Intellectual orientation	Moderate	Positive	Gender, ability, socioeconomic status	Unclear
Interpersonal relations	Weak	Mixed	None	Unclear
Personal adjustment and psychological well-being	Strong	Positive	Socioeconomic status, family situation, religiosity	Small
Maturity and general personal development	No evidence	Unknown	None	Unclear

[a]"Unclear," as used in this table, means we are acknowledging that the studies do not allow such estimates or that evidence, though generally consistent, is still sufficiently complex to make an estimate of effect size hazardous.

Table 8

Summary of Estimated Net Effects of Colleges: *Moral Development*

Outcome	Strength of Evidence	Direction of Effect	Major Rival Explanations Controlled	Magnitude of Net Effect
Use of principled reasoning in judging moral issues	Strong	Positive	Age, precollege differences in moral reasoning, intelligence, socioeconomic status	Unclear[a]
Principled behavior or action	Weak	Positive		Hypothesized effect is indirect and probably small

[a]"Unclear," as used in this table, means we are acknowledging that the studies do not allow such estimates or that the evidence, though generally consistent, is still sufficiently complex to make an estimate of effect size hazardous.

Table 9

Summary of Estimated Long-Term Effects of College: *Socioeconomic Outcomes*

Outcome	Strength of Evidence	Direction of Effect	Major Rival Explanations Controlled	Magnitude of Net Effect
Occupational status	Strong	Positive	Socioeconomic status, aspirations, intelligence	Bachelor's degree confers 1 SD (34 percentile point) advantage over high school diploma
Stability of employment	Moderate	Positive	Socioeconomic status	Unclear[a]; probably large
Career mobility and attainment	Strong	Positive	Initial job level	Unclear
Earnings	Strong	Positive	Socioeconomic status aspirations, occupational status, intelligence, work experience	Bachelor's degree confers 20 to 40 percentage point advantage over high school diploma
Private rate of return	Strong	Positive	Intelligence, costs of education, foregone earnings	Bachelor's degree confers 9.3 to 11% return on investment

[a]"Unclear," as used in this table, means we are acknowledging that the studies do not allow such estimates or that the evidence, though generally consistent, is still sufficiently complex to make an estimate of effect size hazardous.

Table 10

Summary of Estimated Long-Term Effects on College: *Learning and Cognitive Development*

Outcome	Strength of Evidence	Direction of Effect	Major Rival Explanations Controlled	Magnitude of Net Effect
General knowledge	Moderate	Positive	Race, gender, age, initial socioeconomic status, current socioeconomic status, religion, geographical origin	Unclear[a]
General cognitive competencies and skills (e.g., critical thinking and analytical skills, ability to think clearly, oral communication skills)	Moderate	Positive	Age	Unclear

[a]"Unclear," as used in this table, means we are acknowledging that the studies do not allow such estimates or that the evidence, though generally consistent, is still sufficiently complex to make an estimate of effect size hazardous.

Table 11

Summary of Estimated Long-Term Effects of College: *Attitudes and Values*

Outcome	Strength of Evidence	Direction of Effect	Major Rival Explanations Controlled	Magnitude of Net Effect
Aesthetic, cultural, and intellectual values	Moderate	Stable over time	Gender, race, religion, socioeconomic status	Unclear[a]
Value placed on liberal education	Moderate	Positive	Aptitude, employment situation	Unclear
Value placed on liberal education	Moderate	Negative	Aptitude, employment situation	Unclear
Value placed on intrinsic occupational rewards	Strong	Positive	Gender, race, socioeconomic status, precollege values, college GPA	Unclear
Value placed on extrinsic occupational rewards	Strong	Negative	Gender, race, socioeconomic status, precollege values, college GPA	Unclear
Political and social attitudes	Moderate	Stable over time	Aptitude, age, race, gender, religion, socioeconomic status, region, historical period	Unclear; part of effect probably indirect through employment situation
Secularism	Weak	Stable over time	None	Unclear
Gender roles (toward the "modern")	Weak	Positive	Initial attitudes, various background characteristics, occupational experience	Unclear

[a] "Unclear," as used in this table, means we are acknowledging that the studies do not allow such estimates or that the evidence, though generally consistent, is still sufficiently complex to make an estimate of effect size hazardous.

Table 12

Summary of Estimated Long-Term Effects of College: *Psychosocial Changes*

Outcome	Strength of Evidence	Direction of Effect	Major Rival Explanations Controlled	Magnitude of Net Effect
Identity and ego development	Virtually no evidence			
Self-concept: Academic	Strong	Positive	Gender, race, precollege self-concept, achievement, socioeconomic status, degree aspirations, occupational status	Small; stronger among whites than among blacks
Self-concept: Social	Strong	Positive	Gender, race, precollege self-concept, achievement, socioeconomic status, degree aspirations, occupational status	Small; stronger among whites than among blacks
Self-concept: Self-esteem	Strong	Positive	Race, gender, socioeconomic status, ability, precollege self-esteem	Small
Autonomy, independence, and internal locus of control	Moderate	Positive	Gender, race, socioeconomic status, aptitude, precollege locus of control	Unclear,[a] but probably small and perhaps indirect
Authoritarianism, dogmatism, and ethnocentrism	Weak	Stable over time	None	Unclear
Intellectual orientation	Weak	Stable over time; some declines possible	None	Unclear
Interpersonal relations	Weak	Positive	None	Unclear
Personal adjustment and psychosocial well-being	Moderate	Positive	Income, occupational status	Unclear
Maturity and general personal development	Weak	Positive	Unclear	Unclear

[a]"Unclear," as used in this table, means we are acknowledging that the studies do not allow such estimates or that the evidence, though generally consistent, is still sufficiently complex to make an estimate of effect size hazardous.

Table 13

Summary of Estimated Long-Term Effects of College: *Moral Development*

Outcome	Strength of Evidence	Direction of Effect	Major Rival Explanations Controlled	Magnitude of Net Effect
Use of principled reasoning in judging moral issues	Strong	Positive	Precollege level of principled reasoning, regression artifacts	Unclear[a]

[a]"Unclear," as used in this table, means we are acknowledging that the studies do not allow such estimates or that the evidence, though generally consistent, is still sufficiently complex to make an estimate of effect size hazardous.

Table 14

Summary of Estimated Long-Term Effects of College: *Quality of Life Indexes*

Outcome	Strength of Evidence	Direction of Effect	Major Rival Explanations Controlled	Magnitude of Net Effect
Health status	Moderate	Positive	Income, age, prior health status, socioeconomic status	College graduates have 4% advantage in health status and 1.6% advantage in mortality rate over high school graduates[a]
Marital stability	Weak	Positive	Age, age at marriage, job prestige, number of children, income	Probably indirect and small
Family size	Moderate	Positive	Income, family demographic traits	Unclear[b]
Nurturance of children	Weak	Positive	Mother employed	Unclear
Consumer behavior or efficiency	Moderate	Positive	Income	Unclear
Savings and investment efficiency	Moderate	Positive	Age, income, family size, occupation	Unclear
Cultured leisure	Weak	Positive	Income	Unclear
Job satisfaction	Weak	Positive	Age, religious preference	Unclear, but probably small
Marital satisfaction	Moderate	Mixed	Age, age at first marriage, employment outside home, job status	Very small
Subjective well-being (life satisfaction)	Moderate	Mixed	Age, income, job status, socioeconomic status origins	Very small

[a]These estimates were obtained by multiplying by four the advantage attributable to each year of college completed.
[b]"Unclear," as used in this table, means we are acknowledging that the studies do not allow such estimates or that the evidence, though generally consistent, is still sufficiently complex to make an estimate of effect size hazardous.

Table 15

Summary of Estimated Long-Term Effects of College: *Intergenerational Effect*

Outcome	Strength of Evidence	Direction of Effect	Major Rival Explanations Controlled	Magnitude of Net Effect
Educational attainment of children	Strong	Positive	Family income, intelligence, aspirations, race, gender	Unclear;[a] effect may be both direct and indirect and is probably small
Occupational status	Moderate	Positive	Family income, intelligence, aspirations, race, gender	Unclear; effect is probably indirect and small
Daughters entering male-dominated occupation	Moderate	Positive	Family income, academic achievement, aspirations, race	Unclear; effect is probably indirect and small
Earnings of children	Moderate	Positive	Family income, academic achievement, aspirations, race, gender	Unclear; direct effects mixed; effect is probably indirect and small

[a]"Unclear," as used in this table, means we are acknowledging that the studies do not allow such estimates or that the evidence, though generally consistent, is still sufficiently complex to make an estimate of effect size hazardous.

Table 16

Summary of Estimated Between-College Effects: *Two-Year Versus Four-Year Colleges*

Outcome	Strength of Evidence	Direction of Effect	Major Rival Explanations Controlled	Magnitude of Net Effect
Bachelor's degree completion	Strong	Negative for two-year institutions	Academic ability, high school achievement, family socioeconomic status, degree aspirations, college grades, work, age, place of residence	About a 15% or greater disadvantage in likelihood of bachelor's degree completion during a specified time period
Occupational status	Moderate	Negative for two-year institutions	Academic ability, high school achievement, family socioeconomic status, degree aspirations, college grades, educational attainment	Direct effect small and perhaps trivial; most of effect indirect, transmitted by degree completion, and probably small
Earnings	Weak	Inconclusive	Intelligence, educational aspirations, family socioeconomic status, sex, race, educational attainment	Direct effect probably trivial, although disadvantage to two-year institutions may become more pronounced over time; small indirect effect through educational attainment likely but untested

Table 17

Summary of Estimated Between-College Effects: College Quality (Particularly Selectivity and Prestige)

Outcome	Strength of Evidence	Direction of Effect	Major Rival Explanations Controlled	Magnitude of Net Effect
Aesthetic, cultural, and intellectual values	Weak	More positive at selective schools	Gender, socioeconomic status, religion	Unclear,[a] but probably quite small; effect may be somewhat more pronounced when selectivity is combined with private control
Political and social liberalism	Moderate	More positive at selective schools	Gender, socioeconomic status, ability, initial values, various other background variables	Unclear, but probably small; effect may be somewhat more pronounced when selectivity is combined with private control
Secularism	Moderate	More positive at selective schools	Gender, race, socioeconomic status, ability, initial level of religiosity, various other background characteristics	Unclear
Academic self-concept	Moderate	More negative at selective schools	Gender, race, socioeconomic status, ability, initial self-concept, various other precollege characteristics	Unclear, but probably indirect, mediated by GPA
Educational aspirations and educational attainment	Strong	Positive in direction of selectivity, prestige, and financial resources	Initial aspirations, secondary school achievement, family socioeconomic status, college grades, job expectations, college size	Moderate and positive direct effect; small negative indirect effect transmitted through college grades; overall, small positive total effect, accounting for about 1 to 2% of variance
Choice of academic career	Moderate	Positive in direction of college reputation and financial resources	Initial career choice, academic ability, college grades, family socioeconomic status	Unclear, but probably quite small

Table 17 (continued)

Summary of Estimated Between-College Effects: College Quality (Particularly Selectivity and Prestige)

Outcome	Strength of Evidence	Direction of Effect	Major Rival Explanations Controlled	Magnitude of Net Effect
Choice of sex-atypical majors and careers for women	Moderate	Positive in direction of selectivity	Family socioeconomic status, age, marital status, college grades, college type (liberal arts or other)	Small
Entrance into sex-atypical careers for women	Moderate	Positive in direction of selectivity	Race, initial career aspirations, self-concept, secondary school achievement, family socioeconomic status, college gender, college control, college grades, major	Small; perhaps somewhat stronger in non-science careers than in science careers
Career mobility and success	Moderate	Positive in direction of selectivity and prestige	Family socioeconomic status, educational attainment, age, race, gender, college grades, recruitment emphasis of employer	Small
Occupational status in professional career	Moderate	Positive in direction of selectivity	Family socioeconomic status, initial career aspirations, secondary school achievement	Small; unclear whether effect is direct or indirect through educational attainment; evidence for all careers indicates no consistent effect on occupational status
Earnings	Moderate to strong	Positive in direction of selectivity in particular but also prestige and financial resources	Intelligence, family socioeconomic status, achievement motivation, college grades, educational attainment occupational status	Small direct effect slightly larger than 1% of earnings variance, indirect effect through educational attainment may increase this by one-third; only most selective or prestigious colleges may account for this effect

a"Unclear," as used in this table, means we are acknowledging that the studies do not allow such estimates or that the evidence, though generally consistent, is still sufficiently complex to make an estimate of effect size hazardous.

300

Table 18

Summary of Estimated Between-College Effects: College Type

College Characteristic or Outcome	Strength of Evidence	Direction of Effect	Major Rival Explanations Controlled	Magnitude of Net Effects
Private Versus Public Colleges				
Aesthetic, cultural, and intellectual values	Moderate	Positive in the direction of private control	Gender, race, ability, socioeconomic status, degree aspirations, other background traits	Unclear[a]
Educational aspirations and educational attainment	Moderate	Positive in the direction of private control	Family socioeconomic status, secondary school achievement, gender, race, initial occupational aspirations, college selectivity and size, college grades	Small, probably according for no more than 1% of variance
Implementation of career	Moderate	Mixed	Initial career choice, family socioeconomic status, gender, college selectivity	Small tendency for public institutions to significantly enhance implementation of career plans for college teaching and engineering but negatively affect plans for business, law, medicine, nursing
Liberal Arts Colleges				
Women's choice of sex-atypical majors	Moderate	More positive for liberal arts colleges	College selectivity, initial career choice	Small
Value attached to a liberate education	Moderate	More positive for liberal arts colleges	Gender, race, socioeconomic status, ability, initial values	Unclear
Value attached to intrinsic occupational awards	Moderate	More positive for liberal arts colleges	Gender, race, socioeconomic status, ability, initial values	Unclear
Church-Related Colleges				
Secularism	Moderate	Negative in direction of church-related colleges	Initial religious orientation	Small
Humanitarian and altruistic social values	Moderate	More positive at church-related colleges	Sex, race, socioeconomic status, ability, initial values	Unclear, but stronger at church-related schools
Authoritarianism, dogmatism, and ethnocentrism	Weak	Smaller declines at Catholic colleges	Ability	Unclear

[a]"Unclear," as used in this table, means we are acknowledging that the studies do not allow such estimates or that the evidence, though generally consistent, is still sufficiently complex to make an estimate of effect size hazardous.

301

Table 19

Summary of Estimated Between-College Effects: College Size

Outcome	Strength of Evidence	Direction of Effect	Major Rival Explanations Controlled	Magnitude of Effect
Educational attainment	Weak	Negative	Family socioeconomic status, educational aspirations, college selectivity, major, grades, social involvement	Direct effect trivial; small negative indirect effect transmitted through social involvement probably accounting for less than 1% of variance
Occupational status	Strong	Positive	Family socioeconomic status, academic ability, occupational aspirations, college selectivity	Small
Earnings	Strong	Positive	Family socioeconomic status, occupational aspirations, aptitude, college selectivity, college major, grades	Small
Social self-concept	Moderate	Negative	Gender, race, socioeconomic status, ability, degree aspirations, college experiences, other institutional characteristics	Small, indirect

Table 20

Summary of Estimated Between-College Effects: College Racial and Gender Composition

Outcome	Strength of Evidence	Direction of Effect	Major Rival Explanations Controlled	Magnitude of Net Effect
College Characteristic or Racial Composition				
Cognitive development (critical thinking, concept attainment) of black students	Weak	Positive in direction of black colleges	Socioeconomic status, academic aptitude	Unclear[a]
Bachelor's degree completion and educational attainment of Black students	Moderate	Positive in direction of black colleges	Family socioeconomic status, educational aspirations, academic ability, college selectivity and size, college grades	Small direct effect; possibly small indirect effect
Occupational status of black women	Weak	Positive in direction of black colleges	Family socioeconomic status, occupational aspirations, college selectivity and size, college grades, educational attainment	Small
Academic and social self-concepts of black students	Moderate	Positive in direction of black colleges	Gender, socioeconomic status, ability, initial self-concept, aspirations	Unclear; probably small indirect effect but only for black women
Gender Composition				
Educational aspirations and educational attainment of women	Moderate	Positive in direction of women's colleges	Family socioeconomic status, educational aspirations, secondary school achievement, college selectivity, college grades	Small; effect may be both direction and indirect, effect on aspirations probably stronger than effect on attainment
Implementation of career choice for men	Moderate	Positive in direction of men's colleges	Family socioeconomic status, initial career choice	Small positive effect on entering business, law, and the professions in general
Women's choice of sex-atypical careers	Weak	Positive in direction of women's colleges	College selectivity	Unclear
Women's entry into specific sex-atypical occupations (such as medicine, scientific research, engineering	Moderate	Positive in direction of women's colleges	Unclear	Strong overrepresentation of women's college graduates in these fields
Women's achievement of prominence in a field	Moderate	Positive in direction of women's colleges	College selectivity, size, and faculty salary	Moderate to strong overrepresentation of women's college graduates who achieve prominence

[a]"Unclear," as used in this table, means we are acknowledging that the studies do not allow such estimates or that the evidence, though generally consistent, is still sufficiently complex to make an estimate of effect size hazardous.

Table 21

Summary of Estimated Between-College Effects: *College Environments*

Outcome	Strength of Evidence	Direction of Effect	Major Rival Explanations Controlled	Magnitude of Net Effect
Learning (typically on standardized measures such as the Graduate Record Examination)	Moderate	Positive in direction of (1) frequent student-faculty interaction, (2) degree of curricular formal education level	Academic aptitude, major field of study	Very small
Cognitive development (such as critical thinking, adult reasoning skills)	Moderate	Positive in direction of general education emphasis in curriculum	College selectivity	Small to moderate
Educational attainment	Moderate	Positive in direction of (1) cohesive peer environment, (2) participation in college activities, 3) perception of personal concern for student, (4) emphasis on supportive student personnel services	Family socioeconomic status, secondary school achievement, educational aspirations, college size and selectivity	Unclear,[a] but probably small
Aesthetic, cultural, and intellectual attitudes and values	Weak	Positive in direction of campuses high in awareness and scholarship; negative on campuses high in propriety and practicality	None	Unclear
Internal locus of control	Moderate	Positive in direction of cohesive peer environment	Gender, race, socioeconomic status, ability, initial level of internality	Unclear

304

Table 21 (continued)

Outcome	Strength of Evidence	Direction of Effect	Major Rival Explanations Controlled	Magnitude of Net Effect
Authoritarianism and dog-matism	Weak	Negative in direction of schools with liberal campus climate, large proportion of non-conformists, student involvement in class activities, emphasis on intrinsic motivations	Gender, ability, socioeconomic status	Unclear
Personal adjustment and psychological well-being	Weak	Positive in direction of campus with high proportion of "expressive" students classroom participation, emphasis on complex mental activities, intrinsic awards	Gender, socioeconomic status, ability	Unclear
Career choice and career entered	Strong	Positive in direction of "progressive conformity" hypothesis	Initial career choice, major field choice, educational aspirations, academic aptitude, college grades	Small

[a]"Unclear," as used in this table, means we are acknowledging that the studies do not allow such estimates or that the evidence, though generally consistent, is still sufficiently complex to make an estimate of effect size hazardous.

Table 22

Summary of Estimated Between-College Effects: *Geographical and Social Proximity*

Outcome	Strength of Evidence	Direction of Effect	Major Rival Explanations Controlled	Magnitude of Net Effect
Initial job level and promotion rate	Weak	Positive in direction of proximity	College selectivity, age, tenure in firm	Unclear,[a] but probably small

[a]"Unclear," as used in this table, means we are acknowledging that the studies do not allow such estimates or that the evidence, though generally consistent, is still sufficiently complex to make an estimate of effect size hazardous.

Table 23

Summary of Estimated Between-College Effects: *Transfer Between Four-year Institutions*

Outcome	Strength of Evidence	Direction of Effect	Major Rival Explanations Controlled	Magnitude of Net Effect
Educational attainment, occupational status, and earnings	Weak	Negative in direction of transfer	Family socioeconomic status, aspirations, expectations of transfer, selectivity of first college attended, college grades	Moderate negative direct effect on educational attainment; small negative indirect effect on occupational status transmitted through educational attainment; small negative direct and indirect effects on earnings

Table 24

Summary of Estimated Within-College Effects: _Residence_

Outcome	Strength of Evidence	Direction of Effect	Major Rival Explanations Controlled	Magnitude of Net Effect
Aesthetic, cultural, and intellectual values	Moderate	Positive in direction of on-campus residence	Gender, race, socioeconomic status, ability, initial values	Unclear[a]
Sociopolitical attitudes and values	Moderate	Positive in direction of on-campus residence	Gender, race, socioeconomic status, ability	Unclear
Secularism	Moderate	Positive in direction of on-campus residence	Gender, race, socioeconomic status, ability, initial values	Unclear
Self-concepts	Weak to moderate	Positive in direction of on-campus residence	Gender, race, socioeconomic status, ability, initial concept	Unclear, but probably small and indirect via interpersonal relations
Autonomy, independence, internal locus of control	Weak	Positive in direction of on-campus residence	Gender, ability	Unclear
Intellectual orientation	Moderation	Positive in direction of on-campus residence	Gender, ability, initial levels	Unclear, but probably small and indirect, mediated by interpersonal relations and residence environment
Persistence and degree attainment	Strong	Positive in direction of on-campus residence, especially in living-learning center	Gender, ability, socioeconomic status, educational aspirations, high school achievement	Unclear
Moral development	Weak	Positive in direction of on-campus residence	Initial level of moral development	Unclear

[a]"Unclear," as used in this table, means we are acknowledging that the studies do not allow such estimates or that the evidence, though generally consistent, is still sufficiently complex to make an estimate of effect size hazardous.

Table 25

Summary of Estimated Within-College Effects: *Major Field of Study*

Outcome	Strength of Evidence	Direction of Effect	Major Rival Explanations Controlled	Magnitude of Net Effect
Content learning and cognitive development	Strong	Students perform highest on subject matter tests and on measures of general cognitive development most consistent with their academic major	Unclear	Unclear,[a] but probably moderate to large
Academic self-concept	Strong	Positive in favor of sciences, math, technical majors	Gender, race, ability, socioeconomic status, high school achievement, initial self-concept, other precollege traits	Unclear, but departmental environment may be more important than the discipline
Women's entry into sex-atypical occupations	Strong	Positive in direction of high percentage of men in the major (e.g., business engineering, natural sciences)	Age, socioeconomic status, college selectivity, college grades	Unclear, but probably moderate
Earnings	Strong	Positive in direction of business, engineering, and preprofessional majors	Socioeconomic status, race, gender, academic aptitude, college grades, occupational aspirations, educational attainment, college selectivity	Unclear, but probably moderate; also unclear whether earnings advantage extends over one's total career

[a]"Unclear," as used in this table, means we are acknowledging that the studies do not allow such estimates or that the evidence, though generally consistent, is still sufficiently complex to make an estimate of effect size hazardous.

Table 26

Summary of Estimated Within-College Effects: *The Academic Experience*

Outcome	Strength of Evidence	Direction of Effect	Major Rival Explanations Controlled	Magnitude of Net Effect
Knowledge acquisition	Strong	Positive in direction of greater student involvement, individualized instructional strategies, instructor skill, and course structure	Aptitude, motivation; many of the studies of individualized instruction are based on randomized experiments	Individualized instruction produces positive effects of .15 to .49 SD (6 to 19 percentile points) over traditional methods; correlations of course achievement with instructor skill and course structure are about .50 and .47, respectively Small to moderate
Cognitive development	Strong	Positive in direction of greater student involvement, emphasis on inductive learning, academic experiences providing for challenge and/or integration	Academic aptitude, secondary school achievement, socio-economic status	
Sociopolitical and gender role attitudes and values	Weak to moderate	Positive in direction of course work and special programs	Few	Unclear[a]
Academic self-concept	Moderate	Positive in direction of participation in honors program, academic integration with peers and faculty	Gender, race, socio-economic status, ability, aspirations, initial self-concept	Unclear
Relational psychosocial areas (primarily autonomy and independence, nonauthoritarianism, intellectual disposition, general personal development and maturity)	Weak to moderate	Positive in direction of living-earning program participation	Gender, ability, initial levels	Unclear, but may be more indirect than direct, via interpersonal relations and program environment
Moral development	Strong	Positive in direction of instructional interventions stressing dilemma discussion and personality development	Unclear, but studies include several randomized experiments	Dilemma discussion effect size of .51 SD (19.5 percentile point gain); personality development effect size of .41 SD (16 percentile point gain)

[a]"Unclear," as used in this table, means we are acknowledging that the studies do not allow such estimates or that the evidence, though generally consistent, is still sufficiently complex to make an estimate of effect size hazardous.

309

Table 27

Summary of Estimated Within-College Effects: *Interpersonal Involvement*.

Outcome	Strength of Evidence	Direction of Effect	Major Rival Explanations Controlled	Magnitude of Net Effect
Learning and cognitive growth (self-reported)	Moderate	Positive in relation to faculty and (to lesser degree) student interaction	Gender, race, ability, socioeconomic status, degree aspirations, secondary school achievement, major field	Unclear,[a] probably
Aesthetic, cultural and intellectual interests	Weak to moderate	Positive	Openness to change, initial values	Unclear
Occupational values	Moderate	Positive toward intrinsic and away from extrinsic values associated with faculty contact	Gender, race, ability, prior achievements, educational goals, initial values	Unclear
Sociopolitical attitudes and values	Moderate	Positive in relation to peer and faculty contact	Gender, race, ability, socioeconomic status, initial values, degree aspirations other traits	Unclear
Secularism	Weak	Positive in relation to concentration of faculty and peers with same values	Ability, socioeconomic status	Unclear
Identity and ego development	Weak	Positive in relation to contact with the diversity of peers	None	Unclear
Academic and social self-concepts	Strong	Positive in relation to integration in academic and social systems, peers, faculty contact	Gender, race, ability, socioeconomic status, institutional characteristics	Unclear
Intellectual orientation	Moderate	Positive in relation to peer and faculty interaction	Gender, ability, initial level	Unclear

310

Table 27 (continued)

Outcome	Strength of Evidence	Direction of Effect	Major Rival Explanations Controlled	Magnitude of Net Effect
Moral development	Moderate	Positive in relation to peer interactions, contact with divergent perspectives and with peers at higher stages of moral development	Unclear	Unclear
General maturity and personal development	Moderate	Positive in relation to faculty and peer interactiosn	Gender, race, ability, high school, achievement, major, parents' education, degree aspirations	Unclear
Educational aspira-tions, persistence, and attainment	Strong	Positive in relation to peer interactions and out-of-class student-faculty interaction	Gender, secondary school achievement, socioeconomic status, aptitude, educational aspirations, initial institutional and degree commitments, other college experiences	Unclear

[a]"Unclear," as used in this table, means we are acknowledging that the studies do not allow such estimates or that the evidence, though generally consistent, is still sufficiently complex to make an estimate of effect size hazardous.

Table 28

Summary of Estimated Within-College Effects: *Extracurricular Involvement*

Outcome	Strength of Evidence	Direction of Effect	Major Rival Explanations Controlled	Magnitude of Net Effect
Educational persistence and attainment	Moderate	Positive	Gender, ability, high school achievement, socioeconomic status, educational aspirations	Small
Women's choice of sex-atypical careers	Moderate	Positive	Socioeconomic status, secondary school grades, initial occupational aspirations, college grades, college selectivity, educational attainment	Unclear[a]
Social self-concept	Strong	Positive, related to involvement in leadership activities	Gender, race, ability, high school achievement, socioeconomic status, degree aspirations, major, initial self-concept, various other college characteristics, selected institutional characteristics	Unclear

[a]"Unclear," as used in this table, means we are acknowledging that the studies do not allow such estimates or that the evidence, though generally consistent, is still sufficiently complex to make an estimate of effect size hazardous.

Table 29

Summary of Estimated Within-College Effects: *Academic Achievement*

Outcome	Strength of Evidence	Direction of Effect	Major Rival Explanations Controlled	Magnitude of Net Effect
Occupational status	Strong	Positive	Gender, occupational aspirations, socioeconomic status, college selectivity, educational attainment	Small; grades probably account for about 1% of variance; part of effect is indirect via effect on educational attainment
Job performance and career mobility	Moderate	Positive	Socioeconomic status, work experience, college selectivity, educational attainment	Small; grades probably account for no more than 1% of variance
Earnings	Strong	Positive	Socioeconomic status, race, gender, secondary school grades, college selectivity, academic ability educational attainment, occupational status, region of country where employed	Small; grades probably account for about 1% of variance; part of effect is indirect via effect on educational attainment

313

Table 30

Summary of Estimated Conditional College Effects

Outcome	Strength of Evidence	Direction of Effect	Major Rival Explanations Controlled	Magnitude of Net Effect
Effects Conditional on Student Characteristics				
Learning	Moderate	Students high in need for independent achievement or internal locus of control do better in courses stressing self-direction and independent learning; students with high need for conforming or dependent achievement or external locus of control do better in structured, teacher-directed courses	Results based on randomized experiments	Moderate
Cognitive development (formal reasoning)	Weak	Less-advanced reasoners benefit from learning-cycle or inquiry approach to instruction; students advance most via instuctional methods matched to their reasoning level	Initial level of formal reasoning	Unclear[a]
Occupational status	Strong	Nonwhite males derive greater benefits than whites from a bachelor's degree; women derive greater benefits than men from majoring in natural science and technical fields	Socioeconomic status, intelligence, educational aspirations, grades, occupational aspirations	Unclear

Table 30 (continued)

Outcome	Strength of Evidence	Direction of Effect	Major Rival Explanations Controlled	Magnitude of Net Effect
Earnings	Strong	Since about 1970 black and other nonwhite men have derived greater relative earnings benefits from a bachelor's degree than have white men; women derive greater relative earnings benefits than men from each year of college completed and from a bachelor's degree	Socioeconomic status, academic ability, place of residence, years of work experience	Moderate to substantial
Private rate of return	Moderate	White men enjoy somewhat higher private economic rate of return on a bachelor's degree than do nonwhite (primarily black) men, but this gap may be closing; black and other nonwhite women have a higher rate of return on a bachelor's degree than do white women	Unclear	Moderate
Effects Conditional on Institutional Characteristics				
Occupational status	Moderate	College selectivity may have stronger positive impact on occupational status in professional careers than in non-proffesional careers	Socioeconomic status, secondary school achievement, occupational aspirations, race	Small; effect may be both direct and indirect through educational attainment
Earnings	Moderate	College selectivity may have stronger positive impact on earnings for men from relatively high family socioeconomic backgrounds than for men from relatively low family socio-economic backgrounds	Socioeconomic status, educational attainment, occupational status, race	Small

a"Unclear," as used in this table, means we are acknowledging that the studies do not allow such estimates or that the evidence, though generally consistent, is still sufficiently complex to make an estimate of effect size hazardous.

College Outcomes and Student Development: Filling the Gaps

This article discusses current research and literature—most either psychological or sociological—on the college student. Unfortunately, there is little to connect these two divisions. This article discusses the gap and suggests ways to close it. It also discusses two other problems: the monocultural focus of most research and the lack of process models to guide implementation of theory.

Dr. Russell, a newly hired assistant professor, is asked to develop a course on student development theory and research. The course should contain a segment on special student populations. In addition, because the class will be mostly masters' students, it should touch on practical application. Her most recent administrative position was associate dean for academic affairs at a university of 18,000 students where her primary responsibility was to research student admissions and retention, track students within college, and follow the graduates. It has been six years since Russell earned her doctorate, and she does not want to rely on the syllabus from the class she took eight years ago.

Her colleague passes along a syllabus from a course on "The College Student" being taught in a similar program. Flipping to the bibliography, Russell is surprised to recognize few authors. From the list of Gilligan, Perry, King, Kitchener, Kegan, Astin, and Chickering only a few seem familiar. The names she expects—Tinto, Pascarella, Cross, Bean, Pace—are not there.

Realizing that the literature in which she has immersed herself for the past several years might have been "incomplete," she begins to reeducate herself. Again she is dismayed to discover that only a few of the readings mention the special populations whose problems she is to address in her class. She searches for more but finds only scattered articles, for the most part descriptive.

Finally, although Russell finds a few examples of a particular theory being implemented in very specific settings, she finds few "process models" to help her use a particular theory in more general circumstances.

In the past two decades, a great deal of research has focused on the college student. A shift from atheoretical to theoretical studies of college outcomes (satisfaction, progress, persistence, etc.) and the subsequent testing of those theories have spurred research on the topics. Additionally, a change of focus in the student affairs profession has sparked research on the nature of students and how they develop in college. However I find gaps between these two bodies of research; if filled, they could provide broader insights into the college student experience.

Since the early seventies, colleges have gradually relinquished the *in loco parentis* role. Professionals have become less concerned with controlling and limiting student behavior and more concerned with enabling and fostering student development. This shift has led to further exploration of college student development. Additionally, institutional concerns with enrollment and retention have inspired research on student progress and satisfaction.

These relatively recent shifts in focus have yielded seemingly endless knowledge about the college student and the college process. With so much information on the topic, constructing a curriculum to inform practitioners might seem easy. However, closer examination of this literature brings some troublesome observations:

1. There are actually two separate literatures on the college student (sociological and psychological) and few clear links to meaningfully synthesize both the outcomes and the development literature.

2. Much college student literature is monocultural, focusing on white upper- and middle-class students at large residential research universities. Such research does little to inform us about students at nontraditional institutions or about the multicultural populations on most campuses.

3. Too few process models tie directly to specific theory and can be used to guide practice on college campuses.

I will discuss each of these observations in turn and offer some recommendations for researchers and those attempting to incorporate theory in practice.

Two Separate Literatures

Most research on college students is based either on sociology or on psychology. In general, those of us who study student outcomes view the college-going process at the macro level and tend to take a sociological approach in our research. We study students in large aggregates and place them in broad demographic classifications. We assess how these broadly defined groups of students react to their environment and attempt to determine how these variables relate to such outcomes as academic achievement, satisfaction, and persistence.

On the other hand, those of us who study the development of college students view the college-going process at more of a micro level and tend to take more of a psychological approach in our research. We may use one of many student development theories to identify developmental levels or tasks of the students being studied. Usually, as researchers we seek to link the theoretical development of students to specific kinds of campus experiences or activities.

Unfortunately, there is little current overlap in these two literatures. The research on student outcomes seeks to determine which aspects of college life can have positive influences on satisfaction, career choice, persistence, and grade point average. On the other hand, the student development research focuses on the students' development as college students and on what can be done to foster further development.

A few early, ambitious, and well-known studies conceptually and methodologically linked student psychological characteristics with sociological experiences and outcomes (Astin 1968; Feldman and Newcomb 1973). However, since the development of causal models in the study of college students, possible connections between these two bodies of literature have been weak and for the most part, remain unexplored (Stage 1988).

Student Development Research

Theories and research that focus on student development are, for the most part, psychologically based and provide a rich body of information for faculty as well as student affairs practitioners. The most widely used student development theories can be classified into three major families: cognitive theory, psychosocial theory, and typology theory.

Cognitive development theorists like Kohlberg, Gilligan, Perry, King, Kitchener, and Kegan focus on how students reason when faced with decisions (e.g., what thoughts guide a decision about career choice?). Generally, these theories delineate stages in a hierarchy of reasoning with higher levels representing broader, more sophisticated ways of making meaning of the world.

Researchers exploring these theories tend to focus on classifying individuals into stages and determining what causes movement from one stage to another.

The psychosocial theorists include Chickering, Heath, Levinson, and Sheehy. They are more interested in the content or the developmental tasks with which students are dealing (e.g., is the student working on establishing autonomy or on establishing identity?). Researchers operating within these frameworks attempt to identify issues and to explain how such issues are resolved.

Both cognitive development theorists and psychosocial theorists believe that development results from an "optimal mismatch." That is, if a student feels challenged by a situation but also receives sufficient support to meet that challenge, he or she will likely develop. If the challenge is too great, if there is insufficient support, or if there is no challenge, development is unlikely.

Finally, typology theorists include Clark-Trow, Astin, Pace, Holland, and Myers-Briggs. These theorists focus on characteristics of the individual and of the environment, and the fit or lack of fit (interaction) between these two constructs (e.g., is the student an academic type or more of a social type?). Researchers using these theoretical frameworks may use physical, sociological, or perceptual measures of the campus environment. They contrast these measures with measures of a student's needs, personality, or sociological type, or perception of the ideal campus environment to identify discrepancies. These discrepancies then may explain lack of performance, dissatisfaction, or attrition.

As these theories became widely tested, replicated, and understood, researchers as well as college administrators began to recognize and appreciate their value in studying and dealing with college students. Currently these theories form the basis for most research on the development of the college student.

The Student Outcomes Research

During the past fifty years, much of the research in higher education focused on the study of such student outcomes as grade point average (GPA), persistence, intellectual achievement, change of major, and satisfaction with many aspects of the college environment (Ewell 1985; Pace 1984). The field of outcomes research, though not new, has changed radically in the last decade. Before the 1970s, researchers had explored the relationship of many individual variables (gender, socioeconomic status, religion, etc.) to any given outcome (grades, satisfaction, persistence, etc.). Only a few researchers attempted to tie characteristics, attitudes, experiences, and achievements together conceptually (Astin 1968; Feldman and Newcomb 1973). More recently, theorists developed models which provided structure and direction to subsequent research (Bean 1980; Ethington and Wolfle 1986; Pascarella and Staver 1985; Tinto 1975).

Theorists no longer view achievement and satisfaction as simple phenomena that can be predicted from a few easily gathered variables (Pace 1984). Rather they now view these outcomes as constellations of characteristics, attitudes, experiences, and subsequent changes in attitudes which can be depicted graphically. Studies conducted within the scope of the new theoretical frameworks have been replicated and modified so that we can now speak with greater confidence about a few consistent positive influences on persistence, grades, and satisfaction. Important environmental and experiential influences include the residence of the student, the perceived intellectual atmosphere of the campus, contacts with faculty members, perceived value of their education, and academic satisfaction (Tinto 1987). Student aspirations and attitudes about the importance of the college experience also help shape positive college outcomes (Astin 1985).

Despite the general coalescence of knowledge on the topic, a satisfactory explanation of outcomes eludes researchers. They cannot predict with assurance the success or failure, satisfaction or dissatisfaction, persistence or attrition of a student with certain background characteristics and attitudes, studying in a certain environment, and participating at a particular level of campus experiences. Researchers can advise administrators on strategies to promote positive outcomes, but large segments of the population go unaided by such recommendations. Outcomes phenomena seem to be complex webs of interaction that differ from student to student.

Any practitioner attempting to use these two bodies of research to incorporate theory in practice would find little guidance. Marcia Mentkowski and Arthur Chickering (1988) describe several possibilities for such study, but to date only a few recent researchers have begun to explore such links empirically (Pascarella 1987; Stage in press). In contrast, most of us seem to assume that students at widely differing levels of intellectual development will respond similarly to influences of the campus environment. Or we assume that students of widely differing psychosocial types are influenced positively or negatively by similar experiences. So rather than attempting to use developmental or psychosocial types to categorize students for analysis, we use only easily obtained demographic indicators. This method directly contradicts research based on student development theory, which tells us that students of differing psychological makeup respond in various ways to the same environmental stimulations.

A Monocultural Literature

Typically research conducted on college students focuses on the majority, middle- to upper-middle-class students attending a residential university. However, large segments of the population are not majority, and increasing numbers of students commute to and from home. Some work has been done to let us know who these students are, and strategies have been developed to help them negotiate a college campus that may seem alien to them.

Unfortunately most of the psychologically based student development theory is founded in studies of the mainstream college student. Little research has focused on the development of students outside the mainstream culture, although these are frequently the students who need the most help in negotiating a culturally different environment (Manning and Stage 1988).

Fortunately, the sociologically based outcomes research has begun to focus on some of these special populations (Fox 1986; Healy, Mitchell, and Mourton 1987; Pascarella, Smart, and Nettles 1987; Richardson and Bender 1987; Wolfle 1985). As positive as these nascent efforts are, some populations of students (e.g., the learning disabled, homosexuals, native Americans) are not easily identified nor numerous enough to be included in research currently being conducted. For these particular populations, qualitative approaches are probably needed.

Process Models for Practice

Identifying process models to help apply theory to research can prove frustrating. Only a few good process models link research and practice. Donald Blocher (1987) describes three basic types of conceptual frameworks in the counseling profession. First are the basic philosophical assumptions derived from global and abstract representations of human experience. They are empirically untestable but help professionals clarify their values. Second are the scientific theories focusing on and guiding empirical inquiry. And third are the process models, which serve as a guide for those attempting to implement theory.

Blocher described process models as cognitive maps that provide a direct and immediate guide for implementation and specify appropriate action in a given situation. Such models should be evaluated in terms of outcomes. Also important, they should be constantly polished and modified as experience provides more knowledge about their practical usefulness.

Several multi-dimensional process models are useful to guide the development of the college student. The COSPA II cube focuses on differing clientele, roles, and competencies. Similarly, the Colorado State University cube focuses on target, purpose, and method of intervention (see Rodgers 1980). An administrator attempting to solve a campus problem may refer to the Kuh (1984) cube, which requires the identification of disciplinary perspective, intervention theory, and student affairs function. The behavior engineering model (Gilbert 1978) focuses on the interplay between environmental supports and an individual's behavior in three categories: information, instrumentation, and motivation.

These models have provided rich fodder for those who study student development and student affairs organizations. They have also guided many administrators who are informed and sophisticated enough to choose a theory to fit their particular issue. Unfortunately, many of those who work with college students have just begun to explore student development and outcomes. Models with a wide range of possible options might not provide enough guidance for those with limited experience and insight.

At the other extreme, the literature is replete with idiosyncratic articles that discuss implementation of a particular theory at a particular institution with a particular set of problems. Such articles are too specific and do not help identify and match implementation strategies to wider environmental and institutional conditions.

Less experienced practitioners may need process models as defined by Donald Blocher (1987) that outline in a general way how to implement a specific theory and include guides for appraisal, action, and evaluation. Carole Widick and Deborah Simpson (1978) provide an excellent example of the Perry model applied to the college classroom. Similar models focusing on other aspects of the college experience would be useful.

Recommendations

In the midst of these discoveries and complex conditions, Professor Russell, who had thought she would be spending most of her first semester exploring and developing new research ideas, found herself spending more time than she wanted developing her course. Fortunately her efforts provided several options toward which to direct energy and research.

For each of the three problem areas, Professor Russell identified a solution to the short-term problem (information for the class), as well as the long-term problem (focus of research).

Two Separate Literatures

She drew from both bodies of literature in her course on development of the college student. College students generally do not develop where there are no positive outcomes. Those who work with students need to learn which aspects of the campus environment have positive effects on achievement, persistence, and satisfaction. Russell made sure her class read the bodies of research, drew parallels between them, and identified gaps in information.

As a researcher, Russell began to fill in the gap between the two literatures. For example, using student development theory to inform outcomes research, she studied predictors of changes in majors according to John Holland's (1985) framework. She hypothesized that satisfactory campus experiences might be rooted in different activities for an artistic type than for a social type.

Similarly, outcomes research guided a study of student development; possibly studies of developmental growth of students underestimated the importance of peer influences. Russell designed a study to explore the effects of peer pressure on cognitive development of college students.

The Monocultural Literature

To find readings for the class on students outside the mainstream culture, Russell supplemented higher education readings with those from other disciplines. Since the middle seventies, much counseling literature has focused on the problems counseling professionals have in dealing with those who are culturally different from themselves. Those cross-cultural perspectives provided rich resources to better understand students. Psychology, anthropology, and political science also provided insight into the difficulties inherent in negotiating a culturally foreign system and the effects those adjustments might have on student satisfaction and motivation.

Another possibility for Russell was research on the development of particular student populations. Because there were too few nonmajority students to conduct the quantitative multi-variable research traditionally used to predict outcomes, Russell had to shift her research style and "tool up" for a naturalistic study.

Process Models

Russell required students to read the "how we do it" articles as well as the broader, less directive process models. With a firm knowledge of a specific development theory, the class developed its own process models. Linking "scientific theory" to actual practice provided students with a sense of satisfaction and professionalism as well as a more thorough knowledge of the theory being studied.

This third problem presented Russell with a third possibility for research. She began to develop and polish a process model for her "favorite" student development theory. She designed the model to provide more direction for new professionals as well as for older professionals who had trouble applying theory in their daily practice.

Conclusion

We can learn from Russell's experiences. First, we can pay more attention to one another as researchers. It is tempting to focus our attention on those who are testing similar frameworks, operating within the same paradigm, and speaking our language. Unfortunately, this limited focus stifles creativity and reinforces narrow notions of research rather than encouraging us to explore new directions.

Second, research and researchers must be flexible. It is easier to use the same populations, types of variables, and modes of analysis than it is to expand our repertoires. Unfortunately, these self-limiting practices do little to enlarge our knowledge of the development and outcomes we study. To accommodate the non-mainstream students' experiences, which presumably differ from the majority students', we must use more open-ended ways of collecting information. Researchers may need to adopt more of a cultural perspective and focus at first on small numbers of students. Considering a broader range of situations and experiences may lead to new models of development and satisfaction.

Finally, we must work to develop process models with tangible links to practice. These models will enable professionals to use the knowledge that researchers are generating.

Bibliography

Astin, Alexander. *Achieving Educational Excellence.* San Francisco: JosseyBass, 1985.

____. *The College Environment.* Washington, D.C.: American Council on Education, 1968.

Bean, John. "Dropouts and Turnover: The Synthesis and Test of a Causal Model of Student Attrition." *Research in Higher Education* 12, no. 2 (1980): 155–187.

Blocher, Donald. "On the Uses and Misuses of the Term 'Theory.'" *Journal of Counseling and Development* 66 (October 1987): 67–68.

Ethington, Corinna, and Lee Wolfle. "A Structural Model of Mathematics Achievement for Men and Women." *American Educational Research Journal* 23 (Spring 1986): 65–75.

Ewell, Peter, ed. *Assessing Educational Outcomes.* New Directions for Institutional Research, No. 47. San Francisco: Jossey-Bass, 1985.

Feldman, Kenneth, and Theodore Newcomb. *The Impact of College on Students.* San Francisco: Jossey-Bass, 1973.

Fox, Richard. "Application of a Conceptual Model of College Withdrawal to Disadvantaged Students." *American Educational Research Journal* 23 (Fall 1986): 415–424.

Gilbert, Thomas. *Human Competence: Engineering Worthy Performance.* New York: McGraw-Hill, 1978.

Healy, Charles, Judith Mitchell, and Don Mourton. "Age and Grade Differences in Career Development among Community College Students." *Review of Higher Education* 10 (Spring 1987): 247–258.

Holland, John. *Making Vocational Choices: A Theory of Vocational Personalities and Work Environments.* Englewood Cliffs, N.J.: Prentice-Hall, 1986.

Kuh, George. "A Framework for Understanding Student Affairs Work." *Journal of College Student Personnel* 25 (January 1984): 25–38.

Manning, Kathleen, and Frances K. Stage. "Personalizing the College Context from a Cultural Perspective." Paper presented at the Annual Meeting of the National Association of Student Personnel Administrators, St. Louis, Missouri, March 1988. Copy in my possession.

Mentkowski, Marcia, and Arthur Chickering. "Linking Educators and Researchers in Setting a Research Agenda for Undergraduate Education." *Review of Higher Education* 11 (Winter 1987): 137–160.

Pace, Robert. "Historical Perspectives on Student Outcomes: Assessment with Implications for the Future." *NASPA Journal* 22 (Fall 1984): 10–18.

Pascarella, Ernest. "The Development of Critical Thinking: Does College Make a Difference?" *Journal of College Student Development* 30, no.1 (January 1989): 19–26.

Pascarella, Ernest, John Smart, and Michael Nettles. "The Influence of College on Self-concept: A Consideration of Race and Gender Differences." *American Educational Research Journal* 24 (Spring 1987): 49–77.

Pascarella, Ernest, and J. R. Staver. "The Influence of On-campus Work in Science on Science Career Choice in College: A Causal Modeling Approach." *Review of Higher Education* 8 (Spring 1985): 229–245.

Richardson, Richard, and Louis Bender. *Fostering Minority Access and Achievement in Higher Education.* San Francisco: Jossey-Bass, 1987.

Rodgers, Robert. "Theories Underlying Student Development. In *Student Development in Higher Education,* edited by Don Creamer. Cincinnati: ACPA Media, 1980.

Stage, Frances K. "Motivation, Academic and Social Integration, and the Early Dropout. " *American Educational Research Journal,* in press.

_____. "Student Typologies and the Study of College Outcomes." *Review of Higher Education* 11 (Spring 1988): 247–257.

Tinto, Vincent. "Dropout from Higher Education: A Theoretical Synthesis of Recent Research." *Review of Educational Research* 45 (Winter 1975): 89–125.

_____. *Leaving College: Rethinking the Causes and Cures of Student Attrition.* Chicago: University of Chicago Press, 1987.

Widick, Carole and Deborah Simpson. "Developmental Concepts in College Instruction." In *Encouraging Development in College Students,* edited by Clyde Parker. Minneapolis: University of Minnesota Press, 1978.

Wolfle, Lee. "Postsecondary Educational Attainment among Whites and Blacks." *American Educational Research Journal* 22 (Winter 1985): 501–525.

Note

Frances K. Stage is assistant professor of educational leadership and policy studies at Indiana University, Bloomington.

Building Community

John W. Gardner

We know that where community exists it confers upon its members identity, a sense of belonging, and a measure of security. It is in communities that the attributes that distinguish humans as social creatures are nourished. Communities are the ground-level generators and preservers of values and ethical systems. The ideals of justice and compassion are nurtured in communities. The natural setting for religion is the religious community.

The breakdown of communities has had a serious disintegrating effect on the behavior of individuals. We have all observed the consequences in personal and social breakdown. The casualties stream through the juvenile courts and psychiatrists' offices and drug abuse clinics. There has been much talk of the breakup of the nuclear family as a support structure for children. We must remind ourselves that in an earlier era support came not only from the nuclear family but from extended family and community. The child moved in an environment filled with people concerned for his future—not always concerned in a kindly spirit, but concerned. A great many children today live in environments where virtually no one pays attention unless they break the law.

We have seen in recent years a troubling number of very successful, highly rewarded individuals in business and government engage in behavior that brought them crashing down. One explanation is that they betrayed their values for some gratification they couldn't resist (e.g., money, power, sensual pleasure). Another possible explanation is that they had no values to betray, that they were among the many contemporary individuals who had never had roots in a framework of values, or had torn loose from their roots, torn loose from their moorings. Shame, after all, is a social emotion. Individuals who experience it feel that they have transgressed some group standard of propriety or right conduct. But if they have no sense of membership in any group, the basis for feeling ashamed is undermined. And there is an African proverb, "Where there is no shame, there is no honor."

In World War II studies of soldiers in combat, the most common explanation given for acts of extraordinary courage was "I didn't want to let my buddies down." Reflect on the number of individuals in this transient, pluralistic society who have no allegiance to any group, the members of which they would not want to let down.

We know a great deal about the circumstances of contemporary life that erode our sense of community. And we are beginning to understand how our passion for individualism led us away from community. But so far there has been very little considered advice to help us on the road back to community. Many of us are persuaded of the need to travel that road and have no doubt that it exists; but finding it will require that we be clear as to what we're seeking. We can never bring the traditional community back, and if we could it would prove to be hopelessly anachronistic.

The Characteristics of Community

The traditional community was homogenerous. We live with heterogeneity and must design communities to handle it.

The traditional community experienced relatively little change from one decade to the next and resented the little that it did experience. We must design communities that can survive change and, when necessary, seek change.

The traditional community commonly demanded a high degree of conformity. Because of the nature of the world we live in, our communities must be pluralistic and adaptive, fostering individual freedom and responsibility within a framework of group obligation.

The traditional community was often unwelcoming to strangers and all too ready to reduce its communication with the external world. Hard realities require that present-day communities be in continuous and effective touch with the outside world, and our system of values requires that they be inclusive.

The traditional community could boast generations of history and continuity. Only a few communities today can hope to enjoy any such heritage. They must continuously rebuild their shared culture, must consciously foster the norms and values that will ensure their continued integrity.

In short, much as we cherish the thought of the traditional community, we shall have to build anew, seeking to reincarnate some of the cherished values of the old communities in forms appropriate to contemporary social organization.

Most Americans who endorse the idea of community today have in mind communities that strive to exemplify the best of contemporary values, communities that are inclusive, that balance individual freedom and group obligation, that foster the release of human possibilities, that invite participation and the sharing of leadership tasks.

A glance at the contemporary scene reveals diverse kinds of community. Most familiar to us are territorially bounded communities such as towns, suburbs, neighborhoods, and so on, but we must look also at other kinds of community.

Some congregations create what I regard as genuine communities though their members may be scattered over a large metropolitan area. The workplace may constitute a community even though it draws its members from a wide area. Some of the smaller professional and academic fields and some religious orders are communities even though they may be very widely dispersed geographically. Some public schools are communities in the best sense of the word while others are simply geographical locations where young people spend a certain number of allotted hours performing required activities. The same appears to be true of congregations. Some are authentic communities, others are simply locations where unconnected people come together on Sunday. The same contrasts may be found in the workplace.

Wholeness and Belonging

In seeking to explain such differences one is driven to think analytically about the ingredients or characteristics of community. I shall list eight ingredients. The reader is invited to add to the list or define the ingredients in other ways. The important thing at this stage is to get past the generalized idea of community to an understanding of what conditions or circumstances make it real. In order to focus my study I chose four areas for special attention—the city, the workplace, the school, and the church. I shall draw examples from all four, trying not to confuse the reader in the process.

Wholeness incorporating diversity. A community is obviously less of a community if fragmentation or divisiveness exists—and if the rifts are deep it is no community at all. Schools in which faculty and students carry on a kind of trench warfare, congregations divided into cliques, cities in which people of diverse ethnic origins form mutually hostile groups—these are obviously not healthy communities.

We expect and want diversity, and there will be dissension in the best of communities. But in vital communities, cooperation, compromise, and consensus-building will be widely shared pursuits. In the best circumstances such communities will have instruments and processes for conflict resolution. Some cities have created special boards to deal with disputes between groups of citizens. Others have interracial councils and provisions for citizens from one segment of the community to know and work with citizens from other segments. Healthy communities respect diversity but seek common ground and a larger unity.

I have long advocated that in cities, leaders from all segments of the community come together in *networks of responsibility* to set goals and to tackle the city's most pressing problems. The community has a better chance of achieving wholeness if local government collaborates closely and continuously with private sector institutions, profit and nonprofit.

The skills necessary to the resolution of group conflict should be taught in both high school and college. All men and women in positions of leadership, government, or private sector, should be schooled in dispute resolution and all of the antipolarization arts.

A shared culture. The possibility of wholeness is considerably enhanced if the community has a shared culture; i.e., shared norms and values. If the community is lucky (and fewer and fewer are), it will have a shared history and tradition. It will have symbols of group identity, its "story," its legends, and heroes. Social cohesion will be advanced if the group's norms and values are explicit. Values that are never expressed are apt to be taken for granted and not adequately conveyed to young people and newcomers. The well-functioning community provides many opportunities to express values in relevant action. If it believes, for example, that the individual should in some measure serve the community, it will provide many opportunities for young people to engage in such service.

To maintain the sense of belonging and the dedication and commitment so essential to community life, members need inspiring reminders of shared goals and values. A healthy community affirms itself and builds morale and motivation through ceremonies and celebrations that honor the symbols of shared identity and enable members to rededicate themselves. This doesn't mean that they suppress internal criticism or deny their flaws.

One or another form of education about the community, its history, and its purpose is necessary to introduce young people to the shared past and present.

"We" and "They"

Good internal communication. Members of a well-functioning community communicate freely with one another. One of the advantages of the small group is that frequent face-to-face communication is possible. In large systems (cities, corporations) much conscious effort is needed to keep the channels of communication open among all elements of the system, and to combat the "we-they" barriers that impede the flow.

There must be occasions when members gather, there must be meeting spaces. In cities or neighborhoods there must be organizations willing to serve as meeting grounds.

Whatever the type of community, people have to believe that they can have their say. Between manager and worker, governing body and citizens, teacher and students, pastor and parishioners, there must be honest and open two-way communication. Each must understand what the other needs and wants.

In cities, much of the communication will be through the media. Civic leaders and institutions must urge the media toward responsible coverage, but it is a mistake to depend entirely on such urging. Leaders should create an information-sharing network among a wide variety of institutions and organizations. Maximum use should be made of institutions that can serve as neutral conveners—e.g., community foundations, community colleges, universities, churches. A community is strengthened if there are occasions (celebrations, retreats, outings, etc.) on which extensive informal interaction is possible.

Caring, trust, and teamwork. A good community nurtures its members and fosters an atmosphere of trust. They both protect and give a measure of autonomy to the individual. There is a spirit of mutuality and cooperation. Everyone is included.

Such attitudes make it possible to work together on necessary common tasks. Undergirding the teamwork is a widely shared commitment to the common good, an awareness by all that they need one another and must pool their talent, energy, and resources. There is a feeling that when the team wins everybody wins. Tasks that require the sharing of skills and resources foster the habit of collaboration, mutual support, and a willingness to put the good of the team first.

A healthy community deals forthrightly with dissension and "we-they" polarities, accepting diversity and dissent but using all the various mediating, coalition-building, and conflict resolution procedures to find common ground.

It is necessary to add that a community can be too tightly knit, suppressing dissent and constraining the creativity of its members.

Leadership and Participation

Group maintenance and government. A functioning community has institutional provisions for group maintenance or governing. In a corporation it is the board of directors, management, and the chain of command. In a college it is the trustees, administration, faculty council, and student government. In a town or city it is not only the formal governing mechanisms but the nongovernmental leadership exercised through various nonprofit institutions.

One task is the maintenance of some reasonable measure of order and adherence to respected customs and norms. Violence, vandalism, crime, and drugs can destroy every vestige of community—as some urban public schools have discovered to their sorrow. Healthy communities ensure a safe environment for their members.

No less important is the reasonably efficient performance of community services. Community leaders may have the highest of civic ideals, but they also have to ensure that the garbage is collected, the streets maintained, the children educated, and so on. Collaboration between public and private sectors is essential to the performance of some of these tasks.

In a swiftly changing environment, communities and organizations must look ahead. The best of them engage in one or another form of strategic planning and priority setting, not through occasional one-shot "futures" reports but on a regular and continuing basis. In cities, governments and the private sector must collaborate on such forward planning.

Participation and the sharing of leadership tasks. The culture of the healthy community encourages individual involvement in the pursuit of shared purposes. Cities can get significant participation from nongovernmental leaders through hearings, advisory boards, and citizen commissions. Strong neighborhood groups are important; and a wide range of nonprofit civic groups and institutions can play a role.

It is not uncommon in our towns and cities today that the groups most involved in the affairs of the community all come from one or two segments of the community. All segments must participate. In a city or an organization, the possibility of effective participation is increased if everyone is kept informed, and if individuals feel that they have a say. That means the system cannot be autocratically run or excessively centralized. Leaders must devolve initiative and responsibility widely throughout the system. We must never forget that our conception of community involves the participation of mature and responsible individuals. We don't want "community" bought at the price of the individual's mindless submission to the group. The good community will find a productive balance between individuality and group obligation.

Everyone need not participate actively with respect to any given community. We must guard the *right* to participate while recognizing that some will choose not to do so. Individuals expending enormous energies holding their families together may be thankfully passive members of their church congregation. The individual who is an activist in the workplace community may be a passive member of the neighborhood association.

Links to the Future

Development of young people. In a community of the sort we would applaud, the opportunities for individual growth will be numerous and varied for all members. And mature members will ensure that young people grow up with a sense of obligation to the community. Beginning in elementary and high school, boys and girls will learn to take responsibility for the well-being of any group they are in—a seemingly small step but without doubt the first step toward responsible community participation, and for that matter the first step in leadership development. On the playing field, and in group activities in and out of school and college, they will learn teamwork. Through volunteer and intern experiences outside of school they will learn how the adult world works and will have the experience of serving their society. And they will learn that responsible dissent and creative alternative solutions may also serve the community. Every organization serving the community should find ways of involving young people.

Links with the outside world. The sound community has seemingly contradictory responsibilities: it must defend itself from the forces in the outside environment that undermine its integrity, yet it must maintain open, constructive, and extensive relations with the world beyond its boundaries. The school, for example, must be in some respects a haven for its students, capable of shutting out some of the most destructive aspects of city life, but it can maintain itself as a strong institution only through extensive community relations.

Fragmentation and Common Ground

In listing these eight attributes of an ideal community, my interest is not in depicting Utopia. My interest is to get us away from vague generalizations about "community" and to identify some ingredients that we can work on constructively.

I've mentioned cities, neighborhoods, schools, churches, and the workplace. Many universities are to a deplorable degree "non-communities." Government agencies and a great variety of non-profit institutions—museums, charities, cause organizations—have the same problem. The generalizations I have offered apply most easily and readily to social entities of moderate size. Obviously it is difficult to think in the same terms about a huge city, or a nation, or the world. Yet in those far-larger settings the need is even more desperate.

The problem of the typical American city today is fragmentation. The list of the substantive *problems* of the city does not define the city's problem. The city's problem is that it can't pull itself together to deal with any item on the list. It is not a coherent entity. It is broken into segments that have sharply differing purposes, segments that have shown little talent for understanding one another. Or willingness to try.

Any effort by the city to accomplish some larger purpose gets mired in the tensions, cross-purposes, and ultimate stalemate among the segments. The city cannot think like a community nor can it act like one.

The soundest solution to the problem is for leaders from all segments, government and private sector, profit and non-profit, to come together in what I call *a network of responsibility* to think about, talk about, and act in behalf of their city. It happened in Pittsburgh in the 1950s and modern Pittsburgh was born. It happened in New York City in the mid-1970s and the worst fiscal crisis in New York history was solved.

When it happens, there does indeed emerge a constituency for the whole. People come to realize that if the city goes downhill all segments suffer. Obviously all disagreements do not get settled, but the search for common ground achieves some success, and the very fact of searching creates a better climate.

Every institution in the city should have concern for the whole city, and not just concern for its segment of the city or, more commonly, concern solely for itself. Often even the most high-minded organizations have little regard for the community around them. I described the situation facetiously at a national meeting of voluntary organizations recently by saying. "A voluntary group may be profoundly and high-mindedly committed to care of the terminally ill and never notice that the community of which it is a part is itself terminally ill." We must seek to restore a sense of community in our cities; but it may be that the most fruitful approach will be from the ground up, through the more familiar settings I discussed earlier—the school, the church, the workplace, and so on.

How can people work to make their metropolis a community when most of them have never experienced a sense of community in any familiar setting? Men and women who have come to understand, in their own intimate settings, the principles of "wholeness incorporating diversity," the arts of diminishing polarization, the meaning of teamwork and participation will be far better allies in the effort to build elements of community into the metropolis, the nation, and the world.

Developing Learning Communities

CHARLES C. SCHROEDER

Recent reports on the status of higher education—particularly the reports *Involvement in Learning* (Study Group on the Conditions of Excellence in American Higher Education, 1984) and *An American Imperative: Higher Expectations for Higher Education* (Wingspread Group on Higher Education, 1993)—clearly indicate that promoting student learning is the responsibility of both faculty and student affairs educators. The reports broadly conceive student learning to include such outcomes as understanding of self and others, acquisition of knowledge, mastery of content, development of various skills and competencies, and sensitivity to value issues. Many of these learning outcomes could be achieved by intentionally designing residence halls as learning communities. Within such communities, students would learn self-knowledge, self-confidence, and self-worth. These learning communities would foster patience, tolerance, empathy, responsibility, and interpersonal competence. Such humanitarian values as justice, social responsibility, and intercultural understanding would be components of the "implicit" community curriculum. Students would be encouraged to assume a variety of roles, thereby clarifying their values and identifying their strengths and weaknesses. By working together to achieve various community tasks, students would develop decision-making and consensus-building skills. Obviously, many residential experiences promote the achievement of some of these outcomes, albeit some more by default than by design.

The basic premise of this chapter is that learning communities can be developed in residence halls if staff understand the potent impact of peer-group influences on learning and student development. Astin (1992, p. 398) maintains that "the student's peer group is the single most potent source of influence on growth and development during the undergraduate years." Other research has consistently demonstrated that peer-group influences are primary agents in promoting student learning and personal development (Feldman and Newcomb, 1969; Chickering and Reisser, 1993; Pascarella and Terenzini, 1991; Astin, 1977). Unfortunately, staff often fail to link peer-group influences and educational outcomes. Indeed, many traditional approaches to residence education unintentionally create structures that limit student learning and personal development (Schroeder, Nicholls, and Kuh, 1983).

The goal of this chapter is to demonstrate the importance of developing learning communities that maximize peer-group influences. It delineates conditions and principles that foster peer community development, as well as contrasting traditional approaches to residence life with strategies that promote learning communities. A comprehensive example of an effective residential learning community is presented with a description of four principles essential to the development of such communities. Additional examples of learning communities are illustrated, and new perspectives and roles for staff interested in promoting student learning and development are explained.

Community: A Context for Learning and Development

Although "community" is an essential component of promoting learning and student development, no common understanding of its meaning appears to exist among residence educators. For many, community is "traditionally described as a small number of people living in the same area and linked by common values, practices, and goals" (Spitzberg and Thorndike, 1992, p. 7). Some theorists suggest that community encompasses a number of components, including the following: sharing goals, responsibilities, and communication (Mable, Terry, and Duvall, 1977), mutually agreed-on purposes, transcendent themes, and social contracts (Crookston, 1980), and peer-group influence, territoriality, and transcendent values (Tollefson, 1975). It is precisely these components—commonality of purpose, unity, transcendent values, and cohesiveness—that distinguish a community from a traditional residential unit. For example, students living on residence hall floors often have difficulty identifying commonality of purpose and seldom regard themselves as a unified, cohesive group. Distinctions between communities and traditional residential arrangements are relatively transparent. But what features differentiate residential *learning* communities from such common residential arrangements as living-learning centers, special group housing, and theme housing?

Defining Learning Communities

Astin (1985, p. 161) defines learning communities as "small subgroups of students . . . characterized by a common sense of purpose . . . that can be used to build a sense of group identity, cohesiveness, and uniqueness that encourage continuity and the integration of diverse curricular and co-curricular experiences." As compared to other residential arrangements, residential learning communities are ones that "encourage continuity and the integration of diverse curricular and co-curricular experiences." These components of intentionality and integration, as well as the characteristics listed below, make them unique and distinctive from other residential units.

The research literature on residence halls is replete with references to characteristics of such learning communities; however, the central theme in all of this research is student involvement. As students' involvement increases, they benefit more from their educational experiences (Astin, 1977, 1992). Effective learning communities are characterized by a high degree of student influence, control, and ownership. Students *matter*. They are central to the enterprise, and their participation in a variety of roles is essential. According to Schlossberg (1989), involvement and mattering are linked in a critical fashion. She claims that "the creation of environments that clearly indicate to all students that they matter will urge them to greater involvement" (p. 14). Learning communities are also characterized by students who share common interests and purposes, high degrees of social interaction, and social stability that ensures continuity of relationships (Blimling and Schuh, 1981; DeCoster and Mable, 1980; Kuh, Schuh, Whitt, and Associates, 1991).

The research on residence halls has likewise identified additional social and physical environmental factors that must be addressed when developing residential learning communities. Social environmental constraints include diversity of student characteristics, group size, absence of peer support, roommate and floormate incompatibility, and an absence of student influence in governance (Moos, 1979; Schroeder and Jackson, 1987). These constraints can be minimized by systematically matching roommates and floormates on the basis of similar characteristics, encouraging the development of peer governance systems, and ensuring social stability by allowing students to live in their units for as long as they desire.

Certain architectural features can also inhibit the development of effective learning communities. Stark institutional atmospheres, isolated and inaccessible "group rooms," and long and narrow double-loaded corridors often combine to isolate students rather than encouraging their social interaction and group identity (Schroeder, 1980, 1981). Sommer (1969) has referred to traditional residence hall architecture as "hard architecture"—architecture that is impervious to human imprint! Such architectural constraints can be overcome by expecting students to personalize their physical environment by painting and decorating, providing centrally located group lounges, and designating single-room options to reduce density and crowding.

To summarize, residential communities that promote student learning and development are characterized by a high degree of student participation and involvement, control of bounded space, common interests and purposes, high degrees of social interaction and social stability, transcendent values, and student influence. In effective learning communities, students know they matter—their participation and involvement are central to their day-to-day experience.

Strategies That Promote Learning Communities

Traditional approaches to residential life usually disregard the significance of essential conditions that foster learning and personal development—such conditions as the creation of reference groups with common interests, shared and controlled space, transcendent values, and broad-based member involvement. For example, unsystematic and random assignment of students to rooms and floors increases the diversity of student characteristics, thereby limiting students' ability to identify commonalities. The time-consuming and often narrow emphasis of staff on developing student governments rarely ensures broad-based student participation in *governance*. Staff-initiated, top-down programming approaches frequently result in activities that are highly valued by staff but often regarded with minimal interest by residents. As Stamatakos (1991) suggests, these "educational programs" usually reflect the latest whim of pop psychology and are rarely linked to specific academic or educational outcomes. Likewise, as described in Chapter One, requiring resident assistants to conduct a certain number of "developmental programs" each semester seems to have a minimum impact on student learning and personal development. While these programs are often beneficial to particular individuals, often they do not involve students in matters essential and enduring for peer-group development.

In the traditional programmed approach to residence life, efficiency and authority are valued, whereas broad-based student involvement, participation, and influence are actually minimized. Staff exert authority through articulating housing goals, monitoring student adjustment to institutional regulations, and designing programs to facilitate students' attainment of housing goals. Natural interaction among students is compromised; peer association is manipulated through community-building programs designed for students by administrators. Certain policies, particularly those that prohibit students from painting or otherwise personalizing their living environment, discourage individual and group responsibility for the environment. Social stability and long-term enduring relationships are jeopardized by the forced mobility of students that results from certain types of assignment policies, procedures, and practices. As a result, peer-group influences are minimized, since group norms must be renegotiated frequently.

Although the traditional approach to residence life has merit, it has certain limitations as well. First, the approach generally focuses on staff and their interests and preferences as opposed to students' needs and aspirations. Second, since control is primarily vested in staff, there is little broad-based student involvement and influence. The result is that students are often more than willing for staff to do for them, as opposed to assuming individual and collective responsibility for their community. In addition, when responsibility for community development is vested primarily in staff as opposed to students, the environment limits opportunities for learning and personal development. Learning becomes limited to short-term staff interventions instead of day-to-day learning activities in which residents are highly invested. Finally, the traditional approach ends up focusing staff attention and programmatic intervention on the needs of the individual resident—usually to the exclusion of the needs of the group.

A number of outcomes are associated with such traditional approaches. If students are systematically denied opportunities to become involved and influence the direction of their lives in their residence halls, they often choose to leave and seek housing off campus. Other outcomes such as excessive damages, hostile versus supportive interaction, frequent judicial cases, poor academic performance, and lack of personal and group responsibility for behavior are often characteristic of a system that restricts broad-based student participation.

In contrast to traditional residence life approaches, strategies for developing learning communities encourage and require grassroots collaboration and cooperation by individual students on each floor. Students are *expected* to assume responsibility for most aspects of their social and physical environments. Obviously, staff are still needed to facilitate group development; however, their primary role is to create conditions that foster commonality of purpose, student involvement, reference-group formation, and collaborative partnerships with faculty and academic administrators.

Since learning communities are fostered by commonality and consistency of purpose, shared values, and transcendent themes, residence life staff can create conditions that encourage the emergence of these elements. Commonality of purpose can be achieved by organizing students' floor units around transcendent themes like engineering, pharmacy, and natural science or by creating units formed on the basis of other common educational interests. As Astin (1992) suggests, keys to peer-group formation are the creation of common ground on which identification can occur and the provision of opportunities for sustained interaction and the integration of diverse curricular and co-curricular experiences.

The following comprehensive example illustrates how the preceding elements and conditions can be combined to create a unique and effective peer learning community for students with similar academic interests and aspirations.

An Effective Residential Learning Community

During the mid 1970s, engineering enrollments on many campuses experienced dramatic declines. Although a number of factors contributed to the problem, nonpersisting engineers expressed concern over the lack of strong peer-group support and the relatively inactive role of upper-class students in helping new students adjust. These concerns prompted a collaborative effort by Auburn University's School of Engineering and the Housing Department to structure a unique learning community for engineering students.

To address the perceived lack of peer-group support and to organize around the students' commonality of interest in the engineering curriculum, three consecutive floors in a men's residence hall were designated for the learning community. To further facilitate group development, a special lounge was constructed by walling off a previously unused entrance foyer. Wall-to-wall carpeting was added to the lounge, and students were encouraged to construct their own furniture. Remote computer terminals were installed in an alcove of the lounge, and access to the terminals was restricted to engineering residents and their guests by the use of a special key.

Additional design strategies included matching roommates on the basis of complementary personality types (as measured by the Myers-Briggs Type Indicator) and selecting outstanding upper-class engineering students to serve as resident advisers. The roommate matching strategy helped create commonality in the roommate relationship and was important in achieving an appropriate balance of challenge and support in the residential unit. Students were *expected* to actively participate in structuring their physical and social environments. Residents were encouraged, for example, to personalize their living areas by painting; wall papering; paneling; adding plants, posters, and drapes; constructing lofts, bookcases, and other furniture; refinishing doors; plastering ceilings; and replacing fixtures. Room painting included covering the walls with murals, super graphics, caricatures, and slogans. Students also marked the entrance to their engineering lounge by painting the word "Engineers" on the plate-glass window.

A community governance model was implemented to structure the social environment. Residents developed and maintained floor standards and even retained the right to remove a student from the unit if he consistently violated the standards. The limited numbers of highly coveted private rooms were allocated by the residents themselves based on seniority and students' contributions to the floor unit. Students managed their floor funds for projects they deemed worthy of support. Various committees were also formed to handle special tasks, including student recruitment, scholarship, social events, and physical improvements, most of which were designed to ensure the social and academic *integration* of members with the learning community. The student recruitment committee established a recruiting booth on campus during Engineering Day and interviewed prospective residents for the special unit. These interviews were the first steps in creating "anticipatory socialization." They also developed an elaborate orientation program designed to integrate new members through formal and informal rites of passage. The scholarship committee established study hours for the freshmen to ensure that academic goals would be achieved. The social committee distributed football jerseys with "Engineers" emblazoned on the front and encouraged everyone to wear them to classes and special events. This group also organized the engineers' participation in the annual Auburn University blood drive. Traditionally, the engineers had won the award for the highest participation rate among campus living units. The physical improvement committee took responsibility for painting stairwells and hallways as well as supervising the general upkeep of the floors and lounge. This committee also developed a general logo, which was painted at the entrance to each floor. To paraphrase Astin (1985), the committee structures were useful in building the identity and cohesiveness that encouraged continuity and integration of curricular and co-curricular experiences.

In subsequent years, student response to the program was so positive that the learning community was expanded from twenty-seven to fifty-four rooms and occupancy increased from fifty to eighty-six residents. Although residents continued to express high satisfaction with their unique community, increased size appeared to have a detrimental effect on group identity, cohesiveness, and reference-group formation.

One solution to this problem was to place more emphasis on small-group development within the overall community by the creation of a house system. To implement the house concept, one student room within each nine-room house was converted to a group room, which was routinely utilized for peer tutoring, studying, and social interaction. Residents personalized this space by painting, paneling, wall papering , and constructing their own furniture.

To further stimulate a sense of identity within each house, students decided to name their houses after seven of Auburn's most distinguished engineering alumni. House representatives obtained biographical data from the alumni office on twenty-five engineering graduates who had made outstanding contributions to engineering and who represented excellent career role models for aspiring engineers. Following a week of intense debate, seven alumni were chosen for the honor. Among those selected were an astronaut, a past president and chairman of the board of AT&T, a vice president of Eastern Airlines, a renowned chemical engineer and Rhodes Scholar, the president and chairman of the board of TRW Corporation, and two regional presidents of the Bell System. In honor of the distinguished alumni, floors became known as Mattingly House, Shephard House, and so on. A wooden plaque designating the unit (Mattingly House), along with a picture of the distinguished alumnus, was placed at the entrance of each house.

The alumni took an active interest in the engineering students, and many agreed to serve as "alumni in residence" during the year. Alumni also provided direct support to the various units through donations of computer terminals, chemical engineering libraries, furniture, and even monetary gifts.

Results of a longitudinal study indicated that residence in the special learning community was positively associated with a number of educational outcomes. For example, students in the special unit perceived their social climate as emphasizing more involvement, emotional support, academic achievement, and intellectuality than engineering students living on heterogeneous floors. Students in the special unit also achieved significantly higher grade-point averages and persistence rates in engineering than engineers who were not in the special program. Finally, students in the special unit had the highest retention rate of any living units on Auburn University's campus (Schroeder and Griffin, 1977).

Four Essential Principles for Learning Communities

Although the success of the engineering learning community was due to many factors, most of the impact can be explained by the *interaction* effect associated with four essential principles. These principles have been referred to as the four *I's:* involvement, investment, influence, and identity (Schroeder, 1993). In the development of learning communities, the principles are both sequential and cyclical —that is, increased student involvement leads to increased investment, which, in turn, leads to greater influence and eventual identity with the unit. The greater the identity, the greater the involvement, investment, and influence. Since these principles are integral to the establishment of any peer learning community, each element is examined in more depth.

Involvement

A true learning community encourages, expects, and rewards broad-based student involvement. The environment is characterized by an ethic of membership (Kuh, Schuh, Whitt, and Associates, 1991), which impels returning residents to assume major responsibility for orienting and integrating "new" members with the community. The environment is also characterized by a high degree of interaction, with students—*not staff*—assuming a multitude of roles. Members face common problems, share common tasks, and otherwise engage in meaningful activities together. As a consequence, everyone is important, everyone is needed, and everyone matters. Finally, learning communities characterized by a high degree of involvement emphasize supportive interactions, with students naturally helping one another with personal and academic problems.

Investment

Investment is a reflection of psychological ownership. It flows naturally from involvement. Investment is also a consequence of the ethic of care—students clearly care about one another and their group. Boundaries with respect to other groups are clear, and group or institutional property is guarded rather than damaged. Students are simply unwilling to have staff assume responsibility for them—they want to demonstrate their capabilities as the group takes on an ever-widening circle of challenge to enhance the group's status. As evidenced by the engineering learning community example, there are clear variations in status and roles, as well as in longevity of association. Rewards are provided for being a "good" member.

Influence

Influence is essentially a consequence of an ethic of responsibility, where control is vested in group members and students exert maximum influence over their physical and social environments. This principle—influence—is the cornerstone of student governance and a major characteristic of learning communities. In the engineering learning community, residents were expected to personalize their space, recruit and assign members, and develop a social contract whereby group standards were affirmed, both individually and collectively. Interactions are frequent and characterized by gentle confrontation rather than polite or passive-aggressive behaviors, Such groups also exhibit high expectations of one another. Again, in the case of the engineering learning community, residents had established clear goals regarding academic achievement, intramural competition, and participation in social activities. In such units, students feel important, their perspectives are valued, and their contributions are essential to the welfare of the group.

Identity

Learning communities characterized by a high degree of identity are ones that focus on commonalities and transcendent values. Affiliation and identification are a function of commonality of purpose. Students in such communities have shared symbols similar to those exhibited by members of the engineering learning community. In that community, identities were symbolized by wearing engineering jerseys and by marking floor units with house symbols, In such living units, members describe themselves in collective terms such as *we* and *us,* not *I* or *they*, reflecting their emphasis on common purposes and unity.

The four I's are principles *essential* to the development, implementation, and maintenance of learning communities. The principles are more process than content variables—that is, commonality and consistency of purpose (for instance, engineering, agriculture) can vary considerably between and among learning communities, but the four principles should remain relatively constant with regard to the maintenance of these communities.

Additional Examples of Learning Communities

Learning communities can be designed to accomplish a number of important educational objectives (Gabelnick, MacGregor, Matthews, and Smith, 1990). This section highlights a number of examples that accomplish this goal. Although not explicitly stated, the four I's are embedded in each example.

Common Curricular Experiences

One of the more pressing challenges in higher education is to create learning opportunities that provide a degree of coherence and integration for different disciplines. A number of institutions have implemented a variety of approaches for linking courses around a common theme or question so students have opportunities for deeper understanding and integration of the material they are learning, and more interaction with one another and their teachers. The Washington Center (Smith, 1993), for example, has sequenced two classes with the same enrollment and has linked smaller classes to larger ones, providing curricular continuity for students. The center has also sponsored freshman interest groups (FIGs), whereby fifteen triads of courses are offered around "areas of interest." One FIG might focus on prelaw as its "commonality," with students in this group registering for the following *same* three courses: American government, introduction to philosophy (ethics), and fundamentals of public speaking. All of these learning communities have been created outside of the residence halls. They could be even stronger if they were *integrated with* residential living.

Students in large institutions often have the greatest need for reference groups, yet large institutions are composed of huge student bodies with an enormous variety of majors, making it logistically difficult for substantial numbers of resident students to form peer-group relationships based on common interests or on common curricular experiences. The Washington Center model, however, holds promise for addressing this concern. Residence halls in large institutions could create learning communities around such transcendent themes as prelaw, premedicine, natural science, social science, and so on, with students registered for at least three "common courses." Then floor learning communities would develop around these common curricular experiences. Students in such communities would be more likely to help one another with study problems and test preparation and would be more likely to discuss choice of majors and career opportunities. The provision of these courses could be coordinated by faculty teams that would offer a degree of coherence and integration, both within the formal classrooms and as faculty affiliates in the residence hall learning communities. To implement such a program, residence life staff need to develop collaborative partnerships with faculty in particular colleges or departments. Once these partnerships are developed, the registration and course sequencing process is relatively simple. Two examples of this kind of approach are currently underway in the residence halls at the University of Missouri, Columbia. One project focuses on co-enrolling students who live on the same residence hall floors in a minimum of two common courses, usually English, math, psychology, or history. The other project, the Wakonse learning community, emphasizes substantive, ongoing interaction between 10 faculty members and approximately 200 students. Faculty and students participate in common courses in their community and frequently explore a variety of academic and career issues. They also work together in service learning projects and create innovative instructional approaches utilizing computer-enhanced multimedia technology.

Research conducted by the Washington Center on a variety of outcomes of model learning community programs indicates that retention, persistence, degree completion, and achievement have been substantially enhanced. Various active learning approaches have also resulted in increased critical thinking and other forms of intellectual development as well as enhanced student sense of belonging (Smith, 1991). If these results can be obtained through creating learning communities outside the residence halls, the potential educational impact would be even greater if these communities were self-sustaining residential learning communities based on the principles of the four I's and developed around specific academic or curricular themes.

Multicultural Learning Communities

Changing demographics have resulted in significant changes in the composition of student enrollments on many campuses. In particular, the significant increase in the number of African Americans, Hispanic Americans, and Asian Americans has, according to Kuh (1990, p. 85), created "unprecedented challenges to institutions of higher education in general and to student affairs professionals in particular." On many campuses, underrepresented groups band together in ethnic enclaves, maintaining a sense of their own cultural identity and often becoming marginalized in the process. Because of the separation and isolation of members of these groups, many white American students rarely interact with and benefit from associations with people of color. Residential learning communities provide opportunities for natural interaction among diverse students and help students see beyond stereotypes.

Residential learning communities could be structured around multicultural and interracial themes. The learning communities could be intentionally linked to courses that focus on such topics as the history of different cultures, interracial communication, and understanding and appreciation of cultural differences. Students might obtain a fourth academic credit in these classes by participating in a multicultural learning community. As part of the community, students would experience cultural differences in music, food, dress, and other customs. In communities such as these, learning outcomes would include understanding and appreciation of cultural differences, racial understanding, increased cultural awareness, and appreciation of diversity. Students would join the learning community based on their desire to achieve these objectives.

Service Learning Communities

The development of such humanitarian values as justice, altruism, good citizenship, and social responsibility could be achieved by learning communities developed around the theme of service. Although many campuses have encouraged volunteerism through departments of student volunteer programs, the often-fragmented and isolated nature of such programs does not allow for the full academic and social impact on students. This concern is the result of the limited "carry-over" effect that occurs when participation is not coupled with a common residential experience. This limitation can be overcome if learning communities are formed on the basis of supporting ongoing service projects that reflect the collective commitment of residents to altruism, social justice, and community service An example of such a program is the Adams School project at Saint Louis University (Schroeder, 1993). Students living on various floors of a high-rise building chose to "adopt" Adams School, a predominantly African-American, inner-city elementary school located within ten minutes of the campus. Each day students go to Adams to provide tutorial services for approximately fifty youngsters identified by the teachers as needing special, individualized attention. On weekends, students and members of the housing maintenance staff plaster and paint the interior of the school and work with the parents' association to improve other aspects of the school's physical and educational environments.

Many of the college students participating in the Adams School project have decided to change their majors from premedicine and prelaw to such fields as social work and teaching. This service learning experience has enabled these students to clarify their values and identify their various strengths and weaknesses. The experience has also increased their ongoing commitment to community service and civic responsibility.

With national service high on President Clinton's list of priorities, service learning residential communities should be a major component of a residence education program. By involving faculty and integrating certain courses (community psychology, political science, economics) into the learning community program, students will understand the clear connections between classroom and context, between theory and practice, between giving and taking. In such communities, students might engage in various simulations where they assume the role of mayor or city council member, developing and implementing strategies for addressing problems of health care, unemployment, and city services for the poor.

Addressing the Needs of Undecided Students

Institutions of higher learning are increasingly attempting to identify "students at risk." Although students most likely to be characterized as "at risk" are often underprepared students with poor high school grades, low entrance examination scores, and low class rank, increasingly institutions have found that "undecided students" are often at risk as well. Traditionally, undecided students must find their way to the academic advising and/or career planning offices. On presenting themselves, they are usually linked with a counselor who helps them through a process of values clarification, academic and career exploration, and goal setting.

Residential learning communities could be formed on the basis of helping undecided students "decide." Students could be offered a one-year learning community experience with the explicit goal of deciding on a major by the end of the year. Resources such as academic advising, career exploration, and counseling could be *integrated* into the learning community. For example, each week faculty from different academic disciplines could provide brief seminars and dialogue sessions on opportunities in their disciplines. Recent alums could discuss career opportunities associated with those disciplines. A centrally located room could be converted to an academic/career resource center, which might house computer terminals that run software such as SIGI (Systems of Interactive Guidance and Information), a well-respected computer-assisted career search program. Instead of resident advisers, the learning community could be staffed by peer career counselors under the direction of senior staff from the academic advising and career planning and placement centers. The outcomes associated with such a learning community would include skill development in making appropriate academic and career choices, enhanced academic achievement, stability in vocational choice, and increased retention.

Freshman-Experience Learning Communities

With the significant decline in the number of traditional-age college students, many institutions are realizing it is much more cost effective to retain students than to recruit them. As a result, most colleges and universities are providing intrusive academic and social support to freshmen through the creation of special "freshman-year-experience courses" (Upcraft, Gardner, and Associates, 1989). Although these courses are helpful, many lack coherence and substantive integration with other aspects of the freshman experience, and most are operated as an adjunct to the residence hall experience. Residential learning communities can be created to provide the much-needed integration and coherence. For example, students who participate in freshman seminar groups are often assigned to such groups on a random and unsystematic basis. Since students in these groups are rarely assigned common courses, they have few, if any, opportunities to develop ongoing relationships characterized by high degrees of peer support. Instead of randomly assigning students to freshman seminar groups, homogeneous assignments could be developed from floor rosters in the residence halls. For instance, students living on the same floor would be assigned to the same freshman seminar group. Furthermore, using the Washington Center model, these students could be assigned at least two other courses in common, selected from the general education or core requirements of the institution and perhaps team taught by faculty with a particular interest in freshmen. Such a strategy would undoubtedly promote a high degree of social and academic integration, contributing in a meaningful way to enhanced academic achievement, persistence, and greater identification with the institution.

The preceding are but a few examples and strategies for developing learning communities around common purposes and transcendent values. Obviously, numerous other examples could be provided, including learning communities based around the concept of intentional democratic values (Crookston, 1980), values inquiry (Kirby, 1991), and various realms of meaning such as empirical and symbolic modes of inquiry (Shaw, 1975). Regardless of the transcendent values, learning communities should incorporate the following specific principles or themes in their development. Themes one through three are principles characteristic of *both* residential-group communities and learning communities. Themes four through six, however, are associated exclusively with residential learning communities.

1. Learning communities are generally *small*, unique, and cohesive units characterized by a common sense of purpose and powerful peer influences.

2. Student interaction within learning communities should be characterized by the four I's—involvement, investment, influence, and identity.

3. Learning communities involve bounded territory that provides easy access to and control of group space that supports ongoing interaction and social stability.

4. Learning communities should be primarily student centered, not staff centered, if they are to promote student learning. Staff must assume that students are capable and responsible young adults who are primarily responsible for the quality and extent of their learning.

5. Effective learning communities should be the result of collaborative partnerships between faculty, students, and residence hall staff. Learning communities should not be created in a vacuum; they are designed to intentionally achieve specific educational outcomes.

6. Finally, learning communities should exhibit a clear set of values and normative expectations for active participation. The normative peer cultures of learning communities enhance student learning and development in specific ways.

Need for New Perspectives and Roles

Forty years of research on the impact of college on students has clearly demonstrated the centrality of peer influence in promoting student learning and development (Sanford, 1962; Feldman and Newcomb, 1969; Chickering, 1981; Pascarella and Terenzini, 1991; Astin, 1992). Yet, in view of this overwhelming evidence, few housing programs have been designed to fully exploit this important resource. Perhaps one of the most compelling reasons for this neglect reflects traditional housing staff assumptions about students and student learning. If students are viewed as capable, responsible young adults, housing staff will *impel* their broad-based participation in all aspects of their residential experience. At present, such traditional residence hall structures as judicial boards, programming councils, and student government are often simply symbols of involvement. What is needed are expectations, policies, and practices that truly *empower* students, that demonstrate trust in students and their ability to assume major responsibility for their learning and development. If residence life staff utilize the four I's as organizing principles in the design and implementation of learning communities, students will indeed be empowered, because maximum, grassroots participation on their part is absolutely essential.

Perhaps another reason that housing staff have neglected to understand the significance of peer-group influences is that many housing systems have a minimal focus on reference-group development. Programmatic interventions are usually focused at the system or residence hall level as opposed to the smaller, floor-unit group. Furthermore, most residence hall programs focus on individual development (vis-à-vis reliance on Chickering's developmental vectors as the typical entry-level catechism) versus a focus on group or community development. This programming preference is related to the fact that most entry-level student affairs professionals have a background in psychology, not sociology or anthropology. The development and supervision of resident assistants also stress the obligation to focus on individual student development. Perhaps their title should be changed to *community development assistant* and their role changed to that of facilitators of group development. Finally, staff must realize that students' involvement and participation are directly related to group size—that is, as group size increases, opportunities for meaningful participation decline (Barker and Gump, 1964). In the design of learning communities, staff must understand that impact is directly related to group size.

Because of reliance on traditional programmatic approaches that often narrowly focus on individual development, residence life staff have neglected broader perspectives such as campus ecology and environmental management that are essential to the design of learning communities. As previously stated, the development of learning communities involves more than simply assigning students to a unit based on common purpose and transcendent values—it involves creating environmental conditions, both social and physical, that exert a directional influence on student learning and development. Although a multitude of research has demonstrated the powerful impact of environmental influences on student behavior, residence life staff have often neglected to utilize this information in the design of learning communities.

Encapsulated staff roles have also limited opportunities for collaborative partnerships with faculty, staff, and students. Garland (1985) has challenged student affairs staff to become boundary-spanning agents and assume the role of "integrator" by focusing their efforts on integrating student development and institutional development. The integrator role requires housing staff to recognize and respond to major institutional agendas such as promoting active modes of student learning, enhancing academic achievement, supporting multiculturalism, improving retention, and contributing to enrollment management initiatives.

Conclusion

The higher education agenda for the future will be driven by many issues, but three, in particular, stand out—total quality management (TQM), establishing a sense of campus community, and promoting student learning. At first glance, these appear to be separate issues; however, within the context of higher education, there is a great deal of similarity and complementarity between them. With its emphasis on continuous quality improvement, TOM focuses on the question, "What value are we adding to the lives of our students?" Marchese (1993, p. 11) addresses this value issue in stating that "an institution's quality is a function of its contribution to student learning." Learning communities in residence halls can provide the "value-added dimension" by integrating diverse curricular and co-curricular experiences in the service of specific educational outcomes. Furthermore, under the TQM mantle, quality has to be specified and monitored. Translating this TQM principle to residence halls simply means that staff must establish learning communities with clear educational outcomes and use a variety of assessment methods to monitor student progress.

TQM also assumes that people are an organization's greatest resource and that empowering people is what makes a difference in the production of quality. If we value student learning and development, we must also value the important role that students play in the learning process. We must value and affirm broad-based student involvement and participation in the design, development, and maintenance of learning communities, extending our traditional emphasis on student government to embrace a broader and richer conceptualization of student governance.

We must also recognize that student learning is not a spectator sport, and we must evaluate our policies in light of Astin's (1977, p. 298) assertion that "the effectiveness of any education practice or policy is directly related to the capacity of that policy or practice to increase student involvement." Designing learning communities that promote active modes of student learning will also require collaborative partnerships with faculty colleagues, other staff, and students. For too long, student affairs educators have limited their educational impact by keeping their focus within their organizational boundaries. The design of educationally effective learning communities requires residence life staff to leave the comfort, security, and predictability of their bounded organizational space to build linkages with faculty and academic administrators.

In conclusion, residence life staff must assume a broader educational role if they are to contribute to continuous quality improvement, establishing a sense of campus community and promoting student learning. The development of learning communities in residence halls is a primary mechanism for addressing these important higher education agendas.

References

Astin, A. W. *Four Critical Years: Effects of College on Beliefs, Attitudes, and Knowledge.* San Francisco: Jossey-Bass, 1977.

Astin, A. W. *Achieving Educational Excellence: A Critical Assessment of Priorities and Practices in Higher Education.* San Francisco: Jossey-Bass, 1985.

Astin, A. W. *What Matters in College? Four Critical Years Revisited*. San Francisco: Jossey-Bass, 1992.

Barker, R. G., and Gump, P. V. (eds.). *Big School, Small School*. Stanford, Calif.: Stanford University Press, 1964.

Blimling, G. S., and Schuh, J. H. (eds.). *Increasing the Educational Role of Residence Halls*. New Directions for Student Services, no. 13. San Francisco: Jossey-Bass, 1981.

Chickering, A. W., and Associates. *The Modern American College: Responding to the New Realities of Diverse Students and a Changing Society*. San Francisco: Jossey-Bass, 1981.

Chickering, A. W., and Reisser, L. *Education and Identity*. (2nd ed.) San Francisco: Jossey-Bass, 1993.

Crookston, B. B. "A Design for an Intentional Democratic Community." In D. A. DeCoster and P. Mable (eds.), *Student Development and Education in College Residence Halls*. Cincinnati, Ohio: American College Personnel Association, 1980.

DeCoster, D. A., and Mable, P. (eds.). *Student Development and Education in College Residence Halls*. Cincinnati, Ohio: American College Personnel Association, 1980.

Feldman, K. A., and Newcomb, T. M. *The Impact of College on Students*. San Francisco: Jossey-Bass, 1969.

Gabelnick, F., MacGregor, J., Matthews, R. S., and Smith, B. L. *Learning Communities: Creating Connections Among Students, Faculty, and Disciplines*. New Directions for Teaching and Learning, no. 41. San Francisco: Jossey-Bass, 1990.

Garland, P. H. *Serving More Than Students: A Critical Need for College Student Personnel Services*. ASHE-ERIC Higher Education Report No. 7. Washington, D.C.: Association for the Study of Higher Education, 1985.

Kirby, D. J. "Dreaming Ambitious Dreams: The Values Program at LeMoyne College." *AAHE Bulletin*, 1991, 43(6), 9–12.

Kuh, G. D. "The Demographic Juggernaut." In M. J. Barr, M. L. Upcraft, and Associates. *New Futures for Student Affairs: Building a Vision for Professional Leadership and Practice*. San Francisco: Jossey-Bass, 1990.

Kuh, G. D., Schuh, J. H., Whitt, E. J., and Associates. *Involving Colleges: Successful Approaches to Fostering Student Learning and Development Outside the Classroom*. San Francisco: Jossey-Bass 1991.

Mable, P., Terry, M., and Duvall, W. J. "A Model of Student Development Through Community Responsibility." *Journal of College Student Personnel*, 1977, 18(1), 50–56.

Marchese, T. "TQM: A Time for Ideas." *Change*, 1993, 25(3), 10–14.

Moos, R. H. *Evaluating Educational Environments: Procedures, Findings, and Policy Implications*. San Francisco: Jossey-Bass, 1979.

Pascarella, E. T., and Terenzini, P. T. *How College Affects Students: Findings and Insights from Twenty Years of Research*. San Francisco: Jossey-Bass, 1991.

Sanford, N. (ed.). *The American College*. New York: Wiley, 1962.

Schlossberg, N. K. "Marginality and Mattering: Key Issues in Building Community." In D. C. Roberts (ed.) *Designing Campus Activities to Foster a Sense of Community*. New Directions for Student Services, no. 48. San Francisco: Jossey-Bass, 1989.

Schroeder, C. C. "Territoriality: An Imperative for Personal Development and Residence Education." In D. A. DeCoster and P. Mable (eds.), *Personal Education and Community Development in College Residence Halls*. Cincinnati, Ohio, American College Personnel Association, 1980.

Schroeder, C. C. "Student Development Through Environmental Management." In G. S. Blimling and J. H. Schuh (eds.), *Increasing the Educational Role of Residence Halls*. New Directions for Student Services, no. 13. San Francisco: Jossey-Bass, 1981.

Schroeder, C. C. "Conclusion: Creating Residence Life Programs with Student Development Goals." In R. B. Winston, Jr., S. Anchors and Associates, *Student Housing and Residential Life: A Handbook for Professionals Committed to Student Development Goals.* San Francisco: Jossey-Bass, 1993.

Schroeder, C. C., and Griffin, C. R. "A Novel Living-Learning Environment for Freshman Engineering Students." *Engineering Education,* 1977, *67,* 159–161.

Schroeder, C. C., and Jackson, G. S. "Creating Conditions for Student Development in Campus Living Environments." *NASPA Journal,* 1987, *25*(1), 45–53.

Schroeder, C. C., Nicholls, G. E., and Kuh, G. D. "Exploring the Rain Forest: Testing Assumptions and Taking Risks." In G. D. Kuh (ed.), *Understanding Student Affairs Organizations.* New Directions for Student Services, no. 23. San Francisco: Jossey-Bass, 1983.

Shaw, W. B. *The Residence Hall as a Community in Higher Education.* Denver, Colo.: University of Denver Press, 1975.

Smith, B. L. "Assessment That Is Fun, Real, and Stimulating: Washington State's Grass Roots Approach." Paper presented at the annual conference of the American Association for Higher Education, San Francisco, March 1991.

Smith, B. L. "Creating Learning Communities." *Liberal Education,* 1993, *79*(4), 16–21.

Sommer, R. *Personal Space: The Behavioral Basis of Design.* Englewood Cliffs, NJ.: Prentice Hall, 1969.

Spitzberg, I. J., and Thorndike, V. V. *Creating Community on College Campuses.* Albany, N.Y.: State University of New York Press, 1992.

Stamatakos, L. C. "The Great Expectations of Student Affairs and Lessons from Reality: A Contextual Examination." Paper presented at the Virginia Association of Student Personnel Administrators/Virginia Association of College and University Housing Officers Fall Conference, Wintergreen Resort, Va., Oct. 1991.

Study Group on the Conditions of Excellence in American Higher Education. *Involvement in Learning.* Washington, D.C.: U.S. Department of Education, 1984.

Tollefson, A. L. *New Approaches to College Student Development.* New York: Behavioral Publications, 1975.

Upcraft, M. L., Gardner, J. N., and Associates. *The Freshman Year Experience: Helping Students Survive and Succeed in College.* San Francisco: Jossey-Bass, 1989.

Wingspread Group on Higher Education. *An American Imperative: Higher Expectations for Higher Education.* Racine, Wis.: Johnson Foundation, 1993.

Managing Change in a Paradoxical Environment

Margaret J. Barr and Anne E. Gloseth

Higher education in the United States has proved to be extremely adaptable. Even a cursory review of history reveals the many rapid changes that have been embraced by higher education as a whole. New students have been served, curriculum choices have increased, content in courses has been modified, service domains have expanded, institutions have been developed to meet specific needs, technology has become part of the teaching-learning process, and societal expectations for higher education have grown. In one sense, the future will be no different. Change is an inevitable part of any vital educational enterprise.

In some very fundamental ways, however, the future of higher education will be different. First, the pace of change in society has accelerated, and the issues that influence educational change have become increasingly complex (Monat, 1985). Second, the forces of change have increased in both number and power, partially as a result of the information age in which we live. Earlier chapters in this volume have discussed some of the factors that will shape the future tone, style, and direction of colleges and universities. Student bodies will continue to become more diverse in terms of age, gender, race, ethnicity, and socioeconomic status. The legal and regulatory environment of the country will make many more demands on higher education, and technology will continue to be a potent force in shaping human interactions. Finally, the social agendas facing society and education are enormous and will not be easily confronted. "The agenda for higher education has never been more challenging. Colleges and universities must reflect the values of a pluralistic society, provide a forum in which those values can be tested and seek solutions to persistent issues and problems" (National Association of Student Personnel Administrators, 1987, p. 18).

For student affairs, the management of change is particularly important. By history, tradition, and professional values, student affairs professionals are expected to resolve conflicts and to aid groups with competing agendas to reach constructive solutions. Although that role has never been easy, the unpredictability of the future will make it even more difficult. Higher education and student affairs will not be managing change in an atmosphere characterized by agreement on goals, mission, and philosophy. Instead, the future will be filled with choices that must be made between and among legitimate goals. Choices will be difficult because the alternatives that face us are neither inherently good nor inherently bad. Student affairs must assume leadership on campuses during an era when the process of managing change has shifted to the process of managing an environment filled with paradox.

The Question of Paradox

The word *paradox* is most often defined as a contradiction or competition of alternatives, both of which contain truth or rightness or value. Paradoxical issues are most frequently presented in the form of questions. For example, can an institution embrace both the value of equality of access and the value of excellence?

A key skill for student affairs professionals in the future will be the ability to define and recognize paradoxical issues. Paradox is not, however, new to higher education. In fact, paradoxical questions are part of the daily lives of faculty, students, administrators, and staff. In the classroom, such questions are central to the processes of intellectual challenge, creative thinking, and pedagogy.

For example, a vigorous classroom debate on the question of euthanasia will bring forth a number of paradoxical questions with which students must struggle. There are many points of view, and both the rights of an individual person and the rules and laws of society must be weighed in developing an intellectual or personal answer to the question of whether euthanasia is an acceptable solution to problems of illness.

Other examples within the classroom also illustrate the complexities in determining the best course of action. Should we conduct research using animals? How do we determine when life ends? Has our technology in medical care outpaced our ability to provide good and useful alternatives for those we save? These are not abstract questions, and they must be explored if our current and future students are to be able to meet the dilemmas of the future. In campus life, paradoxical questions often relate to the mission of the institution, to the welfare of individuals and groups, and to the relationships among the institution, the larger community, students, faculty, and staff

For example, what is the proper and correct role for the institution when dealing with students who have substance-abuse problems? Should we intervene, or should we ignore the question as long as it does not interfere with their ability to do their academic work? Or should we hold a group responsible for the damage done by its members in the community? Are we correct in assuming that faculty and staff members should be held to a higher standard of conduct than their counterparts are in the larger society? The list of such issues could go on and on. Paradoxical questions arise and must be managed constantly in an academic community.

Some paradoxes are inherent in the higher education enterprise, and others have emerged as results of change in society. Still others are emerging today and will demand increasing attention in the future. Some paradoxes endure regardless of attempts at resolution or changes in time and circumstances, some are resolved or become obsolete because of forces outside the academy, and some arise from the dynamic interaction between the institution and the greater community. All are difficult, all are complex, and all will require time and attention.

Historical Paradoxes. The relationship between the individual and the institution has been a constant source of paradoxical questions in higher education. Some of these historical paradoxes involve issues such as the value of autonomy of the student versus the value of protection of the student, the value of protection of individual freedom of expression and the sometimes competing value of social propriety, and the need to resolve the competing values of personal agendas of campus community members and the sometimes conflicting values of institutional objectives. At times, paradoxes are based in the sensitivity of certain individuals and groups and the pride of other community members in embedded institutional traditions such as mascots. In the sixties and seventies, an overwhelming paradoxical issue for student affairs involved balancing the interests of some members of the campus community in social protest against compelling interests in maintaining an orderly environment. None of these questions has been fully resolved, and they are still present on our campuses today. Any issue of the *Chronicle of Higher Education* bears stark witness to that reality.

The relationship of the individual to the institution also causes a set of ethical questions to emerge for the student affairs professional. For example, what is the responsibility of the professional when students express intention of doing harm to themselves? If the student affairs professional adheres to Kitchener's (1985) ethical principle of respecting autonomy, then mere expression of intention to harm oneself does not warrant action or intervention. If, however, the expression of intention on the part of the student causes distress to others within the community, or if the student involved has a history of suicide attempts, then the professional must consider the ethical principle of doing no harm. The question becomes one of balancing competing values.

Although student rights have been assured through institutional policies and legal cases and statements (American Association of University Professors, 1967), student responsibility is still subject to institutional expectations and disciplinary procedures. The joint goals of freedom and responsibility remain primary though often elusive ideals within the academic community.

An additional historical paradox for student affairs is embedded in its traditional mission of meeting student needs. Balance between providing services to all and concurrently providing attention to individual needs remains difficult to achieve.

Finally, a major paradox remains regarding how student affairs professionals can support freedom of student expression and concurrently meet an institutional objective of maintaining order. Other examples from our recent past that are not yet resolved might also be discussed. All of our historical paradoxical issues bring to student affairs administrators the constant challenge of developing fair and just policies and procedures.

Current Paradoxes. Our historical paradoxes remain with us, and many of the major paradoxes facing higher education are focused on social issues more than on individual matters. The relationship between the greater society and the institution, for example, spawns a number of paradoxes in the area of behavior of students, faculty, and staff. For example, should an individual's behavior be judged in light of campus standards or by those of the larger community? Where do the campus boundaries and limits of authority begin and end? These are not abstract questions; they are very real parts of the work of any student affairs administrator. Resolution of such issues must be made, and not everyone will agree with the decision.

Broader questions also influence the paradoxes of the day. The increased expectations for institutional performance coupled with more limited resources have caused a number of paradoxical questions to surface. Who should be served? What program should be abandoned? Anyone who has faced a budget cut or steady-state funding can testify to the difficulty of resolving such issues. Other competing values arise: academic freedom versus political reality, providing technological training versus human development, creating an autonomous learning environment or a legally bound public service entity, for example. The choice must be both. The dilemma is how.

This decade's overriding paradox, which reflects all other issues, is the question of access versus excellence. The literature mirrors the intensity of the debate—reports, books, and research projects in abundance. Conferences and workshops on the two concepts of access and excellence have proliferated. Legislatures in many states have passed statutes regarding the issue; the number of words, programs, projects, services, and proposed reforms is overwhelming. Yet the paradox of access and excellence remains and is reflected in a number of specific questions that must be resolved if higher education is to move forward. Does affirmative action mean commitment or compliance? Are goals or quotas appropriate? Should higher education provide special admissions programs or equal opportunity? Should achievement be judged only through standardized tests or should other options be considered? The debate is alive and well and will continue as a primary issue in the future.

Emerging Paradoxes. Both the historical and current paradoxes facing higher education provide glimpses of the future. The paradoxical questions of the future will involve both our battered baggage of experience and the possibility of new solutions. Emerging paradoxes will inevitably intensify, so as we glimpse the future, we must employ tools of prediction and prepare to confront a number of new and vexing issues.

One primary tool that we can use to predict the future is the media, which both transmit and create the dilemmas of the present and the future. Careful attention to the hot topics of the day can help each of us prepare for tomorrow. In addition, study of economic forecasts, demographic analyses, historical trends, and changes in technology will provide valuable insights into potential issues that must be resolved.

Access and excellence will continue as the primary issue of higher education and will demand attention and action. The higher education community will need to confront the basic question of whether higher education is a right or an opportunity. The question will not be one of whether the concepts of access and excellence can coexist, but rather one of how these two goals can be accomplished.

The need for cultural sensitivity will intensify in the future and will be accompanied by a backlash that is just beginning to emerge on the college campuses of today. Understanding and appreciating cultural differences will continue to be required for the students and staff of the future. The world, through advances in the media, transportation, and commerce, is continuing to shrink, and the well-prepared individual must be able to function effectively in a wide variety of cultural settings. The emphasis on cultural issues currently is accompanied by reactive behavior on the part of some to the special programs and special attention for ethnic minority groups. Clashes have broken out as students struggle with the rightness and value of affirmative action programs that are much more than mere rhetoric. Finding methods to resolve these intercultural conflicts will remain among the top agendas for the future.

Issues related to personal health and well-being will be part of the future of higher education. Substance abuse, AIDS, and yet unknown diseases will affect the lives of all members of the campus community. The historical paradox of balancing the welfare of the individual and the welfare of the group will reemerge and intensify. In the future, however, there will be an added pressure to resolve these conflicts because the consequences of nonresolution are so much more severe than they have been in the past.

Technology will serve as both a predictor of paradoxical issues and a paradox itself. Nearly every human function in higher education, including teaching, advising, testing, counseling, and student services, will face a technological challenge. The question of whether higher education can provide both technological teaching and human contact is no longer rhetorical. The paradox of technology rests in its ability to open the possibility of learning to many while concurrently threatening many aspects of higher education. With computers, electronic mail, and interactive television becoming more accessible and less expensive, will the college campus really be necessary? With many learners off campus, how can student services be provided for them? Will such services continue to be needed?

Finally, each institution of higher education will have to resolve fundamental questions regarding its mission. The unbridled growth of higher education is at an end, and institutions cannot continue to try to be all things to all people. Making choices among positive alternatives will be difficult and will be the cause of new issues. Clearly, the processes of managing the complex agenda of change that faces us is the challenge of the future.

From any point of view, the future of higher education presents a formidable challenge. The question facing higher education is not one of whether change will occur, but rather one of managing the inevitable changes that will influence our shared, uncertain future. The manner in which we approach managing change may be as important as the final decisions that we reach. "In a pluralistic campus community, the manner in which policies are made, decisions are reached and controversial issues are handled may be as important as the results themselves. Indeed, an institution transmits values to students by the way it approaches policies, decisions and issues" (National Association of Student Personnel Administrators, 1987, p. 15).

Essential Elements in Managing Change

We must consider two sets of essential elements in managing paradox and change. The first set revolves around understanding the environment in which we work. The second focuses on principles that guide our approaches to the task of resolving issues and problems.

Understandings. An essential first step is to understand the mission of a college or university and how that mission may translate into a position on a specific issue. Too often, institutional mission statements are viewed as abstractions and statements of intention rather than action, so we must take time to discuss the specific relationship of an institutional mission statement and the day-to-day processes of decision making and problem resolution on the campus. It is essential that leaders within the academic community understand where the institution stands on certain issues.

Active discussion and debate as part of an ongoing process can help avoid crisis responses to paradoxical questions within the context of the institution.

A second step is embracing a genuine understanding of the ethical dimensions of the profession of student affairs. Although student affairs administrators may not be ethics experts, they must be ethics officers on their campuses. They must see to it that leaders actively engage in examination of the ethical dimensions of their work as they formulate the positions of the institution. Discussion of ethical issues is essential in an educational community where decisions are rarely clearly good or bad, right or wrong. Movement to understanding and a consistent approach to ethical questions permit balance between competing positive interests to be achieved.

Third, understanding the law is essential. Frequently, administrators use the law as a last resort. Sometimes they are forced by students or others to deal with issues on a legal basis. In the past, student affairs educators and faculty often sought to maintain a separation between higher education and the law, but societal changes in the last two decades have made that stance obsolete. Higher education is not an enclave of immunity from the law, and thus legal issues are fundamental to the resolution of many differences on the campus.

On many campuses, policies and procedures have been developed to meet the explosion of mandates, regulations, and compliance requirements. What is too often lost in the process of reaction is the positive value of the partnership between higher education and the law. "Protection of individual rights, ethical and human treatment and responsible actions are principles on which student affairs is founded. The emerging trend toward legalism is in part a response to a lack of adherence to these principles in the past" (Barr, 1988, p. 348). The law can be a powerful tool in conflict resolution, and the astute administrator uses knowledge of the law as a pragmatic force in developing solutions to ongoing problems.

Guiding Principles. There are many principles related to the management of paradoxical situations. Most can be related to three areas: agreement, integrity, and utility.

One of the first principles of resolving conflicts is determination of commonality, common ground, agreements, and ways to cooperate. This principle applies to people, positions, or concepts; the agreements may be goals, limits, procedures, time lines, or decisions. Essential to reaching agreement is the process of inclusion, so it is critical that all who affect, or are affected by, the paradox or issue at hand be included in discussion regarding resolution of the dilemma. All possibilities of action must be explored. In addition, agreement must include openness to further agreements, to new commonalities, and to balance of positions and outcomes.

Integrity involves principles that are too often assumed rather than affirmed. Integrity means demonstrating consistency between beliefs and actions. Implicit in this definition is adherence to behaviors demonstrating honesty, fairness, sensitivity, and a commitment to doing no harm. The simplicity of these words hides the complexity of action based upon such principles when faced with paradoxical issues. Total honesty can sometimes be harmful, fairness to all at times seems impossible, sensitivity is interpretive, and doing no harm involves evaluation. Integrity is in itself a paradox, a continuing struggle for both the institution and the individual.

A third area of principle is utility, a term rarely used with respect to a principle. What is the utility of dealing with a paradox? What can be gained or accomplished? What can be learned? What can be contributed? Is it true that some issues do not need to be addressed but simply ignored until they go away? Perhaps it is. Indeed, not every paradox of life in our society requires attention from higher education or from student affairs. However, many issues that have been ignored, either intentionally or unintentionally, are relevant to the goals of colleges and universities. Again, college administrators have too often confronted paradox as a problem rather than as a possibility. Paradox is a tool for learning, for change, and for progress, regardless of the resolution of the specific issue. Indeed, paradox is often the medium for the message of higher education.

Strategies

Managing change and paradox is a consuming responsibility for student affairs administrators. Once a paradoxical issue or problem is identified, the question becomes one of reaching resolution. Christensen (1980) identified several specific steps in managing changes and placed a strong emphasis on identifying problems, determining problem causes, seeking alternative solutions, and testing those solutions prior to implementing any change. When all factors are reasonably within control, his approach is very useful and is highly recommended. But often we are faced with situations in which not all elements are under our control, emotions run high, and reaching a consensus is difficult, if not impossible. Faced with these circumstances, the following strategies to manage change and paradox may be useful.

Identifying Common Goals. Often when a conflict arises, the first focus is on what separates or otherwise divides the individuals and groups involved. One of the most effective methods of managing change is assisting all parties to identify those issues on which there is agreement and to establish goals on which consensus can be reached. This method involves employment of effective listening and paraphrasing skills to assist all parties in finding out where they can converge instead of divide.

Identifying Patterns. Careful study of institutional history and conflicts can uncover patterns. Certain issues are bound to bring consistent reactions from specific groups or individuals, and if such patterns can be established, communication with these interested parties can be opened before the issue escalates into a crisis. Such an approach may not prevent a crisis, but it can serve as a method to start the process of managing change.

Exercising Patience. When we are faced with a paradoxical situation, patience is genuinely a virtue. Although we may feel that the issue has been resolved and that there is no need to talk about it anymore, some in the community may feel otherwise. The length of time a college student is at the institution is generally much less than that of any administrator or faculty member. Students leave and new students enter the university, so the issue we felt was settled just last year may arise again as a new agenda item for new students. Acknowledgment of this reality helps each of us to maintain perspective.

Setting Limits. Rules, regulations, and approaches to problem solving must be clearly understood by all parties involved in a paradoxical issue. If there are consequences for unscheduled protests, let people know. If there are limits on how often and where parties to the conflict can meet, be honest about those parameters. If there are issues involved that are outside the control of the institution, make them known. To do less invites turmoil and accusations of dishonesty when limits are eventually imposed.

Trying to Work Things Out. Working things out involves bringing people together in dialogue, seeking ways to be fair to all involved, calling upon experts for assistance, spending countless hours in study, analysis, and meetings, and knowing that there is no final or enduring resolution.

Doing More Than Is Needed. Doing extra work may include forming a committee, a task force, or a commission to study the issue; setting timetables for study of the problem; making reports to appropriate legislative bodies, students, faculty, and staff; or giving attention to the problem at the highest possible level within the organization. The extra work involves more people in the final resolution of the issue—more people who then own the solution.

Experiment. The experimental approach is a corollary to the one above. If a report is issued with recommendations for actions, experiment with the proposed solutions and set a time limit for evaluating their effectiveness. Many administrators feel this is a risky approach to solving problems, but it is one that has proved to be successful at many colleges and universities.

Taking Risks. Sometimes, successful management of paradox requires taking risks. Success may mean meeting with groups or individuals who do not have recognized entitlement within the institution. Often it involves taking risks with other administrators and faculty by telling them what they do not want to hear or deal with. It requires being a visible resource, a listener, and a target for those disenchanted with processes or solutions.

Involvement. More than ever before, campuses can and must become places of opportunity for genuine involvement by all community members in resolving the issues of the day. Many studies (Astin, 1977; National Commission on Excellence in Education, 1983) have focused on the concept of involvement as a key ingredient in learning, persistence, and completion of higher education. Student involvement is also crucial to the effective management of paradox and related issues on the campus. It is not enough merely to include students on campus committees and discipline boards. Students must become directly involved in the management of paradox in the residence hall, the classroom, the athletic team room, the newspaper office, and in any context of activity or study on the campus. The campus must be the real world in which real people are dealing with real learning, real dilemmas, and real decisions.

Compromise. One of the most effective tools for dealing with the dilemmas of paradox is compromise. Too often, compromise has been viewed as capitulation rather than as empowerment. Compromise can be a powerful tool for management of paradox because it offers the options of choosing from competing solutions and bringing forth a collaboration of many sides of an issue. Compromise can become the action of first resort—the most viable course for moving on and getting things done for the benefit of all.

Anticipatory Management. Crisis management has become the status quo in higher education and rarely brings permanent resolution to persisting problems. Although crisis management may be inevitable, anticipatory management as a tool is more available than ever before. Issues, dilemmas, and paradoxical challenges that will become parts of the campus milieu are increasingly predictable with continuing advancements in media and technology. College officials can choose to deal with the paradoxical questions of the future, either as crises for reaction or as ongoing challenges for teaching and learning.

Reaching Out. Student affairs efforts include numerous programs of outreach on and beyond the campus. Programs, workshops, and activities are prime methods for reaching students and helping them successfully complete their collegiate experiences. The effective management of paradox requires the expansion of such efforts to the entire campus community and beyond. Sharing data, presenting issues, examining alternatives, and looking to the future must become parts of the domain of student affairs.

But not only students must be involved. Board members, other administrators, faculty, and staff also must become aware of current and emerging issues and begin the process of discussion regarding those issues before they become crises that must be managed. It is time that student affairs professionals "take the lid off" problematic issues and involve others in the challenge of working with the dilemmas of the campus and society.

Doing Nothing. Time will solve the problem. The issue will go away and another will take its place. Certain students will leave, and they may take with them the challenge of contradiction. But choosing this option requires careful thought and understanding of the conditions that surround the issues. It may become the option of either the first or last resort in managing change.

The choice of strategy will depend on the issue at hand, the parties involved, and the potential influence that resolution (or failure to resolve) can have on the academic community. Solutions will not be simple or easy to reach, because the questions we will face do not fall into the category of right or wrong answers. There is usually merit in all of the many sides of the issue. The challenge is to develop solutions that make a positive difference for our institutions.

Summary

The management of change is not an easy task. The problems and dilemmas facing higher education are becoming increasingly complex and reflect the changing values in society. Issues that were once viewed in a rather straightforward manner in the past are now fraught with nuances. As higher education moves into the future, the degree of complexity facing the organization will increase, and the number of paradoxical situations that will need to be managed will grow geometrically. Effective management of change will require student affairs professionals to provide leadership as colleges and universities confront paradoxical and difficult questions and seek to turn difficult situations into opportunities for growth and development for students and institutions.

Within higher education, academic freedom ensures a climate for coexistence of conflicting points of view, of equal but differing values and priorities, of multiple perspectives and infinite possibilities. The campus, however, is more than the academy. Coexistence of paradoxical positions and goals is essential to, but not sufficient for, the management of paradox; a sense of resolution must be achieved.

The chosen strategy for managing change will depend on circumstances, skills, attitudes, and the issues at hand. Successful management of change requires the student affairs professional to be aware of the political realities of the situation while entering the process with a goal of resolving the question. Attention and skill must be brought to the emerging issues of the time, and careful consideration must be given to methods and possible outcomes. To manage change and to make it useful in an environment where many equally important issues and positions are vying for support is a challenge for student affairs now, and it will continue to be so in the future.

References

American Association of University Professors. "Joint Statement on Rights and Freedom of Students." *AAUP Bulletin*, 1967, 52, pp. 365–369.

Astin, A. *Four Critical Years: Effects of College on Beliefs, Attitudes, and Knowledge.* San Francisco: Jossey-Bass, 1977.

Barr, M. J., and Associates. *Student Services and the Law.* San Francisco: Jossey-Bass, 1988.

Christensen, V. R. "Bringing About Change" In U. Delworth, G. Hanson, and Associates, *Student Services: A Handbook for the Profession.* San Francisco: Jossey-Bass, 1980.

Kitchener, K. S. "Ethical Principles and Ethical Decisions in Student Affairs." In H. J. Canon and R. D. Brown (eds.), *Applied Ethics in Student Services.* New Directions for Student Services, no. 30. San Francisco: Jossey-Bass, 1985.

Monat, W. R. "Role of Student Services: A President's Perspective." In M. J. Barr, L. A. Keating, and Associates, *Developing Effective Student Services Programs.* San Francisco: Jossey-Bass, 1985.

National Association of Personnel Administrators. "A Perspective on Student Affairs: A Statement Issued on the Fiftieth Anniversary of *The Student Personnel Point of View.*" Washington, D.C.: National Association of Student Personnel Administrators, 1987.

National Commission on Excellence in Education. *A Nation at Risk: The Imperative for Educational Reform.* Washington, D.C.: U.S. Government Printing Office, 1983.

Promoting Cocurricular Learning

Marcia B. Baxter Magolda

Independence is instilled because in certain situations, there's nobody there to tell you, "That's right; that's wrong. You shouldn't do this; you shouldn't do that." You make your own decisions.

—Gavin

At the outset of Chapter Nine, I described promoting student voice in curricular life through the use of three principles: validating the student as a knower, situating learning in their own experience, and viewing learning as constructing meaning with others. These same principles apply to cocurricular life. In fact, the relational nature inherent in these ideas, so often obscured in academic settings due to the dominance of objectivism, is usually more visible in the cocurricular environment. However, relational learning opportunities are often restricted by the subordinate position that student affairs has historically occupied in the academy. A brief exploration of this situation is necessary to bring to light the assumptions that must be reconsidered if we are to use these three principles to develop student voice in cocurricular life.

When the expansion of the number of students in the early 1900s made it unlikely that faculty could address their total development, responsibilities were divided. "The faculty was charged with intellectual development of students, and such specialists as deans of men and women were assigned responsibility for extracurricular student affairs" (Knock, 1985, p. 15). It was at this juncture that kinds of development other than intellectual, such as aesthetic, affective, or interpersonal, were relegated to the "extracurricular" domain, with the assumption that they could be separated from the intellectual sphere. With such strands of development designated as *extra* (or supplemental), student affairs was assigned a subordinate status from the beginning.

"To be on the margin is to be part of the whole but outside the main body" (Hooks, 1984, p. ix). Hooks's statement describes the dilemma faced by student affairs in light of its historical marginalization. Fenske (1989) describes student services as "a ubiquitous but almost invisible empire in virtually every institution of higher education" (p. 6). *The Student Personnel Point of View* (American Council on Education Studies, 1949) did take a philosophical stance advocating that students be considered as whole beings, whose development in all areas was related. The authors suggested "attention to the student's well-rounded development—physically, socially, emotionally and spiritually, as well as intellectually" (p. 1). Despite this comprehensive perspective, their conceptualization of the role of student affairs was confined to the "other" developmental domains and touched intellectual concerns in only two areas: admitting capable students and providing remedial services to increase academic success. They took a service-oriented approach to the student affairs aspects of development and noted that these could hinder intellectual progress if not effectively addressed. This acceptance of the bifurcation of intellectual and affective development has survived despite considerable challenge by noted writers in the profession. Fenske (1989) recounts repeated attempts dating from the start of the twentieth century to integrate intellectual and affective growth. Many other writers have argued for this integration, and some (for example, Brown, 1972; Miller and Prince, 1976) have articulated specific plans for how it could be achieved. Others (for example, Knefelkamp, 1974; Widick, 1975) provided research data demonstrating that intellectual development could be fostered through the application of student development theory. The conceptualization of new student service roles, particularly the student development educator and the campus ecology manager, held promise for integrating intellectual and affective development. However, Fenske's (1989) contention that most student services professionals continued to accept a complementary role to academic affairs seems true. As recently as 1987, a document to commemorate the fiftieth anniversary of the original 1937 edition of *The Student Personnel Point of View* identified as its first priority: "The academic mission of the institution is preeminent. Colleges and universities organize their activities around the academic experience: the curriculum, the library, the classroom, and the laboratory. The work of student affairs should not compete with and cannot substitute for that academic experience. As a partner in the educational enterprise, student affairs enhances and supports the academic mission" (American Council on Education and the National Association of Student Personnel Administrators, 1987, p. 10). This position appropriately confirms the importance of intellectual development but is narrow in that it limits that development to the curriculum, library, classroom, and laboratory. The partnership is construed as one in which academic affairs stands at the center and student affairs provides service from the margin. As a result, objectivism continues to be endorsed at the center, and relational approaches are relegated to the margin.

This perspective fails to recognize that relational modes of knowing (termed narrative, aesthetic, affective, or interpersonal by various writers) are central to intellectual development. The student stories in this book confirm that this kind of knowing is central to the development of voice for many students. It is also essential to complex ways of knowing. These ideas come as no surprise to many student development educators who have studied the theories evolving in the last twenty years. They know autonomy and interdependency (or the capacity to join others in a relationship that appropriately balances autonomy and dependency) are necessary if the student voice and complex perspectives are to emerge. They know that participation in genuine relationships is a major source of the dissonance that calls upon students to reshape their ways of knowing. Perhaps most importantly, these professionals realize that development of all kinds stems from relational opportunities to interact and experience feedback from others, to differentiate previous perspectives and reintegrate them into new ones and that it is nurtured in contexts offering confirmation, contradiction, and continuity. What these professionals may not realize is that their relational perspective is valid and should be incorporated into the center of the academic enterprise.

Many of the philosophical underpinnings of student affairs support my contention that it should join (not replace) academia at the center. Caring for students is a fundamental concern of student affairs, which has held sacred that students are unique individuals whose differences must be celebrated; student affairs has also emphasized "that the major responsibility for a student's growth in personal and social wisdom rests with the student himself" (American Council on Education Studies 1949, p. 3). Many student affairs divisions have endorsed the recent focus on developing communities in which students care for each other, celebrate diversity, and function interdependently. Kuh and others (1991) concluded that institutions that stress to students their responsibility for their own affairs encourage involvement. These ideas clearly support our three principles: validating students as knowers, situating learning in the students' own experience, and defining learning as jointly constructing meaning. Yet student affairs practice does not always reflect these notions.

I noted earlier Thorne's contention that marginalized groups become silent and invisible. Perhaps this theses explains the contradiction between student affairs practice and the beliefs of professionals in the field. We gave up in loco parentis as a philosophy in *The Student Personnel Point of View* (American Council on Education Studies, 1949). We believe students may take risks, make their own decisions, and manage the outcome in order to develop, even if this behavior creates a disruption of routing campus life. Yet we know that we are accountable to those at the center for "managing" student life in a way that does not interfere with the central mission. Thus, our underlying assumption of student affairs at the margin prohibits us from negotiating a community with our faculty colleagues in which opportunities for development that may be risky can occur. Perhaps being silenced and made invisible explains why student affairs professionals who are so committed to relational approaches choose not to share them with faculty colleagues who could benefit. Changing the basic assumption that student affairs is marginal to the academic mission and that affective development has little to do with intellectual growth is crucial to helping students develop voice and complex ways of knowing. Such a change is crucial to freeing student affairs professionals to implement policies and practices based on the principles I have described. As we explore the role of student affairs in these principles, other underlying assumptions that warrant our attention will emerge as well. The students' stories in Chapter Ten illustrate how these principles relate to the student affairs function. Rather than repeat them here, I often refer to those cited earlier.

Validating the Student as a Knower

As the story lines summarized in Chapter Seven indicated, students with absolute or transitional ways of knowing do not perceive that what they have to say is of great value. Initially, this situation would seem to apply mostly to the academic sphere, but the stories of absolute learners suggest otherwise. Despite their perception of increased independence in everyday life and decision making, they often revealed their reliance on authority. Recall Toni's experience of changing her major four times. Toni felt all alone and totally responsible for her decision. As a result, Toni went to friends, her RA, and then advisers for help. Her mom's absence led to Toni's feeling of independence, but she described what she did on her own as finding authorities to take her mom's place. Toni gave no hint of self-reliance in this important decision. Students like Toni approach career counselors with the assumption that the counselors know more than they do about what they should major in. Peers sometimes took the authority role in other situations, as many students explained how roommates had helped them learn how to live on their own. I want to argue here, as I did in Chapter Nine, that validating students should begin during absolute knowing, rather than waiting for their voices to emerge.

The students' stories about their cocurricular lives show that they found validation in student organization leadership opportunities, work environments, and cross-cultural experiences. Lydia recounted in Chapter Ten how her role as social chair in her sorority helped her "handle certain people under certain conditions." She described learning how to approach people and to "come across like you know what you're talking about." In order to influence her peers, she had to become more adept in both her individual and collective dealings with them. As she told her story, it was clear that, by "coming across as if she knew what she was talking about," she had actually come to see herself as competent. Ned gained similar validation and self-confidence from leadership activities that were new situations for him. He noted that he "came out of all of them pretty well." The connection between self-confidence and autonomous learning is clear in Sean's comments about the effect of his leadership positions. He reported, "It changes how I think about things, how organized I am, the way I see myself in relation to other people." The opportunity to take responsibility for an organization and other people led to Sean's ability to "create something on my own." In that light, his comment about the way he saw himself in relation to other people might refer to seeing himself as a knower.

Students found this same kind of confirmation in their roles as student employees. Stories about work experiences from Chapter Ten demonstrate this point. Gwen described her RA job as pushing her to her limits. Being forced to deal with situations resulted, in Gwen's case, in "doing okay." This outcome confirmed her sense that she could do more than she had imagined. Sheila had a similar experience in her job in the computer lab. She described being around "people who were very science- and math-oriented," through which she learned new things. As a result, Sheila went from believing she was stupid in math and science to stating unequivocally, "I was capable."

Functioning as an authority figure also helped students confirm themselves as knowers. Heather explained how her RA job forced her to "be more outgoing." She said that coming into contact with different problems necessitated that she understand herself in order to help her residents. Carrying out her RA responsibilities forced Heather to view herself as mature and independent, even though she did not feel like that. (Her comments about the problems of shy persons in the classroom, where interaction is required, also support my contention that affective learning is central to intellectual development.) Lowell also learned about himself as a student supervisor in the dining halls. He said, "Dealing with students as an authority figure and controlling your temper—that's probably the hardest thing to do. I've made great strides toward that." His role as an authority figure helped him learn how to function like one.

As we saw in Chapter Ten, the development of voice that comes from viewing oneself as responsible and competent is clear in the student stories about cross-cultural experiences. Marla reported a "sense of being totally on your own—a new culture, language, being absolutely responsible for everything." She found herself in many situations that she had never encountered. She returned from this experience pleased with her ability to figure out how to get out of situations herself. Sheila also valued thinking for herself as a result of what she referred to as going to "some strange place" and coming back and "totally rebuilding" her life. She found this to be a process of self-education. Barry described the same process in his comments about his cross-cultural experience. Recall that Barry's decisions hinged on the question, "All right, if I do this, will I die?" If he thought the answer was no, he would proceed. He described the result of learning "to take risks and handle problems." What is arresting in Barry's story is that he was not always "forced into" new experiences but chose them on the basis of his predictions of survival—in other words, Barry had confidence in his ability to think before these experiences. All three of these stories demonstrate that successful functioning in a new setting helped confirm students as knowers.

Barry's view of himself as an independent thinker before his cross-cultural experience is in contrast to the stories discussed thus far that focus on "forced" contradiction; students described being "pushed," "forced into," and "thrown into" situations. Use of these terms implies that the situation contained significant contradiction. Yet the students reported successful outcomes, which suggest that they were confirmed as knowers. Our understanding of the necessary balance between confirmation and contradiction requires a closer look at their stories. The careful reader has already discovered that the ones I have summarized here came largely from students in independent and contextual knowing; they had probably developed at least some voice previously. Yet a review of the comments of absolute and transitional knowers about organizational and work experiences reveals that the outcomes were friendship and support rather than development of voice. Thus, providing these opportunities is not in itself a sufficient plan for validating all students. Balancing confirmation and contradiction is essential if experiences like those discussed here are to help student voice develop.

Many organizational leadership positions, student affairs opportunities such as resident-adviser positions, and most international exchange experiences are reserved for upper-division students. In the case of leadership and work opportunities, the students with the most individual achievement have a better chance of acquiring these positions. As I think back on my years as a residence hall director, I remember that I always sought the best undergraduate staff members and hall government officers I could find. The ones that I sought were self-confident, could analyze a situation and make a good decision, and could work interdependently with their peers. Placing such students in these positions not only reduced the number of unwise decisions that I then had to deal with but also supposedly served the student population more effectively. Yet my approach meant that I offered opportunities only to those who had already begun to develop a voice. How can we make developmental opportunities available to those who do not yet view themselves as knowers and still balance the need for effective service to students? It seems to me that there are at least three workable solutions to this dilemma.

The first approach entails being more flexible in our expectations of students in organizational leadership roles. By more flexible, I mean less concerned about avoiding uncomfortable situations and more concerned about making them into educational opportunities. Take, for instance, the story about the controversial T-shirt, a version of which has probably occurred on numerous campuses. A student group designed a T-shirt for its members in the spirit of group cohesion and community. Additionally, in the spirit of being clever and creative, they arrived at a design that was interesting and unique. Being caught up in this process, the designers failed to reflect carefully on how the design could be interpreted by others. The T-shirt, which arrived in mass quantities (as T-shirts always do), was offensive to various campus populations.

This scenario is every organization adviser's nightmare. The questions come from administrators. Where was the advisor when the T-shirt was being designed? Did the adviser approve this design? Why did he or she let the group order a T-shirt that had not been approved? And then the students have questions. If we cannot sell or distribute the T-shirts, is the division going to reimburse our organization for the purchase? Why should we be told what we can and cannot do with our money? The outcome of the story usually includes one consistent change: future T-shirt designs must be approved in advance.

The aim of preventing such incidents, particularly when they devalue other student populations, is understandable and justifiable, yet such situations arise every day in many contexts where intervention is not possible. The T-shirt controversy, however, can be turned into an opportunity for education and development. Exploring students' thinking about the design's implications (both with designers and others), assisting students in processing their thinking and feelings, and helping students to hear varying perspectives are opportunities to confirm that students have something valuable to say, to contradict perspectives that are narrowly construed and are insensitive to others, and to support students' struggle to find an acceptable solution. The outcome that would be profitable for future situations would involve staff in an ongoing dialogue with students (in the process of the T-shirt design, for example); dialogue continues the learning experience, whereas approval shuts it down. Dialogue affirms the value of student perspectives without necessarily validating any particular one. Knowing that students often hold ideas that we would like to challenge, we might be wise to watch for these opportunities, rather than to create rules to make sure they do not arise in organized settings. Palmer (1987) suggests that conflict, or "the ability to confront each other critically and honestly over alleged facts, imputed meanings, or personal biases and prejudices" (p. 25), is essential for knowing and makes for a healthy community. Knowing that students are not automatically skilled at this type of confrontation, we ought to look for as many chances to teach and practice it as possible.

A second approach involves broadening student participation beyond leadership and student staff positions. Student leaders and staff routinely complain that they do all the work. Group members who were so enthusiastic at the beginning of the year have disappeared when it is time to implement plans. Although apathy is certainly one explanation, the failure of students to perceive their worth and of leaders to reveal it to them is an equally plausible one. Student leaders are often focused on achieving individually and acquiring confirmation for their own developing voice. This emphasis is particularly true of mastery-, impersonal-, and individual-pattern knowers. Lowell described learning how to "tell people what to do without being bossy. You have to learn how to get people to do what you want them to do without making them angry at you." Lowell emphasized learning to manage people effectively. Effective leadership, according to many experts, involves empowering rather than managing people: "To empower followers means that the leader must share his or her power—converting followers into leaders and being shaped by, as well as shaping, one's followers" (Rogers, 1988, p. 6). If student affairs staff helped student leaders learn how to share their power with others and to engage in mutually beneficial interactions with them, those not yet in leadership positions could be drawn in and experience the validation needed to increase their involvement. This action, of course, requires that student affairs staff treat students in the same way—a central component of the third approach to our dilemma.

The third approach concentrates on confirmation in arenas where all students are "involved" from the outset of their college experience. Living arrangements and student-conduct policy are two such areas that touch all their lives. The stories about living arrangements reveal that validation of individual authority occurred largely in off-campus living arrangements. Many students valued the friendship and support that they received living on campus, but the development of voice was described as a result of having to take responsibility for their everyday life. Alexis's comments from Chapter Ten bear repeating here:

I have some different attitudes about things because I've found living off campus that you have more responsibility. It helps you to budget your time more; it makes everyday life more of a learning experience just in general and about commonsense things. A lot of times your work gets neglected because you have responsibilities, and you have responsibilities to the other people that you live with, too. You don't have any rules. So you have to do more or less what you think is best for yourself all the time. It makes you think about it more.

There are a wealth of insights in Alexis's comments. She had more responsibilities and had to make decisions about how to balance them. She recognized that she had obligations to her housemates that had to be juggled with the rest. She had to decide what was best in the absence of rules, a situation that caused her to reflect more upon her choices. It is important to note that the absence of rules did not translate into doing whatever she wanted. Rather, it translated into wise decisions and a recognition that she had obligations to herself and others. Her autonomy came without the cost of irresponsible behavior. Of course, three hundred students living in a residence hall is quite a different situation from ten students living in a house or two students in an apartment. A complete absence of rules is not feasible in any campus-housing unit. Yet if students are aware, as Alexis was, of their obligations to others with whom they live, their inclusion in discussing group norms within living units could be positive. Most students do not advocate being insensitive to others, harming others, damaging others' property, or creating unsafe living conditions. Group discussions about these matters might result in standards that are closer to staff expectations than they might predict. Students and staff agreeing on living-unit norms would validate students and give them opportunities to take responsibility. There might also be creative ways in which students could assume some of the residence hall duties that are currently undertaken by overburdened resident advisers.

Student participation in student-conduct discussions is another way of fostering self-reliance and independence. Recall Max's complaint about the campus environment: "They baby you—always checking up on you, taking care of you, making sure you do this and that. The rules are the same for upperclass and freshman students." Max does not appear to be arguing for an absence of rules but for expectations appropriate to his maturity. Max would probably feel more affirmed in the campus community if someone listened to his ideas and treated him as an adult who has a reasonable perspective on student behavior. This strategy would be consistent with the philosophy outlined in *The Student Personnel Point of View* (American Council of Education Studies, 1949) that students are responsible for their own growth. It would also constitute a caring approach, in Noddings's (1984) terms. She describes caring as "starting from a position of respect or regard for the projects of the other" and stresses that the one caring "does not abandon her own ethical ideal in doing this" (p. 176). Translated to student affairs, I take this statement to mean that staff would start from a position of respect for students' ideas, yet not abandon their standards about nonnegotiable conduct rules, such as those determined by law or the safety of others. Taking this approach would, of course, increase the risk that things would not always go smoothly. However, the investment of other students in rules of conduct is likely to carry far more weight with those prone to rule violations than the abstract warnings of staff. Engaging students in this kind of dialogue requires changing our assumptions that they will not participate wisely and becoming more comfortable justifying this approach as an educational activity to those at the academic center.

Situating Learning in the Students' Own Experience

What student affairs is responsible for teaching students is less clear cut than it is in academia. *The Student Personnel Point of View* (American Council of Education Studies, 1949) committed student affairs to the physical, social, emotional, and spiritual domains. I have argued that we should also include intellectual development. An entire field of literature is available on how to promote each of these aspects of development. One framework that allows us to discuss how this learning might be situated in students' experience is the Carnegie Foundation for the Advancement of Teaching's (1990) six principles for defining community. Using the student stories to illustrate these principles helps clarify how student affairs can enhance learning in a setting that naturally involves the student's experience. It also offers guidance for how student affairs can move from the margin to the center of educational practice because the conceptualization of community contains the creative tension between objective and relational modes of knowing. *Community* is defined as purposeful, open, just, disciplined, caring, and celebrative.

In advocating a purposeful community, the report calls for members of the community to work together toward educational goals. One avenue for this is an "'out-of-class curriculum' where the intellectual, aesthetic, and social dimensions of campus life thrive" (p. 14). Part of the out-of-class curriculum for Adrian was her student marketing organization. In Chapter Ten, she told us about a promotional campaign that her organization was doing for an actual client. She said, "I have learned more, I think, in that experience that I could ever learn in the classroom." The central point of Adrian's comment seems to be that the experience was real. "We're actually doing what you could be learning" implies that doing and learning are conceived as separate entities. "Doing" connects to Adrian's experience and creates one for her to reflect upon. Andrew's business manager position in a student organization helped him apply what he had learned in class to his organization and to test out ideas to see how they worked. Both Adrian's and Andrew's stories reveal that they were invested in these activities. Organizations that function to integrate learning with students' experience contribute to the educational mission of the community. Drawing on academic experience in these organizations might help more students make the connection.

The principle of an open community dictates that students speak and listen to each other in a way that allows free expression, yet affirms civility. Candace expressed her surprise in her first-year interview that most of her peers had not given any consideration to marriage. In her home town of two hundred, most of her friends were already married and had children. She said that she "learned a lot about people's social values, a lot of things I never really thought existed." She learned these things initially through roommates who were from cities. They shared their experiences and took turns going home with one another. Returning to her home town four years later, she reported wanting to say to people there, "Open your eyes. The world is not like this." Candace's insights came from the fact that she and her roommates, and later other friends, were able to express themselves freely and learn from each other about differences. Tracy reported a similar experience about coming into contact with people who were different. Initially, her reaction was, "When you first look at them, just on appearances, you kind of raise your eyebrow and wonder about them." She later realized that they had many good ideas that she would miss if she did not get to know them. Although Tracy did not say directly how this came about, we know it was through some sort of contact. Somehow, those she wondered about expressed themselves in a way that allowed her to see the value of their ideas. In both Candace's and Tracy's cases, civility (confirmation) was apparently present to balance the free expression (contradiction) of differences. This balance was not apparent in all the stories, however. Lowell reported that "one person called me a name—she was unable to hear my view." Gale used her boy friend to escape her peers because of her frustration at their attempts to impress everyone. Thus, civility and free expression are not automatic but take place in contexts where openness is encouraged by others. The more controversial the topic is—as is the case with racial- or sexual-orientation differences—the less likely that civility and free expression will be balanced.

The possibilities for encountering those from differing backgrounds and cultures abound in cocurricular life. Students live with others, have extensive interactions in organized social groups, work together on tasks in student organizations, interact with peers as student leaders, and play on recreational and organized sports teams. The contradiction stemming from these encounters is inevitable. The confirmation that allows free expression, promotes civility, and facilitates dialogue, so that students can reflect upon their differences, must be created by student affairs staff. So must continuity, as students' exchanges and reflections lead to changes in their perceptions. Creating opportunities for exchange prior to the breakdown of civility is also wise. However, if programming aimed at diversity issues is to be effective, it must be situated in the students' experience. Had a panel of presenters told Candace or Tracy that others have different values or that people cannot be judged by their appearance, their perspectives would not have been changed by the abstract nature of this encounter. Organizing programs in which students can either share experiences that they have already had or create new ones by exploring their differences balances speaking and listening. It also gives students a chance to encounter each other's varying approaches to learning and helps them devise their own.

The principle of a just community extends beyond merely allowing the free expression of diverse opinions in a civil environment to valuing those differences. The Carnegie report (1990) states this idea as honoring the sacredness of each person and pursuing diversity. By her fifth-year interview, Tracy had moved from "accepting people the way they are" to being appreciative of another person with different views. This change occurred as a result of an impromptu discussion with a person who had "some Eastern views" that she met while visiting some friends; Tracy came into contact with a new perspective that she wanted to learn more about. Rob also noted appreciating other perspectives: "I'm not as self-centered as I was in high school." Again, it took the student's own experience to move from self-centeredness, to acceptance, to appreciation.

Most of the instances of coming to value and pursue diversity came about because of interactions with friends. The fact that it was by accident that Tracy met someone who caused her to reassess her opinions attests to the tenuous nature of this experience. Many students who live at the center of campus life will never meet students who live on the margins and vice versa. Establishing activities and programs that involve the perspectives of both groups are needed to bring them together. Encouraging the balance of individual and relational modes of knowing in cocurricular life helps learners within each pattern to encounter the other. Ensuring that groups on the margin are included in student leadership positions is another way to bridge these worlds. Bringing the students together, however, is not enough. Student affairs staff must provide the confirmation needed for these groups to engage in civil and genuine exchanges and must help students learn how to value each other.

A disciplined community is one in which individuals accept their obligations to the group. The Carnegie report (1990), taking alcohol use and abuse as an example, advocated education about alcohol rather than its prohibition. This is advice relevant to other areas as well. Banning particular behaviors attempts to force students to abide by their obligations; it does not help them accept those responsibilities. Assisting students to arrive at their own decisions about their obligations promotes their development and increases the likelihood that they will act on those obligations. Rich's complaint about the visitation policy shows the impact of prohibiting certain activities:

> It's just the principle of saying to twenty-year-olds and nineteen-year-olds, "You can't do this." I don't know where that comes from. Maybe it's my nonconservative approach being from the East, but I can't go down with that. That could be changed.

Rich's issue is not so much about the actual policy as it is that it states, "You can't do this." Anita shares this point of view as she described people taking responsibilities away from her generation:

> Like visitation. I think that if you give people the responsibilities or the privileges to make decisions on their own, they're going to do what's best for them in the end. Maybe they'll go a little crazy for a while, but I think—I don't know. It makes you angry, the visitation thing. I can't see any justifiable reason for it. Supposedly, we live in a democracy. And I think if you took it to a vote, there'd be an overwhelming majority of people who wanted to abolish that. My roommate is completely independent. She pays everything on her own. And for somebody to tell her that she can't do something like that, I think is just really oppressive. It's kind of like, "I'm doing all this proving I'm an adult; I can take responsibility, but I can't have somebody in my room after twelve o'clock." It doesn't coincide with it. It's hard because people are always telling you, "Act like an adult." It's kind of, in a way, you need to be able to learn how to do those things for yourself. College is a time when we should be able to make choices like, "I don't want people making a lot of music around me." I think if you gave people the choices to make for themselves that other people would have respect for each other. And you would learn what's right for you.

Although Anita personally disagrees with the content of the visitation policy, her real point is that students need to learn to make choices, to create their own perspectives as adults. She predicts that students would then accept their obligations. Tonya speaks to this issue from experience:

> The term *in loco parentis*—they seem to go a little overboard in that respect. And it makes me more rebellious, a little more liberal, more determined to break the rules, more determined to do what I'm not supposed to, just because I think they're overstepping their bounds when they try to get you to do it. And it has a lot to do with how I was brought up; my mom didn't really tell me what to do all the time. I had guidelines, and I followed them. When I screwed up, I screwed up pretty badly, but I learned from them. So the conservatism has made me a lot more liberal; I used to be a lot more conservative.

This is clearly a story of policies that have backfired. Tonya is out to break rules because they were imposed on her. She had had the previous experience of making her own decisions and learning from her mistakes. All three students' comments emphasize the need for teaching responsibility to others in a way that includes and relates to them, not by abstract pronouncements of the rules. Helping students negotiate guidelines, make choices, live with the consequences, and reflect on their needs and those of others is the best encouragement of responsibility.

A caring community is necessary to achieve all of the tasks discussed thus far. The Carnegie report notes that "the unique characteristic that make these [the previous four] objectives work, the glue that holds it all together, is the way people relate to one another" (1990, p. 47). The report defines *caring* as the sensitive support of community members for one another and the encouragement of service to others. The relational cocurricular world plays a major part in achieving this goal. Many students talked about the support they received from friends. Hugh's comments in Chapter Ten focused on the importance of being good friends with his seven housemates. The special relationship between Hugh and his housemates provided him with the help he needed. When Leah had a problem, she could also talk to one of her housemates, who listened to her and sometimes diverted her attention by talking about her own concerns. The caring that Leah received from her housemates at times helped her work through her problems or even avoid them. At least, when she pushed them aside, she did so by showing concern for someone else.

Caring for others was sometimes also a way to receive care. Stephanie's story about working at the Oxford Crisis and Referral Center is a good example. She found that she often got overwhelmed by her own problems; she felt "like the whole world's coming down on your shoulders." However, helping someone else provided relief and put her own situation in perspective. Stephanie's service to others had the same effect and kept her in touch with how other people felt, a priority that stemmed from a previous experience:

> Part of the problem with last year, [when] I felt that there was so much tension, was that I had certain friends and acquaintances that really tended to be like that, very into themselves or into their own problems—kind of not caring about the people that were around them as much as what *they* wanted right then. I think it was a reaction to that and to my feeling that I didn't really want to do that; I didn't want to step over other people.

Eileen also volunteered her time to serve others and found it rewarding:

> I'm pretty active at Oxford View Nursing Home up the road. I'm vice president of GAP, which is the grandparent adoption program. It's nice to go there and do bingo and things because they just love—you can just walk in after going through a tornado, and they say, "Oh, you look beautiful." They just love people. And it's nice to go over there; it kind of puts things in perspective every once in a while. Makes you kind of realize how lucky you are and how young you are.

Confirmation like that received by Eileen and Stephanie also came to Hugh, by being a big brother through his finance association, and to Spencer, through being a secretary for a service fraternity. These opportunities to care for others not only helped students find support, but it also undoubtedly helped them to be more sensitive to others. Developing a caring attitude, giving full attention to other people, responding to them in a flexible way that explores possibilities, and cultivating relationships are the characteristics that Noddings (1991) uses to define interpersonal reasoning. These are likely outcomes of experiences like the ones described here.

Stephanie's story makes it clear, however, that not all students are concerned about others. It is an attitude that no doubt evolves from receiving care or experiencing the reward of providing it—a fact that again underscores the importance of situating learning in the students' experience. Hugh commented that although he enjoyed having a little brother, he had not been socialized for it. Mastery-, impersonal-, and individual-pattern learners may need confirmation of their ability to care and opportunities through which they can develop this capacity. Perhaps interpersonal reasoning and caring should be a focus of living-unit programs and educational programming about building relationships. Workshops that teach student organizations how to function might include components on interpersonal reasoning. Experiences like those of Stephanie, Eileen, Hugh, and Spencer, as well as opportunities to volunteer in soup kitchens, build housing for the homeless, and help at-risk youth, should be made more available to students. Contradiction of noncaring attitudes in cocurricular life are also essential to emphasize the importance of care. For example, Lowell found out by being a fraternity house manager that confrontation did not work; he learned through this contradiction to be less confrontational: "Stand by your point, but don't go about it in a bad way. And that's a 'feely' thing; you just have to kind of feel it." Lowell is describing the flexibility of interpersonal reasoning. Certainly, student affairs staff must themselves exhibit concern and interpersonal reasoning in interactions with students to encourage this behavior. Thus, careful attention to students and flexibility in responding to their needs are important. The development of the capacity to care would improve students' ability to work together, speak and listen to each other, appreciate differences, and accept their obligations to others. A caring community makes possible the sixth principle: that communities celebrate their traditions and changes in them. Only in a community that encompasses the first five principles can celebration include both those at the center and those on the periphery.

Defining Learning as Jointly Constructing Meaning

Situating learning in students' own experiences and developing community are still not sufficient for developing student voice. Within these experiences, genuine dialogue among students and staff is necessary to help students create their own identity and their fashion of relating to others in the communities they join. As was the case in teaching, interactions between student affairs staff and students should be seen as shaping both. This perspective agrees with the majority of functions of the student affairs profession. For example, the counselor role is based on appreciating the student's individual perspective and on nonjudgmental interactions; counselors listen to the student rather than using their personal perspective to guide the interaction (Forrest, 1989). The counselor's interpersonal skills are aimed at aiding the development of clients and avoiding establishing power over them. In addition, the belief in genuine interaction with clients underscores that the counseling encounter is the type of mutually transforming dialogue noted by Schniedewind (1987) and Shor and Freire (1987) in Chapter Nine. Similarly, the student development educator views the student as an integral part of the process (Brown, 1989). The student development educator provides experiences to facilitate student development based on an assessment of the student and of the goals that the student and educator mutually determine. Student development educators alter the opportunities they provide as students change, a process that requires an ongoing dialogue. The campus ecology manager focuses on designing environments that also promote student development. Such design is developed on the basis of jointly chosen educational values and goals, student perceptions, and reactions. In all of these roles, the student affairs professional does not minimize her or his expertise but allows it to exist in creative tension with the students' voices. The expertise is not applied to students but offered as part of a dialogue that values their voices.

Constructing meaning jointly with students replaces hierarchical staff-student interactions with heterarchical ones. Rogers (1992) says that educators should "make meaning rather than make rules" (p. 249). She argues, "Making meaning requires a transformative leader to identify and articulate a shared vision, to empower followers, to shape a collaborative culture, to focus on the common good, to model cooperation and to take a multiperspective view" (p. 249). Each of these requirements is relational and involves the acknowledgment of others and of the mutual nature of interaction. Each entails sharing with students how we think, judge, and decide, while offering them an opportunity to engage in the same process. Adopting such an approach means giving up control, or at least the illusion of control, in exchange for joint participation. Not making standard rules means giving up the efficiency and consistency that arise from applying the same rules to everyone and to all situations, the kind of efficiency that is essential for services offered from the margin. Making meaning requires that student affairs practice be designed to promote student voice—the kind of practice based on the educational purpose of the center.

The participation of student affairs professionals in the dialogue would aid student involvement in it. Empowering students would promote their speaking and listening to each other, discovering and accepting their differences to create an open community. A "multiperspective" view would help students appreciate differences, as is necessary in a just community. A focus on the common good, in conjunction with openness and justice, would assist students in accepting their obligations to others to form a disciplined community. A collaborative culture that demonstrates real cooperation promotes caring, celebrates inclusiveness, and includes everyone in striving toward educational goals. To teach students the lessons of community and simultaneously to promote their autonomy, every aspect of cocurricular life should embrace these attitudes. The competition for entrance to student organizations stresses individual achievement; open participation would emphasize inclusion and collaboration. The hierarchical operation of some student organizations gives leaders more power than members; "heterarchical" operation would increase everyone's involvement. Living units should focus on developing collaborative groups that by mutual agreement accept their obligations to others. Making meaning instead of rules would enhance collaboration among student staffs as well. Heterarchical interactions between the student affairs division and student government promotes collaborative rather than adversarial efforts related to conduct expectations and campus activities. These suggestions do not deny the importance of individual achievement or staff authority. They do, however, require that individual achievement and staff authority should not be the priority; instead, they should be placed within a relational context in which they do not supersede the focus on student development. The importance of students' ability to influence their environment and their experience is evident in Gwen's and Mark's comments, two students who (as you recall from Chapter Two) experienced growth to the most complex forms of knowing. Remember this comment of Gwen's in relation to cocurricular involvement. She added:

> You are so the master of your own destiny at college. It's such a time of stretching and growing all the way around. You test the ground and see how it feels in a lot of different areas. And you are trying to fly off cliffs, and you crash a few times, and you soar a few times.

Mark said of his participation in a leadership honor society, "There's a lot of self-determination at Miami, and I liked that a lot." Offering students the opportunity for self-determination, for soaring and crashing, is essential if they are to function in complex ways when they leave college.

Summary

Developing one's voice requires exploration. Thinking in complex ways requires that the individually formed perspective exist and function interdependently, along with individually constructed voices of others. The dual tasks of establishing self and relationships with others is what Kegan (1982) describes as the evolution of the self. Balancing what is part of self versus what is other is an ongoing task that results in truces. Balancing and rebalancing occur as a result of the combination of confirmation, contradiction, and continuity in the environment. Thus, developing voice is more complex than developing an opinion on a specific topic. To develop their own knowledge, students must be able to perceive themselves as autonomous. To engage in complex knowing, they must be able to move beyond autonomy to interdependence.

As students explore who they are and what they believe, experiment with new behaviors, and try new beliefs on for size, support for their ability to choose and reflect upon those choices confirms them as autonomous. Some student choices warrant confirmation, whereas others warrant contradiction. Yet even in the latter case, the student can still be confirmed as a person who is cared for and respected. Giving student opportunities to participate in dialogue in various aspects of their cocurricular life emphasizes both their autonomy and the importance of considering others in a relational context. It also creates opportunities for student affairs staff to process ideas, beliefs, and community values with students that might otherwise occur only by chance. Sharing how staff make choices about their values and behavior can help students struggle with the multitude of decisions that they face in college. Recognizing staff as people who also struggle might help students build trusting relationships with them in which discussion of their ideas could take place.

Contradiction is inherent in participation in a relational community and in genuine dialogue. Students encounter others with different experiences, values, ways of knowing, and patterns within ways of knowing. An environment in which exploration and reflection about the meaning of stereotypes or closed attitudes toward others are confirmed keeps contradiction within the productive range. Too much contradiction threatens students, particularly those whose voices and identities are not yet strong enough to withstand the challenge. Contradiction of an overemphasis on individual achievement automatically occurs when students are in environments where they have to work together, such as living units or organizations. Contradiction of dependence also occurs as students challenge each other to define themselves. Staff can help students work through these contradictions that occur naturally in cocurricular life.

Continuity offers students a support system as they struggle to understand themselves and the nature of their relationships with others. Staff who maintain their connection with students through their various definitions of themselves offer the stability that may not be available from peers or faculty. Constructing meaning together with students helps staff stay attuned to their development in order to adjust the holding environment accordingly.

As is clear in the students' stories, many find the confirmation, contradiction, and continuity that they need through their interactions with peers. This finding might lead some to wonder why student affairs staff should interfere. I would argue, however, that it is surely not wise to expect students to accomplish the daunting task of defining themselves simply by relying on each other. The students in this study struggled for most—or, in some cases, all—of their college life to view themselves as knowers both in academic and cocurricular realms. Although many opportunities for exploration existed, they were often left to their own devices to learn from these experiences. Leaving crucial aspects of development to chance interactions risks that they will not take place or that students will be unable to help each other create new possibilities for making meaning. Staff efforts must reflect an intentional approach to creating opportunities to describe experience, make meaning of it, and create new possibilities for viewing the world and relationships to others. Students are not left to learn the knowledge of their disciplines on their own; they receive guidance from faculty. This comes both in a proactive form, as the instructor prepares a syllabus and course of study, and in a reactive form, as the instructor responds to particular students' needs. In student affairs, our marginal role in education has led to greater focus on reactions—helping students when they struggle and resolving crises as they arise. The roles of student development educator and campus ecology manager call for the proactive stance needed to aid student development in a purposeful way. As is apparent from these students' stories, the mere existence of opportunities is not sufficient to result in complex knowing. They must involve genuine reflection on experience, a component that can be enhanced through staff participation. This approach reflects the type of educational practice that takes place at the core (not the margin) of the educational enterprise. Joining academia at the center of the educational enterprise also requires reconfiguring the partnership between student affairs and academic educators.

Classroom and Context: An Educational Dialectic

Elizabeth S. Blake

The scene is a faculty meeting on a residential campus where the class schedule has traditionally left the late afternoons free for student activities. The motion under discussion would allow classes right through to the dinner hour. The dean of students speaks against the motion. He presents as a clinching argument the idea that co-curricular activities educate the students just as classroom activities do. The faculty responds with restlessness and some obvious hostility, and approves the motion over the dean's opposition.

Change of scene. The vice president for student affairs is discussing an upcoming budget presentation with the chancellor of the university. The agree that more career counseling is needed for undergraduates, especially for the increasing number of women. But the faculty bargaining unit is pushing for higher salaries and more tenure lines in engineering. The vice president rehearses the arguments for adding two career counselor slots to the student affairs budget. Among other points, he states that life planning is as educationally valuable for students as some of the basic courses in the curriculum. The chancellor looks uncomfortable. "You'd better leave that out," she says. "It won't fly."

The line of reasoning used in both cases is all too familiar. People in student affairs, knowing that education is, after all, the mission of their institutions, justify their activities as educational. Yet the more they do this, the less often they convince their faculty colleagues. A persistent gap seems to exist between the two groups of people on campus who work most closely with students. The faculty/nonfaculty separation is a pervasive one throughout college and university structure. It is felt by everyone from groundskeeper to president. The fact that a modern university consists of more than just faculty and students is often ignored. But one might think that professionals in the student affairs area would be in a privileged position in relation to faculty and that a common focus on students would be grounds for mutual understanding. Alas, not so. On some campuses the separation between student affairs professionals—even those who also teach—and the full-time teaching faculty is open and rancorous, on other campuses attempts are made to hide it. Either way, conflicts are there.

In order to survive the next twenty years, our institutions certainly need the collegiality which is at the origin of the word "college" and the unity which is at the origin of the word "university," even if such a recall to linguistic fundamentalism evokes a sad smile from us. Student affairs is here to stay on our campuses. The positions of director of residence, manager of the student union, financial aid officer, director of counseling, and so forth, each require specific expertise today. They are less and less likely to be filled by people who teach at the same time or who, in fact, have ever taught. For the sake of unity, survival, and the quality of the educational experience we offer our students, we need to look at what really does justify the existence of student affairs as an area of endeavor on campus, and why, instead of minimizing the gap between faculty members and student affairs administrators, we may want actually to reinforce our distinctiveness as a source of dialogue.

The issues are hard to pin down and tend to have sensitive personal reverberations. To bring them out into the open, states of affairs will be polarized here which are never so clearly opposite in real life. The point is not to be definitive but to provoke discussion from a new perspective.

Before proceeding, it is important to acknowledge a debt. This paper is the result of one of the longest professional conversations I have ever been involved in as a dean. As an offshoot of the national activities of the Division of Professional Development and Standards of the National Association of Student Personnel Administrators, (NASPA), James J. Ronan, then Dean of Student Affairs at Bentley College in Waltham, Massachusetts, brought together a group a academic deans and deans of students to discuss the relationships between student affairs and academic affairs at a widely disparate assortment of public and private institutions in New England. We met about every two months for two years, 1975 to 1977, and the fifteen or more people who initiated the colloquy dwindled in the end to five: Ronan, Margaret Furman (University of Massachusetts/Boston), Dennis Golden (Framingham State College), John Manning (University of Connecticut), Ridgway Shinn (Rhode Island College), and me (Wellesley College). The line of reasoning of this paper is my own, but many of the ideas were triggered, enhanced, or sharpened by our frank discussions.

An accurate attribution of ideas is impossible and general acknowledgment is hereby expressed. Ronan and Furman each submitted reports back to the NASPA Division of Professional Development and Standards,[1] and Ronan and Shinn conducted a debate at a NASPA conference in 1976, but I do not know of any published follow-up to our unique learning experience. There are insights to be gained from our confrontations, it seems to me, and this paper is an effort to share them more widely.

Classroom and Context

What are the distinctive features of curricular and co-curricular life? In what sense does each contribute to learning? First, it is necessary to state a basic truth that is sometimes obscured: *in a college or university, the formal curriculum is the reason the students are there.* Interaction between student and instructor, i.e., the "classroom," even when it is not physically a place, is central. What goes on outside of class—the context for the classroom experience—is also part of the student's educational immersion, but of itself it is not what makes the university a *university* rather than some other social institution. It may contribute greatly to the student's education, but not *in the same way* as does the formal curriculum. Student activities, and various forms of counseling and advising, involve services which could in fact be offered to any group of people gathered for any purpose: social, religious, recreational, or whatever. It is the formal learning embodied in the curriculum which differentiates the campus community as an institution of higher education from a commune, a church, a club, a camp, or a safari.

A good student affairs program is planned, it does not just happen. It is planned so as to be intensively educational and to integrate its offerings closely with the curricular goals of the institution. But the nature of the learning it promotes is in several ways different from that of the classroom. There is a complementarity involved which is worth exploring.

To make this clear, let us look first at the formal learning situation. Practically anything can go on as a classroom activity and often does. There is no boundary beyond which one can say with assurance that something is *not* a classroom activity, just as one cannot limit the range of what is assigned to the student union building or the residence halls. But, in the case of the classroom, one sort of activity must occur in order for the situation truly to be called formal learning. Formal learning is directed in the end toward manipulating concepts rather than things. Why not just call that thinking? The word "thinking," like the word "education," is too general. It is only certain kinds of thinking which are referred to here. The thrust of formal learning is toward establishing systematic links from the particular to the general, from the concrete to the abstract, from the personal to the objective. Obviously both induction and deduction are used in the classroom, but good teaching tends to start from where the student is: particular, concrete, individual. Thus the characteristic movement of formal education, whether in kindergarten or in post-doctoral seminars, is from known, assimilated (i.e., subjectified) experience toward a new level of objectivity (even in ethical and esthetic matters) and toward the abstraction of general truth and principles.

As an example, students in a course in economics may be asked to look at the use of oil for heating by local home owners and business firms. This provides an immediate, concrete kind of problem. But the reason for studying it is not to get to know the community better or to understand why one family likes their house warmer than another, but to be able to make some useful generalizations about how people's behavior changes in response to changes in price and market conditions. What the instructor expects students to come out with are concepts and principles which can be applied to other instances and to larger economic problems.

The other distinctive characteristic of formal learning is its artificial ordering of experience, the more ordered the better. In teaching a foreign language, one may start by exposing students to large chunks of the language as it is but, very quickly, one begins to pull out examples which illustrate common tendencies, like the endings of verbs or the position of adjectives, so that the students can leap ahead of where they would be if everything had to be absorbed in its unordered form of everyday experience. In the classroom, if the facts are not at some point ordered and if one does not learn to understand and manipulate concepts which can be applied beyond the immediate material presented, it would be hard to say that formal learning has occurred.

The same movement toward concepts and general principles goes on outside the classroom; it is not limited to the curriculum. It is always exciting to see how students' ability to order material and abstract from it on their own increases as they become more and more their own mentors. The point is that whether or not such activity goes on in a given situation outside the classroom does not *define* that situation. It is the reason for being—the *sine qua non*—of formal learning; it is an error to try to make it the reason for being of other campus activities. The student affairs area, in particular, has an almost opposite thrust and justification.

The difference between campus life—as it may be shaped and directed by student affairs personnel—and everyday life outside the campus gates, is not as readily sensed as the difference between the classroom and everyday life. The same sorts of cultural, political, religious, and service activities seem to occur on campus or off, in a kind of organized confusion of intentions, and people's individual reasons for what they do are just as diverse. Is there anything educationally distinctive about the campus context?

If you think about it, campus life differs from ordinary life in the *density* and *accessibility* of the experiences offered during each term or semester. A good campus environment offers concentrated doses of experience, of a marvelous variety of kinds, all available quite freely to the members of the community. There are extraordinary opportunities for learning and growth, some of them formal, most of them informal. Within each semester or quarter, students have access to a quantity and variety of experiences which one would not usually encounter in years of routine home life. This can be true whether one is an undergraduate at seventeen or at seventy. Co-curricular learning can perhaps best be thought of as a sort of *intensified living*. Through exposure to other students, through activities, information, counseling, part-time work, internships, and so on, the personal development of students is encouraged to keep pace with their intellectual development. What goes on in the classroom contributes to personal maturation too, but it is not the reason *for* the classroom. The physics instructor does not teach the laws of theremodynamics to make students more mature. But the personal, societal maturation of students is a concern of the director of residence. It is, in fact, the primary *educational* concern of the director of residence, of the dean of students, and of the other professionals in student affairs.

The general direction of the learning process involved in "intensified living" follows that of our normal dealings with reality. It moves, in other words, from the general to the particular, the abstract to the concrete, the impersonal to the personal. For example, we go to a lecture on campus safety and stop walking home alone at 1:00 A.M. from the library, or a counselor talks about the anguish many students feel while choosing their major and we are relieved to know that our own distress is not unique. The primary effort of counselors and advisors is directed (or should be) toward finding among the institution's options and restrictions a way for each individual student to develop to the fullest. This movement of bringing abstractions and principles down to a personal level is the opposite of what we observed as characteristic of formal learning.

The other defining element of the context in which most American undergraduate formal learning takes place, i.e., campus life, is the acceptability of transient commitment. One can attempt an activity or role on campus and then abandon it for another, usually without personal detriment in the world at large. The campus is a special kind of protected environment. Student activities offer a chance to try out the games of loves and chance, of politics and power, of faith and even of health, apart from the main arena of life where they are played for keeps. This, by the way, is one of the attractions of the campus community for older adults who return to study at a later stage in their lives. The opportunity is a useful one not only for those who are still making their first commitments and mistakes but also for men and women of every age who are making their individual odyssey through what Gail Sheehy has called life's "passages."

There is a further contrast between curricular and co-curricular emphases in learning which may sound like the reverse of what has just been outlined. It arises nonetheless out of the already stated characteristics of each area. In the classroom, although the immediate goal may be training in known skills and modes of thought, the eventual goal of even the most utilitarian of courses is to make people wary of stock answers and bring them to the point where they deal creatively on their own with the material. This is especially true, or should be, of higher education. In this sense higher education is fundamentally subversive. It brings people up to the edges of present knowledge in a field while training them to think independently. It thereby prepares the undermining of the accepted structures and ways of doing things—what the French call the "received ideas"—inherited from the past. The encouragement of independent thinking certainly adds yeast to the mix of our campus activities! On the other hand, students must work together, within commonly agreed-on structures, in order to carry out successful activities and create an enjoyable campus life. Thus there is a sense in which, while the goal of formal learning is very individualistic, even idiosyncratic, the concern of a good student affairs program is to foster a cohesive, workable group existence. In all the various student services, one helps to set up structures and make them work. By necessity one is encouraging students to conform to institutional structures, even as one is also finding ways of mitigating the effects of those structures on each student taken alone.

To summarize, formal learning moves to increase and order the student's conceptual knowledge in a way which can potentially lead to new insights and thereby to societal change. Co-curricular learning, on the other hand, is an intensification of the processes of learning by experience, encouraging personal development commensurate with intellectual sophistication. In contrast to the classroom's encouragement of individualized challenges to accepted ideas, the campus context fosters cooperative effort within the imposed structures of community living.

The danger of polarizing matters in the way we have just done is to make it appear that the content of what occurs in the classroom or outside is necessarily different, which it may not be at all. The material may be exactly the same. Let me suggest two illustrations. A director of student activities spends the morning meeting with student leaders who are preparing a big homecoming weekend. They go over budgets, publicity, contractual arrangements with the guest artists, security, and so on. In the late afternoon the same director, teaching a graduate course in student personnel administration, uses the organization of the homecoming weekend as one of the case studies. As you visualize what that person does in the first role as compared with the second, it is clear that the difference is not in the material but in the approach. Or take the professor of psychology who first teaches her course in counseling psychology and then goes to the college counseling office to counsel students. In both the course and the counseling office one hopes that the students are learning, from themselves and from the psychologist, but how different will be the approach and the expectations!

The generalizations we have made about classroom and context are not limiting or exclusive; they are directed at approach, not content, and they are only an attempt to discern tendencies. What is useful to us as faculty or as student affairs administrators is to realize the almost symmetrically opposite complementarity of our educational functions.

Attributes in Conflict

The preceding discussion on classroom and context makes it seem hardly surprising that different human personalities tend to end up as professors or administrators of student affairs. In caricature the professorial extreme is almost the mirror image of the student personnel administrator extreme.

Of course there was a time in the evolution of many of the older colleges in this country when mentor and monitor were one and the same person. The faculty chose students, taught them, advised them, assisted them with financial or other problems, disciplined them, saw to their exposure to cultural events, and often found them a position at the conclusion of their studies. The twentieth century has brought us to such a degree of specialization that it is unlikely today that a person will be both a regular member of the teaching faculty *and* an administrative officer in student affairs, especially in such areas as financial aid or student union management. Where student affairs administrators are also faculty members, one finds that people will tend to behave differently, even think differently, in their two roles.

In examining those two roles here, the traits will be purposely exaggerated for the sake of contrast. It is not that a different person is involved necessarily but that each role tends to draw upon, and favor, different aspects of personality. The matter is worth examining because of the pervasive difficulties faculty and student affairs people have in discussing professional concerns. Clearly some emotionally charged personal factors are in the background.

The able professional in the student affairs domain has to enjoy students of every style and level of intellectual growth and respond to them as individuals whose entire lives are being reshaped by the educational commitment they have made. The student affairs administrator is drawn to the subjective, experiential side of things, toward immediate problems and events which are important in their particularity. One has to be both practical and gregarious, knowing how to accomplish things *through* others, often in groups. On a rhythm of daily interactions one has to take pleasure in organizing and orchestrating the ephemeral. Two approaches are important in most student affairs jobs: one may be primarily a counselor, as in personal counseling or career development, or one may be primarily a manager. Let us note in passing that faculty members are not primarily either of these. The educational role of a student affairs person is important but it does not, by itself, define one's position as a residence counselor, a foreign student advisor, or whatever. For the chief student affairs administrators, management ability is the key attribute. One must enjoy coordinating, and managing events and people. This is very different from the scholarly mode. One study of a variety of managers, from foremen to hockey coaches to prime ministers, shows that while the folklore would have us believe that the manager is a reflective, systematic planner, the fact is that managers do more reacting than acting. Managerial activities are characterized by "brevity, variety, and discontinuity," and managers tend to be action-oriented people who "dislike reflective activities."[2]

The committed and inspiring faculty member, on the other hand, is expected to have a primary orientation to ideas and reflection, to work with books or experiments or schema, prizing the objective view, reason and proof, detached judgment, originality, esthetic sensibility, exactitude. Social relationships can legitimately be sublimated and forgotten in the exciting pursuit of understanding. The high points of teaching—the "epiphanies," to use James Joyce's term—come when both instructor and students utterly forget themselves and their surroundings in the intensity of their engagement with ideas. The kinds of people who get caught up in teaching—and in the research and writing which back up the best teaching in any field—are allowed by the society at large to remain somewhat apart and ill-adapted if they so choose. A professor can—without harm to professional standing—be shy, withdrawn, not good at handling practical matters, arrogant, self-centered, a loner, a less than active citizen, a sort of social misfit. Most faculty are not that way, but the option is open. Since the dominant American scene is anti-intellectual, as Richard Hofstadter made clear to us years ago,[3] often the only place where the professor enjoys full prestige and honor is within the university. Important to his or her sense of well-being on campus is the feeling of freedom from a too-rigid structuring of the environment.

Clearly the personality tendencies we have sketched can be a source of conflicts between student affairs personnel and faculty. It would be nice if the differences had stimulated constructive dialogue between equals. What has occurred so far on many campuses, unfortunately, is a curious sort of mutual "put-down" at a personal level, leading to mutual avoidance, or worse. One finds people using the defensive strategies of ridicule or the erection of barriers of language and style. Exacerbating the situation is what can be called "the power problem." Actual power, perceived power, and powerlessness exist on both sides. Bringing some of these usually avoided sore points into the open can perhaps help our understanding.

In the roles that they play, both the faculty member and the student affairs administrator are vulnerable to feelings of inferiority which the person in the other role is especially likely to provoke. Each may therefore feel strongly threatened, i.e., "put down," by the other. Successful faculty members are on their own "turf" within the campus confines; as we noted earlier, that is the place—and it may be the only place—where being an intellectual pays off in terms of status and prestige. Outside the university, in the society at large, the same people may be on the defensive, hassled by car salesmen, head waiters, and real estate brokers who would not think of so mistreating the local banker or business person. On campus, professors want full sway, with all the respect and honor which their personal styles may not call forth elsewhere.

The successful administrator of student affairs, on the other hand, is likely to be a "manager" type: entrepreneurial, gregarious, practical, ambitious, at ease socially; in other words, exactly the kind of person from whom the scholar may be trying to take refuge within the university. The epitome of the manager is legitimately installed as dean of student affairs in the very citadel of free inquiry, ready to extend his social mastery, bureaucratic expertise, and love of structure into the professional domain. There looms the very societal put-down which academics had hoped to elude, ready to shame them one more time.

The scholar's reaction of rage and horror is principled as well as personal. It is born out of the instinctive need to defend the territory of free thought and protect the prerogative of being noncon-formist even to the point of turning the world on its ear. The director of student affairs, as a person who especially knows the value of good management, wants the institution to thrive by "running well." "Running well" is apt to mean a strong administrative structure. The faculty member, however, knows the importance of encouraging criticism of the status quo. The tension is a familiar one, mentioned in our discussion of classroom and context, between established social structures which tend to resist change and the mission of higher education not only to preserve and transmit knowledge but to renew it and thereby promote change. A strong administrative structure is always a potential threat to freedom of inquiry. To the faculty member there is always the danger of the university's losing its mission and its soul to its corporate management.

Thus, faculty and student resistance to administrative structure on campus is more than just rebellion against authority. The struggle which goes on is an important one, between the Dionysian and Appollonian forces, if you will, for it indeed has epic proportions. Economic interests tend to be on the side of the status quo in society and to become uneasy when the university insists too much on its creative mission. Faculty and students become uneasy when that mission is impeded inter-nally. An administrator in the student affairs area must walk a fine line between too much structure and not enough. Concern for efficient functioning must not be such as to rule out of existence the professor or student who wants to follow curiosity wherever it leads, since the campus is supposed to be society's haven for such a person. Actually the student affairs person who is a super-manager and the professor who is a born maverick can both be useful to the healthy flourishing of an institution of learning. But one can see why the faculty member may unconsciously find the well-trained and effective student affairs administrator threatening.

Turning to the student affairs administrator, what do we find? All too often we find someone dogged by a sense of inferiority because of a lack of intellectual inclination: well-educated, sympa-thetic to the cause of higher education, supportive of its mission, gifted in the ability to mediate the problems people face in an intellectual community, all of those, yet not having gone the full route out to the frontiers of a field of knowledge often enough and long enough and in a systematic enough way to be a true scholar—or even a very good fake one. Even acquiring a doctorate in student personnel administration, or higher education administration, may not solve the problem if the research emphasis is on "how to" rather than "what." Courses in methods and tactics go against the habits of mind of faculty in the traditional disciplines. Because of this, the person in student affairs—especially someone who has specialized in that field—has a tendency, sometimes uncon-sciously, to hold faculty members in awe. The effect of unfamiliarity with what faculty members are about in their disciplines makes their knowledge seem mysterious and leads to ways of referring to Faculty with a capital "F" in the same rather obsequious way that our society often refers to Scientists with a capital "S." The sense of inequality and of unfamiliarity with the mysteries of what it is that makes teaching and research such an adventure can even cause the student affairs person, out of defensiveness, to criticize and mock faculty for their social shortcomings. This is just what faculty fear that they will do. The mutual "put-down" comes full circle.

But there is more to the matter. At the heart of the "Scientist with a capital 'S'" issue is the fact that scientists usually learn something of literature, history, philosophy, and the arts in the course of becoming scientists whereas humanists—and the rest of us—do not necessarily learn much science. This makes science more mysterious to the nonscientists than humanism is to the scientist. Similarly, teaching and research seem more mysterious to the nonfaculty student affairs person than student affairs seems to the faculty member who, somewhere along the way, has had to acquire some understanding of students, program planning ability, and so forth. Student affairs administrators may hesitate to intrude on the faculty world because of this, while faculty move in and out of the student affairs domain at will, however, lacking in particular expertise they may be. When students are unhappy in the residence halls or there is a security incident during freshman orientation, faculty will claim authority, from their central position with respect to the educational mission of the institution, to criticize the handling of the matter and propose solutions, sometimes without even consulting the student personnel experts.

Using the term "expert" brings up another part of the problem. To what extent is a student affairs administrator an expert, a *professional,* in student affairs? There is a readily identified content and set of professional skills associated with being a university psychiatrist, a college chaplain, or a football coach. Such jobs require a specialized apprenticeship and some form of certification by peers. But one may move into the position of Dean of Students, or Director of Residence, or Advisor for Student Activities from a variety of backgrounds, and the Vice President for Student Affairs of the state university system may be someone with a J.D. or an M.B.A. or a Ph.D. in classics, just as well as a doctorate in student personnel administration.

There is a sense in which any dean, or provost, or president of an institution is not a professional at all. The person takes on a managerial role and thereby moves out from her or his original professional field to become a generalist. Even professional certification in nonprofit business administration is not in itself sufficient to meet the broad demands of a top administrative job. Generalists are extremely valuable amidst the specializing tendencies of a college or university. They deserve respect for the executive and managerial competence they demonstrate. But, strictly speaking, they are professionals by virtue of the field through which they reach their position, not by the position itself.

In the area of student affairs—and what a broad and varied area that can be—confusion is easy between expert and executive. In contrast, the professionalism of faculty is sharply delineated, far more so today than in the days when university contracts stated that a professor could be called on by the trustees to teach any subject! Once again we can see that student affairs people and faculty tend toward two ends of a spectrum, and it is not surprising that misunderstandings about professionalism result. The best solution is not to claim professional standing but to show it. Where there are opportunities for the manager of the student union building or the director of career services to demonstrate to faculty colleagues the importance of new techniques and new bodies of knowledge, and his or her ability to contribute from them usefully to what faculty are trying to accomplish, arguments about professionalism die away. For all the contention that any faculty member can "do" student affairs with the left hand while teaching with the right, few instructors really want to try, especially with the other pressures that are on them today. But it is reasonable for faculty to expect specific knowledge and skills from student affairs administrators and to be able to feel that such skills are being well used.

Various forms of defensiveness arise out of the anxieties which faculty and student affairs administrators provoke in one another by the fact that the areas of strength of the one are so often areas of weakness of the other. The administrator may try to become the scholar he or she basically is not. The faculty member may try unhappily to play the manager's role or may give up all efforts to reach out to students beyond the classroom. Pretense, the use of jargon, withdrawal into a distant superiority are among the unfortunate responses that occur.

Nothing seems to upset faculty from the traditional disciplines more acutely than the vocabulary used in the domain of student affairs. The mixture of terms borrowed from management theory and the behavioral sciences, not always applied precisely, disturbs both those who do not understand and those who fear that they may understand too well. The jargon is viewed as a pretentious smokescreen hiding either superficiality or, far worse, a veritable monster of human control mechanisms. From the faculty member's point of view, too many people in student affairs are too easily taken in by the techniques of applied psychology and computer sociology. Faculty are usually trained skeptics, to whom a person doing research in student personnel administration may seem intellectually gullible. Because of the very difficulty of conducting rigorous analysis in such a field, researchers must prove themselves individually. They are not likely to be accepted automatically into the scholarly fold. For the student affairs administrator whose inclinations are more toward action than scholarship, being a bad scholar leads neither to faculty acceptance nor to the best service to the institution.

Faculty members can be superficial, too, and gullible, especially outside their own areas of expertise. One of the advantages of the Ph.D. is that it allows you to be naive and foolish in everything but your discipline. Sometimes it's a sort of down-curve from the B.A. on. Robert James McCracken once told of some definitions which were circulating at Union Theological Seminary, where many students prepare Bachelor of Divinity or Doctor of Divinity degrees: if you had earned the right to put the initials "B.D." after your name, they stood for Barely Dumb; "D.D." stood, alas, for Definitely Dumb; and "Ph.D."?—Phenomenally Dumb![4] To many worried deans of student affairs today, in touch as they must be with student trends, a lot of faculty currently seem out of touch with the new style of TV-nourished studies they are supposed to teach, lost in their own specialty, too concerned about tenure to teach properly or to carry a share of community burdens, or too secure in tenure to bother. Selfishness, aloofness, tunnel vision, and social insensitivity are all traits among the faculty which rouse the ire of those responsible for making the campus a good learning community for students. The faculty member who tries to move in and run student affairs can also be a problem. Authoritarian ways can lead to revolt, sincerity to indiscretion, and impulsiveness to serious inequities; meanwhile the preparation of lectures is neglected and unreturned student papers lie around in stacks. Being a poor dean, or counselor, or registrar, or whatever, confers little administrative power and less advantage to the institution.

The mention of power brings us to the last aspect of conflict between the commonly seen characteristics of the faculty role and the student affairs role in higher education: the "power problem." A college or university is supposed, in theory, to be a company of scholars, a group of independent professionals banding together to offer instruction. Historically, educational administration has risen out of the faculty. The fact that most institutions today are barely collegial, and that administration has become an entity unto itself, does not affect the central position of the faculty in the operation. As stated earlier, the formal curriculum is the reason students are there. Thus power would appear to rest with the faculty; they determine and teach the curriculum. But the financial base is clearly with the president and the trustees. In many institutions today the administration around the president seems all-powerful and faculty members struggle to keep a share of control through limited participation in governance or through collective bargaining, or both.

Facing this situation, the student affairs professionals are in a curiously ambiguous position. They have less power and prestige than the faculty because they are a step removed from the formal learning process. On the other hand, the dean of students or vice-president for student affairs is often the only university officer other than the president who has an "institution-wide" generalist view. Student affairs executives are chosen for the ability to encompass the institution in its physical arrangements and in its human and intellectual dimensions as it affects all of its publics and are thus in a potentially powerful situation, seeing the larger picture and influencing many actions. They are also advocates for students and responsible for many quasi-legal matters related to students. Student concerns, when pervasive, *have* to become institutional concerns. In addition, student affairs people tend to "embody" the institution to the individual student as they interpret rules, explain procedures, and guide progress. They are usually more immediately accessible than faculty, and their views on educational philosophy may be particularly influential because they are offered outside the teacher/student relationship. Student polls show that students tend to know the student affairs personnel and to have stronger ties to them than to anyone but peers. Student affairs personnel also have potential power through the action of students. Some student affairs administrators can marshal an army of student supporters in a wink and, with their skill in organization and group dynamics, can control that army better than many faculty can handle a freshman laboratory section.

Instinctively, faculty recognize these elements of power in the student affairs situation and resent them. Student affairs administrators are seen as one and the same with the central administration of the institution against which the faculty struggles. From the viewpoint of student affairs, however, the juggernaut of faculty power is always poised to move in—and to leave student affairs out. Collective bargaining sessions may bring new high levels of faculty compensation without a word for staff salaries or benefits, for example. Student affairs people also watch faculty members become increasingly isolated from one another and from their students, and see the institution splitting into many fragments, yet they are unable to change the trend. Both faculty and student personnel administrators feel powerless and angered by their powerlessness.

What with mutual fear, pretense, plays for power and the frustration which accompany them, it is not surprising that the faculty/student affairs relationship is full of friction. From our earlier discussion of characteristic attributes, we can see why there is a pervasive and enduring separation between the two kinds of role. Yet the frictions and the separations may not be a bad thing. In fact the dialectic tension between the two areas could be a source of enrichment for university life. There can only be true dialogue between equals, however. Both faculty and student affairs administrators need to affirm their roles and recognize the importance of the other group to the mission of higher education.

Complementarities

Let us now look at what *could* bring us together. What should we contribute positively to each other and to our institutions? First let us outline some faculty responsibilities and then those of student affairs administrators.

It follows from what we said earlier about the central mission of colleges and universities that the faculty should be accountable for the formal curriculum and, thereby, for the contribution which one particular college or university makes to the world's educational enterprise. We do not often have time, as individual faculty, or even as academic deans, to stand off from the details of our own courses, disciplines, and concerns to contemplate the whole. But we should. What is to be learned in this institution? What are the major questions being asked through the curriculum? To what extent does our curriculum ask questions at all, or does it simply provide answers to questions people have asked in the past?

These are not concerns just for a college of liberal arts. If we are teaching nursing, for example, how do we define that profession? And what kind of program will best prepare nurses still to be competent and able twenty or thirty years from now? If we *are* a liberal arts college, what is our particular definition of the liberal arts? Are we being true to that definition? If we are a state university, are we meeting the needs of the people of our state and, again, how will what we are now teaching people serve them in twenty or thirty years when they are at the peak of their own professional life? These are the kinds of questions which faculty should be asking in relation to the courses they teach and the curricula they establish.

Faculty must also see that curricular concerns are kept central to budget decisions. Do we make the effort that we should to influence university budget decisions more favorably toward the central mission of the institution? Of course it takes an effort to get involved in such matters, but it is part of our responsibility as professionals to do this. The doctor or lawyer who operates independently has to know enough about government regulations, insurance, the cost of supplies, and other such matters to keep his accounts in order and himself afloat financially. There is no reason why faculty members, who are presumably also independent professionals, joined together in the faculty of a university, should feel that they can leave all financial decisions to people who do not teach. They do so at the risk of having educational matters lose their first priority in the institutional structure. After the faculty has asked itself what the curriculum should be, it should then be asking what resources—libraries, media, etc.—are to be available to help answer the questions to which the curriculum addresses itself. Both of these are our responsibilities if we are to preserve freedom of inquiry for future generations.

To say that faculty are accountable in the end for the quality of an institution's curriculum does not mean that faculty are solely responsible for setting it up. It is extremely important that the discussion and decision-making about educational priorities include the central administration, the students, and those in student affairs. It is not simply that the recruiters in the admissions office obviously need to know what the curriculum is and how to explain it when they go out to visit local high schools. Nor is it only that there is a public relations advantage when all employees of an institution of higher education understand its goals and are able to articulate them clearly. It is also that the faculty has something to learn about the curriculum from student affairs personnel. Those who work with and counsel students, who see them in residence halls and extracurricular activities, often have a better sense of the impact of the curriculum as a *whole* on students than any one individual faculty member, or even the faculty taken collectively. The curriculum's "message" as perceived by a given student generation is reflected in discussions of course choices and career plans, of financial aid, of sports, in casual conversation in the dining halls and in student committee work. Good student personnel administrators are alert to perceive the overall effects. They should have the opportunity to report them back accurately to the central administration and the faculty in evaluative discussions. The detail of how this is accomplished—with what committees, when and how—varies among our institutions.

It is also important that they be kept up to date on charges in the curriculum and on the reasoning behind the changes. It is often the people in student affairs who, informally, interpret the courses of study to students, clear up misunderstandings, and give advice. If the institution is to speak to its students in a cohesive way, either the faculty must be as available as the student affairs administrators are, in the residence halls, the student centers, and the advising and counseling offices, or else the faculty must make possible the collaboration of student affairs personnel in the ongoing shaping of the curriculum. At present, students all too often receive conflicting messages, and even incorrect information, because student affairs administrators are too far removed from curricular planning. People trained in student personnel matters are usually good publicists. When they are well informed on curriculum and educational philosophy, they can also help to reduce the "information gap" which haunts our complex institutions. What good does it do to introduce exciting new programs of study if nobody knows about them?

Another thing which faculty should do is to keep pressure on student affairs administrators to limit bureaucracy and encourage innovation. This refers back to our earlier consideration of the tendency of people in student affairs to get caught up in systems and structure. If faculty members themselves are utter conformists, they will not be of help to student affairs here, but at least in theory it is the faculty mission to defend sincere nonconformity. If a new idea is challenged and succumbs, then it probably deserved to succumb, but it is the faculty's responsibility to keep the college or university structure flexible enough so that the more hardy maverick idea, or person, can flourish there. In their teaching, instructors need to be the best possible demonstrators of honest confrontation between new ideas and old, and then insist that the same kind of rigorous, risky, confrontation go on in co-curricular as well as curricular settings.

Now let us turn matters around and see what the professionals in the student affairs area have as educational responsibilities and as expertise to be shared. Here we are thinking primarily of the institution as a whole and of the enrichment of the context in which formal learning takes place, as we described it earlier. The most important educational responsibility of the student affairs administrator, it seems clear, is to know the institution well, along with its particular societal setting—*this* year, *this* location, *these* nearby institutions, *these* times in which to live—and then to help create the most propitious possible context for teaching and learning. There are several aspects to this responsibility.

First and foremost is to know the current students, not in the sense of individual names, but of a sort of evolving group profile. The student population changes over time, often abruptly. From one academic year to another, faculty suddenly feel that they have lost touch, that the teaching process is not working properly. The dean or vice president in charge of student affairs should be a valuable resource for obtaining an overall picture of students, or exemplary insights on special subgroups of students. When an institution, for whatever reason, begins to admit a larger percentage of women, of minorities, of students from abroad, of older students, of the handicapped, or whatever, it is very important that knowledge about the change be communicated to members of the faculty and that guidance be available for those who wish it on new ways of reaching out to the new constituencies. People in the student affairs area are often the ones who know the students best, who are—or should be—alert to changes and who should even try to anticipate them whenever possible. The lowering of the age of majority is an example of a recent change which affected faculty-student relationships and which needed to be anticipated and interpreted with respect to its legal and community implications. When recruiting sources change, when—as is now happening in some places—recruiting is being done in retirement homes as well as in high schools, in suburban "retread" centers as well as in the armed services, the dean of students should be able to anticipate some of the problems that new types of students will bring with them and should assist faculty to prepare themselves in advance. It is also a key role of student affairs administrators to make it possible for students to *succeed* at an institution once they get there.

People in the student affairs area, in touch with their counterparts in many other institutions, should have regional and national information on trends and concerns in the educational world. In addition, while faculty members are keeping up in the disciplines, student affairs administrators should keep up with studies of human development and be ready and qualified to enlighten the rest of the community on problems in student growth and maturation during the college years, especially in those areas which uniquely affect a given college or university. Student affairs personnel may not all do these things today, any more than all faculty members spend time considering the curriculum of their institutions in its totality, but these are things which the logic of our respective roles suggests that we should do.

Student personnel administrators can also contribute to the teaching and learning process in another way, if it can be seen as an enhancement of learning rather than an encroachment on faculty territory. Student services personnel are usually the "get it done people" on campus, those who know how to organize and pull off complex events successfully. As faculty work with more and more complex instructional materials, team teaching situations, audiovisual presentations, televised courses, individualized instruction involving the scheduling of multitudinous small instructional "events" instead of two or three weekly lectures, or whatever, they can make good use of the advice, even the direct assistance, of a student personnel administrator who knows how to get things done. If faculty members know that the student affairs administrators have their own distinctive educational role and will not try to misuse collaboration, there is much that faculty members can usefully draw on in the expertise available from their student affairs colleagues. Faculty can often use instruction in such matters as how to start and lead a discussion, or how to help students to work in teams. Many college instructors have no training in pedagogy or group dynamics and spend frustrating hours trying to make their seminars go smoothly or get student laboratory groups to work together. In faculty development seminars, why not call on student personnel experts? Why not put the chairman of the multisectional introductory political science course in touch with the director of student activities to help design the course? If that proposal sounds unthinkable, it is perhaps a measure of the extent to which our roles have become confused and the separation between us unproductive.

In terms of the college or university as an organization, just as faculty need to keep reminding student personnel managers of the need to allow for nonconformity within their structures, administrators in the student affairs area need to keep reminding both faculty and student that there *are* structures and that equity is best assured by respecting them. Collectively instituted guidelines are almost always preferable to individual and capricious arbitrariness. It is the thankless but necessary task of the dean of student affairs to be even-handed in saying "no" as well as "yes" to students and to try to see that faculty do likewise.

There is a more important sense in which student affairs administrators reinforce the ongoing structure of the institutions they serve. One senses in today's university a kind of general tendency toward fragmentation, the force of entropy at work, if you wish. There are disciplines and subdisciplines, and interdisciplinary and crossdisciplinary programs, each one actively trying to differentiate itself from the others. There are multiple offices and committees and groups and institutes and programs. On the part of the individual—student, instructor, staff member—there is no sense of mastery over the "whole" which is the university, or even over one's own existence with the whole.

In order to gain some feeling of control, people establish territories and isolate themselves within the specialized techniques of their field of interest. As this occurs, who sees to the welfare of the university as a whole? It easily moves more and more in the direction of being the large bureaucratic "machine" which each person individually is trying to avoid. With the increasing complexity of human knowledge and the increasing faculty specialization which accompanies it, it is easy for the disintegrative tendency to take over. One of the few integrative forces left on campus is student affairs. The student affairs vice president, dean, or director, as a generalist, has responsibility for seeing the institution as a whole and interpreting it to students in their individual needs and aspirations. While others are concerned with their specialties, the student affairs counselors and advisors must try to articulate, every day, in every conversation, what the institution is and what it stands for.

This happens whether the counselors involved realize it or not. It is in the nature of the many small actions taken as each student makes his or her way through the complexities of the institution. A student comes in to complain of noise in her hall and ends up challenging the value of doing twenty calculus problems a night. How the dean or counselor responds affects their views of both themselves and their institution. Student personnel administrators are also people who enjoy bringing groups together, initiating dialogue, organizing separate events into cohesive programs. The university should call upon their skills more often in bringing the institution together and in finding the common threads of unity in the diversity of our teaching and scholarship.

These are some of the contributions we can make to each other and to our institutions. The important thing is that members of the faculty, on the one hand, and student affairs people, on the other, must preserve their unique educational point of view, recognizing its identity and its worth. The dialectic, the tension between opposites, is a creative and useful dynamic within an institution. Student affairs people need not become more technically expert or scholarly. They do need to possess identifiable skills and to be articulate apologists for higher education as a whole. Faculty members need not become more managerial and hail-fell-well-met. They do need to be responsible, humane, and independent in working with their students and their material. The identity of student affairs must be asserted and fostered rather than denied. Faculty need to recognize the legitimacy of nonfaculty roles in today's complex colleges and universities, while student affairs administrators need to respect the faculty's specialized educational mission.

Alice M. Rivlin, Director of the Congressional Budget Office, in her address to the American Council on Education in October, 1973, challenged our colleges and universities, now that they are—as she put it—"relieved of the burden of expansion," to concentrate on the quality of education.[5] She echoes what voices within the higher education community have been saying. One way to improve the quality of the college experience without spending more money is to recognize the complementarities of style and skill which faculty and student affairs administrators bring to their work with students, so as to use everyone's talents more fully. Together faculty and student affairs people can do more for the quality of education than they can accomplish separately. This is clear from the conclusions Alexander Astin reaches in his study of the effects of college-going, *Four Critical Years*. He repeats several times that the positive and lasting effects of a college education are in direct proportion to the level of *involvement* of students with their education. The factors which he finds most powerful in encouraging involvement are, first, interaction with faculty, both in the classroom and beyond it, and, second, involvement in the life of the campus, especially through residence on campus but also through part-time work, research projects, athletics, and student activities.[6] Involvement cuts right across the lines of formal and informal learning, just as our joint effort should do. All of us who share responsibility for students must find ways to join and blend our distinctive skills.

In *Blackberry Winter*, Margaret Mead gives her many admirers a lively account of her earlier years. She describes her eager anticipation of going to college: "I approached the idea of college with the expectation of taking part in an intellectual feast," she says, and adds, "In college, in some way that I devoutly believed in but could not explain, I expected to become a person." There we have it: development as a *mind* and as a *person*, fulfillment and transformation. Her first college year went badly, but then, at Barnard College in New York, she found the combination of classroom and context, of intellectual feast and personal development, that met her expectations. The Barnard chapter of the book almost overflows with the activities she got into, the close friends she made, the excitement of finding her career "home" in anthropology. "In the autumn of 1920," she states simply, "I came to Barnard, where I found—and in some measure created—the kind of student life that matched my earlier dreams."[7]

There is a larger and more varied population with college dreams today than in 1920. Not everyone conceives an intellectual feast in the same terms as Margaret Mead, but every prospective student I have talked with wants, and expects, intellectual and personal challenges out of the college experience. Will the life of our campuses—curricular and co-curricular—match the highest dreams of those who come to us? What kinds of learning, formal and informal, will they be able to do? As faculty members and as administrators of student affairs, let us prepare together a good intellectual feast, a powerful transforming experience, so that future Margaret Meads, or Joe Smiths, or Marcia Garcias, can find "and in some measure create" an education that will be the pride of all of us.

Notes

Elizabeth S. Blake is Professor and Academic Dean at the University of Minnesota, Morris.

1. James J. Ronan, "Academic Affairs—Student Affairs: An Analysis of the Relationship," and Margaret L. Furman, "Academic Affairs—Student Affairs: From We-They to Us," position papers developed for the Division of Professional Development and Standards of the National Association of Student Personnel Administrators, in August, 1975 and March, 1977, respectively.

2. Henry Mintzberg. "The Manager's Job: Folklore and Fact," Harvard Business Review, 53 (July–August, 1975), pp. 49–61. The two quotations are from p. 50.

3. *Anti-Intellectualism in American Life* (New York: Knopf, 1963).

4. The story was included in a sermon preached at The Riverside Church, New York City, in the 1950's.

5. W. T. Furniss and D. P. Gardner, eds., *Higher Education and Government: An Uneasy Alliance* (Washington, DC. American Council on Education, 1979), p. 16.

6. Alexander W. Astin, *Four Critical Years* (San Francisco: Jossey-Bass, 1978). See pp. 186–187, 220–241, 256, 260.

7. Margaret Mead, *Blackberry Winter: My Earlier Years* (New York: Simon and Schuster, 1972), pp. 90 and 102, and the chapter between.

On Leadership

John W. Gardner

The Nature of Leadership

Leadership is a word that has risen above normal workaday usage as a conveyor of meaning. There seems to be a feeling that if we invoke it often enough with sufficient ardor we can ease our sense of having lost our way, our sense of things unaccomplished, of duties unfulfilled.

All of that simply clouds our thinking. The aura with which we tend to surround the words *leader* and *leadership* makes it hard to think clearly. Good sense calls for demystification.

Leadership is the process of persuasion or example by which an individual (or leadership team) induces a group to pursue objectives held by the leader or shared by the leader and his or her followers.

In any established group, individuals fill different roles, and one of the roles is that of leader. Leaders cannot be thought of apart from the historic context in which they arise, the setting in which they function (e.g., elective political office), and the system over which they preside (e.g., a particular city or state). They are integral parts of the system, subject to the forces that affect the system. They perform (or cause to be performed) certain tasks or functions that are essential if the group is to accomplish its purposes.

All that we know about the interaction between leaders and constituents or followers tells us that communication and influence flow in both directions; and in that two-way communication, nonrational, nonverbal, and unconscious elements play their part. In the process leaders shape and are shaped. This is true even in systems that appear to be led in quite autocratic fashion. In a state governed by coercion, followers cannot prevent the leader from violating their customs and beliefs, but they have many ways of making it more costly to violate than to honor their norms, and leaders usually make substantial accommodations. If Julius Caesar had been willing to live more flexibly with the give-and-take he might not have been slain in the Senate House. Machiavelli, the ultimate realist, advised the prince, "You will always need the favor of the inhabitants. . . . It is necessary for a prince to possess the friendship of the people."

The connotations of the word *follower* suggest too much passivity and dependence to make it a fit term for all who are at the other end of the dialogue with leaders. I don't intend to discard it, but I also make frequent use of the word *constituent.* It is awkward in some contexts, but often it does fuller justice to the two-way interchange.

Elements of physical coercion are involved in some kinds of leadership; and of course there is psychological coercion, however mild and subtle, including peer pressure, in all social action. But in our culture, popular understanding of the leadership process distinguishes it from coercion—and places those forms involving the least coercion higher on the scale of leadership.

The focus of this book is leadership in this country today. Examples are drawn from other cultures and many of the generations are relevant for all times and places; but the focus is here and now. The points emphasized might be different were I writing fifty years ago or fifty years hence, or writing of Bulgaria or Tibet.

Distinctions

We must not confuse leadership with status. Even in large corporations and government agencies, the top-ranking person may simply be bureaucrat number 1. We have all occasionally encountered top persons who couldn't lead a squad of seven-year-olds to the ice cream counter.

It does not follow that status is irrelevant to leadership. Most positions of high status carry with them symbolic values and traditions that enhance the possibility of leadership. People expect governors and corporation presidents to lead, which heightens the possibility that they will. But the selection process for positions of high status does not make that a sure outcome.

Similarly, we must not confuse leadership with power. Leaders always have some measure of power, rooted in their capacity to persuade, but many people with power are without leadership gifts. Their power derives from money, or from the capacity to inflict harm, or from control of some piece of institutional machinery, or from access to the media. A military dictator has power. The thug who sticks a gun in your ribs has power. Leadership is something else.

Finally, we must not confuse leadership with official authority, which is simply legitimized power. Meter maids have it; the person who audits your tax returns has it.

Leadership requires major expenditures of effort and energy—more than most people care to make. When I outlined to a teenager of my acquaintance the preceding distinctions and then described the hard task of leadership, he said, "I'll leave the leadership to you, Mr. Gardner. Give me some of that power and status."

Confusion between leadership and official authority has a deadly effect on large organizations. Corporations and government agencies everywhere have executives who imagine that their place on the organization chart has given them a body of followers. And of course it has not. They have been given subordinates. Whether the subordinates become followers depends on whether the executives act like leaders.

Is it appropriate to apply to leaders the word *elite?* The word was once applied to families of exalted social status. Then sociologists adopted the word to describe any group of high status, whether hereditary or earned; thus, in addition to the elites of old families and old money, there are elites of performance and profession.

Some social critics today use the word with consistent negative overtones. They believe that elite status is incompatible with an equalitarian philosophy. But in any society—no matter how democratic, no matter how equalitarian—there are elites in the sociologist's sense: intellectual, athletic, artistic, political, and so on. The marks of an open society are that elite status is generally earned, and that those who have earned it do not use their status to violate democratic norms. In our society, leaders are among the many "performance elites."

Leaders and Managers

The word *manager* usually indicates that the individual so labeled holds a directive post in an organization, presiding over the processes by which the organization functions, allocating resources prudently, and making the best possible use of people.

Many writers on leadership take considerable pains to distinguish between leaders and managers. In the process leaders generally end up looking like a cross between Napoleon and the Pied Piper, and managers like unimaginative clods. This troubles me. I once heard it said of a man, "He's an utterly first-class manager but there isn't a trace of the leader in him." I am still looking for that man, and I am beginning to believe that he does not exist. Every time I encounter utterly first-class managers they turn out to have quite a lot of the leader in them.

Even the most visionary leader is faced on occasion with decisions that every manager faces: when to take a short-term loss to achieve a long-term gain, how to allocate scarce resources, whom to trust with a delicate assignment. So even though it has become conventional to contrast leaders and managers, I am inclined to use slightly different categories, lumping leaders and leader/managers into one category and placing in the other category those numerous managers whom one would not normally describe as leaders. Leaders and leader/managers distinguish themselves from the general run of managers in at least six respects:

1. They think longer term—beyond the day's crises, beyond the quarterly report, beyond the horizon.

2. In thinking about the unit they are heading, they grasp its relationship to larger realities—the larger organization of which they are a part, conditions external to the organization, global trends.

3. They reach and influence constituents beyond their jurisdictions, beyond boundaries. Thomas Jefferson influenced people all over Europe. Gandhi influenced people all over the world. In an organization, leaders extend their reach across bureaucratic boundaries—often a distinct advantage in a world too complex and tumultuous to be handled "through channels." Leaders' capacity to rise above jurisdictions may enable them to bind together the fragmented constituencies that must work together to solve a problem.

4. They put heavy emphasis on the intangibles of vision, values, and motivation and understand intuitively the nonrational and unconscious elements in leader-constituent interaction.

5. They have the political skill to cope with the conflicting requirements of multiple constituencies.

6. They think in terms of renewal. The routine manager tends to accept organizational structure and process as it exists. The leader or leader/manager seeks the revisions of process and structure required by ever-changing reality.

The manager is more tightly linked to an organization than is the leader. Indeed, the leader may have no organization at all. Florence Nightingale, after leaving the Crimea, exercised extraordinary leadership in health care for decades with no organization under her command. Gandhi was a leader before he had an organization. Some of our most memorable leaders have headed movements so amorphous that management would be an inappropriate word.

The Many Kinds of Leaders

One hears and reads a surprising number of sentences that describe leaders in general as having such and such attributes and behaving in such and such a fashion—as though one could distill out of the spectacular diversity of leaders an idealized picture of The Leader.

Leaders come in many forms, with many styles and diverse qualities. There are quiet leaders and leaders one can hear in the next county. Some find their strength in eloquence, some in judgment, some in courage. I had a friend who was a superior leader in outdoor activities and sports but quite incapable of leading in a bureaucratic setting.

The diversity is almost without limit: Churchill, the splendidly eloquent old warrior; Gandhi, the visionary and the shrewd mobilizer of his people; Lenin, the coldly purposeful revolutionary. Consider just the limited category of military leadership. George Marshall was a self-effacing, low-keyed man with superb judgment and a limitless capacity to inspire trust. MacArthur was a brilliant strategist, a farsighted administrator, and flamboyant to his fingertips. (Eisenhower, who had served under Macarthur, once said, "I studied dramatics under a master.") Eisenhower in his wartime assignment was an outstanding leader/administrator and coalition builder. General Patton was a slashing, intense combat commander. Field Marshall Montgomery was a gifted, temperamental leader of whom Churchill said, "In defeat, indomitable; in victory, insufferable." All were great leaders—but extraordinarily diverse in personal attributes.

The fact that there are many kinds of leaders has implications for leadership education. Most of those seeking to develop young potential leaders have in mind one ideal model that is inevitably constricting. We should give young people a sense of the many kinds of leaders and styles of leadership, and encourage them to move toward those models that are right for them.

Leaders and History

All too often when we think of our historic leaders, we eliminate all the contradictions that make individuals distinctive. And we further violate reality by lifting them out of their historical contexts. No wonder we are left with pasteboard portraits. As first steps toward a mature view of leaders we must accept complexity and context.

Thomas Jefferson was first of all a gifted and many-sided human, an enigmatic man who loved—among other things—abstract ideas, agriculture, architecture and statecraft. He was a man of natural aloofness who lived most of his life in public; a man of action with a gift for words and a bent for research; an idealist who proved himself a shrewd, even wily, operator on the political scene. Different sides of his nature came into play in different situations.

Place him now in the context of the exhilarating events and themes of his time: a new nation coming into being, with a new consciousness; the brilliant rays of the Enlightenment reaching into every phase of life; the inner contradictions of American society (e.g., slavery) already rumbling beneath the surface.

Finally, add the overpowering impulse of succeeding generations to serve their own needs by mythologizing, idolizing or debunking him. It turns out to be an intricately textured story—and not one that diminishes Jefferson.

It was once believed that if leadership traits were truly present in an individual, they would manifest themselves almost without regard to the situation in which the person was functioning. No one believes that any more. Acts of leadership take place in an unimaginable variety of settings, and the setting does much to determine the kinds of leaders that emerge and how they play their roles.

We cannot avoid the bewhiskered question, "Does the leader make history or does the historical moment make the leader?" It sounds like a seminar question but it is of interest to most leaders sooner or later. Corporate chief executive officers fighting a deteriorating trend in an industry feel like people trying to run up the down escalator. Looking across town at less able leaders riding an upward trend in another industry, they are ripe for the theory that history makes the leader.

Thomas Carlyle placed excessive emphasis on the great person, as did Sidney Hook ("all factors in history, save great men, are inconsequential.") Karl Marx, Georg Hegel, and Herbert Spencer placed excessive emphasis on historical forces. For Marx, economic forces shaped history; for Spencer, societies had their evolutionary course just as species did, and the leader was a product of the process; for Hegel, leaders were a part of the dialectic of history and could not help what they did.

The balanced view, of course, is that historical forces create the circumstances in which leaders emerge, but the characteristics of the particular leader in turn have their impact on history.

It is not possible to understand Queen Isabella without understanding fifteenth-century Europe (when she was born, Spain as we know it did not exist), or without understanding the impact of the Reformation on the Catholic world and the gnawing fear stirred by the Muslim conquests. But many monarchs flourished on the Iberian Peninsula in that historical context; only Isabella left an indelible mark. Similarly, by the time Martin Luther emerged, the seeds of the Reformation had already sprouted in many places, but no one would argue that the passionate, charismatic priest who nailed his ninety-five theses to the church door was a puppet of history. Historical forces set the stage for him, but once there, he was himself a historical force.

Churchill is an even more interesting case because he tried out for leadership many times before history was ready for him. After Dunkirk, England needed a leader who could rally the British people to heroic exertions in an uncompromising war, and the eloquent, combative Churchill delivered one of the great performances of the century. Subsequently the clock of history ticked on and—with the war over—the voters dropped him unceremoniously. When a friend told him it was a blessing in disguise, he growled "If it is, the disguise is perfect."

Forces of history determined his rise and fall, but in his time on the world stage he left a uniquely Churchillian mark on the course of events.

Settings

The historical moment is the broadest context affecting the emergence and functioning of leaders; but immensely diverse settings of a more modest nature clearly affect leadership.

The makeup of the group to be led is, of course, a crucial feature of the context. According to research findings, the approach to leadership or style of leadership that will be effective depends on, among other things, the age level of the individuals to be led; their educational background and competence; the size, homogeneity and cohesiveness of the group; its motivation and morale; its rate of turnover; and so on.

Other relevant contextual features are too numerous and diverse to list. Leading a corporation is one thing, leading a street gang is something else. Thomas Cronin has pointed out that it may take one kind of leadership to start a new enterprise and quite another kind to keep it going through its various phases. Religious bodies, political parties, government agencies, the academic world—all offer distinctive contexts for leadership.

Judgments of Leaders

In curious ways, people tend to aggrandize the role of leaders. They tend to exaggerate the capacity of leaders to influence events. Jeffrey Pfeffer says that people want to achieve a feeling of control over their environment, and that this inclines them to attribute the outcomes of group performance to leaders rather than to context. If we were to face the fact—so the argument goes—that outcomes are the result of a complex set of interactions among group members plus environmental and historical forces, we would feel helpless. By attributing outcomes to an identifiable leader we feel, rightly or not, more in control. There is at least a chance that one can fire the leader; one cannot "fire" historical forces.

Leaders act in the stream of history. As they labor to bring about a result, multiple forces beyond their control, even beyond their knowledge, are moving to hasten or hinder the result. So there is rarely a demonstrable causal link between a leader's specific decisions and consequent events. Consequences are not a reliable measure of leadership. Franklin Roosevelt's efforts to bolster the economy in the middle-to-late-1930s were powerfully aided by a force that did not originate with his economic brain trust—the winds of war. Leaders of a farm workers union fighting for better wages may find their efforts set at naught by a crop failure.

Frank Lloyd Wright said, "A doctor can bury his mistakes. An architect can only advise his client to plant vines." Unlike either doctor or architect, leaders suffer from the mistakes of predecessors and leave some of their own misjudgments as time bombs for successors.

Many of the changes sought by leaders take time: lots of years, long public debate, slow shifts in attitude. In their lifetimes, leaders may see little result from heroic efforts yet may be setting the stage for victories that will come after them. Reflect on the long, slow unfolding of the battles for racial equality or for women's rights. Leaders who did vitally important early work died without knowing what they had wrought.

Leaders may appear to have succeeded (or failed) only to have historians a generation later reverse the verdict. The "verdict of history" has a wonderfully magisterial sound, but in reality it is subject to endless appeals to later generations of historians—with no court of last resort to render a final judgment.

In the real world, the judgments one makes of a leader must be multidimensional, taking into consideration great strengths, streaks of mediocrity, and perhaps great flaws. If the great strengths correspond to the needs of a critical moment in history, the flaws are forgiven and simply provide texture to the biographies. Each leader has his or her own unique pattern of attributes, sometimes conflicting in curious ways. Ronald Reagan was notably passive with respect to many important issues, but vigorously tenacious on other issues.

Leaders change over the course of their active careers as do other human beings. In looking back, it is natural for us to freeze them in that moment when they served history's needs most spectacularly, but leaders evolve. The passionately antislavery Lincoln of the Douglas debates was not the see-both-sides Lincoln of fifteen years earlier. The "national unity" Churchill of 1942 was not the fiercely partisan, adversarial Churchill of the 1930s.

Devolving Initiative and Responsibility

I have already commented on our dispersed leadership and on its importance to the vitality of a large, intricately-organized system. Our most forward-looking business concerns are working in quite imaginative ways to devolve initiative downward and outward through their organizations to develop their lower levels of leadership.

There is no comparable movement in government agencies. But in the nation as a whole, dispersed leadership is a reality. In Santa Barbara County, California, Superintendent of Schools William Cirone is a leader in every sense of the word. A healthy school system requires a vital and involved citizenry. How does one achieve that? Given the aging population, fewer and fewer citizens have children in the schools. How do we keep them interested? Education is a lifelong process. How do we provide for that? These are questions to which Cirone has addressed himself with uncommon energy and imagination.

The leaders of the Soviet Union did not launch the reforms of 1987 because they had developed a sudden taste for grass-roots democracy. They launched them because their system was grinding to a halt. Leader/managers at the lower levels and at the periphery of the system had neither the motivation nor the authority to solve problems that they understood better than the Moscow bureaucrats.

We have only half learned the lesson ourselves. In many of our large corporate, governmental, and nonprofit organizations we still make it all too difficult for potential leaders down the line to exercise initiative. We are still in the process of discovering how much vitality and motivation are buried at those levels awaiting release.

To emphasize the need for dispersed leadership does not deny the need for highly qualified top leadership. But our high-level leaders will be more effective in every way if the systems over which they preside are made vital by dispersed leadership. As I argued in *Excellence,* we must demand high performance at every level of society.

Friends of mine have argued that in view of my convictions concerning the importance of middle- and lower-level leaders, I lean too heavily on examples of high-level leaders. My response is that we know a great deal about the more famous figures, statements about them can be documented, and they are comfortably familiar to readers. No one who reads this book with care could believe that I consider such exalted figures the only ones worth considering.

Institutionalizing Leadership

To exercise leadership today, leaders must institutionalize their leadership. The issues are too technical and the pace of change too swift to expect that a leader, no matter how gifted, will be able to solve personally the major problems facing the system over which he or she presides. So we design an institutional system—a government agency, a corporation—to solve the problems, and then we select a leader who has the capacity to preside over and strengthen the system. Some leaders may be quite gifted in solving problems personally, but if they fail to institutionalize the process, their departure leaves the system crippled. They must create or strengthen systems that will survive them.

The institutional arrangements generally include a leadership team. Often throughout this book when I use the word *leader,* I am in fact referring to the leadership team. No individual has all the skills—and certainly not the time—to carry out all the complex tasks of contemporary leadership. And the team must be chosen for excellence in performance. Loyalty and being on the boss's wavelength are necessary but not sufficient qualifications. I emphasize the point because more than one recent president of the United States has had aides who possessed no other qualifications.

I am attempting in these early chapters to say what leadership is—and no such description would be complete without a careful examination of what leaders do. So next we look at the tasks of leadership.

The Tasks of Leadership

Examination of the tasks performed by leaders takes us to the heart of some of the most interesting questions concerning leadership. It also helps to distinguish among the many kinds of leaders. Leaders differ strikingly in how well they perform various functions.

The following nine tasks seem to me to be the most significant functions of leadership, but I encourage readers to add to the list or to describe the tasks in other ways. Leadership activities implicit in all of the tasks (e.g., communicating, relating effectively with people) are not dealt with separately.

Envisioning Goals

The two tasks at the heart of the popular notion of leadership are goal setting and motivating. As a high school senior put it, "Leaders point us in the right direction and tell us to get moving." Although we take a more complicated view of the tasks of leadership, it is appropriate that we begin with the envisioning of goals. Albert Einstein said, "Perfection of means and confusion of ends seems to characterize our age."

Leaders perform the function of goal setting in diverse ways. Some assert a vision of what the group (organization, community, nation) can be at its best. Others point us toward solutions to our problems. Still others, presiding over internally divided groups, are able to define overarching goals that unify constituencies and focus energies. In today's complex world, the setting of goals may have to be preceded by extensive research and problem solving.

Obviously, a constituency is not a blank slate for the leader to write on. Any collection of people sufficiently related to be called a community has many shared goals, some explicit, some unexpressed (perhaps even unconscious), as tangible as better prices for their crops, as intangible as a better future for their children. In a democracy, the leader takes such shared goals into account.

The relative roles of leaders and followers in determining goals varies from group to group. The teacher of first-grade children and the sergeant training recruits do not do extensive consulting as to goals; congressional candidates do a great deal. In the case of many leaders, goals are handed to them by higher authority. The factory manager and the combat commander may be superb leaders, but many of their goals are set at higher levels.

In short, goals emerge from many sources. The culture itself specifies certain goals; constituents have their concerns; higher authority makes its wishes known. Out of the welter, leaders take some goals as given, and making their own contribution, select and formulate a set of objectives. It may sound as though leaders have only marginal freedom, but in fact there is usually considerable opportunity, even for lower-level leaders, to put their personal emphasis and interpretation on the setting of goals.

There is inevitable tension between long- and short-term goals. On the one hand, constituents are not entirely comfortable with the jerkiness of short-term goal seeking, and they value the sense of stability that comes with a vision of far horizons. On the other hand, long-term goals may require them to defer immediate gratification on at least some fronts. Leaders often fear that when citizens enter the voting booth, they will remember the deferral of gratification more vividly than they remember the reason for it.

Before the Civil War, Elizabeth Cady Stanton saw virtually the whole agenda for women's rights as it was to emerge over the succeeding century. Many of her contemporaries in the movement were not at all prepared for such an inclusive vision and urged her to play it down.

Another visionary far ahead of his time was the South American liberator, Simon Bolivar. He launched his fight in that part of Gran Colombia which is now Venezuela, but in his mind was a vision not only of independence for all of Spain's possessions in the New World, but also a peaceful alliance of the new states in some form of league or confederation. Although he was tragically ahead of his time, the dream never died and has influenced generations of Latin American leaders striving toward unity.

Affirming Values

A great civilization is a drama lived in the minds of a people. It is a shared vision; it is shared norms, expectations, and purposes. When one thinks of the world's great civilizations, the most vivid images that crowd in on us are apt to be of the physical monuments left behind—the Pyramids, the Parthenon, the Mayan temples. But in truth, all the physical splendor was the merest by-product. The civilizations themselves, from beginning to end, existed in the minds of men and women.

If we look at ordinary human communities, we see the same reality: A community lives in the minds of its members—in shared assumptions, beliefs, customs, ideas that give meaning, ideas that motivate. And among the ideas are norms or values. In any healthy, reasonably coherent community, people come to have shared views concerning right and wrong, better and worse—in personal conduct, in governing, in art, whatever. They define for their time and place what things are legal or illegal, virtuous or vicious, good taste or bad. They have little or no impulse to be neutral about such matters. Every society is, as Philip Rieff puts it, "a system of moralizing demands."

Values are embodied in the society's religious beliefs and its secular philosophy. Over the past century, many intellectuals have looked down on the celebration of our values as an unsophisticated and often hypocritical activity. But every healthy society celebrates its values. They are expressed in art, in song, in ritual. They are stated explicitly in historical documents, in ceremonial speeches, in textbooks. They are reflected in stories told around the campfire, in the legends kept alive by old folks, in the fables told to children.

In a pluralistic community there are, within the broad consensus that enables the community to function, many and vigorous conflicts over specific values.

The Regeneration of Values

One of the milder pleasures of maturity is bemoaning the decay of once strongly held values. *Values always decay over time. Societies that keep their values alive do so not by escaping the processes of decay but by powerful processes of regeneration.* There must be perpetual rebuilding. Each generation must rediscover the living elements in its own tradition and adapt them to present realities. To assist in that rediscovery is one of the tasks of leadership.

The leaders whom we admire the most help to revitalize our shared beliefs and values. They have always spent a portion of their time teaching the value framework.

Sometimes the leader's affirmation of values challenges entrenched hypocrisy or conflicts with the values held by a segment of the constituency. Elizabeth Cady Stanton, speaking for now-accepted values, was regarded as a thoroughgoing radical in her day. Jesus not only comforted the afflicted but afflicted the comfortable.

Motivating

Leaders do not create motivation out of thin air. They unlock or channel existing motives. Any group has a great tangle of motives. Effective leaders tap those that serve the purposes of collective action in pursuit of shared goals. They accomplish the alignment of individual and group goals. They deal with the circumstances that often lead group members to withhold their best efforts. They call for the kind of effort and restraint, drive and discipline that make for great performance. They create a climate in which there is pride in making significant contributions to shared goals.

Note that in the tasks of leadership, the transactions between leaders and constituents go beyond the rational level to the nonrational and unconscious levels of human functioning. Young potential leaders who have been schooled to believe that all elements of a problem are rational and technical, reducible to words and numbers, are ill-equipped to move into an area where intuition and empathy are powerful aids to problem solving.

Managing

Most managers exhibit some leadership skills, and most leaders on occasion find themselves managing. Leadership and management are not the same thing, but they overlap. It makes sense to include managing in the list of tasks leaders perform.

In the paragraphs that follow I focus on those aspects of leadership that one might describe as managing without slipping into a conventional description of managing as such. And I try to find terminology and phrasing broad enough to cover the diverse contexts in which leadership occurs in corporations, unions, municipalities, political movements, and so on.

1. *Planning and Priority Setting.* Assuming that broad goals have been set, someone has to plan, fix priorities, choose means, and formulate policy. These are functions often performed by leaders. When Lyndon B. Johnson said, early in his presidency, that education was the nation's number one priority, he galvanized the nation's educational leaders and released constructive energies far beyond any governmental action that had yet been taken. It was a major factor in leading me to accept a post in his Cabinet.

2. *Organizing and Institution Building.* We have all seen leaders enjoy their brilliant moment and then disappear without a trace because they had no gift for building their purposes into institutions. In the ranks of leaders, Alfred Sloan was at the other extreme. Though he sold a lot of automobiles, he was not primarily a salesman; he was an institution builder. His understanding of organization was intuitive and profound.

    Someone has to design the structures and processes through which substantial endeavors get accomplished over time. Ideally, leaders should not regard themselves as indispensable but should enable the group to carry on. Institutions are a means to that end. Jean Monnet said, "Nothing is possible without individuals; nothing is lasting without institutions."

3. *Keeping the System Functioning.* Presiding over the arrangements through which individual energies are coordinated to achieve shared goals sounds like a quintessential management task. But it is clear that most leaders find themselves occasionally performing one or another of the essential chores: mobilizing and allocating resources; staffing and ensuring the continuing vitality of the team; creating and maintaining appropriate procedures; directing, delegating and coordinating; providing a system of incentives; reporting, evaluating and holding accountable.

4. *Agenda Setting and Decision Making.* The goals may be clear and the organization well set up and smoothly operating, but there remain agenda-setting and decision-making functions that must be dealt with. The announcement of goals without a proposed program for meeting them is a familiar enough political phenomenon—but not one that builds credibility. There are leaders who can motivate and inspire but who cannot visualize a path to the goal in practical, feasible steps. Leaders who lack that skill must bring onto their team people who have it.

    One of the purest examples of the leader as agenda setter was Florence Nightingale. Her public image was and is that of the lady of mercy, but under her gentle manner, she was a rugged spirit, a fighter, a tough-minded system changer. She never made public appearances or speeches, and except for her two years in the Crimea, held no public position. Her strength was that she was a formidable authority on the evils to be remedied, she knew what to do about them, and she used public opinion to goad top officials to adopt her agenda.

5. *Exercising Political Judgment.* In our pluralistic society, persons directing substantial enterprises find that they are presiding over many constituencies within their organizations and contending with many outside. Each has its needs and claims. One of the tasks of the leader/manager is to make the political judgments necessary

to prevent secondary conflicts of purpose from blocking progress toward primary goals. Sometimes the literature on administration and management treats politics as an alien and disruptive force. But Aaron Wildavsky, in his brilliant book, *The Nursing Father: Moses as a Political Leader*, makes the point that leaders are inevitably political.

Achieving Workable Unity

A pluralistic society is, by definition, one that accepts many different elements, each with its own purposes. Collisions are inevitable and often healthy—as in commercial competition, in civil suits, and in efforts to redress grievances through the political process. Conflict is necessary in the case of oppressed groups that must fight for the justice that is due them. All our elective officials know the intense conflict of the political campaign. Indeed, one could argue that willingness to engage in battle when necessary is a sine qua non of leadership.

But most leaders most of the time are striving to diminish conflict rather than increase it. Some measure of cohesion and mutual tolerance is an absolute requirement of social functioning.

Sometimes the problem is not outright conflict but an unwillingness to cooperate. One of the gravest problems George Washington faced as a general was that the former colonies, though they had no doubt they were all on the same side, were not always sure they wanted to cooperate. As late as 1818, John Randolph declared, "When I speak of my country, I mean the Commonwealth of Virginia."

The unifying function of leaders is well illustrated in the actions of George Bush after winning the presidential election of 1988. He promptly met with his defeated opponent, Michael Dukakis; with his chief rival for the nomination, Senator Robert Dole; and with Jesse Jackson and Coretta Scott King, both of whom had opposed his election. He asked Jack Kemp, another of his rivals for the nomination, to be Secretary of Housing and Urban Development, and Senator Dole's wife, Elizabeth Hanford Dole, to be Secretary of Labor.

Leaders in this country today must cope with the fragmentation of the society into groups that have great difficulty in understanding one another or agreeing on common goals. It is a fragmentation rooted in the pluralism of our society, in the obsessive specialization of modern life, and in the skill with which groups organize to advance their concerns.

Under the circumstances, all our leaders must spend part of their time dealing with polarization and building community. There is a false notion that this is a more bland, less rigorous task than leadership of one of the combative segments. In fact, the leader willing to combat polarization is the braver person, and is generally under fire from both sides. I would suggest that Jean Monnet, the father of the European Common Market, is a useful model for future leaders. When there were conflicting purposes Monnet saw the possibility of shared goals, and he knew how to move his contemporaries toward those shared goals.

Trust

Much depends on the general level of trust in the organization or society. The infinitely varied and complex doings of the society—any society—would come to a halt if people did not trust other people most of the time—trust them to observe custom, follow the rules, and behave with some predictability. Countless circumstances operate to diminish that trust, but one may be sure that if the society is functioning at all, *some* degree of trust survives.

Leaders can do much to preserve the necessary level of trust. And the first requirement is that they have the capacity to inspire trust in themselves. In sixteenth-century Italy, where relations among the warring kingdoms were an unending alley fight, Machiavelli's chilling advice to the Prince—"It is necessary . . . to be a feigner and a dissembler," or, as another translator renders the same passage, "You must be a great liar and hypocrite" may have been warranted. And, under conditions of iron rule, Hitler and Stalin were able to live by betrayals. But in our society, leaders must work to raise the level of trust.

Explaining

Explaining sounds too pedestrian to be on a list of leadership tasks, but every leader recognizes it. People want to know what the problem is, why they are being asked to do certain things, why they face so many frustrations. Thurman Arnold said, "Unhappy is a people that has run out of words to describe what is happening to them." Leaders find the words.

To be heard above the hubbub in the public forum today, explaining generally requires more than clarity and eloquence. It requires effective access to the media of communication or to those segments of the population that keep ideas in circulation—editors, writers, intellectuals, association leaders, advocacy groups, chief executive officers, and the like.

The task of explaining is so important that some who do it exceptionally well play a leadership roll even though they are not leaders in the conventional sense. When the American colonies were struggling for independence, Thomas Paine was a memorable explainer. In the powerful environmentalist surge of the 1960s and 70s, no activist leader had as pervasive an influence on the movement as did Rachel Carson, whose book *Silent Spring* burst on the scene in 1963. Betty Friedan's *The Feminine Mystique* played a similar role for the women's movement.

Leaders teach. Lincoln, in his second inaugural address, provided an extraordinary example of the leader as teacher. Teaching and leading are distinguishable occupations, but every great leader is clearly teaching—and every great teacher is leading.

Serving as a Symbol

Leaders are inevitably symbols. Workers singled out to be supervisors discover that they are set apart from their old comrades in subtle ways. They try to keep the old camaraderie but things have changed. They are now symbols of management. Sergeants symbolize the chain of command. Parish religious leaders symbolize their churches.

In a group threatened with internal strife, the leader may be a crucial symbol of unity. In a minority group's struggle to find its place, combative leaders—troublesome to others—may be to their own people the perfect symbol of their anger and their struggle.

The top leader of a community or nation symbolizes the group's collective identity and continuity. For this reason, the death of a president produces a special reaction of grief and loss. Americans who were beyond childhood when John F. Kennedy was assassinated remember, despite the passage of decades, precisely where they were and what they were doing when the news reached them. Even for many who did not admire him, the news had the impact of a blow to the solar plexus. And those old enough to remember Franklin D. Roosevelt's death recognize the reaction.

For late eighteenth-century Americans, George Washington was the symbol of all that they had been through together. Thomas Jefferson became such a powerful symbol of our democratic aspirations that for generations politicians fought over his memory. Those who favored Hamiltonian views sought bitterly and unsuccessfully to shatter the Jefferson image. As Merrill Peterson has cogently argued, the man himself lost reality and the symbol took over. In the dark days of the Great Depression, the American impulse to face events in a positive spirit found its symbol in the ebullient Franklin D. Roosevelt.

Outside the political area, Albert Schweitzer, the gifted theologian and musician who in 1913 gave up a comfortable and respected life in his native Germany to spend the remainder of his years presiding over a medical mission in Equatorial Africa, stands as the pristine example of leader as symbol.

Some individuals newly risen to leadership have a hard time adjusting to the reality that they are symbols. I recall a visit with a young college president who had just come into the job fresh from a professorship, with no prior administrative experience. He confided that he was deeply irked by an incident the preceding day. In his first speech before faculty, students, trustees and alumni he had simply been himself—a man of independent mind full of lively personal opinions—and many of his listeners were nonplussed and irritated. They were not interested in a display of idiosyncratic views. They had expected him to speak as their new leader, their symbol of institutional continuity, their ceremonial collective voice. I told him gently that they had expected him to be their spokesman and symbol, and this simply angered him further. "I'll resign" he said, "if I can't be myself!" Over time, he learned that leaders can rarely afford the luxury of speaking for themselves alone.

Most leaders become quite aware of the symbolic aspects of their roles and make effective use of them. One of the twentieth-century leaders who did so most skillfully was Gandhi. In the issues he chose to do battle on, in the way he conducted his campaigns, in the jail terms and the fasting, in his manner of dress, he symbolized his people, their desperate need, and their struggle against oppression.

Needless to say leaders do not always function as benign symbols. In the Iran-Contra affair of 1986–1987 it became apparent that men bound by their oath of office were lying to the public, lying to the Congress of the United States, and lying to one another. To some Americans they became symbols of all the falsehoods and betrayals committed by a distant and distrusted government.

Representing the Group

In quieter times (we love to imagine that there were quieter times) leaders could perhaps concentrate on their own followers. Today, representing the group in its dealings with others is a substantial leadership task.

It is a truism that all of the human systems (organizations, groups, communities) that make up the society and the world are increasingly interdependent. Virtually all leaders at every level must carry on dealings with systems external to the one in which they themselves are involved—tasks of representing and negotiating, of defending institutional integrity, of public relations. As one moves higher in the ranks of leadership, such chores increase.

It goes without saying that people who have spent their careers in the world of the specialist or within the boundaries of a narrow community (their firm, their profession) are often ill-equipped for such leadership tasks. The young potential leader must learn early to cross boundaries and to know many worlds. The attributes that enable leaders to teach and lead their own constituencies may be wholly ineffective in external dealings. Military leaders who are revered by their troops may be clumsy with civilians. The business leader who is effective within the business culture may be lost in dealing with politicians. A distinctive characteristic of the ablest leaders is that they do not shrink from external representation. They see the long-term needs and goals of their constituency in the broadest context, and they act accordingly. The most capable mayors think not just of the city but of the metropolitan area and the region. Able business leaders are alert to the political climate and to world economic trends.

The most remarkable modern example of a leader carrying out the representative function is Charles DeGaulle. DeGaulle has his detractors, but none can fail to marvel at his performance in successfully representing the once and future France-as-a-great-power at a time when the nation itself was a defeated, demoralized, enemy-occupied land. By his own commanding presence, he kept France's place at the table through the dark days. Years later Jean Monnet wrote:

> It took great strength of character for him, a traditional soldier, to cross the great dividing line of disobedience to orders from above. He was the only man of his rank with the courage to do so; and in the painful isolation felt by those Frenchmen who had decided to continue the Allied struggle, DeGaulle's rare example was a source of great moral strength."

Renewing

Leaders need not be renewers. They can lead people down old paths, using old slogans, toward old objectives. Sometimes that is appropriate. But the world changes with disconcerting swiftness. Too often the old paths are blocked and the old solutions no longer solve anything. DeGaulle, writing of France's appalling unpreparedness for World War II, said:

> The Army became stuck in a set of ideas which had had their heyday before the end of the First World War. It was all the more inclined that way because its leaders were growing old at their posts, wedded to errors that had once constituted their glory.

Leaders must foster the process of renewal.

So much for the tasks of leadership. The individual with a gift for building a leadership team may successfully delegate one or another of those tasks to other members of the team. One function that cannot be delegated is that of serving as symbol. That the leader is a symbol is a fact, not a matter of choice. The task is to take appropriate account of that reality and to use it well in the service of the group's goals.

Another function that cannot be delegated entirely is the envisioning of goals. Unless the leader has a sense of where the whole enterprise is going and must go, it is not possible to delegate (or carry out personally) the other functions. To have "a sense of where the whole enterprise is going and must go" is, I am inclined to say, the very core and essence of the best leadership.

In a discussion of the tasks of leadership, a colleague of mine said, "I do not see 'enabling' or 'empowering' on the list. Aren't those the central tasks of leadership?" For those unfamiliar with contemporary discussions of leadership, I should explain that reference to *enabling* or *empowering* has become the preferred method of condensing into a single word the widely held conviction that the purpose of leaders is not to dominate nor diminish followers but to strengthen and help them to develop.

But enabling and empowering are not separable tasks. They require a variety of actions on the parts of leaders. For example:

- Sharing information and making it possible for followers to obtain appropriate kinds of education
- Sharing power by devolving initiative and responsibility
- Building the confidence of followers so that they can achieve their own goals through their own efforts
- Removing barriers to the release of individual energy and talent
- Seeking, finding, and husbanding the various kinds of resources that followers need
- Resolving the conflicts that paralyze group action
- Providing Organizational arrangements appropriate to group effort

Any attempt to describe a social process as complex as leadership inevitably makes it seem more orderly than it is. Leadership is not tidy. Decisions are made and then revised or reversed. Misunderstandings are frequent, inconsistency inevitable. Achieving a goal may simply make the next goal more urgent: inside every solution are the seeds of new problems. And as Donald Michael has pointed out, most of the time most things are out of hand. No leader enjoys that reality, but every leader knows it.

It would be easy to imagine that the tasks described are items to be handled separately, like nine items on a shopping list, each from a separate store. But the effective leader is always doing several tasks simultaneously. The best antidote to the shopping list conception is to look at the setting in which all the tasks are mingled—the complex interplay between leaders and those "led."

Building a Learning Organization

DAVID A. GARVIN

Continuous improvement programs are sprouting up all over as organizations strive to better themselves and gain an edge. The topic list is long and varied, and sometimes it seems as though a program a month is needed just to keep up. Unfortunately, failed programs far outnumber successes, and improvement rates remain distressingly low. Why? Because most companies have failed to grasp a basic truth. Continuous improvement requires a commitment to learning.

How, after all, can an organization improve without first learning something new? Solving a problem, introducing a product, and reengineering a process all require seeing the world in a new light and acting accordingly. In the absence of learning, companies—and individuals—simply repeat old practices. Change remains cosmetic, and improvements are either fortuitous or short-lived.

A few farsighted executives—Ray Stata of Analog Devices, Gordon Forward of Chaparral Steel, Paul Allaire of Xerox—have recognized the link between learning and continuous improvement and have begun to refocus their companies around it. Scholars too have jumped on the bandwagon, beating the drum for "learning organizations" and "knowledge-creating companies." In rapidly changing businesses like semiconductors and consumer electronics, these ideas are fast taking hold. Yet despite the encouraging signs, the topic in large part remains murky, confused, and difficult to penetrate.

Meaning, Management, and Measurement

Scholars are partly to blame. Their discussions of learning organizations have often been reverential and utopian, filled with near mystical terminology. Paradise, they would have you believe, is just around the corner. Peter Senge, who popularized learning organizations in his book *The Fifth Discipline*, described them as places "where people continually expand their capacity to create the results they truly desire, where new and expansive patterns of thinking are nurtured, where collective aspiration is set free, and where people are continually learning how to learn together."[1] To achieve these ends, Senge suggested the use of five "component technologies": systems thinking, personal mastery, mental models, shared vision, and team learning. In a similar spirit, Ikujiro Nonaka characterized knowledge-creating companies as places where "inventing new knowledge is not a specialized activity . . . it is a way of behaving, indeed, a way of being, in which everyone is a knowledge worker."[2] Nonaka suggested that companies use metaphors and organizational redundancy to focus thinking, encourage dialogue, and make tacit, instinctively understood ideas explicit.

Sound idyllic? Absolutely. Desirable? Without question. But does it provide a framework for action? Hardly. The recommendations are far too abstract, and too many questions remain unanswered. How, for example, will managers know when their companies have become learning organizations? What concrete changes in behavior are required? What policies and programs must be in place? How do you get from here to there?

Most discussions of learning organizations finesse these issues. Their focus is high philosophy and grand themes, sweeping metaphors rather than the gritty details of practice. Three critical issues are left unresolved; yet each is essential for effective implementation. First is the question of *meaning*. We need a plausible, well-grounded definition of learning organizations; it must be actionable and easy to apply. Second is the question of *management*. We need clearer guidelines for practice, filled with operational advice rather than high aspirations. And third is the question of *measurement*. We need better tools for assessing an organization's rate and level of learning to ensure that gains have in fact been made.

Once these "three Ms" are addressed, managers will have a firmer foundation for launching learning organizations. Without this groundwork, progress is unlikely, and for the simplest of reasons. For learning to become a meaningful corporate goal, it must first be understood.

What is a Learning Organization?

Surprisingly, a clear definition of learning has proved to be elusive over the years. Organizational theorists have studied learning for a long time; the accompanying quotations suggest that there is still considerable disagreement (see the insert "Definitions of Organizational Learning"). Most scholars view organizational learning as a process that unfolds over time and link it with knowledge acquisition and improved performance. But they differ on other important matters.

Definitions of Organizational Learning

Scholars have proposed a variety of definitions of organizational learning. Here is a small sample:

Organizational learning means the process of improving actions through better knowledge and understanding. C. Marlene Fiol and Marjorie A. Lyles, "Organizational Learning, " *Academy of Management Review*, October 1985.

An entity learns if, through its processing of information, the range of its potential behaviors is changed. George P. Huber, "Organizational Learning: The Contributing Processes and the Literatures," *Organization Science*, February 1991.

Organizations are seen as learning by encoding inferences from history into routines that guide behavior. Barbara Levitt and James G. March, "Organizational Learning," *American Review of Sociology*, Vol. 14, 1988.

Organizational learning is a process of detecting and correcting error. Chris Argyris, "Double Loop Learning in Organizations," *Harvard Business Review*, September–October 1977.

Organizational learning occurs through shared insights, knowledge, and mental models . . . [and] builds on past knowledge and experience—that is, on memory. Ray Stata, "Organizational Learning—The Key to Management Innovation," *Sloan Management Review*, Spring 1989.

Some, for example, believe that behavioral change is required for learning; others insist that new ways of thinking are enough. Some cite information processing as the mechanism through which learning takes place; others propose shared insights, organizational routines, even memory. And some think that organizational learning is common, while others believe that flawed, self-serving interpretations are the norm.

How can we discern among this cacophony of voices yet build on earlier insights? As a first step, consider the following definition:

A learning organization is an organization skilled at creating, acquiring, and transferring knowledge, and at modifying its behavior to reflect new knowledge and insights.

This definition begins with a simple truth: new ideas are essential if learning is to take place. Sometimes they are created de novo, through flashes of insight or creativity; at other times they arrive from outside the organization or are communicated by knowledgeable insiders. Whatever their source, these ideas are the trigger for organizational improvement. But they cannot by themselves create a learning organization. *Without accompanying changes in the way that work gets done, only the potential for improvement exists.*

This is a surprisingly stringent test for it rules out a number of obvious candidates for learning organizations. Many universities fail to qualify, as do many consulting firms. Even General Motors, despite its recent efforts to improve performance, is found wanting. All of these organizations have been effective at creating or acquiring new knowledge but notably less successful in applying that knowledge to their own activities. Total quality management, for example, is now taught at many business schools, yet the number using it to guide their own decision making is very small. Organizational consultants advise clients on social dynamics and small-group behavior but are notorious for their own infighting and factionalism. And GM, with a few exceptions (like Saturn and NUMMI), has had little success in revamping its manufacturing practices, even though its managers are experts on lean manufacturing, JIT production, and the requirements for improved quality of work life.

Organizations that do pass the definitional test—Honda, Corning, and General Electric come quickly to mind—have, by contrast, become adept at translating new knowledge into new ways of behaving. These companies actively manage the learning process to ensure that it occurs by design rather than by chance. Distinctive policies and practices are responsible for their success; they form the building blocks of learning organizations.

Building Blocks

Learning organizations are skilled at five main activities: systematic problem solving, experimentation with new approaches, learning from their own experiences and past history, learning from the experiences and best practices of others, and transferring knowledge quickly and efficiently throughout the organization. Each is accompanied by a distinctive mind-set, tool kit, and pattern of behavior. Many companies practice these activities to some degree. But few are consistently successful because they rely largely on happenstance and isolated examples. By creating systems and processes that support these activities and integrate them into the fabric of daily operations, companies can manage their learning more effectively.

1. Systematic problem solving. This first activity rests heavily on the philosophy and methods of the quality movement. Its underlying ideas, now widely accepted, include:

   - Relying on the scientific method, rather than guesswork, for diagnosing problems (what Deming calls the "Plan, Do, Check, Act" cycle, and others refer to as "hypothesis-generating, hypothesis-testing" techniques).

   - Insisting on data, rather than assumptions, as background for decision making (what quality practitioners call "fact-based management").

   - Using simple statistical tools (histograms, Pareto charts, correlations, cause-and-effect diagrams) to organize data and draw inferences.

Most training programs focus primarily on problem-solving techniques, using exercises and practical examples. These tools are relatively straight-forward and easily communicated; the necessary mind-set, however, is more difficult to establish. Accuracy and precision are essential for learning. Employees must therefore become more disciplined in their thinking and more attentive to details. They must continually ask, "How do we know that's true?", recognizing that close enough is not good enough if real learning is to take place. They must push beyond obvious symptoms to assess underlying causes, often collecting evidence when conventional wisdom says it is unnecessary. Otherwise, the organization will remain a prisoner of "gut facts" and sloppy reasoning, and learning will be stifled.

Xerox's Problem-Solving Process

Step

1. Identify and select problem
2. Analyze problem
3. Generate potential solutions
4. Select and plan the solution
5. Implement the solution
6. Evaluate the solution

Questions to Be Answered

What do we want to change?
What's preventing us from reaching the "desired state"?
How *could* we make the change?
What's the *best* way to do it?
Are we following the plan?
How well did it work?

Expansion/Divergence

Lots of problems for consideration
Lots of potential causes identified
Lots of ideas on how to solve the problem
Lots of criteria for evaluating potential solutions
Lots of ideas on how to implement and evaluate the selected solution

Contraction/Convergence

One problem statement, one "desired state" agreed upon
Key cause(s) identified and verified
Potential solutions clarified
Criteria to use for evaluating solution agreed upon
Implementation and evaluation plans agreed upon
Implementation of agreed-on contingency plans (if necessary)
Effectiveness of solution agreed upon
Continuing problems (if any) identified

What's Needed to Go to the Next Step

Identification of the gap
"Desired state" described in observable terms
Key cause(s) documented and ranked
Solution list
Plan for making and monitoring the change
Measurement criteria to evaluate solution effectiveness
Solution in place
Verification that the problem is solved, or
Agreement to address continuing problems

Xerox has mastered this approach on a company-wide scale. In 1983, senior managers launched the company's Leadership Through Quality initiative; since then, all employees have been trained in small-group activities and problem-solving techniques. Today a six-step process is used for virtually all decisions (see the insert "Xerox's Problem-Solving Process"). Employees are provided with tools in four areas: generating ideas and collecting information (brainstorming, interviewing, surveying); reaching consensus (list reduction, rating forms, weighted voting); analyzing and displaying data (cause-and-effect diagrams, force-field analysis); and planning actions (flow charts, Gantt charts). They then practice these tools during training sessions that last several days. Training is presented in "family groups," members of the same department or business-unit team, and the tools are applied to real problems facing the group. The result of this process has been a common vocabulary and a consistent, companywide approach to problem solving. Once employees have been trained, they are expected to use the techniques at all meetings, and no topic is off-limits. When a high-level group was formed to review Xerox's organizational structure and suggest alternatives, it employed the very same process and tools.[3]

2. Experimentation. This activity involves the systematic searching for and testing of new knowledge. Using the scientific method is essential, and there are obvious parallels to systematic problem solving. But unlike problem solving, experimentation is usually motivated by opportunity and expanding horizons, not by current difficulties. It takes two main forms: ongoing programs and one-of-a-kind demonstration projects.

Ongoing programs normally involve a continuing series of small experiments, designed to produce incremental gains in knowledge. They are the mainstay of most continuous improvement programs and are especially common on the shop floor. Corning, for example, experiments continually with diverse raw materials and new formulations to increase yields and provide better grades of glass. Allegheny Ludlum, a specialty steelmaker, regularly examines new rolling methods and improved technologies to raise productivity and reduce costs.

Successful ongoing programs share several characteristics. First, they work hard to ensure a steady flow of new ideas, even if they must be imported from outside the organization. Chaparral Steel sends its first-line supervisors on sabbaticals around the globe, where they visit academic and industry leaders, develop an understanding of new work practices and technologies, then bring what they've learned back to the company and apply it to daily operations. In large part as a result of these initiatives, Chaparral is one of the five lowest cost steel plants in the world. GE's Impact Program originally sent manufacturing managers to Japan to study factory innovations, such as quality circles and kanban cards, and then apply them in their own organizations; today Europe is the destination, and productivity improvement practices the target. The program is one reason GE has recorded productivity gains averaging nearly 5% over the last four years.

Successful ongoing programs also require an incentive system that favors risk taking. Employees must feel that the benefits of experimentation exceed the costs; otherwise, they will not participate. This creates a difficult challenge for managers, who are trapped between two perilous extremes. They must maintain accountability and control over experiments without stifling creativity by unduly penalizing employees for failures. Allegheny Ludlum has perfected this juggling act: it keeps expensive, high-impact experiments off the scorecard used to evaluate managers but requires prior approvals from four senior vice presidents. The result has been a history of productivity improvements annually averaging 7% to 8%.

Finally, ongoing programs need managers and employees who are trained in the skills required to perform and evaluate experiments. These skills are seldom intuitive and must usually be learned. They cover a broad sweep: statistical methods, like design of experiments, that efficiently compare a large number of alternatives; graphical techniques, like process analysis, that are essential for redesigning work flows; and creativity techniques, like storyboarding and role playing, that keep novel ideas flowing. The most effective training programs are tightly focused and feature a small set of techniques tailored to employees' needs. Training in design of experiments, for example, is useful for manufacturing engineers, while creativity techniques are well suited to development groups.

Demonstration projects are usually larger and more complex than ongoing experiments. They involve holistic, systemwide changes, introduced at a single site, and are often undertaken with the goal of developing new organizational capabilities. Because these projects represent a sharp break from the past, they are usually designed from scratch, using a "clean slate" approach. General Foods's Topeka plant, one of the first high-commitment work systems in this country, was a pioneering demonstration project initiated to introduce the idea of self-managing teams and high levels of worker autonomy; a more recent example, designed to rethink small-car development, manufacturing, and sales, is GM's Saturn Division.

Demonstration projects share a number of distinctive characteristics:

- They are usually the first project to embody principles and approaches that the organization hopes to adopt later on a larger scale. For this reason, they are more transitional efforts than endpoints and involve considerable "learning by doing." Mid-course corrections are common.

- They implicitly establish policy guidelines and decision rules for later projects. Managers must therefore be sensitive to the precedents they are setting and must send strong signals if they expect to establish new norms.

- They often encounter severe test of commitment from employees who wish to see whether the rules have, in fact, changed.

- They are normally developed by strong multifunctional teams reporting directly to senior management. (For projects targeting employee involvement or quality of work life, teams should be multilevel as well.)

- They tend to have only limited impact on the rest of the organization if they are not accompanied by explicit strategies for transferring learning.

All of these characteristics appeared in a demonstration project launched by Copeland Corporation, a highly successful compressor manufacturer, in the mid-1970s. Matt Diggs, then the new CEO, wanted to transform the company's approach to manufacturing. Previously, Copeland had machined and assembled all products in a single facility. Costs were high, and quality was marginal. The problem, Diggs felt, was too much complexity.

At the outset, Diggs assigned a small, multifunctional team the task of designing a "focused factory" dedicated to a narrow, newly developed product line. The team reported directly to Diggs and took three years to complete its work. Initially, the project budget was $10 million to $12 million; that figure was repeatedly revised as the team found, through experience and with Digg's prodding, that it could achieve dramatic improvements. The final investment, a total of $30 million, yielded unanticipated breakthroughs in reliability testing, automatic tool adjustment, and programmable control. All were achieved through learning by doing.

The team set additional precedents during the plant's start-up and early operations. To dramatize the importance of quality, for example, the quality manager was appointed second-in-command, a significant move upward. The same reporting relationship was used at all subsequent plants. In addition, Diggs urged the plant manager to ramp up slowly to full production and resist all efforts to proliferate products. These instructions were unusual at Copeland, where the marketing department normally ruled. Both directives were quickly tested; management held firm, and the implications were felt throughout the organization. Manufacturing's stature improved, and the company as a whole recognized its competitive contribution. One observer commented, "Marketing had always run the company, so they couldn't believe it. The change was visible at the highest levels, and it went down hard."

Once the first focused factory was running smoothly—it seized 25% of the market in two years and held its edge in reliability for over a decade—Copeland built four more factories in quick succession. Diggs assigned members of the initial project to each factory's design team to ensure that early learnings were not lost; these people later rotated into operating assignments. Today focused factories remain the cornerstone of Copeland's manufacturing strategy and a continuing source of its cost and quality advantages.

Stages of Knowledge

Adapted from work by Ramchandran Jaikumar and Roger Bohn

Scholars have suggested that production and operating knowledge can be classified systematically by level or stage of understanding. At the lowest levels of manufacturing knowledge, little is known other than the characteristics of a good product. Production remains an art, and there are few clearly articulated standards or rules. An example would be Stradivarious violins. Experts agree that they produce vastly superior sound, but no one can specify precisely how they were manufactured because skilled artisans were responsible. By contrast, at the highest levels of manufacturing knowledge, all aspects of production are known and understood. All materials and processing variations are articulated and accounted for, with rules and procedures for every contingency. Here an example would be a "lights out," fully automated factory that operates for many hours without any human intervention.

In total, this framework specifies eight stages of knowledge. From lowest to highest, they are:

1. Recognizing prototypes (what is a good product?).

2. Recognizing attributes within prototypes (ability to define some conditions under which process gives good output).

3. Discriminating among attributes (which attributes are important? Experts may differ about relevance of patterns; new operators are often trained through apprenticeships).

4. Measuring attributes (some key attributes are measured; measures may be qualitative and relative).

5. Locally controlling attributes (repeatable performance; process designed by expert, but technicians can perform it).

6. Recognizing and discriminating between contingencies (production process can be mechanized and monitored manually).

7. Controlling contingencies (process can be automated).

8. Understanding procedures and controlling contingencies (process is completely understood).

Whether they are demonstration projects like Copeland's or ongoing programs like Allegheny Ludlum's, all forms of experimentation seek the same end: moving from superficial knowledge to deep understanding. At its simplest, the distinction is between knowing how things are done and knowing why they occur. Knowing how is partial knowledge; it is rooted in norms of behavior, standards of practice, and settings of equipment. Knowing why is more fundamental: it captures underlying cause-and-effect relationships and accommodates exceptions, adaptations, and unforeseen events. The ability to control temperatures and pressures to align grains of silicon and form silicon steel is an example of knowing how; understanding the chemical and physical process that produces the alignment is knowing why.

Further distinctions are possible, as the insert "Stages of Knowledge" suggests. Operating knowledge can be arrayed in a hierarchy, moving from limited understanding and the ability to make few distinctions to more complete understanding in which all contingencies are anticipated and controlled. In this context, experimentation and problem solving foster learning by pushing organizations up the hierarchy, from lower to higher stages of knowledge.

3. Learning from past experience. Companies must review their successes and failures, assess them systematically, and record the lessons in a form that employees find open and accessible. One expert has called this process the "Santayana Review," citing the famous philosopher George Santayana, who coined the phrase

"Those who cannot remember the past are condemned to repeat it." Unfortunately, too many managers today are indifferent, even hostile, to the past, and by failing to reflect on it, they let valuable knowledge escape.

A study of more than 150 new products concluded that "the knowledge gained from failures [is] often instrumental in achieving subsequent successes. . . . In the simplest terms, failure is the ultimate teacher."[4] IBM's 360 computer series, for example, one of the most popular and profitable ever built, was based on the technology of the failed Stretch computer that preceded it. In this case, as in many others, learning occurred by chance rather than by careful planning. A few companies, however, have established processes that require their managers to periodically think about the past and learn from their mistakes.

Boeing did so immediately after its difficulties with the 737 and 747 plane programs. Both planes were introduced with much fanfare and also with serious problems. To ensure that the problems were not repeated, senior managers commissioned a high-level employee group, called Project Homework, to compare the development processes of the 737 and 747 with those of the 707 and 727, two of the company's most profitable planes. The group was asked to develop a set of "lessons learned" that could be used on future projects. After working for three years, they produced hundreds of recommendations and an inch-thick booklet. Several members of the team were then transferred to the 757 and 767 start-ups, and guided by experience, they produced the most successful, error-free launches in Boeing's history.

Other companies have used a similar retrospective approach. Like Boeing, Xerox studied its product development process, examining three troubled products in an effort to understand why the company's new business initiatives failed so often. Arthur D. Little, the consulting company, focused on its past successes. Senior management invited ADL consultants from around the world to a two-day "jamboree," featuring booths and presentations documenting a wide range of the company's most successful practices, publications, and techniques. British Petroleum went even further and established the post-project appraisal unit to review major investment projects, write up case studies, and derive lessons for planners that were then incorporated into revisions of the company's planning guidelines. A five-person unit reported to the board of directors and reviewed six projects annually. The bulk of the time was spent in the field interviewing managers.[5] This type of review is now conducted regularly at the project level.

At the heart of this approach, one expert has observed, "is a mind-set that . . . enables companies to recognize the value of productive failure as contrasted with unproductive success. A productive failure is one that leads to insight, understanding, and thus an addition to the commonly held wisdom of the organization. An unproductive success occurs when something goes well, but nobody knows how or why."[6] IBM's legendary founder, Thomas Watson, Sr., apparently understood the distinction well. Company lore has it that a young manager, after losing $10 million in a risky venture, was called into Watson's office. The young man, thoroughly intimidated, began by saying, "I guess you want my resignation." Watson replied, "You can't be serious. We just spent $10 million educating you."

Fortunately, the learning process need not be so expensive. Case studies and post-project reviews like those of Xerox and British Petroleum can be performed with little cost other than managers' time. Companies can also enlist the help of faculty and students at local colleges or universities; they bring fresh perspectives and view internships and case studies as opportunities to gain experience and increase their own learning. A few companies have established computerized data banks to speed up the learning process. At Paul Revere Life Insurance, management requires all problem-solving teams to complete short registration forms describing their proposed projects if they hope to qualify for the company's award program. The company then enters the forms into its computer system and can immediately retrieve a listing of other groups of people who have worked or are working on the topic, along with a contact person. Relevant experience is then just a telephone call away.

4. Learning from others. Of course, not all learning comes from reflection and self-analysis. Sometimes the most powerful insights come from looking outside one's immediate environment to gain a new perspective. Enlightened managers know

that even companies in completely different businesses can be fertile sources of ideas and catalysts for creative thinking. At these organizations, enthusiastic borrowing is replacing the "not invented here" syndrome. Milliken calls the process SIS, for "Steal Ideas Shamelessly"; the broader term for it is benchmarking.

According to one expert, "benchmarking is an ongoing investigation and learning experience that ensures that best industry practices are uncovered, analyzed, adopted, and implemented."[7] The greatest benefits come from studying *practices*, the way that work gets done, rather than results, and from involving line managers in the process. Almost anything can be benchmarked. Xerox, the concept's creator, has applied it to billing, warehousing, and automated manufacturing. Milliken has been even more creative: in an inspired moment, it benchmarked Xerox's approach to benchmarking.

Unfortunately, there is still considerable confusion about the requirements for successful benchmarking. Benchmarking is not "industrial tourism," a series of ad hoc visits to companies that have received favorable publicity or won quality awards. Rather, it is a disciplined process that begins with a thorough search to identify best-practice organizations, continues with careful study of one's own practices and performance, progresses through systematic site visits and interviews, and concludes with an analysis of results, development of recommendations, and implementation. While time-consuming, the process need not be terribly expensive. AT&T's Benchmarking Group estimates that a moderate-sized project takes four to six months and incurs out-of-pocket costs of $20,000 (when personnel costs are included, the figure is three to four times higher).

Benchmarking is one way of gaining an outside perspective; another, equally fertile source of ideas is customers. Conversations with customers invariably stimulate learning; they are, after all, experts in what they do. Customers can provide up-to-date product information, competitive comparisons, insights into changing preferences, and immediate feedback about service and patterns of use. And companies need these insights at all levels, from the executive suite to the shop floor. At Motorola, members of the Operating and Policy Committee, including the CEO, meet personally and on a regular basis with customers. At Worthington Steel, all machine operators make periodic, unescorted trips to customers' factories to discuss their needs.

Sometimes customers can't articulate their needs or remember even the most recent problems they have had with a product or service. If that's the case, managers must observe them in action. Xerox employs a number of anthropologists at its Palo Alto Research Center to observe users of new document products in their offices. Digital Equipment has developed an interactive process called "contextual inquiry" that is used by software engineers to observe users of new technologies as they go about their work. Milliken has created "first-delivery teams" that accompany the first shipment of all products; team members follow the product through the customer's production process to see how it is used and then develop ideas for further improvement.

Whatever the source of outside ideas, learning will only occur in a receptive environment. Managers can't be defensive and must be open to criticism or bad news. This is a difficult challenge, but it is essential for success. Companies that approach customers assuming that "we must be right, they have to be wrong" or visit other organizations certain that "they can't teach us anything" seldom learn very much. Learning organizations, by contrast, cultivate the art of open, attentive listening.

    5. Transferring knowledge. For learning to be more than a local affair, knowledge must spread quickly and efficiently throughout the organization. Ideas carry maximum impact when they are shared broadly rather than held in a few hands. A variety of mechanisms spur this process, including written, oral, and visual reports, site visits and tours, personnel rotation programs, education and training programs, and standardization programs. Each has distinctive strengths and weaknesses.

Reports and tours are by far the most popular mediums. Reports serve many purposes: they summarize findings, provide checklists of dos and don'ts, and describe important processes and events. They cover a multitude of topics, from benchmarking studies to accounting conventions to newly discovered marketing techniques. Today written reports are often supplemented by videotapes, which offer greater immediacy and fidelity.

Tours are an equally popular means of transferring knowledge, especially for large, multidivisional organizations with multiple sites. The most effective tours are tailored to different audiences and needs. To introduce its managers to the distinctive manufacturing practices of New United Motor Manufacturing Inc. (NUMMI), its joint venture with Toyota, General Motors developed a series of specialized tours. Some were geared to upper and middle managers, while others were aimed at lower ranks. Each tour described the policies, practices, and systems that were most relevant to that level of management.

Despite their popularity, reports and tours are relatively cumbersome ways of transferring knowledge. The gritty details that lie behind complex management concepts are difficult to communicate secondhand. Absorbing facts by reading them or seeing them demonstrated is one thing; experiencing them personally is quite another. As a leading cognitive scientist has observed, "It is very difficult to become knowledgeable in a passive way. Actively experiencing something is considerably more valuable than having it described."[8] For this reason, personnel rotation programs are one of the most powerful methods of transferring knowledge.

In many organizations, expertise is held locally: in a particularly skilled computer technician, perhaps, a savvy global brand manager, or a division head with a track record of successful joint ventures. Those in daily contact with these experts benefit enormously from their skills, but their field of influence is relatively narrow. Transferring them to different parts of the organization helps share the wealth. Transfers may be from division to division, department to department, or facility to facility; they may involve senior, middle, or first-level managers. A supervisor experienced in just-in-time production, for example, might move to another factory to apply the methods there, or a successful division manager might transfer to a lagging division to invigorate it with already proven ideas. The CEO of Time Life used the latter approach when he shifted the president of the company's music division, who had orchestrated several years of rapid growth and high profits through innovative marketing, to the presidency of the book division, where profits were flat because of continued reliance on traditional marketing concepts.

Line to staff transfers are another option. These are most effective when they allow experienced managers to distill what they have learned and diffuse it across the company in the form of new standards, policies, or training programs. Consider how PPG used just such a transfer to advance its human resource practices around the concept of high-commitment work systems. In 1986, PPG constructed a new float-glass plant in Chehalis, Washington; it employed a radically new technology as well as innovations in human resource management that were developed by the plant manager and his staff. All workers were organized into small, self-managing teams with responsibility for work assignments, scheduling, problem solving and improvement, and peer review. After several years running the factory, the plant manager was promoted to director of human resources for the entire glass group. Drawing on his experiences at Chehalis, he developed a training program geared toward first-level supervisors that taught the behaviors needed to manage employees in a participative, self-managing environment.

As the PPG example suggests, education and training programs are powerful tools for transferring knowledge. But for maximum effectiveness, they must be linked explicitly to implementation. All too often, trainers assume that new knowledge will be applied without taking concrete steps to ensure that trainees actually follow through. Seldom do trainers provide opportunities for practice, and few programs consciously promote the application of their teachings after employees have returned to their jobs.

Xerox and GTE are exceptions. As noted earlier, when Xerox introduced problem-solving techniques to its employees in the 1980s, everyone, from the top to the bottom of the organization, was taught in small departmental or divisional groups led by their immediate superior. After an introduction to concepts and techniques, each group applied what they learned to a real-life work problem. In a similar spirit, GTE's Quality: The Competitive Edge program was offered to teams of business-unit presidents and the managers reporting to them. At the beginning of the 3-day course, each team received a request from a company officer to prepare a complete quality plan for their unit, based on the course concepts, within 60 days. Discussion periods of two or three hours were set aside during the program so that teams could begin working on their plans. After the teams submitted their reports, the company officers studied them, and then the teams implemented them.

This GTE program produced dramatic improvements in quality, including a recent semifinalist spot in the Baldrige Awards.

The GTE example suggests another important guideline: knowledge is more likely to be transferred effectively when the right incentives are in place. If employees know that their plans will be evaluated and implemented—in other words, that their learning will be applied—progress is far more likely. At most companies, the status quo is well entrenched; only if managers and employees see new ideas as being in their own best interest will they accept them gracefully. AT&T has developed a creative approach that combines strong incentives with information sharing. Called the Chairman's Quality Award (CQA), it is an internal quality competition modeled on the Baldrige prize but with an important twist: awards are given not only for absolute performance (using the same 1,000-point scoring system as Baldrige) but also for improvements in scoring from the previous year. Gold, silver, and bronze Improvement Awards are given to units that have improved their scores 200, 150, and 100 points, respectively. These awards provide the incentive for change. An accompanying Pockets of Excellence program simplifies knowledge transfer. Every year, it identifies every unit within the company that has scored at least 60% of the possible points in each award category and then publicizes the names of these units using written reports and electronic mail.

Measuring Learning

Managers have long known that "if you can't measure it, you can't manage it." This maxim is as true of learning as it is of any other corporate objective. Traditionally, the solution has been "learning curves" and "manufacturing progress functions." Both concepts date back to the discovery, during the 1920s and 1930s, that the costs of airframe manufacturing fell predictably with increases in cumulative volume. These increases were viewed as proxies for greater manufacturing knowledge, and most early studies examined their impact on the costs of direct labor. Later studies expanded the focus, looking at total manufacturing costs and the impact of experience in other industries, including shipbuilding, oil refining, and consumer electronics. Typically, learning rates were in the 80% to 85% range (meaning that with a doubling of cumulative production, costs fell to 80% to 85% of their previous level), although there was wide variation.

Firms like the Boston Consulting Group raised these ideas to a higher level in the 1970s. Drawing on the logic of learning curves, they argued that industries as a whole faced "experience curves," costs and prices that fell by predictable amounts as industries grew and their total production increased. With this observation, consultants suggested, came an iron law of competition. To enjoy the benefits of experience, companies would have to rapidly increase their production ahead of competitors to lower prices and gain market share.

Both learning and experience curves are still widely used, especially in the aerospace, defense, and electrons industries. Boeing, for instance, has established learning curves for every work station in its assembly plant; they assist in monitoring productivity, determining work flows and staffing levels, and setting prices and profit margins on new airplanes. Experience curves are common in semiconductors and consumer electronics, where they are used to forecast industry costs and prices.

For companies hoping to become learning organizations, however, these measures are incomplete. They focus on only a single measure of output (cost or price) and ignore learning that affects other competitive variables, like quality, delivery, or new product introductions. They suggest only one possible learning driver (total production volumes) and ignore both the possibility of learning in mature industries, where output is flat, and the possibility that learning might be driven by other sources, such as new technology or the challenge posed by competing products. Perhaps most important, they tell us little about the sources of learning or the levers of change.

Another measure has emerged in response to these concerns. Called the "half-life" curve, it was originally developed by Analog Devices, a leading semiconductor manufacturer, as a way of comparing internal improvement rates. A half-life curve measures the time it takes to achieve a 50% improvement in a specified performance measure. When represented graphically, the performance measure (defect rates, on-time delivery, time to market) is plotted on the vertical axis, using a logarithmic scale, and the time scale (days, months, years) is plotted horizontally. Steeper slopes then represent faster learning.

The logic is straightforward. Companies, divisions, or departments that take less time to improve must be learning faster than their peers. In the long run, their short learning cycles will translate into superior performance. The 50% target is a measure of convenience; it was derived empirically from studies of successful improvement processes at a wide range of companies. Half-life curves are also flexible. Unlike learning and experience curves, they work on any output measure, and they are not confined to costs or prices. In addition, they are easy to operationalize, they provide a simple measuring stick, and they allow for ready comparison among groups.

Yet even half-life curves have an important weakness: they focus solely on results. Some types of knowledge take years to digest, with few visible changes in performance for long periods. Creating a total quality culture, for instance, or developing new approaches to product development are difficult systemic changes. Because of their long gestation periods, half-life curves or any other measures focused solely on results are unlikely to capture any short-run learning that has occurred. A more comprehensive framework is needed to track progress.

Organizational learning can usually be traced through three overlapping stages. The first step is cognitive. Members of the organization are exposed to new ideas, expand their knowledge, and begin to think differently. The second step is behavioral. Employees begin to internalize new insights and alter their behavior. And the third step is performance improvement, with changes in behavior leading to measurable improvements in results: superior quality, better delivery, increased market share, or other tangible gains. Because cognitive and behavioral changes typically precede improvements in performance, a complete learning audit must include all three.

Surveys, questionnaires, and interviews are useful for this purpose. At the cognitive level, they would focus on attitudes and depth of understanding. Have employees truly understood the meaning of self-direction and teamwork, or are the terms still unclear? At PPG, a team of human resource experts periodically audits every manufacturing plant, including extensive interviews with shop-floor employees, to ensure that the concepts are well understood. Have new approaches to customer service been fully accepted? At its 1989 Worldwide Marketing Managers' Meeting, Ford presented participants with a series of hypothetical situations in which customer complaints were in conflict with short-term dealer or company profit goals and asked how they would respond. Surveys like these are the first step toward identifying changed attitudes and new ways of thinking.

To assess behavioral changes, surveys and questionnaires must be supplemented by direct observation. Here the proof is in the doing, and there is no substitute for seeing employees in action. Domino's Pizza uses "mystery shoppers" to assess managers' commitment to customer service at its individual stores; L. L. Bean places telephone orders with its own operators to assess service levels. Other companies invite outside consultants to visit, attend meetings, observe employees in action, and then report what they have learned. In many ways, this approach mirrors that of examiners for the Baldrige Award, who make several-day site visits to semifinalists to see whether the companies' deeds match the words on their applications.

Finally, a comprehensive learning audit also measures performance. Half-life curves or other performance measures are essential for ensuring that cognitive and behavioral changes have actually produced results. Without them, companies would lack a rationale for investing in learning and the assurance that learning was serving the organization's ends.

First Steps

Learning organizations are not built overnight. Most successful examples are the products of carefully cultivated attitudes, commitments, and management processes that have accrued slowly and steadily over time. Still, some changes can be made immediately. Any company that wishes to become a learning organization can begin by taking a few simple steps.

The first step is to foster an environment that is conducive to learning. There must be time for reflection and analysis, to think about strategic plans, dissect customer needs, assess current work systems, and invent new products. Learning is difficult when employees are harried or rushed; it tends to be driven out by the pressures of the moment. Only if top management explicitly frees up employees' time for the purpose does learning occur with any frequency. That time will be doubly productive if employees possess the skills to use it wisely. Training in brainstorming, problem solving, evaluating experiments, and other core learning skills is therefore essential.

Another powerful lever is to open up boundaries and stimulate the exchange of ideas. Boundaries inhibit the flow of information; they keep individuals and groups isolated and reinforce preconceptions. Opening up boundaries, with conferences, meetings, and project teams, which either cross organizational levels or link the company and its customers and suppliers, ensures a fresh flow of ideas and the chance to consider competing perspectives. General Electric CEO Jack Welch considers this to be such a powerful stimulant of change that he has made "boundarylessness" a cornerstone of the company's strategy for the 1990s.

Once managers have established a more supportive, open environment, they can create learning forums. These are programs or events designed with explicit learning goals in mind, and they can take a variety of forms: strategic reviews, which examine the changing competitive environment and the company's product portfolio, technology, and market positioning; systems audits, which review the health of large, cross-functional processes and delivery systems; internal benchmarking reports, which identify and compare best-in-class activities within the organization; study missions, which are dispatched to leading organizations around the world to better understand their performance and distinctive skills; and jamborees or symposiums, which bring together customers, suppliers, outside experts, or internal groups to share ideas and learn from one another. Each of these activities fosters learning by requiring employees to wrestle with new knowledge and consider its implications. Each can also be tailored to business needs. A consumer goods company, for example, might sponsor a study mission to Europe to learn more about distribution methods within the newly unified Common Market, while a high-technology company might launch a systems audit to review its new product development process.

Together these efforts help to eliminate barriers that impede learning and begin to move learning higher on the organizational agenda. They also suggest a subtle shift in focus, away from continuous improvement and toward a commitment to learning. Coupled with a better understanding of the "three Ms," the meaning, management, and measurement of learning, this shift provides a solid foundation for building learning organizations.

Notes

David A. Garvin is the Robert and Jane Cizik Professor of Business Administration at the Harvard Business School. His current research focuses on the general manager's role and successful change processes. His last HBR article was "How the Baldrige Award Really Works" (November–December 1991).

1. Peter M. Senge, *The Fifth Discipline* (New York: Doubleday, 1990), p. 1.

2. Ikujiro Nonaka, "The Knowledge-Creating Company," *Harvard Business Review*, November–December 1991, p. 97.

3. Robert Howard, "The CEO as Organizational Architect: An Interview with Xerox's Paul Allaire," *Harvard Business Review*, September–October 1992, p. 106.

4. Modesto A. Maidique and Billie Jo Zirger, "The New Product Learning Cycle," *Research Policy*, Vol. 14, No. 6 (1985), pp. 299, 309.

5. Frank R. Gulliver, "Post-Project Appraisals Pay," *Harvard Business Review*, March–April 1987, p. 128.

6. David Nadler, "Even Failures Can Be Productive," *New York Times*, April 23, 1989, Sec. 3, p. 3.

7. Robert C. Camp, *Benchmarking: The Search for Industry Best Practices that Lead to Superior Performance* (Milwaukee: ASQC Quality Press, 1989), p. 12.

8. Roger Schank, with Peter Childers, *The Creative Attitude* (New York: Macmillan, 1988), p. 9.

9. Ramchandran Jaikumar and Roger Bohn, "The Development of Intelligent Systems for Industrial Use: A Conceptual Framework," *Research on Technological Innovation, Management and Policy*, Vol. 3 (1986), pp. 182–188.

How Involving Colleges Promote Student Learning and Development

GEORGE D. KUH, JOHN H. SCHUH, ELIZABETH J. WHITT AND ASSOCIATES

Imagine a college where students and faculty are actively engaged in the life of the campus community and with one another in teaching and learning. Imagine an institution where students are expected to take, and do assume, responsibility for their learning and personal development. What would such a college look like? What might be some of that institution's characteristics?

Heartland College, Small Town, U.S.A.

When Heartland College (HC) was founded, its mission was to prepare young men and women for a life of leadership and community service. Over the years, the mission has been reinterpreted in the context of the times, but the college's fundamental purposes, and the means used to attain these purposes, have remained consistent. For example, expectations for student performance have always been high. However, the founder, it is told, encouraged students to teach and learn from one another and to take care of one another. Some observers wonder how Heartland is able to maintain high expectations for academic performance and yet encourage the cooperation and mutual respect that characterize relationships among HC students.

Most students, faculty members, and administrators are on a first-name basis. Administrative and professorial titles, when used, are used out of respect, not to acknowledge status differences. Newcomers are neither advantaged or disadvantaged by institutional policies with regard to where they live, study or work. If anything, Heartland seems to go to extraordinary lengths to make certain that members of all groups, particularly groups that have historically been mistreated, such as women and members of racial and ethnic minorities, enjoy the same rights, privileges, and social and educational comfort as white men.

Recognizing that some students who share a cultural heritage often desire to live together, the college has designated cross-cultural living arrangements and centers for group activities for persons from traditionally underrepresented groups. Comfortable indoor space—in residence halls, the union, and the library—is available for small group meetings and encourages informal, spontaneous discussions. However, to use public space on campus, students and others must demonstrate that the activity is related to one or more of the institution's educational purposes. In this sense, Heartland intentionally attempts to blur any perceived distinctions between the goals of the classroom and out-of-class experiences.

As with many colleges, Heartland was intentionally established some distance from a major metropolitan area. This creates both advantages and disadvantages in attaining the college's purposes. Most of the students who attend HC are full-time students for whom college life is their primary role commitment. Also, because virtually all students live on or near the campus, the college uses students' physical proximity to one another and campus facilities to promote learning about and understanding of individual and cultural differences.

Both in-class and out-of-class learning opportunities are plentiful. Indeed, the institution has devoted considerable energy and resources over the past few decades to create opportunities for students to spend time off campus. For example, foreign study opportunities are available through consortia with other colleges with missions similar to that of HC. Internships have been developed in the closest major cities, one of which is the state capital, and at other locations ranging from Washington, D.C., to a nearby American Indian reservation. Most important, a long-standing commitment to public service motivates almost every HC student to spend a summer or part of a semester working in a community agency or a comparable activity.

The well-kept campus seems to blend with its natural surroundings. Plantings include trees and shrubs indigenous to the region as well as some from a Far Eastern country where the college has developed a special relationship with a university. Several outdoor "natural courtyards," carved out of stands of trees, and the nearby college farm allow students to get away for solitary moments of reflection. Campus buildings are not overpowering; no structure stands more than three stories above ground, except for the clock tower on "Old Main." This building has been rebuilt twice, first after a fire in the early years of the college and again following a tornado several decades ago. Almost everyone knows the stories about how the Heartland community rallied and refused to falter after these devastating events.

A high level of interaction occurs among students and faculty member. College policies and practices keep students from being anonymous or unconnected. The routines of campus life and staffing patterns in residence halls keep students in touch with one another. It seems as though every student is involved in at least one of the numerous campus clubs and organizations. Every new year brings several new groups as students organize to pursue their interests.

Heartland is both simple and complicated. Some attribute the college's success to its good fortune in attracting good students and faculty and in creating a physical plant that takes advantage of its rural, but no longer remote, physical setting. Heartland is also a state of mind shaped by decades of history and tradition. Indeed, it has been said that HC works as well as it does because administrators and faculty members do not have to expend a lot of energy monitoring how students spend their time. Students cultures socialize new students about appropriate behaviors and expectations for performance. Perhaps that is why so much effort is devoted to creating opportunities for current students and alumni and alumnae to meet and talk with prospective students about life at Heartland.

Students, faculty, and staff describe Heartland in similar terms. Although they are sometimes critical of certain policies and practices, they are nonetheless animated when talking about "their college." However, their words do not necessarily flow easily. Sooner or later, most say something like, "there's just something about the place."

A cornucopia of events, actions, and beliefs contribute to this shared observation. Heartland's president and senior faculty and administrators often tell stories about the college and link historical incidents to current issues on campus. The values represented in those stories come through clearly in all-campus events such as the opening convocation and commencement. And while the words used by faculty members, staff, and students to describe the college are not unique, they are used in patterns that make interpretation and meaning distinctive to Heartland. It is almost as if you have to be a member of the community to fully understand and appreciate what is going on. In that sense, members of the Heartland family seem to share similar views of teaching and learning and campus life.

Because community members understand what is important and valued at HC, one might expect that the institution has developed a rather lengthy, comprehensive list of policies and procedures to guide faculty, staff, and student behavior. However, just the opposite is the case. Heartland relies on formal and informal socialization activities to teach newcomers—students, faculty, and staff—what is desirable and worthwhile. For students, the introduction to life at Heartland begins with the first admissions brochure, which sets forth in plain language the institution's mission, purposes and expectations for student life. Most prospective students visit the campus; many spend a night or two in a student residence. Once a student is admitted, HC periodically sends information that introduces the new-comer to campus life, including the demands of the academic program and what is expected of members of the HC community. One message in particular is reiterated over and over: students are expected to take responsibility for their learning. Yet the message is conveyed with a tone of caring and deep, sincere interest in the welfare of the individual. In addition, students receive the message that they are expected to participate fully in the life of the community.

Institutional values and the ways in which Heartland policies and practices reinforce its educational priorities are also emphasized to new faculty. Another persistent message is that learning takes place in many forms and forums; students learn from other students as well as faculty members and staff, and faculty members and staff learn from students. Equally important, all groups acknowledge that learning can occur everywhere, both in and out of the classroom.

As with other institutions, Heartland receives more requests from faculty members, students, graduates, and others to develop programs, services, and activities than its resources can support. This sometimes fuels debate and creates tensions. In general, decisions about where and how resources are used adhere to two fundamental principles: the program, service, or activity must contribute to Heartland's mission, and the manner and forums in which decisions are made must allow the views of students and others with a stake in the college to be heard. Taken together, these two principles ensure that the college's educational purposes and philosophy drive the use of finite, precious resources and that the process permits open discussion and debate about institutional values and priorities.

As with any productive enterprise, people are at the heart of Heartland College. Commitment to the ideals and core values of the college runs deep through key members of the administration, faculty, and staff. The caretakers of the HC culture, particularly the president, trustees, and senior faculty and administrators, understand that values decay over time and that if the founding beliefs are to continue to be useful in guiding the college, the institution's values and purposes must periodically be revisited. After all, over a quarter of the students are new to the community each year, and in some years, new tenure track faculty members have made up as much as 15 percent of the faculty.

Because the college takes seriously every admission and employment decision, once an offer is accepted, one immediately becomes, and is expected to act like, a full member of the HC community. But the only way to really learn and understand "the Heartland way" is by being a member of the community. To summarize how well Heartland works, consider the words of a senior just weeks before graduation: "When I visited this place four years ago it felt like home even though I had never been here before and didn't know anybody here. I can't imagine a school that would have been better for me."

In many ways, Heartland is similar to dozens of colleges and universities. Although it is not clear from this description whether Heartland is a small college or a university with many thousands of students, Heartland certainly "feels" small. Heartland is also special because many complementary properties work together to produce a "resonance" between the institution and students as well as among faculty members, administrators, and others. Resonance connotes something qualitatively different from the concept of student-institution fit described in the enrollment management literature. (Hossler, 1984). Certainly, a sense of "fitting in" is important. But Heartland College and others with similar characteristics have fashioned more than just a match. Resonance means that mutually enhancing elements are present that stimulate both the institution and the student to peak performance. Students find peers, faculty members, and staff with whom to work, to challenge and to learn. Student and institution contribute to the growth and development of each other. Students not only feel comfortable at the institution but also are challenged to take advantage of as many leaning opportunities as possible. Similarly, the presence of students who seem to belong there makes the institution stretch to be more than it is and to provide greater challenges and opportunities for student participation as full members of the community. Both the student and institution are stronger, more confident, and more vibrant for their coming together. Thus, resonance connotes a developmentally appropriate—even powerful—relationship between the institution and its students.

Some will asset that places like Heartland College, a composite description of some of the fourteen colleges and universities that participated in this study, are the dinosaurs of American higher education, evolving toward extinction because of the increasing numbers of part-time and older students for whom college is but one, and often not the primary, life role. But many of the characteristics of a Heartland College can be found in different forms in other types of institutions. Consider Metro University.

Metro University, Downtown, U.S.A.

Metro University was founded after World War II when the need to educate returning veterans became obvious to city leaders. In the early years, Metro was essentially a night school offering classes in several high schools in different parts of the city. As enrollments increased, city leaders and state legislators agreed that the university's resources had to be consolidated in one place to provide a broader array of academic programs. The site ultimately selected was in a decaying area of the city.

The development of the Metro campus was met with a fair amount of skepticism and, in some quarters, substantial opposition. Representatives from the other state universities were concerned that Metro would siphon resources and, perhaps, enrollments. To a degree, these concerns were justified. However, Metro is now unlike any other institutions of higher education in the state.

The Metro campus is well kept. Although the campus is surrounded by the city, the boundaries of the campus, while permeable, clearly distinguish the university from the town. At the same time, Metro belongs to the city. Citizens frequently use the term "our" when describing Metro's successful athletic teams. Because the mission of Metro is to respond to the needs of the urban area, city leaders regularly consult with university representatives as economic development plans are made. Faculty members frequently consult with business, industry, and educational groups. Graduate programs are developed to address the economic, social, and health concerns in the city. The university considers itself an integral part of the city, "a citizen of downtown," rather than simply being located there.

For Metro students, attendance at the university is just one, and perhaps not the most important, priority in their lives. Some high school students take advanced mathematics and science classes not available in their curriculum. Most of Metro's students are the first in their family to go to college; many are from economically disadvantaged backgrounds. Other Metro students are teachers, business people, artists, and practicing professionals seeking graduate degrees or technical competence; many take courses at night while pursuing their careers during the day. Any degree the university offers can be earned through evening classes; some classes are also available on weekends and in other parts of the city when the demand is great.

The average age of Metro students is twenty-nine and rising. A substantial proportion have families, homes, and full-time jobs in the city. Indeed, it is difficult to differentiate students from the faculty on the Metro campus. Many of the faculty and students are about the same age, wear the same style of clothes, drive the same kinds of cars, and compete for the best parking places on or near the campus.

Many of the students who attend Metro are at risk; some have academic needs that can be attributed in part to their economic background. It is not surprising, therefore, that many students are insecure about starting classes; they often have low self-concepts and think of themselves as academically disadvantaged. Adult learners, many of whom have been away from academic work for some time, are concerned about keeping up with traditional-age students. Some traditional-age students, conversely, fear that their lack of life experience will put them at a disadvantage in classes with older learners. Faculty know this and intentionally draw on the strengths of all students. Hence, class discussions are often very stimulating and result in rich learning experiences for both older and younger students.

Metro provides a variety of services and resources to help students enroll and stay in college. For example, Metro has scholarships for returning adult learners, mentors for educationally underprepared students, special academic advising for students with poor high school records, tutoring assistance for students who encounter problems in math and science, and child care programs. Admission standards tend to be flexible and most student services are available in the evening.

Because many Metro students are not well prepared for college, every possible effort is made by staff and faculty members to help them succeed. For example, if a Metro student has a disastrous first semester, she or he can, with the approval of an advisor, wipe the record clean and start over. Metro is not a university without standards, however. Academic administrators are quick to point out that much is expected of Metro students; academic standards are not compromised.

Most Metro students have jobs; some work on campus, others off campus. Most work part-time although a substantial number work full-time, particularly those taking evening classes. At any given time, more than a quarter of Metro students participate in cooperative education or internship activities. Strong but hard-won ties between university administrators and faculty members and representatives from local businesses, industries, and service organizations have led to the development of a variety of programs that use the work experience to educational advantage. Indeed, Metro does everything it can to make certain that students' jobs complement their academic and occupational goals. Students receive a quarterly newsletter that includes information and advice about how to apply what they learn in the classroom or laboratory to practical situations.

Most Metro students live at home; in fact, many own their own home! Available residence hall space serves the growing international student population and traditional-age students whose homes are well beyond the city limits. Because of the demands of class and work, it is unusual for students to participate in more than one activity on campus; this activity is often an organization based in an academic department. Students have other important commitments, however. For example, many students are active in civic and religious organizations. Because of students' study and work schedules and family commitments, the biggest challenge for student organizations is to find a time to meet. As a result, it is not uncommon for groups to meet on the weekend or on Friday night. Organizations tend to be small, typically numbering only a dozen or so students, but those members have a keen interest in the activity.

Meeting spaces for faculty members and students and for student organizations were part of the design of campus buildings. For example, space for group study, which is encouraged, is available in virtually all the academic departments and the library. The noon hour is a busy time at Metro; student organization meetings and major events, such as guest speakers, are often scheduled at this time.

Metro administrators and faculty members also realize that, without family support, many students simply could not be successful. Thus, family members are always welcome at Metro events. Metro hosts a "family weekend" to celebrate the contributions of family members—parents, spouses, children—to the success of Metro students. The union frequently sponsors outdoor picnics so that students can get together and visit with one another and faculty members.

Recreational programs cater to the diversity in the Metro student body. While some traditional intramural activities, such as basketball tournaments, are offered, individual and small group recreation are emphasized. Metro students use the recreation building from early morning to late night, lifting weights, using exercise machines, jogging, and taking exercise classes.

Keeping students and faculty members informed is a university priority. The student newspaper cannot compete with the local press, however, so it is published just twice a week. Instead, Metro relies on electronic media such as the campus radio station and its cable television channel. An electronic bulletin board outside the union advertises upcoming activities and events and provides academic information. The word seems to get out, and events are usually quite well attended.

For many students, Metro was their only college option. Indeed, the critical decision for most graduates of the city's high schools is whether to get a job or attend Metro. For most students, a Metro degree will make a significant difference in their lives—in their ability to enjoy life, to be economically productive, and to appreciate the fruits of their labors.

Characteristics Common to Heartland and Metro

Heartland and Metro are very different institutions, but they are similar in some respects. Both have clear institutional missions and educational purposes; campus environments that are compatible with the institutions's mission and philosophy; opportunities for meaningful student involvement in learning and personal development activities; an institutional culture (history, traditions, rituals, language) that reinforces the importance of student involvement; and policies and practices consistent with institutional aspirations, mission and culture. In Chapters Three through Seven, the factors and conditions that characterize Heartland College and Metro University are discussed, drawing on examples from fourteen institutions with different missions, purposes, philosophies, student characteristics, resource bases, and locations. In Chapters Eight through Ten, selected policies and practices are described in some detail in order to understand why and how these policies and practices promote student involvement in out-of-class learning opportunities in large, small, and urban institutions. The term *learning* will be used throughout the remaining chapters to represent the benefits that accrue from student involvement in out-of-class experiences.

A caveat is appropriate. The properties that make up an Involving College cannot be easily separated or isolated. That is, the factors and conditions common to involving institutions work together, in different combinations, toward different purposes, depending on the institutional context and mission, expectations for student and faculty behavior, and desired educational purposes and outcomes. In addition, none of the fourteen institutions exhibited all of the factors and conditions exactly as they are described here. To be useful, these factors and conditions must be interpreted and adapted to the particular purposes, culture, and context of a specific institution. Toward that end, we challenge the reader to think about how the institutional qualities described in the next five chapters are, or could be, manifested in her or his institution.

Conclusions and Recommendations for Creating Involving Colleges

No one of the institutional factors and conditions described in the preceding chapters can ensure involvement and learning on the part of students. Nor can an institution's culture, or student behavior, be easily changed or readily manipulated. However, a high level of student participation in educationally purposeful activities can be promoted if these activities and the policies and practices that support them are compatible with the institution's mission, philosophy, and culture. This chapter presents six conclusions about Involving colleges. Recommendations are offered for institutions interested in creating conditions that seem to promote student learning. Finally, some unresolved issues related to student involvement and some insights from this study about developing a sense of community on campus are discussed.

Conclusion 1: Institutions That Have a Clear Mission, Kept Plainly in View, Encourage Involvement

A clear, coherent mission gives direction to student learning and minimizes confusion and uncertainty about what the institution is and aspires to be. Constant scrutiny is required, however, to keep the institutional mission appropriate within its social and political contexts and meaningful to community members. Goals for what and how students learn are examined, and reexamined, to remain compatible with the institutional mission. Student behavior is assessed and, if necessary, challenged in light of the mission and philosophy.

Recommendations:

1. All members of the campus community should be familiar with and committed to the institution's mission and philosophy.

At Involving Colleges, the most powerful factor in focusing student behavior is the institution's mission and philosophy. The mission should be communicated clearly and consistently in institutional publications, at gatherings of community members, and in the process of welcoming newcomers. Socialization activities send powerful messages about what the institution stands for and create lasting expectations for new (or prospective) students, faculty, and staff.

The chief academic officers (CAO), academic deans, and department chairs should play a primary role in teaching new students and faculty about institutional values regarding student learning. For example, academic administrators can make new faculty aware of the importance of using out-of-class contacts with students to educational advantage. The CAO can recommend that new student orientation include more intellectual activities, such as discussions of books assigned to be read during the summer, and can personally encourage students to become more involved in departmental organizations.

Understanding of, and commitment to, the institutional mission and personal values compatible with the institution's philosophy are particularly important characteristics for student affairs staff. Technical competence in areas such as legal aspects of student-institution relationships, counseling techniques, or conflict resolution is important. However, it is easier to acquire new information than to change values. Technical competence cannot substitute for "fit" between an individual staff member and the institutional ethos.

2. Resist efforts to create a mission that is all things to all people; take pride in and emphasize what is distinctive about the institution.

A distinctive mission not only sets an institution apart from its peers in the eyes of outsiders but also gives community members a shared sense of purpose that guides daily activities and serves as a touchstone for making decisions and establishing policies. New initiatives are evaluated in terms of their compatibility with the mission and philosophy. Are they consistent with "how we do things here" and what is valued? Any change in the mission should occur only after thoughtful reflection and healthy debate, and with thorough understanding of the consequences of a change, not as a result of some educational fad or trend or to avoid conflict.

3. Allocate resources in ways that help the institution attain its mission.

What a college or university values is evident in how, and for what purposes, its resources are allocated. If an institution's mission asserts the importance of encouraging and supporting student learning through out-of-class experiences, a significant portion of its financial and human resources must be directed to that end.

4. Assess the appropriateness and necessity of programs and services in light of the institution's mission and philosophy.

Administrators and faculty can become so involved in the demands of daily events that they do not take time to review whether, or in what ways, their efforts contribute to the accomplishment of the institution's mission. In addition, student activities may monopolize students' time and energy in ways that may or may not have anything to do with the educational purposes of the institution or the learning goals of students themselves.

Campus leaders should examine whether opportunities for involvement and the ways in which community members spend their time are consistent with and promote the institutional mission. If so, the complementarity between mission and community actions should be widely acclaimed and assiduously reinforced. If not, why not? Is the mission no longer viable, or have daily routines taken on a life of their own independent of larger institutional purposes?

5. Institutional advancement personnel should use their contacts with external constituents to teach them about the institution's mission, purposes, and philosophy.

One can learn a great deal about a college from what it says about itself. Prospective students, faculty, and staff need accurate information about what life is like at the college, information that may or may not be provided in institutional publications. For example, do admissions materials portray a picture of campus life that is consistent with the perceptions of current students? Do prospective students seem to expect something other than what they find when they visit campus?

Graduates and other potential donors should also have an accurate picture of institutional priorities. With the help of faculty, students, and student affairs staff, institutional advancement staff should develop publications that clearly communicate the institution's mission and values, articulate expectations for student performance both in and out of the classroom, and—to the extent possible—enable students to be informed sources for their peers who are considering joining the community.

6. Be prepared to deal with the conflict, debate, and discussion likely to characterize colleges and universities into the twenty-first century.

College campuses have always been buffeted by the social, economic, and political turmoil of the outside world. Racism, sexism, poverty, homelessness, abortion, health, and environmental concerns in the United States, as well as struggles of people elsewhere in the world, influence college life and the experiences of students. Increasing diversity of college students will likely increase campus tensions as well as enrich learning. In the process, institutions can become harbingers of the future rather than mirrors of history.

How can colleges and universities effectively meet the challenges of internal and external change and its attendant uncertainty? Up to this point, changes in institutional policies and practices regarding historically underrepresented groups have usually been championed by members of these groups. How will an institution respond when students request or demand changes in institutional policies and practices that enable them to feel understood, respected, and appreciated, rather than alienated and invisible? What changes in policies and practices, consistent with the mission and philosophy, should the *institution* initiate?

On many campuses, unrest is inevitable as institutional agents and students deal with what Steele (1989, p. 49) called the *"politics of difference,* a troubling, volatile politics in which each group justifies itself, its sense of worth, and its pursuit of power, through difference alone." Student affairs staff and faculty are often on the front line and expected to ameliorate campus tensions. However, as institutions evolve from their present state of affairs toward multicultural learning communities, an active role on the part of the president, as the embodiment of institutional mission and values, will be crucial. For example, people of color and women must be active and powerful, not just visible, members of the president's cabinet. Hiring of senior-level administrators alone will not empower women and students of color, but discouraging messages about institutional—and presidential—priorities are sent to members of these groups when the institutional leadership is predominantly white and male.

Conclusion 2: Institutions That Value and Expect Student Initiative and Responsibility Encourage Involvement

A college or university promotes student learning by establishing high expectations for student and faculty performance and tells students, from their contact with the institution, that they will be responsible for their own affairs. When the students are welcomed as full members of the institution (the ethic of membership), they are told, in effect, that they are expected to help the institution attain its mission and participate in running the institution. Involving Colleges expect, and help, students to be responsible for determining policies and rules for residences and holding themselves and one another accountable for maintaining a high quality of campus life. Again, the amount of assistance students should receive from faculty and administration depends on the characteristics of the students and the institution's mission and philosophy.

Recommendations:

1. Create an environment in which students can be responsible.

In order for students to take initiative and be responsible, certain conditions must be present within the institution: trust, care, and support for risk taking as a vehicle for learning. Institutional agents must also be willing to share control of the institution with students and be open to the possibility that there are many ways to achieve institutional purposes, some of which institutional leaders may not have considered. One must keep in mind, too, that any learning process requires patience on the part of both teacher and student. The road to developing student responsibility and self-governance is not likely to be short or smooth, but it is certainly an exciting and worthwhile trip.

2. Spend less time designing and implementing programs and more time encouraging students to take advantage of learning opportunities.

Student affairs staff and faculty should not feel responsible for planning, programming, and organizing all student activities. Do not overstructure or overorganize the out-of-class experience for students; do just enough to enable students to develop and implement their own educational purposeful activities. Experiment with services and programs. Work with students to identify programs and activities that are of debatable utility and suspend them for a year to see if anyone misses them. Use any savings of human or financial resources to concentrate on improving conditions for out-of-class learning.

3.   Recognize and take advantage of the power of the small gesture in encouraging and reinforcing student effort devoted to learning.

As with other powerful learning experiences, there is no substitute for personal contact for encouraging student involvement in educationally purposeful activities. At Involving Colleges, institutional agents and students themselves make many small gestures to one another to encourage effort, such as comments in the margin of an essay acknowledging a salient point, a faculty member's words of encouragement after class, and notes from a staff member to students who have attained personal milestones. The confluence of these expressions of interest in students' welfare make them feel known and valued, and encourages them to stretch themselves, both in and out of the classroom. At a time when a sense of community seems to be unraveling on many college campuses, we would do well to remember that, in many ways, a community is made up of the thousands of small gestures that keep people together and communicate appreciation and belonging. We will come back to this point later in this chapter.

Conclusion 3: Institutions that Recognize and Respond to the Total Student Experience Encourage Involvement

Most colleges and universities are organized to present students with discrete experiences. Different people, at different points in time and in different places (and sometimes with completely different philosophies about what college is for), orient new students, offer advice and counsel, teach classes and labs, get students registered, provide medical care, teach job hunting skills, provide places to live and food to eat, impose degree requirements, and help organize dances and parties.

The fragmentation of universities as organizations is reflected in perceptions of student life: in-class and out-of-class learning are too often treated as separate aspects of undergraduate experience. For example, changing rewards systems encourage faculty members to isolate themselves from students, thus enhancing the attitude that academic and nonacademic aspects of students' lives are, and should be, distinct. Separation of academic and student affairs within the institutional structure can encourage persons within those areas to view their tasks and priorities as distinct and, in some cases, competing.

Students, however, do not think of their lives as bifurcated by the classroom door. For students, college is a stream of learning opportunities: challenges, relationships, discoveries, fun, disappointments, and successes. *Where* these opportunities are encountered is, for the most part, irrelevant; what is important is that students learn. Just as the institution seeks to help students make sense of courses within a major, students yearn to interpret and make sense of all their experiences.

Involving Colleges seems to be aware of the seamlessness of student experience and of the harvest of learning that awaits students from *all* aspects of college life. By envisioning what the total student experience ought to be, and resolving to use the institution's educational resources—curricular and noncurricular, formal and informal—to full advantage to enable that experience, Involving Colleges ignore the perceived, artificial distinctions between what is academic and what is educational and between what are "in-class" and "out-of-class" learning experiences. A college takes a step toward becoming an involving institution when it softens or makes permeable the boundaries between curricular and other student experiences.

Recommendations:

1.   Know your students, how they learn, and the conditions that affect their development.

In many institutions, students' aspirations, backgrounds, abilities, and roles, such as a student, spouse, parent, or worker, have changed dramatically from those of past students, even the recent past. The ways in which these institutions work with and respond to their students must also change—but this can be done effectively only if the institutions know and understand the changes. The effectiveness of faculty, administrators, and staff is enhanced when they recognize and understand differences among individual students and student cultures.

The institutional research office or the student affairs division are likely sources for collection and dissemination of data about students and the quality of student life. Institutional researchers and student affairs staff should obtain up-to-date information about students (characteristics, attitudes, needs, activities) and share this information with faculty, academic administrators, trustees, and the students themselves. A study of student cultures could provide insights into their influence on learning and personal development, and the ways in which student life complements or competes with the educational purposes of the institution. The best source of information about students is the students themselves; any institutional research effort with regard to students and their lives should include interviews with students.

One should be cautious, however, about making generalizations from composite information about student characteristics to individual situations. Every student is unique, with unique needs, interests, and priorities. At the same time, certain subcommunities of students, such as women or African American students or adult learners, have needs specific to their group, needs that are best identified in intensive and extensive interactions with members of their subcommunity.

The student affairs division should be held accountable for articulating and, in collaboration with faculty and others, respond to students' out-of-class needs. Student affairs staff should be able to describe and appreciate the ways in which out-of-class environments and events influence student learning, as well as the institution.

2. Discover the ways in which students spend their time and are influenced by peers, student cultures, and campus life.

In order to recognize and respond to the total experience of students, institutions must first understand the experiences of their students from the point of view of the students themselves. How do students spend their time? With what activities do they fill their lives? How do students decide how to use their time? In what ways do peers and peer cultures affect students' lives and learning? Are students' experiences consistent with the educational purposes of the institution?

On many campuses, the pace of student life is hectic and overwhelming, demanding too much time and energy from students and allowing too few opportunities to think about what they are learning. On other campuses, student life can best be described as boring. In both cases (and all those in between), students may respond by organizing activities that are antithetical to the institution's mission. Social life, including parties and drinking, may become the focus of students' efforts as they seek to escape from the pressures of overinvolvement, or because they cannot think of anything else to do.

Students' experiences can, of course, stray from fulfilling educational purposes in many ways, including overinvestment in a particular activity or many activities, to the extent that a sense of balance is lost. Throughout this book, we have emphasized learning experiences that are educationally purposeful, but there *are* trade-offs associated with high levels of involvement. Some students at Involving Colleges suffer negative effects of overinvolvement, including burnout. Feeling responsibility or pressure to become involved, to take full advantage of the institution's resources, to be actively engaged in one or more activities all the time, can be debilitating. The balancing act becomes even more difficult when a student has a spouse, children, job, or other commitments. It is not surprising that more than a few seniors told us that, after graduation, they would like to take a year off because they were exhausted!

Institutional agents can help ease the stress associated with overinvolvement by being aware of students who appear to be taking on too many responsibilities and helping them examine what constitutes an appropriate balance of effort in different aspects of their lives. Students may need help in weighing the perceived personal and educational benefits of various activities when deciding how to invest their time. When students become aware, and consider the implications of the trade-offs, the collegiate experience more closely approximates life after college, when multiple and often conflictual personal and professional demands are typical. Institutional agents can also assist students by teaching and modeling the importance of, and skills needed for, living a balanced life.

3. Examine what your policies and practices teach students.

Students learn from what an institution *does* just as surely as they learn from what institutional agents *say*; discrepancies between espoused and enacted values may create particularly fruitful teachable moments. What are the social values an institution espouses? How does an institution invest its funds? Is the campus press as free as public statements about the importance of a free press would indicate? Does the common language of the institution, especially the terms used to describe individuals and groups, mirror the espoused values of the institution?

4. Develop a shared vision of the institution and its students.

All institution agents (faculty, academic administrators, student affairs staff) are partners in achieving the institution's educational purposes. This partnership requires a shared vision of the enterprise—what the institution's mission is, who its students are, what sort of education the students should have, what behaviors ought to be expected of students, and what qualities characterize a healthy and effective academic community. A shared vision is forged when faculty, student affairs staff, and others spend time together talking about institutional purposes, about the ways in which the institution's mission and philosophy influence their work, and about students.

The relationship between the chief academic officer (CAO) and the chief student affairs officer (CSAO) is a key to clarifying and reinforcing connections between the curriculum and out-of-class learning opportunities. The CAO will undoubtedly underscore the primacy of the institution's academic mission but should, nevertheless, work with the CSAO, students, and others to discover how the institution's educational purposes can be accomplished in out-of-class learning environments. The priorities of academic and student affairs can complement each other if both acknowledge their common commitment to the institution's mission.

The increasing size and complexity of universities and changing expectations for faculty suggest that student affairs staff on many campuses will play an increasingly prominent role in promoting learning experiences that support the institution's educational purposes. Indeed, at some large institutions, student affairs staff have become the de facto caretakers of the undergraduate experience. Along with a few other administrators and faculty members, student affairs staff model how students can respond effectively to the opportunities and responsibilities present in an academic community. Student affairs staff are more likely than faculty to be present to help students take advantage of the many "teachable moments" that occur out of the classroom.

Conclusion 4: Institutions That Provide Small, Human-scale Environments and Multiple Subcommunities Encourage Involvement

Involving Colleges make creating and maintaining conditions that promote student learning a priority. Learning is promoted when faculty, staff, and students are familiar with one another and have frequent contact. By providing small residences and classes, maintaining effective communication networks, and widely disseminating information, Involving Colleges allow community members to interact easily and comfortably.

At a small college, students probably know several faculty members and administrators who can assist and encourage them to become involved in learning opportunities that fit their abilities and needs. Such relationships between students and faculty or staff are less likely to be found at large institutions. Large institutions can, however, foster interaction among students and between students and faculty and staff, as well as encourage feelings of belonging, through the development and support of subcommunities. A subcommunity provides a niche in which its members can feel comfortable and connected and where they can find others like themselves, whether those "others" be students of color, social activities, biologists, or women. At the same time, a subcommunity can support its members' efforts to participate in the community at large and establish connections with members of other subcommunities.

Recommendations:

1. Reduce physical obstacles to interaction by dividing large facilities into smaller units, increasing the number and span of communication networks and making more effective use of campus space.

In general, small is better. Small residences seem to build a sense of community among residents much more quickly than large residences. Members of a small community can more easily become full participating members of organizations and activities, such as intramurals and student government. This does not mean that large institutions cannot provide "small" environments. We have provided numerous examples of ways in which Involving Colleges—large and small, residential and commuter—have made the most of the advantages of their setting (as well as other aspects of their physical environment) to compensate for any disadvantages and to meet the needs of community members for interaction and solitude.

2. Make sure that safety nets and early warning systems for students in difficulty are in place and operating effectively.

Despite the emphasis placed at many Involving Colleges on student initiative and responsibility, students are not abandoned by these institutions to fend for themselves. Resources to help students are available, although the services and their visibility vary according to student's characteristics and institutional philosophy.

Institutions should find out what academic support systems exist, and assess the extent to which they meet the needs of all students and are compatible with institutional mission and philosophy. One example of an academic safety net is the option to declare academic bankruptcy after a particularly trying semester, similar to the policy in place for first-year students at Wichita State University. For students who came from disadvantaged educational backgrounds, or who have been away from academic work for some years, the possibility of academic bankruptcy may reduce some of the pressure associated with fear of failure.

Student affairs staff are the heart of the early warning systems of Involving Colleges, systems which identify students with problems and—in collaboration with faculty members and students—form the safety nets for them. To expand existing safety nets, new faculty members could be contacted by the chief student affairs officer by letter prior to their arrival and in person by a senior member of the student affairs staff soon after they come to campus. During these contacts, held when new faculty are looking for behavioral cues in their environment about what is important, programs and services available on the campus to help students—and to help faculty help students—can be described. At the same time, student affairs staff establish relationships with new faculty, who now have a contact in student affairs to whom questions can be addressed and students referred.

3. The institution should be a catalyst for multiple subcommunities and cultural pluralism.

Students of color, women, and members of other historically underrepresented groups need support in their efforts to teach others about their background and interests. Although this can be a wearisome task for these students, it is important for achieving understanding and respect for differences among people of all groups. Students in historically underrepresnted groups need the helped of others within the institution to achieve their goals. Some of the most highly sought-after helpers include faculty and staff who are women or people of color, although their minority status can place extensive and intensive demands on their time; the need for more faculty and staff who are people of color and women has already been discussed. The needs of students of historically underrepresented groups are not, however, the exclusive purview of institutional agents who are also members of these groups. All members of the community, and members of all subcommunities, must care for one another.

Some examples of practices that respond to the needs of historically underrepresented groups follow. Many institutions are already doing these things. They are offered in hope that other institutions will recognize the importance of these activities in promoting out-of-class learning by students from these groups.

For Students of Color:

- Assess, perhaps by means of an institutional audit (see Chapter Eleven), the ways in which the needs of students of color are—and are not—being met. On the basis of that assessment, work with students of color to create policies and practices that promote their learning and development.

- Establish recruitment and retention programs for faculty and administrators of color (including those at senior levels) in order to provide a variety of role models for all students.

- Emphasize in word and action, at every opportunity, the importance of a multicultural learning community to the institution's educational purposes.

- Develop orientation workshops for new students of color hosted by currently enrolled students and faculty.

- Create opportunities for students of color to meet regularly with one another and with university administrators to discuss concerns.

- Recruit and train students of color to serve on all major campus governance committees, student government, cultural and social programming boards, and the student newspaper.

- Establish cultural awareness weeks around themes of unity and diversity and observe special holidays and celebrations, such as Black Heritage Month, Cinco de Mayo, and Martin Luther King, Jr.'s birthday.

- Recognize students of color for their service and academic achievements. For other suggestion related to making institutions more hospitable for racial and ethnic minority students, see Fleming, 1984; McHugh, Dalton, Henley, and Buckner, 1988; Moses, 1989; Richardson and Bender, 1987; and Richardson, Simmons, and de los Santos, 1987.

For Women:

The opportunities for women's development at Mount Holyoke are so powerful that we wonder whether some of the enabling elements of the women's college experience can be adapted and incorporated in coeducational institutions, as through single-sex residential units, special theme houses, women' centers, or changes in the curriculum. This may be merely wishful thinking given the domination of most colleges and universities by males and male values. We believe that creating affirming environments for women demands institutional commitment and action, not changes and adaptation on the part of women themselves. Following are our recommendations for women students.

- Assess the campus climate for women: Are women valued or devalued, and in what ways? Are institutional and student resources expended for women's programs and concerns? Are there campus activities or events that are demeaning to, or perpetuate stereotypical roles for, women? Do women serve in senior-level faculty and administrative positions? Are male faculty and administrators supportive of women students? And so forth.

- Establish recruitment and retention programs for female faculty and administrators, including those at senior levels, so that sufficient female role models are available for all students.

- Create leadership development programs for women and encourage women students to seek leadership roles.

- If there is no women's center, create one; if a women's center exists, make sure that it is appropriately funded and emphasized.

- Provide positive feedback to administrators, faculty, and students who take steps to create an affirming environment for women.
- Emphasize in word and action, at every opportunity, the institution's commitment to the education of women (See Hall and Sandler, 1984, and Moses, 1989, for other suggestions.)

For Adult Learners:

- Assess the campus climate for adult learners; do not take for granted that their needs are being met. Are campus services adequately available to them? Are they able to and do they know how to take advantage of opportunities for involvement? Are support services adequate to meet their needs (for example, child care or adult learner support groups)?
- Invite spouses or significant others to orientation programs specifically designed for them.
- Arrange child care for all campus events, such as orientation, especially for those activities at times when children are not in regular child care (nights and weekends).
- Encourage families to attend events by sending special invitations and by offering reduced rates to spouses and children of students.
- Establish a task force to advise decision makers on policies and services, such as advising hours, financial aid policies, office hours, and registration procedures, to increase access for nontraditional students.
- Create programs (one time and ongoing) that meet special needs of older students, such as single-parent support groups, budgeting for college with a family, and balancing academic demands with a job. (See also Schlossberg, Lynch, and Chickering, 1989, for other suggestions related to adult learners).

For Commuters and Part-time Students:

- Establish a communications center and provide a campus mailbox for commuters.
- Send frequent mailings to commuters about campus activities.
- Provide a campus space (other than the library or a campus dining facility) arranged to encourage social interaction so that commuter students can relax and talk informally with faculty and peers.
- Provide easy access to campus events. For example, if there is an all-campus picnic and resident students eat free because of their meal ticket, provide commuters with free or low-cost meals and parking permits.
- Include representatives of special populations on all student government, faculty, and staff committees or task forces. Be sensitive to commuters and students with family commitments; try not to schedule too many meetings that take students away from their families at mealtime.
- Provide peer counselors or student advisers for commuter and part-time students. A resource person who is also a student can provide the kind of information and support that a faculty member or student affairs staff member cannot. (See Jacoby, 1989; and Stewart, 1983, for other suggestions related to commuter and part-time students.)

4. Encourage prospective students to choose a college where they feel they belong and can grow.

Those students who have a choice about where to attend college should recognize that many colleges and universities have a curriculum that will provide them with an education and prepare them for life after college. Some institutions, however, will be better than others in meeting students' unique academic and intellectual needs and motivating them to their best effort.

When visiting a college, prospective students should find out about the nature and number of activities the institution offers for students outside the classroom. Is this a place that will allow them to learn, grow, and develop competence and confidence outside the classroom? With what frequency are opportunities available to hear visiting speakers or take field trips or study abroad? They should determine, as best they can, how important students are at the colleges they are considering; undergraduates and their quality of life are more important at some institutions than at others. Is teaching really important to the faculty? Do professors and students meet together informally, such as over a cup of coffee in the union? Prospective students could ask the tour guide how accessible faculty members are and how difficult or easy it is to get involved in various organizations and activities.

Prospective students should also consider whether they prefer competitive or collaborative styles of working and learning. Some colleges have a competitive ethos, in which students are expected to compete with one another in a variety of settings, both in and out of class. At others, a collaborative ethos prevails, so that students are expected to cooperate with one another, and competition and status differences are actively discouraged.

Most important, prospective students should find out what the institution expects with regard to academic and social performance. At some institutions, students are expected to be responsible for their learning and living activities; at others, institutional agents take a more active role in the lives of students. However, even at the places where students are expected to be responsible, there are usually services that students can use when academic or personal concerns become overwhelming. Prospective students should find out what types of assistance are available, and how helpful current students feel these services are.

One of the most exciting and important aspects of college is the opportunity to have one's views and values challenged and to learn from and about a wide variety of people. One's ability to communicate and work with people who are different in backgrounds, opinions and values will only become more important in the future, so prospective students should seek educational settings that foster experience and skills in tolerance, understanding, and respect. They should get a sense of how the institution and other students treat people from varied cultural and ethnic backgrounds, and how women are viewed and treated by students and institutional agents.

5. Make it clear to students that they are expected to attend orientation.

A college can be an interesting and fun place, but it can also be confusing, especially if students are unaware of where to get answers to their questions, or even what questions to ask. No matter where a student goes to college, he or she will learn a lot about the institution by taking part in the events the institution has planned to introduce new students to college life and what is required to make the most of that particular college.

Institutions might want to consider an extended orientation program, such as a course during the first semester, to use the interest of new students to full advantage and to meet their needs more fully (Upcraft, Gardner, and Associates, 1989). Whether an extended orientation process is appropriate depends, of course, on the needs and goals of the students, as well as the mission, philosophy, and resources of the institution.

6. Encourage students to live on campus for at least one year.

Personal circumstances make living on campus impossible for some students. But for those students who can do so, living among peers for an extended period of time provides innumerable opportunities to learn about themselves and others. Institutions might want to consider ways in which more students can participate in on-campus living, such as residential scholarships, and ways in which commuting students can be included in the residential community, such as residence-based social activities and educational programming.

Conclusion 5: Institutions That Value Students and Take Them and Their Learning Seriously Encourage Involvement

Learning occurs most effectively when students are challenged to reach high, but reasonable, educational goals in an environment in which students are understood and appreciated and which makes manageable the risks inherent in meeting such challenges. High expectations should be established for students, faculty, and others; achievements should be acknowledged, and students, faculty, administrators, and others who contribute to a high-quality campus life should be rewarded.

Recommendations:

1. Make the learning experiences of students, wherever they occur, a priority on the agenda of institutional leaders.

The amount of attention institutional leaders devote to student learning and the quality of campus life is a function of the importance they place on those issues. Of course, merely asserting that the quality of campus life is important does not make it so; actions must accompany the words. Concern for and commitment to students' learning and the quality of their lives should be evident in the words and deeds of institutional leaders, from everyday encounters to long-range plans.

Presidents are expected, when talking with trustees, campus constituencies, state legislators, and the press, to discuss issues that matter, including extraordinary achievements by faculty and students, the institution's future, efforts to retain faculty and recruit students, and plans to enhance collaboration with business and industry. Student learning should also be part of these discussions: What does the institution want and expect its students to learn? How are those expectations communicated? Why is student learning important? How does the institution help students learn? What student learning is taking place?

2. Underscore the importance of student life through symbolic action.

As keepers of the institution's vision, leaders (presidents, academic deans, student affairs staff, senior faculty) use institutional symbols, and other cultural artifacts, to protect and shape community values and assumptions. Because the president serves as the symbolic leader for all members of the campus community, how, where, and to what ends he or she spends time sends strong messages to everyone about what, and who, is valued. For example, the presence of the president, and other institutional leaders at student functions, such as community service events, concerts, or academic honor ceremonies, sends an eloquent message to community members about the importance of students and their activities.

The symbolic ways in which an institution demonstrates that students are valued vary according to the institution's mission and philosophy. Being accessible to students, affirming the importance of students in speeches, meetings, or conversations with community members, knowing students' names, taking time to talk with students about their concerns and interests, and eating with students in their dining halls or interacting with them in their residences and other gathering places are all potentially meaningful symbolic actions on the part of institutional leaders. To *be* meaningful, however, these activities must be viewed by students as genuine—consistent with "the way we do things here"—and not simply for show. Among campus groups, students are the least impressed by symbolic action. Thus, symbolic actions must be reinforced by institutional policies and practices, such as those described in the previous recommendation.

Language is also symbolic action. The words institutional leaders use may convey an assumption of second-class citizenship, or even invisibility, for certain groups of students, faculty, and administrators, or for all students. Language can also encourage or discourage seeing and treating students as responsible and trusted adults. An anecdote to illustrate the point: In explaining the events that led up to the probation of the university's athletic department, a president (nor from any of the institutions in this study) described it as "an adult problem, not a youngster's problem." By using such language, the president inadvertently encouraged institutional agents and students themselves to think of students as lacking the capacity to act like responsible adults.

3. Seek and reward learning-centered faculty members.

Student-centered faculty members (described in Chapter Seven as those who attend student events, serve as advisers to student groups, and regularly interact with students out of class) are no longer in the majority on many campuses, and trying to reverse that trend is probably not realistic for those institutions. Nonetheless, an aspiration to put *learning-centered* faculty members in most undergraduate classrooms seems reasonable. Learning-centered faculty are people who make their love of learning and intellectual inquisitiveness contagious. They create a sense of wonder and excitement in students and view undergraduates as active partners in learning rather than empty and passive vessels to be filled. They challenge students to take full advantage of the institution's resources, including the library, cultural events, and work opportunities both on and off the campus. They have high expectations for student performance and challenge students to discover and use their intellectual capabilities. Learning-centered faculty members treasure knowledge for its own sake and invite students to collaborate on research projects. They also recognize that, for most students, knowledge must be applied to be useful and relevant. For this reason, learning-centered faculty members help students integrate their studies and their lives, in part by relating class material to students' lives and the pressing social issues of our times.

Faculty can also serve as inspiring examples of learners. They illustrate for students the joy of discovery, the rewards of education, and the seamlessness and satisfaction of a learning-centered life. Faculty might, for example, talk about their experiences and reactions to convocations and distinguished lectures and ask students to talk about what they have learned from these events. When a class session has been especially stimulating, faculty members should express appreciation to students; on some campuses, students are too docile or polite to engage faculty in debates or lively discussions about class material. One faculty member told the story about a particularly stimulating class session during which one of her students asked some challenging questions about the material. Several other students approached the faculty member after class to apologize for their peer's "inexcusable, rude behavior!" Of course, many students are uncomfortable speaking in public and need to feel trust and support from the instructor and their peers before they will take intellectual or personal risks in class.

Faculty should focus on intellectual matters when talking with students out of class. While some relaxed conversation may be necessary to develop rapport and trust, student learning seems to be enhanced when faculty members engage students intellectually and relate their in-class and out-of-class experiences to the mission and educational purposes of the institution.

4. Challenge the ethos that encourages faculty and students to avoid meaningful contact with each other.

On some campuses, students and faculty have struck an implicit bargain that says, in effect, "you leave me alone and I will leave you alone." For faculty, this "disengagement compact" has been encouraged by reward systems that favor research over teaching, by the increasing size of institutions, and by efforts to increase institutional status by becoming less like teaching institutions and more like research universities. The student side of the bargain is motivated by the fact that, for too many students intellectual activity and meaningful interaction with faculty are not what college is about. This attitude seems to be exacerbated by students' tendency to view and use college primarily as job training. In addition, students are increasingly likely to hold at least one job while in school in order to purchase items that used to be considered out of the question for college students, such as cars, stereos, computers, compact disc players, television sets, and refrigerators. Most of these possessions somehow get crammed into the dorm room that twenty years ago held two beds and a clock radio. The impact of such amenities, and the jobs that pay for them, on the quality of campus life and student learning ought to be examined.

Conclusion 6: Institutions That Are Able to Generate Feelings of Loyalty and a Sense of Specialness Encourage Involvement

An Involving College is a special place—just ask someone who lives and works there. You may hear examples of ways in which students matter, or outstanding programs or people, or crises that have been weathered. Or you might hear that "there's just something about the place," something that, although intangible, is felt by, and sustains, the community. "Specialness" is found in institutional purposes, values, and history, and is reflected in and affirmed by institutional symbols. Involving Colleges know and celebrate, openly and often, who they are. Their cultures are rich in traditions, language, and stories that keep community values alive so that community members feel that they are part of something truly special.

Recommendations:

1. Discover what makes your institution special and celebrate it.

Institutional self-discovery is necessary both to determine what is special about a college or university and to create an environment to enhance student learning. As we said in Chapter Eleven, make the familiar strange! Review Chapter Eleven and The Involving College Audit Protocol (Resource E) to determine how information from a campus audit might be useful in your setting. Learn as much as you can about your institution's past and present—its history, mission, philosophy, and traditions. The history of the institution and current catalogues and handbooks may provide insights into campus traditions and how these traditions influence student learning. Figure out what messages these events send to students about how to spend their time out of the classroom. Equally useful, and probably more stimulating, will be talking with campus historians, institutional heroines and heroes, emeritus faculty and administrators, graduates and students about what the mission says to and about students. Take a tour of the campus with the institutional historian and architect. Find out why facilities and open spaces are placed where they are and how students use these and other spaces to attain their learning and personal development goals.

A keen sense and appreciation of the past and the traditions that bind various constituencies are essential to discovering the assumptions that undergird the reasons for the institution's existence and the ways in which it achieves its purposes. What makes your institution special? What is distinctive about your institution's mission and philosophy? How are the special qualities of your institution reflected in the out-of-class experiences of students? Recognize that an institution's specialness is as much—if not more—a matter of how people feel about it, and its traditions and history, as it is of its admissions and fundraising success.

2. Leaders should understand and teach institutional cultures.

Senior faculty, administrators, staff, and upper-class students are in the best position to teach the cultures of the institution, including its mission, traditions, symbols, values, assumptions, and beliefs. As with any good teacher, these people must know their material in order to communicate it effectively. This requires that the president, for example, and his or her cabinet, understand the tacit, as well as the obvious, elements of institutional cultures and student subcultures. Campus leaders should become students of the institutional culture, a continuing process of self-discovery described above and in Chapter Eleven. Institutional leaders—or other teachers of culture—should communicate these messages or lessons throughout the institution so that all members can share in the sense of specialness.

3. Create something special.

Some institutions, particularly those that have short histories or have markedly modified their missions within the recent past, may have cultures that lack an abundance of unifying or celebratory rituals, traditions, or symbols. Although the development of cultural richness requires many years, events, and generations of people, a sense of institutional specialness can be created out of the present. Programs and events can easily become traditions; we know of one institution in which a volleyball tournament became an instant tradition when it was designated the "Fifth Annual. . . ." What is important is that the event or activity affirm and celebrate the community's values and purposes.

Every campus has heroines and heroes; make sure that people know about them and that their contributions are periodically heralded. Acknowledgment of student heroes and heroines in particular sends a powerful message that students matter.

The academic year is marked with many milestones—beginnings, endings, achievements, anniversaries—and each offers an opportunity to declare what is special about the institution and its people. Use these times to celebrate the entry of newcomers into the community. Take advantage of these occasions to bring graduates back to the community to affirm the historical continuity—however brief—of the institution. Institutions can be more imaginative about what is considered a milestone or causes for celebration; every institution should find its own ways to express its specialness.

4.   Maintain a sense of perspective and humor about the institution.

Along with a sense of specialness, Involving Colleges do not take themselves too seriously (recall the Stanford Band and Evergreen's "Fighting Geoducks"), a characteristic that enables them to cope with large and small problems with losing sight of what makes them special. Although playful is not a word that is ordinarily used to describe a college or university, some Involving Colleges have developed that quality to remind people to be open to new ideas and new people, and to take pleasure in their work and in one another.

Concluding Thoughts

As we conclude our report of Involving Colleges, two additional matters warrant attention. First, we consider some unresolved issues related to involvement, including the relationship between student characteristics, such as participation in activities in high school or elsewhere, and taking advantage of learning opportunities. Second, we offer some insights from Involving Colleges about establishing, or reestablishing, a sense of community on campus.

Student Involvement Revisited. Students are more likely to take advantage of educationally purposeful out-of-class learning opportunities when both the institution and students devote time, effort, and resources toward this end. Institutional contributions were the focus of this study although, ultimately, the mutually shaping influences of institution and student are not separable. There is, of course, more than can be discovered about how colleges direct their efforts and resources to promoting student involvement in out-of-class learning and personal development opportunities. For example, the out-of-class learning opportunities for students in two-year colleges deserves immediate attention. Also, additional case studies describing in detail how institutions use the factors and conditions described in this book to promote student learning, such as forging relationships with representatives of local business and industry to create employment opportunities, would be informative.

Are students with certain characteristics and experiences more likely to participate in some activities and not others? It is not unusual for students who were active in out-of-class activities in high school to seek similar outlets to express their interests when they get to college. However, students who were not involved in activities, such as musical ensembles, athletics, or student government, in high school or elsewhere sometimes make an effort to get involved when they get to college. Institutions and students could benefit from knowing under what circumstances students without previous experience will attempt to take advantage of out-of-class learning opportunities.

What "involvement" means is also worthy of further investigation. We did not precisely define involvement at the outset of this study because we were interested in identifying the characteristics of natural settings—colleges and universities—which were thought to provide unusually rich, educationally purposeful out-of-class activities for undergraduates. Narrow definitions could have inappropriately constrained our discovery process. The behavior view of involvement (Astin, 1984, 1985; Pace, 1980, 1986)—that involvement can be found in what students do and how much effort they expend in various activities—served our purposes.

Because the concept of involvement is relatively new, it remains somewhat ambiguous, a state of affairs typical in the early stages of the development of a social science construct. When an idea or construct attracts the interest of researchers, there is a period during which its scope and parameters must be examined before precise definitions can be developed (Baird, 1989). Baird suggested that the concept of involvement encompasses dimensions of behavior in addition to that which can be observed. For example, to understand why students actively participated in some activities and not others, aspects of a student's personality, such as motivation and interests, may be relevant.

In addition, involvement probably has a social component. A student may become involved in an activity because of affiliation needs. For example, a student whose friends are actively engaged in a particular activity may begin to participate in that activity in order to spend more time with her or his friends. Some students feel responsible for advancing the status or causes of their group, such as gays and lesbians, students of color, women, or members of a particular political party.

Information about how peers and affinity groups influence student participation in various out-of-class opportunities would be instructive for those interested in encouraging student behavior toward educationally purposeful ends. Clearly, more needs to be learned about individual student variables that influence student involvement and the mutual shaping of student characteristics and institutional factors and conditions that promote student participation in out-of-class learning opportunities.

Insights into Community on Campus. Student out-of-class behavior antithetical to the aims and purposes of higher education is frequently featured in the news media, such as the *New York Times* (Carmody, 1989), and *Newsweek* (Mabry, 1989), as well as the higher education literature (Bresler, 1989). Acquaintance rape and other forms of physical and emotional violence, alcohol abuse, racist incidents, and even a pervasive lack of common courtesy, have become all-too-common lead stories about college student life. In response to these concerns, presidents, trustees, and others have become interested in the quality of campus life (El-Khawas, 1989).

Some observers of higher education (see Carnegie Foundation . . . , 1990) believe that the quality of life for students will improve if a sense of campus community is established. For many institutions of higher education, achieving feelings of community will be difficult. At universities with tens of thousands of students and many student subcommunities (not to mention faculty and staff subcommunities), musing about a campus community may be more the stuff of fond recollections of a bygone era—when colleges were small, homogeneous, and geographically and socially isolated—than a realistic aspiration.

We did not set out to determine the extent to which a sense of community was present at the fourteen institutions in this study. Nonetheless, institutional agents and students often used the word) "community" when describing what was special about their institution. Consider the observation of a Stanford senior a few weeks before graduation: "Be ready for the fact that the university *is* a community. I certainly didn't understand the concept."

Students (and faculty members and administrators) must develop an understanding of the meaning of community and what community may look and feel like in an institution of higher education now and in the future. We believe that by reflecting on the factors and conditions common to Involving Colleges in light of ideals that characterize community, institutional agents can identify ways in which a sense of campus community can be achieved or affirmed.

Gardner (1989) described the qualities that characterize an effective community: wholeness incorporating diversity; shared culture; good internal communication; caring, trust, and teamwork; group maintenance and governance; participation and shared leadership tasks; development of young people; and links with the outside world. All of these qualities can be found in Involving Colleges.

- Good communities incorporate and value diversity.

  We expect and want diversity, and there will be dissension in the best of communities. But in better communities, cooperation, compromise, and consensus building will be widely shared pursuits. In the best circumstances, such communities will have instruments and processes for conflict resolution [Gardner, 1989, p. 76].

Involving Colleges are committed to pluralism in all its forms, and they support the establishment and coexistence of subcommunities that permit students to identify with, and receive support from, people like themselves, so that they can feel comfortable in becoming involved in the larger campus community. However, when subcommunities are allowed to insulate their members from people of different backgrounds and values, they become vehicles for fragmentation and separation, not community building. That is why Involving Colleges also work to develop networks among members of various groups and to promote interaction among students across subcommunities.

- Good communities have a shared culture.

> Social cohesion will be advanced if the group's norms and values are explicit. Values that are never expressed are apt to be taken for granted and not adequately conveyed to young people and newcomers. The well-functioning community provides many opportunities to express values and relevant action. . . . A healthy community affirms itself and builds morale and motivation through ceremonies and celebrations that honor the symbols of shared identity and enable members to rededicate themselves [Gardner, 1989, p. 77].

Evidence from Involving Colleges lends support to Gardner's observations about the necessity of a shared culture (norms, values, symbols of group identify, legends, heroines and heroes) for community on campus. These are institutions that convey their culture by explaining their missions and philosophies through anticipatory socialization and induction activities and clear statements about what the institution expects of students and students can expect of the institution. We have also described the need for presidents, faculty members, staff, trustees, and others to discover their institution's culture in order to determine whether rituals, traditions, ceremonies and other cultural artifacts promote student learning.

- Good communities foster internal communication.

> One of the advantages of the small group is that frequent face-to-face communication is possible. . . . [A] community is strengthened if there are occasions . . . in which extensive, informal interaction is possible [Gardner, 1989, p. 77].

The human-scale qualities of Involving Colleges create opportunities for students to know, work with, and understand faculty, staff and peers. Through assiduous attention to providing small living units and small classes, and maintaining effective communication networks, Involving Colleges create conditions under which frequent face-to-face interaction occurs and information is disseminated to those who need or want to know. Whether it is the chalkboard in the residence hall or house foyer or lavatory, the weekly student newspaper, electronic bulletin boards, mimeographed sheets on the dining-room table, or posters in the campus post office, communication is a priority at Involving Colleges.

- Good communities promote caring, trust, and teamwork.

> A good community nurtures its members and fosters an atmosphere of trust. . . .
> There is a spirit of mutuality and cooperating. Everyone is included [Gardner, 1989, p. 78].

The ethics of care and membership undergirded by invisible safety nets common to Involving Colleges mirror Gardner's qualities of caring, trust, and teamwork. However, in the case of some small colleges or separatist subcommunities, we, like Gardner, observed that "a community can be too tightly knit, suppressing the dissent and constraining the creativity of its members" (p. 78).

- Good communities have group maintenance processes and governance structures that encourage participation and sharing of leadership tasks.

> It is not uncommon . . . that the groups most involved in the affairs of the community all come from one or two segments of the community. All segments must participate . . . everyone need not participate actively . . . we must guard the right to participate while recognizing that some will choose not to do so [Gardner, 1989, p. 79].

Opportunities for student involvement in institutional governance characterize Involving Colleges. Students are, for example, often expected to determine rules and regulations for their living unit's compatible with the mission and values of the institution.

- Good communities foster the development of young people.

Preparing future generations of informed, responsible citizens is, undeniably, one of the fundamental purposes of a college or university. Gardner (1989, p. 80) emphasized the role of out-of-class learning experiences toward this end:

> The opportunities for individual growth will be numerous and varied for all members . . . [O]n the playing field, and in group activities in and out of school and college, they will learn teamwork. Through volunteer and intern experiences outside of school they will learn how the adult world works and will have the experience of serving their society.

An opportunity-rich environment is but one example of the factors and conditions common to Involving Colleges that reflect this quality. Other aspects include policies and practices that give students responsibility for determining how to allocate their money, and "ladders" that provide students with steps to follow to academic success.

- Good communites have links with the outside world.

> The sound community has seemingly contradictory responsibilities: it must defend itself from the forces in the outside environment that undermine its integrity, yet it must maintain open, constructive, and extensive relations with the world beyond its boundaries [Gardner, 1989, p. 80].

An Involving College is, in some respects, a haven for its students, "a place apart" with permeable boundaries. The realities and challenges of the outside world influence teaching and learning and how students spend their time. While some students should, perhaps, be protected for a time from the more destructive forces, such as racism, sexism, and poverty, at work in the larger world, at some point in their education they must have their attitudes, values and knowledge tested on and off the campus. Involving Colleges provide opportunities for students to render service to their communities beyond the campus through local, regional, and international programs. As we have illustrated, Involving Colleges intentionally create opportunities for students to learn firsthand how their education can be used after college by providing, for example, employment opportunities to broaden and enrich the undergraduate experience.

We do not assert that attending to the institutional factors and conditions shared to varying degrees by Involving Colleges will guarantee a strong and positive campus community. However, the process (a campus audit or some other means) through which an institution discovers the degree to which these factors and conditions are present should also provide some insights into what an institution must do to establish, or reestablish, and maintain the qualities associated with good communities.

A Final Word

Educational renewal initiatives in the 1980s emphasized the curriculum, including such perennial issues as what constitutes general education and how learning during college can be assessed (Ewell, 1985). Renewal efforts must also address the quality and frequency of student relationships with faculty, staff, and peers, as well as the contributions of student affairs and other administrative staff who help establish expectations and an appropriate intellectual tone for student cultures (Gaff, 1989). Because "everything that happens on a campus has curricular implications" (Gaff, 1989, p. 14), a college or university must have not only integrity in the curriculum (Association of American Colleges, 1985) but also integrity between the curriculum and the college's ecology (Gaff, 1989). At a college with integrity, institutional policies and practices, both curricular and noncurricular, are consistent with the institution's mission and values.

So we have come full circle, back to the mission and philosophy of the institution as the basis for all that a college or university does, or ought to do. Only through a renewed understanding of what the institution is and aspires to be—its mission—can people learn their role and responsibilities, understand why the institution works the way it does, and develop a shared vision of the institution's future. When all members of a college or university community, including faculty, administrators, trustees, staff, and students, believe that all aspects of the institution's environment contribute to student learning and personal development, the institution can take another step toward realizing its potential and fulfilling its obligation to be a community committed to learning in all forms and forums.

The Political Dimension
of Decision Making

PAUL L. MOORE

In organizational life, the term *politics* may be the most employed and least understood concept among those we use to describe important aspects of our work. For many faculty members and administrators, it has negative connotations, suggesting trickery, manipulation, and self-interest; as a result, it causes some discomfort when used (Block, 1987; Pfeffer, 1981). It is a topic we would prefer to talk about privately or euphemistically. The training of student affairs professionals with its anchors in the helping professions and our focus on the personal development of students may create greater ambivalence for us than others when confronted with "politics." At the same time, however, we understand it to be a necessary and ubiquitous process through which important decisions are made in society and in our institutions. As Appleton (1991, p. 5) notes, "Political behavior is inevitable in every organizational setting, is found at every level in the hierarchy, and intensifies as the decision making possibilities are greater and more important."

Clearly, an understanding of institutional decision making must be a priority for all those who hope to make an influence policies affecting their work and institutions. Whether an institution is large or small, secular or nonsecular, whether it is a research university or community college, an important part of its management involves decision making about direction, strategy, and resource allocation. How these decisions are made is the essence of organizational politics.

One important caveat is that the political approach is not the only useful one in understanding organizations in general and higher education in particular. Bolman and Deal (1984) have identified four major theoretical frameworks with organizations: rational, human resource, political, and symbolic. Each has an interesting perspective that adds to our understanding of organizations. Rational theorists deal with the goals, roles, and technology of organizations. The human resource writers are concerned with the interaction of the needs and capabilities of people with the roles and relationships within organizations. Meaning within organizations is the interest of symbolic theorists. Each approach has its strengths and weaknesses; and although we have emphasized in this chapter the political perspective as being useful to student affairs professionals, it is helpful to acknowledge Pfeffer's (1981, p. 2) caution when speaking of politics and its essential ingredient, power: "While power is something, it is not everything."

The purposes of this chapter are to identify and define key concepts necessary to an understanding of organizational politics, highlight elements of institutions of higher education that distinguish them from other societal institutions and affect their political processes, and suggest political perspectives strategies and tactics for student affairs practitioners.

Basic Concepts

As used in this chapter, *politics* refers to the processes that influence the direction of and allocate resources for an organization. Political behaviors are those designed to shape or determine institutional direction and policy and are as rational or irrational, altruistic or self-serving as the people involved. As we are concerned here with the political processes and activities that occur within colleges and universities, Pfeffer's (1981, p. 7) definition of organizational politics is instructive: "Organizational politics involves those activities taken within organizations to acquire, develop, and use power and other resources to obtain one's preferred outcomes in a situation in which there is uncertainty or dissension about choices."

Key aspects of this definition are power, preferences, and uncertainty. *Power* may be defined as "the ability to produce intended change in others, to influence them so that they will be more likely to act in accordance with one's own preferences" (Birnbaum, 1988, p. 13). *Preferences* suggest what an individual or group would like to see happen within the organization. And *uncertainty* implies that a decision is yet to be made or a direction chosen.

In his study of New York University as a political system, Baldridge (1971, p. 24) describes its major elements: "The broad outline of the political system looks like this: a complex social structure generates multiple pressures, many forms of power and pressure impinge on the decision makers, a legislative stage translates these pressures into policy, and a policy execution phase finally generates feedback in the form of new conflict." Important ideas in this description are differing interests, intergroup disagreement or conflict, use of power in pursuit of interests, efforts to influence decision makers, and decision making itself.

Important Conceptual Considerations

The purpose of this section is to introduce major elements that will help with the discussion of power and politics and perhaps encourage the reader to pursue an independent review of the literature. The intent is not to review in depth all the theoretical concepts that underpin a discussion of organizational politics; excellent discussions of these already exist (Baldridge, 1971; Pfeffer, 1981; Bacharach and Lawler, 1980; and Birnbaum, 1988).

The Political Model

This view of organizations assumes that they are not completely rational and harmonious entities but are composed of constantly shifting coalitions that bargain for desired outcomes and use strategies and tactics designed to influence results. Organizational life is seen as a series of political transactions involving the use of power to obtain resources or achieve other ends (Bacharach and Lawler, 1980). Organizations are not typically homogeneous but rather pluralistic, being composed of all sorts of subgroups and subcultures. Conflicts arising from these differences are natural and are to be expected in political organizations (Baldridge, 1971). Power, differing preferences, conflict, influence, coalitions, negotiation, and compromise are key ingredients in a political system.

To suggest that a college or university is a political system that experiences the use of power, conflict, and mutual influence is not to argue that rational processes, bureaucratic incrementalism, and strong organizational cultural tendencies are not at work or nonexistent. Other methods of making decisions and controlling activity exist that assist with the ongoing activity of an organization. Careful accumulation of information and examination of alternatives frequently inform academic, student welfare, and fund-raising decisions. Organizations will make some decisions based on closely held values, such as those that might be made in an institution with religious roots. And certainly incrementalism will determine many budget allocations.

Political activities tend to be accentuated when normal patterns or processes do not produce coherent direction, strategies, or accepted resource allocations. Active disagreement may be stimulated by external sources, such as an important institutional constituency, or by internal sources, such as a proposal of a new program having perceived negative financial implications for others in the organization. Pfeffer (1981) has identified several elements that produce political activity in organizations; interdependence of the interest groups or actors, goals that are inconsistent, resource scarcity, issues of importance, and decentralized decision making.

The political model assumes that the power of the various participants will determine the outcome. Thus, understanding "who participates in decision making, what determines each player's stand on the issues, what determines each actor's relative power, and how the decision process arrives at a decision" is an important managerial and political consideration (Pfeffer, 1981, p. 28). All groups and individuals are not concerned with all issues. Even when interested, they will exhibit differing levels of intensity and ability to influence a particular decision. And as the results are primarily the consequence of negotiation and compromise, they are rarely the perfect expression of any specific individual or group preferences (Pfeffer, 1981).

Power

Earlier, power was defined as the ability to influence others in such a way that they will more likely do what we prefer. Compared to influence, "power is the potential for influence, and influence is the result of actualized power" (King, 1975, p. 7). Power describes relationships among people that are given particular meaning by the organizational context. Further, the person to be influenced assigns meaning to the behavior or communications that are designed to influence (King, 1975). All relations need not require or manifest the ingredient of power. The organizational setting and the roles of individuals significantly affect the nature and extent of power in the relationship.

French and Raven (1959) identify five bases of power relating to organizational context that describe what groups or individuals use to affect the behavior of others: coercive, reward, expertise, referent, and legitimate power. Some writers have added a sixth: information (Bacharach and Lawler, 1980).

Coercive power suggests the ability to punish, such as dismissal or demotion or, in a group situation, job action by a labor union.

Reward power involves giving something of value (a promotion or raise) if certain behavior is exhibited; in a group situation, it might mean representation on an important board of directors.

Expert power is specialized knowledge about issues or activities of interest to the organization. Examples are the special knowledge of lawyers, medical doctors, and accountants.

Referent power is based on identification with another person, such as the deference shown to charismatic leaders. An example is the credibility often accorded the assistant to a college president.

Legitimate power, sometimes called bureaucratic power, is "power based on rights of control and concomitant obligations to obey" (Bacharach and Lawler, 1980, p. 33). Legitimate power is essentially authorized as ascribed to senior university officers, such as presidents, vice presidents, and deans. By virtue of their positions, they are empowered to make certain decisions and are expected to do so by others.

Legitimate power or authority is not the same as influence. Authority is the ability and right to make and enforce decisions; either one has the right to make decisions or not. Influence, by contrast, is the opportunity for almost anyone in an organization to seek to affect decisions arising from any of the bases of power rather than from organizational right (Bacharach and Lawler, 1980).

Information refers to the opportunity that social actors have to gain information about internal matters or the organization's relations to the environment.

Influence does not occur in a vacuum; it requires both that someone wishes to influence and that someone is willing to be influenced. Writing about social influence and communication, King (1975, p. 12) stated: "For communication and social influence to occur, the receiver must be affected. The receiver assigns meaning to behavior." The bases of power noted above are conceived similarly; someone employs one or a combination of these sources to induce someone else to do something. These processes therefore cannot exist independently of context.

Needs, Motivation, and Expectations

How people behave in an organization reflects in part their motivations for being there, such as pay, prestige, or fellowship, and expectations about how the organization will treat them or respond to certain behaviors on their part (Appleton, 1991). What motivates them and what they expect from an organization are strongly related to their perceived needs. Personal needs may include safety and security, love and affiliation, social esteem and prestige, power and autonomy, self-esteem and competence, and achievement and creativity (Webber, 1979). Needs, motivations, and expectations are as varied as the people who work in an organization and will be influenced by personal values, beliefs, age, experience, gender and ethnicity.

Political, behavior, designed to influence organizational direction and policy through the use of power and other resources, is directly connected to individual motivations and personal or group expectations of the organization. How people respond to efforts to influence them requires that they give meaning to the actions taken, and that meaning is affected and filtered by needs, motivations, and expectations. The exercise of power does not guarantee that the person or group that is to be influenced will respond as hoped. It all depends on the context—individual perceptions, immediate or long-term needs, personal values and beliefs, and the stakes to be won or lost.

Self-Serving Versus Productive Behavior

If the behavior depends in part on the motivations and expectations of the individual, how can an organization elicit behavior that supports its goals? Is self-serving behavior necessarily negative, as some have contended (Block, 1987)? If a person is behaving politically, is that necessarily at odds with institutional goals and culture? How can one distinguish between political activities that support institutional goals and those that do not?

The answer lies in part in the extent to which the political actor's expectations and the results of specific actions are congruent with the goals of the organization.

We know, of course, that the motives of the involved actors and purposes behind particular actions are not always apparent. Organizational politics are consequently complex and ambiguous; things may not be as they appear. Although long-term results may provide definitive answers to questions of motivation and purpose, decisions will be made in the short run based on perceptions of those purposes, whether clearly articulated or not.

Into those judgements are brought all the contextual elements of organizational life—the individual and organizational values, purposes, technologies, histories, and perspectives. Whether or not political behavior is fundamentally self-serving or in the interest of both the individual and organization is frequently a matter of opinion.

Leadership

Influence, and by implication the use of power, is basic to managerial leadership (Webber, 1979). What then is the role of leadership in a political organization? Appleton (1991, p. 13) argues, "The leader must be prepared to use power in an effective manner and to understand the extent to which individual differences and expectations and self-serving political interests will affect the functioning of an organization." Managing the political process and political conflict is at the heart of leadership. (Yates, 1985).

Important Elements of Institutions of Higher Education

If power, influence, and politics exist, are based upon relationships and organizational structures, and are central to administrative life (Pfeffer, 1981; Yates, 1985), then it follows that the practitioner ought to understand the unique aspects of institutions of higher education that shape their political environments.

Goal Diffusion

Colleges and universities typically exhibit a lack of clarity and agreement on institutional goals (Birnbaum, 1988; Baldridge, 1972). Teaching, research, and service are the three most frequently stated goals, but they exist in differing combinations and degrees of emphasis on each campus; moreover, goals may even be assigned a different importance on a single campus. However, other goals may be widely embraced, such as intercollegiate athletics or a particular religion. The result is often a lack of agreed-upon, mutually consistent goals—that is, a number of conflicting or inconsistent goals are accepted. Almost inevitably, such an environment sets the stage for disagreement and competition over institutional direction and the allocation of resources.

Uncertainty of Means or Technologies

Not only are the goals of higher education diffuse, but the means that should be used to educate students are not always clear. Which classroom strategies (lectures, small-discussion seminars, laboratory activity, or independent study) are most productive and when? Many techniques seem to work, but how they create change in students and which ones are best are not known (Birnbaum, 1988). Because our technologies are not clear, major choices about how to allocate resources are often not easily and decisively made. Again, the stage is set for disagreement and political activity.

Dual Control

Another feature of higher education that contributes to political activity is the dual nature of institutional control (Birnbaum, 1988). Responsibility for decision making is vested in an administration, including a board of trustees, a president, and a generally elaborate structure. Simultaneously, responsibility is endowed upon faculty structures, schools, departments, senates, and committees, which make a number of important curricular and personnel decisions. The authority in the former tends to be hierarchical and in the latter professional. Moreover, the two structures are not necessarily clearly defined and integrated; thus opportunity for dissent and conflict abounds.

Structural Uniqueness

Not only do colleges and universities have dual decision-making systems, they are filled with other distinctive features adding ambiguity and complexity to their functioning. As noted above, there is both a management structure and an employee governance structure. In each, labor unions may organize employees in a context structured by complex state government regulations. Outside groups, particularly the federal government, alumni associations, supporters (such as athletic or arts fund-raising groups), and accrediting associations, have their say. And staff and students may be effectively organized and represented in official governance bodies. Clearly, the variety of interests, institutional complexity, and the nature of the decisions-making apparatus, whether direct or advisory, suggest the conditions necessary for a political organization.

Organizational Culture

Culture, according to Schein (1985, p. 9), is "a pattern of basic assumptions—invented, discovered, or developed by a given group as it learns to cope with its problems of external adaptation and internal integration—that has worked well enough to be considered valid and, therefore, to be taught to new members as the correct way to perceive, think, and feel in relation to those problems." Colleges and universities have cultures, as do the structures within them: schools, departments, senates, and groups. In addition, those affiliated with the institution, such as accrediting associations, alumni and support groups and professional associations, exhibit cultural characteristics. The cultures of universities differ from those of other societal institutions as well as from each other. Culture, then, affects how a particular organization reacts to issues of organizational strategy, technology, conflict, communications, socialization and productivity. Culture helps deal with issues of organizational survival and internal functioning (Schein, 1985).

Limits on Leadership

Birnbaum (1988) has analyzed the limitations on leadership in higher education brought about by the organizational, governance, and cultural uniqueness of colleges and universities. Dual decision-making systems, decentralization of academic decision making, the influence of external authorities and interests, and the lack of government on institutional goals—all impose constraints on leadership. It is no wonder that although transformational leadership is almost always desired, it is much less frequently achieved.

Nonetheless, the importance of leadership remains. An understanding of the political dimension of universities is a critical element in providing effective leadership. Strategies and tactics are available to the student affairs leader that can be helpful in managing the political environment for the benefit of students and the institution.

Perspectives and Strategies

The assumption of this chapter is that most of us experience sufficient organizational politics in our daily administrative lives to warrant thinking about ways to improve our effectiveness in dealing with it. The following suggestions may provide some guidance.

The President and Senior Colleagues

Depending on professional level, the term *boss* may be substituted for *president*; the ideas are the same. Although we might wish it were not so, the most important relationship is with the boss. Without a strong or at least respectful relationship, a student affairs leader will struggle with many aspects of his or her responsibility. It is important to take whatever time and do whatever is necessary to secure this relationship, including informing, training, protecting, and supporting senior colleagues. There are, of course, personal and ethical limits that must be understood and acted on, even if it means resignation (Brown, 1991).

Senior colleagues, particular at the vice-presidential level, require attention. Without good, constructive relationships, a sense of teamwork cannot be cultivated, and the normal turf, budget, and policy battles may take on a more partisan tone. Student affairs professionals must recognize their colleagues' biases, strengths, and weaknesses in order to strengthen their relationships, shape their approaches, and protect their interest.

Roles, Issues, and the Institution

To perform well in the political arena, it is critical for those in student affairs to understand thoroughly their role, whether as the chief student affairs officer (Sandeen, 1991) or as a middle manager (Young, 1990; Ellis and Moon, 1991). Being clear about the expectations of one's boss and key constituencies will translate into personal confidence when dealing with the managerial as well as the political dimensions of a position. For example, Brown (1991) sees key aspects of the chief student affairs officer role as being surrogate and shield and defender for the president. Without an appreciation of these expectations, the student affairs vice president may be paralyzed by the conflicting expectations of the president, faculty, and students.

It is equally important to know the issues. Although it is not possible to be aware of all that goes on in a division or large department, it is nonetheless critical to have a good sense of the substance of everything within a job's area of responsibility, especially where criticism or territorial battles are likely.

Following and understanding institutional issues is necessary, whether or not they impinge directly on responsibilities. This practice will be helpful in establishing a reputation as an officer or professional with institutionwide interests and role. Such a perception by others may lead to greater involvement in and influence on the full range of institutional concerns. On the formal side, student affairs officers must keep abreast of relevant current issues through perusal of their professional journals and general publications such as the *Chronicle of Higher Education* and the *Journal of Higher Education*. It may be useful to have a working knowledge of the informal sources followed by other important administrators, such as the publications of the national Association of College and University Business Officers typically reviewed by business and administrative vice presidents.

The Importance of Competence

The power of person competence cannot be overly emphasized. We normally think of competence in relation to student affairs "business" or management, but as a source of power it goes well beyond professional expertise. Professionals in the field must strive to be highly skilled in their work, but that is not sufficient if they are to play a broader institutional role. Political competence, the subject of this chapter, suggests an understanding of power and its uses, of the personal motivations of others in the organization, of the opportunities provided to influence decisions about institutional direction and resource allocation, and the potential of staff work to shape alternatives.

Proper Positioning

One cannot influence decisions unless one is organizationally, professionally, and personally in a position to do so. Opportunities for influencing unit or institutional decisions do not necessarily occur because an individual knows a lot or is recognized as a strong professional by colleagues on other campuses; such opportunities usually occur because that person has taken steps to be known as competent, interested, and involved in the fortunes of his or her unit, division, or institution.

Visibility on the campus, and perhaps in the larger community in which the institution resides, is an important and not-always-understood notion. Being visible simply means attending meetings, socials, and programs of importance to various important constituencies within and without the college or university. Participation may be seen by others as much more beneficial to a program or idea than might be obvious. The positive aspects of visibility can, however, be squandered through overexposure or participation in unimportant activities. One must therefore monitor the importance and frequency of involvement.

Officers in student affairs must keep track of what they and their units accomplish. Acknowledgment of accomplishments serve both as a reinforcement of strong and innovative performance and a method of ensuring that organization efforts are directed toward unit goals.

Accomplishments should also be shared with senior administration officials, colleagues, and faculty members. A performance will be judged with or without information; thus, it is important that others are informed of activities and achievements. Informing others also has the benefit of establishing competence, interest, and involvement in institutional issues and strengthening the ability to participate effectively in the institution's political environment.

Being informed about campus issues and individual responsibilities is, of course, required of those who would influence the course of institutional development. This requirement extends to a clear understanding of institutional history and culture.

Those in the field should also be thoughtful about their public presence—that is, their personal style, which relates to how they do things and how they are perceived by others: "Personal style is the professional demeanor by which each of us is known. It denotes how we behave in our work, as distinguished from what we do" (Appleton, Briggs, and Rhatigan, 1978, p. 139). Style, though rooted in personal characteristics and experiences, can be understood and shaped to enhance effectiveness in the educational and political environment. Do student affairs officers use jargon or language readily understood and accepted by their audiences? Do they and those on their staffs show a level of professionalism appropriate for students, their parents, or trustees? Do they dress in a way that meets the expectations of important constituencies? Are they willing and accomplished public speakers readily available to campus and community groups? The point of these and other similar questions is to argue that one needs to act, look, and see oneself as a major player in institutional decision making and leadership.

Relationships, or Getting to Know Others

Like close ties to the president, relationships with others are essential to effective participation in the political processes of colleges and universities. With the possible exception of legislative activities such as faculty senates, relationships are the best vehicle for building coalitions, resolving conflict, and creating consensus. With such a pivotal function, building and maintaining relationships must be an active concern for student affairs officers.

Brown (1991) refers to the "positive value of gossip," information that gives some hint of situations, motives, or fast-moving events. By working at knowing others, those in student affairs position themselves in key places in the informal communication network of their campus. The information gained can be enormously helpful in countering resistance or informing others of interests or proposals.

Moore (1991) describes a strategy for getting to know and routinely working with academic deans through regular visits or lunches. These periodic contacts need not require agendas other than simply checking in to see how faculty members and students are doing, what issues are developing, and what else might be done. The contact will be appreciated and may build a relationship that will prove mutually beneficial during extraordinary situations.

Time Requirements

It must be clear by now that managing the political dimension of a job can be and frequently is enormously time consuming. The time requirement seems to increase as the organizational level of a position rises; the higher and more central the responsibilities, the greater the opportunities for political activity and the higher the demand on time. In an unpublished study of the political involvement of chief student affairs officers (Moore and Moore, 1991), 74 percent of the 243 responding chief student affairs officers reported that political activities consumed a significant amount of their work time.

Politics is not a function to be managed like budget or planning; it is a backdrop. It is not our work, but it affects our work. Its effect on our time must be accommodated and managed so that it does not overwhelm the requirements of our institutions and our students.

Perhaps politics should be thought of as a consideration—one that must be factored into our efforts at conflict resolution, pursuit of goals, and decision making. In some sense, it is like the notion of student development, which guides and influences much of our work. As such, the time that it takes can be managed so as not to squeeze out other productive activities.

The importance of spending sufficient time on the political process is illustrated by Birnbaum (1988), who writes, "People who spend time on a decision will be disproportionately successful."

Accepting Conflict

Conflict will be more or less present, more or less visible, and more or less a factor in student affairs depending on institutional culture and history and the personalities and motivations of current players. Whatever its degree, however, university administrators must anticipate that conflict over priorities, turf, and resources will occur. It is not unusual or extraordinary.

Differences, and indeed conflict, are necessary ingredients to a political system. This observation implies that student affairs officers must be able to deal with conflict, understand the political system, and know how to operate in it. The marriage of the two, conflict and institutional politics, is a fact that must be considered in confronting problems both between individuals in student affairs and between student affairs personnel and representatives of other areas within the institution.

On a personal level, student affairs officers may not wish to deal with conflict but must have a willingness and strategies to manage it. Individual styles will obviously reflect personal and contextual characteristics.

Fighting, or the Rules of Battle

Inevitably, all administrators will encounter disagreements over territory or resources that will require a struggle. Personal values and style will, of course, determine much of what they do. Nevertheless, there are some points to keep in mind.

Battles should not be fought if they cannot be won. There will be some matters of principle that require a fight even though winning is very unlikely; however, fighting hopeless battles will only dissipate energy and resources. Fighting uses resources, may damage relationships and future interactions, and thus should be engaged in only for important reasons. Personal ego is not such a reason.

It is essential to be well informed. Until preparation is complete, the battle should be postponed. A neutral ground for the conversation should be chosen and privacy ensured. Above all, student affairs officers must maintain their dignity. Fights have consequences, and nothing is worth the loss of one's self-respect and the regard of others.

Integrity

In the final analysis, consistent ethical behavior is the most important strategy. When the battles are over and the dust settles, people will follow leaders of high integrity even when the won-lost record is less than they would hope. To lose integrity is to lose claim to leadership and the support of the boss, staff, and students.

Other Tactics

There are a great number of tactics that might be identified as potentially useful in addition to those formally explored above. Several of these deserve brief mention.

1. The participation of the opposition should be encouraged (Birnbaum, 1988). Participation may help opponents appreciate the real constraints faced by the institution and the consequences inherent in any particular political situation. It may have a tempering effect.

2. Birnbaum (1988) describes another method for dealing with politically sensitive issues. The "garbage can" strategy is based on the notion that new proposals often attract all sorts of unrelated solutions and problems. By increasing the possible solutions, one may reduce the probability that a specific idea or strategy will survive the process. Committees often serve the function of developing so many ideas and solutions that none can get support or be implemented. In addition, sometimes it is strategically important to overload the decision-making system with proposals on various matters. When that occurs and time is limited, chances increase that some proposals will not get through the process of evaluation and decision making by committees and other governance groups.

3. Efforts should be focused on the relevant persons and situations related to an objective. "[The] persons who are there have the power" (Baldridge, 1971, p. 26).

4. Service on committees is crucial; they are where the work gets done (Baldridge, 1971). By being present, doing the work of the committee, and staying until the job is done, student affairs officers will influence what happens.

5. Persistence is vital (Birnbaum, 1988; Baldridge, 1971). Even though a policy is written, the issue may not be settled. Evolving interpretations should be constantly monitored.

6. Management should be unobtrusive (Birnbaum, 1988). Managing small changes without much fanfare may elicit less attention and resistance.

Staff Education

Although many will be reluctant to involve their staffs in the normal political skirmishes, it is important that they understand institutional history and culture. For example, many business schools have faculty consultants in the area of organizational culture who can be quite helpful to student affairs staffs. An informed staff will be more sensitive to issues and interactions that may have political overtones; the result is that the leadership's network is expanded and more consistent organizational responses to political situations can be made. It is also helpful to inform senior staff members of the details of situations either that may cause political disagreement or that invite collaboration with others.

Clear Purposes and Values

A clearly and consistently stated set of purposes and supporting values can help provide a context within which actions and initiatives related to responsibilities can be understood and interpreted. Explicitness is a virtue in itself in that it informs the opinions of others and helps reduce uninformed speculations and the suspicion of secret motivations and agenda. Speculation will always be present in organizations and should therefore be anticipated and countered by information. Actions rooted in core values are more understandable and less subject to misunderstanding.

Explicit and consistently state values and purposes are important not only to external but also to internal audiences, such as the staff or division. Staff members, fully cognizant of organizational values and direction, will act more reliably in pursuit of them and will likely make fewer mistakes that can be seized upon by other interest groups within the organization.

At the same time, it is important that student affairs leaders and staffs work to attain and respond to an institutional perspective. Partisan politics is frequently rooted or finds its voice in narrow matters. Budget requests and program proposals that respond to general institutional goals will more likely gain supporters and ultimate approval and less likely attract opposition because of petty issues. Further, embracing institutional purposes and values signals membership on a team committed to institutional advancement.

Performance

Extremely competent people performing at high levels are more likely to be successful in pursuit of objectives and able to counter opposition to organizational activities and initiatives. A uniformly able staff is an invaluable political asset. Political competence can be encouraged through consistent investment in staff development activities.

Faculty

A widely understood and broadly applicable approach to faculty is an important institutional strategy. Faculty members will be supported by opponents depending on what they know or how they are involved and supported in a given process by student affairs personnel. Importantly, such a strategy must reflect the typical commitments of the faculty, as well as the values and mission of the institution (Bloland, 1991). Managers should think often of faculty in their program planning and evaluation and follow through when faculty participation is secured or interest expressed. (See Chapter Twenty in this volume.)

Staffs should also be encouraged to develop strong relations with academic units through teaching, writing, or consultation. Teaching is the most traditional approach, but consultation on such issues as the handling of difficult students or training on student diversity is increasingly possible. Staff members should be encouraged to respond to faculty concerns quickly and positively, regardless of how insignificant or uninformed the request or question might seem.

Faculties will influence institutional decisions through their senates, institutional standing committees, and school and department governance structures. Although many faculty members may be uninformed about student affairs issues and commitments, they will influence, perhaps negatively, decisions affecting student affairs.

Communication

The student affairs organization must actively communicate with those it would seek to influence. Communication must be consistent, frequent, and of high quality and should originate in all parts of the organization, not just from the top. Each office or function has a constituency with which communication is vital. Its form may be a newsletter, a computer bulletin board, or a personal visit, depending on institutional size and purposes. It may involve the sharing of ideas about common interests through the circulation of articles. Internal articles on student trends or interest can furnish useful information about reentry student characteristics or employment trends. Communication strategies must also contain active opportunities for listening and feedback through an open-door policy, letters to the editor, or a constituent survey.

Ethical Considerations

A number of good resources on ethics are available for the student affairs practitioner (Canon and Brown, 1985; Upcraft and Poole, 1991). It seems, however, that the issue ethical behavior is more important when examining our political roles within the organizations in which we work—perhaps especially because institutions of higher education are committed to the pursuit of truth. The perceived importance of this behavior also stems from our understanding that when we confront institutional politics, we are not necessarily dealing with an idealized good but with a world in which people do not always act nobly.

Yet groups and individuals disagree on institutional direction and resource allocation decisions, attempt to influence decisions that have an impact on themselves or their interests, and exercise power when they do so. Organizational politics are real and ubiquitous and are thus an important aspect of administrative decision making and life. As such, organizational politics must be considered from an ethical perspective. After all, as Appleton (1991) states, it is "the acquisition and right use of power" (p. 6) that ought to be of great interest to the professional operating in the political dimension of administrative life.

Special Considerations

Although institutions and personal situations will provide an array of administrative and political challenges, some deserve special mention to encourage practitioners to think differently or more broadly about them; these include issues of gender, ethnicity, institutional size, and institutional affiliation or sponsorship.

Gender and Ethnicity

There are expected differences in administrative experiences related to gender and ethnicity, but these factors may present special challenges. In a study of female and African-American chief student affairs officers (Mamarchev and Williamson, 1991), respondents reported a number of common issues that affected their ability to manage their political environments. There were perceived differences in the ways that they had been socialized, in the availability of mentors during the formative years of their careers, in familiarity with the territory of senior administration, in their inclusion in some informal social and information-sharing situations, and in others' understanding of their role and competence because of their gender or ethnic background. These situations caused the respondents to find ways to augment their training and experience and to develop strategies to help them cope with a political environment perhaps different from that normally associated with the position held.

Institutional Size

Institutional size clearly affects how one operates, administratively and politically. Size may limit access to decision making, create administrative decentralization and specialization, lessen social interaction, and diminish the accuracy of communication (Smith, 1991). Each of these dimensions will require the tailoring of strategies and tactics designed to influence institutional decision making. Birnbaum (1988) provides an excellent discussion of institutional function based partly on organizational size.

Mission

Institutional sponsorship and therefore mission can have an enormous impact on institutional goals. A Jesuit college, for example, may well have a different social agenda because of a commitment to service than a public, technical university. Private institutions may more vigorously defend their independent status than some other values that public institutions may deem more important, such as broad student access. These differences, as well as those in institutional culture, will also influence the approaches to political systems and situations that student affairs officers will adopt.

Summary

This chapter has argued that the political dimension of institutional life exists and is important, and manageable. The student affairs practitioner will be affected by political struggles about institutional direction, plans for pursuing these purposes, and allocation of resources to implement the plan. It is therefore critical for student affairs administrators to know the history, culture, and people in their institutions and to take into account their colleagues who also wish to influence events. They should know their business, actively participate in institutional life, and be students of the inevitable political processes of their institutions, including the tactics, strategies, and possibilities that are available to them. Institutional politics should be understood, appreciated for its potential and limitations, and practiced as competently as possible.

Certainly, the practice of politics without values is bleak. Lacking a clear sense of fairness, high level of integrity, and commitment to the students, faculty, and institutions we serve, organizational politics can disintegrate to the distasteful, self-serving spectacle too often seen in our political institutions. There is another way—one that understands the processes necessary to create consensus about where we are going and how we will get there but that demonstrates the best values of higher education.

References

Appleton, J. R. "The Context." In P. L. Moore (ed.) *Managing the Political Dimension of Student Affairs.* New Directions for Student Services, no. 55. San Francisco: Jossey-Bass, 1991.

Appleton, J. R., Briggs, C. M., and Rhatigan, J. J. *Pieces of Eight.* Portland, OR.: National Association of Student Personnel Administrators Institute of Research and Development, 1978.

Bacharach, S. B., and Lawler, E. J. *Power and Politics in Organizations: the Social Psychology of Conflict, Coalitions, and Bargaining.* San Francisco: Jossey-Bass, 1980.

Baldridge, J. V. *Power and Conflict in the University.* New York: Wiley, 1971.

Baldridge, J. V. "Organizational Change Processes: A Political Systems Approach." In J. R. Appleton (ed.), *Selected Major Speeches and Excerpts from NASPA's 55th Annual Conference,* Monograph no. 4. Washington, D.C.: National Association of Student Personnel Administrators, Oct. 1973.

Birnbaum, R. *How Colleges Work: The Cybernetics of Academic Organization and Leadership.* San Francisco: Jossey-Bass, 1988.

Block, P. *The Empowered Manager: Positive Political Skills at Work.* San Francisco: Jossey-Bass, 1987.

Bloland, P. A. "Key Academic Values and Issues." In P. L. Moore (ed.), *Managing the Political Dimension of Student Affairs.* New Directions for Student Services, no. 55. San Francisco: Jossey-Bass, 1991.

Bolman, L. G., and Deal, T. E. *Modern Approaches to Understanding and Managing Organizations.* San Francisco: Jossey-Bass, 1984.

Brown, R. M. "Working with the President and Senior Administrators." In P. L. Moore (ed.), *Managing the Political Dimension of Student Affairs.* New Directions for Student Services, no. 55. San Francisco: Jossey-Bass, 1991.

Canon, H. J., and Brown, R. D. (eds.), *Applied Ethics in Student Services.* New Directions for Student Services, no. 30. San Francisco: Jossey-Bass, 1985.

Ellis, H., and Moon, J. "The Middle Manager: Truly in the Middle." In P. L. Moore (ed.), *Managing the Political Dimension of Student Affairs.* New Direction for Student Services, no. 55. San Francisco: Jossey-Bass, 1991.

French, J. R. P., and Raven, B. H. "The Bases of Social Power." In D. Cartwright (ed.), *Studies in Social Power.* Ann Arbor: University of Michigan Press, 1959.

King, S. W. *Communication and Social Influence.* Reading, Mass.: Addison-Wesley, 1975.

Mamarchev, H. L. and Williamson, M. L. "Women and African Americans: Stories Told and Lessons Learned—A Case Study." In P. L. Moore (ed.), *Managing the Political Dimension of Student Affairs.* New Directions for Student Services, no. 55. San Francisco: Jossey-Bass, 1991.

Moore, P. L. "Ideas for the Chief." In P. L. Moore (ed.), *Managing the Political Dimension of Student Affairs.* New Directions for Student Services, no. 55. San Francisco: Jossey-Bass, 1991.

Moore, P. L., and Moore, S. C. "Survey of Political Involvement of Chief Student Affairs Officers." Unpublished data, 1991.

Pfeffer, J. *Power in Organizations,* Marshfield, Mass.: Pitman, 1981.

Sandeen, A. *The Chief Student Affairs Officer: Leader, Manager, Mediator, Educator.* San Francisco: Jossey-Bass, 1985.

Schein, E. H. *Organizational Culture and Leadership: A Dynamic View.* San Francisco: Jossey-Bass, 1985.

Smith, D. G. "Small Colleges and Religious Institutions: Special Issues." In P. L. Moore (ed.), *Managing the Political Dimension of Student Affairs.* New Directions for Student Services, no. 55. San Francisco: Jossey-Bass, 1991.

Upcraft, M. L., and Poole, T. G. "Ethical Issues and Administrative Politics." In P. L. Moore (ed.), *Managing the Political Dimension of Student Affairs.* New Directions for Student Services, no. 55. San Francisco: Jossey-Bass, 1991.

Webber, R. A. *Management: Basic Elements of Managing Organizations.* Homewood, Ill.: Irwin, 1979.

Yates, D., Jr. *The Politics of Management: Exploring the Inner Workings of Public and Private Organizations.* San Francisco: Jossey-Bass, 1985.

Young, R. B. (ed.) *The Invisible Leaders: Student Affairs Mid-Managers.* Washington, D.C.: National Association of Student Personnel Administrators, 1990.

Student Affairs Practitioners as Transformative Educators: Advancing a Critical Cultural Perspective

Robert A. Rhoads and Michael A. Black

A different way of conceptualizing the practice of student affairs work is described, and the benefits of a critical cultural perspective for student affairs practitioners are considered. More specifically, the work of educators who seek to transform institutional cultures and establish an ethic of care and democratic principles as central organizing concepts is examined.

Introduction

Student affairs work has witnessed two distinct waves of theorizing. The first wave was framed by the notion of *in loco parentis* and emphasized student conformity to social custom. The second wave has been characterized by the idea of reforming students by applying developmental theory principally derived from psychological theories of human development. Developmental theory eventually displaced *in loco parentis* as the preeminent philosophy shaping the relationship between students and college professional staff, although remnants of parentalism clearly persist.

A third wave of theorizing about students and student life is under way and can be characterized as a "critical cultural" perspective. Its proponents emphasize the need for professionals to develop a critical awareness of the oppressive effects that different forms of culture have. A critical cultural perspective helps student affairs practitioners understand the power of culture and, in so doing, enables them to engage in campus transformation intended to dismantle oppressive cultural conditions. Practitioners who take such steps can be called "transformative educators."

The idea of transformative educators is based on theories of educational practice most often described as critical pedagogy, which is grounded in a critical cultural perspective that focuses attention on the role teachers might play in creating democratic classrooms in which students struggle to understand how culture and social structure have shaped their lives. The ultimate goal is for students to develop a critical consciousness, engage in social and cultural transformation, and help create a more just and equitable society. The theoretical tenets associated with critical pedagogy as put forth by Freire (1970, 1989), Giroux (1983, 1988), and Hooks (1994), among others, provide helpful insights into to how student affairs practitioners might conduct themselves from a critical cultural perspective. To understand the significance of this perspective, it is helpful to trace the roots of student affairs work.

The First Wave: *In Loco Parentis*

For nearly two centuries, and before the formalization of student services had taken root, college and university staff adhered to the principle of *in loco parentis* (Rudolph, 1962; Veysey, 1965). Dormitory staff and tutors, who doubled as teachers, provided a supportive, protective environment in which students could pursue their academic and religious training without interference or distraction. *In loco parentis* encouraged a relationship between staff and students characterized as one of parent to child, in which college and university staff knew and enforced what was best for students. The controlling aspect of early work with students is captured in Upcraft and Moore's (1990) discussion of evolving theoretical perspectives of student development: "The early colonial colleges believed they had a responsibility to act on behalf of parents for the good of their students. Students were considered children, and the institution their 'parents'" (p. 42). Of course, as Upcraft and Moore pointed out, the average age of college students during the colonial years was about 14, so treating them as children made a great deal of sense. Clearly, the early relationship between staff and students was quite unidirectional, as staff created rules, provided direction, and established consequences for students' behaviors.

The unidirectional relationship between college staff and students continued into the mid-1900s, and it is captured in Mueller's (1961) discussion of the nature of student personnel work. For Mueller, student personnel work was a form of teaching in which the staff focused not only on the "giving of knowledge" but also on taking "responsibility for the student's full use of that knowledge" (p. 49.) The *in loco parentis* notion formed the basis for the relationship between college staff and students, and shaped the development of college communities. Staff often had the final say regarding how student communities were constructed and controlled. In the face of such control by college faculty and staff, students often reacted harshly and violently (Moore, 1978) and at times sought to construct their own communities and subcultures (Horowitz, 1987).

The Second Wave: Developmental Theory

As the influence of *in loco parentis* slowly weakened, the idea of student learning or, as it was later termed, *development*, took on a much broader context. The intellectual and the spiritual growth of students became the primary two areas that student life professionals were concerned with as the field of student affairs began to emerge fully (Stage, 1994). Perhaps no statement about the nature of student affairs responsibilities has been more influential than the *Student Personnel Point of View* (American Council on Education, 1937), which directed student affairs professionals to (a) respond to each student as a whole person, (b) attend to individual differences, and (c) work with students at their level of development.

Despite calls throughout the 1950s for more developmental approaches, no real knowledge base upon which to ground work with students existed. As Widick, Knefelkamp, and Parker (1980) put it: "We [students personnel professionals] did not have theoretical models that could effectively describe college students and provide us with a coherent picture of individual development—a theory on which we could base our practice" (p. 75).

During the late 1960s and throughout the 1970s, research on college students and older adolescents began to inform student affairs work. Developmental theories, derived primarily from psychology and psychology-related fields such as human development, emerged and then influenced the nature and goals of student affairs professionals (Chickering, 1969; Erikson, 1968; Kohlberg 1975; Perry, 1970). Developmental research helped student affairs professionals better structure campus environments to meet the students' needs. A classic example was the work of Sanford (1967), who encouraged student affairs staff to construct campus communities that offered the proper mix of "challenges and supports." As Upcraft and Moore (1990) noted, challenges create a state of incongruence within students, whereas supports help students achieve equilibrium. "Too much challenge is overwhelming; too much support is debilitating. The challenge-support cycle results in growth and change" (p. 46). Later, theorists such as Astin (1984) and Tinto (1987) highlighted the relationship between student involvement in campus life and, respectively, academic performance and persistence.

The work of Gilligan (1982) served as a challenge not only to Kohlberg but to the generalizability of developmental theory, and her efforts marked the crest of a wave of theoretical work that had begun to revolutionize the human development field and the nature of social scientific thought. Most notable perhaps was the work of Kuhn (1970) and Foucault (1970, 1972, 1980), who both raised serious questions about the universality of traditional scientific paradigms and of truth itself. Other work by feminists, Afrocentrists, critical theorists, postmodernists, cultural theorists, and multiculturalists, to name a few also highlighted the shortcomings of "grand theory"—a theory designed to provide a totalizing explanation of human experience or behavior. This revolutionary trend in social scientific thought resulted in the French post-modernist Lyotard (1984) declaring all truisms to be fallacious. Ignoring the irony of his statement, what Lyotard and other radical social theorists called attention to was the need for more localized understandings of human experience, a call echoed by Geertz (1983) and elaborated in his notion of "local knowledge." In the remainder of the paper, some themes that cut across diverse schools of thought are discussed, and a critical cultural perspective is presented.

The Third Wave: A Critical Cultural Perspective

In recent years, student affairs scholars have begun to question conventional approaches to understanding students, student culture, and student life (Upcraft & Moore, 1990). Some have called for a fundamental change in views of campus life and have suggested that greater attention needs to be focused on issues of cultural diversity if more just and equitable college environments are to be constructed. As a result, scholars have advanced a variety of theories to explain human development in more localized terms—that is, by considering the unique experiences of diverse social and cultural groups (Belenky, Clinchy, Goldberger, & Tarule, 1986; Cass, 1979; K. P. Cross, 1988; W. E. Cross, 1991; D'Augelli, 1991; Rhoads, 1994). Other student life scholars have pointed to a changing ethos in the field. For example, Kuh, Whitt, and Shedd (1987) have illustrated distinct differences between conventional and emerging organizational frameworks for student affairs. Emerging frameworks are those that challenge the status quo and seek to change college and university cultures. Likewise, Cheatham (1991) has described the need for a fundamental change in the way campus communities are structured, and he has contended that ethnic minorities' perspectives must be "intentionally incorporated into campus life" (p. 23). Stage and Manning (1992) have presented the "cultural broker" model, in which the goal of building a multicultural campus "is achieved by recognizing and changing the organizational barriers that stand in the way of inclusion" (p. 16).

The student development and student life scholars just cited have alluded to a major change in how the student experience is conceptualized. This change in thinking about students and student life reflects a larger transformation in the social and behavioral sciences that places cultural understanding at the center of theorizing. There are two problems in discussing this changing view of social theory. First, because these ideas are in many ways still evolving, any synthesizing efforts can be only preliminary. Second, because this movement's roots are so diverse, few can agree that connections exist at all. For example, many feminist theorists reject any connection to postmodernists, whom they see as too abstract and at times nihilistic (Ramazanoglu, 1993). Although significant philosophical and political differences exist among diverse theories derived from feminism, postmodernism, and other schools of thought, some connections—such as a focus on culture and power—clearly are evident. Thus, despite the hazards of a synthesizing effort, a more concise conceptualization of this theoretical wave can benefit student affairs practitioners. For the sake of simplicity, four broad camps may be seen as the principal contributors to a critical cultural perspective: feminism, critical theory, postmodernism, and multiculturalism. In what follows, these four schools of thought are discussed, and points of intersection are considered.

Feminism

Gilligan (1982), one of the first to call attention to male-dominated views of human development, highlighted how a sense of connectedness and caring may be fundamental to female development. Other feminists have taken Gilligan's work as a starting point to elaborate views of education and social life based on an ethic of care (Larrabee, 1993). For example, Noddings (1984) contended that education has placed too little attention on issues of caring. She argued that educational settings ought to focus more on developing an environment in which students and teachers engage in ongoing dialogues and a concern for one another is central. Noddings maintained that such an education might then achieve some of the developmental and cognitive ends that are so painfully pursued at present.

Embracing an ethic of care has significant implications for how organizational life is structured. As Ferguson (1984) and Iannello (1992) pointed out, organizations grounded in a sense of connectedness and operating from an ethic of care are less hierarchical and less oriented toward instrumentalism (a perspective stressing nearly every aspect of the organization as a means to some predetermined end). A feminist perspective calls attention to process and the manner in which organizational members relate to one another. An emphasis is placed on democracy and egalitarianism as members strive to create an inclusive organizational community.

Critical Theory

Critical theory has its roots in the Frankfurt School in Germany, where Marcuse, Horkheimer, Adorno, Benjamin, and Habermas advanced critiques of culture and society in an effort to understand the shortcomings of Marxist theorizing (Agger, 1991; Benhabib, 1986; Kellner, 1989). Today, critical theory focuses on advanced modernity's power to limit human justice, equality, and freedom. Critical theorists argue that social and cultural groups compete to legitimize their own versions of social reality (Tierney & Rhoads, 1993). In a capitalist-driven society, groups with the greatest access to capital and cultural capital (Bourdieu, 1986) are best able to define social reality for themselves and for others. This power imbalance limits participatory democracy. The challenge for critical theorists is to unravel the cultural conditions that limit a participatory democracy from taking root. The concept of democracy suggested by critical theorists is best explained in the work of Dewey (1916), who discussed democracy as "Society which makes provision for participation . . . of all its members on equal terms" (p. 105). Thus, the goal is a society in which all people, regardless of their economic and cultural backgrounds have a voice in decisions affecting their lives.

Postmodernism

Unlike critical theorists, postmodernists make few assumptions about what ought to be. Instead, postmodernists embrace a more relativistic view of social life and question all forms of normalcy that they argue are rooted in one group's ability to assume power or legitimacy over another. The concept of power is central to postmodern theorizing (Foucault, 1978, 1980). The challenge of postmodernism is to continually deconstruct aspects of social relations that, through the deployment of power, have emerged as norms, which by their nature privilege some groups and marginalize others. Postmodernists seek to displace normalcy with multiplicity—multiple ways of understanding, knowing, or being. Difference becomes the driving force in a postmodern vision of society (Derrida, 1973). In terms of a critical cultural perspective, postmodernists are most helpful in understanding how various cultures and cultural groups become elevated over others, thus situating some at the center of social life and others at the margins. In rejecting the normalization of culture, especially the normalization of cultural identities, postmodernists provide a vision in which cultural difference is to be embraced and celebrated. Such a view suggests that colleges and universities seek ways to include previously disenfranchised groups in key organizational decisions.

Multiculturalism

Like postmodernists, multiculturalists embrace the idea of cultural difference and seek to build communities where diverse groups and world-views coexist. Following the earlier discussions of the 1960s about "cultural pluralism" and "diversity," multiculturalism has emerged as a philosophical ideal representing much more than an inclusionary practice in which diverse peoples are represented within various institutional arrangements (La Belle & Ward, 1994). Today, the idea of multiculturalism not only relates to the inclusion of diverse peoples, but it also depicts an effort to modify organizational structures and cultures. For example, Hill (1991) maintained that, "Marginalization will be perpetuated . . . if new voices and perspectives are added while the priorities and core of the organization remain unchanged" (p. 45). Likewise, Bensimon (1994) called attention to the need to rebuild colleges and universities in a way that fundamentally alters "structures, practices, and policies that create racial, gender, and sexual hierarchies for the benefit of some at the expense of others" (p. 14). Thus, multiculturalism challenges colleges and universities to be more inclusive and to rethink their work with students.

Points of Intersection

Some common threads that connect the preceding four schools of thought apply to organizational settings such as colleges and universities. All four perspectives speak to the issue of inclusiveness in one form or another. Feminists, through an emphasis on caring and a sense of connectedness, project inclusiveness as an ideal, as do critical theorists through their discussions of democracy. And multiculturalists and postmodernists embrace inclusiveness with their emphasis on accepting, even celebrating, cultural difference.

All four schools of thought envision collaborative decision making as the ideal. Feminists and critical theorists embrace participatory democracy, which demands that organizational members collaborate and discuss key issues; and multiculturalists and postmodernists emphasize that previously marginalized groups be intentionally included in organizational decision making as a means to embrace cultural differences.

Finally, these four schools of thought encourage egalitarian relationships and resist organizational hierarchy. For feminists and critical theorists, hierarchy threatens inclusiveness and a participatory democracy, because organizational status differences often have silencing effects. For multiculturalists and postmodernists, egalitarianism is closely aligned with an accepting attitude toward cultural differences. When majority members of an academic community perceive diverse cultures and cultural groups within that community as legitimate and as equal to their own, then an egalitarian and less-hierarchical climate is more likely to prevail.

Derived from these four schools of thought is an overarching framework for building educational communities rooted in an ethic of care and connectedness, democratic ideals, and respect for diverse cultures and voices. In essence, this is the critical cultural perspective. The remainder of this article is focused on the implications that a critical cultural perspective has for student affairs practitioners.

A Critical Cultural Perspective and the Transformative Educator

In discussing the practical implications of what it means to view students and the educational process from a critical cultural perspective, the work of the theorists Paulo Freire, Henry Giroux, and Bell Hooks stand out. Some classify this work as "critical pedagogy," or in the case of Hooks, "feminist pedagogy" or "engaged pedagogy." For the sake of simplicity, the pedagogical ideas presented in this section that relate to student affairs work are referred to as a "critical cultural practice."

The work of Freire (1970, 1989) calls attention to the notion that a significant goal of education is to eliminate "the oppressive conditions that make it difficult for people to develop into responsible, loving human beings" (Alschuler, 1986, p. 492). Accordingly, a central point of Freire's work is his critique of "banking education," in which the teacher is positioned as the dispenser of knowledge and students as the recipients of the best of what a society has to offer its younger generations. The banking concept of education situates students as passive learners and restricts their ability to achieve *conscientizacao*—critical consciousness. *Critical consciousness* refers to understanding the political, cultural, and economic forces that situate certain individuals and groups on society's margins and taking action to eliminate such oppressive conditions. Just as the banking concept of education instills a passive view of students as learners, enacting a democratic form of pedagogy where students and teachers engage one another in discussions about justice, freedom, and equality challenges students to develop a critical consciousness. "Education as the practice of freedom—as opposed to education as the practice of domination—denies that man is abstract, isolated, independent, and unattached to the world" (Freire, 1970, p. 69). Whereas the banking concept of education encourages students to accept the status quo, education for a critical consciousness encourages students to be concerned about social conditions and involve themselves in cultural change that will create a more democratic society.

Giroux and Hooks are perhaps the two most notable theorists who have built on the work of Freire. Giroux (1988) advances the notion of "teachers as intellectuals"—teachers who bring theoretical and philosophical perspectives to the educational process as a means to create a more just and equitable society. Thus, for Giroux, educators have an obligation to recognize the theoretical implications of their work with students and to create an environment where students have the opportunities to learn about and debate the social, economical, historical, and political forces that limit or enhance democracy.

Like Giroux, Hooks (1994) is concerned with issues related to creating an empowering educational experience: "To teach in a manner that respects and cares for the souls of our students is essential if we are to provide for the necessary conditions where learning can most deeply begin" (p. 13). For Hooks, building democratic educational settings in which all students feel a responsibility to contribute is the central challenge of what she describes as an "engaged pedagogy" (p. 15). Like Freire, Giroux, and other feminist writers, Hooks focuses on education as a potential liberating force in students' lives. Therefore, education must focus not only on forces that limit democracy but also on ways that oppressive conditions might be transformed.

Freire, Giroux, and Hooks have presented an image of a transformative educator who works to establish educational conditions in which students, teachers, and staff engage one another in mutual debate and discourse about issues of justice, freedom, and equality. Such a view of educators has significant implications for student affairs professionals.

The Implications of Student Affairs Practitioners as Transformative Educators

In her application of Freire's work to the field of student affairs, Manning (1994) discussed the role student affairs professionals might play as transformative educators who engage in joint struggle with students to create more democratic communities. Manning was one of the first student affairs theorists to provide a glimpse of what student affairs work might resemble from a critical cultural perspective. In the following seven principles, we advance a vision of how student affairs practitioners might act as transformative educators.

1. *As transformative educators, student affairs practitioners play a crucial role in the way college and university communities are structured.* Typically, student affairs professionals are seen as being concerned primarily with students' out-of-class experiences. However, the campus climate and organizational culture within which students learn and grow include much more than out-of-class experiences. If student affairs

professionals are to have a significant impact on students' overall development, they must be actively involved in shaping the larger academic community. This requires engaging other faculty and staff in campus change.

2. *Building empowering social and cultural settings is central to the work of student affairs practitioners as transformative educators.* Whereas traditional views of student development often emphasize individual development, a critical cultural perspective challenges student affairs professionals to focus on the social and cultural contexts in which student development is presumed to occur. Individuals do not develop in vacuums or "pickle barrels" (Wohlwill, 1973). The assumption is that empowering social settings provide the necessary conditions for students to develop to their fullest potential as community members and as democratic citizens.

3. *As transformative educators, student affairs practitioners contribute to the development of campus communities based on an ethic of care and a commitment to democracy.* Empowerment is made possible when students have opportunities to develop a sensitivity to others as expressed in an ethic of care and openness to cultural differences. Such a community also challenges students to see their connection to others and to society and thus encourages a sense of social responsibility. An empowering student experience can be achieved only when the academic community itself is structured around an ethic of care and a commitment to democracy.

4. *Creating conditions in which diverse students, faculty, and staff can participate fully in campus decision making is central to the work of student affairs practitioners as transformative educators.* A commitment to democratic principles challenges student affairs staff to consider diverse voices in making decisions about organizational life. Transformative educators must therefore challenge organizational gatekeepers to create structures and opportunities so that varied constituencies have representation. Merely having members of diverse groups on campus is not enough; also, they must have opportunities to shape their own experiences through inclusive decision-making structures.

5. *As transformative educators, student affairs practitioners respect cultural differences and encourage others to do the same.* A commitment to caring demands that student affairs professionals accept and respect cultural differences and that they work to help others understand and respect differences. As transformative educators committed to an ethic of care and democratic principles, student affairs professionals must support and protect the rights and liberties of marginalized members of the academic community. This may mean taking unpopular positions such as supporting the rights of lesbian, gay, and bisexual students and staff.

6. *As transformative educators, student affairs practitioners treat students as equals in the struggle to create a more just and caring academic community and society.* From a feminist perspective, hierarchies must be minimized before truly inclusive organizational settings can be built. Thus, student affairs professionals need to foster relationships with students that at times may be best characterized as "engagement with," as opposed to "service for" or "service to." Manning (1994) made this point in her discussion of Freire's potential influence on student affairs.

7. *As transformative educators, student affairs practitioners embrace conflict as an opportunity to transform the academic community.* Because diverse individuals and groups are encouraged to participate in organizational deliberations and decisions, conflicts and disagreements are likely to surface on an ongoing basis. Instead of viewing conflict as a threat to organizational harmony, transformative educators embrace conflict as a way to change the organization. Conflict calls attention to organizational problems and thus serves as an impetus for change. In a community characterized by an ethic of care and a respect for differences, transformation resulting from conflict becomes more likely.

These principles are offered as guides to student affairs professionals who may consider, or perhaps have already considered, what it means to view the transformative dimensions of their work with individual students, student groups, or the larger academic community. These principles are applicable to all areas of student affairs. For example, a residence hall director might choose to embrace these principles as part of his work with a resident assistant staff, as well as with students in his immediate area. To influence the emergence of a more caring and democratic community, he might also choose to become more involved in other areas of the academic community. He might volunteer his services on various committees in which a critical cultural perspective could prove insightful.

A vice president for student affairs might opt to embrace some or all of the principles as a guiding framework in her leadership of a student affairs division. She could have a far-reaching impact if her commitment to creating a more caring and democratic community influenced other student affairs staff, as well as other staff around the campus.

Specific aspects of the student experience might also benefit from a critical cultural perspective. Disciplinary procedures, housing policies, Greek life, athletics, registration, admission practices, and health services might all be transformed through a focus on an ethic of care and participatory democracy. For example, student affairs practitioners who listen to international students' definitions of pain, injury, treatment, and care, which oftentimes differ from Western perspectives, might transform the way in which health care delivery and health education and promotion are conducted.

Conclusion

A critical cultural perspective calls attention to a changing ethos toward how student affairs practitioners understand and work with college students and campus communities. As a third wave in theorizing about college students, a critical cultural perspective challenges all members of an academic community to be more concerned with an ethic of care and a commitment to democratic principles such as justice and equality for all people, regardless of cultural differences. From a critical cultural perspective, student affairs practitioners as transformative educators must continually interpret and reinterpret the organization so they can understand how the organizational culture impedes creation of a caring, democratic community.

The idea of the transformative educator has significant implications for how student affairs practitioners define themselves in relation to students. The role of the student affairs practitioner is to work alongside students and other faculty and staff to transform college and university settings, and a critical cultural perspective offers a theoretical vision of how student affairs professionals can help make significant organizational changes.

References

Agger, B. (1991). Critical theory, poststructuralism, postmodernism: Their sociological relevance. *Annual Review of Sociology, 17,* 105–131.

Alschuler, A. S. (1986). Creating a world where it is easier to love: Counseling applications of Paulo Freire's theory. *Journal of Counseling and Development, 64,* 492–496.

American Council on Education. (1937). *The student personnel point of view* (American Council on Education Studies, Series 1, Vol. 1, No. 3). Washington, DC: Author.

Astin, A. (1984). Student involvement: A developmental theory for higher education. *Journal of College Student Personnel, 25,* 297–308.

Belenky, M. F., Clinchy, B. M., Goldberger, N. R., & Tarule, J. M. (1986). *Women's ways of knowing: The development of self, voice, and mind.* New York: Basic Books.

Benhabib, S. (1986). *Critique, norm, and utopia.* New York: Columbia University Press.

Bensimon, E. M. (Ed.). (1994). *Multicultural teaching and learning: Strategies for change in higher education.* University Park, PA: National Center on Postsecondary Teaching, Learning, & Assessment.

Bourdieu, P. (1986). The forms of capital. In J. G. Richardson (Ed.), *Handbook of theory and research in the sociology of education* (pp. 241–258. New York: Greenwood Press.

Cass, V. C. (1979). Homosexual identity formation: A theoretical model. *Journal of Homosexuality, 4*(3), 219–235.

Cheatham, H. E. (1991). Identity development in a pluralistic society. In H. E. Cheatham (Ed.), *Cultural pluralism on campus* (pp. 23–38). Alexandria, VA: American College Personnel Association.

Chickering, A. W. (1969). *Education and identity.* San Francisco: Jossey-Bass.

Cross, K. P. (1988). *Adults as learners.* San Francisco: Jossey-Bass.

Cross, W. E., Jr. (1991). *Shades of black: Diversity in African-American identity.* Philadelphia: Temple University Press.

D'Augelli, A. R. (1991). Gay men in college: Identity processes and adaptations. *Journal of College Student Development, 32,* 140–146.

Derrida, J. (1973). *Speech and phenomena.* Evanston, IL: Northwestern University Press.

Dewey, J. (1916). *Democracy and education.* New York: Macmillan.

Erikson, E. (1968). *Identity: Youth and crisis.* New York: Norton.

Ferguson, K. E. (1984). *The feminist case against bureaucracy.* Philadelphia: Temple University Press.

Foucault, M. (1970). *The order of things: An archaeology of the human sciences.* New York: Random House.

Foucault, M. (1972). *The archaeology of knowledge and the discourse of language* (A. M. Sheridan Smith, Trans.). New York: Pantheon Books.

Foucault, M. (1978). *The history of sexuality, Volume I: An introduction* (R. Hurley, Trans.). New York: Vintage Books.

Foucault, M. (1980). *Power/knowledge: Selected interviews and other writings, 1972–1977.* New York: Pantheon Books.

Freire, P. (1970). *Pedagogy of the oppressed.* New York: Continuum.

Freire, P. (1989). *Education for critical consciousness.* New York: Continuum.

Geertz, C. (1983). *Local knowledge: Further essays in interpretive anthropology.* New York: Basic Books.

Gilligan, C. (1982). *In a different voice.* Boston: Harvard University Press.

Giroux, H. A. (1983). *Theory and resistance in education: A Pedagogy for the opposition.* South Hadley, MA: Bergin & Garvey.

Giroux, H. A. (1988). *Teachers as intellectuals: Toward a critical pedagogy of learning.* Granby, MA: Bergin & Garvey.

Hill, P. J. (1991). Multiculturalism: The crucial philosophical and organizational issues. *Change, 23*(4), 38–47.

Hooks, B. (1994). *Teaching to transgress: Education as the practice of freedom.* New York: Routledge.

Horowitz, H. L. (1987). *Campus life: Undergraduate cultures from the end of the eighteenth century to the present.* New York: Alfred A. Knopf.

Iannello, K. P. (1992). *Decisions without hierarchy: Feminist interventions in organization theory and practice.* New York: Routledge.

Kellner, D. (1989). *Critical theory, Marxism, and modernity.* Baltimore: Johns Hopkins University Press.

Kohlberg, L. (1975). The cognitive-developmental approach to moral education. *Phi Delta Kappan, 56,* 670–677.

Kuh, G. D., Whitt, E. J., & Shedd, J. D. (1987). *Student affairs work, 2001: A paradigmatic odyssey.* Alexandria, VA: American College Personnel Association.

Kuhn, T. S. (1970). *The structure of scientific revolutions* (2nd ed.). Chicago: University of Chicago Press.

La Belle, T. J., & Ward, C. R. (1994). *Multiculturalism and education: Diversity and its impact on schools and society*. Albany: State University of New York Press.

Larrabee, M. J. (Ed.). (1993). *An ethic of care: Feminist and interdisciplinary perspectives*. New York: Routledge.

Lyotard, J. (1984). *The postmodern condition*. Minneapolis: University of Minnesota Press.

Manning, K. (1994). Liberation theology and student affairs. *Journal of College Student Development, 35*, 94–97.

Moore, K. M. (1978). The war with the tutors: Student-faculty conflict at Harvard and Yale, 1745–1771. *History of Education Quarterly, 18*(2), 115–127.

Mueller, K. H. (1961). *Student personnel work in higher education*. Boston: Houghton Mifflin.

Noddings, N. (1984). *Caring, a feminine approach to ethics and moral education*. Berkeley: University of California Press.

Perry, W. G., Jr. (1970). *Forms of intellectual and ethical development in the college years*. New York: Holt, Rinehart & Winston.

Ramanzanoglu, C. (Ed.). (1993). *Up against Foucault: Explorations of some tensions between Foucault and feminism*. London: Routledge.

Rhoads, R. A. (1994). *Coming out in college: The struggle for a queer identity*. Westport, CT: Bergin & Garvey.

Rudolph, F. (1962). *The American college and university: A history*. New York: Vintage Books.

Sanford, N. (1967). *Where colleges fail*. San Francisco: Jossey-Bass.

Stage, C. (1994). Student development: The evolution and status of an essential idea. *Journal of College Student Development, 35*, 399–412.

Stage, F. K., & Manning, K. (1992). *Enhancing the multicultural campus environment: A cultural brokering approach* (New Directions for Student Services, No. 60). San Francisco: Jossey-Bass.

Tierney, W. G., & Rhoads, R. A. (1993). Postmodernism and critical theory in higher education: Implications for research and practice. In J. C. Smart (Ed.), *Higher education: Handbook of theory and research, vol. IX* (pp. 308–343). New York: Agathon Press.

Tinto, V. (1987). *Leaving college: Rethinking the causes and cures of student attrition*. Chicago: University of Chicago Press.

Upcraft, M. L., & Moore, L. V. (1990). Evolving theoretical perspectives of student development. In M. J. Barr & M. L. Upcraft (Eds.), *New futures for student affairs* (pp. 41–68). San Francisco: Jossey-Bass.

Veysey, L. R. (1965). *The emergence of the American university*. Chicago: University of Chicago Press.

Widick, C., Knefelkamp, L., & Parker, C. A. (1980). Student development. In U. Delworth & G. R. Hanson (Eds.), *Student services: A handbook for the profession* (pp. 75–116). San Francisco: Jossey-Bass.

Wohlwill, J. (1973). *The study of behavioral development*. New York: Academic Press.

Note

Robert A. Rhoads is a Research Associate and Assistant Professor for the Study of Higher Education at Penn State University. Michael A. Black is a doctoral candidate in Higher Education with a minor in Human Development and Family Studies at Penn State University. Funding from the Office of Educational Research and Improvement, U.S. Department of Education under project number R 117G10037. The opinions expressed in this article do not necessarily reflect the positions or policies of OERI or the USDOE.

Managing Education Better: Some Thoughts on the Management of Student Cultures in American Colleges and Universities

John Van Maanen

All desperadoes of the podium know that justifying one's presence on a public platform is a tricky matter. One's words must be sufficiently authoritative to carry weight but not carry so much weight as to sink the whole enterprise. More importantly, a keynote speaker is under some obligation to show that he shares with his audience proper respect for the topics to be considered, in our case, colleges and universities. On this score, I can only say that like most of you I find college life rich, varied, exciting and worthy. In fact, I have so enjoyed college that as a student I managed to attend six of them and as a professor I have almost equaled that count by visitation rights. I regard campus as a far warmer and better place to be than the grim corridors of IBM, US Steel, or General Motors or trapped on the DC shuttle worrying about a governmental agency. I suppose I've come to appreciate university life so thoroughly that for better or worse I am probably now constitutionally unfit for any other employer. While I will have some sharp comments to make about the organization of our mutual association, they are made with a deep and abiding concern and interest in their welfare. Such attraction stems of course from my own values and predilections and on these grounds I launch this late afternoon talk.

Colleges and universities in any society—and, this one, in particular—take on goals that carry enormous ambition and conceit. They have, as many have suggested, an impossible mandate. To offer up a common one: 'Higher education is to fulfill and transform students, to make them smarter, wiser, more skilled and competent in matters of value to the society as well as make them more concerned, enlightened, and complete human beings.' If this vision is shared, as I think it is, the means to its achievement are rather remarkably diverse. Alexis de Tocqueville puts this in comparative perspective by noting in the 1830s: "There are two colleges in England, four in France, ten in Prussia, and 137 in Ohio."

The situation certainly hasn't changed. We now have some 12 to 14 million students in some three to four thousand two-year and four-year institutions. Nobody really knows either the exact body or college count. These institutions offer, as you well know and represent by your presence here, a dazzling, dizzying, altogether mind-boggling display of diversity. To wit, there are the Lutheran colleges of Lake Woebegone, the urban Catholic universities, the elite ivies, the seven sisters, military academies, women's colleges, black colleges, walled-in colleges and colleges without walls; colleges offering hardy vocational programs in business or engineering and colleges promoting, but limping along these days, cultural capital in ancient Greek or modern philosophy. There are also those colleges built around monumental football stadiums with trophy-case shrines and those built around prayer towers or cyclotrons. Each has a unique history, set of traditions, and special sense of worth. To a speaker who claims to speak to the whole of this diversity, such facts are humbling.

Yet, what is clear is that there is a good deal of national pride associated with this situation, largely vested in the numbers of students we manage to pump into and out of these institutions each year. We are probably also the only nation that displays such pride in public by the decals we place on our family cars. So sacred is college that to not put State U or Apache Creek Community College on display when our association warrants it is something of a sacrilege. This point was driven home to me on a recent trip to the west coast where I was told of a student ostracized by peers and upbraided by faculty for rearranging the Stanford University sticker on his car to read Snodfart University.

The basis of such pride and honor seems many times however to be somewhat misplaced, having little to do with the quality of college in the 'fulfill and transform' sense. It rests too often perhaps on that good old American practice of what Veblen labeled "individual display,' the art of being one up on one's neighbor. It speaks also to the intensity, ranking, and rivalry among colleges for the loyalties and affections of the citizenry. "My college is better than your college" being something of a subtext. Much of this status mongering also reflects some hard economic facts whereby some institutions swell and others shrink on the basis of their reputation. From this perspective, it is little surprise that making the Sweet Sixteen of the annual NCAA basketball tournament does far more for the resource base of a college than placing sixteen graduates at Oxbridge colleges as Rhodes Scholars.

All this is to say that a good deal of our talk about college and universities rests on some culturally-specific, economically-constrained and emotionally-laden facts for it is by no means clear just what constitutes the "good college." The criteria are multiple, particularistic, emergent, and, when the chips are down, conflictual. In this light, consider what seems to be something of a growing national hysteria about what many take to be a general decline in the educational quality of American institutions. Much of this worry is directed at the elementary and secondary levels but certainly some of it is reserved for our colleges, large and small. Even the most honored are not spared criticism.

Current concerns are indexed by the formation of National Panels to address educational problems. State legislatures call for the testing of our college grads to assure us that our baccalaureate programs are producing the educated widgets they claim. New presidents and deans are installed in our universities explicitly to recharge educational batteries. Faculty and administrators convene across the land to once again ponder what kinds of distribution requirements, enriched majors, standardized programs, or core curricula are needed to meet the "new" challenges posed by technology, science, languages, or society. This recent unrest and high anxiety seems to me to have little to do with students or university life per se but reflects a kind of face-saving nationalism (and chauvinism) reminiscent of the years following the Russian success with Sputnik. Our curricular marines are now being called out to fix things up and restore our national pride and competitiveness. Predictably, the call is for measurable outputs, no-nonsense leadership, better inputs, tightened-up requirements, remedial programs, doing away with the slack so we can become lean and mean again, more accountability, streamlined course offerings, better instruction, or, put most crudely, "more bang for the buck."

Yet, in all this presumed ratcheting-up of our educational plants and plans, there seems to be precious little attention given to the native's point of view; the natives being our beleaguered and belabored undergraduate students. To understand the native requires more than testing however. It requires us to pause for a moment and consider the possibility, like the Dutch, the French, the Japanese, that cultural matters may well be the integral, dynamic, and primary determinants of student performance, not merely what is left over after the market economy and its attendant social mobility have worked their will. What then can we say of student culture?

We can begin by saying something of their character. I once asked an MIT student of mine to provide a definition for the Institute's culture; without batting an eye, she responded by saying: "Its everything we aren't tested on in the classroom." However little this may be at MIT, it's a damn good answer. It consists of the taken-for-granted patterns of eating, sleeping, socializing; the embraced and disgraced habits of study; the rules of thumb about what activities on campus count as status-enhancing or status-degrading; the norms surrounding what is proper demeanor in and out of the classroom; the loose consensus among students as to what classes are "gut" and what are not; the grapevine gossip that tells students those teachers to take and those to avoid; and so forth. In brief, student cultures offer their members thick and thin guidelines for how to get an education and thus define for students just what an education means. They vary within and between campuses but, rest assured, they will be present.

They are present largely because we, as agents or managers of student lives, bring together large numbers of like-minded people at one time, in one place, there to be "batch-processed," as it were, through a lengthy people-processing sequence marked by specific problems that are best solved collectively rather than individually. The functional utility of student cultures is most clearly seen in the numerous studies of student failure. Such studies demonstrate over and over that those students least likely to graduate or otherwise do well in school are those with the fewest social ties to fellow students. "Fitting in" is as important to success in college as it is anywhere else in the world.

The hard questions we must ask then do not consider the existence of student cultures but concern their vitality, orientation, and lessons students learn in them as a natural consequence of their membership. Are they supporting of our educational ideals? Are they disruptive? More importantly, perhaps, are they open and caring, respectful of others and embracing of values that foster growth and maturity? Or are they closed, exclusionary enclaves of homogeneity, cynical of societal values and concerned only with "making out" in college and beyond? Are they, in the purple prose of *Time* Magazine, "self-policed bastions of stifling conformity and the me-first ethic?"

Needless to say, there are not categorical answers to questions such as these. Some are, some aren't. What *is* categorical is the extent to which college administrators and faculty set the tone for these cultures and, consciously or unconsciously, manage them through a vast number of big and little decisions that quietly direct student life. The message I bring is that if student cultures produce failures of a collective sort, as seems apparent when libraries go unused; soft, unchallenging course loads become the favored means to a degree; sullen, silent students sit listlessly through classes; scholarly traditions go by the wayside; or, when self-indulgent rites of Spring extend from September through June; it makes as little sense to fault the students or their backgrounds for such matters as it does to blame the victims for the rise of urban crime.

This point is occasionally controversial but let me illustrate what I mean by providing a few brief sketches of some problematic areas of student life. These are domains I think vitally important but woefully neglected in our research and discourse on college and universities. There is, as you will see, some bias here since these areas are ones with which I have some personal experience and, hence, emotional recall. But, they do seem to illustrate well the kinds of problems student cultures seem to organize around and if we are to ever manage education better, it seems clear to me that we must learn to address questions such as these.

Consider, first, what happens to students during their pre-enrollment days—when they represent "prospective freshman," highly valued game in these days of scarcity, retrenchment, and declining enrollments. Sociologist regard this period as an anticipatory phase of cultural initiation and note its marked impact on each and every recruit. What do we do to students then before they pass through our hallowed gates?

In a word, we "rush" them. Fairs, telephone campaigns, mass mailings, pamphleteering, alumni contacts, and, somewhat euphemistically, "selection interviews" are a few forms the rush takes. A taste of content of these events and materials can be glimpsed in the ubiquitous recruiting brochure. Those I've peeked at suggest that virtually all college classes are held outside, on warm, sunny days, next to large bodies of water, and presided over by casually attired but serous white males of rugged but youthful appearance, who sit surrounded by adoring students in the shade of a spreading elm. Prospective students who actually show up on campus for the much recommended "personal visit" seem to do little better than brochure readers. I recently witnessed a campus tour that included stops at the underground mini-mall on campus, the student union, the alumni pool, a student pub, a large-screen TV salon, and the steps but not the interior of the library, lecture halls, and faculty office buildings. The tour ended next to a Mr. Money instant cash machine located in the lobby of a towering student dorm.

The distinct impression one gets from such a rush is that education itself doesn't sell very well. We display precious little interest in letting students in on the arcane secretes of just who teaches what to freshmen and just when and where such instructions might take place. "Market share" is apparently the bottom-line and if we squirm at little at such a vulgar characterization, let's all squirm some more by considering an ad for a University Admissions Director that appeared recently in the *New York Times* Education Section asking for resumes from those with a "good speaking voice, telephone skills, and the ability to close."

The facts of the matter are that more and more colleges, public and private, are enrollment or tuition-driven enterprises engaged in a fierce survival game. The current Carnegie Commission Report on Higher Education suggests that fewer than fifty four-year colleges and universities can be considered selective under the most generous criteria of accepting less than half of those who apply. The average acceptance rate in four-year institutions is three out of four with about thirty-five percent being virtually open-door. Little wonder "market share" and the jargon of the biz school has penetrated the admissions office of Shady U.

What does all this mean to a potential recruit? Confusion, of course, since a babble of claims of what Shady U or Beachfront Tech can do for John or Mary fill the air. Claims are exaggerated and the order of the day seems to be inflated expectations as to what college offers its students as well as a general lack of realistic ideas as to what is required of students. Not all of this results from our recruiting practices since the gap between secondary and post-secondary standards appears also to be growing. But, the upshot of this little example is that a fairly chaotic, frantic, high-choice system marks the selection and entry phase of college life.

Such a context serves to set up another illustration concerned with the "reality shock" of the initiatory period of college careers. In many schools, a more poorly managed process is difficult to imagine. Too often, our student newcomers receive the residuals of whatever strengths a particular institution has to offer. Undergraduate, lower-division courses are characterized by their large size, their stiff lecture and recitation format, their standardized materials, their general lack of excitement, and their impersonal evaluation procedures. They are typically taught by low-status, inexperienced faculty as distressed by the classroom situation as the students. This seems true across the mix of institutions notwithstanding a few well-publicized exceptions that essentially prove the rule.

Placed against the high expectations generated by selection practices, the reality shock can be devastating. Turnover statistics bear this out. One of the more distinctive features of the American system of higher education, compared to other systems, is the restlessness and apparent dissatisfaction expressed by students whose academic careers may touch several schools. This is said by one whose Bachelor of Arts degree was earned at five different colleges.

Particularly poignant examples of our failure to treat seriously the old adage about 'first impressions being lasting' are seen during the initial few weeks of campus life for common-denominator freshmen. Few students it seems report any sense of being inducted into or embraced by a special community. Orientation programs seem to be catch-as-catch-can, voluntary affairs that pay little heed to the fact that the first few weeks on campus are critically important in terms of establishing daily routines, setting study patterns, developing local friendships, and forming attitudes about college life. Given that almost thirty percent of all our students are now part-time and more than twice that percentage commute, this failure to manage well the take-off stage of college life is particularly disturbing.

Consider also life-after-entry and the routinization and down-to-earth details of student life. There are 168 hours in the week. If a student attends class an average of 15 of those hours and studies, charitably, two hours for each hour in class, 45 hours in total are given over to academics. Take another 50 hours out for sleeping and eating and we are left with 70 hours unaccounted for by the basics of college. How do students make use of this time? Most, it seems, work. Yet, we are very unlikely to have much data on just who, where, how, and what students do when they work, let alone much data on how it may affect their performance in the classroom. Moreover, if there is a link between education and work it is a most tenuous one, established more on the base of myth and folklore than on any direct evidence. Indirect evidence is not reassuring. Harper's Index, for example, informs us that one of every fifteen Americans now working has worked at McDonald's, the sort of workplace where employees are eligible for a bonus if they manage to last a month on the job. What lessons and what values are transmitted in the youth labor markets today?

Closer to home, today's college students show a marked preference for living on campus. Residential students apparently prefer the convenience, the economy, and social scene of campus life—if, at some college, they are lucky enough not to be warehoused in local hotels and motels, so scarce is dormitory space. Yet, there seems to be widespread ambivalence among college administrators as to just what responsibilities they should take toward student life and behavior. Resident hall management is too often abdicated by administrators who know what is happening within them only when such activity threatens to bring unwanted outside attention. In charge are student personnel officials who, in turn, delegate day-to-day management to Resident Assistants. As an ex-RA, I can attest to the 24-hour a day character of a vastly underrated, underpaid, and difficult job— from finding light bulbs at four AM to birth-control counseling, from cleaning up vomit in the lounge to settling family-like disputes in the co-ed dorms. RA's are typically only a few years the senior of their charges but, in many respects, they are the life-blood of the residential college. They are the priests and police who keep students attending to their studies, to their work, to their friends, and, in extreme cases, to their own lives. I daresay, however, few college professors, deans, institutional researchers, or presidents could identify a single RA on their campus by name.

I do not wish to bypass other variations of student life outside the classroom. The Greek system is back with us again and again there is evidence of its smug, standoffish, selfish character, even if only three-percent of all college students belong to Greek societies. Commuters are still, at best marginal and almost invisible participants on many college campuses and, if drop-out rates are our guide, they remain an endangered species. Enrollment for ethnic and racial minorities are down in most schools and those that remain continue to have the predictably difficult time the numerically few and different have amongst the numerically many and similar.

At any rate, this breathless list of issue areas from the native's point of view is not intended to accomplish much more than remind us just what it might be like to be a student these seemingly placid days. I've picked a few areas of troubling concern because they happen to be favorites of mine. I haven't even mentioned those issues that crowd the pages of our news magazines such as the "you-pick-em" supermarket approach to course design and selection, a tactic that often leaves students befuddled with it all. One of my undergraduates advisees captured this nicely a few years ago by asking quite seriously: "Do I really have to take what I want again next term?" In sum, it appears that for many students who manage to get over the hump of choice and entry, college life boils down to spending four or more years in a youth ghetto. Scrambling for grades in courses of uneven quality and unfathomable sequence, socialized primarily by peers on something of a cultural island that is rarely visited by non-natives.

Too strong? Perhaps I'm not here however to soothe or calm the waters but to stir them up a little. We come now to my sermon along with a few cautionary notes. I'd like to see institutional research rediscover something of its heritage. Pointedly, I'd like to see some institutional research with an edge and concerned less with managerial than student and educational matters. I don't believe college is, at heart, merely a business to be managed calculatively with some cold bottom-line or rate-of-return in mind. To be sure, there is a political economy in which we must all somehow swim and survive and, as such, plans, forecasts, market studies, systems analysis, wage surveys, and estimation procedures play a part. But, there is also much more to whisper in the ear of college administrators than the results of nose count calculus. In particular, we need some indication of what happens to our students during their college years beyond the fact that many of them persist in completing 128 credit hours and gaining a degree. I submit that we don't know very much about student life and culture on our own campus because we don't try very hard to learn. Inputs and outputs are thought to be what counts and, hence, what we measure. We probably know far more about our students before they enter and after they leave than we do while they are with us. I think this short-sighted for if we are to manage education better it is with the process of education itself that we must begin.

Such a process is not captured well by frequencies or statistical summaries. Process entails experience and experience is best captured by narrative. Descriptions of student lives-in-progress are required. On this matter, institutional research, broadly defined, has had considerable past glory. Ted Newcomb, Howard Becker, Edgar Schein, David Riesman, and Burton Clark, to name a few, have all pointed to the distinctive yet varied mix of cultures carried by colleges. A favorite example of mine is Ben Snyder, who, in the mid-sixties, carried out a marvelous little study through the Division of Institutional Research at MIT and added the phrase, "The Hidden Curriculum" to our vocabulary while provoking some much needed change in the way student cultures were treated at the Institute.

What marks these as outstanding examples of institutional research is their ethnographic or descriptive character and serious effort to portray college life from the student's perspective. In these competitive times of cost consciousness and outcome obsessions, students tend to get lost in the shuffle. A sophisticated office of institutional research, however, must think holistically about college life. It must think qualitatively as well as quantitatively, of culture as well as structure, in the language of students as well as managers.

There are no obvious reasons why simple, open, descriptive studies of various student groups can not be developed and distributed such that the pressing and sometimes urgent views of these groups can be heard. We lack not the skill but the will to do such work. Straight-forward ethnographic work of the sort I have in mind here requires only a target group to talk to and some paper and pencil to record what is learned. This is not a high-tech activity and high-powered analytic models do little more than get in the way. Our students are hardly shy, wily natives intent on keeping the anthropologist out of the village. They are more than pleased to speak on matters of personal concern but are left normally with stories only they can tell. I have in mind, of course, more than a take-a-student-to-lunch program but a sort of systematic, on-going, pulse-taking activity whose intention is to describe not prescribe. The foundation here, to twist a phrase, is that there is nothing so practical as a good story.

Ethnographies, be they native, professional, amateur, are what I wish to encourage. Glimpses into the odd corners of our institutions are not only matters of intrinsic interest but are often sparks for creative problem solving and further inquiry. What are our typical campus visits like? How is life lived in Bill-Jim Hall? What is a day in the life of a Hispanic freshmen on a lily-white campus like? These are not statistical questions but questions of value and meaning. Such mundane imponderabilia are the stuff of which college life consists and without knowledge of some of it we surely lose sight of what it is college is about. I have no illusions, of course, about the science of ethnography; it is an art, a craft; but, no less an art or craft than some of our highly-rationalized yet narrow analytic models we seem to spend so much time developing and fine-tuning.

In brief, so much of what passes for information collected and processed by a university about itself is rather empty of meaning since it possesses few obvious connections to everyday life on campus. To be sure, this is an age-old critique but with the astonishing increase in our ability to slice and dice information with our handy-dandy, desk-top computers, we may lose sight of what it all means. I am asking simply that student cultures be taken seriously and we make an effort, however partial and primitive, to try and sketch out some of the concerns that occupy the members of those cultures that, in the final analysis, provide our own justification for a presence on the college campus.

Such work requires some mobility of course. Cultural inquiry takes place on the ground where the objects of our affection are found. It requires listening to and learning from students going about their daily affairs. It might mean, shudder, taking in a class or two; hanging out at the student center for more time than it takes to wolf down a burger; or, gasp, visiting a dorm on a Saturday night. Tactics are however multiple. Surveys, diary methods, intensive interviews, focus groups, archival searches, bull sessions in the halls and quads are all possibilities. A tactic might be borrowed from those anthropologists who make use of spot-reports from native informants. A good deal of ethnography goes on as classroom assignments in many social science, education, and management courses. These could easily be tapped to provide even more. The point is simply that if we really want to get a better feel for what our institutions are currently doing to and for the inmates, there are countless ways of generating the kind of narrative data we need.

That we seldom do so suggests a final and perhaps gloomy point. Maybe we don't really want this information. Maybe if we had it we wouldn't know what to do with it. The history of organizational self-reflection of the sort I've just mentioned is, after all, not all that common. There are several reasons here that bear elaboration.

Educational evaluation, as a field, was captured early on by psychology and, more recently, by various forms of economic analysis. This is not accidental for both fields represent the most "scientific" of our social research disciplines. We all know, however, what has happened as a result. From psychology, we received a testing mentality because the science of what is in people's heads comes complete with a technology for how to unload such knowledge if it is there. From economics, we received various input-output models and the proverbial black box or invisible hand that transforms one to the other. From both, we have been presented with a never ending stream of discoveries on how best to do X, Y, or Z.

The problem, of course, is the speed with which each discovery is replaced by another contradictory discovery. Large classes are in, then out, then in. Zero-based budgeting comes and goes. Forecasting or cost-containment models are adopted and discarded like Cabbage-Patch dolls. It is all a little like child rearing, a science whose experts, on the basis of good evidence, have advised everyone for alternative decades to feed their babies on schedule or on demand.

Why do we accept the authority of such patently fallible traditions? I can only speculate here since I've not done the empirical work to verify it, but, it seems to me that over the years higher education has found itself increasingly in a situation where we have to prove we are being fair and providing the best possible education to our students in the face of substantial and obvious evidence that we are not. Our swoon into the arms of quantitative, scientific, so-called objective techniques coincides with the broad democratization of higher education, the standardization and routinization of education, and its increased competitive character. Time doesn't permit lengthy argument (thankfully) but I suspect the fundamental point is that college and university administrators have promised the moon—'to fulfill and transform'—yet can not really deliver. In the face of being called to task for our shortcomings, we seek to convince skeptics, friends, enemies, legislators, boards, alumni, and, indeed, even ourselves, that our institutions are nonetheless being run on quite rational and defensible grounds. Enter, here, the fair, neutral, beige, scientific, quantitative, and objective planning and evaluating techniques as the culturally-approved means for providing such legitimation and justification.

Subjectivity, sensitivity, and judgment are, however, the keys to the kind of techniques I have in mind for institutional researchers. Alas, these methods run afoul with the legitimation and justification functions of our research because they so often spoil our explanations for just why we sometimes fail—explanations that frequently turn on the alleged inadequacies of the students or the marketplace. It is not venal in the sense that administrators are saying, "Jeez, John, if we let people do descriptive work, they will spoil our excuses," but there is an undeniable element of subterfuge in our coming to terms with the realities of American higher education. This is, I think, part of the reason why we uphold our "scientific techniques" with such zeal and why ethnographic, close to the ground, methods are so disliked.

A somewhat more political point concerns the fact that if we study our institutions inside-out, we will eventually wind up studying everybody. One of the lessons learned from some of the exemplary works I cited before is that student cultures are shaped by a wide array of decisions and non-decisions taken well beyond their borders. If we sniff around a student dorm, for instance, and discover that the faculty have not been seen since the Peloponnesian Wars, the faculty may well become targets for criticism. One of the surprises ethnographies hold in store for people is that all groups on campus are fair game for study. Moreover, members of these groups know well that if people hang around long enough studying what they do all day, sooner or later they will find out things they would prefer not to reveal. Ethnographers, *always and necessarily*, discover such things and their work is profoundly evaluative, no matter how it is sold or explained. The study of student cultures will invariably spin upward and while administrators may not mind studies that point to a few rotten apples, they will have some difficulty with studies that may suggest that the barrel itself is spoiling the apples. Some fun, huh?

Finally, two rather vexing utilization problems are associated with my call for narrative, qualitative research. These matters bring us face-to-face with some issues that surfaced during the brief heyday of field studies in higher education, the 'sixties,' when great hope was placed on the "depth" of ethnographic research and its unarguable closeness to the facts of college life. Administrators, rightly concerned with running a tighter ship, had problems with researchers who stumbled on, for example, drug deals in Founder's Hall, program directors who covered operating expenses by funds allocated for program innovation, or faculty who responded to publication and tenure pressures by simply vanishing from campus for weeks at a time to write at home in the privacy of their studies. Researchers know, however, if they go around telling bosses that the workers are goofing off, there soon will be no workers to study. I do think a far greater sophistication surrounding these matters now exists than in the past. But, it should be clear from the outset that privacy, confidentiality, and a rigorous refusal to scapegoat individuals for institutional failures are moral requirements for the work I have been shamelessly pushing here.

Second, ethnographic, judgmental, student-orientated research is inherently problem-focused but the solutions researchers unearth to the problems studied may not be the ones preferred by decision-makers. Often, our solutions are not seen as "practical." Typically, the problems dug up in ethnographic work are fundamental ones and quite resistant to a so-called quick fix. Here is an example. I once produced a draft of a study I conducted on my own institution, the Sloan School. The faculty and administrators who read it—by and large, only the most concerned and serious of my colleagues—wanted me to make recommendations. For instance, in the report I described (apparently convincingly) how first-year master's students formed tight little conforming and risk-averse groups on the basis of being marched through the coursework at the same speed, in the same order, with the same cohorts, and presented with precisely the same material. The result, since the students were put in the same boat by the faculty and administration, was that individuals wound up doing things together—including homework, tests, term papers, and the like. That appalled the faculty. I explained however that the batch processing model promoted such a response and if they wanted something different they could allow students more choice in when, where, and with whom they take their courses.

My colleagues at this point looked glum. What was wrong? The solution, the program head said, would destroy the ease and economy the current scheduling strategy produced. It would be hard to track students and make sure they fulfilled their requirements on time if we moved away from the block model. Faculty would surely complain because classes would become less standardized and students would be able to make more comparisons among them as to who was teaching well and who was not. My solution might work, but, alas, it wasn't very practical.

This, of course, is the fundamental problem. What the institutional researcher identifies as a cause when working from my ethnographic model may well be something people can't or won't do anything about. Good social research it seems always makes some people uneasy if not angry. But, more optimistically, only work that seriously attempts to get close to its subject matter, student cultures or anything else, produces the sorts of answers that are worth having—the only kind of answers that will work in the long run. The implication of all this is that if we are to manage education better by attending to student life, institutional researchers, like other workers of the field in sociology and anthropology, must learn to live with the critic's curse, namely the slightly marginal status that comes from doing good and reputable work that is viewed by the power holders as somewhat suspicious and dangerous.

But, as long as colleges keep running into failure (and the converse is unimaginable), we must put the pressure on and force decision-makers to look at what they might otherwise prefer not to see. Being members of the very organizations we study helps in this regard for our loyalties can be assumed to flow in the right direction. To live and work inside our colleges and universities is, as I said at the outset, a most attractive, self-enhancing, and worthy situation. To help manage these institutions and try to make them better is certainly a never-ending story but it is a quite noble and downright enchanting one as well.

Thank you.

Prepared for 27th Annual Forum, The Association for Institutional Research, Kansas City, Missouri, May 3, 1987.

The New Scientific Management

Margaret J. Wheatley

In the history of human thought, a new way of understanding or a new frame for seeing the world often appears seemingly spontaneously in widely separated places or from several disciplines at once. Darwin proposed his theory of evolution at the same time that another researcher, working in Malaysia, published very similar ideas. Physicist David Peat has pointed out that the understanding of light as energy evolved in parallel ways in both art and science over the centuries. The sixteenth-century Dutch school of painters drew light for its effects on interior spaces, depicting how it entered rooms through cracks or under doors or was transformed as it passed through colored glass. At the same time, Sir Isaac Newton was studying prisms and the behavior of light as it passed through small apertures. Two hundred years later, J. M. W. Turner painted light as energy, a swirling power that dissolved into many forms; simultaneously, physicist James C. Maxwell was formulating his wave theory in which light results from the swirling motion of electrical and magnetic fields. When Impressionist painters explored light for its effects on dissolving forms, even painting it as discrete dots, physicists were theorizing that light was made up of minuscule energy packets known as quanta (Peat 1987, 31–32; for a detailed exploration of the synchronicity between art and physics, see Schlain 1991).

Very recently, we have witnessed a similar springing forth of parallel concepts in science and business. AT&T began to advertise a world of electronic networks and connectivity at the same time quantum physicists began communicating in earnest to us lay persons about cosmic interconnectivity. Scientists and businesspeople use surprisingly similar language to describe this new world of interconnections. When Levi Strauss CEO Robert Haas told an interviewer that "we are at the center of a seamless web of mutual responsibility and collaboration . . . , a seamless partnership, with interrelationships and mutual commitments," it was easy to hear the voices of physicists in the background (in Howard 1990, 136).

Also in the past few years, a new way of thinking about organizations has been emerging. Whether they be large corporations, microbes, or seemingly inert chemical structures, we are now interested in learning about any organization's "self-renewing" properties. We are searching for the secrets that contribute to vitality and growth both in nature and in our workplaces.

This relationship between business and science goes back many years. Although in many ways Newtonian thinking unwittingly inspired organizational design, science was brought deliberately into management theory and credited with giving it more validity in the era of "scientific management" in the early years of this century. Frederick Taylor, Frank Gilbreth, and hosts of their followers led the efforts to engineer work, creating time-motion studies for efficiencies and breaking work into discrete tasks that could be done by the most untrained workers. Though we may have left behind some of the rigid, fragmented structures created during that time, we have not in any way abandoned science as the source of most of our operating principles. Planning, measurement, motivation theory, organizational design—each of these and more bears the recognizable influence of science.

A few months ago I was in the audience at a social science conference, listening to colleagues report on their research. In each presentation, I was struck by how "scientific" we in the social sciences strive to be. It's as if we're afraid that we might lose our credibility without our links to math and physics. (William Bygrave, trained as a physicist but now a student of organizations, calls this "physics envy" [1989, 16].)

In one conference session, an organizational theorist drew a long formula on the board that captured, he assured us, all of the relevant variables an employee would use to decide on further education. To be fair to this man, I need to say that all of my professional life I have had a deep aversion to formulaic descriptions of human behavior. But I sat there aghast. There was his long string of variables—separate descriptors interacting in precise, mathematical ways—and here was my brain, filled with my recent readings about fuzzy particles that are nothing but temporary connections in the webs of an interrelated universe, moments of meeting that cannot be captured in predictable ways. I was struck suddenly by the joke of it all. We social scientists are trying hard to be conscientious, using the methodologies and thought patterns of seventeenth-century science, while the scientists, traveling away from us at the speed of light, are moving into a universe that suggests entirely new ways of understanding. Just when social scientists seem to have gotten the science down and can construct strings of variables in impressive formulae, the scientists have left, plunging ahead into the vast "porridge of being" that describes a new reality.

We need to link up once again with the vital science of our times, not just because of our historic relationship, but because, by now, scientific concepts and methods are embedded deep within our collective unconscious. We cannot escape their influence nor deny the images they have imprinted on our minds as the dominant thought structure of our society.

Among its new images, science can encourage us to develop a different relationship with discovery. Nobel Prize winner Sir Peter Medawar said that scientists build "explanatory structures, *telling stories* which are scrupulously tested to see if they are stories about real life" (in Judson 1987, 3). I like this idea of storytellers. It works well to describe all of us. We are great weavers of tales, outdoing one another around the campfire to see which stories best capture our imaginations and the experiences of our lives. If we can look at ourselves truthfully in the light of this fire and stop being so serious about getting things "right"—as if there were still an objective reality out there—we can engage in fife with a different quality, a different level of playfulness. Lewis Thomas explains that he could tell something important was going on in an experimental laboratory by the laughter. Surprised by what nature has revealed, we find that things at first always look startlingly funny. "Whenever you can hear laughter," Thomas says, and somebody saying, "But that's *preposterous!*—you can tell that things are going well and that something probably worth looking at has begun to happen in the lab" (in Judson 1987, 71).

Wouldn't we all welcome more laughter in the halls of management? I would be excited to encounter people delighted by surprises instead of the ones I now meet who are scared to death of them. Were we to become truly good scientists of our craft, we would seek out surprises, relishing the unpredictable when it finally decided to reveal itself to us. Surprise is the only route to discovery, the only path we can take if we're to search out the important principles that can govern our work. The dance of this universe extends to all the relationships we have. Knowing the steps ahead of time is not important; being willing to engage with the music and move freely onto the dance floor is what's key.

One of the guiding principles of scientific inquiry is that at all levels, nature seems to resemble itself. For me, the parsimony of nature's laws is further argument why we need to take science seriously. If nature uses certain principles to create her infinite diversity, it is highly probable that those principles apply to human organizations. There is no reason to think we'd be the exception. Nature's predisposition toward self-similarity can be extremely useful. It can even help us evaluate current management practices, providing a guide through the fads and ideas that plague us, directing our attention to those things that have merit at a deeper level. I feel better able to distinguish real nourishment from fast-food guru advice because of my awareness of the directions science is taking. Although I have intimated throughout these essays some of these connections between new science and current management thinking, I'd like to underline a few of them.

To start, there are many critiques offered for the current and growing shift toward participative management. Is this a popular idea that, like so many others, we can wait out, knowing it will pass?

Is it based on democratic principles and therefore nontransferable to other cultures? Is it merely a more sophisticated way to manipulate workers? Or is something else going on? For me, quantum physics answered those questions. I believe in my bones that the movement towards participation is rooted, perhaps subconsciously for now, in our changing perceptions of the organizing principles of the universe. This may sound grandiose, but the quantum realm speaks emphatically to the role of participation, even to its impact on creating reality. As physicists describe this participatory universe, how can we fail to share in it and embrace it in our management practices? Will participation go away? Not until our science changes.

The participatory nature of reality has focused scientific attention on relationships. Nothing exists at the subatomic level, or can be observed, without engagement with another energy source. This focus on relationships is also a dominant theme in today's management advice. For many years, the prevailing maxim of management stated: "Management is getting work done through others." The important thing was the work; the "others" were nuisances that needed to be managed into conformity and predictability. Managers have recently been urged to notice that they have *people* working for them. They have been advised that work gets done by humans like themselves, each with strong desires for recognition and connectedness. The more they (we) feel part of the organization, the more work gets done.

This, of course, brings with it a host of new, relationship-based problems that are receiving much notice. How do we get people to work well together? How do we honor and benefit from diversity? How do we get teams working together quickly and efficiently? How do we resolve conflicts? These *relationships* are confusing and hard to manage, so much so that after a few years away from their MBA programs, most managers report that they wish they had focused more on people management skills while in school.

Leadership skills have also taken on a relational slant. Leaders are being encouraged to include stakeholders, to evoke followership, to empower others. Earlier, when we focused on tasks, and people were the annoying inconvenience, we thought about "situational" leadership—how the situation could affect our choice of styles. A different understanding of leadership has emerged recently. Leadership is *always* dependent on the context, but the context is established by the *relationships* we value. We cannot hope to influence any situation without respect for the complex network of people who contribute to our organizations. Is this a fad? Or is it the web of the universe becoming felt in our work lives?

Participation and relationships are only part of our present dilemmas. Here we sit in the Information Age, besieged by more information than any mind can handle, trying to make sense of the complexity that continues to grow around us. Is information anything more than a new and perplexing management tool? What if physicist John Archibald Wheeler is right? What if information is the basic ingredient of the universe? This is not a universe of things, but a universe of the "nothing" of information, where meaning provides the "software" for the creation of forms (Talbot 1986, 157-58). If the universe *is* nothing more than the invisible workings of information, this could explain why quantum physicists observe connections between particles that transcend space and time, or why our acts of observation change what we see. Information doesn't need to obey the laws of matter and energy; it can assume form or communicate instantaneously anywhere in the information picture of the universe.

In organizations, we aren't suffering from information overload just because of technology, and we won't get out from under our information dilemmas just by using more sophisticated information-sorting techniques. Something much bigger is being asked of us. We are moving irrevocably into a new relationship with the creative force of nature. However long we may drag our feet, we will be forced to accept that information—freely generated and freely exchanged—is our only hope for organization. If we fail to recognize its generative properties, we will be unable to manage in this new world.

This new world is also asking us to develop a different understanding of autonomy. To many managers, autonomy is just one small step away from anarchy. If we are to use it at all, it must be carefully limited. As one manager wryly commented, "I believe in fully autonomous work, as long as it stops at the level below me." Yet everywhere in nature, order is maintained in the midst of change because autonomy exists at local levels. Sub-units absorb change, responding, adapting.

What emerges from this constant flux is that wonderful state of *global* stability. Rather than developing pockets of stability and incrementally building them into a stable organization, nature creates ebbs and flows of movement at all levels. These movements merge into a whole that can resist most of the demands for change at the global level because the system has built into it so much internal motion.

The motion of these systems is kept in harmony by a force we are just beginning to appreciate: the capacity for self-reference. Instead of whirling off in different directions, each part of the system must remain consistent with itself and with all other parts of the system as it changes. There is, even among simple cells, an unerring recognition of the intent of the system, a deep relationship between individual activity and the whole. Could it be possible that nature is guided by something as familiar as Shakespeare's "To thine own self be true"?

More than any other science principle I've encountered, self-reference strikes me as the most important. It conjures up such a different view of management and promises solutions to so many of the dilemmas that plague us: control, motivation, ethics, values, change. And as an operating principle, it decisively separates living organisms from machines. *Star Trek* popularized an effective method for destroying computers; you program them with a self referential statement, e.g., "Prove that your prime directive is not your prime directive" (Briggs and Peat 1989, 67). As the logic turns back on itself in unending iterations, a machine will blow its circuits. Zen masters employ the same technique with koans, but they know that human brains are not machines and that we can be challenged to new levels of thinking by self-referential exercises.

Perhaps self-reference is the best tool of all for leaving behind the clocklike world of Newton. We can use self-reference to sort out the living from the dead—giving us the means to identify the open systems that thrive on autonomous iterations from the truly mechanistic things in organizations that do best at equilibrium. But before we can use self-reference, we need to solve a deeper problem. We need to be able to trust that something as simple as a clear core of values and vision, kept in motion through continuing dialogue, can lead to order.

At the risk of sounding antiquatedly reductionist, I want to make one more speculation. If management practice is ever to be simplified into one unifying principle, I believe it will be found in self-reference. It is not only the science I have read that gives me such assurance. When I look at the shape and meaning of my own life, and how it has evolved with change, I understand the workings of this principle in intimate detail. For me, there is no choice but to take the paths new science has marked. Like all journeys, this one moves through both the dark and the light, the terrors of the unknown and the joys of deep recognition. Some shapes and landmarks are already clear. Others wait to be discovered. No one, especially the scientists, can say where the journey is leading. But the association promises to be fruitful, and I can feel the explorer's blood rising in me. I am glad to feel in awe again.

> "Wisdom is about living harmoniously
> in the universe, which is itself a place of order
> and justice that triumphs over chaos and employs
> chance for its ultimate purpose."
>
> —Matthew Fox

Epilogue

Being Comfortable with Uncertainty

Across the valley, the last colors of this day warm the horizon. Two dimensions move across the land, removing all contours, smoothing purple mountains flat against a rose-radiant sky. A volcano erupted in the Philippines six months ago. Now at every twilight, visiting dust shimmers red in the atmosphere, intensifying the colors of an always intense sky. I sit here, bathed in strange light, embraced by dark magenta mountains.

I move differently in the world these days since traveling in the realms of order and chaos and quantum events. It has become a strange and puzzling place where I cannot rely on what I knew and don't yet feel secured by new sources of confidence. It makes things much more interesting, expecting there to be new ways of working without being able to discern them clearly. In the process of writing this book, of playing with its ideas, and of trying things out with others, I've become aware of how difficult it is *not* to be certain. I've encountered, in myself and others, a desire for these new understandings to translate quickly into reliable and trusty tools and techniques. We are not comfortable with chaos, even in our thoughts, and we want to move out of confusion as quickly as possible.

But the science is helping me understand, among many things, the uses of chaos and its role in self-organization. I think I not only expect chaos now, but I've grown more trusting of it as a necessary stage to greater organization. Recently, I advised a group of students who were taking on an ambitious study of a new subject area, and I noticed a different direction to my advice. They were eager to create a model or framework into which they could slot information. I was intent on letting information do its thing. They wanted to get organized at the start; I wanted them to move into confusion. I urged them to create more information than they could possibly handle. I guaranteed them that at some point the information would self-organize in them, crystallizing into interesting forms and ideas.

Neither they nor I have yet seen the results of their work, but I realize that I have not only the science to support this advice. I also have my own experience. I have worked enough with information—as have you—to recognize how it works with us to organize into new forms. But I needed the science to help me see it. In a similar fashion, I believe each of us can validate many of the strange scientific ideas in this book if we look more carefully at our experiences. What we've been given are some new glasses to help us notice the way things have been working all along.

Ralph Waldo Emerson wrote about life as an ongoing encounter with the unknown and created this image: "We wake and find ourselves on a stair; there are stairs below us which we seem to have ascended, there are stairs above us . . . which go out of sight" (in Eiseley 1978, 214). These stairs of understanding we now are climbing feel different. They are less secure, harder to see, and much more challenging. They require very different things from us.

In our past explorations, the tradition was to discover something and then formulate it into answers and solutions that could be widely transferred. But now we are on a journey of mutual and simultaneous exploration. In my view, all we can expect from one another is new and interesting information. We can *not* expect answers. Solutions, as quantum reality teaches, are a temporary event, specific to a context, developed through the relationship of persons and circumstances. There will be no more patrons, waiting expectantly for our return, just more and more explorers venturing out on their own.

This sounds unnerving—I haven't stopped wanting someone, somewhere to return with the right answers. But I know that my hopes are old, based on a different universe. In this new world, you and I make it up as we go along, not because we lack expertise or planning skills, but because that is the nature of reality. Reality changes shape and meaning because of our activity. And it is constantly new. We are required to be there, as active participants. It can't happen without us and nobody can do it for us.

This is a strange world, and it promises to get stranger. Niels Bohr, who engaged with Heisenberg in those long, nighttime conversations that ended in despair, once said that great innovations, when they appear, seem muddled and strange. They are only half-understood by their discoverer and remain a mystery to everyone else. But if an idea does not appear bizarre, he counseled, there is no hope for it (in Wilbur 1985, 20). So we must live with the strange and the bizarre, even as we climb stairs that we want to bring us to a clearer vantage point. Every step requires that we stay comfortable with uncertainty, and confident of confusion's role. After all is said and done, we will have to muddle our way through. But in the midst of muddle—and I hope I remember this—we can walk with a sure step. For these stairs we climb only take us deeper and deeper into a universe of inherent order.

In Search of the Lost Chord: Applying Research to Planning and Decision Making

LARRY G. BENEDICT

The jury all wrote down on their slates, "She doesn't believe there's an atom of meaning in it," but none of them attempted to explain the paper.

"If there's no meaning in it," said the King, "That saves a world of trouble, you know, as we needn't try to find any. And yet I don't know," he went on, spreading the verses on his knee, and looking at them with one eye; "I seem to see some meaning in them after all. . . ."

Alice's Adventures in Wonderland
Chapter XII: Alice's Experience

Earlier, the authors noted that student affairs practitioners do not systematically use research and, in fact, may actively resist the use of it. They review some of the common complaints that practitioners make as being "too busy," or "it's too expensive." Finally, they argue for the profession to be more research oriented.

In some ways, this clarion call within the profession for improved practice based on research sounds about as realistic as providing homes for the homeless, saving the Brazilian rain forest, or achieving world peace. Everyone is talking about it but not many people are doing much about it. Respected people in the profession continue to advocate for the increased use of research, but it is still not widely practiced. Before one can make the case for expanded use of research, and see the practice become widespread, one needs to understand why practitioners avoid research.

Reasons for Failing to Conduct or Use Research

There are several significant reasons why practitioners do not systematically use research in their practice. Unless the profession understands these reasons and begins to address them directly, it is unlikely that the profession will ever be marked by wide use of research.

Williamson and Biggs (1975) explained that student affairs researchers "find it very difficult to make their research findings meaningful to those who make decisions in colleges or universities" (p. 290). Similarly, Johnson and Steele (1984) reported that student affairs research has little impact at the divisional or institutional level (p. 202). Recently Beeler and Oblander (1989), in a study of student affairs research activities in 570 American colleges and universities, found that research involvement is greatest in assessing the effectiveness of student affairs organizations (p. 9). A compelling case can be made that research activities in student affairs divisions are generally halfhearted, poorly planned, myopic, and ineffective.

Why do student affairs organizations fail to conduct and use meaningful research in their planning and decision making? To begin, attitudes toward research have been poor and are based on some misconceptions. Faced with a decision that needs objective input, decision makers too often make excuses to avoid putting time and energy into research. Matross (cited in Williamson & Biggs, 1975) described three research-inhibiting attitudes:

- Research is too hard for me.
- Research is irrelevant.
- Research is something I don't care to do.

If these attitudes seem simplistic, there are at least four underlying conditions that make them more plausible:

- The language of research is too complex.
- A myth exists that professionals are too busy to do research.
- There is a common misconception that research is too expensive for limited budgets.
- There is unnecessary confusion of roles caused by the use of such labels as "decision maker," "planner," and "evaluator."

Finding Meaning in the Use of Research

There are some steps student affairs practitioners can take to address these conditions. The profession needs to change or simplify the language of research, eliminate the myth of student affairs research as being too time consuming and expensive, better describe the decision-making process, and focus on the concept of improved practice. Until these things happen, like Alice, the profession will not see an atom of meaning in the use of research even though there are many, like the King, who do begin to see some meaning after all.

Simplifying the Language of Research

> *"I only took the regular course," said the Mock Turtle.*
> *"What was that?" inquired Alice.*
> *"Reeling and Writhing, of course, to begin with," the Mock Turtle replied; "and then the different branches of Arithmetic—Ambition, Distraction, Uglification and Derision."*
> *"I never heard of 'Uglification,'" Alice ventured to say. "What is it?"*
> *"Well then," the Gryphon went on, "if you don't know what to uglify is, you are a simpleton."*
> *Alice did not feel encouraged to ask any more questions. . . .*
>
> Alice's Adventures in Wonderland
> Chapter IX: The Mock Turtle's Story

To most of us, confronting a foreign language can be intimidating, scary, confusing, and frustrating, just as Alice's experience in her discussion on learning with the Mock Turtle and the Gryphon. In that discussion Alice confronts many new terms, including "uglification," which she does not understand. Similarly, the language of research can be arcane, obscure, and unintelligible to ordinary mortals. For most students, the required course in research at the master's degree level addresses the language of research in a way that seems divorced from the everyday life of the practitioner. Terms and phrases like "quasi-experimental," "randomization," "control groups," "inferential statistics," "analysis of covariance," "canonical correlations," "multiple regression," and "beta weights" mean about as much to most student affairs professionals as "uglification" means to Alice. Like Alice, many professionals probably feel like "simpletons" when it comes to the language of research.

The language of the research methods course is that of the conclusion-oriented researcher, rather than that of the everyday practitioner or decision maker. It is the language of the experimental researcher and it is this language that can seem so scary and confusing. This language can be contrasted with decision-oriented research (Cronbach & Suppes, 1969). In their classic work, Cronbach and Suppes (1969) sought to understand why educational practice was not being affected by reason to a greater extent than was the case. To help the reader better understand the issue, they described two approaches and tried to explain how each influences educational practice. Conclusion-oriented research seeks to generalize about realities that apply in all or most settings. Decision-oriented research is more concerned with what works in a specific setting, seeking objectivity but limiting its focus to immediate situations.

How does this research notion apply in student affairs administration or student development theory? The answer lies in Chickering's reminder that ". . . in translating any general theory into concrete applications, the specifics of particular contexts, particular combinations of institutional mission, and student characteristics need to be taken into account" (Thomas & Chickering, 1984, p. 394). It is through such research that we gain an understanding of students, their needs, and appropriate planning alternatives at our individual campuses.

For example, the director of the new student program (NSP) is designing a new, overnight orientation program for incoming students. She wants to know what works in overnight programs for traditional-aged students in a metropolitan university. The director does not want or need to design an elaborate new program, randomly assigning some students to the new program, holding some students out as a control, pretesting both groups, making sure that none of the threats to internal and external validity has been violated, etc. One can readily see that faced with such a task, very few if any NSP directors would want to rush into the thicket.

However, the NSP director does want to provide the very best program for her students in her setting. This can be done with simple data collection techniques, in a timely and effective fashion. The data she needs to use in helping make these decisions could be simply gathered by calling some peer institutions which have similar programs. The director does not care if the program she is deciding upon is the best program in the country, or that it works at all universities, or that all traditional-age students in all settings benefit from the program. Rather, she wants to know what will work for her program, with her kinds of students at another institution. It is this message that needs to be communicated to the practitioner. The language and methods of decision-oriented research need to be made widely and simply available to practitioners (Popham, 1975; Bogdan & Biklen, 1982).

As noted, most practitioners have learned whatever research skills they may possess in a conclusion-oriented mode and, therefore, see no connection between those skills and their decision-oriented needs. If practitioners are not taught or do not understand the connection between research and practice, they will never systematically use research. Like Alice, they won't understand the Gryphons and Mock Turtles and will be condemned to wander about Wonderland discouraged about asking anymore questions.

Research is Not Always Time Consuming

"Oh my ears and whiskers, how late it's getting!" said the White Rabbit hurrying down the long passage.

Alice's Adventures in Wonderland
Chapter I: Down the Rabbit-Hole

The fallacy that research is time consuming, perhaps better called an excuse, also stems from the confusion between conclusion-oriented and decision-oriented research. Carefully controlled experimental designs which seek to test hypotheses of universal significance can indeed be expensive. However, these designs go beyond what practitioners typically need. Practitioners need specific information that relates to immediate problems, concerns, and decisions.

Decision-oriented data collection need not be time consuming. Consider, for example, the health educator who must recommend within three days whether condom machines should be installed on campus. The health profession at large is clearly in favor of this program, but in the health educator's campus and community setting condom machines may not be well received. In fact, the administration has denied a request for such installation in the past.

The health educator wants to be on solid ground in dealing with this emotionally charged decision. To make the decision, this practitioner called 10 other universities with similar campus settings, some in similar communities, to see what they were doing; called several vendors to see what their experiences have been; and consulted the American College Health Association (ACHA). Based on this data collection, a decision was made about what to do (install the machines) and how and when to do it (through a coordinated, integrated health education program at the college). This was presented as a comprehensive proposal to the vice president and president who approved it. The program was successful.

This is an actual example. The total staff time required to make the telephone inquiries was perhaps an hour. The time to write the proposal and present it to the administration did not exceed three hours. This was not terribly time-consuming even for very busy people. Furthermore, it worked.

Research Can Be Cost-effective

Decision-oriented research need not be expensive, although it can be made expensive if enough resources are brought to bear. The myth that "we can't afford if" again stems from the misconception that all research designs are elaborate and time consuming. In the example of the condom machines cited above, total cost for the telephone calls was about $15 and the cost of copying the proposal was a few dollars. Even adding indirect costs such as staff time and electricity for the word processing, total costs here were no more than $50. This is not costly even on a shoestring budget.

This is also a good example of the obverse: sometimes an institution can't afford not to do the data collection, for political or educational reasons or because making the wrong decision will prove more costly in the long run. In the condom machine example just cited, an earlier attempt to install them had failed because a convincing case using data had not been made. The decision not to install was made based on a possible "morality" argument or the conventional wisdom on campus about the political climate. Without comparative data from other institutions and information from ACHA, the campus lost nearly two years of the benefits of this particular program.

Another example illustrates how data gathering prevented a potentially dangerous situation. The directors of residence life, police and safety, and health services at one university launched a fire safety prevention program in the residence halls. They decided to survey some residence hall students to see whether their efforts had been successful. The results of this data collection indicated

> that the students surveyed were woefully ill prepared to respond to a fire emergency despite brochures having been distributed, resident assistants and hall directors having informed students about procedures, and so on. In this case, the educational effort was not working and new programming was required. Such programming was developed immediately (Madson, Benedict & Weitzer, 1989, p. 519).

This example clearly illustrates the value of research in planning; it allows the decision maker to take a proactive stance and avoid a problem, rather than reacting to a disaster after it has occurred.

This research was also conducted with a telephone survey at moderate cost. Methods and costs of decision-oriented research are discussed in the next chapter. (See also Madson et al., 1989, for further discussion of these issues.)

The Role of the Generalist Includes Research

The student affairs profession promotes the concept of "generalist" in describing the activities of the student affairs practitioner. Among the skills needed by generalists are the abilities to read, conduct, disseminate, and use research and evaluation. Unfortunately, the labels people used to describe themselves and others often determine how they and others behave. Using language like "decision maker," "planner," or "evaluator" in talking about the use of research can sometimes scare staff from even considering the systematic use of data to improve their decisions. Many student affairs staff do not use such labels to describe themselves, even though much of their activity falls into these functional areas.

Williamson and Biggs (1975) noted that "all student personnel workers can be researchers. Although many are not equipped with statistics or research methodology, they can adopt experimental and empirical attitudes as they deal with complex social behavior" (p. 295). This includes entry-level staff who may often think that department heads and vice presidents are the sole decision makers. Resident directors make decisions about the kinds of programs and activities to sponsor in their halls. Student activities staff make decisions about which events can be scheduled during the year and how much money can be spent on those events. The health educator makes decisions about materials to purchase for National Collegiate Alcohol Awareness Week.

These staff see themselves as "practitioners" rather than "decision makers" even though they continually make decisions. The profession needs to help staff understand that labels are secondary to the task of systematically improving professional practice. Within the profession, student affairs practitioners (generalists, specialists, whatever) need to stay abreast of current research and develop their own skills for gathering and using meaningful data. Only through practice does a practitioner become skillful in applying research to planning and decision making.

The Practitioner as Decision Maker

Student affairs staff do not usually view themselves as researchers, planners, or decision makers. They do view themselves as practitioners, and there is no question that they want to be the very best practitioners they can be.

As they practice delivering service to students, caring for students, supporting students, enhancing student development, and managing the cocurricular experience, student affairs staff continually, almost unconsciously, make decisions. These decisions number in the dozens per day, hundreds per month; perhaps thousands per year. No matter how centralized the organization, decision making is largely decentralized out of necessity.

Curiously, one often hears, "Oh, decision makers work above me on the organizational chart." This is simply not true. Everyone is a decision maker in the language of decision-oriented research, but many do not know it. The last time you bought a car, how did you do it? Did you test drive one or two? Did you read about selected models in an automobile magazine or consumer report? It is likely that you used one of these "research" strategies to gain useful information before making your purchase decision. How many readers have stopped smoking because of something they have heard or read about the effects of smoking? Is that oat bran muffin or oat bran cereal on your table there to reduce your cholesterol?

The point of these examples is that people base many, many decisions on information ("data" in the research language) gathered by themselves or others but don't consciously say, "I am using research results in making the decision to eat oat bran muffins." Student affairs practitioners do the same thing in their professional lives, often as easily as when they shop for a car, change their diets, buy a house, or choose a college to attend. One can describe the subconscious decision-making process:

1. A need or a problem arises: "I need a car."

2. Possible solutions require information: buy a car, lease a car.

3. Information is gathered: about cars, models, maintenance records, safety records, relative costs.

4. A decision is made: to buy a particular car.

Some decisions in our daily lives are made almost automatically, such as brushing one's teeth in the morning or checking the gas gauge prior to buying gasoline. Others are made very deliberately: which comedy team should be sponsored for Winter Carnival, or who will facilitate a workshop on AIDS. Deliberation, by nature, requires information which comes largely from some combination of four sources:

- Personal experience and intuition
- Experience of others: friends, peers, supervisor

- Authority: the literature, the president, Chickering, Astin's research
- Data gathered to describe or inform a specific problem: research

Each of these information sources is appropriate for certain decisions. For example, routine, daily decisions are probably best made using the first category: personal experience and intuition. This style is fast, comfortable, and easy to use. The drawback of this approach is that personal knowledge gained can be quite haphazard or limited, subject to selective memory, and isolated from the knowledge of others.

Relying on the experience of others is also useful in making relatively limited, ordinary, daily decisions. Knowing what other resident assistants (RAs) are doing to enforce quiet hours or how they are enforcing quiet hours can be very helpful for the RA who is looking for suggestions.

The third style, appealing to some external authority or expert can dramatically improve the deliberative decision-making process. For example, one might consult Astin's research and related literature to design programs to improve freshman retention. While this is a step in the right direction, it has some limitations as well:

- the data were gathered on students from all over the country and may not apply to the types of students at a particular institution
- the data interpretation may be biased in the direction of the belief and values of the researcher
- the method of collecting the data may be instructive, but the actual gathering of data must be duplicated or amended at the decision maker's own campus.

The fourth category, the one which is best described as data collection for decision making, is the one which is best suited for the nonroutine decisions which practitioners make. The health educator's decision on the condom machines and the new student program director's decisions about the overnight program are examples of nonroutine decisions to which data-gathering techniques should be applied. This style approaches the problem or decision systematically, asks what information is needed, and then determines how to gather that information. Clearly personal experience is involved to some extent, perhaps reliance on others as well. Often some regional or national information may be gathered. The difference is the focus on the immediate decision needed on a particular campus or in a specific campus setting.

Systematic use of appropriate information will lead to better, more efficient, more effective decisions. This will lead to better practice at all levels in the profession, which in turn becomes a self-perpetuating process when its value is noted.

To paraphrase Blanchard and Johnson (1982), people who produce good work feel good about themselves. People who feel good about themselves produce good work. Our work will be improved by the systematic use of data in our decision-making processes. This, in turn, will improve morale and productivity.

Examples of Decisions Informed by Research

To make this process of data collection and decision making more apparent, it is useful to take a closer look at examples used by the student affairs "researcher" operating behind the mask of "practitioner." The following are actual examples where practitioners have systematically gathered data to inform their decisions. Each decision was effective. All of these "research studies" were done at low cost within a relatively fast time frame. Each "decision maker" felt good about the results of the research which resulted in better service to students and to the respective college or university. These examples are meant to be illustrative and are, therefore, not cluttered with specific details about methods, costs, and procedures.

Health Educator

The university does not have an AIDS policy. It needs to develop one. What should it contain? How should it be developed? How should it be disseminated? Data were gathered and analyzed. A policy was drafted, reviewed by the university's attorney, and adopted.

A new state law requires all entering students to be immunized. The problem is how to implement the law on campus and get students to comply. Data from two similar universities were sufficient to develop procedures to bring the university into compliance with state law.

Orientation Director

A new program for traditional-aged students, including an overnight component, has just been implemented for the first time. Two major changes also included a new role for faculty advisors and a component for parents. Were these changes successful? Data gathered from the faculty indicate that while they liked the new design and felt it was more effective than the prior program, they would like additional training on working with the students in a one-on-one setting. This component will be revised to respond to this need. The parent data indicate there was too much unscheduled time during the first part of the program and that they would like more student interaction. This will be added to the program next year.

Director of Residence Life

The university has four different ID cards: one each for housing, food, the gym, and the library. Food Services is changing the way students are billed and the number of meal options available. This will require new technology which will make the current food ID inoperable. The director of residence life needs to address this change. As a result of his research, a new system was adopted which met the needs of all these constituents. The university will move to one ID card.

Director of Counseling

The director needs to balance the demand for services with staff resources available. The demand for career services has been escalating. The career counseling staff are overwhelmed. The director asks the vice president for more staff. The vice president suggests that the director survey students about their opinions/needs for career counseling services. One result of the study was that a majority of students reported they would prefer initial career counseling in group sessions rather than one-on-one sessions, which was current practice. The director implemented this new mode of delivery. Students were satisfied and much time became available for the career counseling staff, who were also pleased with the new format. It was not necessary to add any new staff.

The counseling director faces the possible need to remove a student from campus because of a psychiatric emergency. However, the university does not have a policy for such a situation. It is a tricky situation fraught with both health and legal liability issues. As a result of very rapid research, a policy was developed which successfully addressed the legal and health issues.

Financial Aid Officer

The office staff have been getting complaints from departments on campus about not being able to hire enough work-study students because the wage bands are too low. After a study of the local job market, wage bands were adjusted to make the university more competitive as an employer.

Admissions Office Counselor

A university has a large number of nontraditional students but its application form (in use for many years) is primarily geared to traditional students, even asking for such inappropriate information as parent address or high school GPA. (This university's typical students are older and many are parents themselves.) The problem is how to develop such a form, what it should contain, and so on. A brief collection of data was used to meet this problem. A different application was designed for nontraditional students, making the university more responsive to the needs of this group.

Dean of Enrollment Management

In the face of a declining pool of 18-year-olds, the dean needs to know a variety of things to help plan the university's enrollment: data on enrollees and nonenrollers, retention, primary and secondary markets, feeder schools, the university's image, etc. This is an example of a very complex study or series of studies needed to formulate an enrollment management plan. While this became a timely process as well as a costly one, it resulted in the university's first enrollment management plan, which was adopted by the campus administration. It was also done at a substantial savings over hiring an external consultant or consulting firm.

These examples have been provided to show the variety of practitioners in student affairs who have used data to improve decisions. In all of the examples except the last one, the data were gathered quickly and inexpensively. In all cases, the policies, activities, and decisions which resulted were effective. Staff did not get hung up on the language of conclusion-oriented research and often did not even use the word research to describe what they did.

In effect, gathering data became a routine problem-solving/decision-making process for these staff. The staff were also pleased and proud of their decisions. This, in turn, should lead them to incorporate data in future decisions.

By avoiding the language of the conclusion-oriented researcher, by eliminating the myths about time and cost elements of research, by avoiding the need for and use of labels, and by focusing on the outcome—improved decisions leading to improved practice—these staff have found meaning in research. Unlike Alice, they did not need to know what uglification and reeling and writhing were and they did not feel like simpletons. Like the King, they have seen some meaning after all.

References

Beeler, K. J., and Oblander, F. W. (1989). A study of student affairs research and evaluation activities in American colleges and universities. Unpublished report. Washington, D.C.: National Association of Student Personnel Administrators, Inc.

Blanchard, K., and Johnson, S. (1982). *The one-minute manager.* New York: William Moore.

Bogdan, R., and Biklen, S. (1982). *Qualitative research in education: An introduction to theory and method.* Boston: Allyn and Bacon.

Cronbach, L. J., and Suppes, P. (eds.). (1969). *Research for tomorrow's schools: Disciplined inquiry for education.* London: Macmillan.

Johnson, D. H., and Steele, B. H. (1984). A national survey of research activity and attitudes in student affairs divisions. *Journal of College Student Personnel,* 25(3), 200–205.

Madson, D. L., Benedict L. G., and Weitzer, W. H. (1989). Using information systems for decision making and planning. In U. Delworth, G. R. Hanson, and Associates (eds.), *Student services: A handbook for the profession.* Second edition. San Francisco: Jossey-Bass Publisher, Inc.

Popham, W. J. (1975). *Educational evaluation.* Englewood Cliffs, N.J.: Prentice-Hall.

Thomas, R., and Chickering, A. W. (1984). Education and identity revisited. *Journal of College Student Personnel,* 25(5), 392–399.

Williamson, E. G., and Biggs, D. A. (1975). Student personnel research. In E. G. Williamson and D. A. Biggs (eds.), *Student personnel work: A program of developmental relationships* (pp. 289–308). New York: John Wiley and Sons, Inc.

Why Student Affairs Needs a Comprehensive Approach to Assessment

JOHN H. SCHUH AND M. LEE UPCRAFT

Those of us who have been involved in the assessment of student affairs services, programs, and facilities over the past few years often get calls from colleagues which go something like this: "Hey, you've been doing assessment stuff for a while. I need some help. We just had a very bad racial incident on our campus and things are very tense. My boss believes we need some data about race relations on our campus, in part because we don't have anything, and in part because we need to do something positive instead of just reacting. Do you have any surveys you might recommend? You know, something 'quick and dirty' we could do to take some of the pressure off."

A second version of this conversation: "We're really on the spot just now. There's a faculty 'Futures Committee' which is asking some tough but very naive questions about certain student services, because our college is going through some rough financial times, and clearly there will be substantial cutbacks. The faculty, of course, has their sights on reducing 'nonessential' student services first. Many services have been targeted for reduction or elimination by the faculty. For example, they ask, 'Why do we need psychological counseling? If students are troubled, let them pay for those services themselves, or get help off campus. After all, we're an educational institution, not a rehabilitation agency.' Do you have a needs assessment survey which would help us convince the faculty that students need psychological services?"

All too often it is the case that, while these problems are real, the solutions are not. Responding to a crisis with a survey is not assessment; it is crisis management. Assessment is a very complex process of which the selection and use of an instrument may be only a part, or no part at all. In reality, the mindless surveying of students in a crisis situation will probably do much more harm than good. Not only will it not solve the problem, but it will destroy the credibility of assessment as an important tool for gathering information about student programs, services, and facilities. Assessment in a crisis situation will also destroy the assessment's potential for determining the worth of such services, programs, and facilities, and communicating this worth to important political constituencies.

For many reasons—which are discussed in more detail later in this chapter—student affairs needs high-quality and comprehensive assessment programs. Unfortunately, among many staff in student affairs, assessment is an unknown quantity at best, or, at the worst, it is misunderstood and misused. It has been our experience that while everyone in student affairs would agree that assessment is important, too often it is considered a low priority and never conducted in any systematic, comprehensive way. And even if it is done, it is often done poorly; as a result, it simply gathers dust on someone's shelf, with little or no impact.

One of the reasons for this situation is the fact that many of us fail to understand why assessment is important in the first place This lack of understanding is compounded by confusion over what we mean by assessment and the assessment process, and how to conduct assessment in ways that are consistent with good practice. Even if all these issues are clear, we may not have a framework within which to develop a comprehensive assessment program.

In this chapter, we discuss the first step in implementing an assessment program: establishing an assessment rationale that all our constituencies will understand—including students, student staff, administrators, faculty, and boards of control, as well as legislators, accreditation agencies, graduates, funding agencies, and the general public. We also (1) review several reasons why assessment is important, for both higher education and student affairs, (2) develop a vocabulary within which to discuss assessment, (3) review the assessment process, (4) discuss some basic principles of good assessment practice, and (5) describe a comprehensive model for assessment in student affairs upon which the rest of the book is based.

Why Assessment in Higher Education?

There are plenty of reasons why higher education should take assessment seriously. Since the 1970s, assessment has become a growing and necessary part of higher education. At first, the assessment "movement" was considered by some to be just another fad that would quickly fade from the scene. They were wrong. In the mid 1980s, several national reports within higher education called for a greater emphasis on assessment in higher education, including the National Institute of Education (NIE) report, *Involvement in Learning* (1984), and Ernest Boyer's Carnegie Foundation report, *College: The Undergraduate Experience in America* (1987).

External pressure also mounted. In 1986, at their annual meeting, the governors from all fifty states declared that they wanted to hold higher education institutions more accountable for the performance of their students. Since that time, forty states have mandated one type of assessment or another, and all regional accreditation associations have adopted criteria for assessment-oriented outcomes (Marchese, 1990).

Tough questions are being asked. What is your college's contribution to student learning? Do your graduates know what you think they know and can they do what your degrees imply? How do you assure that? What do you intend that your students learn? At what level are students learning what you are teaching? Is that the level you intend? What combination of institutional and student effort would it take to get to a higher level of student learning? (Marchese, 1990). What *does* one get out of a college education? What *should* one get out of a college education? What *should* one get out of an education at this institution? How do we know? (Terenzini, 1989).

Just why all the fuss about accountability? For about 350 years, our citizenry accepted as a matter of faith that education was good and that our system of higher education was doing its job, and doing it well. The tremendous rise in enrollment since World War II was testimony to the country's unquestioned faith in the educational, if not economic, benefits of higher education. What happened? What caused the public—and many in higher education—to lose faith?

Many factors have contributed to the current environment. First, there are too many examples of people with college degrees who do not appear to be educated, even in the most basic sense of that term: graduates who are unable to read, write, compute, reason, or do anything else indicative of an educated person. Other graduates come out of college seemingly ill prepared for the world of work, as evidenced by the increasing amount of time spent by employers in training and retraining new college graduates (Wingspread Group, 1993). In other words, the public is gaining the impression that higher education is not producing what it promised, educated persons prepared for the world of work. Thus, accountability becomes an issue.

Second, the public is increasingly dissatisfied because of the rising cost of higher education. For example, from 1973 to 1988, college costs rose more than 200 percent, a pace well ahead of inflation rates for that same period (*Parade*, Mar. 19, 1989). The cost of four years at an Ivy League school is now well over $100,000, and the question being asked is, "Is it worth it?" Even more distressing to students and their families is the declining availability and sufficiency of federal and state grant and loan programs (Astin and others, 1991; Schuh, 1993a). As a result, more students are relying on their families, their savings, and part-time jobs to finance their educations. For example, in 1990, about 80 percent of students said they were getting financial help from their families, compared to 66 percent in 1980 (Astin and others, 1991). So, cost has become a big issue.

Third, there is increasing dissatisfaction with the quality of instruction at many institutions. This dissatisfaction includes large classes, fewer faculty who actually teach, poor academic advising, an emphasis on research at the expense of teaching, failure to do anything about poor teaching, and so forth. In the opinion of many educators at many of our large, public research universities, the learning experience—particularly at the freshman and sophomore level—is largely passive, delivered through lectures and focusing on the memorization of information that is verified through multiple-choice examinations (Upcraft, 1996).

This external dissatisfaction about the quality of higher education has revitalized ongoing efforts within the institution to improve and renewed internal commitment to quality. Signs of this change are the "total quality" efforts cropping up at many institutions. These are based on the principles of total quality management developed by Edwards Deming (1986) and applied to higher education by several others (Teeter and Lozier, 1993; Sherr and Teeter, 1991; Cornesky, McCool, Byrnes, and Weber, 1991). So, quality is an issue.

Fourth, and no less important, are the issues of access and equity in higher education. While higher education has made considerable strides toward becoming more inclusive and diverse by race, ethnicity, gender, disability, sexual orientation, age, socioeconomic status, and other factors, many groups are still underrepresented. Even more alarming is the discrepancy between the success rates of traditionally underrepresented groups and those of the majority. For many underrepresented groups, dropout rates are higher and graduation rates lower. The public, particularly those from underrepresented groups, wants to know why. So, access and equity are issues.

And finally, assessment is now a part of the accreditation of higher education institutions. According to the Commission on Higher Education's *Standards for Accreditation* (1982), one of the criteria for accreditation is outcomes or institutional effectiveness. "The deciding factor in assessing the effectiveness of any institution is evidence of the extent to which it achieves its goals and objectives. The necessity of seeking such evidence continually is inescapable; one of the primary hallmarks of faculty, administration, and governing boards is the skill with which they raise questions about institutional effectiveness, seek answers, and significantly improve procedures in the light of their findings" (pp. 17–18). This moves assessment from the "nice to have if you can afford it" category to the "you had better have it if you want to get accredited" category. So, accreditation is an issue.

Why Assessment in Student Affairs?

A Matter of Survival

As questions of accountability, cost, quality, access, equity, and accreditation combine to make assessment a necessity in higher education, they also make assessment a fundamental necessity in student affairs as well. Are we delivering what we promised, and are we doing so in a cost-effective, high-quality way? Do our services and programs provide access to underrepresented groups and are our campus environments free of bigotry, discrimination, and prejudice? Do our services, programs, and facilities contribute to student learning? These and other questions place an enormous responsibility on student affairs to develop assessment programs which measure the extent to which these overarching institutional goals are being met.

For student affairs, variations on these questions are being asked and new ones posed, both from outside and inside of student affairs. Perhaps the most important of all is this basic question: In an era of declining resources, are student services and programs really necessary? As resources decline and pressures for accountability increase, there is a natural tendency for institutions to reallocate resources to its academic priorities, allocations which are most often narrowly interpreted as support for the faculty, the classroom, the formal curriculum, and those support services that are *clearly* academically related, such as learning support centers and academic advising.

Unfortunately, this narrow academic focus ignores the substantial evidence that the out-of-class environment is an important factor in learning, development, academic achievement, and retention. Also ignored is the substantial evidence that student use of student services, programs, and facilities enhances such outcomes, which are usually interpreted as strictly academic. In short, the fact of student learning and development outside the classroom is not understood among decision makers and seldom taken into account when decisions are made to reallocate resources to narrowly defined academic priorities.

For example, when reviewing the many studies that identify the factors required for persistence and degree completion, Pascarella and Terenzini (1991) concluded that one's level of integration into an institution's social system has significant implications for educational attainment. For example, both involvement in extracurricular activities and the extent and quality of one's social interaction with student peers and faculty have a positive influence on degree attainment, educational aspirations, and graduate school attendance. Living on campus rather than commuting has a strong positive effect on persistence and degree completion, particularly in living-and-learning residence halls, where students' academic and social life are programmatically linked. Participation in orientation programs and freshman seminars have also been positively linked to persistence and degree completion.

Upcraft (1985) reviewed other studies which showed that belonging to student organizations, involvement in social and cultural activities, attending lectures, using campus facilities, and general participation in extracurricular activities are all activities which enhance retention. There is also evidence that the availability and use of student personnel and counseling services is positively related to graduation rates (Hedlund and Jones, 1970).

In spite of this very conclusive evidence, there are strong indications that "student services have borne the brunt of budget cuts. . . . For college administrator, it was a Hobson's choice: to shield academic programs from severe cuts, all other budget categories had to suffer a disproportionate share of reductions" (Cage, 1992, p. A25). Examples include substantial cuts in student activities and support for student government, reduction in career and psychological counseling staff, and outright elimination of programs and services considered less essential, such as legal counseling. In addition, some student services have survived only by initiating fees for such services as placement, health services, student activities, and counseling (Cage, 1992). Another trend is to eliminate selected services and programs, on the assumption that student needs can be met by off-campus and community services. In other words, substantial evidence underscores the contribution of student services and programs to persistence and degree attainment, but that evidence, to date, appears to have had little impact on resource allocations.

As a result, student affairs must respond not only to the more global pressures of accountability, cost, quality, access, and equity but also to internal pressure to justify allocation of resources to program and services that appear to be "nonacademic" and therefore "less essential" to the educational enterprise. Student affairs needs to demonstrate its central role in the academic success of students, and the potentially detrimental effect if student services and programs are curtailed, eliminated, offered differentially depending upon one's ability to pay, or handed off to community agencies which may or may not be prepared to handle students' demands.

Thus, demonstrating the importance of student affairs to the educational enterprise starts with the rationale for our existence. Unfortunately, student affairs is somewhat divided on this point. One view is probably best represented by the National Association of Student Personnel Administrators (NASPA)'s *Perspective on Student Affairs* (1987), in which the first assumption identified is that the academic mission of an institution is preeminent: "Colleges and universities organize their primary activities around the academic experience: the curriculum, the library, the classroom, and the laboratory. The work of student affairs should not compete with and cannot substitute for that academic enterprise. As a partner in the educational enterprise, student affairs enhances and supports the academic mission" (pp. 9–10). In other words, everything we do must somehow contribute to the academic mission of the institution, most often defined as students' academic achievement and retention.

A second perspective is best described as promoting student development. That is, there are certain developmental goals (such as psychosocial development, attitudes and values formation, moral development, and career choice and development) which are related to, but somewhat apart from, academic goals (such as verbal, quantitative, and subject matter competence, and cognitive and intellectual growth). In this view, student affairs assumes the primary responsibility for the achievement of developmental goals, while faculty assume the primary responsibility for the achievement of academic goals. Thus, everything we do in this scenario must somehow contribute to students' development.

The debate over the basic purposes of student affairs has been reignited recently by two very important publications. The first, a position paper developed by the American College Personnel Association titled *The Student Learning Imperative* (1994) argues for a refocusing of the basic mission of student affairs toward the concept of "student learning." We must be concerned not only about affective development and the out-of-class environment but also about cognitive development, both in and out of class. According to this document, "Student Affairs professionals must seize the present moment by affirming student learning and personal development as the primary goals of undergraduate education" (p. 4).

A recent publication goes even further. Bloland, Stamatakos, and Rogers (1994) argue that the uncritical adoption of 'student development' in the 1970s is too narrowly focused on psychosocial development, shifting the role of student affairs away from educating the "whole student." They argue that the mission of higher education consists of learning "not only substantive facts but also values, ethics, an informed way of life and occupational identity, personal and occupational skills— the list goes on—but the focus [should be] on what is learned, not what is developed" (p. 101). On the other hand, the recommended role of student affairs should be more than simply the support of the academic mission of the institution; it should support its educational mission as well.

To complicate matters even further, a third perspective holds that although academic and developmental outcomes are important, other equally important institutional and societal expectations must be addressed first. Providing basic services such as housing and financial aid is absolutely vital to the institution, as opposed to any educational or developmental outcome for which a student affairs office may aim. Students need a place to live, and we assume varying degrees of responsibility in helping them do that, not necessarily because of their educational or developmental interests, but because students will not be able to attend the institution if they do not have affordable, accessible, and livable housing.

Of course, in reality, we do all three: our services and programs contribute to both academic and developmental goals of students and provide basic services to students and other clientele. But it is also true that in an era of declining resources, it is much easier to defend student affairs' contributions to the academic mission of our institutions, or to students' and others' basic physical and financial needs, than to justify our existence strictly on the basis of our contribution to students' developmental goals. Put another way, faculty and upper-level management are more likely to support student affairs services and programs which contribute to academic outcomes such as academic achievement, cognitive development, and retention or provide effective basic services such as financial aid and housing than any contributions they might offer toward meeting developmental goals for students, goals which are somewhat "softer," perhaps less valued, and certainly more difficult to define, achieve, and assess.

By now, our bias should be clear. We believe the primary purpose of student affairs is to contribute to the academic enterprise and to meet the institution's need for basic services. We see student development as a legitimate but less important purpose of student affairs, viable only to the extent that it contributes to students' academic goals. And we see assessment as a way of making the connection between what we do, and how we contribute to the academic mission of our institutions and other institutional expectations. For example, through an assessment study we may find that students increase their interpersonal skills as a result of living in residence halls. That outcome may be important, but it will not do much to justify resource allocation for residence halls. Rather, we should attempt to show that there is a relationship between living in residence halls and such outcome variables as students' academic achievement and retention, or student decisions to select the institution in the first place, live in residence halls in the second place, and return to residence halls in subsequent years. Both of these outcomes (academic success and decisions to live in residence halls) may well be a function of how well students develop interpersonal skills, as well as creating interpersonally supportive residential environments, but it would not be effective to justify residence halls solely on the basis of the development of interpersonal skills; it is more feasible to encourage funding of residence halls on the evidence that the residence hall experience contributes positively to the academic success of students, or to their decision to attend an institution, live in residence halls once they enroll, or return to them in subsequent years.

Without assessment, student affairs is left only to logic, institution, moral imperatives, goodwill, or serendipity in justifying its existence. To be sure, even the most comprehensive and highest-quality assessment is no guarantee that student affairs will survive, but it will go a long way toward making the argument of the importance of student affairs to students and to the institution.

A Matter of Quality

There are many other reasons, besides our survival, why we should have a commitment in student affairs to do assessment. Let's assume that the basic question of the value of student affairs to the institution has been answered affirmatively. There remain many other questions to consider. Even if it is demonstrated that student services, programs , and facilities are essential and needed, a second question is, are they of high quality? To be sure, quality is a somewhat illusive concept, subject to many definitions, depending on who is doing the defining. Generally speaking, high quality requires one to compare one's work against some predetermined standard, which may be absolutely defined (comparing oneself to the Council for the Advancement of Standards in Higher Education or other professional standards or normatively defined (comparing oneself to comparable organizations.

But regardless of the definitions, questions of quality must be asked: Do we have high-quality programs, services, and facilities? How do we define quality, particularly when these definitions will vary from institution to institution, and even among departments within student affairs? What evidence do we have of quality, once properly defined, and what criteria are used to measure it? How do we know if we have improved quality? Assessment is a very important way of linking goals to outcomes, helping define quality, and determining if quality exists in student affairs. It is a fundamental responsibility of student affairs to provide services, programs, and facilities that are of high quality, however quality might be defined and for whomever.

A Matter of Affordability

Another reason for assessment in student affairs is to gauge affordability and cost-effectiveness. The question to be faced goes something like this: "Sure, this program or that service is needed, and there is evidence of their quality, but in an era of declining resources, can we afford them? Can we continue to fund them at current levels?" For example, let's assume that, based on an assessment of student needs, there is abundant evidence that someone should be available to give students legal advice. Let's further assume that, based on a customer satisfaction survey, there is also abundant evidence that legal clients are being very well served by the legal counselor. But let's also say that because this service is offered free of charge to students, it is exorbitantly expensive to the institution, particularly when compared to other student services and the number of students served. What then? A cost-benefit study may well help us decide what to do. It may be that the service is too costly, resulting in a discussion of ways to maintain the service at reduced levels, keep it alive using other resources (such as charging students fees for visits), or eliminate it altogether.

A Matter of Strategic Planning

A fourth reason for developing a comprehensive assessment program is for strategic planning. According to Baldridge (1983), "Strategic planning examines the big issues—the organization's purpose, its mission, its relationship to its environment, its share of the market, its interactions with other organizations. Strategic planning is not concerned with nuts-and-bolts issues. . . . [It] asks the basic questions of institutional health and survival" (p. 175). Assessment contributes to strategic planning by helping define goals and objectives, pointing to critical issues or problems that must be resolved successfully if the organization is to achieve its goals, providing baseline data so that student programs and policies can respond appropriately to students' needs, providing essential feedback about the effectiveness of long-range plans, and pointing to areas where plans must be modified to achieve goals. Assessment is especially important in the early phases of strategic planning, to identify strengths, weaknesses, and opportunities for the future; it is also important in the later stages of planning, when evaluation is important (Jacobi, Astin, and Ayala, 1987).

Assessment, then, can help us decide what we do, as well as how well we do it. For example, let's return to the issue of determining whether or not to continue to offer legal counseling to students. There are several ways assessment can help us make that decision. Is there evidence that legal counseling is a high-priority need for students? Is there evidence that sufficient numbers of students, representing the spectrum of students, use the legal counseling service? Is there evidence that legal counseling is done in a high-quality way? Is there evidence that students who use this service are satisfied with it? What would be the cost of improving this service? All these questions are best answered through systematic assessment, rather than sporadic anecdotal accounts, intuition, piecemeal bits of unrelated information, or no information at all.

A Matter of Policy Development and Decision Making

A fifth question, indirectly related to student services, programs, facilities, is likewise very important: Do we have evidence to support this decision or policy? For example, on what basis did we decide to include sexual orientation in the institution's nondiscrimination clause? What evidence did we cite in the establishment of a center for women students on the campus? Was the decision to rescind our "hate speech" policy based on solid evidence? How do we decide who shall live in on-campus residence halls? And perhaps most important, on what basis do we decide to allocate resources? Thus, policies and decisions, if they are to be developed in a systematic and cogent way, must be driven at least in part by assessment results.

A Matter of Politics

A sixth reason for doing assessment is a practical one, sometimes not related to any of the other questions asked. We do it because someone or some institution of importance wants some information, which makes it politically important to produce. It is part of the "political evaluation" defined later in this chapter. For example, a state legislator, in response to a constituent who thinks residence hall fees are too high, may want to know how many RAs we have, what they do, what they are paid, and how we know they are doing a good job. While this information may be important for a variety of other reasons, we may not have chosen to assess this issue because it was less important than others. So we have to run off and get this information to satisfy a person who might well be very important to the funding or even survival of student affairs.

So there are many reasons why assessment is important for student affairs, including helping to develop a rationale for student affairs, determining and improving the quality of student affairs, analyzing and determining affordability, developing strategic plans, assisting in policy development and decision making, and dealing with political pressures and realities. The questions we are being asked are best answered when we can base them on a comprehensive assessment program. We in student affairs can no longer presume that our jobs are important and effective simply because we think they are or because we've always done them or even because we're doing the right thing. There must be evidence gathered from a comprehensive assessment program to answer these questions.

One more very important issue needs to be addressed at this point. Even if nationally based studies show the importance or effectiveness of student affairs, these studies may not be that important if they are not campus-specific. Tip O'Neill, the late speaker of the House of Representatives, once was reported to have said, "All politics is local." To paraphrase Tip, we believe that "all assessment is local." If our residence halls are unruly and do not contribute to the educational mission of our institution, then all the evidence of the general positive effect of residence halls will not make a difference if we don't have the evidence that good things are happening in *our* residence halls. If our counseling center has no evidence of its effectiveness, even if it is effective, then protecting our counseling centers from resource reductions, or elimination altogether, will be very difficult. If our campus alcohol prevention programs have no evidence of their impact on student knowledge, attitudes, and behaviors, even though there may be some studies reported in the literature which demonstrate such effects, then questions should and will be raised as to whether or not these programs should be continued.

Some Basic Definitions

Before we get too far into the assessment issue, we must provide a common language, because one of the causes of confusion about assessment is terminology. Some terms are used interchangeably ("assessment" and "evaluation"), some phrases are used incorrectly ("statistics show . . ."), and some terms are so vague as to strip them of any commonly accepted meaning ("quality" or "excellence"). So our discussion of assessment in student affairs must be prefaced by developing a common vocabulary.

Let's start with defining the term *assessment*. There are many definitions in the assessment and evaluation literature. One reason for this confusion is whether assessment involves simply gathering data, or if it also includes interpretation and analysis. For example, Astin (1991) defines assessment as "the gathering of information concerning the functioning of students, staff, and institutions of higher education" (p. 2). Others, notably Lenning (1988), would disagree, asserting that assessment involves more than just gathering information. "Assessment refers to gathering *evidence:* gathering data, transforming data so that they can be interpreted, applying analytical techniques, and analyzing data in terms of alternative hypotheses and explanations" (p. 328).

Another conflict regarding assessment is the purpose of assessment. Most would agree one purpose of assessment is the improvement of something, although there is wide disagreement over what it might improve. For example, mainstream academic assessment experts would restrict the term assessment to refer to only those efforts which demonstrate improvement in student learning (Hutchings, and others, 1993; Terenzini, 1989). Others consider this definition too restrictive. For example, Banta (1988) defines assessment as "collecting evidence of (1) student performance on specified measures of development, (2) program strengths and weaknesses, and (3) institutional effectiveness" (p. 1). She argues that we should assess not only what students and graduates know, but what they are able to do with their knowledge, as well as their perceptions of the quality of institutional programs and services. Ewell (1988) agrees, for example, that student survey information can be particularly helpful in gaining broad insights into student perceptions.

But restricting assessment exclusively to student learning and perceptions is also debatable. Institutions of higher education have clientele other than students, and the perceptions of those people are also important. Astin (1991) believes the basic motive for assessment is the functioning of students, staff, and institutions not only for the purposes of student learning, but also for higher education's contribution to knowledge and to the greater society it serves. We prefer an approach which consciously adopts a broad definition of assessment, one that includes and also reaches beyond the collection and analysis of evidence about effectiveness to include *all* parts of the institution. Thus, although evidence for the quality of student learning is a major concern—in general education, for example, and in one's major or professional training—so, too, is evidence of the institution's success in such areas as the cocurricular program and an ethnically diverse campus community.

So what do we make of all these conflicting expert opinions? We can only make an admittedly arbitrary but, we hope, reasoned judgment. Therefore, for the purpose of this book, *assessment is any effort to gather, analyze, and interpret evidence which describes institutional, departmental, divisional, or agency effectiveness.* Effectiveness includes not only assessing student learning outcomes, but assessing other important outcomes as well (cost-effectiveness, clientele satisfaction, meeting clientele needs) for other constituents within the institution (the faculty, administration, governing boards) and outside the institution (alumni, legislators, funding agencies, accreditation agencies).

One further clarification: for the purposes of this book we are not particularly interested in assessing an individual student or other individual clientele outcomes. For example, this book will not cover how to assess an individual for the purposes of deciding his or her admission to an institution, or how to conduct a psychological screening of a potential client in a counseling center. We are interested in these assessments *in the aggregate*. That is, while we may not want information about how an individual prospective student is assessed, we may want to know if, in the aggregate, the students we assess actually persist and graduate. In the context of this book, we may not want information about an individual counseling client, but we may want to know if, in the aggregate, the information gathered in the screening process is actually helpful, on average, in the subsequent therapeutic process.

This definition of assessment is very broad. As will be seen in subsequent chapters, assessment by this definition ranges all the way from keeping track of who uses our services, programs, and facilities to whether or not such offerings have any impact, or the desired impact, on our clientele. It includes student needs assessments, environmental assessments, comparisons to accepted standards or other institutions, and clientele satisfaction with what we offer.

Assessment, however, must be contrasted with but also linked to *evaluation*. Here there is much greater agreement among the experts. Astin (1991) defines evaluation as the utilization of information for institutional and individual improvement. He believes that "there is a fundamental distinction . . . between the information we gather and the uses to which it is put, and that we often forget this distinction when we talk about assessment in higher education. Evaluation . . . has to do with motivation and the rendering of value judgments" (p. 2). Others agree. Ewell (1988) argues that assessment results should be used to make appropriate changes in instruction and support services, and to set the context for an entire range of decisions, from academic advising to the structure of student housing units. He also believes assessment information can be useful in selling a decision once it has been made.

Here again, for the purposes of this book, our arbitrary but reasoned judgment is that *evaluation is any effort to use assessment evidence to improve institutional, departmental, divisional, or agency effectiveness*. While assessment describes effectiveness, evaluation uses these descriptions in order to improve effectiveness, however that might be defined by an institution, department, division, or agency. For example, determining whether or not our admissions criteria predict subsequent persistence and degree completion is assessment. Using that assessment as a rationale for changing admissions criteria is evaluation. Likewise, determining whether or not the information gathered in psychological screening of clients is useful in subsequent therapy is assessment. Using that assessment as a rationale for changing the screening process, or eliminating it altogether, is evaluation.

Having defined evaluation in a general sense leads us to more precise definitions of various types of evaluation. Scriven (1967) was the first to distinguish between *formative* evaluation and *summative* evaluation. Simply put, formative evaluations are those used to improve organizational or institutional effectiveness. Formative evaluations typically focus on improving the processes which potentially lead to increased effectiveness. The admissions and counseling examples used above were clearly formative evaluations, because assessment results were used to improve effectiveness through the improvement of processes. Formative evaluations may also be used to help solve problems and to enhance decision making directed toward improvement.

Summative evaluations are used to determine if a particular organizational activity or function should be continued, enhanced, curtailed, or eliminated. In other words, summative evaluations are conducted for purposes of accountability and strategic planning. In the psychological counseling example, let's suppose that the improvement of the psychological screening process requires more funding because it involves hiring more qualified staff, developing more sophisticated psychometric techniques, and purchasing more computer hardware. Someone may decide that additional resources will be allocated, and the program enhanced. This would be a summative evaluation. On the other hand, someone may decide that such improvements are prohibitively expensive, and that if we can't do screening in a quality and cost-effective way, we shouldn't do it at all. Either we connect prospective clients to therapists without any screening, or eliminate counseling altogether. These evaluations are also summative, but with quite different outcomes.

To these two forms of evaluation Brown and Podolske (1993a) add a third: *political* evaluation, which they define as evaluation that is used to communicate and defend student affairs to potential stakeholders, including professional staff, office staff, faculty, administrators, parents, taxpayers, and funders. To these stakeholders we would add boards of control, state legislators, and the general public (in the instance of public institutions), graduates, foundations, and, of course, the ever-present federal government with its vast array of legislation and regulations. Again, using the admissions example above, a state legislature concerned about admissions standards may require minimum scores on standardized admissions tests for the funding of certain institutions. In this instance, a cutoff score would be established for political rather than summative or formative reasons.

Two other terms also need to be defined: quantitative and qualitative methodologies. *Quantitative methodology* is the assignment of numbers to objects, events, or observations according to some rule (Rossman and El-Khawas, 1987). According to Borg and Gall (1989), "Quantitative researchers attempt to keep themselves from influencing the collection of data. Instruments with established psychometric properties . . . are used to collect data. Statistical methods are used to analyze data and draw conclusions. In other words, quantitative researchers attempt to be objective, meaning that they wish to develop an understanding of the world as it is 'out there,' independent of their personal biases, values, and Idiosyncratic notions" (p. 23). Again, rising the admissions example, the ability to predict college success might involve gathering all the quantifiable data about those variables that are thought to influence persistence and degree completion, such as high school grades, scores on standardized aptitude tests, involvement in high school activities, parents' education and income, etc. These data might then be correlated with subsequent student behavior (dropping out or persisting) to determine which ones, and in which combination, best predict college success.

On the other hand, *qualitative methodology* is the detailed description of situations, events, people, interactions, and observed behaviors; the use of direct quotations from people about their experiences, attitudes, beliefs, and thoughts; and the analysis of excerpts or entire passages from documents, correspondence, records, and case histories (Patton, 1990). According to Borg and Gall (1989), "Qualitative researchers view themselves as a primary instrument for collecting data. They rely partly or entirely on their feelings, impressions, and judgments in collecting data . . . and using their own interpretations in understanding the meaning of data" (p. 23). Using the admissions example, instead of (or in addition to) analyzing some numerical data, admissions personnel might want to interview students who persisted and those who dropped out to determine the extent to which their backgrounds and experiences might have contributed to their success or lack thereof. Variables that seem to predict college success but are difficult to measure (motivation), might be better understood through qualitative measurements.

Another definition is worth mentioning, although it will not be a focus of this book. The term is *research*. In the 1960s and 1970s, it was fashionable to use the term "student affairs research" to refer to assessment and evaluation efforts. The term proved to be confusing, particularly to faculty, who had a much narrower definition of research. When comparing research and assessment, Erwin (1991) argues that although they share many processes in common, they differ at least in two respects. First, assessment guides good practice, while research guides theory and conceptual foundations. Second, assessment typically has implications for a single institution, while research typically has broader implications for student affairs and higher education.

Definitions of other important terms will be introduced as necessary in subsequent chapters. To review, assessment is the gathering, interpreting, and analyzing of evidence of effectiveness, while evaluation is how assessment results are used to improve effectiveness, however that may be defined. We can gather information through qualitative or quantitative methodologies, and we can use assessment results to evaluate student affairs by providing a rationale for our existence, improving quality, determining affordability and guiding policy development and decision making. Assessment can also be used for strategic planning, helping administrators decide, for example, whether or not a particular student service, program, or facility should be enhanced, curtailed, or eliminated. And finally, assessment can meet the demands of those persons and institutions that have influence over what we do.

Principles of Good Practice for Assessment

Before we move to the more specific issues of the assessment process and a model of student affairs assessment, we should consider some general principles of good practice for assessment. In 1991, the American Association of Higher Education Assessment Forum invited twelve practitioners and students of assessment to develop common principles behind good practice for assessing student learning (Hutchings and others, 1993). Although these principles were developed with a focus on assessing student learning, with some adaptation they apply equally well to the assessment of student affairs.

1. *The assessment of student affairs begins with educational values.* Assessment is not an end in itself but a vehicle for organizational effectiveness. Its effective practice, then, begins with and enacts a vision of student affairs we most value. These values should drive not only *what* we choose to assess, but also *how* we do so. When questions about the organizational mission and values are skipped over, assessment threatens to be an exercise in measuring what's easy rather than what is needed.

2. *Assessment is most effective when it reflects an understanding of organizational outcomes as multidimensional, integrated, and revealed in performance over time.* Assessing student affairs is a complex process. It entails supporting the rationale for student affairs, developing evidence of quality and affordability, informing policy development and decision making, guiding strategic planning, and dealing with political realities. Assessment should employ a diverse array of methods, including both quantitative and qualitative approaches. Such an approach aims for a more complete and accurate picture of the effectiveness of student affairs.

3. *Assessment works best when it has clear, explicitly stated goals.* Assessment is a goal-oriented process. It entails comparing intended purposes and expectations derived from the institution's mission, and from the stated purposes and goals of the student affairs. Where student affairs lacks specificity of agreement, assessment as a process pushes student affairs toward clarity about where to aim and which standards to apply; it also prompts attention to where and how organizational goals will be offered and implemented. Clear, shared, implementable goals are the cornerstone for assessment that is focused and useful.

4. *Assessment requires attention to outcomes but also, and just as important, to the processes that lead to them.* Information about outcomes is of high importance, but to improve outcomes, we need to know about the processes that lead to particular outcomes— counseling, advising, educational programming, budgeting, etc. Assessment can help us understand what processes work best under what conditions; with such knowledge comes the capacity to improve the whole organization.

5. *Assessment works best when it is ongoing, not episodic.* Assessment is a process whose power is cumulative. Although an isolated, "one shot" assessment can be better than none, student affairs is best served when assessment entails a linked series of activities undertaken over time. This means tracking the progress of student units or the whole student affairs unit or the whole student affairs organization; it may mean collecting some examples of assessment studies or using the same methods year after year. The point is to monitor progress toward intended goals with the intention of enhancing organizational effectiveness. Along the way, the assessment process itself should be evaluated and refined in light of emerging insights.

6. *Assessment is most effective when representatives from across student affairs and the institution are involved.* Assessment is a way of enacting the many responsibilities of student affairs and the institution. Thus, while assessment efforts may start on a small scale, the aim over time is to involve all people whose interests may be affected by assessment. Student affairs staff play an especially important role, but

assessment's questions cannot be fully addressed without participation by students, student affairs leadership, and others in the educational community. Assessment may also involve individuals from the institution as well as those outside it (graduates, trustees, employers), whose experience can enrich the sense of appropriate aims and standards for organizational effectiveness. Thus understood, assessment is not a task for small groups of experts, but rather a collaborative activity; its aim is wiser, better-informed attention to organizational effectiveness by all parties who have a stake in the organization.

7. *Assessment makes a difference when it begins with issues of use and illuminates questions that people really care about.* Assessment recognizes the value of information in the process of improving student affairs. But to be useful, the information must be connected to issues or questions that people really care about. This implies assessment approaches that produce evidence that the relevant parties will find credible, suggestive, and applicable to the decisions they must make. It means thinking in advance about how the information will be used, and by whom. The point of assessment is not to gather data and return "results"; it is a *process* that starts with the questions of decision makers, that involves them in gathering and interpreting data, and that informs and helps steer the decision makers toward organizational effectiveness.

8. *Assessment should be part of a larger set of conditions that promote change.* By itself, assessment changes little. Its greatest contribution comes on campuses where student affairs is visibly valued and worked at. On such campuses, the push to improve student affairs is a visible and primary goal of leadership; improving student affairs is central to establishing the rationale for student affairs, as well as its quality, affordability, strategic planning, and policy development and decision making.

9. *Through assessment, student affairs professionals meet responsibilities of students, the institution, and the public.* There is a compelling student, institutional, and public stake in assessment. As student affairs professionals, we have responsibilities to the stakeholders who support or depend upon us to provide information about the ways in which our organization meets its goals and expectations. But that responsibility goes beyond reporting such information; our deeper obligation—to ourselves, our students, our institution, and our society—is to provide a high-quality student affairs program. Those to whom educators are accountable have a corresponding obligation to support such attempts at quality enhancement.

The Assessment Process: Some Important Questions

If, as pointed out in the beginning of this chapter, the assessment process does not begin with selecting an instrument, where does it begin? And where does it end? Drawing on the writings of Terenzini (1989), Hanson (1982), Brown and Podolske (1993a), Erwin (1991), and others, we have formulated six basic questions which help define the assessment process, and should be asked *before* the assessment is begun.

1. *Why are we doing this assessment?* What is its basic purpose? Why do we need information in the first place? Are we looking to improve a service? Are we trying to justify the existence of a program? Do we need information to help us make a decision or formulate a policy? Do we need information to satisfy one or more of our clientele? Are we in a crisis where we need some information, and need it fast? Do we need information to determine budget priorities? Or the answer to why we are doing this assessment may be some or all of the above. Answering this "why" question determines in large part the answers to all of the subsequent questions.

2. *What will we assess?* With the "why" question answered, the "what" question must be posted. What information is to be gathered? We may need information about who uses our services, programs, and facilities. We may need information which describes the quality of services, programs, and facilities, or assesses affordability, or guides policy development, decision making, or strategic planning.

3. *How will we assess?* With the "why" and "what" questions answered, the "how" question arises. What methodologies will we use to gather the information we need? Qualitative, quantitative, or both? What will be the source(s) of information? Institutional records? Data collected directly from clientele? Unobtrusive measures? What designs are appropriate to our purposes and what we need to know?

4. *Who will assess?* Here there is always a lot of controversy. Some would argue that those closest to the situation should conduct the assessments and determine their meaning. Others would suggest that assessment, to be objective, should be done by those outside the particular service, program, or facility, but inside student affairs. Still others would suggest that, for complete objectivity, assessment should be done by those outside student affairs, or even outside the institution. All would agree, however, that those who conduct the assessment should be qualified to do so, regardless of their place inside or outside the institution.

5. *How will the results be analyzed?* In other words, how will the information gathered be analyzed and interpreted? Information, in and of itself, tells us very little. The interpretation and analysis of data, however, does tell us something, and we need to give careful consideration to this process. What does a specific piece of information mean? How do specific pieces of information fit together? What is the context within which the information is being interpreted?

6. *How will the results be communicated and to whom?* These two questions are very much interrelated, because the plan for communicating assessment results will be determined, in part, by the target audiences for whom the assessment is intended. We recommend multiple formats for various internal and external audiences when reporting results, rather than one comprehensive report for all intended readers. A typical report, regardless of the length and intended audience, should include an executive summary, the purpose, design, and results of the study, and any recommendations the investigators have to offer. The timing of communicating results is also very important and must be considered.

To summarize, it is important to ask these questions for every assessment study *before* it is done, and the answers must be communicated to all those who may be involved in or influenced by the assessment. To do anything less compromises the assessment process, not to mention the ethics of assessment.

Using Assessment Results: Evaluation

So the vice president for student affairs has just received an assessment report on how participants assessed the educational programs conducted by the health education office. It was a very good assessment, taking into account all of the components identified in the previous section. The conclusion reached was that while students know about these programs, they attend them very sparingly, and those who do attend are mostly white females. What now? How will this report be used? What is the process by which the results are applied to the organization? Who will determine how these results will be used? In other words, are these results to be used for *formative* reasons, *summative* reasons, *political* reasons, or one or more of the above?

These are very important questions because how the results will be used (how these educational programs are evaluated) may be critical in gaining the cooperation of those who might be affected. Nothing creates more resistance from students and staff than the suspicion that assessment results will be used to "get" an individual, program, or service. *How assessment results will be used is very important and must be clearly stated before an assessment study is begun.* It is also very important to involve those who will be affected from the very beginning of the assessment process.

There is, however, a very perplexing problem with regard to the use of assessment studies. Sometimes it is difficult to limit a particular assessment to its original purpose(s). That is, while we may gather certain data for the expressed purpose of quality improvement (formative evaluation), once the information is out, it may be used by "unfriendly critics" as ammunition to reduce or eliminate a program, service, or facility (summative evaluation). Likewise, one never knows when formative evaluations will be used by other important clientele for political purposes. In this sense, in spite of good intentions, one can never really be sure that a particular assessment will be used exclusively for formative evaluations.

A Comprehensive Assessment Model

So, all of these issues must be addressed. But how? What are the components of a comprehensive model of assessment, how are they defined, and why are they important? The reader will find elements of this model in virtually all the examples presented in this book, though at times packaged slightly differently!

The first component of a comprehensive student affairs assessment is *keeping track of who uses student services, programs, and facilities.* How many clients use services, programs, and facilities, and how are they described by gender, race, ethnicity, age, class standing, residence, and other demographic variables? Are there clients other than students who must be counted and described?

This component is very important because if our intended clientele do not use our services, programs, or facilities, then our intended purposes cannot be achieved. The first thing to consider is numbers; if too few of our intended clientele use our services, programs, and facilities, then we have a problem. For example, if very few students attend our alcohol education programs, we must reassess what we are doing and why. If we have a problem filling our residence halls, we must reassess what we are doing and why.

However, sheer numbers do not tell us the whole story. Even if programs, services, and facilities are well used in terms of critical numbers, the users or participants must be representative of our student population. For example, a few years ago a health center at a major university discovered that while the total number of patients seen was reasonable, a closer analysis revealed that virtually no African American students were using the health service, in spite of the fact that African American students represented 6 percent of the student population. This assessment result was then used as a basis for reassessing the services and programs offered, and marketing them specifically to African American students. Within two years, African American students were not only using health services in proportion to their representation in the student population, but in some instances their use of the facility exceeded that proportion. Similar analyses might be made by gender, class standing, place of residence, age, and other demographic variables.

The second component of this model is *the assessment of student and other clientele needs.* The basic principle that we should meet the needs of our clientele is a good one, and well supported in the literature. For example, much of the thrust of various "total quality" efforts focus on "customer" needs as the main ingredient in quality improvement (Deming, 1986). While describing students and other users of our services as "customers" is offensive to some educators, it is a good idea to abide by the basic principle that whatever services, programs, and facilities we offer must meet the needs of our clientele.

Assessing the needs of student and other clientele is not easy, and there are many questions to be answered. What kinds of services, programs, and facilities do students and other clientele need, based on student and staff perceptions, institutional expectations, and research on student needs? How do we distinguish between clientele "wants" and "needs." What are the ways of determining if the services, programs, and facilities we offer "fit" with our clientele? Are some of our offerings obsolete? Are additional or different kinds of services, programs, and facilities needed?

The third component of this assessment model is *clientele satisfaction.* Of those persons who use student services, programs, and facilities, what is their level of satisfaction? What strengths, weaknesses, and suggestions for improvement do they identify? Would they come back? Would they recommend us to a friend? Clientele satisfaction is important for obvious reasons: if they are not satisfied, they won't use the service, program, or facility again, and they will not recommend them to friends and colleagues. Getting clientele to use what we offer is the first step; providing what we offer in ways that satisfy our clientele is the second step, and we must be able to assess their level of satisfaction.

The fourth component is *assessing campus environments and student cultures*. While assessing individual use, needs, and satisfaction is important, it is also important to take a look at their collective perceptions of campus environments and student cultures within which they conduct their day-to-day lives.

The fifth component of this comprehensive assessment model is *assessing outcomes*. Of those persons who use our services, programs, and facilities, is there any effect on their learning, development, academic success, or other intended outcomes, particularly when compared with nonusers? Can programmatic interventions be isolated from other variables which may influence outcomes, such as background, characteristics, and other experiences? These kinds of studies are very difficult to design, implement, and interpret, but in some ways they attempt to answer the most fundamental question of all: Is what you are doing having any effect, and is that effect the intended one?

The sixth component is *comparable institutions assessment*: How does the quality of services, programs, and facilities compare with "best in class" comparable institutions? Again, the "total quality" literature (Deming, 1986) would support the notion that one important way of assessing quality is to compare oneself to other institutions which appear to be doing a better job with a particular service, program, or facility. One purpose would be to discover how others achieve their results, and then to translate their processes to one's own environment. The key to this assessment component is to select comparable institutions which have good assessment programs, rather than going by anecdotal or reputational evidence. Also, one must select comparable institutions with great care, because institutions vary greatly, and selecting the wrong institutions could result in "apples and oranges" comparisons.

The final component of this model is *using nationally accepted standards to assess*. How do our services, programs, and facilities compare to accepted national standards, such as those developed by the Council for the Advancement of Standards for Student Services/Development Programs, various national and regional accrediting agencies, and professional organizations?

Conclusion

There are many reasons why assessment is important to both higher education and to student affairs. Institutions must respond to both internal and external pressures to improve what we are doing, and to demonstrate that what we do is what we say we do.

External pressures from legislatures, funding agencies, accreditation agencies, and the general public, among others, have moved assessment from an option to a necessity. It is clear that higher education must be more accountable for its accessibility, cost-effectiveness, quality, and results.

As part of the educational enterprise, student affairs must also respond to these pressures and others. Internally, questions about whether or not student affairs should exist or not are being raised, along with questions about affordability, quality, and effectiveness. Assessment can provide some of the answers to these questions, as well as support strategic planning and policy development and decision making. Assessment can also provide some of the answers in dealing with political realities and institutional expectations.

It is our contention that we do this by following good assessment practices, asking the right questions before we do assessment, and using a comprehensive assessment model that includes keeping track of who uses what we offer, determining how satisfied they are with what we offer, determining if what we offer meets their needs and has an impact, gathering their collective perceptions of their environments and cultures, and comparing how well we do with other comparable institutions and accepted national standards.

The Case for Flexibility in Research and Assessment of College Students

FRANCES K. STAGE

As we move toward the beginning of a new century, it is important that our visions of higher education, reflected in research and assessment of the college campus, move with us. Many of those who seek to understand and describe the campus environment present a limited vision of the world. By conditioning or by habit, they turn to the surveys, standardized instruments, and structured interviews despite an abundance of useful, creative, and eye-opening research techniques. This chapter focuses on the limitations of relying on only a few ways of collecting information, and provides a justification for learning new and creative ways to increase our knowledge of college and university students and the student experience. The chapter also provides a brief introduction to some issues of research design and basic definitions as well as suggestions for further reading.

The Literature to Date

Research on college and university students has been conducted extensively throughout the 20th century (Blandin, 1909; Greenleaf, 1952; Minnesota University, 1924; Olin, 1909), and it has shown a remarkable evolution in terms of quantitative methodological sophistication. The earliest studies reported percentages or examined simple correlations of one factor with another (Cooper, 1928; Cummings, 1949; Iffert, 1958). Gradually authors moved to speculations about conceptual relationships and, eventually, to attempts at explanation of those relationships (Bean & Metzner, 1985; Pascarella, Ethington, & Smart, 1988; Terenzini & Wright, 1987; Tinto, 1975). Currently, some authors urge researchers to move beyond explanation of what is happening today and focus research toward attempts to influence future possibilities (e.g., Gage, 1989; Stage, 1990; Stage & Kuh, 1992). This perspective, critical theory, may be helpful to those seeking new ways to gather data on their campuses and to effect change in those environments.

Despite this evolution in the ways that quantitative data are analyzed, changes to approaches to data collection do not evolve as readily. Many of those who currently practice in the field of student affairs have only superficial knowledge of the various techniques that may be used to collect data on college and university students. Thus they understandably limit themselves in approaching data collection (typically a standardized questionnaire, locally designed survey, or structured interview) despite the benefits of using other methods. Further, because of this lack of knowledge, they may be uncomfortable reading research that employs alternative techniques.

With the development of the assessment movement in the United States has come an attendant dissatisfaction with traditional, standardized measures of student growth and development in higher education institutions (Banta, Lambert, Pike, Schmidhammer, & Schneider, 1987; Ewell, 1988; Terenzini, 1989). The earliest assessments of campus outcomes were based on research on student outcomes and persistence. Such assessments were viewed as "action research" conducted by institutional research offices (Ewell, 1988). Today, there are powerful instruments such as Pace's (1984) College Student Experiences Questionnaire (CSEQ), the ACT College Outcomes Measures Project (COMP), and the Educational Testing Service's Academic Profile based on the work of these early, campus-specific assessment efforts.

Unfortunately, the information provided by these instruments does not always completely satisfy our needs to learn about the college student experience. Fortunately, we can elicit other kinds of information easily. Administrators, researchers, and professionals need to understand the alternatives that exist for the collection of data on the college student experience. Additionally, there is a need for consumers of such information to discern high quality research and assessment.

Alternative methods of data collection are not new; Komarovsky (1953), Leon (1975), and Perry (1970) employed nonquantitative measures in their studies of college students. During the 1980s a continual discussion raged about the merits of new perspectives from which to evaluate, research, and describe (Fry, Chantavanich, & Chantavanich, 1981; Keller, 1986; Lincoln, 1986; Rist, 1977; J. K. Smith, 1983; M. L. Smith, 1986). Descriptions of these various perspectives are provided at the end of this chapter.

Despite the availability of many options for data collection, however, inflexibility reigns. Whether attempting to conduct an assessment or research, most rely solely on surveys and standardized tests even though there are limitations inherent in these particular methods of data collection. Kuh, Bean, Bradley, and Coomes (1986) analyzed articles on college students in seven journals over a 14-year period. For those researchers who collected information from students, the overwhelming method of choice was the survey. An examination of the last 5 years of the *Journal of College Student Development* (1986–1990) revealed that of those articles that described collected data, 231 out of 263, or 88%, were based on surveys or questionnaires. These survey and questionnaire methods usually require quantitative analyses and reporting of results. Only occasionally do they include reporting qualitative information as well. Articles based on only qualitative techniques are rare (Downey & Wantz, 1990).

In our efforts to talk in quantitative terms, we strip away idiosyncrasies that are important to understanding the college student experience (Parker, 1977; Stage, 1989). By stripping away those idiosyncrasies, we imply that anything that is important to know about students on our campus can be reduced to numbers. Details about students, their personal lives, and the influences on the college experience are lost. This approach produces limitations that result in gaps between those who gather information and the student affairs practitioners who use it—and who cannot ignore details about college students' lives. These limitations have been extensively discussed (Caple & Voss, 1983; Conrad, 1989; Keller, 1986; Lincoln, 1986; Strange, 1983). In ignoring or losing important information that could be gained through less traditional research techniques, our work is often not useful to administrators, educators, and policy makers.

Through the 1980s, other methods began to appear with greater frequency in the higher education and student affairs literature. Techniques for conducting research on college students became increasingly diverse. The variety of methods includes ethnographic interviews (Belenky, Clinchy, Goldberger, & Tarule, 1986; Gilligan, 1982; Milne, 1989; Tierney, 1990), the case study (Manning, 1989; Whitt, 1989), the phenomenological interview (Attinasi, 1989), and nonreactive measures (Heikinheimo & Shute, 1986). Increasingly, those who study college students have discovered that many of their most burning questions could not be answered through simple quantitative approaches to data collection and analysis.

Reasons for Increasing Our Flexibility

A recent experience serves to illustrate one of a number of invalidity problems inherent in survey methods. Like many of those whose major enterprise is collecting and interpreting data, I am inclined to respond to requests for responses to others' data collection. I ask many people to participate in my data collections; the least I can do is reciprocate. Recently however, I stopped about one-third of the way through a survey. I had already spent 30 minutes answering detailed questions and could not justify another hour to complete the task. I returned the partially completed survey knowing that it would probably not be used. I could not help wondering about what kind of sample the researcher might get—those who are incredibly persistent about completing tasks they begin or those who have a large amount of leisure time and choose to spend it filling out surveys.

Such self-selection (deciding whether or not to complete a questionnaire) is only one of the problems that comes with relying exclusively on survey data (unless one is collecting information from a captive group of students who must participate, and that brings its own set of problems). Assumptions inherent in sole reliance on surveys, structured interviews, and standardized instruments include (a) everything important to consider can be obtained through the survey (questionnaire, structured interview) format; (b) whoever constructed the instrument knows exactly what is important to ask college students; (c) students who participate in the data collection are representative, for example, of all college students in the nation, at this type of college, on this campus; (d) students are equally adept at responding to multiple choice, fill in the blank, verbal response, or open-ended survey questions; and (e) the information sought is not available elsewhere. A discussion of each assumption follows:

- *Everything important to consider can be obtained through the survey, questionnaire, or interview format.* A researcher once said, "If I can't measure it, it doesn't exist." Although few researchers display such hubris today, those who collect data from college students seem to hold this notion. The corollary for the study of college students might be "If it can't be asked on a survey, questionnaire, or quick interview, it's unimportant." Clearly, the method of choice for those seeking information about college students and their experiences has been the survey. As campus issues become more complex and students more diverse, the quick answer becomes less useful.

- *The designer of the instrument knows exactly what is important to ask about the college student experience and therefore can construct an instrument designed to ask specific questions about those things.* How many of us have conducted an interview with a student, expected to hear one thing, and ended up in a discussion that took a totally different direction? As we become more experienced as administrators, we are carried farther from the perspective of our own undergraduate days. Additionally, it is becoming increasingly likely that not all the students we seek to understand share a common background and culture. Assessment and research should be open to the possible emergence of hidden issues, new themes, and unpredicted discoveries.

- *Students who participate in this data collection are representative, for example, of all college students in the nation, at this type of college, on my campus.* There is no guarantee that the students who are accessible to those distributing an instrument or conducting an interview, and who ultimately respond, are representative. Analysis shows that if participation is voluntary, respondents are more likely to be White, female, traditional-age college students. Unless the data collection effort is compulsory, or care is taken to ensure a representative sample, the results may not reflect the sentiments of the population. Those who are most interested or enthusiastic about a topic are more likely to respond, thus giving an unbalanced view of campus life.

  For example, suppose admissions office staff want information about prospective students in their geographic location for recruiting and promotional programming. A mail survey of randomly selected local high school juniors and seniors might seem like the obvious solution. However, the aim is to learn about students who are uninterested in college in general, or in the college in particular. These are precisely the students least likely to return the survey. Conducting focus groups of local high school students who are not planning to attend college or of students who have committed to other colleges and universities may produce more useful information.

- *All students are equally adept at responding to multiple choice, fill in the blank, verbal response, or open-ended survey questions.* It is widely known that there are differences in students' verbal and written skills and that some students are more adept than others at moving successfully through a standardized test battery (Powell & Steelman, 1984). An attempt to assess students' cognitive growth that relies solely on responses to a structured interview may underestimate "value added" for some students. Similarly, relying on changes in standardized instrument scores, such as using equations for intellectual growth calculated from incoming Scholastic Aptitude Test and senior year Graduate Record Exam scores, could produce exaggerated or underestimated results for students who have test anxiety. Open-ended responses may accurately reflect the opinions of many students; however, opinions of low verbal and English-as-a-second-language (ESL) students may go unreported or misinterpreted.

- *The information sought is not available elsewhere.* Given the current climate of assessment, evaluation, and data storage and retrieval on college campuses, it is possible that much of the information sought has already been collected. Additionally, in this climate of scarce resources, existing databases could be used, and important new information could be collected and analyzed through less traditional means. For example, to examine campus safety we could conduct a document analysis of campus police records and record responses of focus groups of students discussing the issue. A career development office's analysis of trends in employment since 1970 could examine historical information from office archives and conduct surveys of current students rather than conduct an expensive mail survey of alumni. Campus data systems for financial aid, registrar's records, the campus newspaper, and student activities records are also examples of the rich depositories of information waiting to be utilized.

Although not all the assumptions just discussed cause problems every time data are collected, just one or two of them can result in consistent sources of invalidity in our most widely used ways of learning about the college and university student experience. Through a wider use of qualitative approaches, we can move research and assessment of college and university students beyond the status quo and expand student affairs literature beyond what we have learned through overuse of the same traditional methods.

Definitions

Definitions helpful to readers of this publication and germane to any discussion of a variety of approaches to data collection include the following:

- *authenticity and trustworthiness*—techniques to assure the faithfulness of emergent paradigm constructions to the respondents' knowledge
- *emergent paradigm*—a view of the world that recognizes multiple realities and mutual causality and results in research that is time- and context-bound
- *naturalistic perspective*—a view that seeks to elucidate phenomena within their natural contexts
- *positivistic perspective*—a view seeking bits of knowledge as integral parts of one whole that is ultimately completely describable and controllable
- *postpositivistic perspective*—a view of the world that seeks bits of knowledge in an attempt to understand portions of an underlying reality
- *qualitative methods*—techniques employing description of the constructs of interest (such as interviewing, document analysis, observation)
- *quantitative methods*—measures requiring that a numerical or other evaluative symbol be assigned to the construct of interest

- *validity*—the extent to which a measure or observation describes what it is purported to describe.

The traditional mode of data collection in education is quasi-experimental. From this perspective, also called positivistic, researchers exert a high degree of control over the conditions of data collection as well as the questions asked, hence limiting the information collected. For example, researchers studying retention from a positivistic perspective may include only students from a highly selective university in their sample, controlling the conditions of data collection. Additionally, they may collect the information through a questionnaire, thus limiting the type and scope of information collected.

Less traditional approaches to data collection exert less control over the conditions of the data collection and/or the information collected. At the logical opposite from positivistic research designs are those conducted from the constructivist or naturalistic perspectives. Here the researcher exerts little control over conditions as well as little control over the information collected. Rather than control, the researcher seeks an understanding of the phenomenon under study from the respondent's perspective. Instead of being concerned with issues of validity, the researcher is concerned with issues of authenticity and trustworthiness. For example, researchers studying retention from the naturalistic perspective probably include a purposive sample of a small number of students and choose ethnically diverse students attending a particular institution. They conduct open-ended interviews with students to seek details of the students' lives. They may ask them to describe their lives on campus, what is important to them at college, who provides support, what presents frustration. The questions asked are open ended and free ranging. The case study or final report requires a technique that is descriptive and interpretive. No attempt is made to generalize. The reader of the report is free to learn vicariously from the detailed descriptions and interpretations of each student. For further descriptions of this perspective see Guba and Lincoln, 1981; Lincoln and Guba, 1985; and Spradley, 1979.

It should be noted that *approach to data collection* or *perspective* is not synonymous with *method* or *technique*. Using a qualitative method does not guarantee adoption of the emergent paradigm. We can be quite positivistic while conducting an interview. For example, in conducting interviews of students' moral decision making, a researcher may attend only to mentions of legal rights and ignore references to responsibility toward others. Similarly, employing a quantitative method does not mean that we are positivistic. For example, a researcher could conduct a case study of students with learning disabilities at a particular college through ethnographic interviews of 12 students; but quantifying certain information, such as noting that 9 of the 12 experienced difficulty conveying their disabilities to faculty members, does not make the research positivistic. It is in the researcher's and respondent's mutual constructions of their experience that place the study within the emergent paradigm framework.

These perspectives and ideological debates cannot be discussed fully here. The interested reader is encouraged to pursue these dilemmas through references cited throughout this chapter, in discussions with colleagues, and through attending pertinent sessions at professional meetings. It is hoped that this publication will lead to an expansion of our knowledge about the college student and result in richer and more useful information.

Further Reading

In addition to the references listed at the end of this chapter, readers who are interested in topics not covered here (for example, critical incidents analysis, single subject design, secondary data analysis) may want to consult publications such as Sage's Applied Social Research Methods series or Qualitative Research Methods series. Further, both the New Directions for Institutional Research and the New Directions for Research in the Behavioral and Social Sciences series contain discussions of many relevant research issues.

References

Attinasi, L., Jr. (1989). Getting in: Mexican Americans' perceptions of university attendance and the implications for freshman year persistence. *Journal of Higher Education, 60*, 247–277.

Banta, T. W., Lambert, E. W., Pike, G. R., Schmidhammer, J. L., & Schneider, J. A. (1987, April). *Estimated score gain on the ACT COMP exam: Valid tool for institutional assessment?* Paper presented at the annual meeting of the American Educational Research Association, Washington, DC.

Bean, J. P., & Metzner, B. S. (1985). A conceptual model of nontraditional undergraduate student attrition. *Review of Educational Research, 55*, 484–540.

Belenky, M., Clinchy, B., Goldberger, N., & Tarule, J. (1986). *Women's ways of knowing: The development of self, voice, and mind.* New York: Basic Books.

Blandin, I. M. (1909). *History of higher education of women in the South prior to 1870.* New York: Neale.

Caple, R. B., Voss, C. H. (1983). Communication between consumers and producers of student affairs research. *Journal of College Student Personnel, 24*, 38–42.

Conrad, C. F. (1989). Meditations on the ideology of inquiry in higher education: Exposition, critique, and conjecture. *Review of Higher Education, 12*(3), 199–220.

Cooper, L. B. (1928). A study in freshman elimination in one college. *Nation's Schools, 2*(3), 25–29.

Cummings, E. C. (1949). Causes of student withdrawals at DePauw University. *School & Society, 70*, 152–153.

Downey, J., & Wantz, G. (1990). *An examination of research methods employed in the Journal of College Student Development.* Unpublished manuscript.

Ewell, P. T. (1988). Outcomes, assessment, and academic improvement: In search of usable knowledge. In J. Smart (Ed.), *Higher education: Handbook of theory and research* (Vol. 5). New York: Agathon.

Fry, G., Chantavanich, S., & Chantavanich, A. (1981). Merging quantitative and qualitative research techniques: Toward a new research paradigm. *Anthropology and Education Quarterly, 12*(2), 145–158.

Gage, N. L. (1989). The paradigm wars and their aftermath: A "historical" sketch of research on teaching since 1989. *Educational Researcher, 18*, 4–10.

Gilligan, C. (1982). *In a different voice.* Cambridge, MA: Harvard University Press.

Greenleaf, E. A. (1952). *A comparison of women at Indiana University majoring in three different colleges.* Unpublished doctoral dissertation, Indiana University, Bloomington.

Guba, E., & Lincoln, Y. S. (1981). *Naturalistic evaluation.* Beverly Hills, CA: Sage

Heikinheimo, P. S., & Shute, J. C. M. (1986). The adaptation of foreign students: Student views and institutional implications. *Journal of College Student Personnel, 27*(5), 399–406.

Iffert, R. (1958). *Retention and withdrawal of college students.* Washington, DC: U. S. Department of Health, Education, and Welfare.

Keller, G. (1986). Free at last? Breaking the chains that bind educational research. *Review of Higher Education, 10*(2), 129–134.

Komarovsky, M. (1953). *Women in the modern world: Their education and their dilemmas.* New York: Irvington.

Kuh, G. L., Bean, J. P., Bradley, R. K., & Coomes, M. D. (1986). Contributions of student affairs journals to the literature on college students. *Journal of College Student Personnel, 27*(4), 292–304.

Leon, D. (1975). Chicano college dropouts and the educational opportunity program: Failure after high school. *High School Behavioral Science, 3*, 6–11.

Lincoln, Y. S. (1986). A future-oriented comment on the state of the profession. *Review of Higher Education, 10*(2), 135–142.

Lincoln, Y. S., & Guba, E. (1985). *Naturalistic inquiry*. Beverly Hills, CA: Sage.

Manning, K. (1989). *Campus rituals and cultural meaning*. Unpublished doctoral dissertation, Indiana University, Bloomington.

Milne, N. V. (1989). *The experiences of college students with learning disabilities*. Unpublished doctoral dissertation, Indiana University, Bloomington.

Minnesota University. (1924). Report of the Survey Commission VI: Student mortality. *Bulletin of the University of Minnesota, 4*, 27.

Olin, H. R. (1909). *The women of a state university: An illustration of the workings of coeducation in the Middle West*. New York: Putnam.

Pace, C. R. (1984). *Measuring the quality of college student experiences*. Los Angeles: University of California, Higher Education Research Institute.

Parker, C. A. (1977). On modeling reality. *Journal of College Student Personnel, 18*, 419–425.

Pascarella, E. T., Ethington, C. A., & Smart, J. C. (1988). The influence of college on humanitarian/civic involvement values. *Journal of Higher Education, 59*(4), 412–437.

Perry, W. G. (1970). *Forms of intellectual and ethical development in the college years: A scheme*. New York: Holt, Rinehart and Winston.

Powell, B., & Steelman, L. C. (1984). Variations in state SAT performance: Meaningful or misleading? *Harvard Educational Review, 54*(4), 389–412.

Rist, R. C. (1977). On the relations among educational research paradigms: From disdain to detente. *Anthropology and Education Quarterly, 8*, 42–49.

Smith, J. K. (1983). Quantitative versus qualitative research: An attempt to clarify the issue. *Educational Researcher, 12*, 6–13.

Smith, M. L. (1986). The whole is greater: Combining qualitative and quantitative approaches in evaluation studies. In D. Williams (Ed.), *Naturalistic evaluation* (New Directions for Program Evaluation, No. 30). San Francisco: Jossey-Bass.

Spradley, J. P. (1979). *The ethnographic interview*. New York: Holt, Rinehart and Winston.

Stage, F. K. (1989). College outcomes and student development: Filling the gaps. *Review of Higher Education, 12*(3), 293–304.

Stage, F. K. (1990). Research on college students: Commonality, difference, and direction. *Review of Higher Education, 13*(3), 249–258.

Stage, F. K., & Kuh, G. D. (1992). Student development in the college years. In B. Clark & G. Neave (Eds.), *Encyclopedia of higher education*. Oxford: Pergammon Press.

Strange, C. C. (1983). Human development theory and practice in student affairs: Ships passing in the daylight? *NASPA Journal, 21*(1), 2–8.

Terenzini, P. T. (1989). Assessment with open eyes: Pitfalls in studying student outcomes. *Journal of Higher Education, 60*(6), 644–664.

Terenzini, P. T., & Wright, T. M. (1987). Students' personal growth during the first 2 years of college. *Review of Higher Education, 10*(3), 259–271.

Tierney, W. G. (1990). *The worlds we create: Organizational aspects of Native-American participation in postsecondary education*. Unpublished manuscript, Pennsylvania State University, Center for the Study of Higher Education, University Park.

Tinto, V. (1975). Dropout from higher education: A theoretical synthesis of recent research. *Review of Educational Research, 45*, 89–125.

Whitt, E. (1989). *"Hit the ground running": Experiences of new faculty at a school of education at a research university*. Unpublished doctoral dissertation, Indiana University, Bloomington.

PART IV

PROFESSIONAL DEVELOPMENT IN COLLEGE STUDENT AFFAIRS ADMINISTRATION

Part Four focuses on issues important to the initial and ongoing development of student affairs professionals. Issues addressed in this section are (1) development of new professionals, (2) professional ethics, and (3) involvement in professional associations and activities.

Making the Transition to a Professional Role

Margaret J. Barr

Acceptance of a first professional position in student affairs brings with it many questions, concerns, and emotions. Among the questions are those related to competence, achievement, relationships with new colleagues, satisfaction, and enjoyment. Each professional new to student affairs encounters a range of problems and concerns about the future. The process of transition and change brings with it both doubt and anxiety.

In this chapter, the broad professional and personal issues influencing success in a first, crucial professional position will be discussed. False beliefs concerning work in student affairs and higher education will be identified. Finally, suggestions will be presented to assist new student affairs professionals to gain mastery of their new role.

A caveat is in order at this point. Not everything suggested in this chapter will be applicable to all new professionals. Readers must critically assess the ideas and suggestions presented and evaluate what has the most meaning for them. The institutional context, professional training, personal experience, and personal style of the professional will all influence the decisions that need to be made. The goal of this chapter is to discuss common concerns involved in a transition to a new role and to have readers begin the process of identifying concerns and developing strategies to confront their own set of issues.

Professional Issues

At a minimum, six professional issues must be addressed as a transition is made to a new position and to a professional role. These include: obtaining and using needed information, establishing expectations for performance, confronting the question of translating theory to practice, mapping the environment, establishing positive relationships with students, and continuing professional growth.

Obtaining and Using Information

As a new professional, a great deal of information will need to be mastered in a relatively short period of time. Some of that information will relate to the specific terms and conditions of employment, including employee benefits, retirement systems, insurance, educational benefits, and parking. Even though the content of the position is primary, do not ignore the need for good solid information regarding conditions of employment. Take the time to read and understand all the information received. Do not be afraid to ask questions and get clarification, if necessary. For example, inadvertently parking in an inappropriate space could cause conflicts with potential colleagues, and not understanding expectations for participation in faculty/staff orientation activities could create a negative first impression.

A second, but equally critical base of information revolves around questions of how to get started in the new position. Some divisions of student affairs have established comprehensive orientation programs for new staff. If employed in an institution where such a program exists, take full advantage of such orientation (Baier, 1985). Usually such programs will cover the history and philosophy of the institution and the student affairs unit, critical policies and procedures, organizational responsibilities, and sources of help.

If, however, such a program does not exist, orientate yourself to the who, what, when, and where of the institution and the division. Initiative is required, but a great deal of information is available in most institutions to assist with that task. Read the catalog, course schedule, written policies and procedures, and old files. Ask colleagues about what is unclear. Seek out individuals who have been in the institution for some time and listen carefully to what they say. Study the organizational chart and learn the names of key players and actors in the institutional setting. Show interest in others and take the initiative in establishing relationships with them. Try to suspend judgment about the appropriateness of what is going on until a full and complete set of information is available on which to base a response.

Establishing Expectations

Administrative superiors and colleagues all have explicit and implicit expectations for performance. Stamatakos (1978) reminded new professionals to "Regularly ask yourself, 'Am I doing what my supervisor expects of me? What concrete or other evidence do I have that I am/am not satisfying my supervisor's expectations of me?'" (p. 325). Further, Stamatakos indicates that a job description is only a guide to what is expected. "The expectations of how a professional is to behave will have a great influence on how well the tasks defined can be accomplished" (Scher and Barr, 1979, p. 532). Clarity is essential and the new professional often must take the initiative to assure that their work performance meets expected standards. A number of expectations, however, are relatively easy to understand and can be applied in every professional setting. These include keeping your supervisor informed (Stamatakos, 1978); understanding the legal and organizational limits on your authority to act (Barr, 1988); meeting deadlines and following procedures (Pembroke, 1984); and producing accurate, thoughtful, well-planned work (Barr and Keating, 1985).

Other staff members also have expectations for the performance of a new colleague. Often these are even less readily discerned than those of a supervisor. Young (1985) indicated student affairs practitioners come into the field from a variety of academic backgrounds and experiences, and such differences may influence expectations. Ostroth (1981), however, indicates that most student affairs staff members are hired because of skills related to interpersonal communication, cooperation, and the ability to work with others.

Although great variation in background may exist among potential staff colleagues, the common skills delineated by Ostroth provide a new professional with a unique opportunity to learn from colleagues. A great deal can be learned from both observing and listening. Determine agency norms for office hours, attendance at events, dress, and demeanor through both observation and questioning. Listen carefully to both what is said and not said at staff meetings. Ask questions and elicit advice and assistance from your new staff colleagues. Often diametrically opposed points of view will surface regarding any specific person or issue. Judgments will also be required, although such judgments should not be made in haste. A decision to follow or reject institutional norms can only be made when institutional norms are known. Any decision will have consequences for the staff member's future within the organization (Scher and Barr, 1979, p. 531). Finally, request both positive and negative feedback and then attempt not to get defensive when the feedback is forthcoming. Peers and colleagues can provide a great deal of assistance in the process of achieving success in a new position.

Theory to Practice

Practitioners who emerge from a strong, theory-based program often experience dissonance between theory and actual practice in their first practitioner setting. Young (1985) indicated that this dissonance can even begin to emerge during practice and internship experiences. What is learned in the classroom at times may not seem relevant or even valued in the new professional setting.

Stamatakos (1978) indicated that new professionals experience conflict because they know "what should or ought to be done and what is not being done" (p. 326). Often a major philosophical conflict arises for the new professional and frustration results. Some new professionals experience frustration with the theory-to-practice debate from an entirely different perspective. Usually this latter group includes individuals who come to student affairs from a different academic background. They become just as confused when they join an organization steeped in human development theory, and the organization uses that theory base to make decisions. Even conversations seem foreign to them as their colleagues discuss vectors, stages, and the like. Whether the frustration arises from a perceived difference between theory and practice, a perceived lack of knowledge on the part of new colleagues, or lack of a theory base on the part of the new professional, frustration will result.

The translation of human development or other theories to practice is difficult at best. The astute new professional proceeds very slowly and attempts to identify individuals who share beliefs or can help the new professional gain the skills and competencies needed to start on the translation process. If a new professional is in an environment where program efforts are either theoretical or merely based on tradition, there are positive steps which can be taken. Stamatakos (1978) suggested that a new professional (a) identify supporting elements; (b) identify obstacles; (c) assess the importance of those elements to the task; (d) determine the need for change; (e) develop a program proposal; and (f) present it in a positive, nonthreatening manner (p. 326). Knefelkamp and Wells (1983) cautioned that the use of theory really begins with practice and with asking pragmatic questions about the needs of students and effectiveness of professional practice. They further warned that "one cannot translate theory directly into practice. There is a critical middle step in the process: translating the theory into accurate characteristics of particular students in a particular environment" (Knefelkamp and Wells, 1983, p. 326).

The best advice to the new professional regarding this issue is to watch, observe, and assimilate prior to assuming that theory is not being used in your new environment. Once the needed data base is established, carefully develop a supporting framework to meet the goal of providing quality services for students.

Mapping the Environment

In addition to learning information about the institution, be able to apply that information in an effective manner. A new professional needs to get beyond the superficial and find out who really makes decisions and what the norms of behavior are within the institution.

Study the organizational chart and develop a private version identifying key assistants, secretaries, and others who provide access and information in the system (Barr and Keating, 1979). Observe others and ask questions with great frequency and precision.

To be successful in any position in higher education, horizons need to be extended beyond a specific job or agency. Actively work at understanding the "big picture." Stamatakos (1978) admonished young professionals, for example, to cultivate faculty. His advice is worth following, for not only are new friends and support systems developed, but understanding begins to emerge regarding the complexity of the institutional climate. Get involved in the life of the institution as well as the specific position or agency. Attend concerts, plays, lectures, and meetings. Such behavior will increase both knowledge and effectiveness as a student affairs administrator. With work, commitment, and dedication, a new professional will soon be able to differentiate between the crucial, the important, the necessary, and the irrelevant elements in the new environment.

Positive Relationships with Students

Most new professionals spend a great deal of their professional life working with students in both formal and informal settings. Thus, a critical element for professional success is establishing positive and productive working relationships with students. Often, this is easier said than done! Some new professionals over identify with students and do not clearly differentiate their professional role with students. Other new professionals fall into the trap of over identifying with their professional role and tend to structure their relationships with students in a rigid and authoritarian manner. Either extreme in behavior causes problems for both the new professional and for the students.

Monat (1985) indicated that he expects student affairs professionals "to speak up for students but never down to them" (p. 126). This is sound advice. Achieving a clear professional identity in your relationships with students is not an easy task, but one which must be mastered if professional success is to be achieved.

Some fairly simple guidelines seem to work best. First, identify someone on the campus who appears to have established positive working relationships with students and observe them. Second, identify both the written and unwritten rules of behavior on the campus and discuss them with both supervisors and your professional colleagues. Seek clarity on such questions as staff attendance and procedures. Third, define your role, the limitations in that role, and communicate that information to students. For example, as an advisor to a student organization, what are the limits of your authority? If an advisor can veto actions, students need to understand that the possibility exists for you to exercise your authority. Fourth, never promise students more than can be delivered. For instance, a promise of confidentiality may not be met under certain conditions. The ethical principles of your professional association will provide helpful guidance in this important area. Finally, be consistent, honest, and predictable in any relationships with students. Students are astute judges of people and can quickly sense insincerity. Students should reasonably expect that a professional be consistent and straightforward in a relationship.

Each new professional will need to develop their own personal style in relating to students. That style will be shaped, in part, by institutional practices, institutional rules, and the ethical codes of conduct governing professional practice.

Continued Professional Growth

One of the expectations an institution should have of all student affairs professionals is to "be intellectually and professionally active" (NASPA, 1988, P. 16). The methods of remaining active will vary from individual to individual. Active membership in a professional organization such as the National Association of Student Personnel Administrators (NASPA), the American College Personnel Association (ACPA), or one of the professional specialty groups such as the Association of College Unions International (ACUI) or the Association of College and University Housing Officers International (ACUHO-I) is a good first step. Journals and newsletters will provide information about current issues. Announcements of professional development opportunities on the state, regional, and national levels will also be available and may be of value.

One relatively easy way to assure professional growth is to keep up-to-date on issues and new practices in student affairs through professional reading. Journals, books, and newsletters are all sources of ideas and information that can be put to use in your professional practice. Keeping up-to-date on current issues in higher education through regular perusal of *The Chronicle of Higher Education* is equally important. Current knowledge assists in making positive contributions as the institution faces new challenges in the years ahead.

Invest both time and personal money, if necessary, in your future as a student affairs professional. Attend workshops and conferences. New material will be learned and connections with other professional colleagues will be developed. Take the risk of submitting a program idea and making a presentation at a conference. Testing ideas with colleagues is a certain way to assure continued professional growth.

Local staff development programs also provide a viable option for continued professional growth. Whether such opportunities are offered on institutional, divisional, or departmental level, take the initiative to get involved and participate in such programs. At the very least, an extended network of persons on campus interested in similar issues will be established. More than likely, however, new knowledge will be gained or skills and competencies developed.

Finally, consider resuming a formal educational degree program. The structured institutional learning experiences can help a new professional remain intellectually active and professionally aware.

However, the decision to pursue advanced studies (e.g., doctoral degree, special certification) may crucially affect a professional's career and educational advancement. Some significant considerations are financial (e.g., tuition and lack of a regular paycheck), disruption of continuous full-time work, family concerns, and the timing related to gaining practical experience and professional growth in one's career.

False Beliefs

There are a number of false beliefs that can influence our effectiveness as student affairs professionals. Some of these false beliefs center around the political nature of the higher education enterprise.

The first is a deeply held belief that worthwhile concepts should and will be supported. Barr and Keating (1979) cautioned that, in addition to a concept being worthwhile, concept criteria must be cost effective, consistent, and in line with institutional priorities.

Second, some believe that opposition to ideas and concepts is due to bad intentions on the part of the other party (Barr and Keating, 1979). This is not necessarily true. Sometimes individuals see the world from a different perspective and have different information than those proposing the idea. Before bad intentions are assumed, try to understand the source of the opposition. The concern expressed by others may indeed be legitimate.

Third, some feel that outside pressure should have no influence on professional practice, but both internal and external forces have a real and very direct influence on higher education institutions and student affairs (Barr, 1985). For example, drug abuse is of national concern and cannot be ignored by colleges and universities. National political issues such as the threat of war have long influenced higher education institutions. Changes in the law and interpretation of the law will affect both policies and procedures. No institution or student affairs agency is immune to outside influences, and astute professionals learn to effectively deal with such pressures when they occur.

Fourth, many student affairs professionals feel they should and can understand the pressures faced by their administrative superior (Barr and Keating, 1979). As higher education becomes more complex, many administrators are dealing with new pressures. Expectations of resource management and planning are examples. Sometimes it is impossible to understand all the pressures, and it is not necessary to do so.

Fifth, there is a temptation to believe that details are not important. While it is necessary to understand the larger implications of professional practice, the astute new staff member recognizes that the big picture is filled with details. Successful programs and interventions only occur when all the details are taken care of in a timely and efficient manner. Mastery of planning and program implementation skills requires attention to detail.

Sixth, many believe a negative decision is forever (Barr and Keating, 1979). Several factors influence decisions, including key actors in the process, the current context, timing, and political currents flowing on and off the campus. The astute professional attempts to determine the reasons for a negative decision and then strives to modify their proposal, resubmitting the idea when all factors are more positive.

Other false beliefs which can influence professional practice probably exist. The important point is that new professionals should be cautious about making assumptions about people, systems, or institutions before gathering all the facts.

Suggestions for Practice

Several concrete steps are available to new professionals to maximize their success in a new position.

Seek a mentoring relationship. Young (1985), Barr and Keating (1979), and others asserted that a positive mentoring relationship has great potential. Identifying such potential mentors is not an easy task and a relationship must be developed through mutual trust and loyalty. One person may not be able to provide the full range of guidance that is needed and may not be directly available on campus. In fact, some individuals, both on and off campus, may be able to provide support and direction in specific areas. Such relationships must never be one-sided. A person seeking help can also provide valuable information and perspective to a mentor. Seasoned professionals can help new professionals learn and grow, and intentionality is needed for developing and nurturing such growth producing professional relationships.

Develop new interests. Balance is needed between personal and professional lives. Expanded interests help to maintain perspective, provide stimulation, and give a needed respite from the pressures of work. Scher and Barr (1979) suggested trying something you have always wanted to do, whether it is mastery of a skill or studying a subject. Outside involvement helps an individual gain and keep a perspective on the professional task.

Take care of yourself. The popular press is filled with descriptions of workaholics. Becoming a workaholic is easy in student affairs because hours are erratic and the work is interesting. Therefore developing personal support networks is critical and should be a priority (Barr and Keating, 1979). In addition, personal, physical, and mental health concerns cannot be ignored.

Maintain friendships. One of the inevitable costs of moving to a new position is separation from friends and relatives. Work at keeping those relationships alive and active through letters and phone calls. During the process of change, support is needed and will not occur without intentional effort.

Maintain a sense of humor. A good, healthy sense of humor helps many through difficult times. Research also indicates that happier people feel less stress and work more effectively with others. Work should be enjoyable and a sense of humor helps maintain that enjoyment.

Be true to yourself. Stamatakos (1978) and Scher and Barr (1979) admonished new professionals to be true to themselves as they go about their work. The advice of the Hebrew sage Hillel is particularly relevant, "If I am not for myself, who is for me?" (Goldin, 1962). "Self-worth as a professional and as a person is closely related to the honesty and enthusiasm we manifest in the practice of our profession" (Stamatakos, 1979, p. 330). Each professional will need to determine if the current environment meets essential needs and supports important values. If not, then a decision to leave must be made in a professional and responsible manner.

Summary

The transition to a new professional position in student affairs is filled with excitement, challenge, and change. Inevitably, problems and frustrations will emerge. Success will come to those who exercise their skills and are patient as they encounter new people, problems, opportunities, and challenges. The key to success lies in the ability of the new professional to assume a new role in a positive, straightforward manner and to be slow in making assumptions about people, programs, and policies.

References

Baier, J. (1985). Recruiting and training competent staff. In M. J. Barr and L. A. Keating (Eds.), *Developing effective student services programs* (pp. 212–33). San Francisco: Jossey-Bass Publishers.

Barr, M. J. (1985). Internal and external forces influencing programming. In M. J. Barr and L. A. Keating (Eds.), *Developing effective student services programs* (pp. 62–82). San Francisco: Jossey-Bass Publishers.

Barr, M. J. (1988). *Student services and the law: A guide for practitioners.* San Francisco: Jossey-Bass Publishers.

Barr, M. J., and Keating, L. A. (1979). No program is an island. In M. J. Barr and L. A. Keating (Eds.), *New directions for student services: Establishing effective student services programs* (p. 7). San Francisco: Jossey-Bass Publishers.

Barr, M. J., and Keating, L. A. (Eds.). (1985). *Developing effective student services programs*. San Francisco: Jossey-Bass Publishers.

Goldin, G. (Ed.). (1962). *Ethics of the fathers*. New York: Hebrew Publishing Company.

Knefelkamp, L., and Wells, E. (1983). Translating student development theory into practice for student affairs personnel. Unpublished manuscript.

Monat, W. (1985). Role of student services: A presidential perspective. In M. J. Barr and L. A. Keating (Eds.), *Developing effective student services programs* (p. 126). San Francisco: Jossey-Bass Publishers.

National Association of Student Personnel Administrators. (1988). *A perspective on student affairs*. Washington, D.C.: Author.

Ostroth, D. (1981). Competencies for entry level professionals: What do employers look for when hiring new staff? *Journal of College Student Personnel, 22,* 5–11.

Pembroke, W. J. (1985). Fiscal restraints on program development. In M. J. Barr and L. A. Keating (Eds.), *Developing effective student services programs* (pp. 83–109). San Francisco: Jossey-Bass Publishers.

Scher, M. A., and Barr, M. J. (1979). Beyond graduate school: Strategies for survival. *Journal of College Student Personnel, 19,* 325–330.

Stamatakos, L. C. (1978). Unsolicited advice for new professionals. *Journal of College Student Personnel, 19,* 325–30.

Young, R. D. (1985). Impressions of the development of professional identity: From programs to practice. *NASPA Journal, 23*(2), 50–60.

Supervision and Evaluation: Selected Topics for Emerging Professionals

JOHN H. SCHUH AND WAYNE CARLISLE

Fuhrmann (1987), in describing careers in higher education compared with those in the corporate world, stated:

> A career is a sequence of work-related positions occupied throughout a person's life. It reflects the individual's needs, motives, and expectations, as well as societal and organizational expectations and constraints. A successful career is one in which the individual and organizational perspectives have been meshed through appropriate role adjustments, developments, and changes in response to both individual and organizational characteristics. Research in corporations has shown that a worker's performance is facilitated when organizational values and individual values are compatible and when individual growth is encouraged. Human resource professionals in the corporate world are charged with the task of assuring the best possible fit between organizations and individual values, and they actively intervene in both organizational and individual planning to assure the best matches. We in academia need to do the same. (p. 24)

This chapter takes the position that supervision and evaluation have not received adequate attention as key elements for a career in student affairs. Few practitioners have received adequate preparation as supervisors or evaluators, and frequently pay little attention to those roles after entering the field. Perhaps as frustrating for many student affairs professionals is the tendency for some practitioners to fail to provide consistent, on-going supervision and evaluation to subordinates, on the one hand, while expecting or demanding more thorough supervision and evaluation for their own career development.

To learn more about various aspects of student affairs administration, a good place of reference is the *CAS Standards and Guidelines for Student Services/Development Programs* (CAS, 1986). In regard to supervision and evaluation, the standards state: "All functional areas must have a regular system of staff selection and evaluation, and must provide continuing professional development opportunities for staff. . . ." (CAS, 1986, p. 6). This statement requires staff evaluation, but provides neither direction for performing the function nor guidance for appropriate supervision.

The question then becomes, How will the supervision and evaluation functions in student affairs be carried out? Who is responsible for them? And perhaps even, why should staff members be evaluated at all?

Both the supervisor *and* the staff member are responsible for these functions and the process should not be viewed as a passive one. This process involves a great deal of personal interaction, and all parties can and should use evaluation information in considering career development.

498

Although administrators are increasingly being held accountable for their subordinates' careers (Kaye, 1981), individuals are responsible for their own career development and young professionals who expect supervisors to plan career development for them are naive.

Individuals should continually negotiate how they wish to be supervised and evaluated. Needs for information, clarity of responsibility, feedback and direction differ from person to person throughout the developmental stages. Maccoby (1988) referred to people who are keenly aware of their need for new skills, changing responsibilities, opportunities for success and failure, and in-depth performance reviews as *self-developers.* These people represent an increasing proportion of the work force. Their principle loyalties are to the quality of their work and to the opportunity for meaningful and rewarding work. They are not, therefore, as loyal to organizations or institutions as has been the ideal and frequently are not interested in traditional upward mobility.

For the self-developers in student affairs, opportunities must be provided for professional development, flexible responsibilities, and in-depth performance reviews. If the trends in corporate work are in fact reflected in student affairs, even more emphasis on supervision and evaluation will be required.

Supervision

In the business community the term "supervisor" frequently refers only to first line managers who work with classified, union, or production personnel. To supervise implies that the employee must be watched, judged, motivated, or taught (Phillips, 1985). For purposes of this chapter, the term supervision is used in a broader sense to include any relationship where one person has the responsibility to provide leadership, direction, information, motivation, evaluation, or support for one or more persons. In student affairs, many terms are used when referring to the person to whom a practitioner reports including boss, manager, budget review officer, director, dean, department head, and even a few terms that may be best not printed. In this chapter, the *supervisory relationship* is defined as the interaction that transpires as one staff member provides opportunities, structure, and support to another.

Motivation Issues

Over the years motivation has been considered an important factor in employee productivity, and employees have operated either by fear or as a result of fresh enthusiasm (Blake & Mouton, 1981). In effect, "people tend to do the things for which they are rewarded and to avoid what is not rewarded" (Blake & Mouton, 1985, p. 139). The competent administrator's task is to understand various theories of motivation and apply them in ways that are consistent with the organization's mission. Peterson and Tracy (1979) have summarized three theories of motivation.

Conditioning Theory. This simple theory of motivation states that behavior is driven by needs, and that if needs are satisfied by a particular action, then the behavior tends to be repeated. Rewards or punishments must closely follow particular behavior so that positive behaviors are encouraged and negative ones are discouraged.

Expectancy Theory. Put in elementary terms, expectancy theory indicates that the strength of any particular action is motivated by what the person expects to gain from that action. If people expect to gain large rewards from a particular action, they will work hard toward that end. If the benefits are perceived to be limited, so will be the effort.

In a student affairs setting, if the advisor to a student group expects to get little reward from attending meetings of the organization, he or she may attend few of the meetings. On the other hand, if the advisor expects to be recognized in a major way for the efforts expended on behalf of the organization, such as an opportunity to attend a national conference or personal gratification through interpersonal relationships with members of the organization, the advisor may put in tremendous effort on the organization's behalf

Motivator-hygiene Theory. This theory is drawn from the work of Herzberg (Herzberg, Mausner, & Snyderman, 1959) who suggested that some factors associated with work will facilitate employees' enjoying their efforts, while the absence of others will cause them to become dissatisfied. Recognition, responsibility, and a sense of achievement were perceived to be satisfiers, while pay, working conditions, and job security were dissatisfiers. Peterson and Tracy (1979) indicated that Herzberg's theory has not been supported by research entirely, although it appears to be congruent with Maslow's (1954) hierarchy of needs and McGregor's (1960) Theory Y of management. Theory X and Theory Y are ways of viewing individuals in the context of organizational life. The central principle of organization which derives from Theory X is that of direction and control through the exercise of authority—what has been called the "scalar principle." The central principle of organization which derives from Theory Y is that of integration—the creation of conditions such that the members of the organization can achieve their own goals best by directing their efforts toward the success of the enterprise (McGregor, 1960). Hersey and Blanchard (1982) warned that one should avoid assuming that Theory X is bad and that Theory Y is good. Theory X and Theory Y are simply different ways of viewing human behavior. Regardless of whether a practitioner subscribes to a particular theory, what is most important is that she or he realize that no consensus exists about how to motivate people. Practitioners in supervisory roles need to adopt an approach that is consistent with their values and beliefs, and try to develop ways of working with staff members that are congruent with the theory of motivation to which they subscribe and which has been tested and proved to produce desired results consistently.

Supervisory Styles

While the suggestion has been that every practitioner needs to develop a personal supervisory style, and will work with colleagues who possess very different styles, several classical styles are worth examining. Peterson and Tracy (1979) have identified three of these.

> **One-dimensional Supervision.** This general style assumes that leadership follows a continuum that ranges from the highly autocratic to the laissez-faire. On the one end of the supervisory continuum is the very directive leader who makes all the decisions for subordinates leaving no room for individual decision making or initiative. At the other end, the supervisor provides staff members with little structure or pressure.

> **Two-dimension Leadership.** Two dimensions of supervisory behavior references include initiating structure, which deals with activities like assigning work, encouraging overtime work, criticizing poor work, and exerting pressure toward greater effort, and consideration, which involves helping behaviors, such as helping others with personal problems, being receptive to disagreements, and consulting with subordinates about change. This approach has been so pervasive that it was influential in the development of Blake and Mouton's Managerial Grid (1974) and Hersey and Blanchard's Life Cycle Leadership Theory (1977).

> **Facilitating Development.** Behaviors that facilitate development include such activities as designing challenging jobs, assigning challenging tasks, and asking subordinates to set high goals. At the other end of the continuum are behaviors that do not facilitate development, such as designing jobs that are overly simple or impossible to accomplish, encouraging poor quality work in order just to get finished, or rejecting all ideas from subordinates. Clearly these behaviors destroy good morale and discourage staff members from putting forth strong efforts on behalf of the organization.

As with motivation theory, no specific supervisory theory will meet all needs of all employees, so one must select elements that can be used to develop a theory that fits his or her personality, the composition of the staff and the particular work setting. Entry-level practitioners, in many cases, supervise at least two types of staff members: paraprofessionals and clerical/technical. At a minimum, the entry level practitioner needs to recognize that the motivation for work by members of these two groups varies considerably and require distinctive supervisory approaches. Paraprofessionals, such as orientation leaders, peer counselors, or resident assistants, work for a variety of reasons that complement their academic curricula, but the primary reason that they are on campus is to complete their courses of study. In short, work is a supplementary activity. Clerical and technical staff members, on the other hand, are associated with the campus community because of their employment. Their views of work, and their expectations of supervisors are considerably different from those of their paraprofessional colleagues. A host of implications are suggested by this dichotomy, and the new professional must plan carefully when interacting with these different employee groups. As supervision of professional staff increases during a career, continued adjustment to individual developmental needs becomes even more crucial.

After establishing a personal style of supervision, the next step is to examine the elements essential to supervisory effectiveness.

Elements of Supervisory Success

Elements that promote supervisory success according to Peterson & Tracy (1979), are briefly discussed.

Managerial Philosophy. Organizations have explicit and implicit philosophies that guide how they will be managed. Some organizations are direct and autocratic, whereas others appear unfocused and laissez-faire. In a college's student affairs division, much of the administrative philosophy will depend on the chief student affairs administrator (CSAA) and the campus' chief executive officer (president or chancellor). If the CSAA decides that an autocratic organization is best, then that will be the pervasive philosophy. That is not to imply that some departure from this approach may occur within various departments, but what will be rewarded in the CSAA's eyes is a supervisory style consistent with that person's philosophy. By and large, research findings do not tend to support a highly autocratic approach. Job satisfaction studies suggest that giving people independence in deciding how to go about their work increases job satisfaction (Teas, 1981). Most likely professionals will encounter a wide variety of managerial philosophies during the course of their careers.

Staff Needs and Values. Even though a CSAA has a philosophy of management that tilts in one direction, that does not mean that other staff members cannot have countervailing needs and values. Possibly the CSAA may view the world from one perspective while staff members view it from another. When this occurs, middle managers often find themselves in awkward positions. As a result, a certain degree of compromise on the part of all concerned may be required, if the organization is to effectively accomplish its mission. For example, the CSAA may believe that the agenda for the division places student growth as the organization's highest priority, while some staff members believe that controlling student behavior is paramount. Consequently, compromises are needed, and the middle managers must interpret what the leader needs while simultaneously identifying the needs of each staff member and responding to those needs in individual ways. This juggling act is not easy, but it is an important component of effective supervision. Perhaps the key to success here is supervisor flexibility and the ability to understand the motives and values that drive fellow staff members.

Career Development

Part of a supervisor's responsibility is to provide opportunities for staff members' career development. Open communication about individual goals is crucial before the supervisor can provide opportunities for skill building, information gathering, and formal or informal education. The evaluation process can provide the supervisor with knowledge about areas of weakness that can be strengthened through a career development plan. Opportunities for inservice education in functional areas other than the one to which a practitioner is assigned are fairly rare. More commonly encouragement and training opportunities are provided for upward mobility within the assigned functional area. A broader view of career development by both practitioners and supervisors can provide greater flexibility in assigning responsibilities and training opportunities across the student affairs spectrum.

Private enterprise corporations are increasingly offering career development programs for employees (Barkhaus, 1983). The primary goals of these programs are to increase employees' work satisfaction and productivity, to help the organization change, and to retain the most valued employees. Likewise, student affairs leaders can increase the provision of career development opportunities for staff members. To utilize the institution's career services staff members as resources and to encourage continuing education on campus is particularly appropriate. Because professional career development programs are at a premium on college campuses, an important procedure is for new staff members to request the establishment of systematic career development programs.

Mentoring

While many articles exist in the business literature about mentoring relationships, far less has been published in the higher education and student affairs literature (Kelly, 1984). A definition of **mentor** was proffered by Moore and Salimbene (cited in Kelly, 1984) who stated that a mentor is "a more experienced and powerful individual who guides, advises, and assists in any number of ways the career of a less experienced, often younger, upwardly mobile protégé in the context of a close professionally-centered relationship usually lasting one year or more" (p. 50).

Purposes of Mentoring Relationships

Kram (1986) identified two broad categories that subsume the purposes of a mentoring relationship: career functions and psychosocial functions.

Career Functions. Five functions are included in the career category. (1) *Sponsorship functions* are those related to opening doors of opportunity. This might mean that the mentor provides introductions to specific activities and people in a professional organization or on campus. (2) *Coaching functions* refer to "teaching a person the ropes." This includes providing information and feedback on performance. How well did the meeting go with students? What could be done to improve one's performance? (3) *Protection* is provided by the mentor for dealing with problems that are outside one's span of control or personal experience. The mentor may act as a buffer in this kind of situation. (4) *Exposure* means that one is provided special opportunities to grow. For instance, one might accompany the mentor to a meeting with the vice president or president and simply act as an observer. Not only would one have a chance to learn from this experience, but he or she would be introduced to others as a competent person whose career is on the move. (5) Finally, the mentor may *assign challenging tasks* that provide opportunities to develop work skills beyond what would normally be expected.

Psychosocial Functions. Included in this category are such activities as role modeling, counseling, acceptance and confirmation. (1) When mentors serve as role models they demonstrate attitudes, behaviors, and skills that will aid in developing competence, confidence, and clearer professional identity. (2) Counseling refers to the provision of opportunities for mutual reflection on professional dilemmas, ethical concerns, and other sensitive issues that one encounters. The mentor can provide advice and guidance, and the new professional's role is to sort out the various approaches that might be taken so that one's behavior is compatible with one's belief system.

A new professional's self-confidence will be strengthened when the mentor provides continuing support, respect, and admiration. These functions are characterized as acceptance and confirmation.

Good Mentors

Not everyone can be or desires to be a good mentor. Normally, the decision to enter into a mentor-protégé relationship is mutual, but it is entirely possible that the protégé will have to initiate the contact with the potential mentor even though mentoring is currently seen as being a much more important component in managers' job descriptions than ever before (Derr, 1986). What, then, are the characteristics of good mentors? Odiorne (1984) suggested five qualities that characterize good mentors.

When looking for a mentor one should look for a person with these five qualities and make sure that the person is an individual who is not too exacting, hostile, overly judgmental, or punitive (Odiorne, 1984). These last four characteristics can be destructive to a mentoring relationship.

Excellence. Good mentors are winners themselves in the sense that they tend to have been successful in their own professional endeavors. There is no value in imitating a loser, so young practitioners should find a person who has been very successful and they will be on the right track to finding a mentor.

Excellent Example. The person who serves as a good mentor realizes that she or he will be serving as an example. Good mentors behave in ways worthy of emulation.

Supportive. Good mentors are supportive in their work with subordinates. They are patient, slow to criticize, and willing to work with those who are less well developed in their careers.

Delegators. Top candidates for mentors are those who are not afraid to delegate tasks to colleagues and are not threatened by others who exhibit talent and initiative. The good mentor provides support for the protégé who has been unsuccessful, and provides plenty of praise for those who have been successful.

Feedback. Finally, the good mentor provides periodic, detailed, and honest feedback to the protégé.

Issues Related to Gender

Kram (1986) listed a series of issues related to gender and mentoring relationships. This is an extraordinarily sensitive subject, and while the hope is for change in the future, the present situation is replete with problems. Among the problems listed by Kram were the following: (1) Increasing intimacy and sexual attraction frequently characterize these relationships. (2) Both men and women tend to rely on traditional sex role stereotypes in these relationships. (3) Frequently cross-gender mentoring relationships are unsatisfactory to the junior person and at times to the senior person as well. (4) Cross-gender relationships are open to public scrutiny and may be viewed with suspicion. Rumors, innuendo, and gossip may result from a cross-gender relationship. (5) Peers may resent these relationships as well. Possibly women may run the risk of resentment if they appear to be the "chosen" one of a senior male in the organization.

Suggestions for dealing with these issues, which are built on an awareness that this kind of relationship is very sensitive, include travel arrangements, social occasions, and non-work related activities must be evaluated in terms of appearances. While same-gender mentor relationships are less likely to have these concerns, all mentoring relationships should be based on the career development of the junior person. Both persons need to acknowledge the professional limits of the relationship. One should not conclude that problems will automatically result from a cross-gender mentoring relationship. What is important to note, however, is that this kind of relationship requires particularly clear communication, extra preparation, and a mutual awareness of its sensitive nature.

Issues Related to Race

Odiorne (1984) indicated that barriers do continue to exist for members of minority groups who seek mentoring relationships with those outside their racial groups. One would hope that such is a vestige of the past, but he wrote that some people "simply can't see themselves doing anything special for a minority person" (1984, p. 141). That is a lamentable social commentary. Beginning minority practitioners should seek mentors from senior student affairs staff members (regardless of race) who are inclined to base supervision on competence and potential. Members of minority groups are placed in an extraordinarily difficult situation if they feel that they must compromise their values to "fit in" with other staff members. Odiorne suggested that an alternative would be to use networks, support groups, and caucuses as vehicles for networking. These groups can focus on social and professional barriers that group members will be required to overcome if they are to be successful in their careers.

Ethical Issues

A number of ethical issues are involved in the mentoring process. Odiorne (1984) put forward these cautions and caveats: (1) Favoritism is not mentoring. (2) The mentoring relationship should be temporary not permanent, and should be reviewed at least annually. (3) Gratitude, repayment, or services should not be extracted from a protégé. (4) The protégé should be worthy of the relationship. Not all people should be on a fast track for promotion, and there is no point in a mentor entering into such a relationship unless the protégé can benefit from it. (5) Having more than one protégé at a given time is better for all concerned. This is a way of avoiding charges of the mentor playing favorites or entering into a special relationship with one person to the detriment of others on the staff (For additional discussion of these issues, see Chapter 17).

Evaluation

Evaluation is a particularly complex issue with much literature devoted to it; consequently, only the more salient issues for the young professional are addressed here. For the purposes of this discussion, the evaluation of a student affairs practitioner by a qualified supervisor is the primary referent. Other forms of evaluation exist including peer reviews, client feedback, and program and departmental reviews. Because of space limitations, however, discussion is limited to supervisor-supervisee evaluations alone.

Business Models and Theories

Business approaches to evaluation are diverse and rapidly changing as management theory, competition, and managers influence decision. In general, business leaders use evaluation techniques more frequently and take the process more seriously than do most higher education administrators. While significant differences do exist between the settings and the goals in areas of measurable progress, compensation, and promotion, features of evaluation can be learned from the corporate community and transferred to higher education. Penn (1979, p. 152) noted that: "A division or department of student affairs with sound staff evaluation procedure recognizes the value of people, helps staff feel they are being treated fairly, and demonstrates a commitment of the effective delivery of services and programs as well as the utilization of human resources."

Two trends in the work place make supervision and evaluation especially crucial. One trend is an increase in the amount of discretion employees have in how they do their work, and the other trend is an increase in the expectation that work is a primary means to promote personal growth and satisfaction (Yankelovich & Immerwahr, 1984). Higher education professions have long held work discretion and personal growth as important values, but are experiencing increased pressures to plan for them more systematically in supervision and evaluation procedures. Many student affairs practitioners view higher education as a particularly attractive employment setting precisely because of these factors. However, as businesses increasingly provide similar opportunities, the desirability edge for higher education settings will lessen and thereby require increased efforts on the part of CSAAs to articulate the advantages of their work environment to emerging professionals.

Naisbeth and Aburdene (1985) stated that organizations that create the most nourishing environments for personal growth will attract and retain the most talented people. What follows then is that a thorough, fair, and developmental approach to supervision and evaluation will help create the kinds of environments most conducive to personal growth.

In white collar careers, Americans are experiencing an ever increasing desire for self-determined expectations and standards for performance (Hallett, 1987). This approach assumes collaboration, the opportunity to provide ideas, and the evaluation of the supervision being provided. Participative management approaches change the whole concept of supervision and increase the time that needs to be committed to the process.

The evaluation of college personnel, including student affairs staff members, is often more complicated than for positions in business settings. Responsibilities of student affairs practitioners frequently are not clearly defined; require interactive support; and often cross office, department, or unit distinctions (Lynton & Elman, 1987). These factors make the evaluation processes more difficult and crucial for effective performance. In many instances the clearest messages sent by supervisors are what they elect to evaluate (Waterman, 1987). The employee rightfully assumes that the criteria for evaluation must reflect those things that are most important. Therefore what becomes imperative is that supervisors provide accurate information about the relative importance (weighting) of the areas to be evaluated. In higher education, administrators usually define the goals and boundaries whereas discretion for how task responsibilities will be accomplished usually is assigned to the individual. Since discretion is so broad, clarity of goals and boundaries is even more important than in more structured environments.

Higher education institutions and student affairs practice obviously are different in many respects from the business world, and those differences are often the reason individuals choose the profession. Based on Belker (1978), business management emphasizes aspects of evaluation that differ from what is commonly experienced in student affairs.

1. In business, compensable factors are often used to measure exactly how an employee performs the specific tasks that the organization decides are most important. In student affairs, a much broader approach is used to decide how a staff member is meeting the goals and standards.

2. In business, retention is more often a goal for evaluation than it is in student affairs. Even though keeping the best people is important, student affairs leaders also encourage career development that includes helping staff members move to positions in other settings. In business, that help would either never be offered or would be a thinly veiled way of removing an unwanted employee.

3. Compensation issues are much different since most colleges do not rely on merit or bonus systems. In business, frequent direct compensation rewards are often based on performance. The private sector has such tools as bonuses, year-end gifts, and special perquisites to reward employees for exceptional service. Most institutions of higher education simply cannot match these rewards. In student affairs success or failure is often measured by verbal or written comments with an indirect relationship to salary or promotion.

4. Higher education usually provides more opportunity for upward evaluation. Student affairs practitioners more often influence how they are supervised and evaluated than for their counterparts in business. Student affairs staff members often have direct access to supervisors' written evaluations, a practice uncommon in most businesses.

5. Supervisors in business may not be particularly well trained to do evaluations, but they are usually offered more and better training than is common in student affairs programs. The whole evaluation process also tends to be better organized and endorsed in the business world.

Purposes of Evaluation

A number of purposes have been identified for the evaluation process. Two principal reasons for performance appraisals were reported by Watson (1981) as being judgmental and developmental. The *judgmental issues* are related to pay, promotion, training needs, demotions, and separations. *Developmental issues* refer to such categories as improving individual performance, selection, placement, and training policies and practices. Peterson and Tracy (1979) viewed the purposes of evaluation in much the same way, although they were more straightforward in their characterizations. They indicated that evaluations are conducted to determine wages and salaries and to make career decisions. Evaluations are conducted for multiple reasons, including resources planning and development and human resources administration (Caruth, Noe, & Mondy, 1988; Tyer, 1983). Brown (1988) defined evaluation (or performance appraisal) as "the process of assessing and recording staff performance for the purpose of making judgments about staff that lead to decisions" (p. 6).

The supervisor and the employee need to acknowledge which of the purposes are intended in the evaluation process. Organizations and their individual supervisors frequently have different goals for the evaluation process.

One area of evaluation that is frequently overlooked is its use for initiating change. The evaluation process can be a way to encourage change that the organization desires. For example, a student affairs division may desire to move toward a goal of more leadership training opportunities for students. Each director of a functional area might then be expected in the evaluation process to discuss ways the department has contributed to that general goal. Group participation in deciding appropriate ways to implement changes to meet the goal is crucial. The inclusion of a particular goal in the evaluation process clearly sends a message of the significance for the expectation for change. Kanter (1985) presented reasons why individuals may resist change including uncertainty about goals, fear of more work, fear of failure, loss of control, and surprise. The clearer the information about the changed expectations and the greater the participation in collaborative goal setting, the greater the chances for success.

Benefits of Evaluation

A number of benefits directly result from conducting routine employee evaluations. Morrisey (1983) categorized the benefits into two groups: loss avoided and value added. *Losses avoided* refer to problems that are averted and *value added* to that which is enhanced by conducting evaluations. The organization, the supervisor, and the employee can all gain from the evaluation process. The organization is likely to avoid litigation and can reduce employee turnover while developing more motivated employees and improving the internal communications of the organization. Even though no evaluation procedure guarantees that litigation by employees can be avoided, having direct observations of work performance in writing in an employee's file can help provide a record for the inspection of disinterested third parties, such as members of a jury or a judge. Each evaluation ought to focus on specific work related behaviors. Some of these might reflect on the fact that an employee is chronically late to work, or fails to complete tasks in a reasonable time frame, or abuses sick leave or vacation time. Matters of opinion are harder to document, including such factors as whether or not the person is pleasant over the telephone, or conveys a professional image to the public. Careful, systematic evaluations also may reduce conflicts and avoid misunderstandings about what the job entails. The employee is more likely to obtain a clear picture of the supervisor's expectations and gain greater personal satisfaction from the employment situation when the criteria for evaluation are clearly stated and communicated.

An Effective Evaluation System

Caruth, Noe, and Mondy (1988) identified eleven characteristics of an effective evaluation system. Their ideas are helpful for developing a system designed to meet the needs of an organization as well as the needs of individual staff members. The characteristics listed hereafter provide the basis of an effective system.

Formal. An effective system is formal, with written policies and procedures. A copy of the written material is made available to all those subject to the evaluation system.

Job Related. The evaluation that is conducted pertains to the job itself, and not to extraneous factors such as personal characteristics, family matters, or hobbies. Blake and Mouton added that "the importance of rewarding contribution based on merit remains undiminished" (1985, p. 136).

Valid. The standards established measure what they purport to measure.

Reliable. The appraisal system consistently yields the kind of information that is desired. Excellent performance should generate excellent evaluations, and poor performance should consistently lead to poor evaluations.

Open Communication. The evaluation interview provides a formal process whereby the supervisor and staff member can exchange ideas on the staff member's performance, but that does not substitute for routine feedback or interaction between them. Infrequent, formal discussions are not sufficient to meet the needs of either person.

Trained Appraisers. The fact that a person functions in a supervisory role is not an adequate reason to believe that the person is an expert evaluator. A good system will provide periodic training so that supervisors' evaluation skills are finely honed.

Ease in Use. The evaluation system should be easy to use and free of complexities. In fact, it should be based firmly on standards and measurements that result in greater validity and reliability.

Employee Access. Employees should have access to evaluation results and be provided with copies of written materials or have access to files where the materials are kept. If employees cannot see the written results, the process may become suspect.

Review Mechanism. As is the case in the military an automatic review of the performance evaluation should be done by the next level of supervision in the organization. This will provide a check of the process to assure fairness and equity.

Appeal Process. If an employee disagrees with the results of an evaluation, an appeal should be available. The appeals process protects employees from being treated unfairly, and also ensures that supervisors will do their jobs more conscientiously.

Brown (1988) has offered further criteria for defining an effective performance appraisal system in student affairs: (1) The staff to be evaluated should be involved with the evaluators in developing and evaluating the system. (2) A purpose statement for the system, which links the system to the units mission, should be developed and communicated. (3) Job standards provide the guidelines for determining what is an "adequate" performance. (4) Evaluators and staff members engage in an ongoing process of setting goals and providing feedback rather than depending solely on end-of-the-year review sessions. (5) The central orientation of the system is on education and developmental processes.

Student Affairs Staff Evaluation Components

Only general evaluation characteristics have been identified to this point. The following represents a list of more specific evaluation components that are integral to an evaluation system in student affairs. A sound performance appraisal instrument or tool should:

- be based on an accurate position description;
- be specific to tasks;
- coincide with academic term or annual reports;
- use a broad Likert-type scale of from 5 to 7 points;
- include weighting of responsibilities;
- include both ongoing job responsibilities and ad hoc projects that arose or were implemented during the evaluation period;
- be related to office, division, and institutional goals;
- be interactive, with about one half of the evaluation focusing on employee self-evaluations, comments, and future plans; and
- include a section concerning how the employee feels about the quality of supervision.

A future direction for business that would be beneficial if adopted by student affairs is described by Peters (1988, p. 283) as "achieving flexibility by empowering people." Listening to employees' ideas and concerns, involving more people in decision making, and creating more team projects are all increasingly suggested by management experts. Increased responsibility for self-management and cooperative work relationships should be hallmarks for student affairs. Unfortunately, turf protection, hierarchy of decisions, and bureaucracy still are prevalent.

Student affairs could improve its supervision and evaluation processes by providing clearer and more complete information, listening to staff concerns and suggestions, giving increased responsibility to individual and project teams, and recognizing excellence. The cost in time to improve these areas is repaid many times over in staff satisfaction, retention, and productivity. The financial cost may be minimal since recognition can be individual or public, and compensation changes are not necessarily expensive. A sample evaluation instrument that can be used in student affairs divisions is presented in Figure 1.

Types of Evaluation Instruments

A number of different approaches are available for conducting evaluations, and the content contained in these instruments can vary widely. A study of state-wide performance appraisals conducted by Feild and Holley (1975) indicated that more than 40% of the respondents were interested in such variables as quality and quantity of work, initiative, and human relations. Other factors that have been examined on appraisal forms are judgment, job knowledge, work habits, dependability, organizing and planning, and supervisory ability. Tyer (1983) identified eight different types of evaluation formats.

1. *Rating Scales.* This approach requires the evaluator to check a box or place a mark along a continuum which describes a particular characteristic of the employee. It is the most common approach, but is ambiguous and subjective in nature. The definition is left to the supervisor which can create problems (Odiorne, 1984). Feild and Holley (1975) found that 62% of 39 respondents used this format.

2. *Essay Reports.* The essay requires that the evaluator prepare an open-ended report on the employee. If the evaluator does not prepare a thoughtful report, then this approach will not work well. On the other hand, it forces the evaluator to reflect on the employee's performance and results. Thirteen percent of the respondents to the Feild and Holley (1975) survey reported using essay reports.

3. *Checklist.* In this situation the evaluator checks those statements that describe an employee from a list of statements. This approach is more person-based than performance-based.

4. *Critical Incidents.* This is an approach that uses anecdotal records that are kept on employees. The supervisor lists positive and negative incidents that pertain to certain aspects of the employee's work. This can be very time consuming, but pertains to actual behaviors and performance rather than personal characteristics.

5. *Forced Choice.* From a list of positive and negative statements about an employee, the supervisor is asked to make an evaluation. It is easy to administer but does not provide much useful feedback to the employee.

6. *Ranking.* This is fairly easy to complete, and can be conducted in a number of ways. Employees can be ranked from best to worst in a department, or they can be paired by comparing each employee with every other employee.

7. *Forced Distribution.* This is a variation on the ranking approach. Employees are ranked by percentiles or quartiles, for example. The major problem with this kind of approach is that the criteria for placing employees in various categories often is unclear, which can lead to employee suspicion and morale problems.

8. *Management by Objectives (MBO).* This approach refers to the supervisor and employee mutually agreeing upon a set of objectives that are quantifiable and measurable. This approach, while expensive, focuses on results. Hollmann (1979) observed that superiors must learn how to accurately assess and respond to the numerous factors determining how frequently feedback should be provided to each subordinate. According to Odiorne (1984) MBO Is the most complex system, but is worth the effort in terms of outcomes.

One other type of evaluation instrument worth noting is behaviorally anchored rating scales (BARS). BARS work well on lower-level jobs where requirements are well known, but are less helpful for professional and managerial positions (Odiorne, 1984). This approach was particularly attractive in some management circles, but research findings indicated that very little reason exists to believe that BARS are superior to alternative evaluation instruments (Schwab, Heneman, & DeCotis, 1979).

Student Affairs

Goals

A comprehensive and fair review of each student affairs member's performance of responsibilities is the primary objective. The purposes of evaluation are to provide opportunity for clarifying expectations, giving constructive criticism, setting professional growth objectives, and giving support for quality performance.

Components

The evaluation should primarily focus on the position description and the quality of performance of assigned tasks. Both standard expectations for normal ongoing responsibilities *and* additional expectations of yearly goals and new expectations should be evaluated. The weighting of components must be clear prior to initiating the evaluation process. The supervisor and the staff member should both complete evaluation forms and should share equally in oral discussions about progress.

Timing

Supervision assumes regular discussion of performance. Formal evaluations should be conducted at least yearly with a semi-annual format best for new professionals or newly hired staff. The best procedure is to combine the evaluation process with a review of current year goals, and the preliminary setting of goals and professional development plans for the next period.

Suggested Format

Name: _____

Title: _____

Date: _____

Period Evaluated: _____

Score Rating Definitions

5	Excellent	Performance is consistently well above expectations.
4	Above average	Performance is above acceptable level.
3	Average	Performance is acceptable.
2	Below Average	Performance is below acceptable expectations.
1	Unsatisfactory	Significant improvement is required.

I. Ratings On Individual Factors

Using the Rating Definitions, indicate the appropriate numerical rating and enter comments under each factor which follows. If the factor does not apply, enter N.A. in the Rating Column.

Rating

_____ A. **Work Accomplishment.** Accomplishment of primary mission of position or function, achieving results in a timely fashion.
Comments: _____

_____ B. **Communication:** Oral and written expression, keeping associates informed, maintaining appropriate relationships; persuasiveness.
Comments: _____

_____ C. **Decision-making:** Promptness; clarity, quality, consideration of all facts, willingness to assume responsibility.
Comments: _____

_____ D. Planning **and** Organizing: Developing plans; establishing priorities; completion and follow-up of assigned tasks. Organizing work to complete responsibilities.
Comments: _____

Figure 1. Sample Evaluation System.

_____ E. **Problem-solving:** Analytical ability; resourcefulness, overall awareness of cost implications; anticipating problems and solving them early.
Comments: _____

_____ F. **Initiative and Creativity:** Suggesting new approaches to problems, originality of approach; desire for new responsibility.
Comments: _____

_____ G. **Budgeting:** Setting realistic budget: effective use of people and funds; careful planning for new financial resources.
Comments: _____

_____ H. **Delegation of Responsibility:** Delegating authority in unit; ensuring effective coordination of subordinate units, supervisors and employees.
Comments: _____

_____ I. **Leadership:** Motivating subordinates to work in harmony for unit goals and objectives; ability to gain confidence and respect. Selection, training, and development of staff .
Comments: _____

_____ J. **Overall Performance Rating:**
Comments: _____

II. Yearly Goals And Adaptations

Rating

_____ A. Performance of current year individual goals.
Comments: _____

_____ B. Performance on contributions to unit and/or student affairs goals for the evaluation period.
Comments: _____

_____ C. Ability to adapt to and perform unexpected tasks that arose during the evaluation period.
Comments: _____

_____ D. Contributions to the profession through associations, presentations and writing.
Comments: _____

_____ E. Contributions to the college and local community.
Comments: _____

III. Strengths, Improvement Needed, And Action Plan

1. Describe the person's most significant strengths: _____
2. Describe the Person's development needs: _____
3. Identify specific professional development goals that are to be accomplished in the coming year and the support that will be provided to meet those goals: _____

IV. General Comments

1. Staff Member
   By my signature below, I confirm that this evaluation report has been discussed with me, however, it does not indicate my agreement or disagreement with the results except as I have commented here. Comments: _____
   Staff Member's Signature _____
   Date: _____

2. Supervisor Summary Comments: _____
   Supervisor's Signature _____
   Date: _____
   Position Description Reviewed: Date: _____
   (If changes made, please attach revised position description and forward to the Vice President of Student Affairs).

Figure 1. Continued

Difficulties In Evaluation

A number of problems are associated with evaluation, which can, in fact, seriously damage the value of the process.

Evaluator Errors. The person conducting the evaluation can make a number of mistakes, which affect the evaluation adversely. Common problems in this general classification include lack of the skills required of evaluators, the difference between day-to-day management skills and employee development skills, and the different frames of reference brought to the evaluation process (Tyer, 1983). Additionally, the "halo and horns effects" can influence the process. The *halo effect* is the tendency for the supervisor to place a positive aura or halo over the rating of a subordinate, while the *horns effect* refers to the tendency to rate people lower than their performance actually justifies (Odiorne, 1984).

Fortunato and Waddell (1981) pointed to several other evaluator errors, including leniency (supervisors being lenient to avoid facing the unpleasant task of confronting an employee), evaluating on the basis of potential (rating on the basis of the employee's potential rather than actual accomplishments), and associating (assuming an employee is proficient in all areas of responsibility because some are done very well). Other evaluator errors include tendencies to rate all employees as average, make a best guess, exhibit personal biases (Caruth, Noe, & Mondy, 1988), *and* not evaluating a staff member as being extremely good or bad, even when the performance is actually at such a level (Watson, 1981).

Instrumental Errors. If the instruments used in the appraisal have flaws, obviously barriers will be present to effective appraisals (Tyer, 1983). Establishing effective standards and measurements is difficult and challenging, but this must be accomplished if the performance of employees is to be measured accurately (Caruth, Noe, & Mondy, 1988). Other errors occur when goals or standards are not clearly articulated or understood before the evaluation occurs (Watson, 1981).

Process Problems. Tyer (1983) identified a number of problems related to the evaluation process. Among these are the tendencies to try to achieve too many objectives with a single evaluation instrument, some of which may be in conflict with others such as combining career development with salary adjustments, to be excessively formal, view evaluation as an annual activity, and to play the *zero-sum game*. The zero-sum game refers to the view that if one employee moves toward the top of the organization, then another must move down the ladder. In this regard, Penn (1979) added that "The primary goal of the [evaluation feedback] session should be to encourage improved performance, not to discourage or alienate the employee. Also, as noted earlier, the evaluation interview is not the time to discuss issues concerning salary adjustment or employee benefits" (p. 159).

Organizational Climate. Tyer (1983) referred to one other category of barriers to effective evaluation as those associated with the organizational climate. "Climate is determined importantly by characteristics, conduct, attitudes, expectations of other persons, by sociological and cultural realistics" (Gibson, Ivancevich, & Donnelly, 1973, p. 313).

Misconceptions about Performance Standards

Phillips (1985) identified a number of misconceptions about performance standards. "Performance standards represent a type of goal-setting process. In simple terms, a written performance standard is defined as a statement of the conditions that will exist when a job has been or is being satisfactorily performed" (p. 126). One's work will highly likely be evaluated against performance standards. "People are rewarded primarily for their contributions to goal attainment. Work habits and personal characteristics are relevant only to the extent that they influence or are related to organizational goals" (Penn, 1979, p. 156). For example, the change in emphasis of a department might be reflected in performance standards. In the recreational sports department, because of an increasing number of older students, the emphasis may change from providing an intramural program based on competitive teams and tournaments to more individualized fitness programs. Staff responsible in that area may have their performance goals adjusted to reflect the change in emphasis of the department. Among the problems that are associated with performance standards are the following (Phillips, 1985):

1. failure on the part of staff to realize the advantages of standards,
2. supervisors becoming overly involved in the mechanics of the process and forgetting the purpose of performance standards,
3. viewing performance standards as a mechanism for identifying failure,
4. failure to set realistic standards against which performance can be judged,
5. taking shortcuts so as to manipulate the evaluation process,
6. developing so many standards that the process becomes confused, and/or
7. hoping that the standards are a fad or gimmick and that they will go away.

Without appropriate standards of performance, the evaluation process will be badly flawed and unsuccessful. Therefore, whether one is being evaluated or serving as an evaluator, one needs to work diligently in setting appropriate standards and working toward making the total process successful.

Legal Considerations

A number of legal considerations are important to the evaluation process that should be recognized by everyone concerned with the evaluation process. Odiorne (1984) Indicated that a number of groups may not legally be discriminated against. That is not to say that it is acceptable to discriminate against members of non-protected groups, but the force of law makes it criminal to discriminate against racial minorities including African-Americans, Native Americans, and those of Hispanic descent; women; older workers; and the handicapped. Depending on state and local laws, Vietnam-era veterans also may have certain protected rights, as may homosexuals. Some states are moving toward passing "comparable worth" legislation, which means that employees doing work of a certain worth should be paid the same as the employees performing different, but similarly-valued work. How far this concept will extend is not clear but supervisors and practitioners alike should know the laws of their jurisdiction and the implications such legislation has for supervision.

In the final analysis the recommendation is that the most useful guidelines are for supervisors to treat all staff members fairly, to be aware of any special legal requirements incumbent upon members of their jurisdiction, and to seek help from the institution's legal counsel should questions arise, (See Chapter 13 for further discussion of the legal issues related to employment.)

Civil Service Issues

Those employed in private colleges will not be confronted with the requirements of the state civil service commission or a similar body. Obviously, this does not mean that staff members should be treated poorly because they are not state employees. What it does mean is that supervisors will not encounter legislated aspects of supervising public employees. Morrisey (1983) pointed out "that there are some significant differences in the way performance appraisals must be handled in the public sector when compared to the private sector" (p. 26). Among these differences are substantially more media attention, elected officials focusing on state-assisted institutions, relationships with employee unions, and taxpayer revolt. Although beginning professionals seldom have to address these issues, to realize that significant distinctions do exist between public and private institutions and that one's work will be affected accordingly is important.

Equity Issues

Supervisors must conduct both supervision and evaluation as equitably as possible. Since everyone is subject to both positive and negative bias, the more objective the expectations and evaluations the better. Included in the process is the necessity for providing challenging work in conjunction with support for success. Low expectations are as discriminatory as an inequitable set of performance measurements. Caution is particularly necessary when gender, race, and age differences add to the supervisor's need to understand individual goals, skills, and preferences. To act on the assumption that one can be more straight forward in providing constructive criticism to male staff members denies female staff members an equal opportunity to receive clear signals, to grow toward the goals, and to learn the "system." In some situations, another level of supervision may need to be added to insure equity.

Equity should not be construed to mean literally that the same expectations and responsibilities exist for everyone. All supervision and evaluation should be individualized, but the criteria for individualization should be based on skill, potential, experience, and goals rather than on gender, age, or any other personal circumstance.

A further equity problem can occur in the area of mentoring or sponsorship, a topic addressed earlier. Because the process of mentoring may be (usually is) initiated by a supervisor, the decision regarding who is singled out for special time and attention is of concern. While subjective criteria are unavoidable, the selection should be based on observed potential, past performance, individual goals and motivation, and the opportunities available to provide the staff person with experiences that will benefit his or her career progress.

Training Supervisors to Conduct Evaluations

Even in student affairs settings where a fair, complete evaluation process is used, a major problem may occur when those responsible for the supervision are not trained to implement the evaluations. At the point of hiring and at every promotion (change of responsibility) the supervisor needs to be taught the importance of and the process of implementing the evaluation system. Inconsistent evaluations among supervisors or between departments are unfair and a major cause of low staff morale. A seminar on conducting the evaluations should be offered annually and a team consisting of staff members at all levels should review the entire evaluation process at least every three years. A corollary to the process is that all candidates for positions in a student division should be clearly informed about the supervision and evaluation processes in use.

Summary

Information has been presented on issues and trends in supervision and evaluation. The responsibility for the quality and content of the supervision and evaluation processes is mutually shared by the institution, the student affairs division, the individual supervisor, and the individual staff member. Excellent supervision and evaluation contribute to work satisfaction, productivity, employee retention, and staff cooperation.

Student affairs staff members expect broad discretion to determine how they will accomplish their responsibilities and significant involvement in setting task priorities. They deserve clear information on the performance expectations and the relative significance of each responsibility. Student affairs professionals should take leadership in adapting recent trends in human resource management to higher education.

Ethical and professional considerations must be considered in designing a fair and equitable evaluation system. Training of supervisors is crucial for consistent application of performance reviews.

References

Barkhaus. R. (1983, Summer). Career development in the corporation. *Journal of College Placement*, pp. 29–32.

Belker, L. B. (1978). *The first-time manager*. New York: AMACOM.

Blake, R. R., & Mouton, J. S. (1974). *The managerial grid*. Houston: Gulf.

Blake, R. R., & Mouton, J. S. (1981). *Productivity: The human side.* San Francisco: Jossey-Bass.

Blake, R. R., & Mouton, J. S. (1985). *The managerial grid III,* Houston: Gulf.

Brown. R. D. (1988). *Performance appraisal as a tool for staff development.* New Directions for Student Services (No. 43). San Francisco: Jossey-Bass.

Caruth, D. L., Noe, III, R. M., & Mondy, R. W. (1988). *Staffing the contemporary organization.* New York: Quorum.

Council for the Advancement of Standards for Student Services/Development Programs (CAS) (1986). *CAS standards and guidelines for student services /development programs.* Washington. D. C.: Author.

Derr, C. B. (1986). *Managing the new careerists.* San Francisco: Jossey-Bass.

Field, H. S., & Holley, W. H. (1975). Performance appraisal—An analysis of state-wide practices. *Public Personnel Management 4*(3), 145–150.

Fortunato, R. T., & Waddell, D. G. (l981). *Personnel administration in higher education.* San Francisco: Jossey-Bass.

Fuhrmann. B. (1987). Career paths in higher education: Lessons from the corporate world. *National Forum, 67*(1), 22–24.

Gibson, J. L., Ivancevich, J. M., & Donnelly, Jr., J. H. (1973). *Organizations: Structure, process, behavior.* Dallas: Business publications.

Hallett, J. J. (1987). *Worklife vision: Redefining work for the information economy.* Alexandria, VA. American Society for Personnel Administrators.

Hersey, P. & Blanchard, K. (1977). *Management of organizational behavior: Utilizing human resources (3rd ed.).* Englewood Cliffs, NJ: Prentice-Hall.

Hersey, P. & Blanchard, K. (1982). *Management of organizational behavior: Utilizing human resources (4th ed.).* Englewood Cliffs, NJ: Prentice-Hall.

Herzberg, F., Mausner, B., & Snyderman, B. B. (1959). *The motivation to work.* New York: Wiley.

Hollmann, R. W. (1979). Applying MBO research to practice. In P. S. Greenlaw (Ed.). *Readings in personnel management* (pp. 140–147). Philadelphia: Saunders.

Kanter, R. M. (1985, April). Managing the human side of change. *Management Review,* pp. 52–56.

Kaye, B. L. (1981). Up is not the only way. *Supervisory Management.* 25 (2), 2–9.

Kelly, K. E. (1984). Initiating a relationship with a mentor in student affairs. *NASPA Journal, 21*(3) , 49–54.

Kram, K. F. (1986). Mentoring in the workplace. In D. T. Hall (Ed.), *Career development in organizations* (pp. 160–201). San Francisco: Jossey-Bass.

Lynton, E., & Elman, S. (1987). New priorities for the university. San Francisco: Jossey-Bass.

Maccoby, M. (1988). *Why work: Leading the new generation.* New York: Simon & Schuster.

Maslow, A. H. (1954). *Motivation and personality.* New York: Harper.

McGregor, D. (1960). *The human side of enterprise.* New York: McGraw-Hill.

Morrisey, G. L. (1983). *Performance appraisal in the public sector.* Menlo Park, CA: Addison-Wesley.

Naisbeth, J., & Aburden, P. (1985). *Re-inventing the corporation.* New York: Warner.

Odiorne, G. S. (1984). *Strategic management of human resources.* San Francisco: Jossey-Bass.

Penn, J. R. (1979). Staff evaluation. In G. D. Kuh (Ed.). *Evaluation in student affairs* (pp. 149–160). Cincinnati, OH: ACPA Media.

Peters, T. (1988). *Thriving on chaos: Handbook for a management revolution.* New York: Knopf.

Peterson, R. B., & Tracy, L. (1979). *Systematic management of human resources.* Menlo Park, CA. Addison-Wesley.

Phillips. J. J. (1985). *Improving supervisors' effectiveness*. San Francisco: Jossey-Bass.

Schwab, D. P., Heneman, III, H. G., & DeCotts, T. A. (1979). Behaviorally anchored rating scales: A review of the literature. In P. S. Greenlaw (Ed.), *Readings in personnel management* (pp. 148–159). Philadelphia: Saunders.

Teas, R. K. (1981). A test of a model of department store salespeople's job satisfaction. *Journal of Retailing 57*(1), 3–25.

Tyer, C. B. (1983). Employee performance appraisal: Process in search of a technique. In S. W. Hays and R. C. Kearney (Eds.). *Public personnel administration: Problems and prospects* (pp. 118–136). Englewood Cliffs. NJ: Prentice Hall.

Waterman. R. H. (1987). *The renewal factor: How the best get and keep the competitive edge*. New York: Bantam Books.

Watson, C. E. (1981). *Results-oriented managing: The key to performance*. Menlo Park, CA: Addison-Wesley.

Yankelovich, D., & Immerwahr, J. (1984). The emergence of expressivism will revolutionize the contract between workers and employers. In L. Chiara & D. Lacey (Eds.), *Work in the 21st century* (pp. 11–24). Alexandria. VA: American Society for Personnel Administration.

Suggested Readings

Baird, L. S., Beatty, R. W., & Schneier, C. E. (Eds.). (1982). *The performance appraisal sourcebook*. Amherst, MA: Human Resources Development Press.

Brown, R. D. (1988). *Performance appraisal as a tool for staff development*. New Directions for Student Services (No. 43). San Francisco: Jossey-Bass.

Council for the Advancement of Standards for Student Services/Development Programs (CAS). (1986). *CAS standards and guidelines for student services/development programs*. Washington, D. C.: Author.

Fortunato, R. T., & Waddell, D. G. (1981). *Personnel administration in higher education*. San Francisco: Jossey-Bass.

Morrisey, G. L. (1983). *Performance appraisal in the public sector*. Menlo Park, CA. Addison-Wesley.

"Don't Drink the Water?": A Guide to Encountering a New Institutional Culture

Elizabeth J. Whitt

Introduction

Last May, Janet completed her master's degree in college student personnel administration at Midwestern State University. Her involvement in student government there as an undergrad led to her interest in student affairs work. Janet's graduate program provided a thorough grounding in student development theory and she was able to put that in-class learning into practice in her role as grad advisor in a hall of 1200 students.

During the job-hunting season Janet found her "ideal job"—Director of Residence Life and Student Activities at a small independent college in the Northeast. She had been looking for a "generalist" position in a setting where she could be actively and broadly involved in students' growth and development. During her first three months at the college, however, Janet has found herself in several encounters with students, faculty, and other administrators which have left her confused and frustrated. Most recently, no faculty have responded to her request for volunteers to serve as "secret holiday elves" for residence hall floors. She wonders what happened to her "ideal job" and expresses frustration to her grad school friends about the college's lack of concern for students.

Janet's situation is, of course, not unusual. In the first issue of Connections, Oblander and Strange (1989) examined the first-year experiences of new student affairs professionals. The newcomers described encountering challenges to their expectations, assumptions, and beliefs—challenges to their understanding of student affairs work, to their expectations of themselves and their colleagues, and to their professional and personal values. In addition, newcomers felt like outsiders, unfamiliar with the local language and isolated in their status as "new kid on the block." To a great extent, the experiences of newcomers, including their fit with, and investment in, the new institution, were found to be mediated by aspects of institutional culture, including values, norms, traditions, history, and so forth.

The purpose of this article is to provide new professionals with some guidelines for learning about and developing an understanding—and appreciation—of the cultures in which they now (or are about to) work. A brief description of cultural definitions and perspectives is followed by a discussion of the implications of institutional cultures for newcomers. Finally, a list of suggestions for a "traveler" in a new culture is offered.

An Overview of Cultural Perspectives

"Culture" is complicated to talk about and understand, in part because there are so many different ways of defining what the word means and what the concept encompasses. The concept of culture has roots in many disciplines, including anthropology, sociology, and social psychology, and each has its own definition of what culture means and how it should be studied (Kuh & Whitt, 1988). Organizational culture has been variously defined as the assumptions and understandings that guide daily life in the workplace (Deal & Kennedy, 1983); the shared philosophies, assumptions, values, expectations, attitudes, and norms that bind a group of people (Kilmann, Saxton, Serpa, & Associates, 1985); and the means developed within an organization to cope with problems in its environment (Schein, 1985). For the purpose of this article, institutional culture is defined as

> the collective, mutually shaping patterns of norms, values, practices, beliefs, and assumptions that guide the behavior of individuals and groups in an institution of higher education and provide a frame of reference within which to interpret the meaning of events and actions on and off campus (Kuh & Whitt, 1988, p. 13).

The culture of an institution of higher education (IHE) is evident in its traditions, stories, ceremonies, history, myths, heroines and heroes, interactions among members, policies and practices, symbols, mission and philosophy, and the curriculum (Clark, 1984). These and other artifacts are what we usually think of when we hear the phrase "institutional culture"—what we can see, what is most obvious about the culture of an institution, including Commencement, Homecoming, stories told about the founder and the crises weathered in the early years of the school, the mascot and motto, and welcoming speeches from the President to new students and their parents.

Artifacts of culture are founded on, and illustrate, the basic values of the institution (Schein, 1985). That welcome speech may emphasize to new students the importance of hard work in class and involvement in out-of-class activities. Homecoming may demonstrate the value placed on lifelong commitment to the college on the part of alumni/ae and the importance of including current students in the planning and implementation of university-wide events. The faculty rewards system may illustrate a commitment to teaching or the values of research and publication.

Undergirding cultural artifacts and values are basic assumptions and beliefs (Schein, 1985)—"the core of culture" (Kuh & Whitt, 1988, p. 25). These assumptions strongly influence what the members of a culture believe to be important, how they spend their time, what they expect from one another and themselves, and how they act and interact. It is the fundamental nature of institutional assumptions and beliefs to be implicit in the life of the institution and tacit in the hearts and minds of its people. As a result, these assumptions are very difficult to identify by participants, especially newcomers. In the following section, the interaction between newcomers and the institution's culture will be discussed in more detail.

A college or university's culture is also influenced by the size, type (public or private, church-related), and the age of the institution. In any case, the culture of an IHE provides the people within it with ways to make meaning of institutional events and activities; create internal and external images; evoke loyalty and commitment; and develop and maintain a deep belief in the value of the institution that sustains its people in times of crisis (Clark, 1980).

Encountering a New Culture

Oblander and Strange (1988) asserted that the perceptions and perspectives of newcomers regarding the new institution are greatly influenced by their experiences in previous institutional cultures. Similarly, Van Maanen (1984) stated that "people carry culture with them." (p. 217). For example, the beliefs, assumptions, values, and attitudes developed in undergraduate and graduate school and prior employment settings affect newcomers' understanding of, and response to, the events, requirements, tasks, values, and assumptions encountered in the new institution.

Similarities and differences between prior and new institutional cultures can affect the ease with which newcomers can figure out and adapt to the new "way we do things—and see things—

around here" (Van Maanen & Schein, 1979). Thus, the newcomer is simultaneously learning, living, and shaping the culture of the new institution.

Newcomers face additional challenges in trying to learn about and understand the culture of a new institution because of the nature of institutional cultures. For example, what is referred to or thought of as an institution's culture may, in fact, be many cultures (Kuh & Whitt, 1988; Morgan, 1986). A college is made up of many groups, including students, faculty, administrators, and staff, each of which may have its own set of values and beliefs, and some of which may compete with the values of other groups or of the institution as a whole. Faculty and student affairs administrators may have similar or different beliefs about what the mission of the institution is and what the needs of students are. The faculty subculture (if it can be described as such) may be further subdivided by differing commitments to teaching and research and different levels of commitment to involvement with students outside of class. Student affairs administrators may differ in their understanding of and belief in the usefulness of student development theories, or in their perceptions of how to facilitate student growth outside of class. The student subculture may, in fact, be many subcultures, including residence hall groups, Greek groups, and groups defined by race, ethnicity, lifestyle preference, political beliefs, or career goals. In addition, the culture of a college or university is surrounded and influenced by the cultures of its external environment, including the local community, state, and region, as well as the society at large (Kuh & Whitt, 1988). Economic, social, political, geographical, and other conditions affect attitudes about the financing of higher education; expectations of IHEs and their faculty, staff, and students; and so forth.

Finally, while institutional culture is a source of stability and continuity (Kuh & Whitt, 1988), it is also always evolving, influenced by changes in the expectations, beliefs, and values of members of the institution—and the addition of new members—as well as changes in the external environment (Morgan, 1986). Also, because institutional culture develops slowly and is founded on the basic assumptions and values of its participants, the culture may be so taken for granted by people in the institution that it has become invisible to them (Kuh & Whitt, 1988). As a consequence, attempts on the part of newcomers to figure out those assumptions and values, as well as the artifacts that provide evidence of institutional culture, are further complicated.

This discussion of some of the challenges newcomers face in trying to figure out and understand the culture of their new work setting is not intended to discourage attempts to do so. Although the process is complicated, it _can_ be accomplished. In the next section, some suggestions to facilitate that process are offered.

"Travel" Tips

Morgan (1989) has described moving into a new organization as being somewhat like moving to a new country. Newcomers to an IHE encounter a new language, a new set of daily routines and practices, new cultural artifacts, values, and assumptions, and a new way of looking at themselves. Newcomers may also experience "culture shock," the physical and psychological effects of finding differences between expectations and reality (Rhinesmith, 1975). At the same time, newcomers have the opportunity to learn about a new place and a new group of people while learning more about themselves.

The metaphor of being a foreign visitor, a stranger in a strange country, is continued in the following "travel hints," suggestions for anyone who wants to learn about and understand the culture of a new institutional setting.

1. Read the Guidebooks Before You Leave Home.

Read as much about the new culture in advance as you possibly can. Some documents, such as job descriptions and manuals, long-range plans, goal and mission statements, and admissions materials, will probably be made available to you as part of the recruitment and hiring process. Other potentially fruitful sources of information about a college include institutional histories, student newspapers, alumni/ae publications, student affairs brochures, residence hall handbooks, and publications for new students (especially those by current students) (Whitt & Kuh, 1989). The purpose of reading these documents is to learn about the mission, history, and traditions of the institution, as well as to get a sense of how it portrays itself to outsiders as well as people within the college. Newcomers might find it useful to think about the messages communicated in these documents and the institutional values the messages reflect. What do institutional materials say about what it is like to be a member of the culture? What do these documents indicate is important to the people in the institution? What, if any, questions do you have as a result of reading the documents?

2. Identify Your Own Cultural "Baggage."

That is, try to understand your own values, assumptions, and beliefs and the ways in which they have been shaped by your previous cultures, including cultures of other colleges or universities and the culture of the student affairs profession as communicated during your graduate studies. What, for example, are your professional values and your assumptions about student affairs work—what such work includes, what role student affairs work should play in a college or university, how it should be done and by whom, and for what purposes? What are your beliefs about the purposes of higher education, and about the ways in which students should be treated? What assumptions and expectations do you have about how someone in your new position—and in your new office or division—should spend her or his time? You may also find it useful to think about your values about work, about relationships and interactions among people with whom you work, about relationships and interactions between student affairs staff and faculty and between student affairs staff and students. How have those values been influenced by your graduate and undergraduate experiences? And what are your impressions about the values and assumptions about these matters held by people in your new institution?

Of course, some of these questions have to do with fit between you and your new organization and ought to be asked during the process of deciding whether or not to take the job. That is not to imply that you ought to look for a new work setting that is exactly like that to which you have been socialized as a graduate student. You should, however, be aware of differences (or potential differences) and have some idea about what implications those differences have for your work.

To some extent, you can become aware of the cultural lenses you wear—the cultural values and assumptions you carry with you—only after you move to a new place and encounter the "daily realities" (Morgan, 1989, p. 157) of that place. This process of self-understanding is not, then, something for which you can completely prepare yourself in advance of your "trip." But understanding that you *are* wearing cultural lenses—whether you know how they influence your ability to see or not—can be very helpful in learning about and adjusting to a new culture.

3. Get to Know the Natives.

The best source of information about a culture is, of course, the people in that culture. Talk to people about their lives in the culture. Ask questions. Get as many perspectives as possible about what the institution is about, what the elements of the culture are, why things are the way they are, and so on. The more different points of view about a culture you can obtain, the more accurate a picture you can develop and the more effectively you can get to know and understand that culture.

4. Find a Guide.

Find someone who is willing to "show you around," literally and figuratively, someone who is willing to take you under his or her wing, talk to you about "how we do things here," and answer your questions with honesty and appreciation for what it is like to be a newcomer. Your guide might be your supervisor, another staff member, or someone who is also relatively new to the institution. Although students are a very valuable source of information about a college or university, avoid using a student as your guide; you need a guide who can help you learn what it means to be a student affairs professional in that institution. In fact, you may do well to have more than one guide so that you can obtain more than one person's perspective on the institution, how things work there, what student affairs staff do, and how they ought to act.

5. Experience Local Color.

There are obvious occasions—convocations, reunions, Oktoberfest, Spring Fling, commencements, awards ceremonies, induction and orientation events, recruitment activities—at which the culture of the institution is very clearly on display and you can get a sense of the richness of its history and traditions. Events at which the President speaks, or when outsiders are present to hear about the institution, or when faculty gather to affirm the institution's academic purposes offer excellent opportunities to learn about and understand cultural symbols.

6. See the Sights.

You will probably be most concerned, at first, about getting a sense of the physical environment—where your office is, where to pick up a paycheck, where the copy machine is, and so on. You may not be aware, however, that the physical environment of an institution also reflects its culture, including the values and beliefs of participants (Kuh & Whitt, 1988). The location, design, and maintenance of campus buildings; the availability of gathering places and open space; and the amount of space for use and control by students can provide evidence of the value the institution places on student and community life (Kuh, Schuh, Whitt & Associates, forthcoming).

In addition to the physical environment, the "sights" of a culture also include the ways in which people act and interact. Observing activities, events, and other behavior can provide many insights into an institution's culture. As was stated in the previous "hint," some events or times of the academic year, such as New Student Orientation, Homecoming, or Commencement, can be particularly fruitful sources of information; at these times, the values of the institution are made explicit in ceremonies, traditions, and the words and stories of institutional leaders (Whitt & Kuh, 1989).

7. Take Side Trips.

This "hint" is a corollary to number 6. Evidence of, and messages about, a culture can also be found in less colorful or special events; daily activities and routine interactions, such as staff meetings, classes, and meal times, can also say much about the culture of the institution (Morgan, 1986; Whitt & Kuh, 1989). In fact, it may be the case that the values expressed or demonstrated at special events may be only espoused and not enacted in the daily lives of people in the institution. How do people spend their work time? Are office doors usually closed or open? Who interacts with whom and how? Who speaks at staff meetings and what do they say? How do staff and faculty interact with students? How do students interact with one another? Do people speak to one another in hallways and on sidewalks? When problems arise, what is at issue and how are problems resolved? And what do these behaviors say about the values and assumptions of the institution?

8. Learn the Language.

Every culture—an institution, a profession—has its own language. The language of that culture, including expressions and words and their meanings within that cultural context, encourage feelings of belonging or exclusion and reflect and communicate cultural values and assumptions (Kuh & Whitt, 1988). For example, the language of The Evergreen State College (Washington) is the language of an "alternative" institution committed to personal freedom, political and social activism, and egalitarianism. The College motto is *Omnia Extares*, roughly translated as "Let it all hang out"; faculty and students refer to themselves as "younger learners and older learners" (Kuh et al; in press). Other aspects of an institution's language include acronyms (GSB, ASUN, SAB, and so on), course numbers, and names of heroines, heroes, and campus buildings.

Also part of the language of an institution's culture are terms of respect—or disrespect—for groups and individuals within the culture. The words used to refer to racial, ethnic, and lifestyle groups and women vary by institution, region, and, perhaps, student cohort (Kuh et al; in press). It is important to know and acknowledge the names by which people want to be called.

It is also important to be aware of the language of subcultures, such as that of student affairs staff. The student affairs profession has a terminology—or jargon—to describe its work and values: "the student personnel point of view," "caring abut the whole student," "student development," "developmental programs," "CAS Standards," and so on. The student affairs staff in your new setting may or may not be familiar with and/or use this language. Also, other staff and faculty may not understand or appreciate student affairs terminology; the use of jargon may, in fact, create barriers to achieving common educational purposes by highlighting differences and obfuscating communication.

9. Seek Storytellers.

Stories, such as those about heroines and heroes or past achievements and crises, can be a very useful source of information about "how we do things around here" (Morgan, 1989). Stories convey cultural expectations and values, as well as institutional history and mission, and include both explicit and implicit lessons abut how people ought to behave—"scripts" for newcomers (Morgan, 1989, p. 161). For example, the story is told at Stanford University of how, when approached by a messenger with a request to meet with Leland Stanford, Senior, about becoming president of the new university in California, David Starr Jordan (then President of Indiana University) insisted on finishing the class he was teaching. This story is intended to illustrate the commitment to teaching that is part of Stanford's history (Kuh et al, in press).

Most campuses have an historian. This may be someone who is formally appointed to that role, such as an archivist, or a person, such as a senior faculty or staff member or alumna/us, who has been at the institution for a long time. It would be worth your while to talk to that person to hear the culture's stories, get a sense of its history, and of the ways in which the past has shaped the present. In addition, many colleges and universities have written institutional histories that can provide information and insight for newcomers.

10. Ask for Directions.

Don't hesitate to ask questions when you need information or don't understand something. Do not assume that you know what is to be done and how. You may have experience at being a Director of Student Activities, but you may not know exactly what that role means and how it should be performed in your new institution. It may be the case, for example, that faculty expect to be invited to student events—a practice that was not acceptable at your previous institution. You may have received thorough socialization to being a student affairs professional in your graduate program, but you may not be aware of the implicit rules of professional behavior, such as what is or is not to be considered confidential or how one is expected to behave in interactions with students, at your new institution. You can learn some of these rules and expectations only after violating them—some mistakes are to be expected!—, but if you are aware that such rules are likely to exist, you can ask about them before stumbling over them.

11. Phone Home.

You may find it useful to talk to colleagues in other institutions, in order to re-connect with broader professional values and to perform "reality checks" on your impressions of what you hear and see in the new culture. Such conversations can help you to step back and get a more complete and accurate picture of the institution. Morgan (1989) asserted that newcomers to a culture are uniquely qualified to obtain a wholistic cultural perspective because they take less for granted and see what is probably invisible to insiders. You may find that talking to someone outside the institution enables you to see more clearly what it is that you think you see. You may, for example, have received contradictory information about "the way we do things here." It may be helpful to talk about those differences in order to make sense of them.

Similarly, you may find that other newcomers are an effective source of support and provide a non-threatening place to ask questions and voice frustrations or confusion. The experiences or questions that you encounter may be shared by other newcomers and you may help one another to figure out the new culture by sharing your impressions. There is potential danger, however, in using only newcomers for support or information as that may hinder your learning about and becoming integrated into the new setting. In addition, it is possible to "phone home" too often; think of the adjustment problems of the new student who goes home every weekend and calls home every night!

12. Travel with an Open Mind.

Chaffee and Tierney (1988) recommend learning about a new institutional culture "in the same way [you] learn to know a valued friend" (p. 4)—slowly, patiently, and putting aside judgments and evaluations. Respect and appreciate the uniqueness of the new culture and do not assume that, because something—a practice or tradition or value—is different than what you are used to or what you expect, it is wrong or bad; learn and understand what that practice or value means in the institutional context in which it occurs (Whitt, forthcoming).

13. Don't Expect to Change the Culture.

As was mentioned previously, culture is a force for stability and continuity, and, therefore, elements of culture are resistant to change, especially by outsiders or newcomers. As people are perhaps more likely to accept feedback from friends, so, too, are cultures more likely to accept feedback from their members (Kuh & Whitt, 1988). Traditions and practices develop over time as a means to bind members of a community with shared meanings and values, and so are likely to be strongly protected from interference. This does not mean that institutional cultures or their artifacts cannot and do not change; they do, however, change slowly. There is, perhaps, a balance between understanding and becoming part of a culture and accepting all of its elements as not needing alteration.

Conclusion

The process of learning about a new institutional culture is also a process of learning how to do one's job effectively. Over time, the new culture becomes one's own; what is new or different becomes less obvious as its elements, values, and assumptions are incorporated into one's own system of beliefs. The extent to which this occurs and the time the process takes varies, depending on the newcomer's openness, insightfulness, and flexibility and the nature of the new setting (whether that be an entire institution or a division thereof)—its size, complexity, the strength and clarity of its culture, and the character of its members. However, with open-mindedness and patience, newcomers *can* learn to understand and appreciate the culture of their new "country."

References

Chaffee, E. E., & Tierney, W. G. (1988). *Collegiate culture and leadership strategies*. New York: American Council of Education/Macmillan Publishing.

Clark, B. R. (1980). *Academic culture*. Yale Higher Education Research Group Report No. 42. New Haven, CT: Institution for Social and Policy Studies, Yale University.

_____. (1984). *The higher education system: Academic organization in cross-national perspective*. Berkeley, CA: University of California Press.

Deal, T. E., & Kennedy, A. A. (1982). *Corporate cultures*. Reading, MA: Addison-Wesley.

Kilmann, R. H., Saxton, M., Serpa, R., & Associates (Eds.) (1985). *Gaining control of the corporate culture*. San Francisco: Jossey-Bass.

Kuh, G. D., Schuh, J. H., Whitt, E. J., & Associates (in press). *Involving colleges: Encouraging student learning and personal development through out-of-class experiences*. San Francisco: Jossey-Bass.

Kuh, G. D., & Whitt, E. J. (1988). *The invisible tapestry: Cultures in American colleges and universities*. ASHE-ERIC Higher Education Report Series, No. 1. Washington, DC: Association for the Study of Higher Education.

Morgan, G. (1986). *Images of organization*. Beverly Hills, CA: Sage.

Morgan, G. (1989). *Creative organization theory: A resource book*. Newbury Park, CA: Sage.

Oblander, D., & Strange, C. C. (1989, Fall). Jumping in: Case studies of the first year in the profession. *Connections, 1*, 4–7.

Rhinesmith, S. (1975). *Bring home the world*. New York: AMACOM.

Schein, E. H. (1985). *Organizational culture and leadership*. San Francisco: Jossey-Bass.

Van Maanen, J. (1984). Doing new things in old ways: The chains of socialization. In J. L. Bess (Ed.), *College and university organization: Insights from the behavior sciences* (pp. 211–247). New York: New York University Press.

Van Maanen, J., & Schein, E. H. (1979). Toward a theory of organizational socialization. In B. M. Staw (Ed.), *Research in organizational behavior* (Vol. 1) (pp. 209–264). Greenwich, CT: JAI Press.

Whitt, E. J. (in press). Making the familiar strange: Discovering culture. In G. D. Kuh (Ed.), *Using cultural perspectives in student affairs*. Alexandria, VA: ACPA Media.

Whitt, E. J., & Kuh, G. D. (1989). *Qualitative methods in higher education research: A team approach to multiple site investigation*. Paper presented at the Annual Meeting of the Association for the Study of Higher Education, Atlanta.

Note

Elizabeth J. Whitt is Assistant Professor, Department of Professional Studies in Education, Iowa State University.

Statement of Ethical Principles and Standards

AMERICAN COLLEGE PERSONNEL ASSOCIATION

Preamble

The American College Personnel Association (ACPA), a Division of the American Association for Counseling and Development (AACD), is an association whose members are dedicated to enhancing the worth, dignity, potential, and uniqueness of each individual within post-secondary educational institutions and thus to the service of society. ACPA members are committed to contributing to the comprehensive education of the student, protecting human rights, advancing knowledge of student growth and development, and promoting the effectiveness of institutional programs, services, and organizational units. As a means of supporting these commitments, members of ACPA subscribe to the following principles and standards of ethical conduct. Acceptance of membership in ACPA signifies that the member agrees to adhere to the provisions of this statement. This statement is designed to complement the AACD Ethical Standards (1988) by addressing issues particularly relevant to college student affairs practice. Persons charged with duties in various functional areas of higher education are also encouraged to consult ethical standards specific to their professional responsibilities.

Use of This Statement

The principal purpose of this statement is to assist student affairs professionals in regulating their own behavior by sensitizing them to potential ethical problems and by providing standards useful in daily practice. Observance of ethical behavior also benefits fellow professionals and students due to the effects of modeling. Self-regulation is the most effective and preferred means of assuring ethical behavior. If, however, a professional observes conduct by a fellow professional that seems contrary to the provisions of this document, several courses of action are available.

Initiate a Private Conference

Because unethical conduct often is due to a lack of awareness or understanding of ethical standards, a private conference with the professional(s) about the conduct in question is an important initial line of action. This conference, if pursued in a spirit of collegiality and sincerity, often may resolve the ethical concern and promote future ethical conduct.

Pursue Institutional Remedies

If private consultation does not produce the desired results, institutional channels for resolving alleged ethical improprieties may be pursued. All student affairs divisions should have a widely-publicized process for addressing allegations of ethical misconduct.

Contact ACPA Ethics Committee

If the ACPA member is unsure about whether a particular activity or practice falls under the provisions of this statement, the Ethics Committee may be contacted in writing. The member should describe in reasonable detail (omitting data that would identify the person(s) as much as possible) the potentially unethical conduct or practices and the circumstances surrounding the situation. Members of the Committee or others in the Association will provide the member with a summary of opinions regarding the ethical appropriateness of the conduct or practice in question. Because these opinions are based on limited information, no specific situation or action will be judged "unethical." The responses rendered by the Committee are advisory only and are not an official statement on behalf of ACPA.

Request Consultation from ACPA Ethics Committee

If the institution wants further assistance in resolving the controversy, an institutional representative may request on-campus consultation. Provided all parties to the controversy agree, a team of consultants selected by the Ethics Committee will visit the campus at the institution's expense to hear the allegations and to review the facts and circumstances. The team will advise institutional leadership on possible actions consistent with both the content and spirit of the ACPA Statement of Ethical Principles and Standards. Compliance with recommendations is voluntary. No sanctions will be imposed by ACPA. Institutional leaders remain responsible for assuring ethical conduct and practice. The consultation team will maintain confidentiality surrounding the process to the extent possible.

Submit Complaint to AACD Ethics Committee

If the alleged misconduct may be a violation of the AACD Ethical Standards, the person charged is a member of AACD, and the institutional process is unavailable or produces unsatisfactory results, then proceedings against the individual(s) may be brought to the AACD Ethics Committee for review. Details regarding the procedures may be obtained by contacting AACD headquarters.

Ethical Principles

No statement of ethical standards can anticipate all situations that have ethical implications. When student affairs professionals are presented with dilemmas that are not explicitly addressed herein, five ethical principles may be used in conjunction with the four enumerated standards (Professional Responsibility and Competence, Student Learning and Development, Responsibility to the Institution, and Responsibility to Society) to assist in making decisions and determining appropriate courses of action.

Ethical principles should guide the behavior of professionals in everyday practice. Principles, however, are not just guidelines for reaction when something goes wrong or when a complaint is raised. Adhering to ethical principles also calls for action. These principles include the following.

Act to Benefit Others

Service to humanity is the basic tenet underlying student affairs practice. Hence, student affairs professionals exist to (a) promote healthy social, physical, academic, moral, cognitive, career, and personality development of students; (b) bring a developmental perspective to the institution's total educational process and learning environment; (c) contribute to the effective functioning of the institution; and (d) provide programs and services consistent with this principle.

Promote Justice

Student affairs professionals are committed to assuring fundamental fairness for all individuals within the academic community. In pursuit of this goal, the principles of impartiality, equity, and reciprocity (treating others as one would desire to be treated) are basic. When there are greater needs than resources available or when the interests of constituencies conflict, justice requires honest consideration of all claims and requests and equitable (not necessarily equal) distribution of goods and services. A crucial aspect of promoting justice is demonstrating an appreciation for human differences and opposing intolerance and bigotry concerning these differences. Important human differences include, but are not limited to, characteristics such as age, culture, ethnicity, gender, disabling condition, race, religion, or sexual/affectional orientation.

Respect Autonomy

Student affairs professionals respect and promote individual autonomy and privacy. Students' freedom of choice and action are not restricted unless their actions significantly interfere with the welfare of others or the accomplishment of the institution's mission.

Be Faithful

Student affairs professionals are truthful, honor agreements, and are trustworthy in the performance of their duties.

Do No Harm

Student affairs professionals do not engage in activities that cause either physical or psychological damage to others. In addition to their personal actions, student affairs professionals are especially vigilant to assure that the institutional policies do not: (a) hinder students' opportunities to benefit from the learning experiences available in the environment; (b) threaten individuals' self-worth, dignity, or safety; or (c) discriminate unjustly or illegally.

Ethical Standards

Four ethical standards related to primary constituencies with whom student affairs professionals work—fellow professionals, students, educational institutions, and society—are specified.

1. *Professional Responsibility and Competence.* Student affairs professionals are responsible for promoting students' learning and development, enhancing the understanding of student life, and advancing the profession and its ideals. They possess the knowledge, skills, emotional stability, and maturity to discharge responsibilities as administrators, advisors, consultants, counselors, programmers, researchers, and teachers. High levels of professional competence are expected in the performance of their duties and responsibilities. They ultimately are responsible for the consequences of their actions or inaction.

As ACPA members, student affairs professionals will:

1.1 Adopt a professional lifestyle characterized by use of sound theoretical principles and a personal value system congruent with the basic tenets of the profession.

1.2 Contribute to the development of the profession (e.g., recruiting students to the profession, serving professional organizations, educating new professionals, improving professional practices, and conducting and reporting research).

1.3 Maintain and enhance professional effectiveness by improving skills and acquiring new knowledge.

1.4 Monitor their personal and professional functioning and effectiveness and seek assistance from appropriate professionals as needed.

1.5 Represent their professional credentials, competencies, and limitations accurately and correct any misrepresentations of these qualifications by others.

1.6 Establish fees for professional services after consideration of the ability of the recipient to pay. They will provide some services, including professional development activities for colleagues, for little or no remuneration.

1.7 Refrain from attitudes or actions that impinge on colleagues' dignity, moral code, privacy, worth, professional functioning, and/or personal growth.

1.8 Abstain from sexual harassment.

1.9 Abstain from sexual intimacies with colleagues or with staff for whom they have supervisory, evaluative, or instructional responsibility.

1.10 Refrain from using their positions to seek unjustified personal gains, sexual favors, unfair advantages, or unearned goods and services not normally accorded those in such positions.

1.11 Inform students of the nature and/or limits of confidentiality. They will share information about the students only in accordance with institutional policies and applicable laws, when given their permission, or when required to prevent personal harm to themselves or others.

1.12 Use records and electronically stored information only to accomplish legitimate, institutional purposes and to benefit students.

1.13 Define job responsibilities, decision-making procedures, mutual expectations, accountability procedures, and evaluation criteria with subordinates and supervisors.

1.14 Acknowledge contributions by others to program development, program implementation, evaluations, and reports.

1.15 Assure that participation by staff in planned activities that emphasize self-disclosure or other tentatively intimate or personal involvement is voluntary and that the leader(s) of such activities do not have administrative, supervisory, or evaluative authority over participants.

1.16 Adhere to professional practices in securing positions: (a) represent education and experiences accurately; (b) respond to offers promptly; (c) accept only those positions they intend to assume; (d) advise current employer and all institutions at which applications are pending immediately when they sign a contract; and (e) inform their employers at least thirty days before leaving a position.

1.17 Gain approval of research plans involving human subjects from the institutional committee with oversight responsibility prior to initiation of the study. In the absence of such a committee they will seek to create procedures to protect the rights and assure the safety of research participants.

1.18 Conduct and report research studies accurately. They will neither engage in fraudulent research nor will they distort or misrepresent their data or deliberately bias their results.

1.19 Cite previous works on a topic when writing or when speaking to professional audiences.

1.20 Acknowledge major contributions to research projects and professional writings through joint authorships with the principal contributor listed first. They will acknowledge minor technical or professional contributions in notes or introductory statements.

1.21 Not demand co-authorship of publications when their involvement was ancillary or unduly pressure others for joint authorship.

1.22 Share original research data with qualified others upon request.

1.23   Communicate the results of any research judged to be of value to professionals and not withhold test results reflecting unfavorably on specific institutions, programs, services, or prevailing opinion.

1.24   Submit manuscripts for consideration to only one journal at a time. They will not seek to publish previously published or accepted-for-publication materials in other media or publications without first informing all editors and/or publishers concerned. They will make appropriate references in the text and receive permission to use if copyrights are involved.

1.25   Support professional preparation program efforts by providing assistantships, practica, field placements, and consultation to students and faculty.

As ACPA members, preparation program faculty will:

1.26   Inform prospective graduate students of program expectations, predominant theoretical orientations, skills needed for successful completion, and employment of recent graduates.

1.27   Assure that required experiences involving self-disclosure are communicated to prospective graduate students. When the program offers experiences that emphasize self-disclosure or other relatively intimate or personal involvement (e.g., group or individual counseling or growth groups), professionals must not have current or anticipated administrative, supervisory, or evaluative authority over participants.

1.28   Provide graduate students with a broad knowledge base consisting of theory, research, and practice.

1.29   Inform graduate students of the ethical responsibilities and standards of the profession.

1.30   Assess all relevant competencies and interpersonal functioning of students throughout the program, communicate these assessments to students, and take appropriate corrective actions including dismissal when warranted.

1.31   Assure that field supervisors are qualified to provide supervision to graduate students and are informed of their ethical responsibilities in this role.

2.   *Student Learning and Development.* Student development is an essential purpose of higher education, and the pursuit of this aim is a major responsibility of student affairs. Development is complex and includes cognitive, physical, moral, social, career, spiritual, personality, and educational dimensions. Professionals must be sensitive to the variety of backgrounds, cultures, and personal characteristics evident in the student population and use appropriate theoretical perspectives to identify learning opportunities and to reduce barriers that inhibit development.

As ACPA members, student affairs professionals will:

2.1   Treat students as individuals who possess dignity, worth, and the ability to be self-directed.

2.2   Avoid dual relationships with students (e.g., counselor/employer, supervisor/best friend, or faculty/sexual partner) that may involve incompatible roles and conflicting responsibilities.

2.3   Abstain from sexual harassment.

2.4   Abstain from sexual intimacies with clients or with students for whom they have supervisory, evaluative, or instructional responsibility.

2.5   Inform students of the conditions under which they may receive assistance and the limits of confidentiality when the counseling relationship is initiated.

2.6 Avoid entering or continuing helping relationships if benefits to students are unlikely. They will refer students to appropriate specialists and recognize that if the referral is declined, they are not obligated to continue the relationship.

2.7 Inform students about the purpose of assessment and make explicit the planned use of results prior to assessment.

2.8 Provide appropriate information to students prior to and following the use of any assessment procedure to place results in proper perspective with other relevant factors (e.g., socioeconomic, ethnic, cultural, and gender related experiences).

2.9 Confront students regarding issues, attitudes, and behaviors that have ethical implications.

3. *Responsibility to the Institution.* Institutions of higher education provide the context for student affairs practice. Institutional mission, policies, organizational structure, and culture, combined with individual judgment and professional standards, define and delimit the nature and extent of practice. Student affairs professionals share responsibility with other members of the academic community for fulfilling the institutional mission. Responsibility to promote the development of individual students and to support the institution's policies and interests require that professionals balance competing demands.

As ACPA members, student affairs professionals will:

3.1 Contribute to their institution by supporting its mission, goals, and policies.

3.2 Seek resolution when they and their institution encounter substantial disagreements concerning professional or personal values. Resolution may require sustained efforts to modify institutional policies and practices or result in voluntary termination of employment.

3.3 Recognize that conflicts among students, colleagues, or the institution should be resolved without diminishing appropriate obligations to any party involved.

3.4 Assure that information provided about the institution is factual and accurate.

3.5 Inform appropriate officials of conditions that may be disruptive or damaging to their institution.

3.6 Inform supervisors of conditions or practices that may restrict institutional or professional effectiveness.

3.7 Recognize their fiduciary responsibility to the institution. They will assure that funds for which they have oversight are expended following established procedures and in ways that optimize value, are accounted for properly, and contribute to the accomplishment of the institution's mission. They also will assure equipment, facilities, personnel, and other resources are used to promote the welfare of the institution and students.

3.8 Restrict their private interests, obligations, and transactions in ways to minimize conflicts of interest or the appearance of conflicts of interest. They will identify their personal views and actions as private citizens from those expressed or undertaken as institutional representatives.

3.9 Collaborate and share professional expertise with members of the academic community.

3.10 Evaluate programs, services, and organizational structures regularly and systematically to assure conformity to published standards and guidelines. Evaluations should be conducted using rigorous evaluation methods and principles, and the results should be made available to appropriate institutional personnel.

3.11 Evaluate job performance of subordinates regularly and recommend appropriate actions to enhance professional development and improve performance.

3.12   Provide fair and honest assessments of colleagues' job performance.

3.13   Seek evaluations of their job performance and/or services they provide.

3.14   Provide training to student affairs search and screening committee members who are unfamiliar with the profession.

3.15   Disseminate information that accurately describes the responsibilities of position vacancies, required qualifications, and the institution.

3.16   Follow a published interview and selection process that periodically notifies applicants of their status.

4. *Responsibility to Society.* Student affairs professionals, both as citizens and practitioners, have a responsibility to contribute to the improvement of the communities in which they live and work. They respect individuality and recognize that worth is not diminished by characteristics such as age, culture, ethnicity, gender, disabling condition, race, religion, or sexual/affectional orientation. Student affairs professionals work to protect human rights and promote an appreciation of human diversity in higher education.

As ACPA members, student affairs professionals will:

4.1   Assist students in becoming productive and responsible citizens.

4.2   Demonstrate concern for the welfare of all students and work for constructive change on behalf of students.

4.3   Not discriminate on the basis of age, culture, ethnicity, gender, disabling condition, race, religion, or sexual/affectional orientation. They will work to modify discriminatory practices.

4.4   Demonstrate regard for social codes and moral expectations of the communities in which they live and work. They will recognize that violations of accepted moral and legal standards may involve their clients, students, or colleagues in damaging personal conflicts and may impugn the integrity of the profession, their own reputations, and that of the employing institution.

4.5   Report to the appropriate authority any condition that is likely to harm their clients and/or others.

Reference

American Association for Counseling and Development. (1988). Ethical Standards. Alexandria, VA: Author.

Note

As revised and approved by ACPA Executive Council, July 1989.

Standards of Professional Practice

NATIONAL ASSOCIATION OF STUDENT PERSONNEL ADMINISTRATORS

The National Association of Student Personnel Administrators (NASPA) is an organization of colleges, universities, agencies, and professional educators whose members are committed to providing services and education that enhance student growth and development. The association seeks to promote student personnel work as a profession which requires personal integrity, belief in the dignity and worth of individuals, respect for individual differences and diversity, a commitment to service, and dedication to the development of individuals and the college community through education. NASPA supports student personnel work by providing opportunities for its members to expand knowledge and skills through professional education and experience. The following standards were endorsed by NASPA at the December 1990 board of directors meeting in Washington, D. C.

1. Professional Services

Members of NASPA fulfill the responsibilities of their position by supporting the educational interests, rights, and welfare of students in accordance with the mission of the employing institution.

2. Agreement with Institutional Mission and Goals

Members who accept employment with an educational institution subscribe to the general mission and goals of the institution.

3. Management of Institutional Resources

Members seek to advance the welfare of the employing institution through accountability for the proper use of institutional funds, personnel, equipment, and other resources. Members inform appropriate officials of conditions which may be potentially disruptive or damaging to the institution's mission, personnel, and property.

4. Employment Relationship

Members honor employment relationships. Members do not commence new duties or obligations at another institution under a new contractual agreement until termination of an existing contract, unless otherwise agreed to by the member and the member's current and new supervisors. Members adhere to professional practices in securing positions and employment relationships.

5. Conflict of Interest

Members recognize their obligation to the employing institution and seek to avoid private interests, obligations, and transactions which are in conflict of interest or give the appearance of impropriety. Members clearly distinguish between statements and actions which represent their own personal views and those which represent their employing institution when important to do so.

6. Legal Authority

Members respect and acknowledge all lawful authority. Members refrain from conduct involving dishonesty, fraud, deceit, and misrepresentation or unlawful discrimination. NASPA recognizes that legal issues are often ambiguous, and members should seek the advice of counsel as appropriate. Members demonstrate concern for the legal, social codes and moral expectations of the communities in which they live and work even when the dictates of one's conscience may require behavior as a private citizen which is not in keeping with these codes/expectations.

7. Equal Consideration and Treatment of Others

Members execute professional responsibilities with fairness and impartiality and show equal consideration to individuals regardless of status or position. Members respect individuality and promote an appreciation of human diversity in higher education. In keeping with the mission of their respective institution and remaining cognizant of federal, state, and local laws, they do not discriminate on the basis of race, religion, creed, gender, age, national origin, sexual orientation, or physical disability. Members do not engage in or tolerate harassment in any form and should exercise professional judgment in entering into intimate relationships with those for whom they have any supervisory, evaluative, or instructional responsibility.

8. Student Behavior

Members demonstrate and promote responsible behavior and support actions that enhance personal growth and development of students. Members foster conditions designed to ensure a student's acceptance of responsibility for his/her own behavior. Members inform and educate students as to sanctions or constraints on student behavior which may result from violations of law or institutional policies.

9. Integrity of Information and Research

Members ensure that all information conveyed to others is accurate and in appropriate context. In their research and publications, members conduct and report research studies to assure accurate interpretation of findings, and they adhere to accepted professional standards of academic integrity.

10. Confidentiality

Members ensure that confidentiality is maintained with respect to all privileged communications and to educational and professional records considered confidential. They inform all parties of the nature and/or limits of confidentiality. Members share information only in accordance with institutional policies and relevant statutes when given the informed consent or when required to prevent personal harm to themselves or others.

11. Research Involving Human Subjects

Members are aware of and take responsibility for all pertinent ethical principles and institutional requirements when planning any research activity dealing with human subjects. (See *Ethical Prin-*

ciples in the Conduct of Research with Human Participants, Washington, D. C.: American Psychological Association, 1982.)

12. Representation of Professional Competence

Members at all times represent accurately their professional credentials, competencies, and limitations and act to correct any misrepresentations of these qualifications by others. Members make proper referrals to appropriate professionals when the member's professional competence does not meet the task or issue in question.

13. Selection and Promotion Practices

Members support nondiscriminatory, fair employment practices by appropriately publicizing staff vacancies, selection criteria, deadlines, and promotion criteria in accordance with the spirit and intent of equal opportunity policies and established legal guidelines and institutional policies.

14. References

Members, when serving as a reference, provide accurate and complete information about candidates, including both relevant strengths and limitations of a professional and personal nature.

15. Job Definitions and Performance Evaluation

Members clearly define with subordinates and supervisors job responsibilities and decision-making procedures, mutual expectations, accountability procedures, and evaluation criteria.

16. Campus Community

Members promote a sense of community among all areas of the campus by working cooperatively with students, faculty, staff, and others outside the institution to address the common goals of student learning and development. Members foster a climate of collegiality and mutual respect in their work relationships.

17. Professional Development

Members have an obligation to continue personal professional growth and to contribute to the development of the profession by enhancing personal knowledge and skills, sharing ideas and information, improving professional practices, conducting and reporting research, and participating in association activities. Members promote and facilitate the professional growth of staff and they emphasize ethical standards in professional preparation and development programs.

18. Assessment

Members regularly and systematically assess organizational structures, programs, and services to determine whether the developmental goals and needs of students are being met and to assure conformity to published standards and guidelines such as those of the Council for the Advancement of Standards for Student Services/Development Programs (CAS). Members collect data which include responses from students and other significant constituencies and make assessment results available to appropriate institutional officials for the purpose of revising and improving program goals and implementation.

Caring

Nel Noddings

The German philosopher Martin Heidegger (1962) described care as the very Being of human life. His use of the term is very broad, covering an attitude of solicitousness toward other living beings, a concern to do things meticulously, the deepest existential longings, fleeting moments of concern, and all the burdens and woes that belong to human life. From his perspective, we are immersed in care; it is the ultimate reality of life.

Heidegger's full range of meanings will be of interest as this exploration continues, but the meaning that will be primary here is relational. A *caring relation* is, in its most basic form, a connection or encounter between two human beings—a carer and a recipient of care, or cared-for. In order for the relation to be properly called caring, both parties must contribute to it in characteristic ways. A failure on the part of either carer or cared-for blocks completion of caring and, although there may still be a relation—that is, an encounter or connection in which each party feels something toward the other—it is not a *caring* relation. Even before I describe the contributions of carer and cared-for, one can see how useful this relational definition is. No matter how hard teachers try to care, if the caring is not received by students, the claim "they don't care" has some validity. It suggests strongly that something is very wrong.

In *Caring* (1984), I described the state of consciousness of the carer (or "one-caring") as characterized by engrossment and motivational displacement. By engrossment I mean an open, nonselective receptivity to the cared-for. Other writers have used the word "attention" to describe this characteristic. Iris Murdoch (1970), for example, discussed attention as essential in moral life, and she traced the concept to Simone Weil. Weil placed attention at the center of love for our neighbors. It is what characterizes our consciousness when we ask another (explicitly or implicitly), "What are you going through?" Weil wrote:

> This way of looking is first of all attentive. The soul empties itself of all its own contents in order to receive into itself the being it is looking at, just as he is, in all his truth. Only he who is capable of attention can do this. (1951, p. 115)

To say that the soul empties itself of all its own contents in order to receive the other describes well what I mean by engrossment. I do not mean infatuation, enchantment, or obsession but a full receptivity. When I care, I really hear, see, or feel what the other tries to convey. The engrossment or attention may last only a few moments and it may or may not be repeated in future encounters, but it is full and essential in any caring encounter. For example, if a stranger stops me to ask directions, the encounter may produce a caring relation, albeit a brief one. I listen attentively to his need, and I respond in a way that he receives and recognizes. The caring relation is completed when he receives my efforts at caring.

As carer in the brief encounter just described, I was attentive, but I also felt the desire to help the stranger in his need. My consciousness was characterized by motivational displacement. Where a moment earlier I had my own projects in mind, I was now concerned with his project—finding his way on campus. When we watch a small child trying to tie her shoes, we often feel our own fingers moving in sympathetic reaction. This is motivational displacement, the sense that our motive energy is flowing toward others and their projects. I receive what the other conveys, and I want to respond in a way that furthers the other's purpose or project.

Experiencing motivational displacement, one begins to think. Just as we consider, plan, and reflect on our own projects, we now think what we can do to help another. Engrossment and motivational displacement do not tell us what to do; they merely characterize our consciousness when we care. But the thinking that we do will now be as careful as it is in our own service. We are seized by the needs of another.

What characterizes the consciousness of one who is cared for? Reception, recognition, and response seem to be primary. The cared-for receives the caring and shows that it has been received. This recognition now becomes part of what the carer receives in his or her engrossment, and the caring is completed.

Some critics worry that my account puts a tremendous burden on the carer and very little on the recipient of care. But we must keep in mind that the basic caring relation is an encounter. My description of a caring relation does not entail that carer and cared-for are permanent labels for individuals. Mature relationships are characterized by mutuality. They are made up of strings of encounters in which the parties exchange places; both members are carers and cared-fors as opportunities arise.

Even in the basic situation, however, the contribution of the cared-for is not negligible. Consider the mother-infant relationship. In every caring encounter, the mother is necessarily carer and the infant cared-for. But the infant responds—he or she coos, wriggles, stares attentively, smiles, reaches out, and cuddles. These responses are heartwarming; they make caregiving a rewarding experience. To see just how vital the infant's response is to the caring relation, one should observe what happens when infants cannot respond normally to care. Mothers and other caregivers in such situations are worn down by the lack of completion—burned out by the constant outward flow of energy that is not replenished by the response of the cared-for. Teachers, too, suffer this dreadful loss of energy when their students do not respond. Thus, even when the second party in a relation cannot assume the status of carer, there is a genuine form of reciprocity that is essential to the relation.

The desire to be cared for is almost certainly a universal human characteristic. Not everyone wants to be cuddled or fussed over. But everyone wants to be received, to elicit a response that is congruent with an underlying need or desire. Cool and formal people want others to respond to them with respect and a touch of deference. Warm, informal people often appreciate smiles and hugs. Everyone appreciates a person who knows when to hug and when to stand apart. In schools, all kids want to be cared for in this sense. They do not want to be treated "like numbers," by recipe—no matter how sweet the recipe may be for some consumers. When we understand that everyone wants to be cared for and that there is no recipe for caring, we see how important engrossment (or attention) is. In order to respond as a genuine carer, one does have to empty the soul of its own contents. One cannot say, "Aha! This fellow needs care. Now, let's see—here are the seven steps I must follow. "Caring is a way of being in relation, not a set of specific behaviors.

I have put great emphasis on caring as relation, because our temptation is to think of caring as a virtue, an individual attribute. We do talk this way at times. We say, "He is a caring person," or even, "She is really a caring person, but she has trouble showing it." Both of these comments capture something of our broad notion of care, but both are misleading because of their emphasis on caring as an individual virtue. As we explore caring in the context of caregiving—any long-term unequal relation in which one person is carer and the other cared-for—we will ask about the virtues that support caring. But for now, it is important not to detach carers from caring relations. No matter how much a person professes to care, the result that concerns us is the caring relation. Lots of self-righteous, "caring" people induce the response, "she doesn't really care about me at all."

Even though I will often use the word *caring* to apply to relations, I will also need to apply it to capacities. The uses should be clear in context. I want to avoid a concentration on judgment or evaluation that accompanies an interpretation of caring as an individual virtue, but I also want to acknowledge that people have various capacities for caring—that is, for entering into caring relations as well as for attending to objects and ideas.

When we discuss teaching and teacher-learner relationships in depth, we will see that teachers not only have to create caring relations in which they are the carers, but that they also have a responsibility to help their students develop the capacity to care. What can this mean? For Heidegger care is inevitable; all aware human beings care. It is the mark of being human. But not everyone develops the capacity to care for others in the way described above. Perhaps very few learn to care for ideas, for nonhuman life, for objects. And often we confuse the forms of caring and suppose caring to be a unitary capacity that transfers easily from one domain to another.

Simone Weil is a good example of an outstanding thinker who seems to have believed that intellectual caring and interpersonal caring are closely related. In the essay from which the earlier passage was extracted, Weil observed that the study of geometry requires attention and that attention so learned could increase students' concentration in prayer. Thence, we may suppose, Weil concluded that closer connection in prayer would produce more sensitive interpersonal relations; that is, she believed that intellectual attention could be transferred to interpersonal attention. This is doubtful. Evidence abounds that people can attain high levels of intellectuality and remain insensitive to human beings and other living things. Consider the Nazi high command or the fictional Professor Moriarty (Sherlock Holmes's nemesis) who attended lovingly to his orchids but was evil incarnate in the human domain. So the varieties of care need analysis.

Unequal caring relations are interesting not only in the human domain but also in the realm of nonhuman animals. It is doubtful whether any animal can be a carer with respect to humans (although there are those who have argued the case for dogs), but many animals are responsive cared-fors, and taking care of animals can be a wonderful way to learn caring. In our interaction with animals, we also have an opportunity to study the forms of response that we value. Some animals respond with intelligence, and we usually value that. Some respond with affection; they like to be stroked, cuddled, held, or scratched. Still others respond vocally. All of these responses affect us and call forth a caring attitude. Further, certain physical characteristics that suggest the possibility of a valued response also affect us. Most of us feel sympathy for baby seals threatened by hunters, because they look as though they might respond in the ways mentioned. Creatures that are slimy, scaly, or spiny rarely evoke a sympathetic response in us. The nature of our responses will be seen as important when we consider the roots of ethical life.

In another sense of care, human beings can care about ideas or objects. An approach to education that begins with care is not, as I pointed out earlier, anti-intellectual. Part of what we receive from others is a sense of their interests, including intellectual passions. To enhance a student's understanding and skill in a given subject is an important task for teachers, but current educational practices are riddled with slogans and myths that are not very helpful.

Often we begin with the innocent-sounding slogan mentioned earlier, "All children can learn." The slogan was created by people who mean well. They want teachers to have high expectations for all their students and not to decide on the basis of race, ethnicity, sex, or economic status that some groups of children simply cannot learn the subject at hand. With that much I agree.

But I will argue that not all individual children can learn everything we might like to teach them. Further, the good intentions captured in the slogan can lead to highly manipulative and dictatorial methods that disregard the interests and purposes of students. Teachers these days are expected to induce a desire to learn in all students. But all students already want to learn; it is a question of *what* they want to learn. John Dewey (1963) argued years ago that teachers had to start with the experience and interests of students and patiently forge connections between that experience and whatever subject matter was prescribed. I would go further. There are few things that all students need to know, and it ought to be acceptable for students to reject some material in order to pursue other topics with enthusiasm. Caring teachers listen and respond differentially to their students. Much more will be said on this highly controversial issue in later chapters. For now it is enough to note that our schools are not intellectually stimulating places, even for many students who are intellectually oriented.

Few students learn to care for ideas in school. Perhaps even fewer learn to care for objects. I am not talking about mere acquisitiveness; this seems to be learned all too well. I am talking about what Harry Broudy (1972) called "enlightened cherishing" and what the novelist and essayist John

Galsworthy (1948) called "quality." This kind of caring produces fine objects and takes care of them. In a society apparently devoted to planned obsolescence, our children have few opportunities to care lovingly for old furniture, dishes, carpets, or even new bicycles, radios, cassette players, and the like. It can be argued that the care of many tools and instruments is a waste of time because they are so easily replaced. But one wonders how long a throwaway society can live harmoniously with the natural environment and also how closely this form of carelessness is related to the gross desire for more and more acquisitions. Is there a role for schools to play in teaching care of buildings, books, computers, furniture, and laboratory equipment?

Caring for ideas and objects is different from caring for people and other living things. Strictly speaking, one cannot form a relation with mathematics or music or a food processor. The cared-for cannot feel anything for us; there is no affect in the second party. But, oddly, people do report a form of responsiveness from ideas and objects. The mathematician Gauss was "seized" by mathematics. The poet Robert Frost insisted that "a poem finds its own way" (see the accounts in Noddings & Shore, 1984). And we know that well-tended engines purr, polished instruments gleam, and fine glassware glistens. The care we exert induces something like a response from fields of ideas and from inanimate objects. Do our students hear enough—or anything at all—about these wondrous events?

Finally, we must consider Heidegger's deepest sense of care. As human beings, we care what happens to us. We wonder whether there is life after death, whether there is a deity who cares about us, whether we are loved by those we love, whether we belong anywhere; we wonder what we will become, who we are, how much control we have over our own fate. For adolescents these are among the most pressing questions: Who am I? What kind of person will I be? Who will love me? How do others see me? Yet schools spend more time on the quadratic formula than on any of these existential questions.

In reviewing the forms of care, it becomes clear that there is a challenge to care in schools. The structures of current schooling work against care, and at the same time, the need for care is perhaps greater than ever.

The Debate in Ethics

No discussion of caring today could be adequate without some attention to the ethic of care. In 1982 Carol Gilligan published her now famous *In a Different Voice*, describing an alternative approach to moral problems. This approach was identified in the voices of women, but Gilligan did not claim that the approach is exclusively female, nor did she claim that all women use it. Still, the avalanche of response from women who recognized themselves in Gilligan's description is an impressive phenomenon. "This is me," many women said. "Finally someone has articulated the way I come at moral problems."

Gilligan described a morality based on the recognition of needs, relation, and response. Women who speak in the different voice refuse to leave themselves, their loved ones, and connections out of their moral reasoning. They speak from and to a situation, and their reasoning is contextual. Those of us who write about an ethic of care have emphasized affective factors, but this is not to say that caring is irrational or even nonrational. It has its own rationality or reasonableness, and in appropriate situations carers draw freely on standard linear rationality as well. But its emphasis is on living together, on creating, maintaining, and enhancing positive relations—not on decision making in moments of high moral conflict, nor on justification.

An ethic of care—a needs- and response-based ethic—challenges many premises of traditional ethics and moral education. First, there is the difference of focus already mentioned. There is also a rejection of universalizability, the notion that anything that is morally justifiable is necessarily something that anyone else in a similar situation is obligated to do. Universalizability suggests that who we are, to whom we are related, and how we are situated should have nothing to do with our moral decision making. An ethic of caring rejects this. Next, although an ethic of care puts great emphasis on consequences in the sense that it always asks what happens to the relation, it is not a form of utilitarianism; it does not posit one greatest good to be optimized, nor does it separate means and ends. Finally, it is not properly labeled an ethic of virtue. Although it calls on people to be carers and to develop the virtues and capacities to care, it does not regard caring solely as an individual attribute. It recognizes the part played by the cared-for. It is an ethic of relation.

In moral education an ethic of care's great emphasis on motivation challenges the primacy of moral reasoning. We concentrate on developing the attitudes and skills required to sustain caring relations and the desire to do so, not nearly so much on the reasoning used to arrive at a decision. Lawrence Kohlberg (1981) and his associates, following Plato and Socrates, have focused on moral reasoning. The supposition here is that moral knowledge is sufficient for moral behavior. From this perspective, wrongdoing is always equated with ignorance. Gilligan explicitly challenged Kohlberg's scale or hierarchy of moral reasoning (suggesting a powerful alternative developmental model), but others of us have challenged the whole idea of a developmental model, arguing that moral responses in a given individual may vary contextually at almost any age. (The language used to discuss what one is doing and why may, of course, depend on intellectual development, but moral behavior and its intellectual articulation are not synonymous.)

Moral education from the perspective of an ethic of caring has four major components: modeling, dialogue, practice, and confirmation (Noddings, 1984). Modeling is important in most schemes of moral education, but in caring it is vital. In this framework we are not trying to teach students principles and ways of applying them to problems through chains of mathematical reasoning. Rather, we have to show how to care in our own relations with cared-fors. For example, professors of education and school administrators cannot be sarcastic and dictatorial with teachers in the hope that coercion will make them care for students. I have heard administrators use this excuse for "being tough" with teachers—"because I care about the kids of this state"—but, of course, the likely outcome is that teachers will then turn attention protectively to themselves rather than lovingly to their students. So we do not tell our students to care; we show them how to care by creating caring relations with them.

There is a second reason why modeling is so vital. The capacity to care may be dependent on adequate experience in being cared for. Even while a child is too young to be a carer, he or she can learn how to be a responsive cared-for. Thus our role as carer is more important than our role as model, but we fill both simultaneously. We remind ourselves when we are tempted to take short cuts in moral education that we are, inevitably, models. But otherwise, in our daily activities we simply respond as carers when the need arises. The function of modeling gets special attention when we try to explain what we are doing and why in moral education. But the primary reason for responding as carers to our students' needs is that we are called to such response by our moral orientation.

Dialogue is the second essential component of moral education. My use of the term *dialogue* is similar to that of Paulo Freire (1970). It is not just talk or conversation—certainly not an oral presentation of argument in which the second party is merely allowed to ask an occasional question. Dialogue is open-ended; that is, in a genuine dialogue, neither party knows at the outset what the outcome or decision will be. As parents and teachers, we cannot enter into dialogue with children when we know what our decision is already made. It is maddening to young people (or any people) to engage in "dialogue" with a sweetly reasonable adult who cannot be persuaded and who, in the end, will say, "Here's how it's going to be. I tried to reason with you. . . ." We do have to talk this way at times, but we should not pretend that this is dialogue. Dialogue is a common search for understanding, empathy, or appreciation. It can be playful or serious, logical or imaginative, goal or process oriented, but it is always a genuine quest for something undetermined at the beginning.

Dialogue permits us to talk about what we try to show. It gives learners opportunities to question "why," and it helps both parties to arrive at well-informed decisions. Although I do not believe that all wrongdoing can be equated with ignorance, I do believe that many moral errors are ill-informed decisions, particularly in the very young. Thus dialogue serves not only to inform the decision under consideration; it also contributes to a habit of mind—that of seeking adequate information on which to make decisions.

Dialogue serves another purpose in moral education. It connects us to each other and helps to maintain caring relations. It also provides us with the knowledge of each other that forms a foundation for response in caring. Caring (acting as carer) requires knowledge and skill as well as characteristic attitudes. We respond most effectively as carers when we understand what the other needs and the history of this need. Dialogue is implied in the criterion of engrossment. To receive the other is to attend fully and openly. Continuing dialogue builds up a substantial knowledge of one another that serves to guide our responses.

A third component of moral education is practice. Attitudes and "mentalities" are shaped, at least in part, by experience. Most of us speak regularly of a "military mind," a "police mentality," "business thinking," and the like. Although some of this talk is a product of stereotyping, it seems clear that it also captures some truth about human behavior. All disciplines and institutional organizations have training programs designed not only to teach specific skills but also to "shape minds," that is, to induce certain attitudes and ways of looking at the world. If we want people to approach moral life prepared to care, we need to provide opportunities for them to gain skills in caregiving and, more important, to develop the characteristic attitudes described earlier.

Some of the most fascinating work in contemporary feminist theory is devoted to the study of women's experience and its articulation. It seems likely that women's traditional experience is closely related to the moral approach described in ethics of care. Women, more often than men, have been charged with the direct care of young children, the ill, and the aged. They have been expected to maintain a pleasing environment, to look after the needs of others, and to mediate disputes in ordinary social situations. If we regard this experience as inseparable from oppression, then we might agree with Nietzsche that what I am describing is merely "slave mentality." But if we analyze the experience, we find considerable autonomy, love, choice, and consummate skill in the traditional female role. We may evaluate the experience as essential in developing fully human beings.

Women have learned to regard every human encounter as a potential caring occasion. In nursing theory, for example, Jean Watson (1985) defined the moment in which nurse and patient meet as a "caring occasion." It is not just that the nurse will provide care in the form of physical skills to the patient. Rather, it is a moment in which each must decide how to meet the other and what to do with the moment. This is obviously very different from defining a medical encounter as a problem-solving event. Problem solving is involved, of course, but it is preceded by a moment of receptivity—one in which the full humanity of both parties is recognized—and it is followed by a return to the human other in all his or her fullness.

If we decide that the capacity to care is as much a mark of personhood as reason or rationality, then we will want to find ways to increase this capacity. Just as we now think it is important for girls as well as boys to have mathematical experience, so we should want both boys and girls to have experience in caring. It does not just happen; we have to plan for it. As we will see, such planning is complex and loaded with potential pitfalls.

Some schools, recognizing the needs just discussed, have instituted requirements for a form of community service. This is a move in the right direction, but reflection produces some issues to worry about. The practice provided must be with people who can demonstrate caring. We do not want our children to learn the menial (or even sophisticated) skills of caregiving without the characteristic attitude of caring. The experience of caregiving should initiate or contribute to the desired attitude, but the conditions have to be right, and people are central to the setting. This is a major point, to which I will return.

Next, practice in caring should transform schools and, eventually, the society in which we live. If the practice is assimilated to the present structures of schooling, it may lose its transformative powers. *It* may be transformed—that is, distorted. If we were to give grades for caregiving, for example, students might well begin to compete for honors in caring. Clearly, then, their attention could be diverted from cared-fors to themselves. If, on the other hand, we neither grade nor give credit for such work, it may inevitably have second-class status in our schools. So long as our schools are organized hierarchically with emphasis on rewards and penalties, it will be very difficult to provide the kind of experience envisioned.

The fourth component of moral education from the perspective of caring is confirmation. Martin Buber (1965) described confirmation as an act of affirming and encouraging the best in others. When we confirm someone, we spot a better self and encourage its development. We can do this only if we know the other well enough to see what he or she is trying to become. Formulas and slogans have no place here. We do not set up a single ideal or set of expectations for everyone to meet, but we identify something admirable, or at least acceptable, struggling to emerge in each person we encounter. The person working toward a better self must see the attribute or goal as worthy, and we too must see it as at least morally acceptable. We do not confirm people in ways we judge to be wrong.

Confirmation requires attribution of the best possible motive consonant with reality. When someone commits an act we find reprehensible, we ask ourselves what might have motivated such an act. Often it is not hard to identify an array of possible motives ranging from the gross and grubby to some that are acceptable or even admirable. This array is not constructed in abstraction. We build it from a knowledge of this particular other and by listening carefully to what she or he tells us. The motive we attribute has to be a real, a genuine possibility. Then we can open our dialogue with something like, "I know you were trying to help your friend . . ." or "I know what you're trying to accomplish. . . ." It will be clear that we disapprove of this particular act, but it will also be clear to the other that we see a self that is better than this act. Often the other will respond with enormous relief. *Here is this significant and percipient other who sees through the smallness or meanness of my present behavior a self that is better and a real possibility.* Confirmation lifts us toward our vision of a better self.

It is worth repeating that confirmation cannot be done by formula. A relation of trust must ground it. Continuity is required, because the carer in acting to confirm must know the cared-for well enough to be able to identify motives consonant with reality. Confirmation cannot be described in terms of strategies; it is a loving act founded on a relation of some depth. When we turn to specific changes that should occur in schooling in order to meet the challenge to care, I will put great emphasis on continuity. Not all caring relations require continuity (some, as we have seen, are brief encounters), but teaching does require it.

Confirmation contrasts sharply with the standard mode of religious moral education. There we usually find a sequence of accusation, confession, penance, and forgiveness. The initial step, accusation, causes or sustains separation. We stand in moral judgment and separate the other from ourselves and the moral community. In contrast, confirmation calls us to remain in connection. Further, accusation tends to produce denial or rationalization, which we then feel compelled to overthrow. But the rationalization may in fact be an attempt on the part of the accused to find that possible motive and convey it to us, the accuser. Because we have to reject it in order to proceed with confession, penance, and forgiveness, offenders may never understand their own true motives. This sequence also depends heavily on authority, obedience, fear, and subordination. We can be harsh or magnanimous in our judgment and forgiveness. Our authority is emphasized, and the potential power of the offender's own moral struggle is overlooked.

I do not mean to suggest that there is never a place for accusation and confession in moral education. It is not always possible for us to find a motive that is morally acceptable; sometimes we have to begin by asking straight out, "Why did you do that?" or "How could you do such a thing?" But it is gratifying how often we really can see a better self if we look for one, and its identification is a first step in its realization.

This whole way of looking at ethics and moral education challenges not only parts of the religious tradition but also the ideas of Freud and like-minded theorists. Freud believed that our sense of morality develops out of fear. The superego, Freud said, is an internalization of authority— of the father's voice—and its establishment results from resolution of the oedipal conflict. Sons fear castration by the father if they disobey or compete with him. Resolution of this desire to rebel and compete involves acceptance of the father's power and authority, and the superego (Freud's guide to acceptable behavior) takes up residence within the son. This account of moral development led Freud to conclude that women must be morally inferior to men. Because girls need not fear castration (having been born in that dread condition), their moral voice never attains the strength and dependability of men's.

Recent criticisms of Freud suggest that more attention should be given to the preoedipal period. Nancy Chodorow (1978) has theorized that girls and boys develop different psychological deep structures because females are almost exclusively the primary caregivers for both. Girls can find their gender identity without separating from their mother and, hence, develop a relational personality structure and perhaps even a relational epistemology or way of knowing (Keller, 1985). Boys, however, must construct their gender identity in opposition to all that is female. Here we have the possible roots of the different moral voices described by Gilligan. We will consider other alternatives as well.

Eli Sagan (1988) has also suggested that moral development begins and is strongly affected by preoedipal life. Without rejecting the Freudian framework entirely, Sagan recommends a shift in emphasis. If we give due weight to early childhood, we see that conscience (a sense of right and wrong, not mere internalization of authority) develops as much out of love and attachment as out of fear. Further, the primary fear is not of harm and punishment but, rather, of disappointing a loved parent and, at worst, losing that parent's love. This is a major challenge to masculinist psychology and a suggestion compatible with an ethic of caring and the model of moral education outlined here. Love, caring, and relation play central roles in both ethics and moral education.

I want to suggest that caring is the very bedrock of all successful education and that contemporary schooling can be revitalized in its light. Before describing a broad plan to make caring central in education, I need to explain why the current ideal is inadequate. Liberal education has been the Western ideal for centuries. Even when it is poorly funded in comparison with technical and professional education, it is still the ideal that puts pressure on precollegiate education. It is the form of education—done well or poorly—that most of us experienced. What is wrong with it, and why should it be rejected as a model of universal education?

The Role of Professional Associations

Elizabeth M. Nuss

Professional associations have an important function in American higher education. The purpose of this chapter is to demonstrate to student affairs professionals how these organizations can help them enhance or develop their administrative and professional skills. The chapter provides a brief history of professional associations and describes what they are and do. It reviews the wide variety of forms of participation and the ways that involvement in a professional association may vary over the span of a career. Suggestions about how to become involved, tips for managing time commitments and personal resources, and issues related to affiliation in multiple associations are discussed.

The chapter gives examples of many professional associations but is *not* intended to be a definitive summary of the universe of professional associations. The sample listing is included for illustrative purposes only. Moreover, the chapter does not advocate membership in any particular organization. As should be evident from the following discussion, decisions about which professional associations to join and when to join them are based on the reader's current professional goals, talents, and institutional needs. Nevertheless, participation in these organizations is the hallmark of a professional. At a minimum, anyone intending a serious career in student affairs should be a member of at least one professional association.

Brief History of Professional Associations

Professional associations have many objectives. They seek to advance understanding, recognition, and knowledge in the field; to develop and promulgate standards for professional practice; to serve the public interest; and to provide professionals with a peer group that promotes a sense of identity. The oldest American professional society still in existence is the American Philosophical Society, founded by Benjamin Franklin in 1743. Of the nearly 21,000 national associations, there are approximately 1,217 educational associations (American Society of Association Executives, 1988). As societies grow and become technically and socially more complex and specialized, associations are created to represent those specialized interests (Bloland, 1985).

The founding of the major student affairs professional associations follows the history and development of higher education and the profession itself. Student affairs as a distinct entity emerged in the early 1900s as a result of alterations in the nature and purpose of public higher education and changes in the American professorate. Deans of men and deans of women were appointed to resolve student problems and to administer campus discipline systems (National Association of Student Personnel Administrators, 1987). In 1916, the first formal program of study in vocational guidance was offered at Teachers College, Columbia University (National Association of Student Personnel Administrators, 1987). The increased size and specialization of higher education fostered the establishment of appropriate professional associations to articulate the shared concerns of each institutional group (Bloland, 1985). The fact that many student services in the early 1900s were organized by gender also influenced the development of the professional associations.

The National Association of Deans of Women (NADW) was organized in 1916. Since its founding, the organization has focused its mission on serving the needs of women in education. In 1956, NADW became the National Association of Women Deans and Counselors (NAWDC). In 1972, a decision was made to change the group's name and purpose; the organization became NAWDAC—the National Association of Women Deans, Administrators, and Counselors (Sheeley, 1983). In 1991, the organization's name was changed to the National Association of Women in Education (NAWE) to reflect more accurately its contemporary scope and focus.

In January 1919, a meeting, referred to as the Conference of Deans and Advisers of Men, was held at the University of Wisconsin. That meeting is now recognized as the founding of the National Association of Deans and Advisers of Men (NADAM). After two earlier attempts (1948 and 1949) failed, the organization officially adopted NASPA (National Association of Student Personnel Administrators) as its name in 1951. This broadened the base of the association, and for the first time NASPA began to recruit members (Rhatigan, 1991).

The American College Personnel Association (ACPA) traces its founding to 1924, when it began as the National Association of Appointment Secretaries (NAAS) (Sheeley, 1983; Bloland, 1972). The title of appointment secretary referred to persons who assisted in placing teachers and other college graduates. NAAS's first meeting in 1924 was held jointly with NADW. In 1929, NAAS's name was changed to National Association of Placement and Personnel Officers to reflect its broader professional role. In 1931, the name was again changed, to ACPA (Bloland, 1972). Bloland (1972) describes the historical cooperative relationships among these three major associations.

A sample listing (not by any means a complete one) of some other national higher education and student affairs associations and their founding dates is included in Table 1. The list provides a historical context for the development of the different associations and provides familiarity with the acronyms frequently used. For complete information, consult the *Encyclopedia of Associations* (Burek, 1992).

It should also be noted that over time many regional or state associations developed independently of the national organizations. Examples include the Western Deans and the Pennsylvania Association of Student Personnel Administrators.

Roles of Professional Associations

The mission of each organization describes the fundamental reasons for its existence, establishes the scope of its activities, and provides its overall direction. Like many other social institutions, these purposes evolve and change over time. It is also true that like a college or university, an association's mission may or may not be explicit or readily understood by its members or a wider professional audience. One of the marks of excellence in a voluntary association is the degree to which its mission is clearly articulated and serves as a guidepost for determining the appropriateness of the association's activities (Independent Sector, 1989). For example, the mission of NACUBO (National Association of College and University Business Officers) is "to promote sound management and financial administration of colleges and universities and to anticipate the issues affecting higher education" (Hines, 1982, p. 109). In 1991, NASPA reconsidered its mission statement as a part of the strategic planning process. The revised mission states, "The National Association of Student Personnel Administrators (NASPA) enriches the education experience of all students. It serves colleges and universities by providing leadership and professional growth opportunities for the chief student affairs officer and other professionals who consider higher education and student affairs issues from an institutional perspective" (p. 2). The financial and human resources of most associations are limited. As board members consider alternative programs and services, choices must be made among several desirable options. Determinations should be based on how centrally related the particular program or service is to the organization's mission.

Generally, associations are described by both their mission and scope. They may be local, regional, statewide, national, and international. They may be an organization composed of individual members, institutional members, or both. The specific types of services and programs offered may vary. As a general rule, most professional associations perform the following functions:

Table 1

A Sample Listing of Professional Associations by Year of Founding.

Association	Year
Association of American Universities (AAU)	1900
American Association of Collegiate Registrars and Admissions Officers (AACRAO)	1910
Association of College Unions—International (ACU-I)	1914
National Association of Women in Education (NAWE)	1916
American Council on Education (ACE)	1918
National Association of Student Personnel Administrators (NASPA)	1919
American Association of Community and Junior Colleges (AACJC)	1920
American College Health Association (ACHA)	1920
Association of Governing Boards of Universities and Colleges (ABG)	1921
American College Personnel Association (ACPA)	1924
National Association of College Admission Counselors (NACAC)	1937
National Orientation Directors Association (NODA)	1947
Association of International Educators (NAFSA)	1948
National Association of College and University Business Officers (NACUBO)	1950
American Association for Counseling and Development (AACD)	1952
Association of College and University Housing Officers—International (ACUHO-I)	1952
National Association of Personnel Workers (NAPW)	1954
American Association of State Colleges and Universities (AASCU)	1961
National Association of State Universities and Land Grant Colleges (NASULGC)	1962
National Association of Independent Colleges and Universities (NAICU)	1967
National Association for Campus Activities (NACA)	1968
National Association for Student Financial Aid Administrators (NASFAA)	1968
American Association of Higher Education (AAHE)	1969
Council for the Advancement and Support of Education (CASE)	1974
Association for Student Judicial Affairs (ASJA)	1987

Source: Adapted from Burek, 1992.

conduct research; publish and disseminate research, information, and opinions; provide educational training and professional development programs; advocate on behalf of public policy or broad professional issues affecting members; assist members with career development issues; promulgate standards for professional preparation and practice; and create opportunities for professional peers to interact (American Society of Association Executives, 1988).

Professional associations are governed by their members and exist to serve their interests and needs. Most associations are legally incorporated nonprofit entities. The formal rules and structure for governance are various and are described in documents such as the articles of incorporation, constitutions, or bylaws. A governing board—composed of elected and/or appointed individuals—has the fiduciary responsibility to govern the association in compliance with the published bylaws.

A key characteristic of most student affairs professional associations is the degree to which their operations are managed by volunteers. Organizations such as NASPA, NAWE, ACUHO-I (Association of College and University Housing Officers-International), and others have small office staffs (fewer than ten full-time employees or the equivalent) that provide administrative services and assistance to the hundreds of volunteers responsible for program development and execution.

Professional associations are funded primarily by member dues; fees for programs, services, and publications; and corporate or foundation grants.

Like other organizations, associations are distinctive for many reasons, including those attributable to organizational culture. That culture is constantly evolving, incorporating changes in the beliefs, values, and attitudes of society as well as those of the members (Kuh, Schuh, Whitt, and Associates, 1991). The culture of the association determines in large measure how the governing board, staff, and volunteers behave, regardless of written policies (Independent Sector, 1989). Examples of organizational culture might include the dominant values espoused by the association, such as the degree to which volunteers have responsibility for program development, the emphasis placed on service to members, and the priority assigned multicultural participation and involvement.

Many associations collaborate on issues of common concern. For example, the American Council on Education (ACE) coordinated the Washington Higher Education Secretariat, composed of over thirty higher education associations based in Washington, D.C. NACUBO coordinates the Council of Higher Education Management Associations. Many of the organizations listed in Table 1 are members of one or both of these coordinating councils.

Reasons for Belonging to a Professional Association

Why do institutions and individuals belong to professional associations? There are a host of answers, but based on my conversations with colleagues, the majority of reasons fall into one of the following categories: opportunities for professional growth, a means to benefit from the services and programs provided, a chance to test professional competencies, a desire to join with others of similar interest to influence the future direction of the association or profession, and a professional sense of obligation to help advance the status of the profession and fund programs that assist it. Bloland (1985) argues that colleges and universities join the higher education associations based in Washington, D.C., because they need to have their case presented to Congress and the administration.

There are many different forms of participation and involvement, ranging from consumer to board member. These and the typical skills and time commitments required are summarized below.

Consumer

A consumer is an individual who is not a member but may (for example) periodically read the publications in the library; purchase a publication or audiotape; subscribe to a teleconference as a staff development tool; or attend a state, regional, or national conference.

Member

A member is a professional who has joined the association and receives copies of newsletters, journals, and other publications. The member follows the news of the association and responds to surveys on professional issues. These individuals have an opportunity to influence the direction and priorities of the association and are able to attend conferences or purchase resource materials and services at reduced costs. They may also volunteer and serve in a variety of leadership roles.

Contributor

A contributor may or may not be a member of the association. Working alone or in conjunction with colleagues, the contributor submits program proposals for workshops or conferences, makes presentations, prepares newsletter articles, or submits research results for publication. These tasks require good oral presentation and written communication skills and a solid conceptual understanding of research and the professional issues being addressed. The time commitment will depend on the scope and nature of the project.

Volunteer

A volunteer is a member who agrees to assist with an activity, project, or program. The assignment may be for as little time as one hour or an ongoing assignment that requires a considerable investment of time and expertise (such as service on a committee). A volunteer must have an ability to handle independent tasks as well as work as a team member. Examples of possible jobs include posting signs; planning programs; helping with registration, newsletter preparation, or surveys; conducting research; and recruiting members.

Coordinator

The coordinator is a member responsible for planning, coordinating, and directing the efforts of other volunteers and colleagues to deliver a program, event, or service. The assignment may be on a project, local, state, regional, or national level and usually requires involvement for six to eighteen months. The work typically involves coordination, administration, supervisory, interpersonal, and communication skills. Financial management skills may also be necessary. Because committee members may be located across the country, being a coordinator requires an ability to interact with and motivate others in person, on the telephone, and in written form. Possible assignments may include editing publications, chairing committees, planning educational programs, and coordinating commissions or networks.

Governance

A member can be elected or appointed to an advisory board or the governing board. This person is responsible for establishing major policies and long-range planning. It is work requiring understanding of budget and finance, a significant time commitment, and an appreciation of the important and emerging issues in the profession.

In summary, the major reasons why professionals join and become involved with associations are (1) to enhance their own professional development, (2) to make a contribution to the association, and (3) to help the profession. Individuals can assist their own professional development through all the forms of participation described above. However, making a contribution to the association and profession requires membership at a minimum and usually participation as either a contributor or a volunteer or in a governance capacity.

Involvement over the Career Life Cycle

It may be helpful to think about a career in student affairs as a life cycle. During the course of the cycle, we may be at various points or playing many different roles. Consider the student affairs professionals in a typical student affairs division. There are graduate assistants with varying amounts of previous professional experience, new professionals, persons who have made a career transfer from another field or discipline, midlevel professionals, senior student affairs officers, faculty members, and perhaps several retired staff members. In addition to their professional assignments, each of the individuals may have family responsibilities, may be involved in community or church activities, or may be working on an advanced degree. All of these factors influence the degree to which they are able to participate or interested in participating in professional associations and the types of involvement that they seek.

The examples listed below describe categories of participation and involvement for student affairs professionals.

Consumer and Member

Sally is a graduate assistant with limited time and financial resources. She is a resident director and a member of ACHUO-I. She subscribes to the NAWE journal *Initiatives* and reads other publications as required for her course work. Next year she plans to join ACPA so she can attend the annual conference and participate in career services.

Consumer, Member, Contributor, and Volunteer

Jim is a doctoral student who has three years' previous professional experience as a Greek adviser. Prior to returning to graduate school, he was a member of ACPA's Commission IV (student activities) and edited its newsletter. As a result, his writing and publication skills improved considerably. This year he joined NASPA and plans to attend the regional conference. He and his faculty adviser have submitted a program proposal and hope to present it at the regional conference.

Consumer, Member, Contributor, and Volunteer

George is the director of the counseling center. He is a member of AACD (American Association for Counseling and Development), ACPA, and APA (American Psychological Association). In the past fifteen years, he has served in numerous volunteer roles, has made frequent presentations at conferences, and has published his research regularly. Because of the demands of his current position and budget restrictions, he will not be able to attend any professional conferences this year. He has, however, agreed to serve as a reviewer of program proposals for the conference.

Member

Alice has recently been named director of the outdoor recreation program in the student center. Her previous professional experience was as a high school coach. She plans to maintain her membership in the National Intramural/Recreational Sports Association and has recently joined the Association of College Unions—International to learn more about the union field. Alice hopes to attend the summer institute sponsored by the association this year.

Member, Contributor, Volunteer, and Governance Participant

Sue has been a faculty member and a student affairs professional for twenty-five years. She has served as editor of the *NASPA Journal* for three years, was director of the research division, was director of the NASPA summer institute, and served as a member of the board of directors for both NASPA and NAWE. In 1985, she was elected president of ACPA, and she has recently agreed to be the program chair for the upcoming annual conference.

Consumer and Member

Bill is the dean of students and has been a student affairs professional for ten years. He has been a member of ACUHO-I, ACPA, and NASPA. He now has administrative responsibility for financial aid and the student health service. He has recently joined the National Association for Student Financial Aid Administrators and plans to accompany the health center director to the American College Health Association conference next year. Occasionally, he also attends the annual ACE meeting with the president of the college.

These are just a few examples of how participation and involvement in professional associations may vary over the course of a career. These examples are based on the patterns of contemporary professionals. Think about your own pattern of involvement and participation. How does it compare to these examples or to the experiences of your colleagues and other professionals whom you respect?

The Role of Associations in Professional Development

Professional associations provide programs and services designed to enhance their members' understanding of contemporary issues and to develop their professional skills. Though the benefits derived from participation often depend on the type of individual involvement, the potential positive outcomes are significant. The most often cited benefits are summarized below.

Colleagues

The reason members give most frequently for joining or belonging to the association is the opportunity it offers for professional networks. Individuals encounter colleagues and make friends with whom to exchange ideas, perspectives, and concerns beyond the scope of their current work. The professional is able to interact with individuals in similar types of institutions and to compare ideas on programs and services, as well as to gain a broader perspective on issues from professionals in other types of institutions and parts of the country. Someone who moves from a small liberal arts college in New England to a public four-year college in the Southwest may have an automatic network of colleagues as a result of involvement in professional associations.

For many members of underrepresented ethnic groups and women, participation in professional associations creates valuable contacts. In cases where few women or ethnic minorities are employed on a campus, the organization provides connections to valuable role models and colleagues with similar interests and concerns.

The social nature of professional associations is also a legitimate advantage of involvement. Friendships and personal relationships develop during graduate school, in employment settings, and as a result of professional work. As people move to different institutions and regions of the country, professional associations furnish opportunities for continued interactions and get-togethers. Individuals often develop strong friendships with those with whom they have served on committees or in other volunteer roles.

Opportunities for Understanding

The simple act of getting away from a single campus environment is important in gaining new perspectives. The chance to consider issues from the perspective of others is invaluable. For example, their current campus assignment may be in the area of health education, but individuals can learn more about residence life issues through participation in different professional associations. Staff members are also able to broaden their understanding of different types of institutions and the issues that they confront.

Ongoing Professional Development

Participation in professional associations creates access to the latest professional developments through publications and conferences. As a contributor or volunteer, an individual is able to expand and test a repertoire of skills and experiences beyond those required in a current assignment. It may be possible to perform duties and tasks not included in a full-time position. Many professionals gain the necessary experience and training for broader or more responsible career roles as a result of association involvement. Further, they also have a chance to establish a professional reputation beyond an individual campus as a result of their contributions.

Orientation to the Profession

New professionals and persons who transfer into student affairs from another career field receive an important orientation to the relevant issues and literature through participation in association-sponsored programs. Many chief student affairs officers are appointed to the leadership roles from faculty positions. The professional associations provide important opportunities to gain conceptual grounding as well as advice from more experienced colleagues.